DAVID BUSCH'S
Nikon® Z5 II
GUIDE TO
DIGITAL PHOTOGRAPHY

DAVID D. BUSCH

David Busch's Nikon® Z5 II Guide to Digital Photography
David D. Busch

Project Manager: Jenny Davidson
Technical Editor: Doug Klostermann
Layout: Bill Hartman
Cover Design: Mike Tanamachi
Indexer: Valerie Haynes Perry
Proofreader: Mike Beady

ISBN: 979-8-88814-427-5
1st Edition (1st printing)

© 2025 David D. Busch

All images © David D. Busch unless otherwise noted

Rocky Nook, Inc.
1010 B Street, Suite 350
San Rafael, CA 94901
USA
www.rockynook.com
info@rockynook.com
(415) 747-8756

Represented in the E.U. by:
Rheinwerk Verlag GmbH
Rheinwerkallee 4
53227 Bonn
Germany
service@rheinwerk-verlag.de

Distributed in the UK and Europe by Publishers Group UK
Distributed in the U.S. and all other territories by Publishers Group West

Library of Congress Control Number: 2025936756

This book is printed on acid-free paper.
Printed in Korea

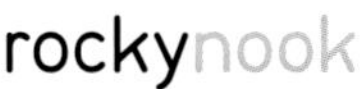

For Cathy

Acknowledgments

Thanks to everyone at Rocky Nook, including Scott Cowlin, managing director and publisher, for the freedom to let me explore the amazing capabilities of the Nikon Z5 II camera in depth. I couldn't do it without my veteran production team, overseen by project manager, Jenny Davidson. Also, thanks to Doug Klostermann, technical editor; Bill Hartman, layout; Valerie Haynes Perry, indexing; Mike Beady, proofreading; Mike Tanamachi, cover design; and my agent, Carole Jelen, who has the amazing ability to keep both publishers and authors happy.

About the Author

With more than 3 million books in print, **David D. Busch** is the world's #1 selling digital camera guide author, and the originator of popular digital photography series like *David Busch's Pro Secrets* and *David Busch's Quick Snap Guides*. He has written more than four dozen hugely successful guidebooks and compact guides for Nikon digital cameras, dozens of additional user guides for other camera models, as well as many popular books devoted to photography. As a roving photojournalist for more than 20 years, he illustrated his books, magazine articles, and newspaper reports with award-winning images. He's operated his own commercial studio, suffocated in formal dress while shooting weddings, and shot sports for a daily newspaper and an upstate New York college. His photos and articles have been published in magazines as diverse as *Popular Photography, Rangefinder, Professional Photographer,* and hundreds of other publications. He's also reviewed dozens of digital cameras for CNet Networks and other CBS publications. His advice has been featured on National Public Radio's *All Tech Considered.*

When About.com named its top five books on Beginning Digital Photography, debuting at the #1 and #2 slots were Busch's *Digital Photography All-In-One Desk Reference for Dummies* and *Mastering Digital Photography.* He's had as many as five of his books listed in the Top 20 of Amazon.com's Digital Photography Bestseller list—simultaneously! Busch's 350-plus other books published since 1983 include bestsellers like *Digital SLR Cameras and Photography for Dummies.*

Busch is a member of the Professional Photographers of America, and the Cleveland Photographic Society (www.clevelandphoto.org), which has operated continuously since 1887. Visit his Facebook group *David D. Busch Photography Guides.*

Contents

CHAPTER 7

Custom Settings Menu 217

CHAPTER 8

Playback Menu 275

CHAPTER 9

The Setup, Network, Retouch, and My Menus — 287

CHAPTER 10

Introduction to Video — 333

CHAPTER 11
Focus on Lenses   369

Preface

With the new Nikon Z5 II, the company has redefined what you can expect from an "entry-level" camera. Nikon's most affordable full-frame mirrorless model packs an impressive range of high-end features into a compact body. An action photographer's dream camera, the Nikon Z5 II can take photos at an astonishing 30 frames per second and even capture action that happened *before* you pressed the shutter release down all the way, with its pre-capture buffering. Super-responsive autofocus can search for, detect, and lock focus on the eyes, faces, and torsos of people, birds, dogs, cats, animals, and other difficult-to-track subjects, including planes, trains, and motorcycles. An innovative focus-stacking feature provides stunning depth-of-field for deep-focus macro images. The Z5 II's pixel-shift capabilities can capture a series of shots that can be merged to produce amazing 96-megapixel images.

Best of all, the Z5 II looks and handles like the Nikons we love, with controls and menus that veteran Nikon owners will find comfortably familiar and new users will grow to appreciate as they explore the latest enhancements. Every photo enthusiast will easily master the camera's capabilities, even though the sheer number of features and options can be daunting. The only thing standing between you and pixel proficiency is the lack of a comprehensive manual. Complete instructions for the Z5 II are available online only, downloadable as a massive PDF.

Everything you need to know is in the manual somewhere, but you don't know where to start, nor how to find the information you really need to master your camera. In addition, the camera manual doesn't offer much guidance on the principles that will help you master digital photography. Nor does it really tell you much about how mirrorless shooting might differ from the kinds of digital photography you may already be used to. If you're like most enthusiasts, you're probably not interested in spending hours or days studying a comprehensive book on digital photography that doesn't necessarily apply directly to the enhanced features of your camera.

What you really need is a guide that explains the purpose and function of the camera's basic controls, available lens options, and most essential accessories from the perspective of mirrorless cameras. It should tell you how you should use them, and *why*. Ideally, there should be information about the exciting features at your disposal, how to optimize image quality, when to use exposure modes like Aperture- or Shutter-priority, and the use of special autofocus modes. In many cases, you'd prefer to read about those topics only after you've had the chance to go out and take a few hundred great pictures with your new camera. Why isn't there a book that summarizes the most important information in its first two or three chapters? This is that book.

If you can't decide on what basic settings to use with your camera because you can't figure out how changing ISO or white balance or focus defaults will affect your pictures, you need this guide. I won't talk down to you, either; this book isn't padded with dozens of pages of checklists telling you how to take a travel picture, a sports photo, or how to take a snapshot of your kids in overly simplistic terms. There are no special sections devoted to "real-world" recipes here. All of us do 100 percent of our shooting in the real world! So, I give you all the information you need to cook up great photos on your own!

Introduction

The Nikon Z5 II is a particularly welcome entry in the company's versatile mirrorless camera lineup. Ostensibly an entry-level model for budding photo enthusiasts, it nevertheless incorporates many of the features of Nikon's more advanced models, providing plenty of features to grow into in a more affordable, more compact package.

Nikon's own downloadable PDF manual is filled with information, but there's really very little about *why* or *when* you should use particular settings or features. I've tried to make *David Busch's Nikon Z5 II Guide to Digital Photography* different from your other camera learn-up options, and more efficient than those YouTube videos that make you sit through irrelevant discussions to get to the one piece of information you're really looking for. The visual roadmap sections in Chapter 1 use larger, color pictures to show you where all the buttons and dials are, and the explanations of what they do are longer and more comprehensive. You'll find tips and techniques for using all the features of your Nikon camera, along with recommendations on how to select the best autofocus mode, shutter speed, f/stop, or flash capability to take eye-catching, compelling photos.

Best of Both Worlds

I first began writing Nikon camera guides more than 20 years ago, starting with the venerable Nikon D70, long before Kindle and other ebook formats became as important as they are today. The trend to electronic publishing has been beneficial to photographers who like to keep a copy of one of my books on their phone or tablet for ready reference in the field or viewing on their computer. At the same time, interest in traditional printed books like these has remained strong, because illustrated how-to publications really lend themselves to casual browsing, jumping from page to page, and examining visual examples in detail. The latest fiction best-seller looks great on your smartphone's small screen; a reference guide may not.

So, while the bulk of printed camera guides—including those from Nikon itself—have largely been replaced by PDFs, I've insisted on offering both traditional manuals and Kindle/ebook versions so you can choose to purchase the format you really need, or both, if you prefer. In addition, electronic publishing provides the opportunity to produce hybrid books like this one, which has the same essential information in both printed and ebook formats, while retaining the ability to present updates, as required, when new equipment is introduced or Nikon makes changes through additional firmware releases.

David Busch's Nikon Z5 II Guide to Digital Photography offers the exact same descriptions, advice, tricks, and techniques two different ways, in both print and digital formats:

- **Printed Version.** The printed version of this book includes 11 chapters that guide you through setting up and learning your Z5 II's controls, features, and menus, while helping you master the basics of exposure, autofocus, use of flash, and the camera's video features. Separate chapters and sections on the Photo Shooting, Video Recording, Custom Settings, Playback, Setup, and Network menus include my recommendations on how to work with each entry, along with suggestions on when you should—or should not—use each option. I also include a detailed how-to chapter on the Z5 II's video features, which Nikon has optimized for content creators and vloggers, as well as traditional videographers.

In addition, those who have the printed version can also download one additional chapter containing the kind of material that often needs frequent updating—something that can best be done quickly, efficiently, and seamlessly through electronic publishing. Your "bonus" material can be found in Chapter 12, which provides troubleshooting information and descriptions of bug fixes and new features included in future updates for the Z5 II. It also includes step-by-step information for fine-tuning the autofocus of certain lenses. As electronic downloads, I'll be able to revise this material quickly as new hardware and firmware releases are introduced.

- **Electronic eBook Version.** The digital version of this book will always include all 12 chapters, both the 11-chapter main publication, as well as the digital chapter (and any additional add-ons that may be offered), available for download by those who buy only the printed version. If you choose to get the electronic version only, you'll always have access to the most up-to-date version of this guide in ebook form.

How To Download the Digital Material

Those who purchase the printed version can download the digital Chapter 12 by navigating to the following URL. You can retrieve the latest chapters at any time for viewing on your smartphone, tablet, computer, or other device.

https://rockynook.com/nikon-z5-ii/

Who Am I?

After spending many years as the world's most successful unknown author, I've become slightly less obscure in the past few decades or so, thanks to a horde of camera guidebooks and other photographically oriented tomes. You may have seen my photography articles in the late, lamented *Popular Photography* magazine. I've also written about 2,000 articles for magazines like *Rangefinder*, *Professional Photographer*, and dozens of other photographic publications. You may have attended one of the workshops or presentations I've given at groups ranging from camera clubs to meetings of the Professional Photographers of America organization to which I belong.

But, first, and foremost, I'm a photojournalist who made my living in the field until I began devoting most of my time to writing books. Although I love writing, I'm happiest when I'm out taking pictures. Recently, I spent two weeks traveling Route 66 in the USA, returned to Europe to recapture images of the continent's rich history and culture, and made my first visit to New Zealand. You'll find photos of some of these visual treasures within the pages of this book.

Like all my digital photography books, this one was written by a Nikon devotee with an incurable photography bug who has used Nikon cameras professionally for longer than I care to admit. Over the years, I've worked as a sports photographer for an Ohio newspaper and for an upstate New York college. I've operated my own commercial studio and photo lab, cranking out product shots on demand and then printing a few hundred glossy 8 × 10s on a tight deadline for a press kit. I've served as a photo-posing instructor for a modeling agency. People have actually paid me to shoot their weddings and immortalize them with portraits. I even prepared press kits and articles on photography as a PR consultant for a large Rochester, NY company, which older readers may recall as an industry giant. My trials and travails with imaging and computer technology have made their way into print in book form an alarming number of times, including dozens dealing with scanners and a broad range of photographic topics.

Like you, I love photography for its own merits, and I view technology as just another tool to help me get the images I see in my mind's eye. But, also like you, I had to master this technology before I could apply it to my work. This book is the result of what I've learned, and I hope it will help you master your Nikon camera, too.

In closing, I'd like to ask a special favor: let me know what you think of this book. If you have any recommendations about how I can make it better, contact me directly at questions@dslrguides.com. Send your comments, suggestions on topics that should be explained in more detail, or, especially, any typos. I really value your ideas and appreciate it when you take the time to tell me what you think! Most of the organization and some of the content of the book you hold in your hands came from suggestions I received from readers like yourself. If you found this book especially useful, tell others about it. Visit https://www.amazon.com/David-Buschs-Digital-Photography-Camera/dp/B0F47GRGPH and leave a positive review. Your feedback is what spurs me to make each one of these books better than the last. Thanks!

Your Setup Guide and Quick Start

1

If you're like me, the first thing you probably did when you extracted your Z5 II from the box was attach a lens, power up the beast, and begin taking photos through a tentative trial-and-error process. If you're a veteran Nikon shooter, you probably found many of the controls and menus very similar to what you're used to. But now that you've taken a few hundred (or thousand) photos with your new Nikon Z5 II, you're ready to learn more. To help you begin shooting as quickly as possible, this chapter is divided into three main parts that will provide you with everything you need to know, but were afraid to ask:

- **Part I: Setup Guide.** This is the section that will help you hit the ground running, with a list of all the things you need to do to get your Z5 II up and running as you master the main controls and learn menu anatomy and touch-screen features.
- **Part II: Visual Roadmap.** This section is an illustrated guide to the location of all the Z5 II's controls and components, and how to use them.
- **Part III: Operations Quick Start.** Here, you'll quickly learn how to set your camera's Release mode, Exposure mode, Focus mode, Autofocus-area mode, and other basic settings. I'll cover just the basics here, with references to the chapters that cover each of these essential tools in depth.

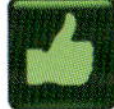

TIP In this book, you'll find short tips labeled **My recommendation** or **My preference**, each intended to help you sort through the available options for a feature, control, or menu entry. I'll provide my preference, suitable for most people in most situations. I don't provide these recommendations for every single feature, and you should consider your own needs before adopting any of them.

Part I: Setup Guide

The following sections provide a basic pre-flight checklist that you need to complete before you spread your wings and take off. I'm going to tell you just what you absolutely *must* understand, accompanied by some interesting tidbits that will help you become acclimated to your Z5 II. You don't have to memorize everything you see. Just relax, follow a few easy steps, and then go out and begin taking your best shots—ever.

Your Out-of-Box Experience

The Nikon Z5 II comes in an impressive box filled with stuff, including lots of paperwork. The most important components are the camera and lens (if you purchased your Z5 II with a lens), battery, USB cable, and, if you're the nervous type, the neck strap. You'll also need a memory card or two, plus spares, as they are not included.

At a minimum, the box should contain the following components:

- **Nikon Z5 II digital camera.** Check out the camera immediately, making sure the back-panel LCD monitor isn't scratched or cracked, the access doors open properly, and, when a charged battery is inserted and lens mounted, the camera powers up and reports for duty.

- **Lens (optional).** At its introduction, the Z5 II was available *only* as an unadorned body or with one or more "kit" lenses, including the compact 24-50mm f/4-6.3 and a versatile 24-200mm f/4-6.3 zoom. Nikon retailers will probably offer *other* lenses as part of a kit in the future, and most will readily package this camera with the lens of your choice, often at a savings over buying them individually.

- **USB cable UC-E25.** This is a Type-C cable (the easy-insert kind that doesn't require a specific orientation). You can use this cable to transfer photos from the camera to your computer (I don't recommend that because direct transfer uses a lot of battery power), to charge its batteries, to upload and download settings between the camera and your computer (highly recommended), and to operate your camera remotely using the optional Nikon NX Studio or Nikon Camera Control Pro software.

  My recommendation: This cable has USB Type-C connectors at both ends for use with computers that have a USB Type-C port or if you plan to use a charger compatible with the USB C Power Delivery specification. *However*, if your computer has only USB A ports for USB 2.x and USB 3.x connections, you'll need to buy a USB-C-to-USB-A cable, as one is *not* included with your Z5 II.

- **Rechargeable Li-ion battery EN-EL15c.** You'll need to charge this 7.0V, 2280 mAh (milliampere hour) battery before use, as described shortly. You'll want a second EN-EL15c battery as a spare (trust me), so buy one as soon as possible.

- **AN-DC26 neck strap.** Nikon provides you with a neck strap emblazoned with the Nikon Z logo. It's not very adjustable, and, while useful for showing off to your friends exactly which nifty new camera you bought, it can also alert observant unsavory types that you're sporting a higher-end model that's worthy of their attention.

  My recommendation: I never attach the Nikon "steal me" strap to my camera. I personally prefer third-party conventional straps over holsters, slings, chest straps, or any support that dangles my camera upside down from the tripod socket and allows it to swing around too freely when I'm on the run.

- **BF-N1 body cap.** The body cap keeps dust from infiltrating your camera when a lens is not mounted. Always carry a body cap (and rear lens cap) in your camera bag for those times when you need to have the camera bare of optics for more than a minute or two. (That usually happens when repacking a bag efficiently for transport, or when you are carrying an extra body or two for backup.) The body cap/lens cap nest together for compact storage.

- **DK-29 rubber eyecup.** This is the round rubber eyepiece that comes installed on the viewfinder of the Z5 II. It slides on and off the viewfinder. ProMaster and a few other companies offer replacement eyecups in shapes that some find more comfortable.

- **BS-1 accessory shoe cover.** This little piece of plastic protects the electrical contacts of the "hot" shoe on top of the Z5 II. You can remove it when mounting an electronic flash or other accessory, and then safely leave it off for the rest of your life. I've never had an accessory shoe receive damage in normal use, even when not protected. The paranoid among you who use accessories frequently can keep removing/mounting the shoe cover as required. Note that Nikon also offers a BS-3 shoe cover ($10) with better weather sealing to protect the hot shoe if you're working in damp environments.

My recommendation: Find a safe place to keep it between uses, or purchase replacements for this easily mislaid item. The previous low-cost source for these covers has gone out of business, so I've imported a stock of them, in both standard and bubble-level versions, which I'll send you for a few bucks. (Visit www.laserfairepress.com for more details.) I also can supply spare rear lens caps and body caps if you need one. I get this stuff for my personal use, and it's cheaper to just buy them in bulk and offer the extras to readers.

- **User's manuals.** The skimpy printed User Guide provided with the camera provides only basic information. A 928-page Reference Guide is available online from Nikon support in HTML and PDF versions.

  My recommendation: The URL for Nikon's online support varies, depending on your country; it's simpler to just Google "Nikon Z5 II manual PDF" to find a downloadable version of the reference guide that you can store on your laptop, on a USB stick, or other media in case you want to access this reference when the paper version isn't handy.

- **Warranty and registration card.** Don't lose these! You can register your Nikon Z5 II by mail or online (in the USA, the URL is www.nikonusa.com/register), and you may need the information in this paperwork (plus the purchase receipt/invoice from your retailer) should you require Nikon service support.

There are a few things Nikon classifies as optional accessories, even though you (and I) might consider some of them essential. Here's a list of what you *don't* get in the box but might want to think about as an impending purchase. I'll list them roughly in the order of importance:

- **SD Memory card.** Cards are an "optional" accessory because Nikon doesn't have the slightest idea of what capacity or speed card you prefer, so why charge you for one?

  My recommendation: The Z5 II's 24-megapixel image files each amount to roughly 11.3MB for JPEG Fine and up to 28.6MB for Lossless Compressed 14-bit NEF (RAW) files. Size your cards accordingly; I typically rely on 128GB and 256GB SD cards, although I do own several 512TB and 1TB cards that come in handy when I travel. Larger, faster cards are especially useful for shooting video.

  The Z5 II's dual-memory card slots support SD, SDHC, and SDXC memory cards, plus both UHS-I and the faster UHS-II specification. It's unlikely you'll still have any of the older, slow, SD or SDHC cards, as the newer SDXC cards (particularly their fast UHS-II versions) are now the standard, and available in sizes up to 2TB. The latest SDUC type you may have heard of allows capacities up to 128TB but must be used only in devices specifically designed for them (the Z5 II isn't one of them).

- **Extra EN-EL15c battery.** As a mirrorless model, the Z5 II's sensor and electronic viewfinder and/or LCD monitor are energized anytime the camera is powered up, so you may note that you are getting fewer shots per charge than you may be used to. Nikon says that if you shoot with the viewfinder only, you can expect to get as many as 380 images before you'll need to swap batteries (when using Energy Saving Mode, described in Chapter 9); if using the slightly less energy-hungry LCD monitor, up to 390 shots should be possible in Energy Saving mode. You should be able to capture 85 minutes of video with either display.

At least one extra battery is virtually mandatory. Fortunately, you can use the previous model EN-EL15, EN-EL15a, and EN-EL15b batteries used in many older and current Nikon models, with several caveats. The older versions of the EN-EL15 battery, marked with a *Li-ion 01* designation to the left of the hologram on the cell's bottom, are not fully compatible with the Z5 II, and will, in fact, show less capacity than they really contain when used. The newer EN-EL15 version (marked *Li-ion 20*) and latest EN-EL15a/b/c batteries do not have this problem.

Note: In addition, third-party versions of the EN-EL15/EN-EL15a/b batteries *may not work* in the Z5 II at all. (The camera reports a "dead" battery even if it's fully charged.) Finally, only EN-EL15b and EN-EL15c versions can be charged internally. The others require a separate charger (see below).

- **Battery charger.** *The Nikon Z5 II does not come with a separate charger!* You'll either need to charge your battery internally by connecting a power source to the camera's USB-C port or by purchasing a separate charger. Without an external charger, if you want to use your camera while the battery is being refreshed, you'll be tied to that power source. Not good. Worse, *only* the EN-EL15c and EN-EL15b batteries can be charged internally.

  One option is the Nikon EH-8P charging AC adapter. Plug this small, square "wall wart" into an AC outlet and connect the Type-C USB connector cable to the USB port of the Z5 II and you can recharge the EN-EL15c battery of the camera internally while the camera is turned off. It can be used to supply power to the camera for taking pictures, if you set USB Power Delivery to On in the Setup menu, as described in Chapter 9.

  My recommendation: You can pick up the EH-8P if you feel the need, but you can do the same thing with any Type-C USB cable and an external USB source that outputs 27W (e.g., 9V/3A) of power. However, keep in mind that most computers and cheap chargers may not be able to provide enough power to charge your battery efficiently. You definitely need a charger capable of providing the minimum of 27W of power that internal charging requires. Your best bet is a Power Delivery-compatible wall charger or power bank. Nikon has tested and recommends the Anker PowerCore+ 26800 PD 45-watt power bank, which is estimated to provide four full battery charges.

  I prefer separate PD chargers that plug into the wall for charging batteries internally or units like the optional Nikon MH-32 external charger, or third-party equivalents. These external chargers allow you to rejuvenate your one battery while you are shooting with an additional battery installed in the camera.

- **Nikon NX Studio and Nikon ViewNX-i software.** You can download a free copy of these software utilities from Nikon's website. Nikon stopped packing a CD-ROM with its cameras at roughly the same time CD-ROMs really ceased being a thing.

- **Camera Control Pro 2 software/Nikon NX Tether.** These are utilities you can use to operate your camera remotely from your computer. Nikon charges extra for Camera Control Pro 2, but NX Tether is a free download. You'll find them invaluable if you're hiding near a tethered, tripod-mounted camera while shooting, say, close-ups of hummingbirds. There are lots of applications for remote shooting, and you may need Camera Control Pro 2 or NX Tether to operate your camera.

My recommendation: You may already own and be proficient with Adobe Lightroom, which does an excellent job for tethered shooting, or DxO Labs' Capture One. Buy a suitably longer USB-C cable, too.

- **Add-on Speedlight.** Like all Nikon's full-frame Z-mount cameras to date, the Z5 II does not have a built-in electronic flash. If you do much flash photography at all, consider an add-on Speedlight as an important accessory.

  My recommendation: An add-on flash can serve as the main illumination for your picture, diffused or bounced and used as a fill light, or, if you own several Speedlights, serve as a remote trigger for an off-camera unit. At around $250, the Nikon SB-500 has the most affordable combination of reasonable power, compact size, and features, including a built-in LED video light. If you need more power, the Speedlight SB-700, SB-910, or SB-5000 also offer more flexibility. I'll provide more information on electronic flash in Chapter 4.

- **Remote control.** When you want to take a photo at the exact moment you desire (and not when the self-timer happens to trip) or need to eliminate all possibility of human-induced camera shake, you need a wireless remote control or a plug-in release cord.

  My recommendation: Your Z5 II is compatible with the Nikon wireless remote (ML-L7), a Bluetooth device that has two function buttons that can be defined to start playback or launch menus. I'll show you how to use the Wireless Remote Connection (ML-L7) entry in Chapter 9, as well.

  Alternatively, you can opt for the MC-DC3 wired remote release. Note that the latter uses a 3.5 mm stereo mini-pin headphone jack that does double-duty for connecting to a remote control, unlike the older MC-DC2 wired remote (and third-party substitutes) which used a special connection found on many previous Nikon Z-series cameras but is not included with the Z5 II.

  The Z5 II can usually discern whether a headphone or the MC-DC3 remote control is plugged in when the Connector Function entry in the Setup menu is set to Auto Switch (as described in Chapter 9). If not, you can manually specify Headphone within the entry.

  Finally, the Z5 II is also compatible with third-party Bluetooth remote controls. Nikon has officially certified the SmallRig SR-RG2 Wireless Shooting Grip, an extensible "handle" that screws into the Z5 II's tripod socket and can be converted into a tabletop tripod. It has built-in focus/shutter and REC buttons, a tele/wide zoom rocker, and one customizable C button.

- **HDMI audio/video cable.** The Z5 II can be connected to a high-definition television or monitor and can export its video output to an external recorder. You'll need to buy an HDMI (high-definition multimedia interface) cable with a standard (Type A) HDMI connector on one end (to connect to your display or recorder) and an HDMI micro (Type D) connector on the other end to plug into the camera. No HDMI cable is included with the camera.

- **Power battery pack MB-N14.** Lots of photographers consider a battery pack/vertical grip to be an essential item. The pack holds two EN-EL15c batteries and increases the number of shots and video recording time by approximately 1.9X. Its adapter replaces your camera's internal battery, so you end up with two (not three) power cells. This battery grip is also compatible with earlier Nikon Z6 III and Z7 II/Z6 II cameras.

It provides the same level of environmental sealing as the Z5 II, and its internal batteries can be recharged using an external adapter. Many find a grip of this sort makes a compact camera like the Z5 II more comfortable in their hands. It includes main and sub-command dials, a multi selector, Fn button, and AF-ON button for vertical shooting.

If you already own the Nikon MB-N11 version used with the Z7 II and Z6 II, it is compatible with the Z5 II as well. The fit is slightly different, and the MB-N11 requires the earlier EH-7P charger instead of the latest model EH-8P. (The MB-N14 can be charged with either.) Theoretically, the original MB-N10 pack should work as well (I haven't tried it), but that device has no control buttons; it's more of a battery holder than actual vertical grip. You can bet that third-party suppliers are busy designing compatible grips for the Z5 II, too.

My recommendation: Hold out for the MB-N14. Many people love third-party grips from Meike, Neewer, Vivitar, and others, at a cost somewhat less than Nikon asks for its MB-N14. However, most people like to clamp their add-on grips onto the camera and remove them only rarely. If you intend to make a battery grip part of your permanent setup, the Nikon model will be better made, more rugged, and guaranteed to work seamlessly with your camera.

- **SC-28 TTL flash cord.** Allows using Nikon Speedlights off-camera, while retaining all the automated features. The SC-29 TTL flash cord is similar, and has its own infrared autofocus-assist lamp, which *does not work with mirrorless cameras.* If you already own the SC-29, fine, but there is no need to pay extra for a feature that you cannot use.

My recommendation: If you intend to work with an external flash extensively, you'll definitely want to use it off camera. Either of these cables will give you that flexibility. Wireless flash operation (described in Chapter 4) is more versatile but requires more setup and has a steeper learning curve. With a flash cord, you just connect the cable to your camera and flash and fire away.

Initial Setup

Many basic functions will be covered in the next few sections and can be mastered quickly, especially if you already know how to navigate your Z5 II's menu system and perform tasks like setting the clock and formatting a memory card. If you need some help, skip over those steps until you've read the "Mastering the Main Controls" and "Menu Anatomy" sections later in this chapter.

Charging the Battery

To charge the battery, use the optional EH-8P AC adapter, or connect the supplied USB-C cable to a suitable third-party charger, preferably a USB-C PD charger meeting the Power Delivery specification. A full charge can take up to 2 hours and 30 minutes.

You can check the Setup menu's Battery Info entry to make sure the battery is fully charged. If not, one of three things may be the culprit: 1.) the actual charging cycle sometimes takes longer than you (or the charger) expected; 2.) the battery is new and needs to be "seasoned" for a few charging cycles, after which it will accept a full charge and deliver more shots; 3.) you've got a defective battery. The last is fairly rare, but before you start counting on getting a particular number of exposures from a battery, it's best to make sure it's fully charged, seasoned, and ready to deliver.

Because Li-ion batteries don't have a memory, you can top them up at any time. However, their capacity when fully charged will eventually change over time. Once in a while, it's a good idea to use a battery until it is fully discharged and then recharge it beyond the normal charging time. It's also best to not store a battery for long periods either fully discharged or completely charged in order to maintain its longevity. If you own several (as you should), you'll probably want to rotate them to even the electronic wear and tear.

Setting the Clock

The camera's clock settings are stored in internal memory powered by a rechargeable battery that's not accessible to the user. It is recharged whenever a removable battery is installed in the battery compartment, and two days of normal use will recharge the internal battery enough to power the clock for about a month. The camera is normally sold without its main battery installed, so you'll probably see a clock icon the first time you power it up. In addition, if you store your camera for a long period without a charged main battery, the "clock" battery may go dead and "forget" your time/date/zone settings. It will recharge when a fresh battery is inserted, and you'll need to set the clock again.

When you receive your camera, it's likely that its internal clock hasn't been set to your local time, so you may need to do that first. You'll find complete instructions for setting the four options for the date/time (time zone, actual date and time, the date format, and whether you want the camera to conform to Daylight Saving Time) in Chapter 9. However, most Z5 II users can perform this step without instruction. Just press the MENU button, use the multi selector (a thumb-friendly directional pad located to the immediate right of the back-panel LCD monitor), highlight the main menu icons on the left side of the screen, and then scroll down to the Setup menu. Next, press the multi selector button to the right and scroll down to Time Zone and Date choice, and press right again. The options will appear on the screen that appears next. Keep in mind that you'll need to reset your camera's internal clock from time to time, as it is not 100 percent accurate.

Format/Insert a Memory Card

Formatting is the process that removes any existing information from a memory card and replaces it with a fresh file system structure using the correct DCF (Design rule for Camera File system) structure, including the DCIM (Digital Camera Images) folder to store your images. The DCIM folder can include subfolders for each different camera type you use, so the same SD card can be used in multiple cameras—including those made by different vendors. Images taken by other Nikon cameras, or even those produced by Canon, Sony, or other manufacturers can co-exist on the same card.

To insert your card, slide the door on the back-right edge of the body toward the back of the camera to release the cover, and then open it. You should only remove a memory card when the camera is switched off, or, at the very least, when the yellow-green memory access light (shown in Figure 1.1) that indicates the camera is writing to the card is not illuminated.

Inside the compartment, you'll find two card slots. You can use one card, or two. The camera will operate even if only one of the slots is occupied. Insert the memory card with the label facing the back of the camera, oriented so the edge with the contacts goes into the slot first. The card can be removed just by pressing it inward; it will pop out far enough that you can extract it.

Always let the Z5 II format your memory card using the Setup menu entry. Format with your computer only as a last resort to revive a card that has failed. There are three ways to create a blank memory card for your Z5 II, and two of them are wrong. Here are your options, both correct and incorrect:

- **Transfer (move) files to your computer.** When you transfer (rather than copy) all the image files to your computer from the memory card (either using a direct cable transfer or with a card reader), the old image files are erased from the card, leaving the card blank. Theoretically. Unfortunately, this method does *not* remove files that you've labeled as Protected (by pressing the *i* button during Playback and selecting Protect from the screen that pops up), nor does it identify and lock out parts of your memory card that have become corrupted or unusable since the last time you formatted the card. Therefore, I recommend always formatting the card, rather than simply moving the image files, each time you want to make a blank card. The only exception is when you *want* to leave the protected/unerased images on the card for a while longer, say, to share with friends, family, and colleagues.
- **(Don't) Format in your computer.** With the memory card inserted in a card reader or card slot in your computer, you *can* use Windows or Mac OS to reformat the memory card. Don't! The operating system won't necessarily install the correct file system. The only way to ensure that the card has been properly formatted for your camera is to perform the format in the camera itself.
- **Setup menu format.** To use the recommended method to format a memory card, press the MENU button, use the up/down buttons of the multi selector to choose the Setup menu (which is represented by a wrench icon), press right to navigate to the Format Memory Card entry, press OK, and select Yes from the screen that appears. Press OK to begin the format process.

  My recommendation: I always use the Setup menu format before each shoot, as long as the images thereon have already been transferred to my computer. Nothing is worse than beginning a session and discovering that your memory card is almost full and contains images you don't want to delete to make room for new shots. If you neglected to bring along an extra memory card, you may have some difficult decisions to make.

Diopter Correction

Pull out the dial on the right side of the viewfinder housing, rotate it to adjust, then push it back in to lock the setting. Adjustment is available from −4 to +2 correction. If more than one person uses your camera, and each requires a different diopter setting on the camera itself, you can save a little time by noting the number of clicks and direction (clockwise to increase the diopter power; counterclockwise to decrease the diopter value) required to change from one user to the other.

Mounting the Lens

If your Z5 II has no lens attached, select the lens you want to use and loosen (but do not remove) the rear lens cap. After that, remove the body cap by rotating the cap away from the release button. You should always mount the body cap when there is no lens on the camera because it helps keep dust out of the interior of the camera. The body cap also protects the sensor from damage caused by intruding objects (including your fingers, if you're not cautious).

Mount the lens on the camera by matching the alignment indicator on the lens barrel with the raised white bump on the camera's lens mount. Rotate the lens toward the shutter release until it seats securely. If the lens hood is bayoneted on the lens in the reversed position, twist it off and remount facing outward. A lens hood protects the front of the lens from accidental bumps, and reduces flare caused by extraneous light arriving at the front element of the lens from outside the picture area.

SWITCHING FROM VIEWFINDER TO MONITOR

The camera has a sensor located just above the viewfinder window. When it detects you've brought the camera up to your eye, it switches its display from the LCD monitor to the viewfinder, and then back again when you remove the camera from your eye. You can change this default behavior, as I'll explain in Chapter 9, or manually switch between them using the Monitor Mode button located on the left side of the viewfinder.

Mastering the Main Controls

Now that your Z5 II is ready to go, your first step will be to master the main controls, which you'll use for navigating menus, reviewing images, and performing other functions. Most of them will require the MENU button and the multi selector and some other controls. I'll be saving some descriptions for the comprehensive "Visual Roadmap" sections later in this chapter. Figure 1.1 shows the location of the key navigational controls on the Nikon Z5 II. You'll want to learn these controls first:

- **Main and sub-command dials.** The main command dial and sub-command dial are located on the rear and front of the camera, respectively, and located at the top of the figure and within the inset at top right. The main command dial is used to change settings such as shutter speed, while the sub-command dial adjusts an alternate or secondary setting. For example, in Manual exposure mode, you'd use the sub-command dial to change the aperture, while the main command

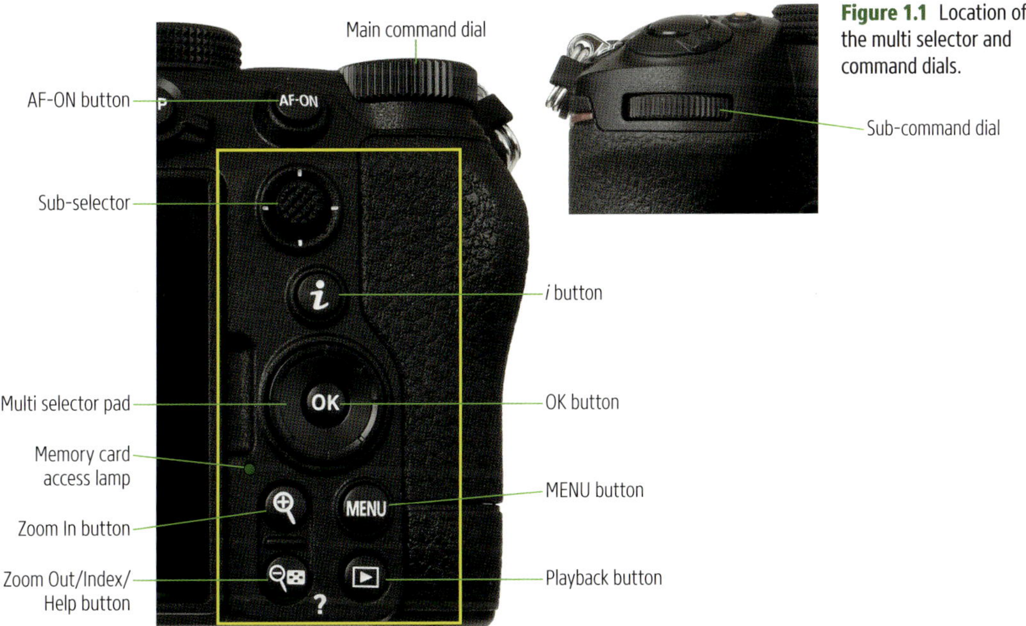

Figure 1.1 Location of the multi selector and command dials.

dial is used to change the shutter speed. (In both cases, the dial is "active" for these adjustments only when the camera's exposure meter is on, until the "Standby Timer" runs out.) The meter will automatically go to sleep after an interval (you'll learn how to specify the length of time in Chapter 7), and you must wake the camera (just tap the shutter-release button) to switch the meter back on and activate the main and sub-command dials.

You can swap functions of the main and sub-command dials, reverse the rotation direction, choose whether the aperture ring on the lens or the sub-command dial will be used to set the f/stop, and activate the main command dials to navigate menus and images. You'll learn about these Custom Settings menu options in Chapter 7.

- **MENU button.** It requires almost no explanation; when you want to access a menu, press it. To exit most menus or to confirm and exit in some cases, press it again.
- **Multi selector pad/directional controls.** This joypad-like disk can be shifted up, down, side to side, and diagonally for a total of eight directions. It is used for several functions, including AF point selection, scrolling around a magnified image, trimming a photo, or setting white balance bias along the green/magenta and blue/amber (yellow) axes. Within menus, pressing the up/down arrows moves the on-screen cursor up or down; pressing toward the right selects the highlighted item and displays its options; pressing left cancels and returns to the previous menu or changes the value of a setting.

  The multi selector is used extensively for navigation (for example, to travel through menus, to advance or reverse display of a series of images during picture review, or to change the kind of photo information displayed on the screen). It can also be used to choose one of the user-selectable focus areas on the viewfinder and LCD monitor displays.
- **OK (multi selector center) button.** The center button (as well as the right directional button) can be used to select a highlighted item from a menu. (I find pressing the right directional button faster and easier.) The center button also can function as an OK/Enter key. Like many other controls, it can be redefined; in this case, use Custom Setting f2. I'll explain those customization options in Chapter 7.
  - **Shooting mode.** In AF-area modes in which you can specify the initial focus point, pressing the OK button resets the focus point to the center of the frame.
  - **Menu mode.** When working with menus, the OK button selects the highlighted menu option (same as the right arrow button).
  - **Playback mode.** Press to turn zoom on or off. Repeated presses toggle between those two modes only; zoom magnification does not change. To adjust magnification, use the Zoom In and Zoom Out buttons, described shortly.
- **Sub-selector.** The sub-selector can be moved like a joystick or pressed as if it were a button. When pressed inward it locks focus or exposure (as an AE/AF lock button) by default, but it can also be redefined to a variety of other behaviors with Custom Setting f2: Custom Controls (Shooting).

  When tilted in joystick fashion, the sub-selector is a convenient control for positioning the focus point, for navigating menu screens, and scrolling playback functions. Unlike the sub-selector *button* mode, the joystick behaviors are locked in and *cannot* be redefined to perform some other action.

Other key components on the right side of the Z5 II you'll want to learn are also pictured in Figure 1.1. They are as follows:

- **Zoom In button.** This button can be used in four different modes:
  - **Playback mode.** Press to zoom in on an image when in full-screen view, to increase the zoom ratio (from 16X to 24X up to 32X, depending on your Image Size setting), or to decrease the number of thumbnails when in index view (described shortly). **Note:** You can also zoom in and out in playback mode using "squeeze" and "stretch" gestures on the touch screen, similarly to the techniques used with smartphones. I'll explain zooming and other playback options in an upcoming section.
  - **Shooting mode 1.** Press to zoom in while focusing, and to increase the zoom ratio.
  - **Shooting mode 2.** When a power zoom lens, such as the Nikkor Z 28-135mm f/4 PZ is mounted, this button changes the focal length of the lens, zooming to the maximum setting as you press.
  - **Video playback mode.** Press to increase the volume of the playback audio.
- **Zoom Out/Index/Help button.** This button has separate Playback/Video Playback, Shooting, and Menu mode functions:
  - **Playback mode.** Press this button to change from full-screen view to 4, 9, or 72 thumbnails. Press the Zoom In button to go the other way back to full screen and magnified views.
  - **Video playback mode.** Press to decrease the volume of the playback audio.
  - **Shooting mode 1.** Press to zoom out of a magnified image.
  - **Shooting mode 2.** With power zoom lenses, this button changes the focal length of the lens, zooming out to the minimum setting as you press.
  - **Menu mode.** When working with many menu items, if you see a ? icon appear in the upper-right corner of the screen, pressing this button produces a concise Help screen. The screen includes tips on how to make the relevant setting with the highlighted menu item. The Help screen may have several pages you can scroll through using the up/down buttons. Press this button again to exit Help.
- **Playback button.** Press this button to review images you've taken, using the controls and options I'll explain in the next section. To remove the image display, press the Playback button again, or simply tap the shutter-release button.
- **AF-ON button.** Press this button to activate the autofocus system without needing to partially depress the shutter release. This control, used with other buttons, allows you to lock exposure and focus separately. Lock autofocus by pressing the shutter release halfway or by pressing the AF-ON button.
- **_i_ button.** Pressing this button in Photo or Video Shooting modes summons the _i_ menu. A total of 12 adjustments can be accessed from the _i_ menu, but you can replace any entry you don't use much with another function of your choice, using Custom Setting f1: Customize _i_ menu (for Photo mode) or Custom Setting g1: Customize _i_ menu (for Video mode), as described in Chapter 7. I'll show you how to use the _i_ menus in the section that follows.
- **Memory card access lamp.** This yellow-green LED is located just to the southwest of the multi selector pad. When lit or blinking, this lamp indicates that a memory card is being accessed.

Using the *i* Menus

The Z5 II has four different *i* menus, which are pop-up displays that provide fast access to some of the most frequently used functions. There are separate *i* menus for Photo Shooting, Video Recording, Still Photo Playback, and Video Playback.

The Photo Shooting and Video Recording *i* menus each have a total of 12 functions, arrayed across the bottom, and seen in Figure 1.2, left and right. Seven of them are the same in either mode, with substitutions for five entries (boldfaced and marked with asterisks in the list below). During Playback, the *i* menus differ when viewing still photos and video clips, as seen in Figure 1.3, left and right. Some functions, such as Filtered Playback, Filtered Playback Criteria, Choose Slot and Folder, Protect/Unprotect All, and Slide Show are common to both. Others are available only when viewing stills or videos.

Note that some entries can change depending on other settings. For example, there are nine different "Select for Upload…" entries that allow choosing files to upload to a smart device, computer/FTP server, or Nikon Imaging Cloud, and these may appear only when you are connected to the relevant destination.

Photo Shooting *i* Menu Functions (see Figure 1.2, left):

- **Top Row:** Set Picture Control, White Balance, Image Quality, Image Size, AF-Area Mode/Subject Detection, and Focus Mode.

  Bottom Row: Tone Mode, Vibration Reduction, Custom Controls (Shooting), Metering Mode, Airplane Mode, and View Memory Card Information.

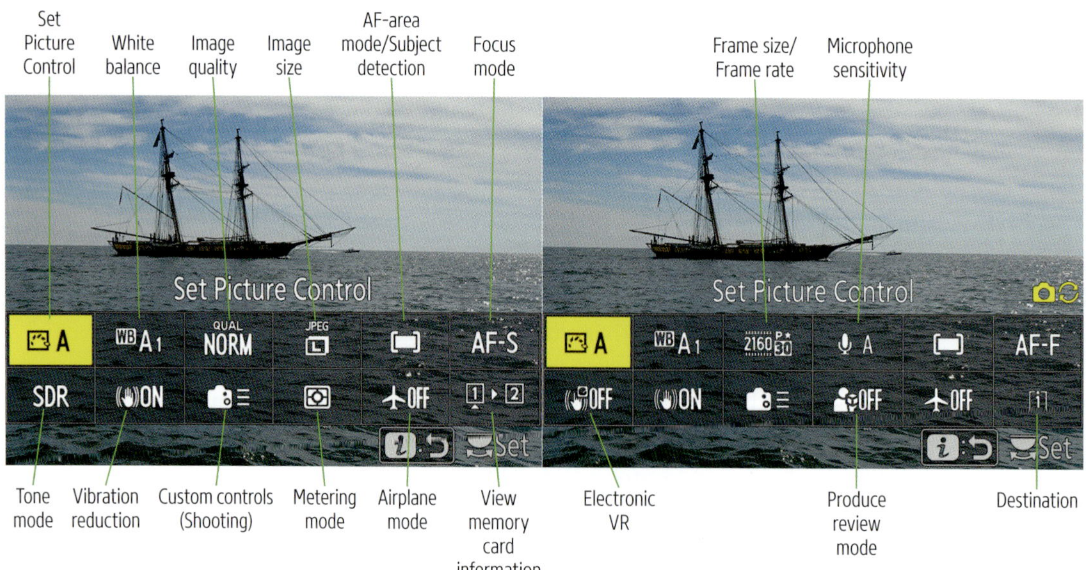

Figure 1.2 Photo Shooting (left) and Video Recording (right) *i* menus.

Video Recording *i* Menu Functions (see Figure 1.2, right):

- **Top Row:** Set Picture Control, White Balance, **Frame Size/Frame Rate** *, **Microphone Sensitivity** *, AF-area mode/Subject Detection, and Focus Mode.

  Bottom Row: Electronic VR *, Vibration Reduction, Custom Controls, **Product Review Mode** *, Airplane Mode, and **Destination** *.

Still Photo Playback *i* Menu Functions (see Figure 1.3, left):

- **Still Photo Playback:** Manage Series, Rating, Select for Upload to Smart Device, Filtered Playback, Filtered Playback Criteria, Record Voice Memo, Retouch, Jump to Copy on Other Card, Choose Slot and Folder, Protect, Unprotect All, IPTC, Side-by-Side Comparison, Slide Show

Video Playback *i* Menu Functions (see Figure 1.3, right):

- **Video Playback:** Rating, Filtered Playback, Filtered Playback Criteria, Volume Control, Trim Video, Choose Slot and Folder, Protect, Unprotect All, Slide Show, Playback Speed

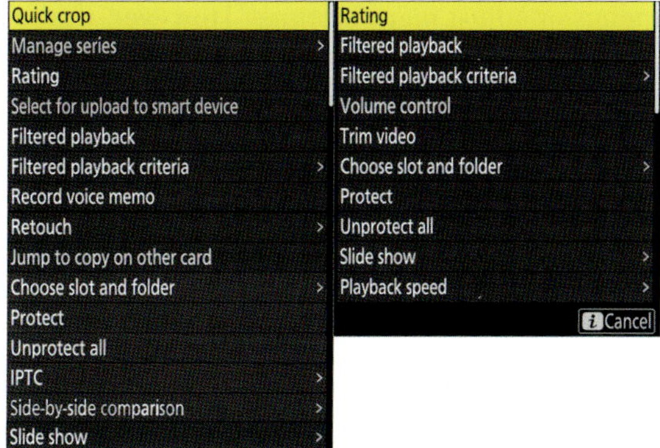

Figure 1.3 Still Photo Playback *i* menu (left). Video Playback *i* menu (right).

Note: Some *i* menu items in the Still Photo version may be hidden or replaced. Quick Crop doesn't appear when RGB histograms are displayed. The Select for Upload to Smart Device entry may be replaced with options for uploading to Nikon Imaging Cloud, a computer, or FTP server if those destinations are selected.

To use the Photo Shooting or Video Recording *i* menus, just follow these steps:

1. **Press the *i* button.** Then use the directional controls to highlight the function you want to use.

2a. **Simple adjustments.** While the function is highlighted, rotate the main command dial until the option you want is highlighted. Then press the *i* button again to confirm or exit.

   or

2b. **Optional adjustments.** When the function is highlighted, press the OK button. A settings screen will pop up, and you can use either the main command dial or directional buttons to make your selection. If you use this method, you can invoke some additional options:

   - **Set Picture Control.** Highlight the Picture Control you want and press the down directional button to customize its settings, as described in Chapter 5.
   - **White balance.** Press the down button to fine-tune the highlighted white balance setting using the main command and sub-command dials.
   - **AF-area mode/Subject Detection.** You can choose the AF-area mode *and* choose subject-detection options for modes that use that texture, using the main command and sub-command dials, as described in Chapter 3.
   - **Custom Controls.** The Custom Controls sub-menu, explained in Chapter 7, appears.

3. **Press the *i* button.** Press the *i* button again to confirm and exit.

The Still Photo Playback and Video Playback *i* menus summon traditional non-graphic menus shown in Figure 1.3. I'll explain how to use each of them in Chapters 8 (for still photos) and 10 (for video clips).

Touch Screen

The LCD monitor supports a number of touch operations. For example, you can use it to navigate menus or adjust many settings. However, the touch screen can be especially useful during image playback and when shooting to adjust settings, specify a focus point, or to trip the shutter. You can specify which touch features are available using the Setup menu's Touch Controls entry, as described in Chapter 9. The main gestures you can use with the screen are shown in Figure 1.4:

- **Flick left/right (Playback mode).** Quickly move a single finger a short distance from side to side across the monitor. During playback, a flick to the right or left advances to the next or previous full image. Note that if a second finger or other object is also touching the monitor, it may not respond, or, instead, cause the image to zoom.
- **Flick left/right/up/down (magnified playback).** If you've zoomed in during playback, you can scroll around within the image by moving a single finger across the screen in left, right, up, or down directions. (See Figure 1.4, top left.)
- **Finger slide (magnified playback).** Instead of flicking, you can press down on the screen and slowly slide your finger in any direction to move to any area within a magnified image.
- **Double-tap zoom.** During playback, double tap a full image to quickly zoom in the maximum amount. Double tap again to return to full-image view. If you're looking at 4, 9, or 72 thumbnails instead, a double-tap jumps immediately to full-image view.

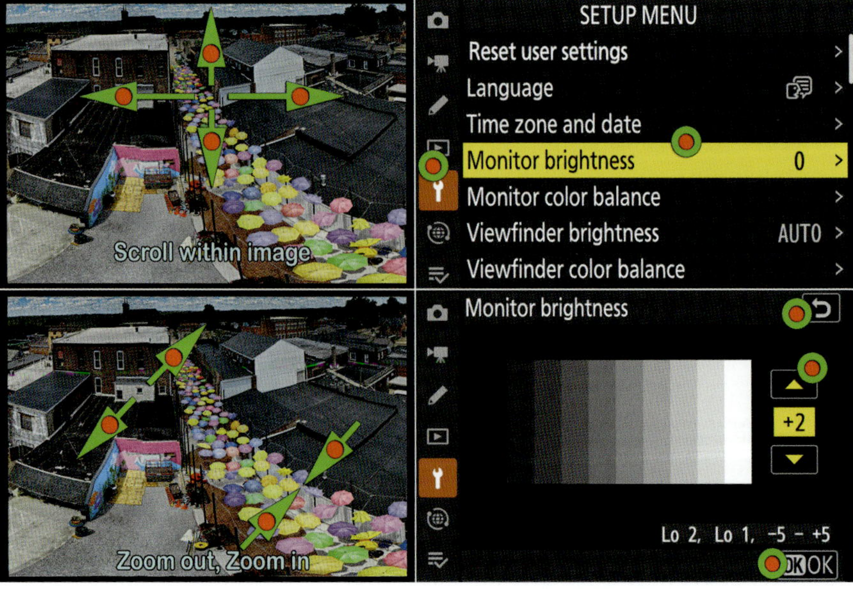

Figure 1.4 Flick or slide your finger across the touch screen to scroll from side to side, up, or down (top left). Pinch or spread two fingers to zoom in and out (bottom left). Tap menu tabs, entries, and settings to make adjustments (top and bottom, right).

- **Flick up (Playback).** During picture review of a full image, an upward flick can perform any one of five different tasks (or None) using Custom Setting f14: Full-frame Playback Flicks, as described in Chapter 7. They include:
  - **Rating.** One specific rating, from zero to five stars (or Candidate for Deletion), will be given to the currently displayed image.
  - **Select for Upload to Computer.** The current image will be assigned for transfer using all methods, including FTP.
  - **Select for Upload (FTP).** The current image will be assigned for transfer using FTP.
  - **Protect.** The flicked image will be marked as Protected. A second flick will Unprotect it.
  - **Voice Memo.** The voice memo recorded for the displayed image using the Record Voice Memo option of the Playback *i* menu will be played back.
  - **None.** Upward flicks are ignored.
- **Flick down (Playback).** Custom Setting f14: Full-frame Playback Flicks can be used to assign the same tasks available for Flick Up.
- **Flick Advance Direction.** Use this Custom Setting f14 option to change from the default right-to-left gesture to advance to the next image during playback to the reverse (left to right). **Note:** The *labels* in the menu entry both read Left-Right; it is only the *arrows* separating the two words that flip direction.
- **Spread/pinch.** Spread apart two fingers to zoom into an image during playback or pinch them together to zoom out. (See Figure 1.4, bottom left.)
- **Tap.** Touch the screen with a single finger to make a menu adjustment. (See Figure 1.4, top and bottom right.) For example, you can tap an up/down or left/right triangle to increase or decrease a setting, such as monitor brightness. Menu options with only On/Off choices can be toggled by tapping the entry (it's not necessary to hit the on/off icon).

  When Touch Shutter/Touch AF is activated, tapping the screen locates the focus point at the tapped location and takes a picture when you remove your finger from the screen. When Touch Shutter is deactivated, tapping the screen simply relocates the focus point. (You'll find a Touch Shutter icon at the left side of the LCD monitor screen that allows you to cycle among Touch AF, Touch Shutter/Touch AF, Move Focus Point, and Off.)

Here's a summary of the things you can do with the touch screen using the gestures described above:

- **In Playback mode:**
  - **Navigate among images one by one.** You can flick the left or right screen to advance to the previous or next image during full-frame (non-zoomed) playback.
  - **Advance quickly.** In full-frame playback, touch the bottom of the display to produce a frame advance bar, which you can drag to scroll quickly forward and back among your images.
  - **Zoom in or out.** Double tap on the touch screen to zoom in or out of an image under review. Use pinch and stretch to zoom in and out.
  - **Relocate zoomed area.** You can slide a finger around the monitor to reposition the zoomed area.
  - **View thumbnails and movies.** You can navigate among index thumbnails and movies with taps.

- ■ **In Photo mode (when using the LCD monitor):**
  - **Select a focus point.** In both Photo and Movie modes, you can tap a location on the touch screen to specify a focus point.
  - **Take pictures.** In Photo mode, if the monitor is active, you can tap the touch screen and lift your finger to take a picture without pressing the shutter-release button. A quick tap can set the focus point and capture an image with one gesture. (However, you can't begin video capture with a tap.) The touch focus/shutter functions can be enabled/disabled using the Touch Controls entry in the Setup menu.
  - **Adjust settings.** Some settings, such as shutter speed, aperture, ISO sensitivity, and *i* menu adjustments can be activated by tapping their icons or sliders. When adjustments are available, a white rectangle is drawn around the indicator that can be accessed by touch. You will see up/down and left/right triangles used to adjust increments, or other icons for various functions. After you make your change, you can tap OK or a return arrow to confirm and return to the previous screen.
  - **Navigate menus.** Personally, I often find the touch screen a little clumsy for navigating menus. You can scroll quickly up or down with an upward or downward swipe (using the tiny scroll bar on the right isn't necessary), but the menu bars and icons can be a bit too small on the 3.2-inch screen to be tapped with precision by those with large fingers. You still must press the MENU button to produce the menus, tap the main menu tab at the left of the screen, tap the specific item, and then choose among its options. Most of the time the multi selector directional buttons are a lot faster.
  - **Enter text.** When working with a text-entry screen (for example, to enter copyright information in the Setup menu), you can tap the on-screen keyboard to enter your text. That's *much* faster than the alternative—using the directional buttons to tediously move the highlighting from one character to another.

As noted, you can disable touch functions entirely or enable them for playback functions only (and thus disabling touch menu navigation) in the Setup menu, as described in Chapter 9. In addition, you can turn the Touch Shutter/AF feature off by tapping an icon that appears at the left side of the screen during viewfinder and movie shooting.

Because the screen uses static electricity, it may not respond when touched with gloved hands, fingernails, or when covered with a protective film. The Touch Controls screen does have a glove mode that improves response for winter shooters who don't want to lose fingers to frostbite. I have a glass screen over my Z5 II's monitor, and it works just fine; your experience may vary, depending on the covering you use. Don't use a stylus, pen, or sharp object instead of a finger; if your fingers are too large, stick to the physical controls such as the buttons or dials.

A TOUCH OF SCREEN

Throughout this book, when telling you how to use a touch-compatible feature, I'm going to stick to referring to the physical buttons and dials, for the benefit of those who prefer to use the traditional controls and to avoid having to repeat that you can use either the touch screen or the physical controls. From time to time, I'll remind you that a particular function can also be accessed using the touch screen.

Menu Anatomy

If you used any Nikon digital SLR or mirrorless camera before you purchased your Z5 II, you're probably already familiar with the basic menu system. Navigating among the various menus is easy and follows a consistent set of rules. The simple example shown in Figure 1.5 shows you virtually everything you need to know. Just press the MENU button on the lower-right corner of the Z5 II's back panel to access the main menu screens, then follow these steps:

1. **Choose a top-level menu.** The left-most column on the menus screen seen at left in the figure has a stack of top-level menu icons. When that column is selected, you can scroll up and down using the sub-selector joystick or the multi selector's up/down buttons. When you enter a menu's entry list, each icon's highlighting will change from gray to the color associated with that menu, and a banner across the top of the screen displays the menu's name. Starting from the top, they are:

   - **Still Camera (Green).** Photo Shooting menu.
   - **Video Camera (Olive Green).** Video Recording menu.
   - **Pencil (Red).** Custom Settings menu.
   - **Playback (Blue).** Playback menu.
   - **Wrench icon (Orange-Brown).** Settings menu.
   - **Globe (Purple).** Network menu.
   - **Checklist (Taupe).** My Menu.

2. **Enter top-level menu.** When you arrive at the tab you want to work with, use the multi selector's right directional button or the sub-selector joystick to move into the column containing that menu's choices. The currently selected menu option will be highlighted in yellow, as shown in the figure. **Note:** You can also press the OK button or the multi selector to move into a high-lighted top-level menu's entries, but it's usually simpler to just press the right directional button, because you'll be using the multi selector's directional buttons to navigate the menus anyway.

3. **Toggle controls.** Nikon has streamlined many entries that have only On or Off options, providing a quick-access toggle, represented by the Link VR to Focus Point entry at left in the figure. To switch states, you can tap the entry on the touch screen or highlight the entry and press either the OK or right directional button.

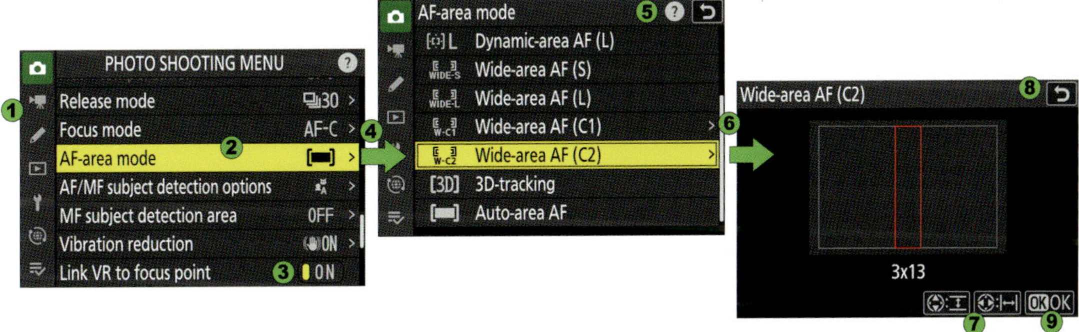

Figure 1.5 The multi selector's navigational buttons are used to move among the various menu entries shown here.

4. **Select a menu entry.** Use the up/down buttons to scroll among the entries. A scroll bar appears at the far right of the screen, with a position slider showing the relative position of the currently highlighted entry. To work with a highlighted menu entry, press the OK button, or, more conveniently, just press the right directional button on the multi selector. Any additional screens of choices will appear (see Figure 1.5, center). You can move among the options using the same controls.

5. **Get Help.** If you're not sure what an option does, any time a question mark appears at upper right in a screen, press the Help/Zoom Out/Index button to view a screen with a brief description.

6. **Select your option.** Many settings offer no additional adjustments, and you can select the highlighted option by pressing the right directional button or the OK button. When a > symbol appears, press the right directional button to move on to the next screen.

7. **Additional adjustments.** Entries that have additional adjustments will have appropriate controls indicated on the screen, as shown at right in Figure 1.5. In this example, you're told you can use the up/down and left/right directional buttons to change the dimensions of the red selection box.

8. **Change your mind.** Many screens have a "return" arrow in the upper-right corner. Select or tap it on the LCD screen to retreat to *the most recent* screen. (You won't return to the main menu.)

9. **Confirm your choice.** In general, when you're finished making adjustments, you can activate your setting by pressing the OK button or, sometimes, by pressing the left or right directional buttons on the multi selector. Some functions require scrolling to a Done menu choice or include an instruction to set a choice using some other button. If you don't follow the required procedure to exit, you may end up not actually confirming the adjustment you intended to make.

You can exit the menu system entirely at any time by tapping the shutter-release button. The multi selector left button usually backs you out of the current screen and pressing the MENU button again usually does the same thing.

TIP

- **Returning to an entry.** The camera "remembers" the top-level menu and specific menu entry you were using the last time the menu system was accessed, so pressing the MENU button brings you back to where you left off. So, if you were working with an entry in the Custom Settings menu's Metering/Exposure section, then decided to take a photo, the next time you press the MENU button the Custom Settings menu and the Metering/Exposure entry you last used will be highlighted. Even better, if you scroll up or down to a different main menu heading, you'll find the entry you last used with that menu highlighted as well.

- **Accessing a frequently used entry.** If you use the same menu items over and over, you can create a My Menu listing of those entries. Or, if you'd rather have a rotating listing of the last 20 menu items you accessed, you can convert My Menu to a Recent Settings menu instead. I'll show you exactly how to do that in Chapter 9.

MENU DISPLAYS

The figures in this book illustrating menu options are for easy reference only and may not correspond exactly to what you see on your camera's display. The Nikon Z5 II menus scroll continuously with listings at the bottom of the screen partially cut off, rather than in neat pages. For clarity, I have trimmed the menu screens so that each figure shows a complete set of menu options. In addition, none of the entries are grayed out in any of the figures; in real life, some will conflict with others and cannot be displayed as shown.

Working with Information Displays

The good news is that mirrorless cameras like your Nikon Z5 II are able to include a great deal more information in their displays during shooting or image review than their dSLR counterparts. The bad news is that all that data can be obtrusive, especially when you're trying to compose an image in the viewfinder or on the rear LCD monitor. Fortunately, you have a great deal of control over which bits of information are displayed, and you can create your own customized screens that will display as much or as little as you desire, and cycle among them using the DISP button. I'll show you exactly how to do that using the Custom Monitor/Viewfinder Shooting Display options in Chapter 7, and the Playback Display Options entry in Chapter 8.

The next sections will introduce you to the basic displays you can view while composing/capturing still photos, and when reviewing the images you took during playback.

Shooting Mode Displays

In Photo and Video Recording modes, much of the important shooting status information is shown on the electronic viewfinder and LCD monitor displays. In either Shooting mode, you can press the DISP button to cycle through the available views. As I noted above, you can define five different monitor shooting displays and four unique viewfinder shooting displays, using Custom Settings d19 and d20.

Keep in mind that while both the viewfinder and LCD have customizable displays, they are *separate* and you are free to define different sets of information icons to each. In addition, the way the icons are displayed is slightly different. The viewfinder display arrays information at black bars at the top and bottom of the screen, rather than overlaid onto the image area of the frame. That gives you a less-cluttered canvas on which to compose your image. The LCD, in contrast, overlays everything on the image frame, as seen in Figure 1.6. That alone provides a good reason for carefully customizing your displays. Note that the figure shows only some of the possible icons that can be displayed, and that not all icons will be visible at all times.

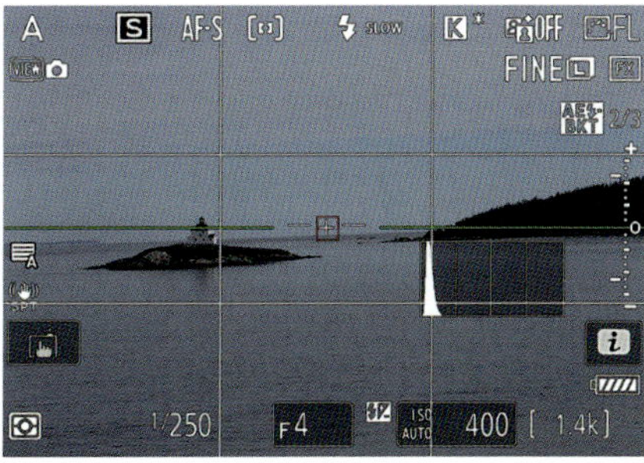

Figure 1.6 Typical Photo mode LCD information display.

One additional text-/graphics-only screen is available for the LCD monitor only and is seen in Figure 1.7. It shows not only exposure information, but, arrayed in two rows at the bottom of the screen, icon indicators display key settings, such as current picture control, white balance, focus mode, and metering mode. It's often smart to allocate this screen to the LCD monitor as a reference while relying on a different display in the viewfinder.

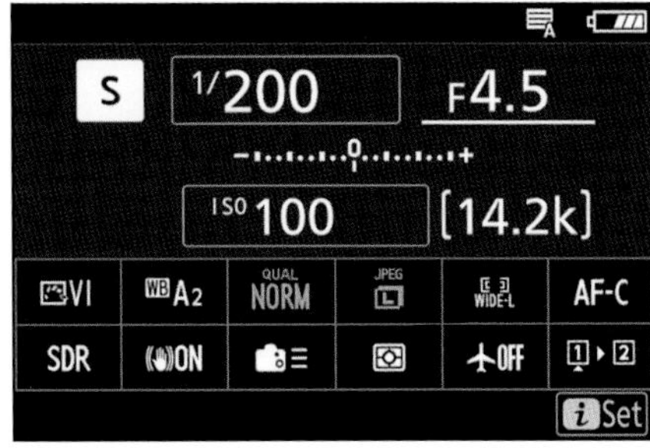

Figure 1.7 The Photo Shooting Information screen is displayed only on the LCD monitor.

The graphics screen cannot be customized by the user, as it is set up to do triple duty, with three different useful functions:

- Serves as an informational screen, providing data such as current exposure settings, shooting mode, battery level, and number of exposures remaining, along with the status of the 12 settings available from the *i* menu.
- Allows *changing* the shutter speed and/or aperture, plus ISO sensitivity using the touch screen controls.
- Acts as a gateway to the Photo Shooting version of the *i* menu. You can tap the *i* set icon on the touch screen, or press the *i* button to access any of the 12 *i* menu settings. The default indicators and adjustments available were shown earlier in Figure 1.2. After you've highlighted an icon, the command dials can be used to make a setting.

A more complete reference for your camera's shooting mode displays can be seen in Figure 1.8, which includes the basic array of icons available for the Nikon Z5 II's rear LCD monitor, and the viewfinder icons are similar to those displayed on the LCD.

Using the Photo Data Displays

When reviewing an image on the viewfinder or monitor displays, your camera can supplement the image itself with a variety of shooting data, ranging from basic information presented at the bottom of the display, to a series of text overlays that detail virtually every shooting option you've selected. There is also a display for Location (GPS) Data if you're using a GPS device, such as a linked smartphone, and two views of histograms. I'll explain how to work with histograms in the discussion on achieving optimum exposure in Chapter 2. However, this is a good place to provide an overview of the kind of information you can view when playing back your photos.

You can change the *types* of information displayed using the Playback Display Options entry in the Playback menu. There you will find checkboxes you can mark for both basic photo information (overexposed highlights and the focus point used when the image was captured) and detailed photo information (which includes an RGB histogram and various data screens). You must mark any unchecked box to enable that type of information display. I'll show you how to activate these info options in Chapter 8 and provide more detailed reasons why you might want to see each type of data when you review your pictures. This section will simply show you the type of information available. Most of the data is self-explanatory.

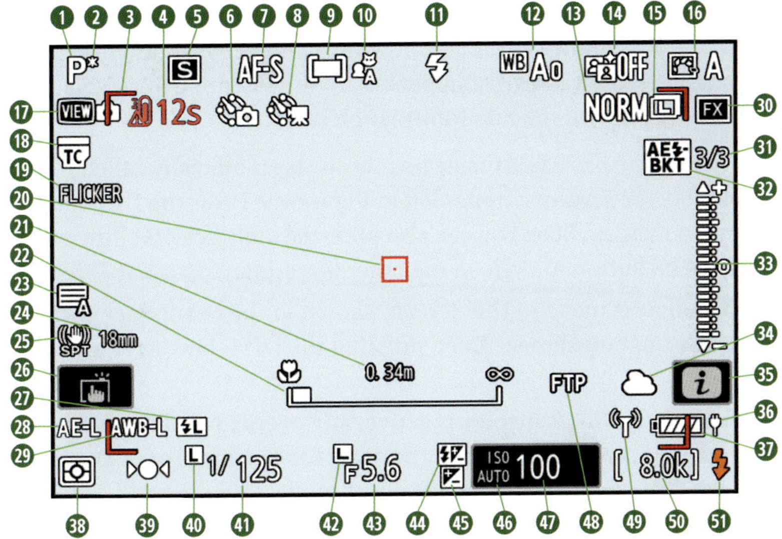

1 Shooting mode

2 Flexible program indicator

3 Out-of-focus indicator (Auto-area AF)

4 Temperature warning

5 Release mode

6 Interval-timer photography indicator
Time-lapse icon
"No memory card" indicator

7 Focus mode

8 Time-lapse video indicator

9 AF-area mode

10 Subject detection

11 Flash mode

12 White balance

13 Image quality

14 Active D-Lighting

15 Image size

16 Picture Control

17 View mode

18 "Lens built-in teleconverter enabled" indicator

19 FLICKER icon

20 Focus point

21 Distance between the camera and the focus position

22 Focus distance indicator

23 Shutter type
Silent mode

24 Focal length

25 Vibration reduction indicator

26 Touch shooting

27 FV lock indicator

28 Autoexposure (AE) lock

29 Auto white balance (AWB) lock

30 Image area

31 Number of shots in exposure and flash bracketing sequence
Number of shots in WB bracketing sequence
Number of shots in ADL bracketing sequence
HDR strength
Number of shots in multiple exposure

32 Exposure and flash bracketing indicator
WB bracketing indicator
ADL bracketing indicator
HDR indicator
Multiple exposure indicator
Pixel shift indicator

33 Exposure indicator
• Exposure
• Exposure compensation
• Auto bracketing

34 Nikon Imaging Cloud connection status
Remote camera connection status

35 *i* icon

36 USB power delivery

37 Battery indicator

38 Metering

39 Focus indicator

40 Shutter speed lock icon

41 Shutter speed

42 Aperture lock icon

43 Aperture

44 Flash compensation indicator

45 Exposure compensation indicator

46 ISO sensitivity indicator
Auto ISO sensitivity indicator

47 ISO sensitivity

48 FTP connection status

49 Wi-Fi connection indicator
Bluetooth connection indicator
Airplane mode

50 Number of exposures remaining
Camera control mode display

51 Flash-ready indicator

Figure 1.8 LCD Monitor icon reference.

To change to any of these views while an image is on the screen in Playback mode, press the DISP button or up/down buttons. Figure 1.9 shows how the camera cycles among the various screens, from the File Information screen shown at upper left, to the Picture Only display at lower left, after which the cycle begins again with the File Information screen:

- **File Information screen.** The basic full-image review display is officially called the File Information screen and looks like the screen at upper left in Figure 1.9. Press the DISP button to advance to the next information screen. **Note:** You can also press the multi selector down to move to the next screen or press the up button to cycle in the other direction.

- **Exposure Data.** You'll next move to this screen, shown in the next panel to the right, with only basic exposure information shown. Keep pressing the DISP button to advance to the screens that follow.

- **Highlights.** When the highlights display is active, any overexposed areas will be indicated by a flashing black outline around the edges of the overexposed image area. As I am unable to make the printed page flash, you'll have to check out this effect for yourself. You can visualize what

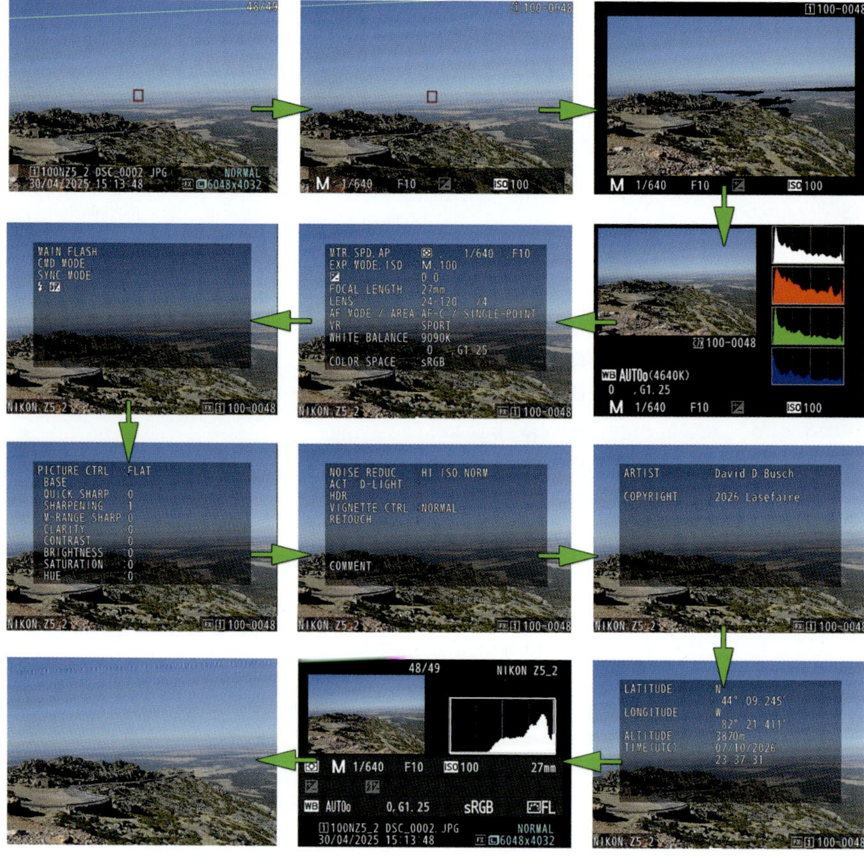

Figure 1.9 The Photo Information screen cycle.

these "blinkies" look like in the figure, as they are most easily discerned as the black splotches off in the distance.

- **RGB Histogram.** Another optional screen is the RGB Histogram. I'm going to leave the discussion of histograms for Chapter 2.

- **Shooting Data.** These are a series of screens that collectively provide everything else you might want to know about a picture you've taken. Note that each screen may not show all the information that can be displayed on that screen, and that all the screens may not appear. Only the data and screens that apply to your image will be shown. For example, the GPS screen appears only if a picture has GPS information embedded in it; the Artist/Copyright screen is shown only if you have chosen to embed that information in your image file. (I'll show you how to do that in Chapter 9.) The six main screens include:
  - Exposure, lens, and autofocus/VR information.
  - Flash exposure information.
  - Picture Control adjustments.
  - Noise reduction, Active D-Lighting, Retouching, Comments, and other information.
  - Artist information and copyright notices, if enabled.
  - GPS data is displayed if the image was taken using a GPS device.

- **Overview Data.** This screen, shown at bottom center in the figure, provides a smaller image of your photo but offers more information, including a luminance (brightness) histogram, metering mode used, lens focal length, exposure compensation, flash compensation, and lots of other data that's self-explanatory.

- **Picture Only.** When None is selected in the Playback Options entry, you can view a clean, uncluttered screen with no overlays, as seen at bottom left in the figure.

Part II: Visual Roadmap

In the Setup Guide, I already introduced the main buttons, dials, and other controls located on the back-right panel of your Z5 II. Now it's time to master the other components found on the front and side panels and bottom of the camera. If you've used any Nikon digital camera previously, even if this is your first mirrorless model, you may find your Z5 II comfortably familiar in shape and placement of many of the controls. Your camera has been right-sized to fit in the hand, with all the buttons, dials, and knobs needed for the most frequently adjusted functions arranged for easy access. If you want to operate your camera efficiently, you'll need to learn the location, function, and application of all these controls.

You'll also find this "roadmap" section a good guide to the rest of the book, as well. I'll try to provide as much detail here about the use of the main controls as I can, but some topics (such as autofocus and exposure) are too complex to address in depth right away. So, I'll point you to the relevant chapters that discuss things like setup options, exposure, use of electronic flash, and working with lenses with the occasional cross-reference.

Front View

This is the side seen by your subjects as you snap away. For the photographer, though, the front is the surface your fingers curl around as you hold the camera, and there are really only a few buttons to press, all within easy reach of the fingers of your left and right hands. There are additional controls on the lens itself. You'll need to look at several different views to see everything. Figure 1.10 shows the front of the camera with the lens removed. The components are as follows:

- **AF-assist illuminator/Self-timer/Red-eye reduction lamp.** This green LED lights up when needed during focusing under dim lighting to provide some additional illumination that can be helpful when focusing on subjects within a few feet of the camera. It also blinks as a self-timer countdown indicator and can provide a burst of light to contract your subject's pupils to reduce red-eye effect.

- **Sub-command dial.** This dial is used to change shooting settings, as described in the Setup Guide. When settings are available in pairs (such as shutter speed/aperture), this dial will be used to make one type of setting, such as aperture, while the main command dial (on the back of the camera) will be used to make the other, such as shutter speed.

- **Electronic contacts.** These 11 contact points mate with matching points on the bayonet mount of the lens itself and allow two-way communication between the camera and lens for functions like aperture size and autofocus information.

- **Sensor.** This is where the magic happens. Never touch or press against the sensor, to avoid damaging the protective surface of the sensor itself.

- **Function 1 (Fn1) button.** The default function for this button is white balance, but you can assign a new behavior using Custom Setting f2: Custom Controls (Shooting), described in Chapter 7.

Figure 1.10

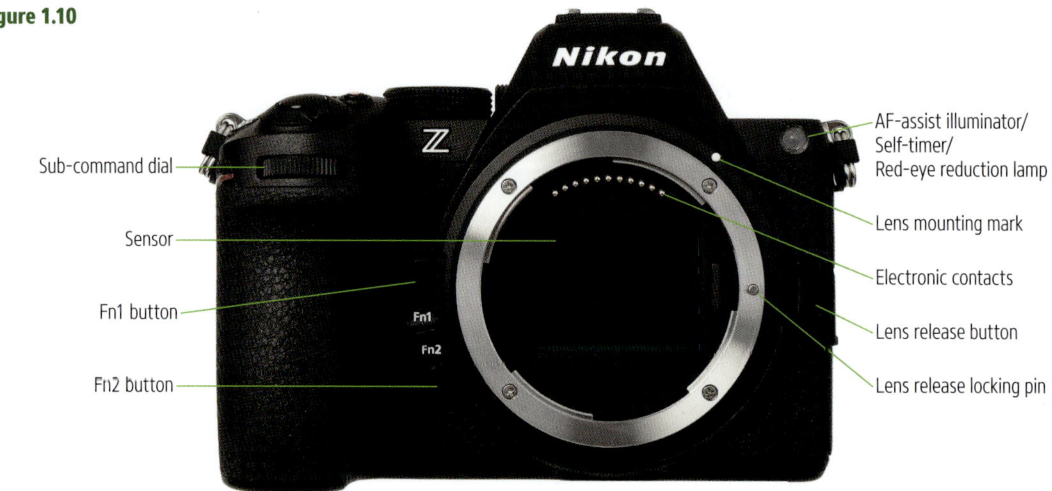

Hold down this button and rotate the main command dial to choose from these settings (explained in more detail in Chapter 5):

- **Auto variations.** When WB A_0, A_1, or A_2 appear, with the Fn1 button still held down, rotate the sub-command dial to choose from A_0 (Keep white), A_1 (Keep overall atmosphere), or A_2 (Keep warm lighting colors).
- **Natural Light Auto.**
- **Direct Sunlight.**
- **Cloudy.**
- **Shade.**
- **Incandescent.**
- **Fluorescent.** When this is highlighted, rotate the sub-command dial to select Cool-white, Day white, or Daylight.
- **Flash.**
- **K.** Rotate the sub-command dial to specify a color temperature from 2,500K–10,000K.
- **Preset Manual.** Use the sub-command dial to activate presets Pre_1 to Pre_6 as described in Chapter 5.

- **Function 2 (Fn2) button.** By default, this button adjusts focus mode (AF-S, AF-C, AF-A, Manual focus) with the main control dial and AF-area mode (Pinpoint AF, Single-point AF, Dynamic-area AF [Small/Medium/Large], Wide-area AF [Small/Large/Custom 1, Custom 2], 3D-tracking AF, Subject-tracking AF, or Auto-area AF). These are all described later in this chapter and in Chapter 3.
- **Lens mount.** This precision bayonet mount mates with the matching mount on the back of each compatible lens. The Z-mount is held on the camera using four screws that provide a secure attachment to the body, but not *too* secure. Their mounting holes are shallow enough to allow the bayonet mount to pop off if you drop the camera on the lens (which avoids even worse damage to the camera body itself). But don't worry, the mount is more than secure enough for everyday use, even with the heaviest lenses.
- **Lens mounting mark.** Align this mark on the camera body with the corresponding mark on the lens when attaching to the camera.
- **Lens release button.** Press this button to retract the locking pin on the lens mount so a lens can be rotated to remove it from the camera.
- **Lens release locking pin.** This pin slides inside a matching hole in the lens to keep it from rotating until the lens release button is pressed.

Side View

You'll find more controls on the other side of the camera, shown in Figure 1.11. The main points of interest shown include:

- **Monitor mode button.** Press this button multiple times to cycle among the available monitor modes, which I'll describe in detail in Chapter 9:
  - **Automatic Display Switch.** The active display always switches from the monitor to the viewfinder when you place your eye or anything else up to the viewfinder, and switches to the LCD when the sensor no longer detects an object.
  - **Viewfinder Only.** The monitor is disabled, and the viewfinder is used exclusively for shooting, navigating menus, or image playback.

- **Monitor Only.** The viewfinder is disabled, and display is directed to the LCD monitor only.
- **Prioritize Viewfinder 1/2.** With these power-saving options, when you're shooting pictures, the display is directed to the viewfinder exclusively; it turns on when you move your eye to the EVF and turns off when you remove your eye.

- **Neck strap eyelet.** Attach your neck strap to this mounting point and its counterpart on the other side.

- **External microphone connector.** Although the camera has built-in microphones on top, if you want better quality (and want to shield your video clip soundtracks from noises emanating from the camera and/or your handling of it), you can plug in an accessory mic, such as the Nikon ME-1, here.

- **Headphone/Remote control connector.** Plug in your headphones or other audio device here using a stereo miniplug to monitor your sound as you record, or to listen to the audio when playing back a video clip. As I noted in the Setup Guide, this 3.5mm jack doubles as a connector for a wired remote control. While the Z5 II can recognize the MC-D3 and shift into remote control mode, it may not identify all headphones, in which case you should change from Auto Switch to the Headphone setting in the Connector Function entry in the Setup menu.

- **HDMI connector.** I already advised you to purchase an HDMI Standard (Type A) to HDMI Micro (Type D) cable to connect to an external video recorder, monitor, or HDTV. If you have a high-resolution television or monitor, it's worth the expenditure to be able to view your camera's output in all its glory. And if you want to use a video recorder, a good cable will be worth its weight in gold.

- **USB connector.** Plug in the USB cable included in the box and connect the other end to a USB port in your computer to transfer photos, to upload Picture Control settings, or to upload/download other settings between your camera and computer. This USB 3 Type-C connector is also used for charging the Nikon Z5 II's battery internally.

- **Charge lamp.** This LED will glow yellow when the battery is being charged.

Figure 1.11

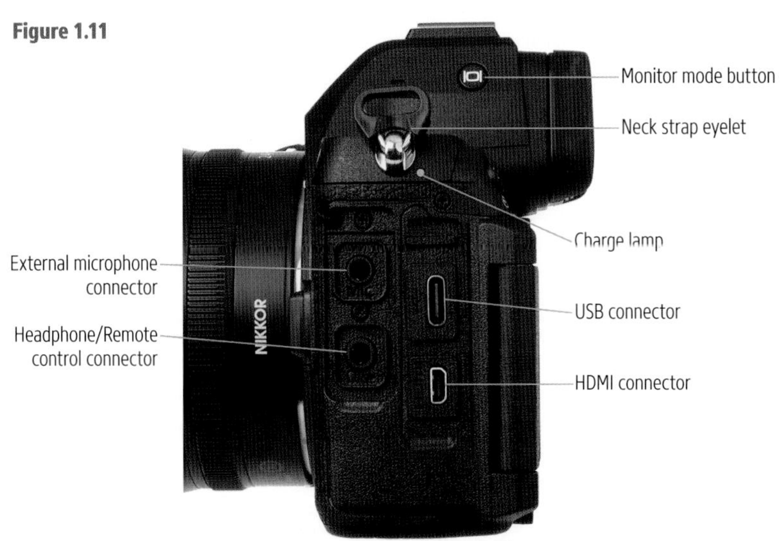

Rear View (Top)

You'll most often be viewing your camera from the angle shown in Figure 1.12. That's where most of the controls reside, and I've divided it into three regions for discussion. I'm going to start with the top surface, highlighted in the figure inside a green box:

- **Focal plane mark.** This indicator shows the *plane* of the sensor, for use in applications where exact measurement of the distance from the focal plane to the subject is necessary. (These are mostly scientific/close-up applications.)

- **Speaker.** Sounds generated by the Z5 II emerge here.

- **Accessory shoe.** Slide an electronic flash into this mount when you need supplementary on-camera illumination. A dedicated flash unit, like the Nikon SB-5000, can use the multiple contact points shown to communicate exposure, zoom setting, white balance information, and other data between the flash and the camera. You can also mount other accessories on this shoe, such as an external stereo microphone.

- **Stereo microphones.** This pair, located on either side of the viewfinder hump, captures sounds when shooting video.

- **Diopter adjustment control.** Rotate this knob to adjust the viewfinder for your vision, as described earlier.

- **Power switch.** Rotate this switch clockwise to turn on the camera.

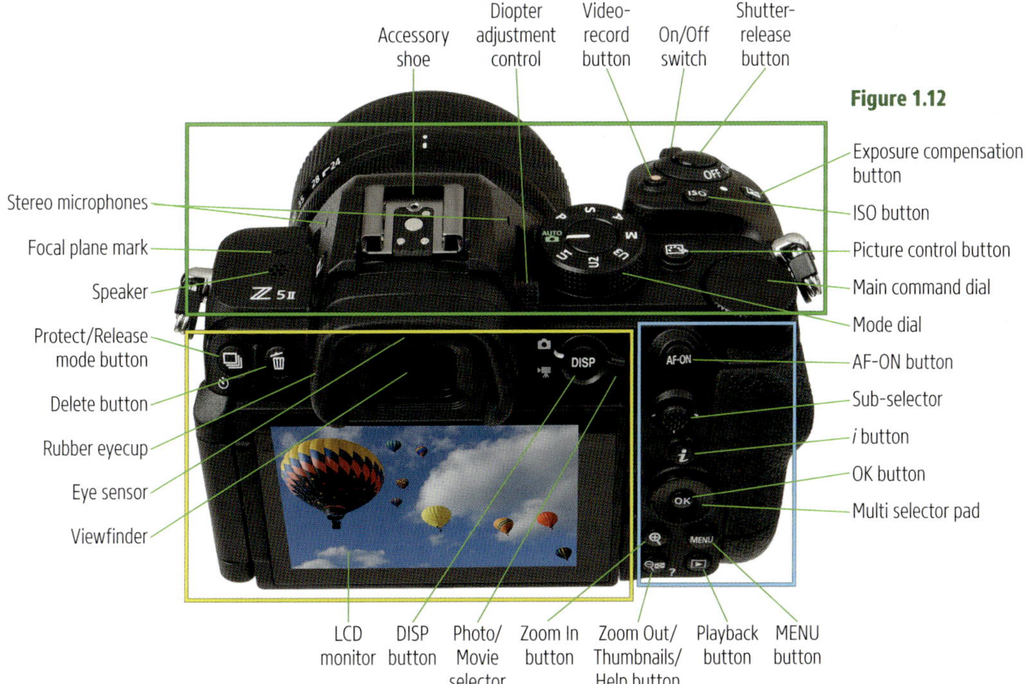

Figure 1.12

- **Shutter-release button.** Partially depress this button to activate the exposure meter (and the main and sub-command dials that adjust metering settings), and focus (unless you've redefined the focus activation button, as outlined in Chapter 7). Press all the way to take the picture. Tapping the shutter release when the camera has turned off the autoexposure and autofocus mechanisms reactivates both. When a review image is displayed on the back-panel color monitor, tapping this button removes the image from the display and reactivates the autoexposure and autofocus mechanisms.

- **ISO button.** Hold this button and rotate the main command dial until the ISO value you want is shown in the viewfinder, and on the monitor. The sub-command dial turns Auto ISO on or off.

- **Exposure compensation button.** Hold down this button and spin the main command dial to add or subtract exposure when using Program, Aperture-priority, or Shutter-priority modes. (In Manual mode, the exposure remains the same, but the "ideal" exposure shown in the electronic analog display is modified to reflect the extra/reduced exposure you're calling for.) The exposure compensation amount is shown in the viewfinder and rear display as plus or minus values.

  Values from –5 EV to +5 EV are available in Photo mode, with –3 EV to +3 EV available in Video Recording mode. You can adjust the increment from the default 1/3 stop to 1/2 or 1.0 stops using Custom Setting b2.

- **Video record button.** When the Photo/Video selector is in the Video position, you can press this button to begin video capture; press a second time to stop. This button has no default function in Photo mode, but you can assign a behavior using Custom Setting f2, as described in Chapter 7.

- **Mode dial.** Spin this dial to choose from five exposure modes (Auto, Programmed auto, Shutter-priority, Aperture-priority, and Manual exposure) or any of three user-definable groups of settings, labeled U1, U2, and U3. The Auto mode is for simple point-and-shoot photography with the camera making all the decisions. I'll explain all these in the Operations Quick Start section that follows.

- **Picture Control button.** This button provides a quick way to change the look of your still photos or videos using the Z5 II's Picture Control feature. This is probably a nod to content creators/vloggers who want to add special looks to their work on the fly. Press the button once (no need to hold it down) and use the left/right directional controls to highlight a particular Picture Control. The effect will appear on the display as you scroll. Press the down button to bring the complete Picture Control adjustment screen, described in Chapter 5.

- **Main command dial.** In the Setup Guide, I described how the main command dial works in tandem with the sub-command dial on the front of the camera to change settings and will not repeat that information here.

Back Panel

The main controls on the right side of the back panel of the camera are highlighted with a blue box in Figure 1.12. They include the AF-ON button, sub-selector, *i* button, multi selector pad, OK button, MENU button, and Zoom In, Zoom Out/Thumbnails/Help, and Playback buttons. I provided an overview of their functions in the Setup Guide at the beginning of this chapter and won't repeat that information here. Highlighted inside the yellow box in Figure 1.12 are the elements you interact with most, clustered around that large, bright 3.2-inch swiveling LCD monitor.

Your key components are as follows:

- **Protect/Release mode button.** In shooting mode, you can press and hold the Release mode button down while rotating the main command dial to choose from the available single-shot and continuous shooting modes. I'll describe each of them in the "Choosing a Release Mode" section later in this chapter. In Playback mode, press this button to protect the current image from accidental deletion. Images will still be removed when the memory card is formatted, however.

- **Delete button.** Press to erase the image shown on the LCD monitor. A display will pop up on the LCD monitor asking you to press the Delete button once more to delete the photo or press the Playback button to cancel.

- **Photo/Movie selector.** Switches the camera from Still Photo Shooting mode to Movie mode.

- **Viewfinder/Rubber eyecup.** You can frame your composition by peering into the 3690K-pixel (Quad VGA) OLED electronic viewfinder, which shows 100 percent of your image frame at 0.8X magnification. It's surrounded by a soft, removable rubber frame that seals out extraneous light when pressing your eye tightly up to the viewfinder, and it also protects your eyeglass lenses (if worn) from scratching. Your eye can be up to 21mm away from the viewfinder window (the "eyepoint") and still view the entire focus screen area.

- **Eye sensor.** Detects when your eye (or anything else) approaches the viewfinder window (anything closer than about two inches in my tests).

- **DISP button.** Shows or hides informational displays in the LCD monitor or viewfinder. Press to cycle among the available displays in Photo, Video, and Playback modes.

- **LCD monitor.** The 3.2-inch LCD monitor has a 2100K-dot TFT touch-sensitive screen with a 170-degree viewing angle that allows you to see the screen clearly even from the side or slightly above. It provides a 100 percent view of what the sensor sees.

  It swings out and tilts so you can position the camera down low (say, for macro shots of flowers), up high for a periscope view in both landscape and portrait orientations, and reverses to face your subject in selfie mode. (See Figure 1.13.) In the latter configuration, the camera displays a reversed image (like a mirror) and icons that allow you to tap to adjust exposure compensation or activate a self-timer or video delay mode. An icon representing Product Review mode appears when shooting video. Again, another feature content creators/vloggers will appreciate.

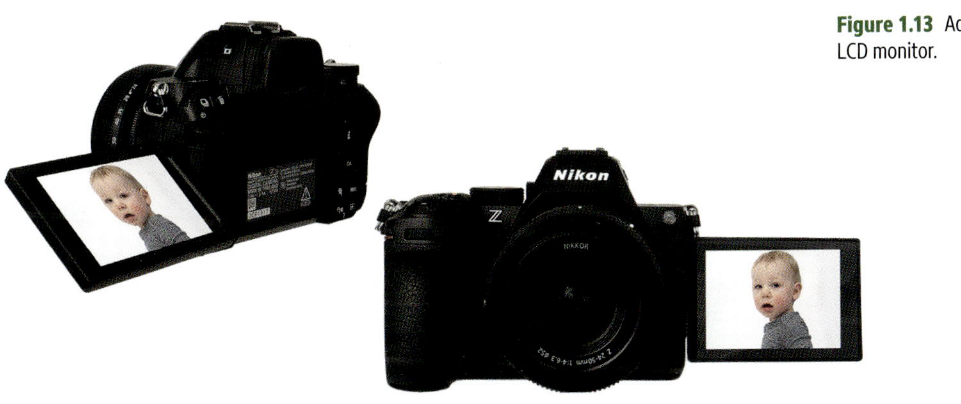

Figure 1.13 Adjustable LCD monitor.

Underneath Your Camera

There's not a lot going on with the bottom panel of your camera. Your most frequently accessed component will be the battery chamber door, which can be opened by sliding its latch. The door can be removed when attaching the optional MB-N14 Power Battery Pack, which holds two EN-EL15c batteries and provides more juice to run your camera to take more exposures with a single charge along with a complete set of vertical controls. The tripod socket accepts other accessories, such as quick-release plates that allow rapid attaching and detaching the camera from a matching platform affixed to your tripod and video cages. (See Figure 1.14.)

Figure 1.14

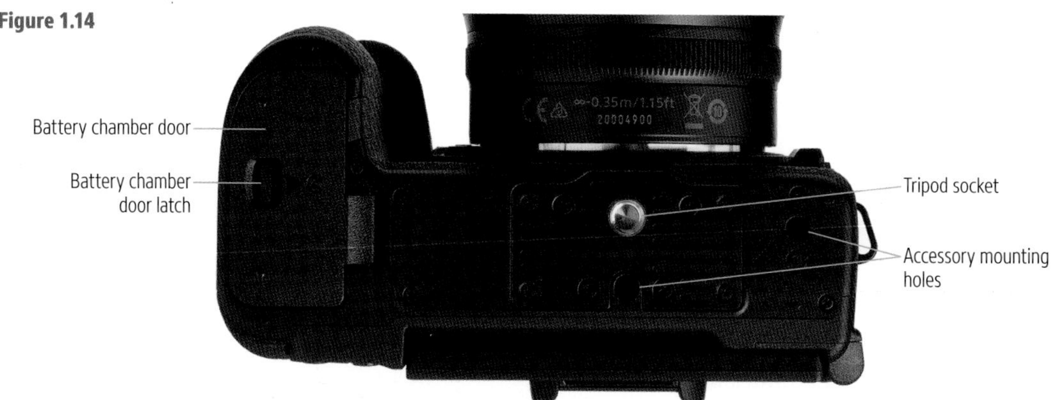

Attaching the MB-N14 Power Battery Pack

The Nikon MB-N14 Power Battery Pack is an optional vertical grip/battery pack accessory. It holds two EN-EL15c batteries (replacing the single battery normally housed in the camera's grip). It contains a duplicate set of controls for vertical shooting, including a Fn button, shutter-release button, multi selector, AF-ON button, main command dial, and sub-command dial. (See Figure 1.15.)

Although the attractions of the mirrorless cameras are their relatively smaller size and lighter weight, many photographers prefer the ergonomics of a vertical grip, particularly when the camera is rotated

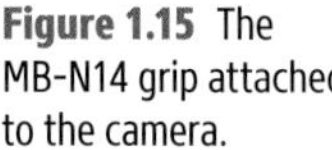

Figure 1.15 The MB-N14 grip attached to the camera.

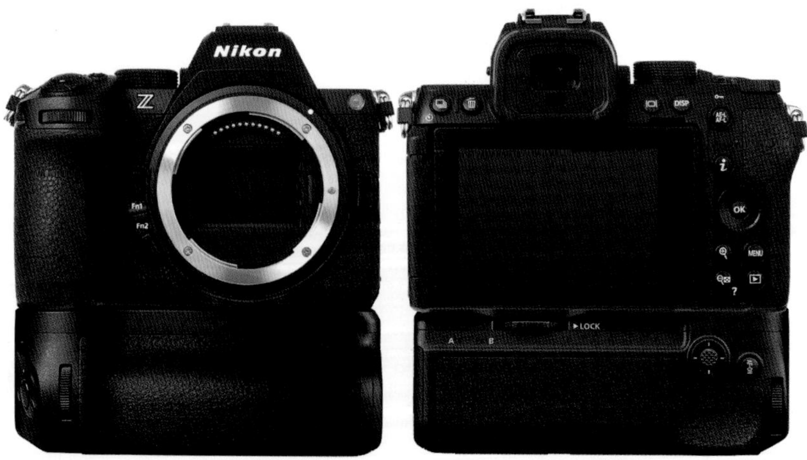

90 degrees to shoot in portrait orientation. The MB-N14 is a distinct improvement over some earlier Nikon grips, because it offers that full set of controls, the ability to recharge its batteries while still attached to the camera, and convenient hot-swapping of one of the batteries while the camera is still powered up. The latter two features are great for time-lapse and interval shooting. To attach the MB-N14 grip, just follow these steps:

1. **Turn off the camera.** Then, remove the camera's battery.

2. **Remove the camera's battery chamber door.** Open the door and tilt it at approximately a 60-degree angle. That will align the two hinge pins with slots, so you can gently slide the door off. The inner chamber with contacts for both battery and control signals can be seen at the bottom of the compartment in Figure 1.16.

3. **Remove contact cap from the grip.** This protects the contacts from damage while the grip is not attached.

4. **Store battery chamber cover.** There is a handy recess in the MB-N14 grip to store the battery door when it's detached from the camera.

5. **Disable controls.** A lock switch is concentric with the grip's shutter-release button. Rotate it to the L position to avoid activating the camera before you are ready to take a picture.

6. **Lower the camera onto the grip.** The extension goes in the battery compartment, and the tripod screw on the attachment wheel mates with the camera's tripod socket.

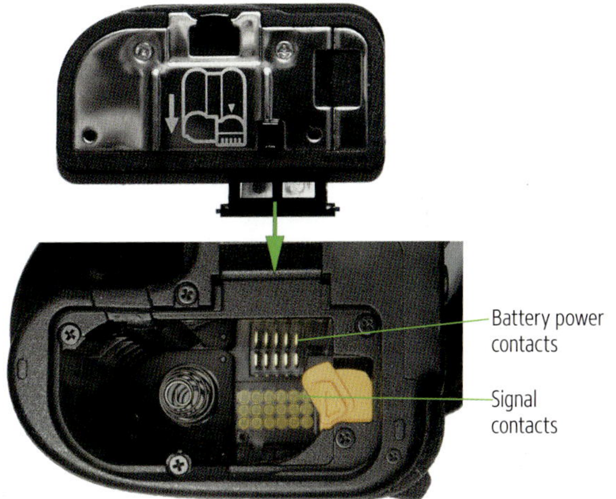

Figure 1.16 Detach the battery compartment door.

7. **Secure the grip to the camera.** Rotate the attachment wheel to the right until the grip is firmly attached. The MB-N14 has its own tripod socket on the bottom so you can still mount the camera/grip on a tripod.

8. **Open battery holder-chamber cover.** Slide the latch on the end of the grip toward the back of the camera and open the door. Inside, you'll find a slide-out battery holder.

9. **Insert one or two batteries in the holder.** If you are using only one battery, it can be placed in either position. If you are using two batteries, the one in the outermost chamber A will be used first; when it is exhausted, the camera will switch to the battery in the innermost chamber B. You can replace the chamber A battery at any time, even while using the camera continuously.

10. **Recharge batteries in the grip (optional).** The batteries in the grip can be recharged without removing them. You'll find a USB Power Delivery connector under a cover on the end of the grip opposite the controls. The batteries will charge while the camera is turned off, or, the camera is on and the standby timer has elapsed. There are two charge lamps on the back panel marked A and B. They illuminate to indicate which battery is being charged and will turn off when charging is complete.

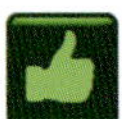

NOTE When using the MB-N14 grip, the status of the battery in use is shown on the shooting display and control panel. The shooting display also shows an icon indicating which battery (A or B) is in use. The Battery Info entry in the Setup menu provides information on battery age and battery level.

Lens Components

Not all Nikon lenses include all of the features shown in Figure 1.17, but the Nikkor Z 100-400mm f/4.5-5.6 VR S lens shown provides a good example. Components shown in the figure include:

- **Lens hood mounting mark.** Lenses use this to mount the lens hood, lining up a matching mark on the hood with this *lens hood alignment indicator,* a dot on the edge showing how to align the lens hood with the bayonet mount.

- **Filter thread (not shown).** Most lenses have a thread on the front for attaching filters and other add-ons. Some F-mount lenses, such as the AF-S Nikkor 14-24mm f/2.8G ED lens, have no front filter thread, either because their front elements are too curved to allow mounting a filter and/or because the front element is so large that huge filters would be prohibitively expensive. Some of these front-filter-hostile lenses allow using smaller filters that drop into a slot at the back of the lens.

- **Focus ring.** This is the ring you turn when you manually focus the lens, or fine-tune autofocus adjustment. The amount of focus change per degree of rotation can be fine-tuned using Custom Setting f10, as explained in Chapter 7. The location of the focus ring may vary, depending on the lens.

- **Control ring.** This ring can be assigned the Focus function if you find its position more convenient. By default, it is used to open and close the aperture in Aperture-priority and Manual exposure modes, but a variety of other behaviors are available using Custom Setting f2. The responsiveness of the control ring can be adjusted using Custom Setting f11.

- **Zoom ring/Zoom scale.** Turn this ring to change the zoom setting, using the zoom scale as reference.

- **Lens function ring.** If present, this ring, by default, recalls the last focus position. Custom Setting f2 allows you to define some other behavior, such as Save Focus Position, Switch Eyes, or Aperture control. Separate definitions can be assigned for clockwise and counterclockwise rotation.

- **Lens function buttons.** Depending on the lens, you may find one or more buttons labeled L-Fn or L-Fn2, which can be assigned specific behaviors. For example, the Nikkor 24-120 f/4 S has just one L-Fn button, while the 100-400mm f/4.5-5.6 VR S has one L-Fn and four L-Fn2 buttons. Separate functions are available for the L-Fn and L-Fn2 buttons. By default, the L-Fn button serves as an AE/AL lock, and the L-Fn2 as an AF-ON button.

- **Lens information panel/Display button.** The OLED (organic light emitting diode) display (if present) illuminates to provide information when mounted and the camera is powered up. Pressing the DISP button cycles among three different info screens:
  - Focus distance, Minimum focus index, Depth-of-field
  - Current focal length
  - Current aperture

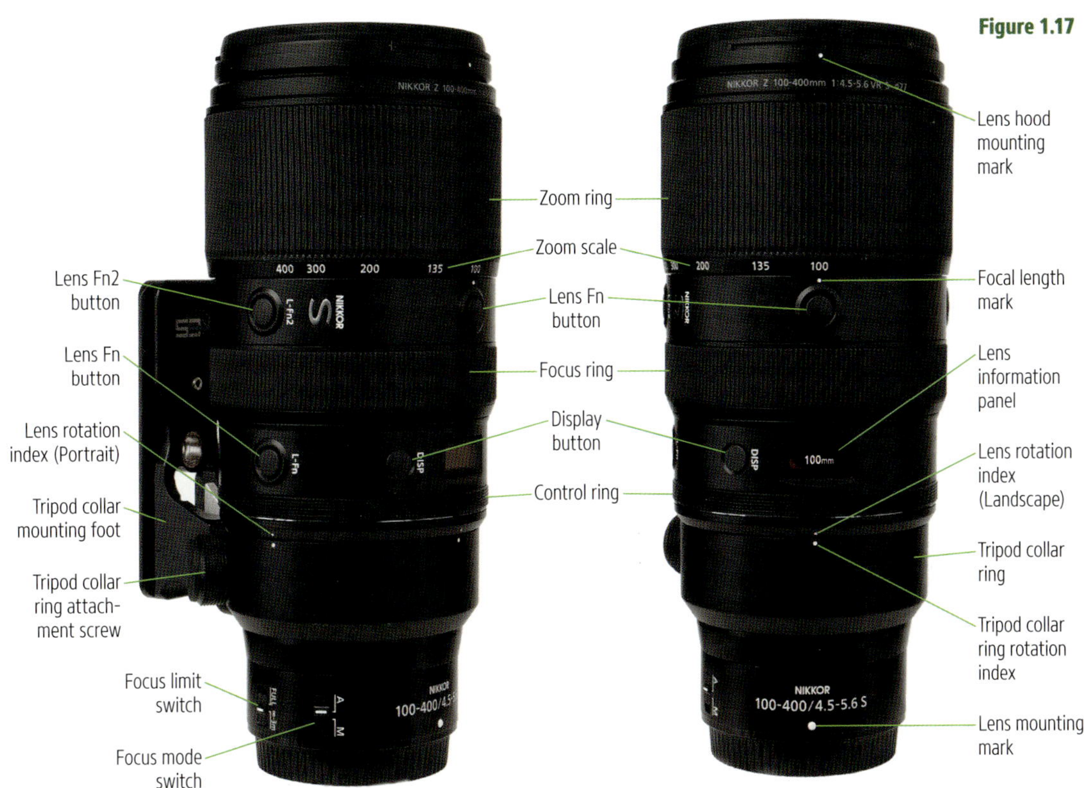

- **Tripod collar ring/rotation index/attachment screw.** The tripod collar is a thick rotating ring near the base of the lens, locked at any position with an attachment screw that can be backed all the way out if you want to remove the tripod collar and mounting foot entirely. Lens rotation indexes are guides that mark 90-degree positions for landscape and portrait mode camera orientations. A security slot for attaching an anti-theft cable can be found inside the attachment screw of some lenses.

- **Tripod collar mounting foot.** This foot is used to attach the lens to a tripod or other support, providing a safer mount with better weight distribution than using the tripod socket on the bottom of the camera. Nikon doesn't like to pay royalties for the right to include the industry-standard Arca-Swiss compatible quick-release foot, so the first thing I do when I get a Nikon lens that includes a tripod collar is purchase the Kirk Photo replacement foot, shown in the figure. (Really Right Stuff also makes an excellent replacement.)

- **Focus mode switch.** Allows you to change from automatic focus to manual focus. Note that if you've set manual focus using the camera's controls, the Autofocus setting of this switch will be ignored.

- **Focus limit switch.** Choose Full to allow focusing on subjects from infinity to the lens' closest focus distance. The "Distance" setting (which varies from lens to lens) limits focus from infinity down to a specific distance. For example, that value is 9.85 feet (3 meters) with the 100-400mm f/4.5-5.6 VR S and 16 feet (5 meters) with the Nikkor 70-200mm f/2.8 VR S lens.

- **Electronic contacts (not shown).** These metal contacts pass information to matching contacts located in the camera body, allowing a firm electrical connection so that exposure, distance, and other information can be exchanged between the camera and lens.
- **Rubber lens-mount gasket (not shown).** This seal *helps* (emphasis mine) prevent water or dust from entering the camera when the lens is mounted. It does not make a lens completely water-resistant.

Part III: Operations Quick Start

When faced with a manual packed with in-depth discussions of how to use every feature and option, you may not know where to start. Don't panic. The next few sections provide a quick-start overview on how to make the most important settings with your camera. There will be plenty of time to master everything the Z5 II is capable of. Meanwhile, you can quickly learn how to set your camera's release mode, exposure mode, focus mode, autofocus-area mode, and other basic settings. I'll cover just the most important aspects here, with references to the other parts of the book that explain these essential features in depth.

Choosing a Release Mode

The release mode determines when and how often a picture is taken in single shots, continuously, or after a self-timer has elapsed. If you're a late-comer moving to the interchangeable-lens photography world from a point-and-shoot model, you might have used one that labels these options as drive modes, a term that dates back to the film era when cameras could be set for single-shot or "motor drive" (continuous) shooting modes. There are seven release modes, which I'll describe shortly.

Hold the Release mode button down and rotate the main command dial to select any of the main release modes. Some have options, which you can access by rotating the sub-command dial.

- **Single shot.** In single-shot mode, one picture is taken each time you press the shutter-release button down all the way. If you press the shutter and nothing happens (which is very frustrating!), you may be using a focus mode that requires sharp focus to be achieved before a picture can be taken. This is called focus-priority and is discussed in more detail under "Choosing a Focus Mode," later in this chapter.
- **Continuous L (Low).** Captures a series of images as long as the shutter release is held down. When this option is highlighted, you can also rotate the sub-command dial to specify a frame rate from 1 to 7 frames per second. The chosen frame rate is shown in an additional line on the display as you make your selection. I use Continuous L when slicing a scene into tiny fragments of time isn't necessary or desirable (say, I'm bracketing in multi-shot bursts, or don't want a zillion versions of a scene that really isn't changing that fast).

  My recommendation: I find Continuous low-speed, set to 2 fps, to be particularly useful for street photography and photojournalism applications. Because the speed is so slow, you can use it like single frame most of the time and capture a single image by pressing the shutter-release button once and then lifting your finger. But if you find a subject that merits a more rapid-fire approach, you can keep the shutter-release button pressed down, and fire off several shots sequentially. That's faster than switching from single to continuous mode, and you can avoid the intrusive, distracting "machine-gun" approach.

- **Continuous H (High).** The Z5 II captures images at roughly 9.4 frames per second (or up to 10 frames per second in silent mode). Maximum frame rates are achieved in AF-C focus mode, in Manual exposure mode, and shutter speeds of 1/250th second or faster. Speeds may slow in silent mode, when using flash or Photo Flicker Reduction, at slower shutter speeds, and with very small f/stops (typically f/16 or smaller).

- **Continuous H (extended).** A series of images are taken at up to 14 fps (or 15 fps in silent mode).

- **C15/C30.** With these high-speed frame capture modes, you can choose even faster frame rates of 15 or 30 fps to grab pictures with JPEG/HEIF Normal image quality and Large size. As you might expect, this ultra-high-speed mode has some limitations, which you can read about in Chapter 5.

  These modes are used with your Z5 II's "time travel" capabilities, when you want to store images buffered in memory *before* you actually press the shutter release down all the way. You'll need to activate Custom Setting d3: Pre-Release Capture options, described in Chapter 7, and then select the C15 or C30 release modes.

- **Self-timer.** If you want to set a short delay before your picture is taken, you can use the self-timer. When setting the self-timer, you can rotate the sub-command dial and choose delays of 2s, 5s, 10s, or 20s. You can also choose these parameters in the Self-timer entry, Custom Setting c2 (as described in Chapter 7), as well as the number of shots taken after the delay and the interval between each of those shots.

  Once the self-timer has been selected as the release mode, press the shutter-release button to lock focus and start the timer. In AF-S autofocus mode, if the camera is unable to focus, the timer may not begin. The green self-timer lamp on the front of the camera will blink and the beeper will sound (unless you've silenced it in the menus) until the final two seconds, when the lamp remains on. If you've turned Beep on in the Camera Sounds entry of the Setup menu, an annoying chirp will let you know the timer is active and will increase in speed during the last two seconds.

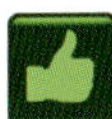

TIP If you plan to join the scene when working with the self-timer, consider using manual focus so the camera won't refocus on your fleeing form and produce unintended results. (Nikon really needs to offer an option to autofocus at the *end* of the self-timer cycle.) An alternative is to use an optional wireless remote, including the ML-L7.

Nikon's SnapBridge app also allows you to control your camera remotely from a smart device app running on your iOS or Android phone.

SHOOTING MOVIES

But if you want to get started shooting movies right away, it's easy. Just rotate the Photo/Movie selector switch (located on the back of the camera to the immediate right of the viewfinder window) to the Movie position and press the button with the red dot on the top-right panel, southwest of the shutter-release button. Press the button again to stop shooting. That's it!

Selecting an Exposure Mode

Available exposure modes include four manual and semi-automatic modes, including Programmed auto (or Program mode), Shutter-priority auto, Aperture-priority auto, and Manual exposure mode. These modes allow you to specify how the exposure settings are selected, for greater creative control. Just rotate the mode dial on the top-right shoulder of the Z5 II to select what Nikon likes to call "shooting" mode. A fully automatic mode is also available, and three User settings, marked U1, U2, and U3, which allow you to retrieve previously stored groups of settings. You'll be using these semi-automatic/manual modes most often:

- **P (Programmed auto).** This mode allows the camera to select the basic exposure settings, but you can still override those choices to fine-tune your image, while maintaining metered exposure, as I'll explain in Chapter 2.

- **S (Shutter-priority).** This mode is useful when you want to use a particular shutter speed to stop action or produce creative blur effects. Choose your preferred shutter speed by rotating the main command dial when the meter is active, and the camera will select the appropriate f/stop for you. Shutter speeds of up to 1/8000th second are available.

- **A (Aperture-priority).** Choose when you want to use a particular lens opening, especially to control sharpness or how much of your image is in focus. Specify the f/stop you want using the sub-command dial when the meter is "awake" (tap the shutter-release button to activate the meter, if necessary), and the camera will select the appropriate shutter speed for you.

- **M (Manual).** Select when you want full control over the shutter speed and lens opening, either for creative effects or because you are using a studio flash or other flash unit not compatible with the automatic metering when using an attached electronic flash. Use the main command dial and sub-command dial when the exposure meter is active to specify the shutter speed and f/stop (respectively).

As I noted, in addition to the PSAM modes described above, your camera has one automatic mode: Auto (represented by a green camera icon on the mode dial). In Auto mode, the camera chooses shutter speed, aperture, white balance, and other settings, which will be grayed out and unavailable in the menus. The three user settings (U1, U2, and U3) can store frequently used parameters for quick recall with the Save User Settings entry in the Setup menu, as explained in Chapter 9. These include many Photo Shooting and Video Recording menu options, Custom Settings, PSAM shooting modes, shutter speed, aperture, and exposure compensation.

Choosing a Metering Mode

The metering mode determines how exposure is calculated. You might want to select a particular metering mode for your first shots, although the default Matrix metering is probably the best choice as you get to know your camera. I'll explain when and how to use each of the four metering modes later.

Select your Metering mode from the Metering entry of the Photo Shooting and Video Recording menus:

- **Matrix metering.** The standard metering mode; the camera attempts to intelligently classify your image and choose the best exposure based on readings from the sensor.
- **Center-weighted metering.** The camera meters the entire scene but gives 75 percent of the emphasis to the central area of the frame. You can change the size of the area. The default Standard setting measures about 12mm; you can choose Small to switch to a smaller 8mm area. Or, select full-frame averaging instead. (Access Custom Setting b5, as I'll describe in Chapter 7.) You can specify whether the metered area is shown or hidden on the LCD monitor or in the viewfinder using Custom Settings d19 and d20.
- **Spot metering.** Exposure is calculated from a smaller 4mm central spot, about 1.5 percent of the image area, centered on the current focus point, except when Auto-area AF is chosen for the AF-area mode (described shortly); the center focus point will be used instead.
- **Highlight-weighted metering.** Despite its icon (a "spot" accompanied by an asterisk), this is not a spot metering variation. Highlight-weighted metering uses a matrix measuring system to emphasize the highlights of an image, retaining detail in the brightest areas.

Choosing a Focus Mode

You can easily switch between automatic and manual focus by moving the A/M, AF/MF, or M-AF/MF switch on your lens (if present). You can select the autofocus mode (*when* the camera measures and locks in focus) and autofocus pattern (*which* of the available autofocus points are used to interpret correct focus). Use the *i* menu to specify focus mode. I explained how to access the *i* menu earlier in this chapter. You can select from the following modes:

- **(AF-C) Continuous-servo autofocus.** This mode, sometimes called *continuous autofocus*, sets focus when you partially depress the shutter button (or other autofocus activation button), but continues to monitor the frame and refocuses if you or your subject has moved. This is a useful mode for photographing sports and moving subjects. Focus- or release-priority can be specified for AF-C mode using Custom Setting a1.
- **(AF-S) Single-servo autofocus.** This mode, sometimes called *single autofocus*, locks in a focus point when the shutter button is pressed down halfway (there are other autofocus activation button options, described in Chapter 3). The focus will remain locked until you release the button or take the picture. This mode is best when your subject is relatively motionless. As you'll learn in Chapter 7, you can use Custom Setting a2 to specify that a picture will not be taken unless sharp focus is achieved (*focus-priority*), so that it will go ahead and snap a photo while still adjusting focus (*release-priority*).
- **(AF-A) AF mode auto-switch.** Available only when the photo/video selector switch is set to the photo position, this mode uses AF-S for stationary subjects, and changes to AF-C mode if your subject is moving or begins moving.

- **Manual focus.** In this mode, you select the focus plane by rotating the focus ring on the lens.
- **(AF-F) Full-time AF.** This additional mode is available only when the photo/video selector switch is set to the video position. The camera adjusts focus continually (no need to press the shutter release), displaying the current focus point in red. When you press the shutter release down half-way, focus will lock and the focus point will turn green.

Choosing the Autofocus Area Mode

The Z5 II uses up to 299 different focus points to calculate correct focus. Nikon allows you to choose which points to use with its Autofocus-area mode options. One or more points are selected automatically by the camera or chosen by you. I'll show you exactly where these focus areas are located and tell you how to use them in Chapter 4. Use the *i* menu to specify AF-area mode:

- **Pinpoint AF (AF-S only).** The camera uses a small point to calculate focus. Use this for precise focus on a specific area. This mode is not available when shooting movies.
- **Single-point (AF-S or AF-C).** The camera focuses on a point you select, using the multi selector directional buttons. This mode is good for non-moving subjects.
- **Dynamic-area (Small/Medium/Large) (AF-C only).** You select the focus point, but if the subject moves from the selected area, it will use information from the surrounding points. It's often the best AF-area mode for moving subjects.
- **Wide-area AF (Small).** Calculates focus from a larger area than Single-point AF and is best for stationary subjects that occupy more space in the frame.
- **Wide-area AF (Large).** Calculates focus from an even larger zone and can achieve accurate focus on subjects that may be located in a wider area of the frame.
- **Wide-area AF (C1/C2).** You can choose the height and width of the area using the up/down and left/ right directional buttons, with 77 different combinations available in Still Photography mode, and 66 available for video. I'll show you these in Chapter 3.
- **3D-tracking (AF-C only).** The camera follows a subject you specify by moving the focus point to the subject and pressing the shutter-release button halfway to start tracking.
- **Subject-tracking AF (Video only).** The camera follows a subject you specify by moving the focus point to the subject and pressing the shutter-release button halfway to start tracking.
- **Auto-area AF (AF-S or AF-C).** The camera chooses a focus point without input from you, rapidly detecting likely subject matter, especially humans. If a portrait subject is detected, faces will be indicated by a yellow border.

Adjusting White Balance and ISO

If you like, you can custom-tailor your white balance (color balance) and ISO sensitivity settings. To start out, it's best to set white balance (WB) to Auto$_0$, and ISO to ISO 200 for daylight photos, and to ISO 400 for pictures in dimmer light. (Don't be afraid of ISO 1600 or even higher, however; the camera does a *much* better job of producing low-noise photos at higher ISOs than earlier generations.)

You can set either now:

- **White balance.** Hold down the Fn1 (White Balance) button, located on the front of the camera. Then rotate the main command dial to specify your choice. Additional options are available for some settings with the sub-command dial. I'll explain those in detail later in this chapter.

  - **Auto variations.** When WB A_0, A_1, or A_2 appear, with the WB button still held down, rotate the sub-command dial to select (or retain) A_0 (Keep White/Reduce Warm Colors), which is the default auto white balance setting. The other two partially or fully preserve the warm color cast produced by incandescent lighting, as I'll explain in Chapter 5.
  - **Natural Light Auto.**
  - **Direct Sunlight.**
  - **Cloudy.**
  - **Shade.**
  - **Incandescent.**
  - **Fluorescent (Cool-white, Day white, and Daylight varieties).**
  - **Flash.**
  - **K Choose color temperature.**
  - **Preset manual.**

- **ISO.** To set ISO, press the ISO button on the top-right shoulder just aft of the On/Off switch, and rotate the main command dial until the ISO value you want is displayed in the viewfinder and monitor. Rotate the sub-command dial to turn Auto ISO on or off.

Reviewing the Images You've Taken

Your camera has a broad range of playback and image review options, including the ability to have all the images in a burst "stacked" so you can review only the first shot in a series rather than pore through them all one by one. I'll cover these in more detail in Chapter 8. For now, you'll want to learn just the basics. Here is all you really need to know at this time:

- **Press the Playback button to review images.** Press the Playback button (marked with a white right-pointing triangle) at the bottom-right corner of the back of the camera to display the most recent image on the LCD monitor. Press the Playback button again or just tap the shutter-release button to exit playback view.

- **Previous/Next image.** Press the multi selector left or right to review additional images. Press right to advance to the next image or left to go back to a previous image. You can also use the main command dial.

- **Change amount/type of information.** Press the multi selector button up or down or the DISP button to change among overlays of basic image information or detailed shooting information.

- **Zoom In/Zoom Out.** Press the Zoom In button repeatedly to zoom in on the image displayed; the Zoom Out button reduces the image. A thumbnail representation of the whole image appears in the lower-right corner with a yellow rectangle showing the relative level of zoom. At intermediate zoom positions, the yellow rectangle can be moved around within the frame using the multi selector.

- **Press to delete current image.** Some mistakes should never see the light of day. Press the Trash button to erase the currently displayed image. A Delete? message will appear. Press Trash again to confirm, or the Playback button to cancel.

- **Protect an image.** Press the Release mode button to protect the current image from accidental deletion. Images will still be removed when the memory card is formatted, however.
- **Access Playback *i* menu.** This summons a quick-access menu that lets you apply a rating to an image, choose pictures to upload to a smart device, sort through images by attributes, define those attributes, record and attach voice memos to an image, or retouch pictures. I'll address all of these in detail in Chapter 8.

Playing Back Images

Reviewing images is a joy, whether you use the big 3.2-inch color LCD monitor or the viewfinder (which is especially handy for viewing images in bright light under which the monitor may tend to wash out).

Here are the basics involved in reviewing images on the camera's displays (or on a monitor or screen you have connected with a cable). You'll find more details about some of these functions in the chapters that I point you to. This section just lists the must-know information.

- **Start review.** To begin review, press the Playback button at the lower-right corner of the back of the camera. The most recently viewed image will appear on the display.
- **Playback folder.** If you have more than one folder on your memory card, you can change which folder is used for playback by starting playback with the Playback button and then pressing the *i* button and selecting Choose Slot and Folder. Press the right directional button, select the slot (any slots containing an empty memory card will be grayed out), and then press the right directional button again to choose from a list of available folders. Press the right directional button again to activate that slot/folder.

  You can also select the active folder using the Playback Folder option (choose NZ5_2, All, or Current) in the Playback menu. You can create and activate a *new* folder (or change the default name to something else) using the Storage Folder entry in the Photo Shooting menu. See Chapter 5 for more information on both options.
- **View thumbnail images.** To change the view from a single image to 4, 9, or 72 thumbnails, follow the instructions in the "Viewing Thumbnails" section that follows.
- **Zoom in and out.** To zoom in or out, press the Zoom In or Zoom Out buttons, following the instructions in the "Zooming the Playback Display" section, next. (It also shows you how to move the zoomed area around using the multi selector pad.)
- **Move back and forth.** To advance to the next image, press the right edge of the multi selector pad; to go back to a previous shot, press the left edge. When you reach the beginning/end of the photos in your folder, the display "wraps around" to the end/beginning of the available shots. **Note:** You can assign a special behavior to the sub-command dial such that rotating it skips ahead either 10 or 50 images, or advance by other parameters, such as rating. See the discussion of Custom Setting f3 (Customize Controls Playback > Sub-dial Frame Advance) in Chapter 7 for more information.
- **See different types of data.** To change the type of information about the displayed image that is shown, press the up and down portions of the multi selector pad.

- **Remove images.** To delete an image that's currently on display, press the Trash button once, then press it again to confirm the deletion. To select and delete a group of images, use the Delete option in the Playback menu to specify particular photos to remove, as described in more detail in Chapter 8.
- **Cancel playback.** To cancel image review, press the Playback button again, or simply tap the shutter-release button.

Zooming the Playback Display

The Playback display zooms in and out of preview images using the procedure that follows:

1. **Zoom in.** When an image is displayed (use the Playback button to start), press the Zoom In button to fill the screen with a slightly magnified version of the image. When viewing on the monitor, you can also press the multi selector center button, tap the touch screen twice, or touch two fingers to the LCD monitor and spread them apart to enlarge the image.

2. **Continue zooming.** A navigation window appears in the lower-right corner of the LCD monitor showing the entire image. Keep pressing to continue zooming in to the maximum of 32X enlargement (with a full-resolution large image in FX format). (Medium and Small images can be enlarged up to 24X and 16X, respectively.)

3. **Zoomed area indicated.** A yellow box in the navigation window shows the zoomed area within the full image. (See Figure 1.18.) The entire navigation window vanishes from the screen after a few seconds, leaving you with a full-screen view of the zoomed portion of the image.

4. **Move zoomed area around.** Use the multi selector buttons to move the zoomed area around within the image. The navigation window will reappear for reference when zooming or scrolling around within the display. You can also slide one finger around the touch screen to move the zoomed area.

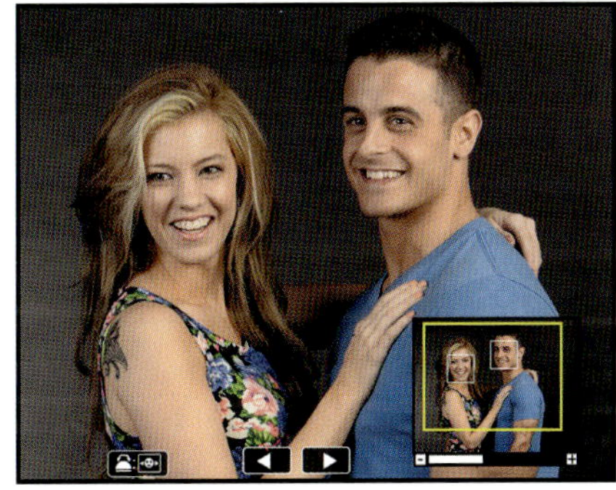

Figure 1.18 Playback zoom.

5. **Find faces.** To detect faces, rotate the sub-command dial while an image is zoomed. Up to 35 faces will be detected by the camera, indicated by white borders in the navigation window. Rotate the sub-command dial or tap the on-screen guide (seen at the lower-left bottom edge in the figure) to move highlighting to the individual faces.

6. **Review same area on another image.** Use the main command dial or tap the left/right triangles at the bottom of the touch screen to move to the same zoomed area of the next/previous image. This allows you to compare a detail in a series of similar shots. I often use the capability to see if a spot in an image is a dust spot (it shows up in the same place in other images) or just an artifact found in a single image.

7. **Zoom out.** Use the Zoom Out button to zoom back out of the image.

8. **Exit.** To exit zoom in/zoom out display, keep pressing the Zoom Out button until the full screen/full image/information display appears again. Or, just tap the shutter-release button halfway or press the Playback button to exit playback entirely.

Viewing Thumbnails

The camera provides other options for reviewing images in addition to zooming in and out. You can switch between single image view and 4, 9, or 72 reduced-size thumbnail images on a single display.

Pages of thumbnail images offer a quick way to scroll through a large number of pictures quickly to find the one you want to examine in more detail. The camera lets you switch quickly with a scroll bar displayed at the right side of the screen to show you the relative position of the displayed thumbnails within the full collection of images in the active folder on your memory card. Use the Zoom In and Zoom Out/Thumbnail buttons or the pinch and spread gestures with two fingers on the touch screen to increase or decrease the number of thumbnail indexes shown.

Here's how to work with thumbnail images:

- **Add thumbnails.** To increase the number of thumbnails on the screen, press the Zoom Out button or pinch the touch screen. The camera will switch from single image to 4 thumbnails to 9 thumbnails to 72 thumbnails. (The display doesn't cycle back to single image again.)
- **Reduce number of thumbnails.** To decrease the number of thumbnails on the screen, press the Zoom In button or use the spread gesture on the touch screen to change from 72 to 9 thumbnails to 4 thumbnails, or from 4 to single-image display. Continuing once you've returned to single-image display starts the zoom process described in the previous section.
- **Change folder.** When viewing images, press the *i* button to produce the dialog box (shown earlier in Figure 1.3) that includes an option to choose the folder of the memory card that contains the images you want to view.
- **Switch between thumbnails and full image.** When viewing thumbnails, you can quickly switch between thumbnail view and full-image display by pressing the OK button in the center of the multi selector, or by double tapping the thumbnail image on the touch screen.
- **Retouch an image/thumbnail.** When an image or thumbnail is viewed, press the *i* button to access the options screen that includes a Retouch option for that image (described in Chapter 9).
- **Change highlighted thumbnail area.** Use the multi selector to move the yellow highlight box around among the thumbnails, or, preferably, use the monitor and a single finger on the touch screen to scroll back and forth or to select a particular thumbnail. Note that *touching* a thumbnail moves the highlighting to that thumbnail, while *tapping* the highlighted thumbnail produces a full-screen view of the image.
- **Protect and delete images.** When viewing thumbnails or a single-page image, press the *i* button and choose Protect to preserve the highlighted image against accidental deletion (a key icon is overlaid over the thumbnail image; return to the *i* menu to remove protection).
- **Exit image review.** Tap the shutter-release button or press the Playback button to exit image review. You don't have to worry about missing a shot because you were reviewing images; a half-press of the shutter-release button automatically brings back the camera's exposure meters, the autofocus system, and, unless you've redefined your controls or are using manual focus, cancels image review.

Nailing the Right Exposure | 2

The Nikon Z5 II has an exceptional amount of intelligence when it comes to calculating the correct exposure for a wide variety of scenes. Even so, you are smarter—and more creative. The more you shoot, the more ways you'll discover how to improve your camera's picture-taking decisions and, even when to *ignore* them when you want to create a particular look or effect. For example, when you shoot with the main light source behind the subject, you end up with *backlighting*, which can result in an overexposed background and/or an underexposed subject. The exposure system recognizes backlit situations nicely, and, in most cases, can properly base exposure on the main subject using the default Matrix metering mode, producing a decent photo.

But as a creative photographer there will be many instances where you would rather *not* have automatic correction for backlighting. What if you *want* to underexpose the subject to produce a silhouette effect? The camera does a poor job of exposing intentional silhouettes and will end up producing unwanted detail in what should have been inky black areas of your image. Fortunately, the camera has metering modes and other exposure options that allow you to produce the image you are looking for. If you're looking for an extensive exposure range, features like the camera's built-in HDR and Active D-Lighting can fine-tune your exposure as you take photos, preserving detail in the highlights and shadows as required. Your camera also has the capability of *fine-tuning* exposure separately for each of the metering modes, so you can consistently add or subtract a little exposure to suit your creative tastes.

In the next few pages, I'm going to give you a grounding in exposure concepts, either as an introduction or as a refresher course, depending on your current level of expertise. When you finish this chapter, you'll understand most of what you need to know to take well-exposed photographs creatively in a broad range of situations.

Getting a Handle on Exposure

In the most basic sense, exposure is all about light. Correct exposure brings out the detail in the areas you want to picture, providing the range of tones and colors you need to create the desired image. Poor exposure can cloak important details in shadow or wash them out in glare-filled featureless expanses of white. However, getting the perfect exposure requires some intelligence—either that built into the camera or the smarts in your head—because digital sensors can't capture all the tones we are able to see. If the range of tones in an image is extensive, embracing both inky black shadows and bright highlights, we often must settle for an exposure that renders most of those tones—but not all—in a way that best suits the photo we want to produce.

As the owner of a Z-series mirrorless camera, you're probably well aware of the traditional "exposure triangle" of aperture (quantity of light, light passed by the lens), shutter speed (the amount of time the shutter is open), and the ISO sensitivity of the sensor—all working proportionately and reciprocally to produce an exposure. The trio is itself affected by the amount of illumination that is available to work with. So, if you double the amount of light, increase the aperture by one stop, make the shutter speed twice as long, or boost the ISO setting 2X, you'll get twice as much exposure. Similarly, you can increase any of these factors while decreasing one of the others by a similar amount to keep the *same* exposure.

Working with any of the three controls always involves trade-offs. Larger f/stops provide less depth-of-field, while smaller f/stops increase depth-of-field and decrease sharpness through a phenomenon called diffraction. Shorter shutter speeds do a better job of reducing the effects of camera/subject motion, while longer shutter speeds make that motion blur more likely. Higher ISO settings increase the amount of visual noise and artifacts in your image, while lower ISO settings reduce the effects of noise. (See Figure 2.1.)

The three legs of the triangle all work proportionately and reciprocally to produce an exposure. If you double the amount of light, double the size of the aperture opening, make the shutter speed twice as long, or double the ISO sensitivity, you'll get twice as much exposure. Similarly, you can reduce any of these and reduce the exposure when that is preferable.

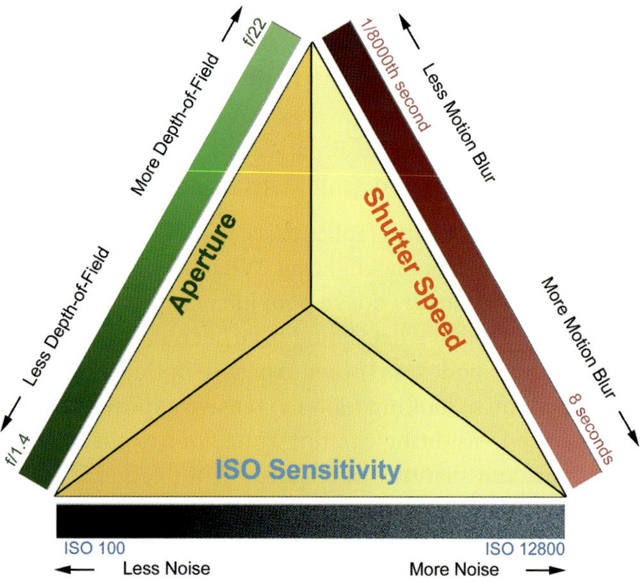

Figure 2.1 The traditional exposure triangle includes aperture, shutter speed, and ISO sensitivity.

F/STOPS AND SHUTTER SPEEDS

The lens aperture, or f/stop, is a ratio, much like a fraction, which is why f/2 is larger than f/4, just as 1/2 is larger than 1/4. However, f/2 is actually *four times* as large as f/4. (If you remember your high school geometry, you'll know that to double the area of a circle, you multiply its diameter by the square root of two: 1.4.)

Lenses are usually marked with intermediate f/stops that represent a size that's twice as much/half as much as the previous aperture. So, a lens might be marked: f/4, f/5.6, f/8, f/11, f/16, with each larger number representing an aperture that admits half as much light as the one before. Of course, you can also set *intermediate* apertures, such as f/6.3 and f/7.1, which fall between f/5.6 and f/8.

Shutter speeds are actual fractions (of a second), but the numerator is omitted, so that 60, 125, 250, 500, and so forth represent 1/60th, 1/125th, 1/250th, and 1/500th. To avoid confusion, Nikon uses quotation marks to signify longer exposures: 2", 2.5", 4", and so forth representing 2.0-, 2.5-, and 4.0-second exposures, respectively.

As we'll see, however, changing any of those aspects in P, A, or S mode does not change the exposure. The camera also makes adjustments when you do so, in order to maintain the same exposure. That's why Nikon provides other methods for modifying the exposure in those modes.

Equivalent Exposure

Most commonly, exposure settings are made using the aperture and shutter speed, followed by adjusting the ISO sensitivity, if it's not possible to get the preferred exposure (that is, the one that uses the "best" f/stop or shutter speed for the depth-of-field or action stopping we want).

One of the most important aspects in this discussion is the concept of *equivalent exposure*. This term means that exactly the same amount of light will reach the sensor at various combinations of aperture and shutter speed. Whether we use a small aperture (large f/number) with a long shutter speed or a wide aperture (small f/number) with a fast shutter speed, the amount of light reaching the sensor can be exactly the same. Table 2.1 shows equivalent exposure settings using various shutter speeds and f/stops; in other words, any of the combination of settings listed will produce exactly the same exposure.

TABLE 2.1 Equivalent Exposures

SHUTTER SPEED	F/STOP	SHUTTER SPEED	F/STOP
1/30th second	f/22	1/1000th second	f/4
1/60th second	f/16	1/2000th second	f/2.8
1/125th second	f/11	1/4000th second	f/2
1/250th second	f/8	1/8000th second	f/1.4
1/500th second	f/5.6		

When the camera is set for Programmed-auto (P), the metering system selects the correct exposure for you automatically, but you can change quickly to an equivalent exposure by spinning the main command dial until the desired equivalent exposure combination is displayed, with an asterisk appearing next to the P when you're using this "Flexible Program" feature. You can make Flexible Program adjustments more easily if you remember that you need to rotate the command dial toward the left when you want to increase the amount of depth-of-field (DOF) or use a slower shutter speed;

F/STOPS VERSUS STOPS

In photography parlance, *f/stop* always means the aperture or lens opening. However, for lack of a current commonly used word for one exposure increment, the term *stop* is often used. In this book, when I say "stop" by itself (no *f/*), I mean one whole unit of exposure and am not necessarily referring to an actual f/stop or lens aperture. So, adjusting the exposure by "one stop" can mean changing to the next shutter speed increment (say, from 1/125th second to 1/250th second) or the next aperture (such as f/4 to f/5.6). Similarly, 1/3-stop or 1/2-stop increments can mean either shutter speed or aperture changes, depending on the context. Be forewarned. Exposure increments are also referred to as EV (exposure value) adjustments, particularly when using *exposure compensation*, as described later in this chapter in the "Making EV Changes" section.

rotate to the right when you want to reduce the depth-of-field or use a faster shutter speed. The need for more/less DOF and slower/faster shutter speed are the primary reasons you'd want to use Flexible Program. This program shift mode does not work when you're using flash.

In Aperture-priority (A) and Shutter-priority (S) modes, you can change to an equivalent exposure, but only by adjusting either the aperture with the sub-command dial in A mode (the camera chooses the shutter speed) or shutter speed with the main command dial in S mode (the camera selects the aperture). I'll cover all these exposure modes later in the chapter.

Calculating Exposure

Exposure is measured using a specific area of the frame, using a pattern that you can select (more on that later). It's based on the assumption that each area being measured reflects about the same amount of light as a neutral gray card that reflects a "middle" gray. That assumption is necessary, because different subjects reflect different amounts of light. In a photo containing, say, a white cat and a dark gray cat, the white cat might reflect five times as much light as the gray cat. An exposure based on the white cat will cause the gray cat to appear to be black, while an exposure based only on the gray cat will make the white cat washed out.

This is more easily understood if you look at some photos of subjects that are dark (they reflect little light), those that have predominantly middle tones, and subjects that are highly reflective. Figure 2.2 shows three separate portraits of a human (not a cat) that include a simplified test card with black, gray, and white patches, illustrating how different exposure measurements actually do affect an exposure:

- **Correctly Exposed.** At left in Figure 2.2, exposure was calculated by measuring the light reflecting from the middle-gray patch. The exposure meter in the camera sees an object that it thinks is a middle gray, calculates an exposure based on that, so the patch in the center of the strip is rendered at its proper tonal value. Best of all, because the resulting exposure is correct, the black patch at left and white patch at right are rendered properly as well.

  If your Z5 II bases its exposure on a subject that averages that "ideal" middle gray, you'll end up with similar (accurate) results. The camera's exposure algorithms are concocted to ensure this kind of result as often as possible, barring any unusual subjects (that is, those that are backlit or have uneven illumination).

- **Overexposed.** At center in Figure 2.2, exposure was calculated based on metering the leftmost, black patch. The light meter sees less light reflecting from the black square than it would see from a gray middle-tone subject, and so figures, "Aha! I need to add exposure to brighten this subject up to a middle gray!" That lightens the "black" patch, so it now appears to be gray.

  But now the patch in the middle that was *originally* middle gray is overexposed and becomes light gray. And the white square at right is now seriously overexposed and loses detail in the highlights, which have become a featureless white. Our human subject is similarly overexposed.

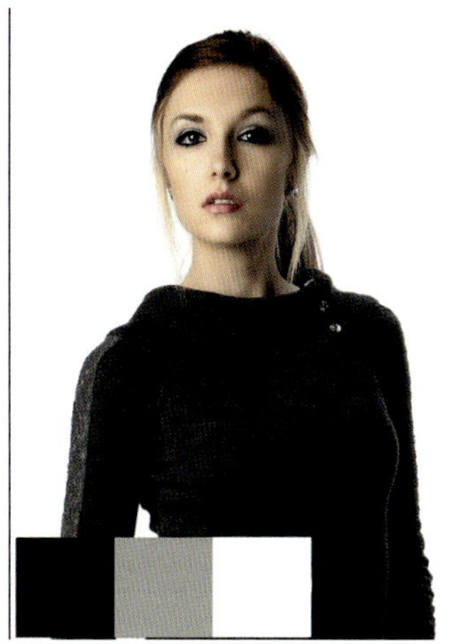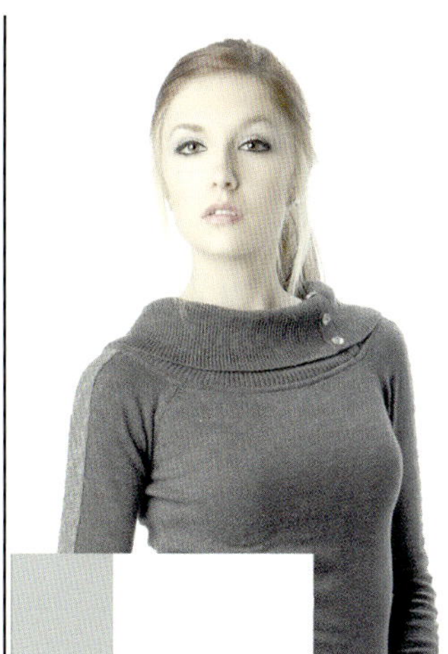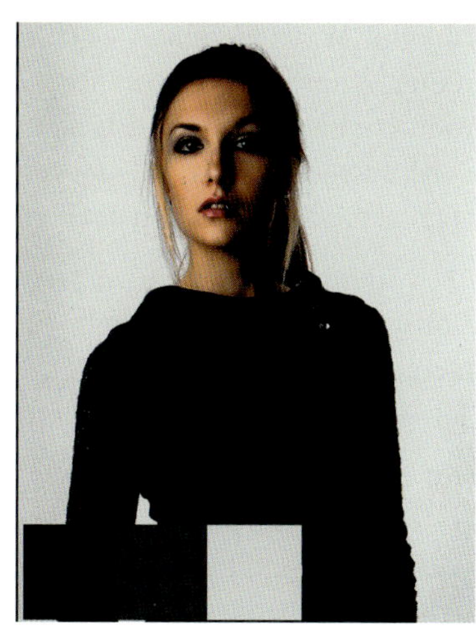

Figure 2.2 Exposure calculated from the middle-gray patch produces a correct exposure for all three patches and the subject (left). Exposure measured from the black patch yields an overexposed image (center). Exposure calculated from the white patch produces underexposure (right).

- **Underexposed.** At right, the light meter has measured the illumination bouncing off the white patch and tries to render *that* tone as a middle gray. A lot of light is reflected by the white square, so the exposure is *reduced*, bringing that patch closer to a middle-gray tone. The patches that were originally gray and black are now rendered too dark. Clearly, measuring the gray card—or a substitute that reflects about the same amount of light—is the only way to ensure that the exposure is precisely correct.

Metering Mid-Tones

As you can see, the ideal way to measure exposure is to meter from a subject that reflects 12 to 18 percent of the light that reaches it. If you want the most precise exposure calculations, the solution is to use a stand-in. Any mid-tone subject—including green grass or a rich, medium-blue sky—also reflects about 12 to 18 percent of the light. Metering such an area should ensure that the exposure for the entire scene will be correct or close to correct for average subjects.

ORIGIN OF THE 18 PERCENT "MYTH"

Why are so many photographers under the impression that camera light meters are calibrated to the 18 percent "standard," rather than the true value, which may be 12 to 14 percent, depending on the vendor? You'll find this misinformation in an alarming number of places. I've seen the 18 percent "myth" taught in camera classes; I've found it in books and even been given this wrong information from the technical staff of camera vendors. (They should know better—the same vendors' engineers who design and calibrate the cameras have the right figure.)

The most common explanation is that during a revision of Kodak's instructions for its gray cards in 1977, the advice to open up an extra half stop was omitted, and a whole generation of shooters grew up thinking that a measurement off a gray card could be used as is. Kodak restored the proviso in 1997, it's said, but by then it was too late.

In some very bright scenes (like a snowy landscape or a lava field), you won't have a mid-tone to meter. Another substitute for a gray card is the palm of a human hand (the backside of the hand is too variable). But a human palm, regardless of ethnic group, is even brighter than a standard gray card, so you need to add one additional stop. That is, if your meter reading is 1/500th of a second at f/11, use 1/500th second at f/8 or 1/250th second at f/11 instead. (Both exposures are equivalent.)

Or, you might want to resort to using an evenly illuminated gray card mentioned earlier. Small versions are available that can be tucked in a camera bag. Place it in your frame near your main subject, facing the camera, and with the exact same even illumination falling on it that is falling on your subject. Then, use the Spot metering function (described in the next section) to calculate exposure.

But the standard Kodak gray card reflects 18 percent of the light while, as I noted, your camera is calibrated for a somewhat darker 12 percent tone. If you insisted on getting a perfect exposure, you would need to add about one-half stop more exposure than the value provided by taking the light meter reading from the card. Of course, in most situations, it's not necessary to do this. Your camera's light meter will do a good job of calculating the right exposure, especially if you use the exposure tips in the next section. But I felt that explaining exactly what is going on during exposure calculation would help you understand how your camera's metering system works.

The light meters built into your camera are calibrated at the factory and can only be changed using the Fine-Tune Optimal Exposure option (Custom Setting b6). But if you use a hand-held incident or reflective light meter, you *can* calibrate it, using the instructions supplied with your meter. Because a hand-held meter *can* be calibrated to the 18 percent gray standard (or any other value you choose), my rant about the myth of the 18 percent gray card doesn't apply.

MODES, MODES, AND MORE MODES

Call them modes or methods, the Z5 II seems to have a lot of different sets of options that are described using similar terms. Here's how to sort them out:

- **Metering method.** These modes determine the *parts of the image* within the sensor that are examined in order to calculate exposure. The camera may look at many different points within the image, segregating them by zone (Matrix metering); examining the same number of points, but giving greater weight to those located in the middle of the frame (Center-weighted metering); evaluating only a limited number of points in a limited area (Spot metering); or adjusting exposure to preserve detail in highlights (Highlight-weighted metering).
- **Exposure method.** These modes (Program, Aperture-priority, Shutter-priority, or Manual) determine *which* settings are used to expose the image. The camera may adjust the shutter speed, the aperture, or both, or even ISO setting (if Auto ISO is active), depending on the method you choose.

Choosing a Metering Method

The Z5 II has four different schemes for evaluating the light received by its exposure sensors: Matrix, Center-weighted, Spot, and Highlight-weighted. Select the mode you want from the *i* menu, or Photo Shooting and Video Recording menus. Or, if you frequently use one metering method, but occasionally like to switch to another method on the fly, you can redefine one of the camera's buttons, such as the video recording button, to shift to your alternate mode with the twirl of a command dial. The button can be programmed to cycle among Matrix metering, Center-weighted metering, Spot metering, or Highlight-weighted metering when a command dial is rotated (as discussed in Chapter 7), using Custom Setting f2.

I've done this as a way to compare the exposure settings of the four metering methods while composing a single image in the viewfinder. I've also found the capability useful when I'm, say, working with Matrix metering and want to zero in on a particular area of the frame temporarily using Spot metering.

Your camera calculates exposure by measuring the light that passes through the lens and strikes the sensor. These pixels are said to be able to detect light over a range of –4 to +17 EV at ISO 100. That translates into exposures from sixteen minutes at f/16 to 1/2000th second at f/16.

In everyday terms, 0 EV represents the illumination you might see outdoors at night under a full moon, while the brightest daytime scene you're likely to encounter (a snow scene in full daylight) would be 16 EV. Your camera is able to *detect* photons under an extremely broad EV span—three stops dimmer than full moonlight, and one stop brighter than a daylight snow scene. However, the ability to *capture* images is limited to a much smaller range. Note that the sensor's dynamic range (the tones it can preserve in your final image) is less than the full range of tones it can *detect*. It's easy to get these two separate aspects confused.

Figure 2.3 shows examples of how Matrix metering, Center-weighted metering, Spot metering, and Highlight-weighted metering measure exposure. The figure shows the icons that appear in the lower-left corner of the viewfinder and LCD displays (left); a representation of the area being metered (center); and an example of typical subject matter for each method (right).

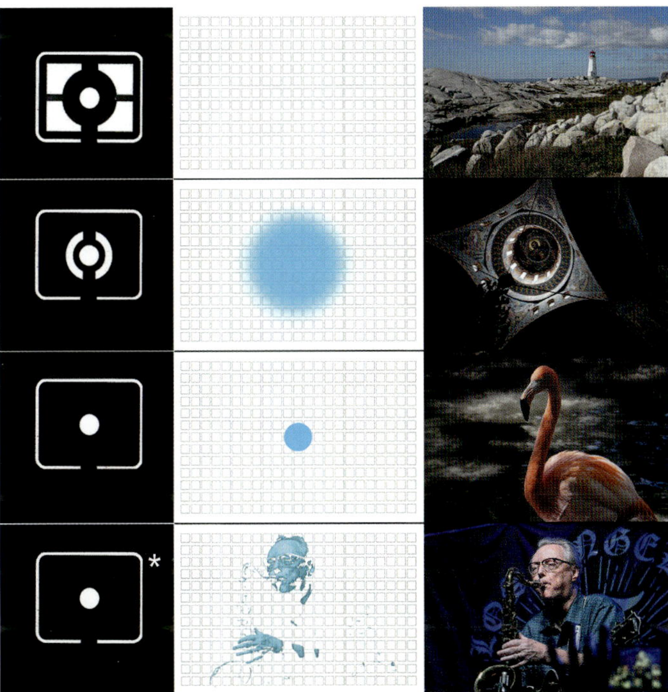

Figure 2.3 Top to bottom: Matrix, Center-weighted, Spot, and Highlight-weighted metering icons.

Matrix Metering

For Matrix metering mode, the camera reads the light falling on the sensor and compares the brightness of many areas using a matrix array. Then, the camera evaluates the differences between the many zones and compares them with a built-in database representing actual images, to make an educated guess about what kind of picture you're taking. For example, if the top sections of a picture are much lighter than the bottom portions, the algorithm can assume that the scene is a landscape photo with lots of sky. However, if there is a lighter area in the center of the frame, and the camera detects skin tones, it will assume that you're shooting a portrait and not a landscape photo and expose for the human subject. A typical image suitable for Matrix metering is shown at top right in Figure 2.3.

Matrix metering mode can often recognize many types of bright scenes and automatically increase the exposure to reduce the risk of a dark photo. This is useful when your subject is a snow-covered landscape or a close-up of a bride in white. Granted, you may need to use a bit of exposure compensation, but often, the exposure will be close to accurate without it. Matrix metering is most successful with light-toned scenes on bright days and when humans are in the frame. When shooting in dark, overcast conditions, it's more likely to underexpose a scene of that type.

Exposure meters have long used brightness to calculate correct exposure. The advanced exposure technology uses other information to make more intelligent settings. These factors include:

- **Patterns.** The camera compares exposure across the entire sensor with a database of tens of thousands of picture types, looking for differences among pixels and similarities to images in the database. When it finds a match, it uses that information as a basis for its recommended exposure. If the contrast in a scene is high enough that the sensor probably won't be able to preserve detail in both highlights and shadows, in most cases, the camera will favor the highlights. As you'll learn later in this chapter, once highlights are lost, they are gone forever, but it is sometimes possible to retrieve data in shadow areas. If you are shooting RAW, the exposure setting and other adjustments can often boost information in darker areas.

- **Faces.** By default, the Z5 II adjusts its matrix metering calculations when a face is detected within the frame to provide the best rendition of faces, even if the result is an improperly exposed background. You can partially disable this bias by disabling Custom Setting b4 (Matrix Metering Face Detection), but the camera will still use face tones within the frame to set exposure.

- **Colors.** The camera can enhance its readings based on the colors detected in the frame. Large areas of blue in the upper part of the image can be deemed to be sky, greens can be reasonably assumed to be foliage, and the presence of skin tones readily indicates human beings.

- **Autofocus area.** Whether you or the camera selects which autofocus zone is used, the exposure system assumes, logically, that the part of the image that is in focus contains your subject matter.

- **Distance and focal length.** The distance and focal length supplied by your Z-mount lenses is used to better calculate what kind of scene you have framed. For example, if you're shooting a portrait with a longer focal-length lens focused to about 5 to 12 feet from the camera, and the upper half of the scene is very bright, the camera assumes you would prefer to meter for the rest of the image and will discount the bright area. However, if a wide-angle lens is attached and focused at infinity, the camera can assume you're taking a landscape photo and take the bright upper area into account to produce better-looking sky and clouds.

Matrix metering is best for most general subjects, because it is able to intelligently analyze a scene and make an excellent guess of what kind of subject you're shooting a great deal of the time. The camera can tell the difference between low-contrast and high-contrast subjects by looking at the range of differences in brightness across the scene. Because the camera has a fairly good idea about what kind of subject matter you are shooting, it can underexpose slightly when appropriate to preserve highlight detail when image contrast is high. (It's often possible to pull detail out of shadows that are too dark using an image editor, but once highlights are converted to white pixels, they are gone forever.)

CAUTION If you're using a strong filter, including a polarizing filter, split-color filter, or neutral-density filter (particularly a graduated neutral-density filter), you should switch from Matrix metering to Center-weighted, because the filter can affect the relationships between the different areas of the frame used to calculate a Matrix exposure. For example, a polarizing filter produces a sky that is darker than usual, hindering the Matrix algorithm's recognition of a landscape photo. Extra-dark or colored filters disturb the color relationships used for color Matrix metering, too.

Center-weighted Metering

In this mode, the exposure meter emphasizes an area in the center of the frame to calculate exposure. With Center-weighted metering, you end up with conventional metering without any "intelligent" scene evaluation. (See Figure 2.3, second row from the top.) The light meter considers brightness in the entire frame but places 75 percent of the emphasis on a large area in the center of the frame (shown in blue), on the theory that, for most pictures, the main subject will not be located far off-center. The remaining 25 percent of the exposure is based on the rest of the frame.

Of course, Center-weighted metering is most effective when the subject in the central area is a midtone. Even then, if your main subject is surrounded by large, extremely bright or very dark areas, the exposure might not be exactly right. (You might need to use exposure compensation, a feature discussed shortly.) However, this scheme works well in many situations if you don't want to use one of the other modes, for scenes like the one shown in the figure. This mode can be useful for close-ups of subjects like flowers, or for portraits. You can adjust the size of the area assigned the greatest weight using Custom Setting b5, as described in Chapter 7.

Your choices include Small (with an 8mm circle), Standard (the default, with a 12mm circle), and Average, which is the same as the old-time full-frame averaging systems. By default, the camera will show a translucent gray circle in the display that represents the size of the center-weighted area in display configurations 1–3 (which cycle through when you press the DISP button). You can disable/enable the circle (which Nikon calls the Center-weighted area) using the Custom Monitor/Viewfinder Shooting Display entries: d19 and d20.

Spot Metering

Spot metering is favored by those of us who have used a hand-held light meter to measure exposure at various points (such as metering highlights and shadows separately). However, you can use Spot metering in any situation where you want to individually measure the light reflecting from light, midtone, or dark areas of your subject—or any combination of areas. This mode is useful if you have the time to make careful measurements and calculate your exposure based on them. Note that Spot metering is not available in Video Recording mode; Matrix metering will be used instead.

This mode confines the reading to a limited 4mm area in the viewfinder, making up only 1.5 percent of the image, as shown by the blue circle in Figure 2.3 (third row down from the top). The circle is centered on the *current focus point* (which can be *any* of the available focus points, *not* just the center one shown in the figure), *but is larger than the focus point*, so don't fall into the trap of believing that exposure is being measured only within the viewfinder indicators that represent the active focus point. This is the only metering method you can use to specify exactly where to measure exposure within the frame. However, if you have selected Auto-area AF, only the center focus point is used to spot meter.

You'll find Spot metering useful when you want to base exposure on a small area in the frame. If that area is in the center of the frame, so much the better. If not, you'll have to make your meter reading for an off-center subject using an appropriate focus point and then lock exposure by pressing the shutter release halfway. This mode is best for subjects where the background is significantly brighter or darker.

If you Spot meter a very light-toned area or a dark-toned area, you will get underexposure or over-exposure respectively; you would need to use an override for more accurate results. On the other hand, you can Spot meter a small mid-tone subject surrounded by a sky with big white clouds or by an indigo blue wall and get a good exposure. (The light meter ignores the subject's surroundings, so they do not affect the exposure setting.) That would not be possible with Center-weighted metering, which considers brightness in a much larger area.

Using Spot Metering

Matrix and Center-weighted metering basically have few options to worry about. They are both affected by exposure compensation changes and Custom Setting b6: Fine-Tune Optimal Exposure adjustments. Spot metering, on the other hand, can benefit from your input in selecting the spot used. Here are some considerations to keep in mind:

- **Moving the spot.** Remember that you don't move the metering spot itself; the current *focus* spot is used. So, you must be using an AF-area mode that allows changing the location of the AF area, which happens to be any of the AF-area modes *except* Auto-area AF. In that mode, the center focus point is *always* used as the metering spot, and you cannot change it.

- **Choosing a compatible AF-area mode.** You can use the *i* menu to cycle among the AF areas. The available modes differ depending on the focus mode you've chosen. All these AF-area modes will allow you to switch the AF point to any of the available focus areas in the display:
  - **AF-S focus mode:** Pinpoint AF, Single-point AF, Wide-area AF (Small, Large, C1, C2).
  - **AF-C focus mode:** Single-point AF, Dynamic-area AF (Small, Medium, Large), Wide-area AF (Small, Large, C1, C2), 3D-tracking.
  - **Manual focus mode:** Only Single-point AF is available. **Note:** With manual focus, the camera does not autofocus, of course; the position of the focus point is used only for the electronic rangefinder and Spot metering functions. You can find information on all the focus and AF-area modes in Chapter 3.

- **Wrap around.** You'll use the multi selector's directional buttons to move the AF point around within the display—and the metering spot with it. The focus point's movement will stop at the left/right/top/bottom edges *unless* you've turned on focus point wrap-around in Custom Setting a9.

- **When using Auto-area AF.** If you've selected Auto-area AF, the center focus point will always be used when Spot metering—*even if the camera selects a different point for the autofocus function.* That's actually a positive: since in Auto-area AF mode you don't know what the focus spot will be until you press the shutter release halfway, it's *good* to know that the camera will be using the center spot. While Spot metering is most useful when not using Auto-area AF, it still functions, albeit in a less flexible way.

- **Reminder: When the focus point moves, the spot metering point moves, too.** If you're using Dynamic-area AF and continuous autofocus (AF-C, described in Chapter 3), the camera may move the focus point you originally selected and base focus on the surrounding focus points. *The metering area will tag along.*

A good example of a scene where you might want to use Spot metering is shown at right in Figure 2.3, third row from the top, which shows a flamingo amidst a very dark background. The illumination might have fooled both Matrix and Center-weighted metering (although Center-weighted might have come close), but Spot metering allowed taking a reading directly from the bird's plumage. While I preferred Spot metering in this case, another option might have been Highlight-weighted metering, described next.

Highlight-weighted Metering

In this metering mode, the exposure system examines your entire scene, just as it does using Matrix metering. It is *not* a spot metering mode, despite its icon, which is the same as the spot icon, with an asterisk added. With this mode, the Expeed 7 processor seeks out non-specular highlight areas of your image and bases exposure on a setting that will keep those highlights from being overexposed. Less emphasis ("weight") is given to non-highlight areas. That's why Highlight-weighted *might* have worked for the flamingo image, but it's actually better suited for images in which the highlights are spread over a larger area of the frame. This metering mode does not use the current focus point as the base point for its calculations.

So, if you're shooting spotlit performers on-stage at a concert or play, the camera is able to calculate the correct exposure using the performers, and ignoring, for the most part, the dark surroundings. You'd have your choice of measuring exposure in Spot mode, as described in the previous section, placing the metering spot on the dancer's face or shirt, or, you could select Highlight-weighted metering and allow the camera to identify the performer when figuring exposure. Your results might be similar with either, depending on how well you "placed" the Spot area and how cleverly the system sorts out your subject from the background. I tend to use Spot metering when the area I want to meter is clearly defined and Highlight-weighted metering when there is a range of highlights that I'd like to preserve, as in the photo of Billy Zoom, from the LA punk band X, shown in Figure 2.3, bottom.

Choosing an Exposure Method

Your Z5 II offers five different methods for choosing the appropriate aperture and shutter speed, all available using the mode dial on the right shoulder of the camera. One of these, Auto, labeled with a green camera icon, is a beginner-friendly point-and-shoot mode that not only selects the two exposure parameters, but makes other settings, including white balance and autofocus modes for you.

Auto is fine for beginners and quick shots, but if you need more creative control over your images, you'll want to work with one of the Z5 II's four semi-automatic/manual options instead. You can choose among Aperture-priority, Shutter-priority, Program, or Manual options by rotating the mode dial to the Manual, Aperture-priority, Shutter-priority, or Program positions. Your decision on which is best for a given shooting situation will depend on things like your need for lots of (or less) depth-of-field, a desire to freeze action or allow motion blur, or how much noise you find acceptable in an image. Each of the exposure methods emphasizes one aspect of image capture or another. This section introduces you to all four.

Aperture-Priority

In Aperture-priority (A) mode, you specify the lens opening used, and the camera will set a suitable shutter speed appropriate for the aperture and the ISO sensitivity in use. If you change to a smaller aperture, from f/5.6 to f/11, for example, the camera will automatically set a longer shutter speed to maintain the same exposure, using guidance from the built-in light meter. (I discussed the concept of equivalent exposure earlier in this chapter and provided the equivalent exposure settings in Table 2.1.)

Aperture-priority is especially good when you want to use a particular lens opening to achieve a desired effect. Perhaps you'd like to use the smallest f/stop possible (such as f/22) to maximize depth-of-field (DOF) in a close-up picture. Or, you might want to work with a large f/stop to throw everything except your main subject out of focus, as in Figure 2.4. Maybe you'd just like to "lock in" a particular f/stop because it's the sharpest available aperture with that lens. Or, you might prefer to use, say, f/2.8 on a lens with a maximum aperture of f/1.4, because you want the best compromise between shutter speed and sharpness.

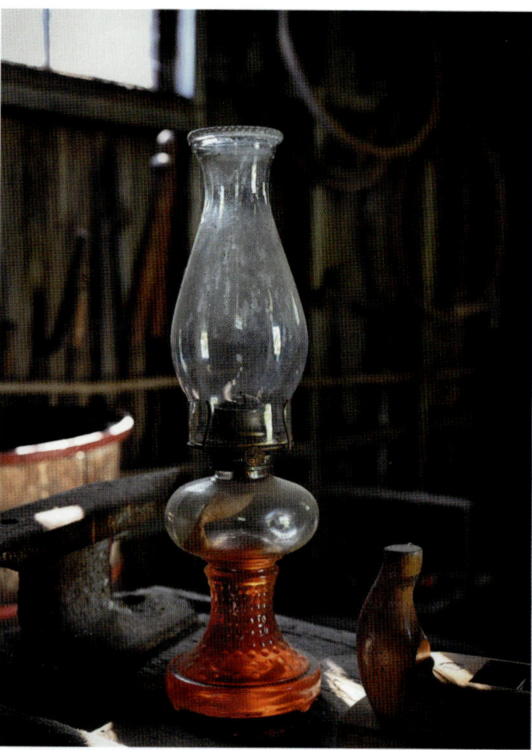

Figure 2.4 Use Aperture-priority to "lock in" a large f/stop when you want to blur distracting elements, or emphasize the main subject in the photo, in this case an antique lantern.

Aperture-priority can even be used to specify a *range* of shutter speeds you want to use under varying lighting conditions, which seems almost contradictory. But think about it. You're shooting a soccer game outdoors with a telephoto lens and want a relatively high shutter speed, but you don't care if the speed changes a little should the sun duck behind a cloud. Set your exposure method to A, and adjust the aperture until a shutter speed of, say, 1/1000th second is selected at your current ISO setting. (In bright sunlight at ISO 400, that aperture is likely to be around f/11.) Then, go ahead and shoot, knowing that your camera will maintain that f/11 aperture (for sufficient depth-of-field as the soccer players move about the field), but will drop down to 1/750th or 1/500th second, if necessary, should the lighting change a little.

When the shutter speed indicator in the display blinks, that indicates that selecting an appropriate shutter speed at the selected aperture is not possible, and that over- and underexposure will occur at the current ISO setting. That's the major pitfall of using Aperture-priority: you might select an f/stop that is too small or too large to allow an optimal exposure with the available shutter speeds. For example, if you choose f/2.8 as your aperture and the illumination is quite bright (say, at the beach or in snow), even your camera's fastest shutter speed might not be able to cut down the amount of light reaching the sensor to provide the right exposure. Or, if you select f/8 in a dimly lit room, you might find yourself shooting with a very slow shutter speed that can cause blurring from subject movement or camera shake. Aperture-priority is best used by those with a bit of experience in choosing settings. Many seasoned photographers leave their camera set on A all the time. The exposure indicator scale in the display indicates the amount of under- or overexposure.

When to use Aperture-priority:

- **General landscape photography.** Aperture-priority is a good tool for ensuring that your landscape is sharp from foreground to infinity, if you select an f/stop that provides maximum depth-of-field.

  If you use Aperture-priority mode and select an aperture like f/11 or f/16, it's your responsibility to make sure the shutter speed selected is fast enough to avoid losing detail to camera shake, or that the camera is mounted on a tripod. One thing that new landscape photographers fail to account for is the movement of distant leaves and tree branches. When seeking the ultimate in sharpness, go ahead and use Aperture-priority, but boost ISO sensitivity a bit, if necessary, to provide a sufficiently fast shutter speed, whether shooting hand-held or with a tripod.

- **Specific landscape situations.** Aperture-priority is also useful when you have no objection to using a long shutter speed, or, particularly, *want* the camera to select one. Waterfalls are a perfect example. You can use Aperture-priority mode, set your camera to ISO 100, use a small f/stop, and let the exposure system select a longer shutter speed that will allow the water to blur as it flows. Indeed, you might need to use a neutral-density filter to get a sufficiently long shutter speed. But Aperture-priority mode is a good start.

- **Portrait photography.** Portraits are the most common applications of selective focus. A medium-large aperture (say, f/5.6 or f/8) with a longer lens/zoom setting (in the 85mm to 135mm range) will allow the background behind your portrait subject to blur. A *very* large aperture (I frequently shoot wide open with my Nikkor Z 85mm f/1.8 S lens) lets you apply selective focus to your subject's *face*. With a three-quarters view of your subject, as long as his or her eyes are sharp, it's okay if the far ear or hair is out of focus.

- **When you want to ensure optimal sharpness.** All lenses have an aperture or two at which they perform best, providing the level of sharpness you expect to find. That's usually about two stops down from wide open and thus will vary depending on the maximum aperture of the lens.

- **Close-up/Macro photography.** Depth-of-field is typically very shallow when shooting macro photos, and you'll want to choose your f/stop carefully. Perhaps you might want to use a wider stop to emphasize your subject. Or, you might need the smallest aperture you can get away with to maximize depth-of-field. Aperture-priority mode comes in very useful when shooting close-up pictures, too. Because macro work is frequently done with the camera mounted on a tripod, and your close-up subjects, if not living creatures, may not be moving much, a longer shutter speed isn't a problem. Aperture-priority can be your preferred choice.

Shutter-Priority

Shutter-priority (S) is the inverse of Aperture-priority: you choose the shutter speed you'd like to use, and the metering system selects the appropriate f/stop. Perhaps you're shooting action photos, and you want to use the absolute fastest shutter speed available; in other cases, you might want to use a slow shutter speed to add some blur to an action photo that would be mundane if the action were completely frozen. Shutter-priority mode gives you some control over how much action-freezing capability your digital camera brings to bear in a particular situation.

Take care when using a slow shutter speed such as 1/8th second or slower, because you'll get blurring from camera shake unless you're using vibration reduction or have mounted the camera on a tripod or other firm support. Very high shutter speeds (the maximum is 1/8000th second) require a lot of light.

You'll also encounter the same problem as with Aperture-priority when you select a shutter speed that's too long or too short for correct exposure under some conditions. As in Aperture-priority mode, it's possible to choose an inappropriate shutter speed. If that's the case, the aperture number in the display will blink.

When to use Shutter-priority:

- **To reduce blur from subject motion.** Set the shutter speed to a higher value to reduce the amount of blur from subjects that are moving. The exact speed will vary depending on how fast your subject is moving and how much blur is acceptable. You might want to freeze a basketball player in mid-dunk with a 1/1000th second shutter speed or use 1/200th second to allow the spinning wheels of a motocross racer to blur a tiny bit to add the feeling of motion.

- **To add blur from subject motion.** There are times when you want a subject to blur, say, when shooting waterfalls with a one- or two-second exposure in Shutter-priority mode.

- **To add blur from camera motion when *you* are moving.** Say you're panning to follow a pair of relay runners. You might want to use Shutter-priority mode and set a 1/60th second shutter speed, so that the background will blur as you pan with the runners. The shutter speed will be fast enough to provide a sharp image of the athletes, while reducing their distracting background to a blur. For Figure 2.5, I was panning to follow the relay runner and shot at 1/30th second to allow the background to blur.

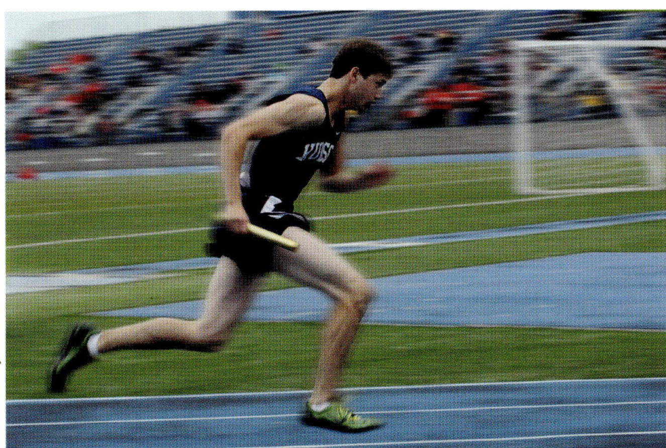

Figure 2.5 Shutter-priority allows you to specify a speed that will render a moving subject like this relay runner reasonably sharp as you pan.

- **To reduce blur from camera motion when *you* are moving.** In other situations, the camera may be in motion, say, because you're shooting from a moving train or auto, and you want to minimize the amount of blur caused by the motion of the camera. Shutter-priority is a good choice here, too.
- **Landscape photography hand-held.** If you can't use a tripod for your landscape shots, you'll still probably want the sharpest image possible, especially when shooting a scene in which gusts of wind may cause foliage to flutter. Shutter-priority can allow you to specify a shutter speed that's fast enough to reduce or eliminate the effects of camera shake. Just make sure that your ISO setting is high enough that the camera will select an aperture with sufficient depth-of-field, too.
- **Concerts and stage performances.** I shoot a lot of concerts with my 70-200mm f/2.8 lens and have discovered that, when vibration reduction is taken into account, a shutter speed of 1/180th second is fast enough—along with vibration reduction—to eliminate camera shake that can result from hand-holding the camera with this lens, and also to avoid blur from the movement of all but the most energetic performers. I use Shutter-priority and set the ISO so the camera will select an aperture in the f/4-5.6 range.

Programmed Auto Mode

Program mode (P) uses the camera's built-in smarts to select the correct f/stop and shutter speed using a database of picture information that tells it which combination of shutter speed and aperture will work best for a particular photo. If the correct exposure cannot be achieved at the current ISO setting, the shutter speed and aperture will blink in the display. You can then boost or reduce the ISO to increase or decrease sensitivity.

The recommended exposure can be overridden if you want. Use the EV (exposure value/exposure compensation) setting feature to add or subtract exposure from the metered value. And, as I mentioned earlier in this chapter, in Program mode you can rotate the main command dial to change from the recommended setting to an equivalent setting (as shown previously in Table 2.1) that produces the same exposure but using a different combination of f/stop and shutter speed.

This is called "Flexible Program" by Nikon. Rotate the main command dial left to reduce the size of the aperture (going from, say, f/4 to f/5.6), so that the camera will automatically use a slower shutter speed (going from, say, 1/250th second to 1/125th second). Rotate the main command dial right to use a larger f/stop, while automatically producing a shorter shutter speed that provides the same equivalent exposure as metered in P mode. An asterisk appears next to the P in the viewfinder/monitor display, so you'll know you've overridden the default program setting. Your adjustment remains in force until you rotate the main command dial until the asterisk disappears, or you switch to a different exposure mode, or turn the camera off.

Making EV Changes

Sometimes you'll want more or less exposure than indicated by the metering system. Perhaps you want to underexpose to create a silhouette effect or overexpose to produce a high-key look. It's easy to use the camera's exposure compensation system to override the exposure recommendations. Press the exposure compensation (EV) button on the top panel (just southeast of the shutter release). Then rotate the main command dial right to add exposure and left to subtract exposure. The EV change you've made remains for the exposures that follow, until you manually zero out the EV setting. The EV plus/minus icon appears in the display to warn you that an exposure compensation change has been entered. You can increase or decrease exposure over a range of plus or minus five stops. Remember to zero out your setting when finished.

Custom Setting b3: Easy Exposure Compensation, as described in Chapter 7, streamlines the operation. Choose On, and you don't have to hold down the EV button; rotating the main or sub-command dials alone changes the EV value when using Program, Aperture-priority, Shutter-priority, or Manual exposure modes. Select On (Auto Reset) instead, and dialed in compensation is canceled when the standby timer expires or the Z5 II is powered down. Use that option to make a single EV change that isn't "sticky" and doesn't carry over to the next exposure.

When to use Program mode:

- **When you're in a hurry to get a shot.** The camera will do a pretty good job of calculating an appropriate exposure for you, without any input from you.
- **When you hand your camera to a novice.** Set the camera to P, hand the camera to your friend, relative, or *trustworthy* stranger you meet in front of the Eiffel Tower, point to the shutter-release button and viewfinder, and say, "Look through here, and press this button."
- **When no special shutter speed or aperture settings are needed.** If your subject doesn't require special anti- or pro-blur techniques, and depth-of-field or selective focus aren't important, use P as a general-purpose setting. You can still make adjustments to increase/decrease depth-of-field or add/reduce motion blur with a minimum of fuss.

Manual Exposure

Part of being an experienced photographer comes from knowing when to rely on your camera's automation (with P mode), when to go semi-automatic (with S or A), and when to set exposure manually (using M). Some photographers actually prefer to set their exposure manually, as the camera will be happy to provide an indication of when its metering system judges your manual settings provide the proper exposure, using the analog exposure scale at the bottom of the display.

Manual exposure can come in handy in some situations. You might be taking a silhouette photo and find that none of the exposure modes or exposure compensation features give you exactly the effect you want. Set the exposure manually to use the exact shutter speed and f/stop you need. Or, you might be working in a studio environment using multiple flash units. The additional flash units are triggered by receiver devices (gadgets that set off the flash when they sense the light from another flash unit, or, perhaps from a radio or infrared remote control). Your exposure meter doesn't compensate for the extra illumination, so you need to set the aperture manually.

Because, depending on your proclivities, you might not need to set exposure manually very often, you should still make sure you understand how it works. Fortunately, the camera makes setting exposure manually very easy. Just rotate the mode dial to change to Manual mode, and then turn the main command dial to set the shutter speed, and the sub-command dial to adjust the aperture. The exposure scale in the viewfinder shows you how far your chosen setting diverges from the metered exposure.

METERING WITH OLDER LENSES

You may use the FTZ or FTZ II adapter to mount older lenses that lack the CPU chip that tells the Nikon camera what kind of lens is mounted. These lenses can still be used with Aperture-priority and Manual exposure modes only, assuming you've entered the Non-CPU Lens Data in the Setup menu, as described in Chapter 9. If the camera knows the maximum aperture of the lens, you can set the aperture using the lens's aperture ring, and, in Aperture-priority mode, it will automatically select an appropriate shutter speed. In Manual mode, you can set the aperture, and the analog exposure scale in the viewfinder will indicate when you've set the correct shutter speed manually.

When to use Manual exposure:

- **When working in the studio.** If you're working in a studio environment, you generally have total control over the lighting and can set exposure exactly as you want. The last thing you need is for the camera to interpret the scene and make adjustments of its own. Use M, and shutter speed, aperture, and (as long as you don't use ISO Auto) the ISO setting are totally up to you.
- **When using non-dedicated flash.** When working with flash units that are not compatible with the Nikon Creative Lighting System (CLS), particularly studio flash plugged into the PC/X flash terminal found on the AS-15 Sync Terminal adapter attached to the Z5 II's hot shoe, the camera has no clue about the intensity of the flash, so you'll have to dial in the appropriate aperture manually.
- **If you're using a hand-held light meter.** The appropriate aperture, both for flash exposures and shots taken under continuous lighting, can be determined by a hand-held light meter, flash meter, or combo meter that measures both kinds of illumination. With an external meter, you can measure highlights, shadows, backgrounds, or additional subjects separately, and use Manual exposure to make your settings.
- **When you want to outsmart the metering system.** Your metering system is "trained" to react to unusual lighting situations, such as backlighting, extra-bright illumination, or low-key images with murky shadows. But what if you don't *want* a well-exposed image? Manual exposure allows you to produce silhouettes in backlit situations, wash out all the middle tones to produce a luminous look, or underexpose to create a moody or ominous dark-toned photograph.

- **When you want to select shutter speed and aperture.** Aperture- and Shutter-priority give you auto-exposure while allowing you to lock in a preferred shutter speed or aperture—but not both at the same time. Manual exposure makes it possible to specify both and *retain* autoexposure capabilities. All you have to do is activate ISO Auto. The camera will keep the shutter speed and aperture you want but raise or lower the sensitivity setting to provide an appropriate exposure.

- **When you want extra-long exposures.** In Manual mode, you can specify speed longer than the 30 seconds provided by the automated modes, including Time and Bulb. The Z5 II's Extended Shutter Speeds feature allows timed shots of up to 900 seconds in Manual exposure mode.

Adjusting Exposure with ISO Settings

As I mentioned above, another way of adjusting exposures is by changing the ISO sensitivity setting. Sometimes photographers forget about this option, because the common practice is to set the ISO once for a particular shooting session (say, at ISO 100 for bright sunlight outdoors, or ISO 800 when shooting indoors) and then forget about it. Your Z5 II's sensor is actually set up for that, using a *dual gain* system that establishes two different "base" ISOs optimized for those kinds of lighting conditions, as I'll explain in the next section.

So, with modern cameras, higher ISO settings needn't be considered "bad" or "necessary evils." Changing the ISO is a valid way of adjusting exposure settings, particularly with a camera like the Z5 II, which produces good results at ISO settings that created grainy, unusable pictures with earlier models.

Indeed, I find myself using ISO adjustment as a convenient alternate way of adding or subtracting EV (Exposure Value—another way of representing one stop of exposure) when shooting in Manual mode, and as a quick way of choosing equivalent exposures when in Program, Shutter-priority, or Aperture-priority modes. For example, I've selected a Manual exposure with both f/stop and shutter speed suitable for my image using, say, ISO 200. I can change the exposure in 1/3-stop increments by holding down the ISO button located on the top-right shoulder of the camera, and spinning the main command dial one click at a time. The difference in image quality/noise at ISO 200 is negligible if I dial in ISO 160 or ISO 125 to reduce exposure a little or change to ISO 250 or ISO 320 to increase exposure. I keep my preferred f/stop and shutter speed but still adjust the exposure. (And, as I noted earlier, if ISO Auto is active, I can even allow the camera to set the exposure automatically using the f/stop and shutter speed I want.)

Or, perhaps, I am using Shutter-priority mode and the metered exposure at ISO 200 is 1/500th second at f/11. If I decide, on the spur of the moment, I'd rather use 1/500th second at f/8, I can press the ISO button and spin the main command dial to switch to ISO 100. Of course, it's a good idea to monitor your ISO changes, so you don't end up at ISO 6400 accidentally. An ISO indicator appears in the display to remind you what sensitivity setting has been dialed in.

ISO settings can, of course, also be used to boost or reduce sensitivity in particular shooting situations. The Z5 II has basic ISO settings from ISO 100 to ISO 64000, plus "extended" Hi settings up to Hi 1.7 (ISO 204800 equivalent) and Lo settings down to Lo 1.0 (ISO 50 equivalent). It can also adjust the ISO *automatically* as appropriate for various lighting conditions. When you choose the Auto ISO sensitivity settings (Auto ISO) in the Photo Shooting menu, as described in Chapter 5, the camera adjusts the sensitivity dynamically to suit the subject matter, based on minimum shutter speed and ISO limits you have prescribed. You should use Auto ISO cautiously if you don't want the camera to use an ISO higher than you might otherwise have selected.

Fortunately, the camera includes several useful wrinkles in its Auto ISO arsenal. You can set limits, specifying both a *maximum sensitivity* (for both ambient exposures and flash) and a *minimum* shutter speed. If Auto ISO is active (it will be indicated in the display), the camera will never select an ISO you deem to be too high. Moreover, if your exposure will result in a speed slower than the minimum you set (thereby risking blur from subject motion and/or camera movement), the camera will switch to a higher ISO setting to allow using the minimum shutter speed or faster.

As I'll explain in Chapter 5, you can ask the camera to choose an appropriate minimum shutter speed for you—it will generally use the *1/focal length* formula (e.g., 1/200th second for a 200mm lens) to set the minimum, or you can tell the camera to depart from that formula and use a faster or slower shutter speed instead to accommodate the amount or lack of blur you find acceptable in a given situation. I'll show you how to fine-tune the ISO minimum shutter speed parameter in Chapter 5.

Dealing with Noise

One reason that higher ISO settings are regarded as detrimental is that they can produce extra contrast and undesirable visual noise, a random grainy effect that robs your image of detail. What you may not realize is that the ISO setting is not the only culprit when it comes to the creation of visual noise. Indeed, the worst noise effects are a function of exposure, not ISO. There are three common types of noise in images. S*hot noise* is a random fluctuation in intensity when photons are captured by the sensor. *Read noise* is produced by electronic circuits of the sensor as the signal is converted to digital format, is not affected by shutter speed, and actually is worse at lower ISO settings. *Embedded noise* is caused by imperfections in the sensor.

The only thing you really need to know is that, in practical use, your Z5 II treats all noise created as resulting either from long exposure or higher ISO settings, as evidenced by the separate ISO reduction features for each found in the Photo Shooting and Video Recording menus, where you can specify High, Normal, or Low reduction, or turn it off entirely.

High ISO noise appears as a result of the amplification needed to increase the sensitivity of the sensor. While higher ISOs do pull details out of dark areas, they also amplify non-signal information randomly, creating noise. Because noise reduction itself tends to soften the grainy look while robbing an image of detail, you may want to disable the feature if you're willing to accept a little noise in exchange for more details.

A similar noisy phenomenon occurs during long time exposures, which allow more photons to reach the sensor, increasing your ability to capture a picture under low-light conditions. However, the longer exposures also increase the likelihood that some pixels will register random phantom photons, often because the longer an imager is "hot," the warmer it gets, and that heat can be mistaken for photons. There's also a special kind of noise that CMOS sensors like the one used in the Z5 II are potentially susceptible to. CMOS imagers contain millions of individual amplifiers and A/D converters, all working in unison. Because these circuits don't necessarily all process in precisely the same way all the time, they can introduce something called fixed-pattern noise into the image data.

The Long Exposure NR setting in the Photo Shooting menu activates taking a second, blank exposure, and comparing the random pixels in that image with the photograph you just took. Pixels that coincide in the two represent noise and can safely be suppressed. This noise reduction system, called *dark frame subtraction,* effectively doubles the amount of time required to take a picture, and is used only for exposures longer than one second. Noise reduction can reduce the amount of detail in your picture, as some image information may be removed along with the noise. So, you might want to use this feature with moderation. You can also apply noise reduction to a lesser extent using Photoshop, and when converting RAW files to some other format, using your favorite RAW converter, or an industrial-strength product like Photo Ninja (www.picturecode.com) to wipe out noise after you've already taken the picture.

Minimizing High ISO Noise

Fortunately, Nikon's electronics geniuses have done an exceptional job minimizing noise from all causes in the camera, and you don't have to rely exclusively on the Photo Shooting menu's noise reduction features. One innovation in recent years has been the introduction of *dual-gain sensors.* Digital sensors have always had a "base" ISO, typically around ISO 100, with higher settings produced by increasing the gain, or amplification, of the signal. As with every electronic system, additional amplification results in deterioration of the signal-to-noise ratio, producing an effect similar to opening your car windows and then having to turn up the volume on your radio in a fruitless attempt to counter the increased external noise.

The dual-gain sensor of the Z5 II has a traditional low base setting of ISO 100, which is your best bet when light is abundant. The sensor's circuitry can amplify the signal in the range 2X–8X to give you ISO 200, 400, 640, and other settings even though it loses some precision in capturing fine shadow detail, like an analog bathroom scale, which can show you how many pounds you've gained, but not necessarily how many ounces are involved.

A second base ISO 800 is also available, and that level of gain can also be multiplied to produce even higher ISO settings. These go up to ISO 64000, and can be further extended through additional processing up to Hi 1.7 (effectively 204800). Those higher settings are best used under dim lighting conditions or when important detail is found in shadow areas. At the higher base ISO, the Z5 II is able to detect small differences in brightness, like a postal scale that can measure fractions of an ounce. Just as a typical postal scale is lousy at measuring heavy objects, ISO settings of ISO 800 and higher are less adept at handling large quantities of light. That's why you're better off, noise-wise and exposure-wise, using lower ISO settings in bright daylight.

Bracketing

Bracketing is a method for shooting several consecutive exposures using different settings as a way of improving the odds that one will be exactly right. Alternatively, bracketing can be used to create a series of photos with slightly different exposures (or white balances) in anticipation that one of the exposures will be "better" from a creative standpoint. For example, bracketing can supply you with a normal exposure of a backlit subject; one that's "underexposed," producing a silhouette effect; and a third that's "overexposed" to create still another look.

The Z5 II can bracket exposures precisely, and bracket white balance and Active D-Lighting (described later in this chapter) as well. While WB bracketing is sometimes used when getting color absolutely correct is important, autoexposure bracketing is used much more often. When this feature is activated, the camera takes a series of consecutive photos: starting with the metered "correct" exposure, then progressing to shots with less exposure, and additional shots with more exposure, using an increment of up to +3/−3 stops. In A mode, the shutter speed will change, while in S mode, the aperture will change as the bracketed exposures are made.

Bracketing can also be done in Manual exposure mode by locking in one shutter speed—say, 1/125th second—then taking a series of three photos by varying the f/stop from f/8 to f/11 to f/16. Or, if keeping the same depth-of-field range were more important than action-stopping, you could set the aperture to f/11 and adjust the shutter speed from 1/60th to 1/125th to 1/250th second. In practice, smaller than whole-stop increments are used for greater precision, and it's common to capture more than three shots in a bracketing sequence.

Setting up autoexposure bracketing parameters is trickier than it needs to be, but you can follow these steps:

1. **Choose bracketing order.** With Custom Setting e7 you can select [Normal] MTR > Under > Over or Under > MTR > Over bracket orders. I prefer the latter (Underexposure, Metered exposure, Overexposure), as it makes certain types of manual HDR exposures easier to work with when the frames are captured in order of increasing exposure.

2. **Turn Auto bracketing on.** Navigate to the Auto Bracketing entry of the Photo Shooting menu and press the right directional button. The screen shown at left in Figure 2.6 will appear. Enable Auto Bracketing On/Off (the top option in the list).

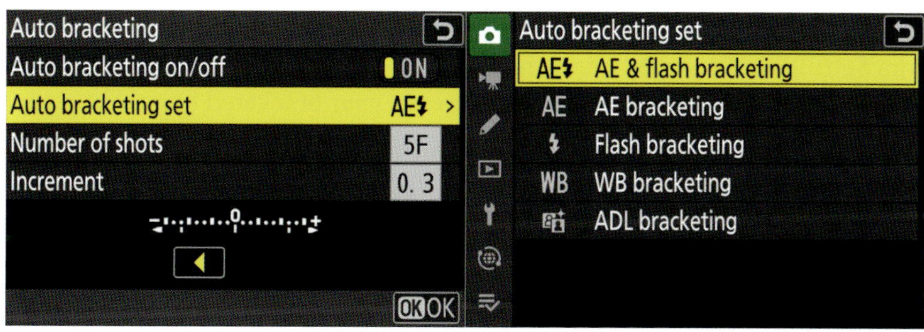

Figure 2.6 Choose Auto bracketing set, plus number of shots and increment (left). Then select the Auto bracketing set (right).

3. **Choose type of bracketing.** Next, highlight Auto Bracketing Set and press the right directional button to access the screen shown at right in Figure 2.6. Select the type of bracketing you want to do. You can select autoexposure and flash, autoexposure only, flash only, white balance only, and ADL bracketing. Press OK to return to the previous screen.

4. **Select number of bracketed exposures.** Highlight Number of Shots and use the multi selector left/right buttons or touch screen to choose 3-, 5-, 7-, or 9-shot bracket sets centered around the metered exposure.

5. **Choose bracket increment.** Next, select Increment, and use the left/right buttons or touch screen to choose the exposure increment. The size of the increments will reflect the value selected in Custom Setting b2 (EV Steps for Exposure Control), as described in Chapter 7. That is, if you've selected 1/3 EV, the bracketing increments will be 0.3, 0.7, 1.0, 1.3, 1.7, 2.0, 2.3, 2.7, and 3.0 EV. If you've specified 1/2 EV or 1 EV, the bracketing increments will be 0.5, 1.0, 1.5, 2.0, 2.5, and 3.0 or 1.0, 2.0, and 3.0, respectively.

   Note: If you select an increment of 2 EV or higher, then the number of shots in the bracketed set that you specified in Step 4 is limited to 3 or 5. If you had chosen 7 or 9 shots in Step 4, the camera will automatically change the setting to 5 shots.

6. **Disable Auto ISO.** I always disable Auto ISO when bracketing exposures, in order to limit the adjustments to f/stop and shutter speed using the increments I've selected. If Auto ISO is enabled, bracketing will still take place as directed, but the camera may make an ISO change rather than adjust f/stop or shutter speed, which may not be what you want, as described next.

7. **Choose exposure mode.** If you're using selective focus techniques or producing a set of exposures for later HDR processing, you may want the focus point and aperture to remain constant during the bracket sequence. In that case, Aperture-priority should be your preferred exposure mode. Or, you may want to avoid shutter speeds that are too slow because the scene you are capturing includes moving subjects. Choose Shutter-priority and bracketing will change only the aperture (as long as Auto ISO has been disabled).

   Manual exposure can be used for bracketing, too. If you plan on shooting in Manual exposure mode, you can specify how bracketing is performed using Custom Setting e6. Your choices are flash/shutter speed, flash/shutter speed/aperture, flash/aperture, flash/ISO sensitivity, or flash only. White balance and ADL bracketing are not available in Manual exposure mode.

8. **Frame and shoot.** As you take your photos, the camera will vary exposure, flash level, or white balance for each image, based on the bracketing "program" you selected, and in the order you specified in Custom Setting e6. In Single-frame mode, you'll need to press the shutter-release button the number of times you specified for the exposures in your bracketed burst. I've found it easy to forget that I am shooting bracketed pictures, stop taking my sequence, and then wonder why the remaining pictures in my defined burst are "incorrectly" exposed. To avoid that, I often set the camera to one of the two continuous shooting modes, so that all my bracketed pictures are taken consecutively as the shutter release is held down. The camera will stop when the sequence is complete.

9. **Turn bracketing off.** When you're finished bracketing shots, remember to return to the Auto Bracketing entry and select Off for the Auto Bracketing On/Off option, as the setting remains in effect when you power down the camera and subsequently turn it on again.

ACTIVATING BRACKETING

Once you've set up the type of bracketing you want to use, as described next, taking a bracketed set of exposures is easy. When bracketing is active, to quickly initiate exposing a set, just press a defined Bracketing Burst button. (Use Custom Setting f2 as described in Chapter 7 to assign the Bracketing Burst behavior to a button.) Once the defined button is pressed and held down, all shots in the set will be taken each time you press and hold the shutter-release button, even if the camera is set for Single Frame release mode. However, note that if bracketing is initiated using a defined button, and a Continuous release mode is set, the camera will not stop automatically at the end of a sequence. It will continue to capture series of shots until you release the button.

White Balance Bracketing

White balance bracketing is available only when you're not shooting RAW images. One snap, and you get 3, 5, 7, or 9 JPEG images at the quality level you specified, bracketed as you directed. Very slick. As you might guess, WB bracketing is applied only to JPEG files; you can't specify WB bracketing if you've chosen RAW or RAW+JPEG. RAW files are always created unmodified and will be converted according to the white balance settings you opted for in the camera when the photo is imported into your image editor (however, you can make white balance changes during importation).

White balance bracketing produces JPEG files that vary, not by f/stops (which is the case with exposure bracketing), but by units called *mireds* (micro reciprocal degrees) that are used to specify color temperature. You don't really need to understand mireds at all, other than to know that WB bracketing varies the color temperature of your images by 5 mireds for each shot taken in the bracket set.

Changes are made only in the amber-blue range; bracketing isn't applied to the green-magenta color bias. In addition, if you want to change the relative *color temperature* used for images, you'll need to work with the Choose Color Temperature option in the White Balance entry of the Photo Shooting/Video Recording menus. I'll go into a little more detail on that later in this chapter.

Meanwhile, to activate White Balance bracketing, just follow these steps:

1. **JPEG/HEIF only.** Make sure you've selected a JPEG/HEIF-only setting in the Image Quality entry of the Photo Shooting menu.

2. **Specify WB Bracketing.** In the Auto Bracketing entry of the Photo Shooting menu, choose WB Bracketing as your bracketing set.

3. **Choose number of shots.** In the Auto Bracketing screen, after you've chosen WB Bracketing, scroll down to Number of Shots and select how many bracketed exposures you want. Select 3, 5, 7, or 9 (use the right directional button) and the camera will take the specified number of shots, in the amber and blue directions, equally spread on either side of the zero point of the amber-blue scale.

4. **Select increment.** You can choose increments—the spread of the bias, measured in mireds—of 1, 2, or 3 between individual shots. For example, if you choose 5 as your number of shots and an increment of 2, the sequence will include one neutral shot, plus two biased by 5 and 10 mireds in both amber and blue directions.

ADL Bracketing

To initiate Active D-Lighting bracketing, select it from the Auto Bracketing Set option of the Auto Bracketing entry in the Photo Shooting menu and select number of shots and amount, as described next. As with exposure bracketing, you can trigger a burst with one press of the shutter release if you've defined a Bracketing Burst button.

To bracket Active D-Lighting, first use the Auto Bracketing Set option to specify ADL Bracketing, then scroll down to the Number of Shots and Amount options. The Amount (strength) adjustments vary, depending on how many shots you've specified:

- **2 (Number of shots).** Only two shots will be taken, using the option you specify by scrolling down to the Amount box. The available pairs are Off/Auto, Off/Extra High, Off/High, Off/Normal, and Off/Low.
- **3-5 (Number of shots).** You can choose 3, 4, or 5 shots, with strength settings available in the Amount box:
    - **3 shots:** Off, plus Low and Normal. (You cannot change these.)
    - **4 shots:** Off, plus Low, Normal, and High. (You cannot change these.)
    - **5 shots:** Off, plus Low, Normal, High, and Extra High. (You cannot change these.)

As with exposure, flash, and WB bracketing, remember to turn off ADL bracketing when you no longer want to use it. Once set, it is automatically invoked each time you take a picture until disabled.

Flash Bracketing

You can capture bracketed sequences using an external flash attached and powered up. The way in which the flash contributes to the bracketed exposures is determined by the Auto Bracketing Set option in the Auto Bracketing item in the Photo Shooting menu. There are three choices, shown earlier in Figure 2.6, right and listed below:

- **AE & flash bracketing.** During the sequence, both ambient exposure and flash exposure are varied individually to produce the bracketed set. Use this setting if you want the camera to adjust the flash output to match changes in ambient exposure during the sequence.
- **AE bracketing.** Only the ambient exposure is bracketed. The flash output is not changed from shot to shot.
- **Flash bracketing.** Ambient exposure is not bracketed, but the flash output is varied to produce the bracketed set.

Working with HDR

High Dynamic Range (HDR) photography is quite the rage these days, and entire books have been written on the subject. It's not really a new technique—film photographers have been combining multiple exposures for ages to produce a single image of, say, an interior room while maintaining detail in the scene visible through the windows.

It's the same deal in the digital age. Suppose you wanted to photograph a dimly lit room that had a bright window showing an outdoors scene. Proper exposure for the room might be on the order of 1/60th second at f/2.8 at ISO 200, while the outdoors scene probably would require f/11 at 1/400th second. That's almost a 7 EV step difference (approximately 7 f/stops) and well beyond the dynamic range of any digital camera, including the Z5 II.

Until sensors gain much higher dynamic ranges (which may not be as far into the distant future as we think), special tricks like Active D-Lighting and HDR photography will remain basic tools. With the Z5 II, you can create in-camera HDR exposures, or shoot HDR the old-fashioned way—with separate bracketed exposures that are later combined in a tool like Photomatix or Adobe's Merge to HDR image-editing feature. I'm going to show you how to use both.

HDR Overlay

I've been surprised at how well Nikon has solved the hand-held auto HDR problem, because there are two stumbling blocks that, at least theoretically, should lead to less-than-awesome results. First, while your camera can generate HDR images for you on the fly, there is the tendency to put the feature to work under non-optimal conditions; specifically, impromptu hand-held situations. If you've done any traditional HDR, you know that the technique works best when the camera is mounted on a tripod, so that the bracketed exposures are virtually identical except for the exposure itself. Although all HDR software can correct for slight camera movement and align images that are slightly out of register, the results I've gotten have not been great. I expected hand-held HDR to be comparable. However, Nikon's implementation does an excellent job.

The second theoretical weakness of the HDR feature is the limitation of combining just two shots to arrive at the final image. The best traditional HDR photos I've produced have involved at least three shots, and more frequently five or more, each separated by a stop of exposure. The camera takes two shots, total, and combines them. Despite these speed bumps, I've been pleased with my results.

Your Nikon Z5 II's in-camera HDR feature is simple, not particularly flexible, but still surprisingly effective in creating high dynamic range images. It's also remarkably easy to use. Although it combines only two images to create a single HDR photograph, it can often produce images that are as good as those created using the manual HDR method I'll describe in the section after this one.

It's often tricky to capture detail in both highlights and shadows in a single image, because the number of tones, the *dynamic range* of the sensor, is limited. The human eye has a "dynamic range" of up to 30 stops; typical digital cameras can capture 10 to 12 stops worth of tones in JPEG mode, and up to 14 stops if you're processing RAW files. If you need more tones, HDR is one way of overcoming the inherent limitations of the sensor.

Figure 2.7 illustrates how the two shots that the HDR feature merges might look. There is a three-stop differential between the underexposed image at left, and the overexposed image at center. The in-camera HDR Overlay feature is able to combine the two to derive an image similar to the one shown in Figure 2.7, right, which has a much fuller range of tones.

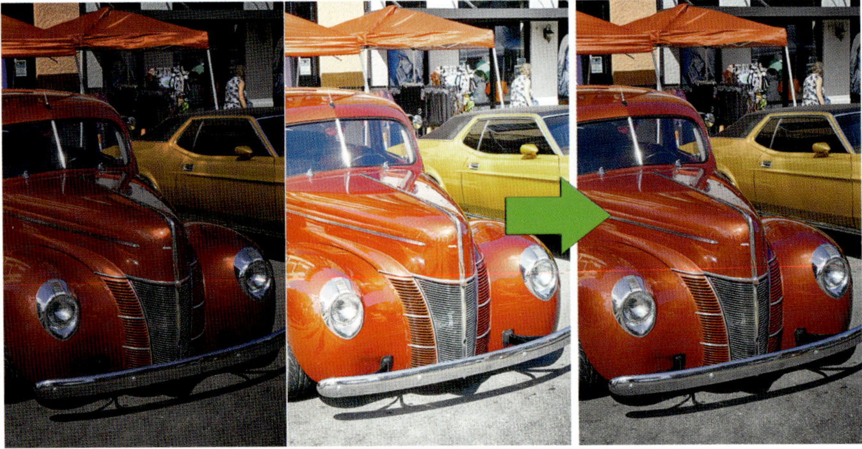

Figure 2.7 The under-exposed image (left) can be combined with the overexposed image (center) to produce the merged HDR image (right).

To use HDR Overlay, just follow these steps. The feature cannot be used simultaneously with photo flicker reduction, bracketing features, multiple exposure, focus shift shooting, interval-timer series, or time-lapse photography. The fastest continuous shooting rates (C15 or C30), as well as Bulb and Time exposures are also incompatible.

1. **Activate the menu.** Press the MENU button and navigate to the Photo Shooting menu, represented by a camera icon.

2. **Scroll down to HDR Overlay.** Press the right multi selector button. A screen appears with three choices: HDR Mode, HDR Strength, and Save Individual Pictures (RAW). (See Figure 2.8, left.)

3. **Turn on HDR.** Choose HDR Mode, press right, and select either On (series) if you want to shoot multiple HDR photos consecutively or On (single photo) to take a single HDR image and then shut the feature off. Choose OFF to disable the feature. Press OK to confirm. (See Figure 2.8, center.)

4. **Set strength.** Choose HDR Strength. Select Auto (the camera chooses the EV differential based on how contrasty it deems your scene to be). Auto is a good choice for your initial experiments if your camera is set for Matrix metering. If you've chosen Center-weighted or Spot metering, the Auto option uses Normal, instead.

   To fine-tune the strength, you can choose Extra High, High, Normal, or Low. Use stronger settings for higher-contrast subjects, and a lower value for lower-contrast subjects. Press OK to confirm. (See Figure 2.8, right.)

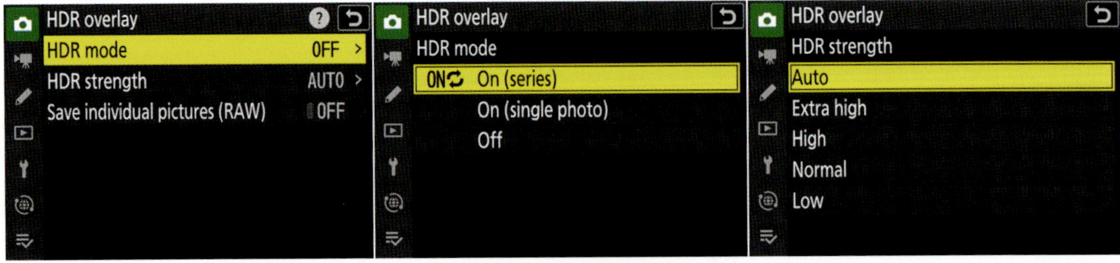

Figure 2.8 Choose HDR parameters.

Watch for haloing effects: HDR can cause haloing around the boundaries of areas within an image. If you see this "glowing" look in image review, change to a lower HDR strength.

5. **Save Individual Images (optional).** Ordinarily, the camera captures two images, combines them to produce an HDR shot, and then deletes the individual images. Turn Save Individual Pictures (RAW) on, and the camera will store a Large RAW version of each shot (even if you are in JPEG Only mode and have not selected RAW or Large image quality/size). You'll have the intermediate images available for editing/tweaking on your computer.

6. **Set Aperture-priority mode.** You want exposure to be adjusted by changing the shutter speed, rather than using a different aperture, in order to keep your depth-of-field the same for each shot.

7. **Ready to go.** You'll know the camera is in HDR mode when an indicator (HDR H, HDR A, etc.) appears at the bottom of the viewfinder display and the right side of the LCD screen. If your current display mode doesn't include the indicator, press DISP until it appears.

8. **Take your shot.** Although you can shoot HDR hand-held, you'll get the best results with the camera mounted on a tripod, and with subjects that don't display a lot of motion. Note that because the camera tries to align shots, even if there is slight camera movement, some portion of the images at the edges will be cropped out. You're better off using a tripod for Auto HDR, even though it does a decent job handheld.

Bracketing and Merge to HDR Pro

If your credo is "If you want something done right, do it yourself," you can also shoot HDR manually, without resorting to the camera's HDR mode. Instead, you can capture individual images either by manually bracketing or using the auto bracketing modes, described earlier in this chapter. Then, use Photoshop's Merge to HDR Pro feature (or similar features found in other image editors) to combine them.

Just take several pictures, some exposed for the shadows, some for the middle tones, and some for the highlights. The exact number of images to combine is up to you. The images should be as identical as possible, except for exposure. So, it's a good idea to mount the camera on a tripod, use a remote release, and take all the exposures in one burst. Just follow these steps:

1. **Set up the camera.** Mount the camera on a tripod.

2. **Set the camera to shoot a bracketed burst with an increment of 2 EV or 3 EV.** This was described earlier in this chapter.

3. **Choose an f/stop.** Set the camera for Aperture-priority and select an aperture that will provide a correct exposure at your initial settings for the series of manually bracketed shots. *And then leave this adjustment alone!* As I noted earlier, you don't want the aperture to change for your series, as that would change the depth-of-field. You want the camera to adjust exposure *only* using the shutter speed.

4. **Choose manual focus.** You don't want the focus to change between shots, so set the camera to manual focus, and carefully focus your shot.

5. **Choose RAW exposures.** Set the camera to take RAW files, which will give you the widest range of tones in your images.

6. **Take your bracketed set.** Press the button on the remote (or carefully press the shutter release or use the self-timer) and take the set of bracketed exposures.

7. **Continue with the Merge to HDR Pro steps listed next.** You can also use a different program, such as Photomatix, if you know how to use it.

DETERMINING THE BEST EXPOSURE DIFFERENTIAL

How do you choose the number of EV/stops to separate your exposures? You can use histograms, described later in this chapter, to determine the correct bracketing range. Take a test shot and examine the histogram. Reduce the exposure until dark tones are clipped off at the left of the resulting histogram. Then, increase the exposure until the lighter tones are clipped off at the right of the histogram. The number of stops between the two is the range that should be covered using your bracketed exposures. You can learn more about histograms in the section following this one.

The next steps show you how to combine the separate exposures into one merged HDR image. The sample images in Figure 2.9 (left) show the results you can get from a three-shot bracketed sequence. The images were taken from a hill above Florence, Italy, in the Piazzale Michelangelo, a square that is actually a glorified parking lot with a fancy name (and a fantastic view).

1. **Copy your images to your computer.** If you use an application to transfer the files to your computer, make sure it does not make any adjustments to brightness, contrast, or exposure. You want the real raw information for Merge to HDR Pro to work with.

2. **Activate Merge to HDR Pro.** Choose File > Automate > Merge to HDR Pro.

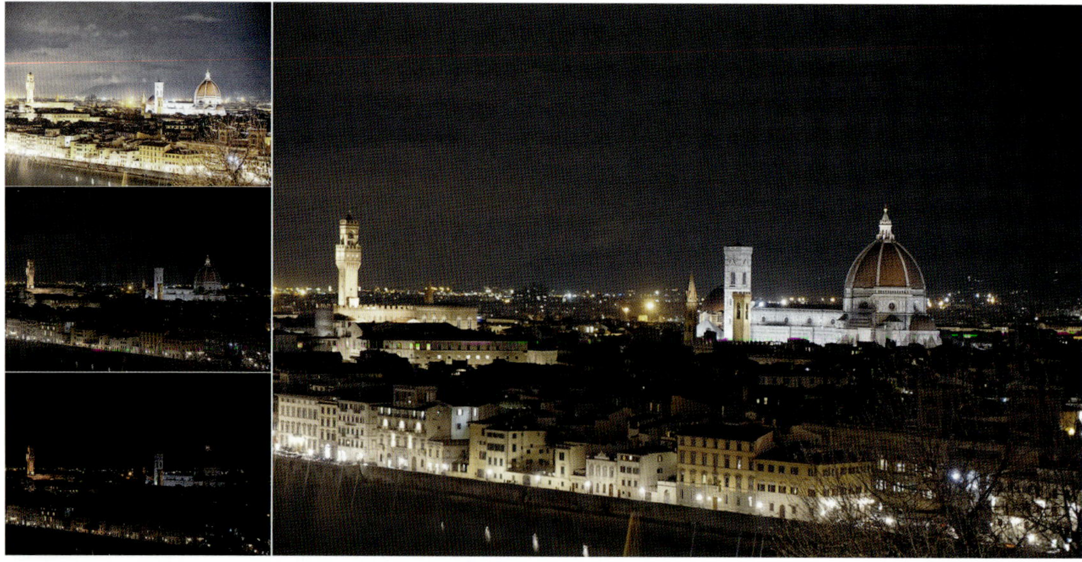

Figure 2.9 Left: Three bracketed photos should look like this. Right: You'll end up with an extended dynamic range photo like this one.

3. **Select the photos to be merged.** Use the Browse feature to locate and select your photos to be merged. You'll note a checkbox that can be used to automatically align the images if they were not taken with the camera mounted on a rock-steady support. This will adjust for any slight movement of the camera that might have occurred when you changed exposure settings.

4. **Choose parameters (optional).** The first time you use Merge to HDR Pro, you can let the program work with its default parameters. Once you've played with the feature a few times, you can read the Adobe help files and learn more about the options than I can present in this non-software-oriented camera guide.

5. **Click OK.** The merger begins.

6. **Save.** Once HDR merge has done its thing, save the file to your computer.

If you do everything correctly, you'll end up with a photo like the one shown in Figure 2.9 (right).

What if you don't have the opportunity, inclination, or skills to create several images at different exposures, as described? If you shoot in RAW format, you can still use Merge to HDR, working with a *single* original image file. What you do is import the image into Photoshop several times, using Adobe Camera Raw to create multiple copies of the file at different exposure levels.

For example, you'd create one copy that's too dark, so the shadows lose detail, but the highlights are preserved. Create another copy with the shadows intact and allow the highlights to wash out. Then, you can use Merge to HDR to combine the two and end up with a finished image that has the extended dynamic range you're looking for.

Fixing Exposures with Histograms

While you can often recover poorly exposed photos in your image editor, your best bet is to arrive at the correct exposure in the camera. However, you can't always judge exposure just by simply looking at the preview or review image on your display, as ambient light may make the monitor difficult to see, and the brightness level set for the monitor and viewfinder in the Setup menu may affect the appearance of the image. Instead, you can use a histogram, which is a chart shown on the camera's display that shows the number of tones that have been captured at each brightness level. Histograms are available in real time on your display as you shoot and in the review image during playback, but they are available only when enabled.

- **Photo and Movie modes.** For still and movie shooting, the histogram can be activated by using the Custom Monitor/Custom Viewfinder Shooting Display entries of the Custom Settings menu. I'll explain how to do this in Chapter 7. The histogram appears at lower right in both displays. The LCD screen version is shown at left in Figure 2.10.

- **Playback.** To see histograms during image review, check the Histogram box in the Playback Display Options entry of the Playback menu (discussed in Chapter 8). The camera offers four histogram variations in two screens: one histogram that shows overall brightness levels for an image (see Figure 2.10, center) and an alternate version that also shows brightness (also called *luminance*) but offers additional histograms that separate the red, green, and blue channels of your image into separate graphs (see Figure 2.10, right).

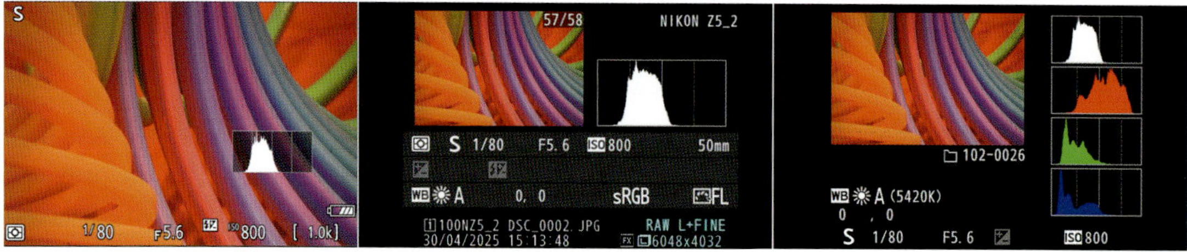

Figure 2.10 In Photo and Video Recording modes, the histogram appears in your live view image when enabled (left). Histograms are available on two different screens during playback (center and right).

Tonal Range

Histograms help you adjust the tonal range of an image, the span of dark to light tones, from a complete absence of brightness (black) to the brightest possible tone (white), and all the middle tones in between. Because all values for tones fall into a continuous spectrum between black and white, it's easiest to think of a photo's tonality in terms of a black-and-white or grayscale image, even though you're capturing those tones in three separate color layers of red, green, and blue.

Because your images are digital, the tonal "spectrum" isn't really continuous: it's divided into discrete steps that represent the different tones that can be captured. Figure 2.11 may help you understand this concept. The gray steps shown range from 100 percent gray (black) at the left, to 0 percent gray (white) at the right, with 20 gray steps in all (plus white).

Along the bottom of the chart are the digital values from 0 to 255 recorded by your sensor for an image with 8 bits per channel (8 bits of red, 8 bits of green, and 8 bits of blue equal a 24-bit, full-color image). Any black captured would be represented by a value of 0, the brightest white by 255, and the midtones would be clustered around the 128 marker. The actual information captured may be "finer" and record, say, 0 to 4,094 for an image captured with a 14 bits per channel NEF (RAW) file.

Grayscale images (which we call black-and-white photos) are easy to understand. Or, at least, that's what we think. When we look at a black-and-white image, we think we're seeing a continuous range of tones from black to white, and all the grays in between. But, that's not exactly true. The blackest black in any photo isn't a true black, because *some* light is always reflected from the surface of the print, and if viewed on a screen, the deepest black is only as dark as the least-reflective area a computer monitor can produce. The whitest white isn't a true white, either, because even the lightest

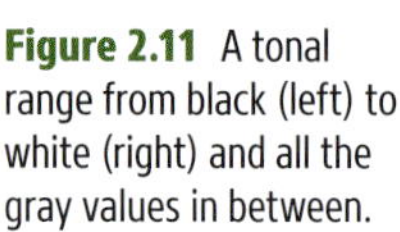

Figure 2.11 A tonal range from black (left) to white (right) and all the gray values in between.

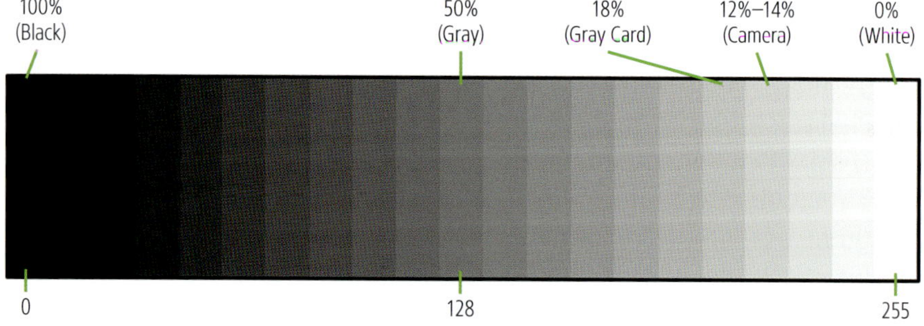

areas of a print absorb some light (only a mirror reflects close to all the light that strikes it), and, when viewing on a computer monitor, the whites are limited by the brightness of the display's LCD or LED picture elements. Lacking darker blacks and brighter, whiter whites, that continuous set of tones doesn't cover the full grayscale tonal range.

The full scale of tones becomes useful when you have an image that has large expanses of shades that change gradually from one level to the next, such as areas of sky, water, or walls. Think of a picture taken of a group of campers around a campfire. Since the light from the fire is striking them directly in the face, there aren't many shadows on the campers' faces. All the tones that make up the *features* of the people around the fire are compressed into one end of the brightness spectrum— the lighter end.

Yet, there's more to this scene than faces. Behind the campers are trees, rocks, and perhaps a few animals that have emerged from the shadows to see what is going on. These are illuminated by the softer light that bounces off the surrounding surfaces. If your eyes become accustomed to the reduced illumination, you'll find that there is a wealth of detail in these shadow images.

This campfire scene would be a nightmare to reproduce faithfully under any circumstances. If you are an experienced photographer, you are probably already wincing at what is called a *high-contrast* lighting situation. Some photos may be high in contrast when there are fewer tones, and they are all bunched up at limited points in the scale. In a low-contrast image, there are more tones, but they are spread out so widely that the image looks flat. Your digital camera can show you the relationship between these tones using a *histogram*.

Histogram Basics

Histograms are a simplified display of the numbers of pixels at each of 256 brightness levels, producing an interesting "mountain range" shape in the graph. Although separate charts may be provided for brightness and the red, green, and blue channels, when you first start using histograms, you'll want to concentrate on the brightness histogram.

Each vertical line in the graph represents the number of pixels in the image for each brightness value, from 0 (black) on the left to 255 (white) on the right. The vertical direction measures that number of pixels at each level. That range isn't a fixed number; it changes to accommodate the scene.

Although histograms are most often used to fine-tune exposure, you can glean other information from them, such as the relative contrast of the image. Figure 2.12, top, is a simplified rendition of the upper half of the Overview screen, with an image having normal contrast. In such an image, most of the pixels are spread across the image, with a healthy distribution of tones throughout the midtone section of the graph. That large peak at the right side of the graph represents all those light tones in the sky. A normal-contrast image you shoot may have less sky area, and less of a peak at the right side, but notice that very few pixels hug the right edge of the histogram, indicating that the lightest tones are not being clipped because the histogram graph is only getting close to the right edge of the histogram window, but has not gone past it.

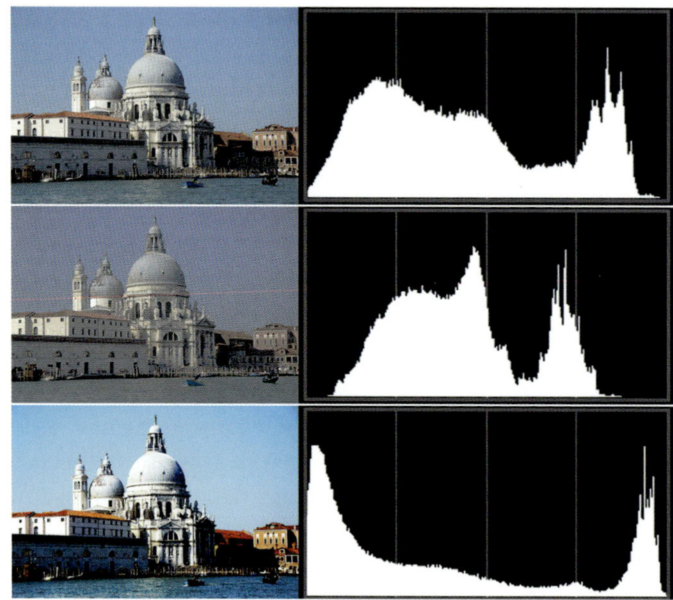

Figure 2.12 Top: This image has fairly normal contrast, even though there is a peak of light tones at the right side representing the sky. Center: This low-contrast image has all the tones squished into one section of the grayscale. Bottom: A high-contrast image produces a histogram in which the tones are spread out.

With a lower-contrast image, like the one shown in Figure 2.12, center, the basic shape of the previous histogram will remain recognizable but gradually will be compressed together to cover a smaller area of the gray spectrum. The squished shape of the histogram is caused by all the grays in the original image being represented by a limited number of gray tones in a smaller range of the scale.

Instead of the darkest tones of the image reaching into the black end of the spectrum and the whitest tones extending to the lightest end, the blackest areas of the scene are now represented by a light gray, and the whites by a somewhat lighter gray. The overall contrast of the image is reduced. Because all the darker tones are actually a middle gray or lighter, the scene in this version of the photo appears lighter as well.

Going in the other direction, increasing the contrast of an image produces a histogram like the one shown in Figure 2.12, bottom. In this case, the tonal range is now spread over the entire width of the chart, but, except for the bright sky, there is not much variation in the middle tones; the mountain "peaks" are not very high. When you stretch the grayscale in both directions like this, the darkest tones should become darker and the lightest tones should become lighter. But that may not be possible, because shades that might have been gray before can change to fully black or completely white as they are moved toward either end of the scale, and once that happens, they can't become blacker or whiter.

The effect of increasing contrast may be to move some tones off either end of the scale altogether, while spreading the remaining grays over a smaller number of locations on the spectrum. That's exactly the case in the example shown. The number of possible tones is smaller, and the image appears harsher.

Understanding Histograms

The important thing to remember when working with the histogram display in your camera is that changing the exposure does *not* change the contrast of an image. The curves illustrated in the previous three examples remain exactly the same shape when you increase or decrease exposure. I repeat: the proportional distribution of grays shown in the histogram doesn't change when exposure changes; it is neither stretched nor compressed. However, the tones as a whole are moved toward one end of the scale or the other, depending on whether you're increasing or decreasing exposure. You'll be able to see that in some illustrations that follow.

So, as you reduce exposure, tones gradually move to the black end (and off the scale), while the reverse is true when you increase exposure. The contrast within the image is changed only to the extent that some of the tones can no longer be represented when they are moved off the scale. To change the *contrast* of an image, you must do one of four things:

- **Change the contrast setting** using the menu system. You'll find these adjustments in your camera's Picture Controls menus, as explained in Chapter 5.
- **Use your built-in shadow-tone "booster."** As previously discussed, Active D-Lighting (or plain old D-Lighting applied after the fact from the Retouch menu) can also adjust contrast.
- **Alter the contrast of the scene itself,** for example, by using a fill light or reflectors to add illumination to shadows that are too dark, or light-*blocking* tools, such as "anti-reflectors" called *gobos* (because they "go between" subjects and light sources).
- **Attempt to adjust contrast in post-processing** using your image editor or RAW file converter. You may use features such as Levels or Curves (in Photoshop, Photoshop Elements, and many other image editors), or work with HDR software to cherry-pick the best values in shadows and highlights from multiple images.

Of the four of these, the third—changing the contrast of the scene—is the most desirable, because attempting to fix contrast by fiddling with the tonal values is unlikely to be a perfect remedy. However, adding a little contrast can be successful because you can discard some tones to make the image more contrasty. However, the opposite is much more difficult. An overly contrasty image rarely can be fixed because you can't add information that isn't there in the first place.

What you *can* do is adjust the exposure so that the tones *that are already present in the scene* are captured correctly. Figure 2.13, top, shows the histogram for an image that is badly underexposed. You can guess from the shape of the histogram that many of the dark tones to the left of the graph have been clipped off. There's plenty of room on the right side for additional pixels to reside without having them become overexposed. So, you can increase the exposure (either by changing the f/stop or shutter speed, or by adding an EV value) to produce the corrected histogram shown in Figure 2.13, center.

Conversely, if your histogram looks like the one shown in Figure 2.13, bottom, with bright tones pushed off the right edge of the chart, you have an overexposed image, and you can correct it by reducing exposure. In addition to the histogram, there is a Highlights option, which, when activated, shows areas that are overexposed with flashing tones (often called "blinkies") in the review screen. Depending on the importance of this "clipped" detail, you can adjust exposure or leave it alone. For

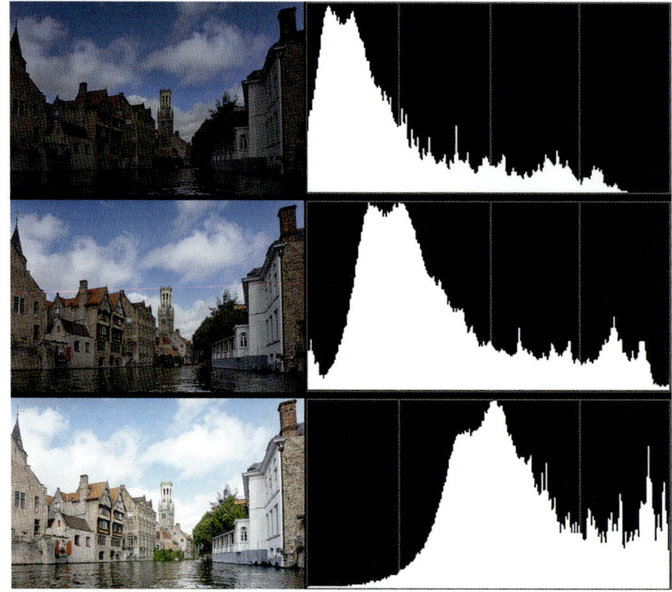

Figure 2.13 Top: A histogram of an under-exposed image may look like this. Center: Adding exposure will produce a histogram like this one. Bottom: A histogram of an overexposed image will show clipping at the right side.

example, if all the dark-coded areas in the review are in a background that you care little about, you can forget about them and not change the exposure, but if such areas appear in facial details of your subject, you may want to make some adjustments.

In working with histograms, your goal should be to have all the tones in an image spread out between the edges, with none clipped off at the left and right sides. Underexposing (to preserve highlights) should be done only as a last resort, because retrieving the underexposed shadows in your image editor will frequently increase the noise, even if you're working with RAW files. A better course of action is to expose for the highlights, but, when the subject matter makes it practical, fill in the shadows with additional light, using reflectors, fill flash, or other techniques rather than allowing them to be seriously underexposed.

A traditional technique for optimizing exposure is called "expose to the right" (ETTR), which involves adding exposure to push the histogram's curve toward the right side *but not far enough to clip off highlights.* The rationale for this method is that extra shadow detail will be produced with a minimum increase in noise, especially in the shadow areas. It's said that half of a digital sensor's response lies in the brightest areas of an image and so requires the least amount of amplification (which is one way to increase digital noise). ETTR can work as long as you're able to capture a satisfactory amount of information in the shadows.

Exposing to the Right

It's easier to understand exposing to the right if you mentally divide the histogram into fifths (unfortunately, the camera's histogram uses quarters instead). And, for the sake of simplicity and smaller numbers, assume you're shooting in 14-bit RAW. Any 14-bit image can record a maximum of 16,383 different tones per red, green, or blue channel. However, each fifth of the histogram does *not* encompass 3,277 tones (one-fifth of 16,383).

Instead, the right-most fifth, the highlights, shown in Figure 2.14, accounts for fully *half* of the different captured tones. Moving toward the left, the next fifth represents one quarter of the available levels, followed by one-eighth, one-sixteenth, and, in the left-most section where the deepest shadows reside, only 1/32nd different tones are captured. When processing your RAW file, there are only roughly 500 tones to recover in the shadows, which is why boosting/amplifying them increases noise. (The effect is most noticeable in the red and blue channels; your sensor's Bayer array has twice as many green-sensitive pixels as red or blue.)

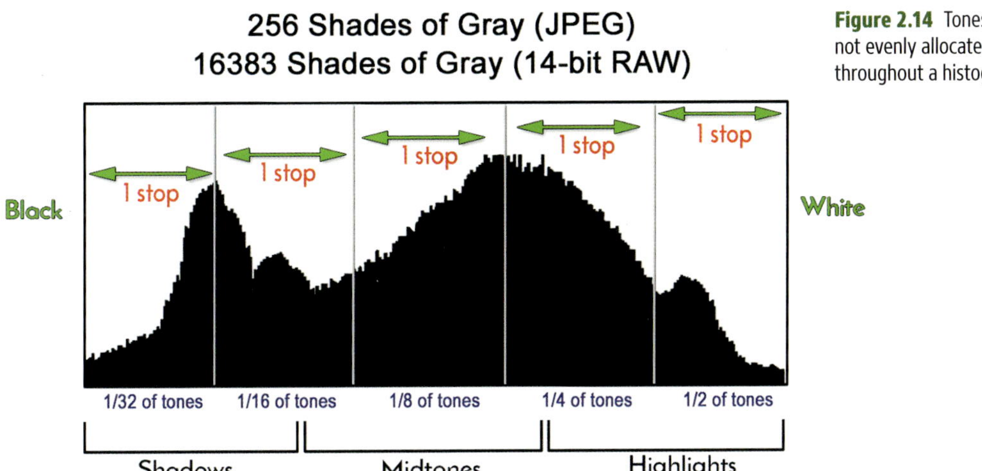

Figure 2.14 Tones are not evenly allocated throughout a histogram.

Instead, you want to add exposure—as long as you don't push highlights off the right edge of the histogram—to brighten the shadows. Because half of the tones are available in the highlights, even if the RAW image *looks* overexposed, it's possible to use your RAW converter's Exposure slider (such as the one found in Adobe Camera Raw) to bring back detail captured in that surplus of tones in the highlights. This procedure is the exact opposite of what was recommended for film of the transparency variety—it was fairly easy to retrieve detail from shadows by pumping more light through them when processing the image, while even small amounts of extra exposure blew out highlights. You'll often find that the range of tones in your image is so great that there is no way to keep your histogram from spilling over into the left and right edges, costing you both highlight and shadow detail. Exposing to the right may not work in such situations. A second school of thought recommends *reducing* exposure to bring back the highlights, or "exposing to the left." You would then attempt to recover shadow detail in an image editor, using tools like Adobe Camera Raw's Exposure slider. But remember, above all, that this procedure will also boost noise in the shadows, and so the technique should be used with caution. In most cases, exposing to the right is your best bet.

Dealing with RGB Channels

The more you work with histograms, the more useful they become. One of the first things that histogram veterans notice is that it's possible to overexpose one channel even if the overall exposure appears to be correct. For example, flower photographers soon discover that it's really, really difficult to get a good picture of a red rose, like the one shown at left in Figure 2.15. The exposure looks

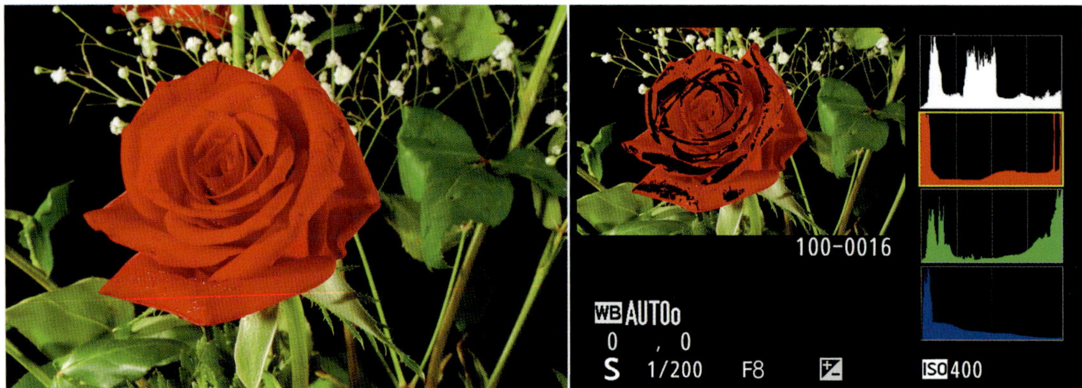

Figure 2.15 It's common to lose detail in bright red flowers because the red channel becomes overexposed even when the other chan-nels are properly exposed (left). The RGB histograms show that both the red and green channels are overexposed, with tones extending past the right edge of the chart (right).

okay—but there's no detail in the rose's petals. Looking at the histogram (see Figure 2.15, right) shows why: the red channel is blown out. If you look at the red histogram, there's a peak at the right edge that indicates that highlight information has been lost. In fact, the green channel has been blown, too, and so the green parts of the flower also lack detail. Only the blue channel's histogram is entirely contained within the boundaries of the chart, and, on first glance, the white luminance histogram at top of the column of graphs seems fairly normal.

Any of the primary channels—red, green, or blue—can blow out all by themselves, although bright reds seem to be the most common problem area. More difficult to diagnose are overexposed tones in one of the "in-between" hues on the color wheel. Overexposed yellows (which are very common) will be shown by blowouts in *both* the red and green channels. Too-bright cyans will manifest as excessive blue and green highlights, while overexposure in the red and blue channels reduces detail in magenta colors. As you gain experience, you'll be able to see exactly how anomalies in the RGB channels translate into poor highlights and murky shadows.

The only way to correct for color channel blowouts is to reduce exposure. As I mentioned earlier, you might want to consider filling in the shadows with additional light to keep them from becoming too dark when you decrease exposure. In practice, you'll want to monitor the red channel most closely, followed by the blue channel, and slightly decrease exposure to see if that helps. Because of the way our eyes perceive color, we are more sensitive to variations in green, so green channel blowouts are less of a problem, unless your main subject is heavily colored in that hue. If you plan on photograph-ing a frog hopping around on your front lawn, you'll want to be extra careful to preserve detail in the green channel, using bracketing or other exposure techniques outlined in this chapter.

Fine-Tuning Exposure

When all else fails—that is, when you find your camera *consistently* over- or underexposes when using a particular exposure mode—you can recalibrate the camera to produce images more to your liking. This setting is a powerful adjustment that allows you to dial in a specific amount of exposure adjustment that will be applied, invisibly, to every photo you take using each of the metering modes. No more can you complain, "My camera always underexposes by 1/3 stop!" If that is actually the case, and the phenomenon is consistent, you can use this custom menu adjustment to compensate.

Exposure compensation is usually a better idea (does your camera *really* underexpose that consistently?), but this setting does allow you to adjust your camera's behavior yourself. Your dialed-in modifications will survive a two-button reset. However, you have no indication that fine-tuning has been made, so you'll need to remember what you've done. After all, you someday might discover that your camera is consistently *over*exposing images by 1/3 stop, not remembering that you've made the adjustment. To fine-tune your exposure:

1. **Select fine-tuning.** Choose Custom Setting b6: Fine-Tune Optimal Exposure from the Custom Settings menu.

2. **Consider yourself warned.** In the screen that appears, choose Yes after carefully reading the warning that Nikon insists on showing you each and every time this option is activated. The screen shown in Figure 2.16, left, appears.

3. **Select metering mode to correct.** Choose Matrix metering, Center-weighted metering, Spot metering, or Highlight-weighted metering by highlighting your choice and pressing the multi selector right button.

4. **Specify amount of correction.** Press the up/down buttons to dial in the exposure compensation you want to apply. (See Figure 2.16, right.) You can specify compensation in increments of 1/6 stop, half as large a change as conventional exposure compensation. This is truly *fine-tuning*.

5. **Confirm your change.** Press OK when finished. You can repeat the action to fine-tune the other three exposure modes if you wish. To return your settings to your defaults, simply repeat the process and dial in 0 correction for the desired mode.

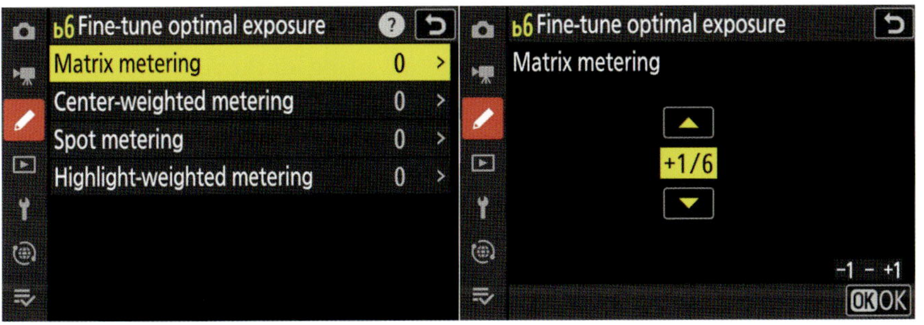

Figure 2.16 Fine-tune optimal exposure.

Interval Photography

There are two ways to capture a series of photos at intervals: manually and using the Z5 II's automatic interval photography mode. As you might expect, the manual method is labor-intensive and time-consuming. If you have the patience and motivation, you can take individual photos from approximately the same location at intervals of days, weeks, or months. One project I've started is to take photos at different times of the year, creating a series of landscape images that show the same scene in spring, summer, fall, and winter.

Construction sites also make interesting subjects for shots captured manually to document the work in progress. They can move at a snail's pace for large structures, or quite quickly in the case of home construction. For best results, try for a consistent viewpoint. It's likely you'll want a set of images taken from the same perspective so you can easily compare the progress of the construction. That can be tricky, and it requires some planning. You'll need to record the position of your camera so you can replicate it on subsequent visits.

Choose an appropriate time of day. For "progress" shots, sunny weather at midday will provide the most contrast, with shadows helping to make the details of the construction clearly visible. Early morning and late afternoon shots produce long shadows that can either be distracting or part of the composition if you want to use them creatively. Keep in mind that the weather may not always cooperate. At times, there may be no sunny days at critical times.

Automated interval photography is generally the most practical for sequences of a few hours to a day. For Figure 2.17, I pointed my camera out my office window in Florida, hoping to use Interval Timing Shooting to catch some manatees. I left the camera running for hours, capturing the three images shown in the figure. I've also used interval shooting for images of sunsets. Typically, I aim the camera at the horizon and set it to shoot a three-shot bracket with a 3.0-stop increment. Then, I set the interval to capture an image every 10 seconds.

The Z5 II's built-in interval photography feature allows you to take pictures for up to 9999 intervals in bursts of as many as nine shots, with a delay of up to 24 hours between shots/bursts, and an initial start-up time of as long as 24 hours from the time you activate the feature. That means that if you want to photograph a rosebud opening and would like to photograph the flower once every two minutes over the next 16 hours, you can do that easily. If you like, you can delay the first photo taken by a couple hours, so you don't have to stand there by the camera waiting for the right moment. This next section will tell you everything you need to know to capture images using the camera's built-in intervalometer—whether you intend to use the resulting still photos as such, or plan to combine them into a home-brewed time-lapse movie, as described shortly.

Before you start:

1. **Check your time.** The camera uses its internal clock to activate, so make sure the time has been set accurately in the Setup menu before you begin.
2. **Check release mode.** You don't need to set the camera for continuous shooting. The camera will take the specified number of shots at each interval regardless of release mode setting, with one exception: if Self-timer is selected, the sequence will be unable to start.

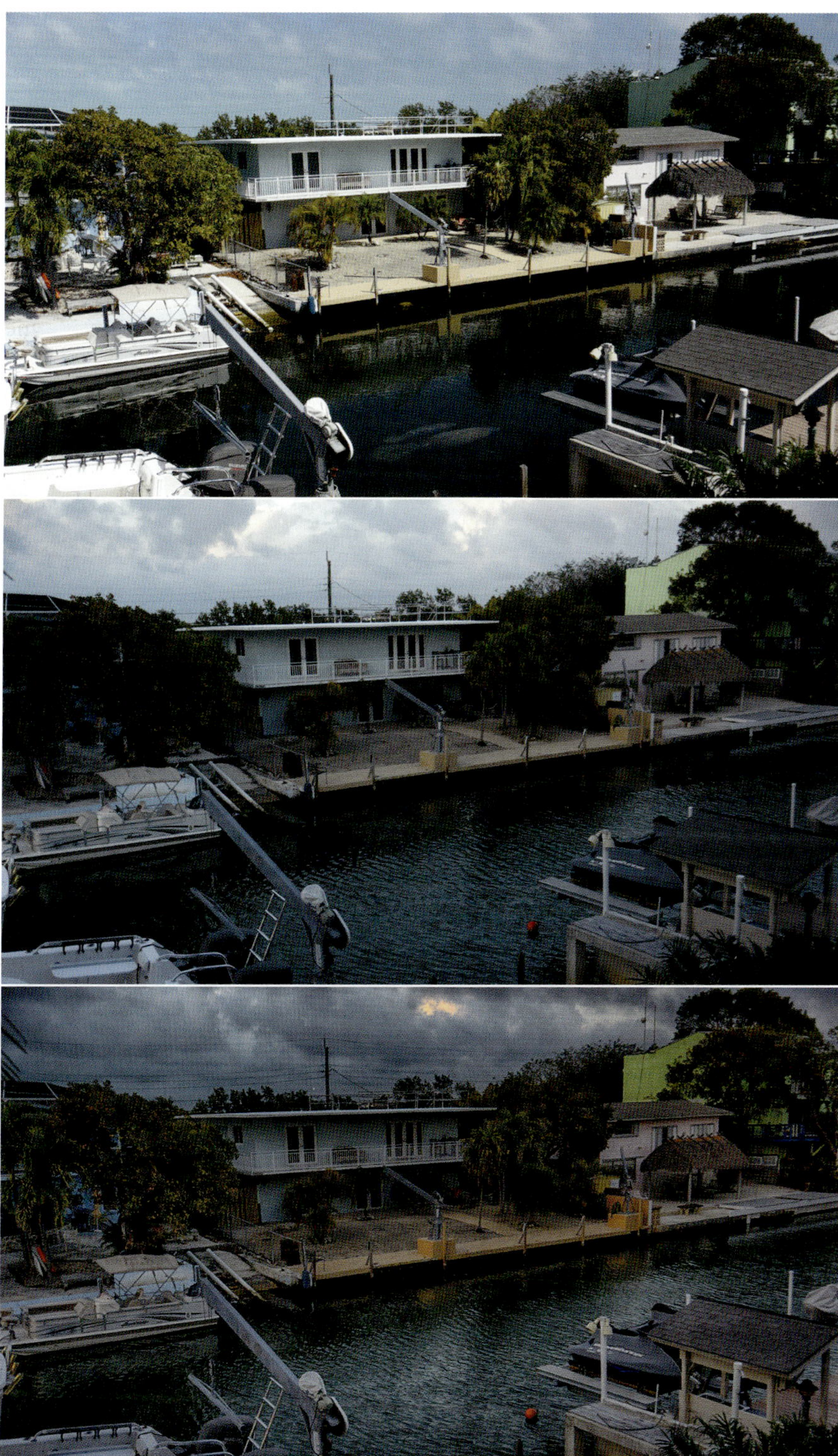

Figure 2.17 One of my time-lapse photos captured a mother manatee and her calf swimming by (top); the other exposures produced interesting variations on a static scene.

3. **Turn off bracketing.** You can certainly bracket exposures while performing interval photography—but it's *not* done with the Photo Shooting menu's Auto Bracketing feature. You must set up bracketing using the Interval Timer Shooting entries options. If conventional auto bracketing in the Photo Shooting menu is enabled, that feature will be *disabled* for interval shooting.

4. **Position camera.** Mount the camera on a tripod or other secure support.

5. **Fully charge the battery.** You might want to connect the camera to an external power source if you plan to shoot long sequences. Although the camera more or less goes to sleep between intervals, some power is drawn, and long sequences with bursts of shots can drain power even when you're not using the interval timer feature.

6. **Make sure the camera is protected** from the elements, accidents, and theft.

When you're ready to go, set up the camera for interval shooting:

1. **Access feature.** Choose Interval Timer Shooting from the Photo Shooting menu. The screen shown in Figure 2.18 will appear. Although Start is the option at the top, save it for last. Unless you're simply repeating an interval sequence you have already set up, you'll need to make the settings listed below first.

2. **Specify a starting time.** Highlight Choose Start Day/Time and press the right directional button. A screen appears allowing you to choose either Now (to begin interval shooting immediately after you finish making your settings and select Start) or Choose Day/Time. (See Figure 2.19, upper left.)

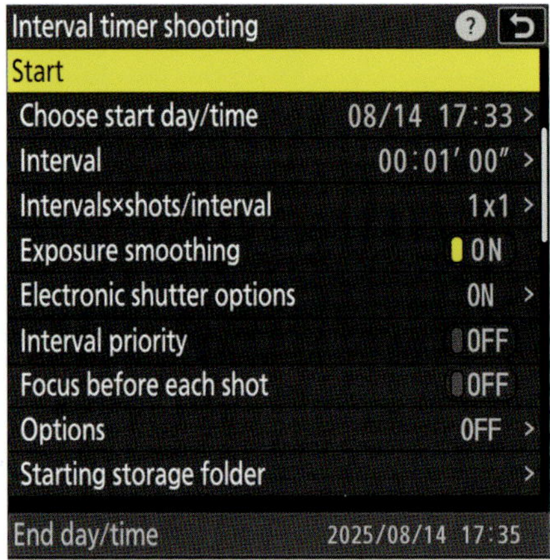

Figure 2.18 Interval timer shooting options.

To set a start time in the future, highlight Choose Day/Time and press the right directional button. A screen appears that allows entering a Start Date, H (Hour), and M (Minute). (See Figure 2.19, upper right.) You can set the current date, or up to seven days in the future. Hours are available in 24-hour format. Press OK when you've specified the start time.

3. **Set the interval between exposures.** Scroll down to the Interval entry and press the right directional button to produce the screen shown in Figure 2.19, lower left. Use the left/right directional buttons to move among hours, minutes, and seconds, and use the up/down directional buttons to choose an interval from one second to 24 hours. Press the OK button when finished to move back to the main screen.

4. **Select the spacing and number of shots.** Highlight Intervals × Shots/Interval and press the right directional button to access the screen shown at lower right in Figure 2.19. Use the left/right directional buttons to highlight the number of intervals (that is, how many times you want the camera activated) and the number of shots taken after each interval has elapsed (as many as nine images taken at each activation). The total number of shots to be exposed overall will be shown

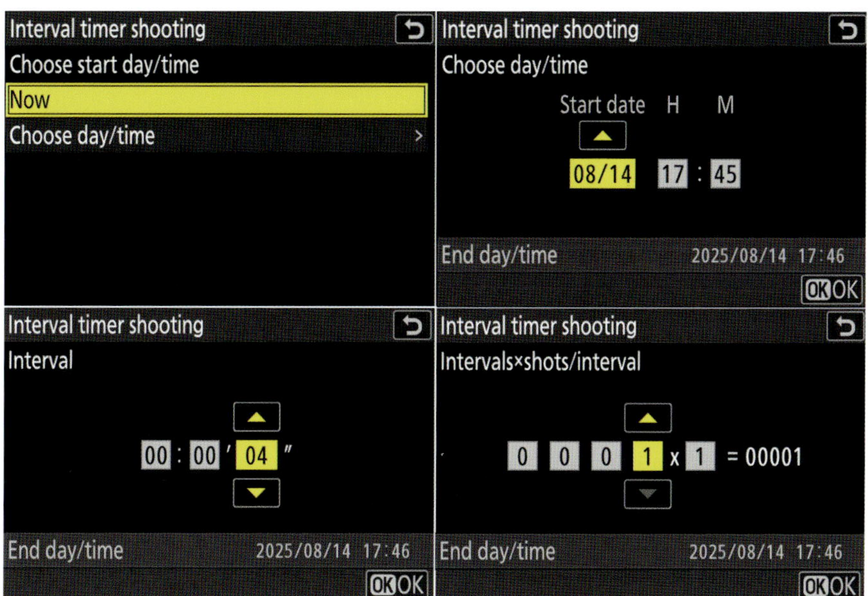

Figure 2.19 Choose starting day/time (top). Select interval and shots per interval (bottom).

at far right once you've entered those two parameters. You can highlight each number column separately, so that to enter, say, 250 intervals, you can set the 100s, 10s, and 1s columns individually (rather than press the up button 250 times!). You can select up to 9,999 intervals, and 9 shots per interval for a maximum of 89,991 exposures with one interval shooting cycle. Press OK to return to the main screen. **Tip:** Your memory card won't hold 89,991 exposures at full resolution!

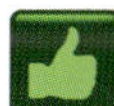 **TIP**   The interval cannot be shorter than the shutter speed; for example, you cannot set one second as the interval if the images will be taken at a shutter speed of two seconds or longer.

5. **Specify Exposure Smoothing.** You can turn this feature on or off. When activated, the camera will adjust the exposure of each shot to match that of the previous shot in P, S, or A mode. So, if you want the shutter speed to remain the same for each image (and don't care if the aperture is adjusted), use Shutter-priority mode. If you'd rather lock in your selected aperture (say, to keep the same depth-of-field), use Aperture-priority mode. Smoothing can also be used in Manual mode, but, of course, the camera won't vary either the shutter speed *or* aperture. You must have set ISO Sensitivity to Auto, to allow the camera to conform exposures by adjusting the ISO instead. Press OK to confirm.

6. **Electronic Shutter Options.** You can choose to use the Z5 II's electronic shutter, which is a useful option if you'd prefer to capture your images in quiet/stealth mode, or if you fire off a lot of shots, machine-gun style (say, for sports) and want to save wear and tear on the mechanical shutter. When the e-shutter is active, you can select volume levels from 0 (off) to 3.

7. **Set Interval Priority.** Interval Priority can be set to On or Off. This parameter handles situations in which the shutter speed automatically selected in Program or Aperture-priority ends up being longer than the interval between shots. Perhaps you're shooting outdoors, and daylight has

waned into night and a shutter speed of, say, two seconds is required even though your selected interval is one second.

- **Interval Priority On:** The camera takes the picture at the specified interval anyway, even though the image may be taken at a shorter shutter speed and, therefore, underexposed. You can avoid the underexposure by activating Auto ISO Sensitivity and selecting a minimum shutter speed that is shorter than the interval time. In that case, the camera will increase the ISO setting (if necessary) to produce the correct exposure using the automatically selected shutter speed.

- **Interval Priority Off:** The chosen interval is lengthened to allow a correct exposure.

8. **Focus Before Each Shot.** Choose On to tell the camera to focus before each new exposure. Use this option if your subject is likely to move or, more commonly, a different subject is in the frame for some or all exposures. For example, if you were recording passersby on a busy street, some might be closer to the camera than others. **Note:** The camera will use Release Priority for AF-S or AF-C focus, regardless of your Custom Setting a1 or a2.

9. **Options.** Additional options are available here, as seen in Figure 2.20, left. They include Auto-exposure Bracketing and Time-Lapse Video. You can choose one or the other, then follow the steps listed in Step 10a or 10b. The default is Off, which disables both.

10a. **AE Bracketing (optional).** As I noted earlier, you must set up exposure bracketing for interval shooting here, rather than using the Photo Shooting menu's Auto Bracketing entry. Two parameters are available, as seen in Figure 2.20, center:

- **Number of shots.** The number of shots in each bracket sequence is set as with Auto Bracketing. You can choose three or two shots bracketed either under or over the metered exposure (–3/+3 and –2/+2), or 3, 5, 7, or 9 shots with the exposures spread equally between under- and overexposure. The exposure scale at the bottom of the screen shows the distribution of the exposures.

- **Increment.** Select an increment of 0.3, 0.5, 0.7, 1.0, 1.3, 1.5, 1.7, 2.0, 2.3, 2.5, 2.7, or 3.0 stops. (If you choose 7 or 9 shots, the increments are limited to 0.3 to 1.7.) The exposure scale at the bottom of the screen will display the relative size of the increment selected. Once you've defined your bracketed set, the Intervals × Shots/Interval display will change to reflect the number of shots taken at each interval. (See Figure 2.20, right.)

10b. **Time-lapse Video (optional).** The camera will save the still photos captured in your interval sequence *and also assemble a time-lapse movie.* The movie options for Interval Timer shooting's video are similar to those used with the Time-lapse Video entry. You can choose Video File Type, Frame/Size/Rate, and Destination, as described in the next section.

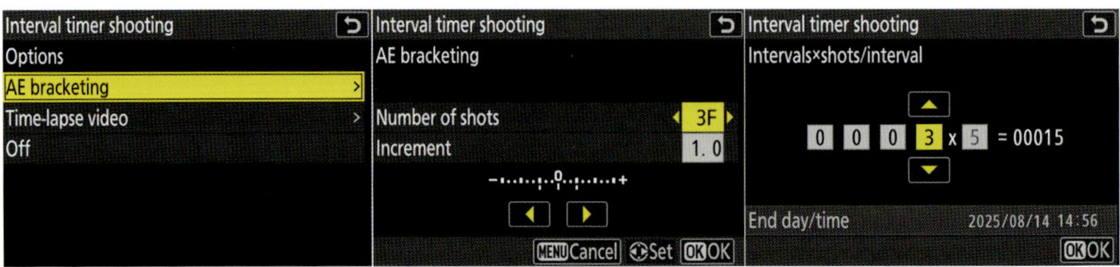

Figure 2.20 Autoexposure bracketing settings.

11. **Starting Storage Folder.** Highlight New Folder and press the right directional button to tell the camera to create a new folder for each time-lapse sequence. This allows you to easily keep your sequences separate in their own folders. If you've chosen New Folder, you can also activate Reset File Numbering, which resets the numbering of each sequence to 0001 when a new folder is created. It's handy to have each sequence numbered separately.

12. **Activate shooting.** When all the parameters have been entered, scroll to the Start option at the top of the menu and press OK. If you've selected Now under Start Options, then interval shooting will begin immediately. If you chose a specific date/time instead, the appropriate delay will elapse before recording begins. Leave your camera turned on (and connected to an external power source if necessary).

    Once you activate interval shooting, a blinking "timer" clock icon will appear on the viewfinder/ LCD displays.

PAUSE OR CANCEL INTERVAL SHOOTING

While interval shooting is underway, you can review the images already taken using the Playback button. The monitor will clear automatically about four seconds before the next interval begins. Press the OK button between intervals (but not when images are still being recorded to the memory card) or choose the Interval Timer Shooting menu entry and select Pause. Interval shooting can also be paused by turning the camera on or off. To resume the Interval Timer Shooting menu again, press the multi selector right button, and choose Restart. You may also select Off to stop the shooting entirely.

Time-Lapse Video

Time-lapse cinematography is relatively new. Invented in the early 1950s by John Ott, the technique caught the public eye when he used it for a sequence in an Academy Award-winning nature film by Walt Disney. A film documenting the building of Disneyland in California was probably the first use of time-lapse photography to picture construction progress in movie form. Who today hasn't marveled at a time-lapse photograph of a flower opening, a series of shots of the moon marching across the sky, or one of those extreme time-lapse picture sets showing something that takes a very, very long time, such as a building slowly under construction?

The Z5 II provides three different ways to capture time-lapse video rather than just a series of still pictures. One requires a little work on your part, but the other two are highly automated. I'll explain the differences between them and then show you how to use either of the two automated methods:

- **Do it yourself.** You gain more flexibility and some options if you capture the individual frames using the camera's Interval Timer and then combine them in a video editor to produce a finished movie. Depending on the power of your video editor, you may be able to crop and manipulate your images to create a professional-level video with up to 8K resolution.

- **Interval sequence plus video.** Interval Timer Shooting is fully capable of automatically creating a video from the sequence frames you capture, using Step 10b as described above. Use that mode when you want stills and a video. It's convenient for shorter video clips to accompany the individual frames, as the interval timer retains all the shots you capture *and* creates a .MOV or .MP4 video clip.

- **Video only.** If all you want is video, the Z5 II's Time-Lapse Video entry is in some ways simpler to use. You don't (can't) stipulate a start time, and instead of specifying a particular number of shots, you indicate the desired length of the finished video. I'll provide a more detailed description of this method next.

If you've mastered interval photography, shooting time-lapse video to allow the camera to capture the individual frames and assemble them into a movie for you is a snap! The settings screen is similar to the one for interval shooting, with some additional options. The key entries, shown in Figure 2.21, include:

- **Start.** Unlike the similar Interval Timer shooting entry, Time-Lapse Video has no Start Options. Make your other settings, select Start, and time-lapse photography will begin automatically about three seconds later. Be sure to double-check your settings before triggering the camera.

- **Interval.** Select an interval between frames; use a longer value for slow-moving action, such as a flower bud unfolding. You might want to experiment and choose a time between shots of one minute or longer. Some blooms mature faster than others. Use a shorter value for movies, say, depicting humans moving around at a comical pace for a Charlie Chaplin-like effect. This parameter can be set from 1 second to 10 minutes.

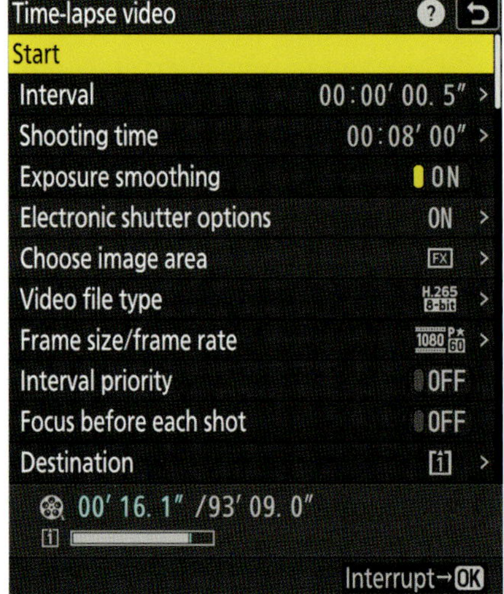

Figure 2.21 Time-lapse video options.

- **Shooting Time.** You can specify how long the camera will continue to capture frames at the interval you specified. The shortest time you can select is one minute, while the longest period you can capture is 23 hours, 59 minutes. That should be plenty for most applications. Andy Warhol's 1963 flick *Sleep* was only 5 hours, 20 minutes long!

The information bar (seen at the bottom of Figure 2.21) displays the length of your finished movie (in cyan) and the maximum length possible given the remaining capacity of your memory card in gray. A graphic below the text represents the amount of storage left. If the movie length is displayed in red instead of cyan, there is not enough space on the memory card for a video of that length.

- **Exposure Smoothing.** You can turn exposure smoothing on or off. When activated, the camera adjusts the exposure of each frame to match that of the previous frame in P, S, or A mode. That avoids sudden changes in exposure modes other than Manual exposure (which, of course, will remain at your manual settings throughout). Smoothing can also be used in Manual mode, but, of course, the camera won't vary either the shutter speed *or* aperture. You must have set ISO Sensitivity to Auto to allow the camera to compensate appropriately for changes in brightness. Press OK to confirm.

- **Electronic Shutter Options.** You can choose to use the Z5 II's electronic shutter, which is a useful option if you'd prefer to capture your images in quiet/stealth mode. When the e-shutter is active, you can select volume levels from 0 (off) to 3.

- **Choose Image Area.** You can select FX-based movie format or DX-based movie format (both cropped to the 16:9 aspect ratio of HD video, of course).

- **Video File Type.** You can choose to create your video in 8-bit .MOV format or 8-bit .MP4 format. I'll explain the difference between the two in Chapter 10, but the most important one here is that .MP4 allows creating *only* Full HD (1920 × 1080) resolution videos. (See Figure 2.22, left.)

- **Frame Size/Frame Rate.** Here you can select the frame size and frames per second setting for your time-lapse movie. As noted, only 1920 × 1080 videos at 60/50p, 30/25p, and 24p frame rates are available for .MP4 movies. If you've selected .MOV as your file type, then FHD (1920 × 1080) and 4K (3840 × 2160) resolutions are available at 60/50p, 30/25p, and 24p frame rates. (See Figure 2.22, right.)

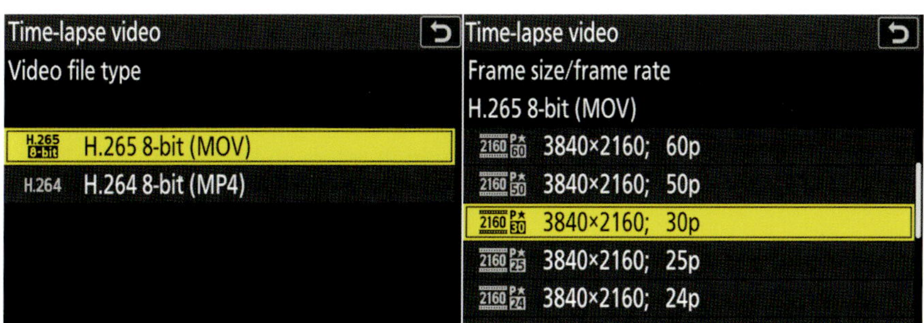

Figure 2.22 Choosing video file type and frame size/rate.

- **Interval Priority.** This setting is similar to its intervalometer counterpart, as explained previously. It takes care of situations in which the shutter speed automatically selected in Program or Aperture-priority ends up being longer than the interval between shots. When enabled, the camera captures the movie frame at the specified interval, giving it priority even though the image may be taken at a shorter shutter speed and underexposed.

  To compensate, activate Auto ISO Sensitivity, and select a minimum shutter speed that is shorter than the interval time. The camera will boost ISO to allow exposure at the correct interval. When disabled, the camera increases the interval you specified to allow correct exposure. However, with some subjects, the increased time may be visible in the finished movie as a jump or delay.

- **Focus Before Each Shot.** Choose On to tell the camera to focus before each new exposure. Use this option if your subject is likely to move or, more commonly, a different subject is in the frame for some or all exposures. For example, if you were recording passersby on a busy street, some might be closer to the camera than others.

- **Destination.** Choose either Slot 1 or Slot 2.

Star Trails

Star trails are another great application for both long exposures and interval shooting. You can shoot the night sky using long exposures with your camera mounted on a tripod. However, because of the rotation of the Earth, longer exposures will record the apparent motion of the celestial objects through the sky, producing a light trail. If you use a very, very long exposure, the light trail will record as continuous streaks, centered around Polaris (the North Star) in the northern hemisphere and Sigma Octantis (which is, unfortunately, too dim to be easily seen with the naked eye) in the southern hemisphere. If you activate Extended Shutter Speeds, you can record night shots as long as 15 minutes.

Such long exposures can result in excessive noise and sensor overheating, so it's more common for photographers to take a series of individual exposures and combine them to produce a single star trail image. If you want your stars to appear as reasonably sharp points, you'll need to keep the exposure short enough that their movement in the sky isn't apparent. Fortunately, there's a simple formula you can use to calculate that exposure time—the "500 Rule." Divide 500 by the focal length of your lens to determine the longest exposure (in seconds) before stars start to produce a blurred trail. For example, with a 50mm lens, the longest exposure would be 10 seconds (500 divided by 50). Capturing the complete canopy of stars generally requires a wider viewing perspective. With the 16mm wide-angle setting, exposures could be as long as roughly 30 seconds.

For Figure 2.23, I set my camera to ISO 200 and used a basic exposure of 30 seconds at f/5.6. I selected an interval of 32 seconds and 170 total exposures, which totals about 90 minutes. Noise reduction was OFF! Then, I followed these steps, using Photoshop:

1. **Transfer files to a folder.** Select a folder on your computer and copy all your files to that location.
2. **In Photoshop.** Choose Files > Scripts > Load Files into Stack.
3. **Browse to folder.** Click the Browse button and navigate to the folder where your images are stored.
4. **Click OK.** Photoshop will create a file with one layer for each of your captured images.
5. **Select All layers.** Then click Layer Blending Options from the Layers palette and choose Lighten.
6. **Flatten image.** You'll want to flatten your image (the multi-layer file will be huge!). You'll end up with an impressive star trail image.

Figure 2.23 Capturing a star trail.

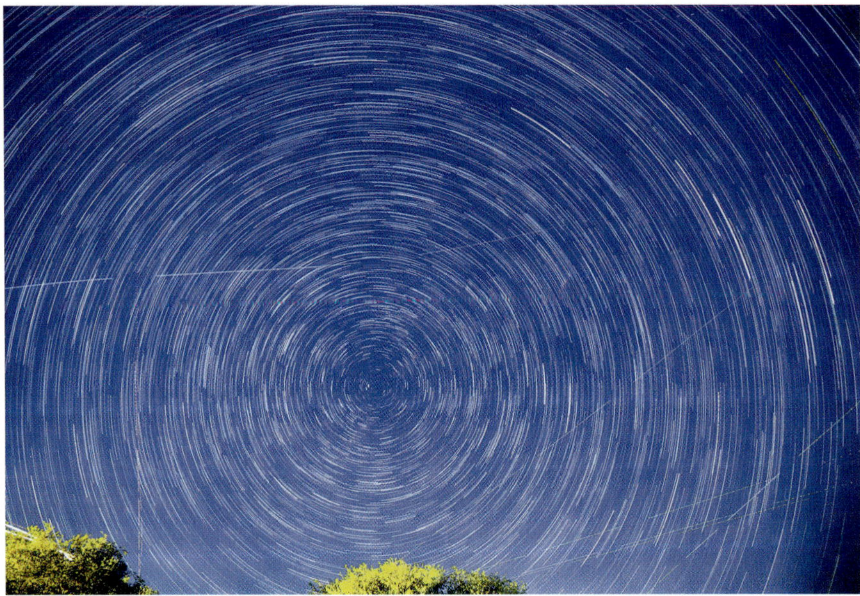

Mastering the Mysteries of Focus 3

Modern digital cameras like the Z5 II can identify potential subject matter, lock in on human faces, animals, birds, vehicles, and airplanes, and automatically focus faster than the blink of an eye. Usually. Of course, sometimes a camera's AF will zero in on the *wrong* subject, become confused by background pattern, or be totally unable to follow a fast-moving target like a bird in flight.

One key problem is that the camera doesn't have any way of determining, for certain, what subject you want to be in sharp focus. It may select an object and lock in focus with lightning speed—even though the subject is not the one that's the center of interest of your photograph. Or, the camera may lock focus too soon, or too late. While Nikon has given us faster and more precise autofocus systems, with many more choices, it's common for the sheer number of options to confuse even the most advanced photographers.

Nobody likes to get bogged down in 100-page chapters that try to cover every possible aspect of a subject in a convoluted way. So, this chapter is going to concentrate on the essential information you need to master the Z5 II's amazing autofocus and manual focus features, without multiple side-trips explaining complicated or little-used options. Indeed, Nikon has scattered focus-oriented settings among three different top-level menus. I've found that separating the "how to" lessons like those in this chapter from the reference material has proved to be the best way to explain complex topics. Here's a quick guide to finding the information you need:

- **Autofocus/Manual Focus features.** In this chapter, I'm going to introduce your camera's extensive roster of focus options and tell you how to use them. I'll cover how focus works, how to deploy all the individual focus and focus point modes, tracking, subject detection, and available focus aids. I'm also going to describe useful techniques like trap focus, back-button focus, and focus stacking.

- **Focus feature reference.** In Chapter 5, you'll find more detail about the specific menu options for AF Subject Detection, AF-area mode, and Focus Mode functions, which are all located in the Photo Shooting menu.

- **Custom Settings reference.** Chapter 7 contains comprehensive listings of the thirteen autofocus/manual focus options in the Custom Settings menu.

- **Setup Fine-Tuning.** AF Fine-tuning and retaining focus position are addressed in Chapter 9's Setup menu discussions. I explain all the options and provide an overview of AF Fine-tuning in that chapter, but it's a function you will rarely (or never) need to perform, so I'm including step-by-step instructions for using it in Chapter 12. That chapter is included in the ebook versions of this guide, and available for download as a PDF file, as described in the Introduction to this book.

How Focus Works

Simply put, focus is the process of adjusting the camera so that parts of our subject that we *want* to be sharp and clear are, in fact, sharp and clear. We can allow the camera to focus for us, automatically, or we can rotate the lens's focus ring manually to achieve the desired focus. Manual focusing is especially problematic because our eyes and brains have poor memory for correct focus. That's why your eye doctor conducting a refraction test must shift back and forth between pairs of lenses and ask, "Does that look sharper—or was it sharper before?" in determining your correct prescription. Too often, the slight differences are such that the lens pairs must be swapped multiple times.

Similarly, manual focusing involves jogging the focus ring back and forth as you go from almost in focus, to sharp focus, to almost focused again. The little clockwise and counterclockwise arcs decrease in size until you've zeroed in on the point of correct focus. What you're looking for is the image with the most contrast between the edges of elements in the image.

Your autofocus mechanism, like all such systems found in modern cameras, also evaluates these increases and decreases in sharpness, but it is able to remember the progression perfectly, so that autofocus can lock in much more quickly and, with an image that has sufficient contrast, more precisely. Unfortunately, while the autofocus system finds it easy to measure degrees of apparent focus at each of the focus points in the viewfinder, it doesn't really know with any certainty *which object* should be in sharpest focus. Is it the closest object? The subject in the center? Something lurking *behind* the closest subject? A person standing over at the side of the picture? Using autofocus effectively involves telling the camera exactly what it should be focusing on.

As the camera collects focus information from the sensors, it then evaluates it to determine whether the desired sharp focus has been achieved. The calculations may include whether the subject is moving, and whether the camera needs to "predict" where the subject will be when the shutter-release button is fully depressed, and the picture is taken. The speed with which the camera is able to evaluate focus and then move the lens elements into the proper position to achieve the sharpest focus determines how fast the autofocus mechanism is. Although the AF system will almost always focus more quickly than a human eye, there are types of shooting situations where that's not fast enough. For example, if you're having problems shooting a sport with many fast-moving players because the autofocus system manically follows each moving subject, a better choice might be to switch Autofocus modes or shift into Manual and prefocus on a spot where you anticipate the action will be, such as a goal line or soccer net.

You'll be using a *hybrid* autofocus system, using two technologies called contrast-detection autofocus (CDAF) and phase-detection autofocus (PDAF). I'm going to provide a quick overview of contrast detection first, and then devote much of the rest of this chapter to the complexities of phase detection.

Contrast Detection

Contrast detection is very easy to understand, and is illustrated by Figure 3.1, a close-up of the side of an old barn. At left in the figure, the transitions between the edges found in the siding and foundation are soft and blurred because of the low contrast between them. Whether the edges are horizontal, vertical (like the siding), or diagonal doesn't matter in the least; the focus system looks only for contrast between edges, and those edges can run in any direction at all.

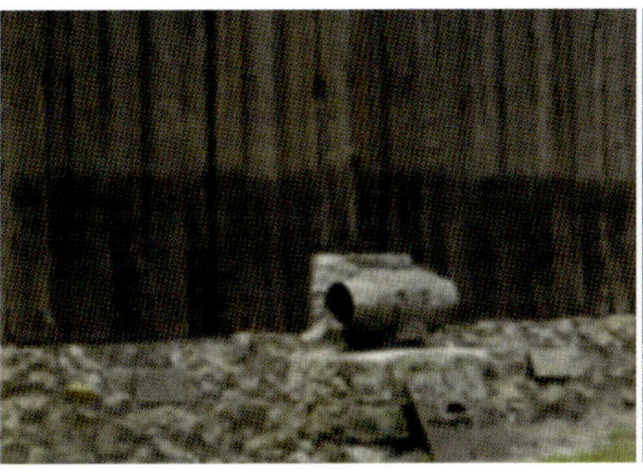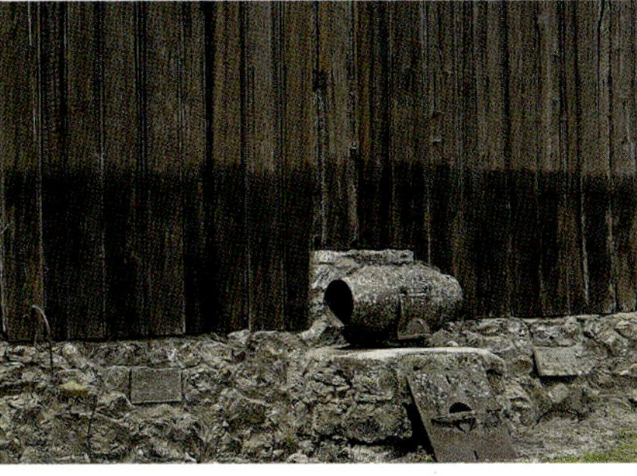

Figure 3.1 Focus in contrast-detection mode evaluates the increase in contrast in the edges of subjects, starting with a blurry image (left) and producing a sharp, contrasty image (right).

At right in Figure 3.1, the image has been brought into sharp focus, and the edges have much more contrast; the transitions are sharp and clear. Although this example is a bit exaggerated so you can see the results on the printed page, it's easy to understand that when maximum contrast in a subject is achieved, it can be deemed to be in sharp focus. Although achieving focus with contrast detection is generally slower, there are several advantages—and disadvantages—to this method:

- **Works with more image types.** Any subject that has edges will work with CDAF.
- **Focus on any point.** With contrast detection, any portion of the image can be used to focus: you don't need dedicated AF sensors. Focus is achieved with the actual sensor image, so focus-point selection is simply a matter of choosing which part of the sensor image to use. It's easy to move the focus point around to virtually any location. Because a smaller area of the sensor can be used to focus, the camera uses contrast detection to confirm focus when the autofocus area mode is set to Pinpoint AF. (I'll explain AF-area modes later in this chapter.)
- **Potentially more accurate.** Contrast detection is clear-cut. The camera can clearly see when the highest contrast has been achieved, as long as there is sufficient light to allow it to examine the image produced by the sensor. However, some "hunting" may be necessary. As the camera seeks the ideal plane of focus, it may overshoot and have to back up a little, then re-correct if the new focus plane is not optimal. However, once CDAF settles on the ideal focus plane, the results are generally very accurate. Contrast detection is an excellent way of fine-tuning focus that has been achieved through PDAF. As noted, the Z5 II can use contrast detection when the AF-area mode is Pinpoint AF, especially in AF-S focus mode, or under low-light conditions.

Phase Detection

Phase detection is much more rapid than contrast detection. The challenge is to make its operation as accurate as possible. Digital SLRs have always used PDAF, with an array of tiny autofocus sensors located in the "floor" of the mirror box, and a small portion of the illumination directed downward to the autofocus sensor array. That separate AF sensor in the dSLR is replaced by a large number of phase-detect autofocus points embedded in the Z5 II's imaging sensor, as shown in Figure 3.2.

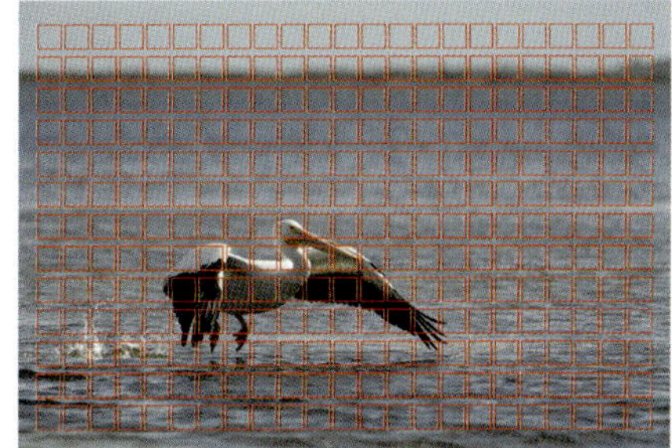

Figure 3.2 The boxes represent the 299 AF areas when using Auto-area AF.

There are 299 areas available (arranged in a 23 × 13 matrix) when using Auto-area AF, and 273 areas (a 21 × 13 array) in other autofocus area modes.

The phase-detection pixels in the camera's sensor have a mask covering half of the pixel on one side, with a nearby laterally displaced phase-detection pixel masked on the opposite side. The effect is to create two different "views," each arriving from opposite sides of the lens. This pair of images functions exactly like the rangefinders used for surveying and in rangefinder-focusing cameras like the venerable Leica M series. The two images are separated when out of focus, and then brought together to achieve sharp focus, as shown from top to bottom in Figure 3.3. **Note:** Using some pho-

tosites as AF sensors doesn't rob your camera of resolution; the phase-detect sensors are actually *dual-pixel* photosites and are used to collect *both* autofocus and image information. In addition, your Z5 II has 24.5 *million* pixels available to create an image; assigning some to double duty has no effect on image quality.

This process determines when the image pair are "in phase" and aligned. The rangefinder approach of phase detection indicates exactly how out of focus the image is, and in which direction (focus is too near, or too far) thanks to the amount and direction of the displacement of the split image. The system can quickly and precisely snap the image into sharp focus and match the lines.

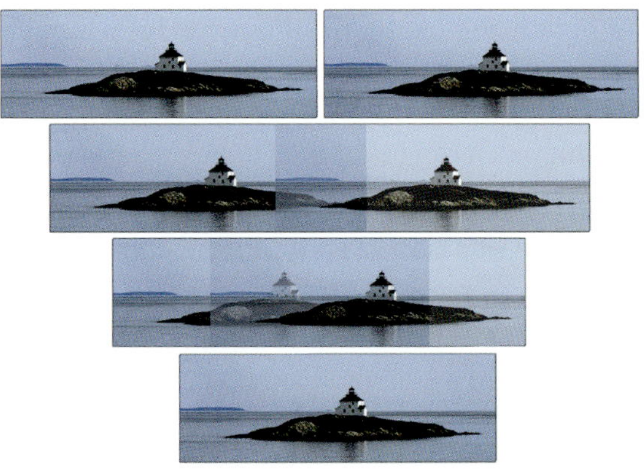

Figure 3.3 In phase detection, parts of an image are split in two and compared (top). When the image is in focus, the two halves of the image align, as with a rangefinder (bottom).

The PDAF sensors are all *line sensors,* which means they work best with features that transect the sensor either perpendicularly or at an angle, as visualized in Figure 3.4, left. It's easy to detect when the two halves of the vertical lines of the weathered wood are aligned. (See Figure 3.4, center.) However, when the same sensor is asked to measure focus for, say, horizontal lines that don't split up quite so conveniently, or, in the worst case, subjects such as the sky (which may have neither vertical nor horizontal lines), focus can slow down drastically. One such scenario is pictured in Figure 3.4, right.

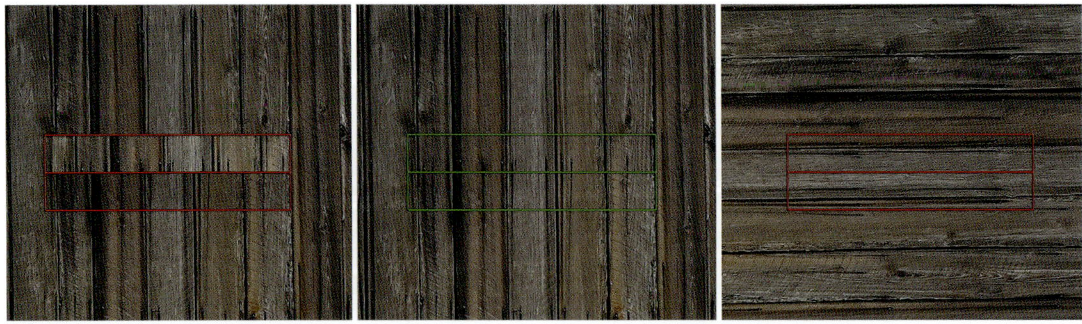

Figure 3.4 When an image is out of focus, the split lines don't align precisely (left). Using phase detection, the camera is able to align the features of the image and achieve sharp focus quickly (center). Horizontal lines aren't ideal for horizontally oriented sensors and require vertical contrast detection to achieve final focus (right).

Once the focus plane has been achieved using the line sensors of the phase-detect system, the camera is able to use contrast detection to fine-tune focus, if necessary. The combination provides the speed of PDAF with the accuracy of CDAF.

All dSLRs perform autofocus using the lens's largest f/stop, which means that lenses with a maximum aperture smaller than f/5.6 or f/8 can't use autofocus at all. Your Z5 II doesn't have that limitation: it always autofocuses at the *aperture you've set* if it is f/5.6 or wider. That reduces the possibility of focus shift that can result from focusing at one aperture and taking the actual photo at a different aperture (and different depth-of-field characteristics). However, if your selected f/stop is smaller than f/5.6, the Z5 II will use f/5.6 anyway.

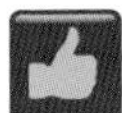 **TIP** If you find the horizontal line AF sensors (which are most sensitive to vertical lines) have difficulties focusing on a subject that is predominated by horizontal features, rotate the camera at least 45 degrees and lock focus, then return to your previous orientation. Obviously, this works best with subjects that aren't moving.

Your Z5 II's phase-detect system offers one final bonus: reducing/eliminating the need for AF fine-tuning (although the option still exists in the Setup menu). In contrast, a dSLR's separate AF mechanism has a half-dozen different components that can potentially be out of alignment; with mirrorless cameras only the lens/lens mount and sensor planes need to be perfectly lined up.

Focus and Depth-of-Field

You know that increased depth-of-field brings more of your subject into focus. But more depth-of-field also makes autofocusing (as well as manual focusing) more difficult because the contrast is lower between objects at different distances. To make things even more complicated, many subjects move around in the frame, so that even if the camera is sharply focused on your main subject, it may change position and require refocusing. An intervening subject may pop into the frame and pass between you and the subject you meant to photograph. You (or the camera) have to decide whether to lock focus on this new subject or remain focused on the original subject. Finally, there are some kinds of subjects that are difficult to bring into sharp focus because they lack enough contrast to allow the camera's AF system (or our eyes) to lock in. Blank walls, a clear blue sky, birds-in-flight, or other subject matter may make focusing difficult.

If you find all these focus factors confusing, you're on the right track. Focus is, in fact, measured using something called a *circle of confusion*. An ideal image consists of zillions of tiny little points, which, like all points, theoretically have no height or width. There is perfect contrast between the point and its surroundings. You can think of each point as a pinpoint of light in a darkened room. When a given point is out of focus, its edges decrease in contrast and it changes from a perfect point to a tiny disc with blurry edges (remember, blur is the lack of contrast between boundaries in an image). (See Figure 3.5.)

If this blurry disc—the circle of confusion—is small enough, our eye still perceives it as a point. It's only when the disc grows large enough that we can see it as a blur rather than a sharp point that a given point is viewed as out of focus.

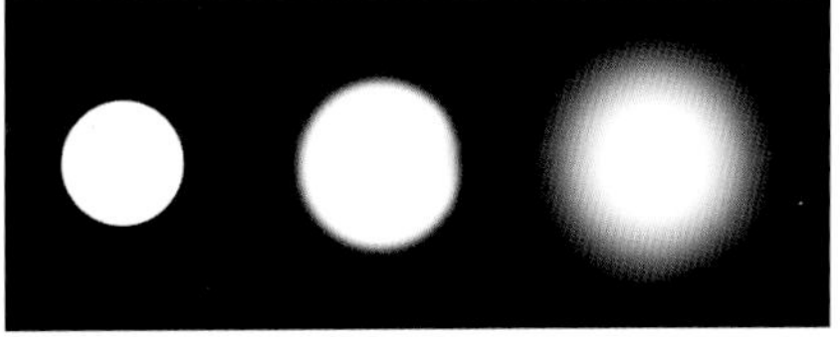

Figure 3.5 When a pinpoint of light (left) goes out of focus, its blurry edges form a circle of confusion (center and right).

You can see, then, that enlarging an image, either by displaying it larger on your computer monitor or by making a large print, also enlarges the size of each circle of confusion. Moving closer to the image does the same thing. So, parts of an image that may look perfectly sharp in a 5 × 7–inch print viewed at arm's length, might appear blurry when blown up to 11 × 14 and examined at the same distance. Take a few steps back, however, and it may look sharp again.

Technically, there is just one plane within your picture area, parallel to the back of the camera (or sensor, in the case of a digital camera), that is in sharp focus. That's the plane in which the points of the image are rendered as precise points. At every other plane in front of or behind the focus plane, the points show up as discs that range from slightly blurry to extremely blurry. In practice, the discs in many of these planes will still be so small that we see them as points, and that's where we get depth-of-field. Depth-of-field is just the range of planes that include discs that we perceive as points rather than blurred splotches. The size of this range increases as the aperture is reduced in size and is allocated roughly one-third in front of the plane of sharpest focus, and two-thirds behind it. The range of sharp focus is always greater behind your in-focus subject than in front of it. (See Figure 3.6.)

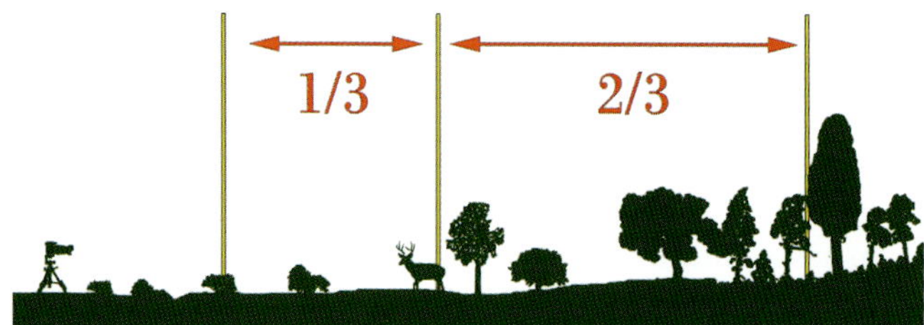

Figure 3.6 The range of sharp focus is greater behind your in-focus subject than in front of it.

Bringing the AF System into Focus

Autofocus can sometimes be frustrating for the new digital photographer. That's because correct focus plays a greater role among your creative options with a digital camera, even when photographing the same subjects. Most point-and-shoot digital cameras and smartphones have sensors that are much tinier than the sensor in the camera. Those smaller sensors require shorter focal length lenses and zoom settings, which have, effectively, more depth-of-field.

The bottom line is that with the average point-and-shoot camera or smartphone, *everything* is in focus from about one foot to infinity and at virtually every f/stop. Unless you're shooting close-up photos a few inches from the camera, the depth-of-field is prodigious, and autofocus is almost a non-factor. Of course, some of the latest phones have multiple lenses, extra-large f/stops (with reduced depth-of-field), and intelligent algorithms that can process images to produce selective focus effects and blurry backgrounds.

Your Z5 II needs no special tricks to achieve similar effects, because, as a full-frame model, it uses longer focal length lenses, so there is less depth-of-field. That's a *good* thing, creatively, because you have the choice to use selective focus to isolate subjects. But it does make the correct use of autofocus more critical. To maintain the most creative control, you have to choose three attributes:

- **How much is in focus.** Generally, by choosing the f/stop used, you'll determine the *range* of sharpness/amount of depth-of-field. The more extensive the DOF, the "easier" it is for the autofocus system's locked-in focus point to be appropriate (even though, strictly speaking, there is only one actual plane of sharp focus). With less depth-of-field, the accuracy of the focus point becomes more critical, because even a small error will result in an out-of-focus shot.

- **What subject is in focus.** The portion of your subject that is zeroed in for autofocus is determined by the autofocus zone that is active, and which is chosen either by you or by the Nikon camera (as described next). For example, when shooting portraits, it's actually okay for part of the subject—or even part of the subject's face—to be slightly out of focus as long as the eyes (or even just the *nearest* eye) appear sharp.

- **When focus is applied.** For static shots of objects that aren't moving when focus is applied, it doesn't matter as much. But when you're shooting sports, or birds in flight, or children, the subject may move within the viewfinder as you're framing the image. Whether that movement is across the frame or headed right toward you, timing the instant when autofocus is applied can be important.

Choice of which f/stop to use is totally up to you and depends on just how much depth-of-field you want for an image, whether it's very little (in order to apply selective focus techniques) or a great deal (for deep-focus effects or to make sure challenging subjects remain sharply focused). What subject is in focus, and when focus is applied are determined by your use of your Z5 II's autofocus settings and controls, including these:

- **Autofocus mode and priority.** This governs *when* during the framing and shooting process autofocus is achieved. Should the camera focus once when activated, or continue to monitor your subject and refocus should the subject move? (AF-S or AF-C?) Is it okay to take a picture even if sharp focus isn't yet achieved, or should the camera lock out the shutter release until the image is sharp?

- **Autofocus point selection.** This aspect controls how the camera selects which areas of the frame are used to evaluate focus. Point selection allows the camera (or you) to specify a subject and lock focus in on that subject. Choosing the right AF-area mode is the key here.

- **Autofocus activation.** When should the autofocus process *begin*, and when should it be locked? This aspect is related to the autofocus mode but uses controls that you can specify to activate and/or lock the autofocus process.

As the camera collects information from the sensors, it then evaluates the data to determine whether the desired sharp focus has been achieved. The calculations may include whether the subject is moving, and whether the camera needs to "predict" where the subject will be when the shutter-release button is fully depressed, and the picture is taken.

The speed with which the camera is able to evaluate focus and then move the lens elements into the proper position to achieve the sharpest focus determines how fast the autofocus mechanism is. Although your Z5 II will almost always focus more quickly than a human, there are types of shooting situations where that's not fast enough. For example, as I mentioned, if you're having problems shooting sports because the camera's autofocus system follows each moving subject, a better option might be to switch autofocus modes or shift into manual and prefocus on a spot where you anticipate the action will be, such as a goal line. At night football games, for example, when I am shooting with a telephoto lens almost wide open under dim lighting, I sometimes focus manually on one of the referees who happens to be standing where I expect the action to be taking place (say, a halfback run or a pass reception).

Focus Mode and Priority

Choosing the right focus mode (AF-S, AF-C, AF-A, or Manual) is another key to focusing success. (Your camera also has an additional focus mode, AF-F—full-time autofocus in Video mode—as explained in Chapter 10.) To save battery power, when shooting stills, your camera doesn't start to focus the lens until you partially depress the shutter release or AF-ON button (or some other button you have assigned the AF-ON function to using Custom Setting f2). But, autofocus isn't some mindless beast out there snapping your pictures in and out of focus with no feedback from you after you press that button. There are several settings you can modify that return at least a modicum of control to you. Your first decisions should be whether you set the camera to AF-S, AF-C, or manual focus, and whether to use focus-priority or release-priority (described soon).

You can easily specify AF-S, AF-C, AF-A, or Manual focus: hold down the Fn2 button and rotate the main command dial or just press the *i* button and access Focus mode, located by default at the far right in the top row of the *i* menu. If you have a lot of time on your hands, use the Focus mode entry in the Photo Shooting or Video Recording menus.

Autofocus Mode

This choice determines *when* your camera starts to autofocus, and what it does when focus is achieved. In still photo mode, automatic focus is not something that happens all the time when your camera is turned on. As I mentioned, to save battery power, your camera generally doesn't start to focus the lens until you partially depress the shutter release, AF-ON button, or another button assigned the AF-ON behavior.

Single-Servo Autofocus (AF-S)

In this mode, also called *Single Autofocus*, focus is set once and remains at that setting until the button is fully depressed, taking the picture, or until you release the shutter button without taking a shot. The Z5 II focuses very quickly, relying only on phase detection. As mentioned earlier, contrast-detect correction is applied only when using the Pinpoint AF area mode, or when the camera's low-light AF feature (see the sidebar below) is enabled.

LOW-LIGHT AF

All digital cameras find autofocusing in low-light environments a challenge. One aid is Custom Setting d11: Starlight View (Photo Lv). Autofocus may take longer. You may also be able to improve autofocus performance for subjects that are within the range of about three feet to nearly 10 feet (1 to 3 meters) with the built-in AF-assist illuminator lamp on the front of the camera, which is activated by default but may be disabled using Custom Setting a11.

For non-action photography, this setting may be your best choice, as it minimizes out-of-focus pictures (at the expense of spontaneity). The drawback here is that you might not be able to take a picture at all while the camera is seeking focus; you're locked out until the autofocus mechanism is happy with the current setting. As described in Chapter 5, you can set AF-S mode to use either focus-priority (the default) or release-priority using Custom Setting a2.

When sharp focus is achieved, the user-specified focus point (or the points selected by the camera in Auto-area AF mode) will turn green. You'll hear a beep (if not disabled using Beep Options in the Setup menu, as described in Chapter 9) and the camera is set to focus-priority. By keeping the shutter button depressed halfway, you'll find you can reframe the image while retaining the focus (and exposure) that's been set. You can also press the sub-selector (which is assigned the AE-L/AF-L function by default) to lock exposure and autofocus plane. If the camera is unable to focus, the focus point will flash red. Because of the small delay while the camera zeroes in on correct focus, you might experience slightly more shutter lag. This mode uses less battery power.

Using the directional controls, you can select any of the available focus areas in this AF mode when your Autofocus Area setting (described shortly) is set to Single-point AF, any of the four variations of Wide-area AF, or virtually anywhere within the focus area encompassed by the boxes in Figure 3.2 when Pinpoint AF is active. AF-S is the mode to use if you want to place the focus point within your frame with accuracy. One advantage is that you can place your subject within the focus area (no matter where it is in the frame), then press the shutter release halfway to lock focus, and then reframe, and focus will remain at the plane you focused on.

Continuous-Servo Autofocus (AF-C)

This is the mode to use for sports and other types of photography with fast-moving subjects. In this mode, once the shutter release is partially depressed, the camera sets the focus but continues to monitor the subject, so that if it moves or you move, the lens will be refocused to suit. Focus and exposure aren't really locked until you press the shutter release down all the way to take the picture. You'll find that AF-C produces the least amount of shutter lag of any autofocus mode when set to release-priority: press the button and the camera fires, even if sharp focus has not quite been achieved. It also uses the most battery power, because the autofocus system operates as long as the shutter-release button is partially depressed.

When using AF-C, the active focus areas are shown in red, as with AF-S mode. However, when you press the shutter release halfway down (or press an AF-ON button), when the camera achieves sharp focus, by default you won't see a green box or hear a beep as confirmation. That can be a *good* thing. If that were the case, since AF-C constantly refocuses as long as the shutter release is held down halfway (or AF-ON button is depressed), you'd be treated to a barrage of beeps and constantly flickering green indicator until the picture is taken. If you see your subject has gone out of focus and the camera doesn't quickly recover, just release the button and press again to restart the focusing process. If you'd prefer to see the green focus confirmation indicators, you can activate it using Custom Setting a10: Focus Point Display > AF-C In-Focus Display. You'll learn how to customize focus point display for manual focus, Dynamic-area AF assist, and 3D-tracking, too, in Chapter 7.

Continuous-servo autofocus uses a technology called *predictive focus tracking*, which allows the camera to calculate the correct focus if the subject is moving toward or away from the camera at a constant rate. It uses either the automatically selected AF point (in Auto-area AF mode) or the point you select manually to set focus. As described in Chapter 7, you can set AF-C mode to use release-priority (the default) or focus-priority using Custom Setting a1.

Automatic Autofocus (AF-A) (Still Photo Mode Only)

This mode, also known as *AF-A*, is available only when the Video/Photo selector is set to the Photo position. The Z5 II starts out in AF-S mode but will switch to AF-C mode if your subject starts to move. It's useful for unpredictable subjects, say, a pet canine that appears to be in repose, but which may perk up and dash off when it's spotted a squirrel.

Full-time Autofocus (AF-F) (Video Mode Only)

This mode, also known as *AF-F*, is available only in Video mode. You don't need to activate focus with a button: the camera adjusts focus continually as your subject moves. Focus locks only when the shutter release is pressed halfway. Obviously, this mode uses the most juice.

Focus-Priority versus Release-Priority

One autofocus aspect that's often misunderstood is the concept of *priority*. The camera allows you to choose either focus-priority or release-priority, which determines whether it delays taking a picture until sharp focus is achieved when the shutter release is pressed down all the way, or whether it takes a picture immediately. You can use Custom Settings a1: AF-C Priority Selection and a2: AF-S Priority Selection to specify your choice.

- **Focus-priority.** This is the default setting for the AF-S autofocus mode. When enabled, the camera will not take a picture when you press the shutter release down all the way until focus is confirmed. This may cause a slight delay, *but only if the camera has not yet finished the autofocus process.* In practice, there are three possibilities:
  - **In AF-S mode:** If you've already pressed the shutter release halfway to lock in focus, the camera will go ahead and take your photo with no further delay.
  - **In AF-S mode:** If you haven't pressed the shutter release halfway—say, you press down all the way in one continuous motion—there may be a delay until the camera confirms focus. This delay may be very short if your subject can be easily focused using your current AF-area mode, or somewhat longer if achieving sharp focus (say, with a subject that's low in contrast against its background) is problematic. Note that focus-priority can reduce continuous shooting frame rates while the camera waits for the AF system.
  - **In AF-C mode:** If you've set AF-C mode to focus-priority (which I don't recommend), the camera will continuously focus and refocus as long as the shutter release is held down halfway. That will usually translate into only a minimal delay when the shutter button is finally fully depressed to take the picture.
- **Release-priority.** This is the default setting for AF-C autofocus mode. When active, the camera will take a picture as soon as the shutter release is pressed down all the way, *even if sharp autofocus has not been confirmed.* Sports, action, and wildlife photographers use release-priority almost exclusively, because capturing the decisive moment takes precedence over getting the sharpest possible photo. But don't make the mistake of thinking that release-priority will produce a large number of slightly out-of-focus photos. The majority of the time, this setting will produce sharp photos even though the AF system has not yet been able to *confirm* focus. The image may, indeed, be sharply focused, even if the camera hasn't had time to confirm it.

I like to stick with release-priority for AF-C mode, because it has less impact on continuous shooting speeds. In general, AF-C will lock in focus for the first shot in a continuous sequence and subsequent exposures in the series won't really require much adjustment of focus. You could use focus-priority in AF-C mode when *not* shooting continuously and the sharpest focus possible was required. Release-priority provides no special advantages for AF-S mode (especially if you prefocus by pressing the shutter button halfway), so I don't use it.

- **Focus+Release.** Nikon actually has the name for this option backward: priority is given to *release* (not focus) initially, but under dim lighting or with low-contrast subjects, the Z5 II will shift to focus-priority for the first shot in a sequence, then continue in release-priority mode. Use this for continuous shooting, so the camera will take a little extra time focusing for the first shot. It will then capture the remaining images in the sequence using the same focus point, but will refocus, as necessary, if it can. The Focus+Release option is available only for Custom Setting a1: AF-C Priority Selection; only Release or Focus priority is available for AF-S mode.

Full-time Autofocus (AF-F) (Movie Mode Only)

This mode is available only in Movie mode. You don't need to activate focus with a button: the Z5 II adjusts focus continually as your subject moves. Focus locks only when the shutter release is pressed halfway. You can turn off continuous focusing temporarily by holding down a button assigned to the AF-ON function. Obviously, this mode uses the most juice. Because changing the focus plane while capturing video can be intrusive, AF-F is slower, but focus speed and tracking can be fine-tuned using Custom Settings g5 and g6.

Manual Focus

The fastest way to change to Manual focus is to hold down the Fn2 button and rotate the main command dial, which will cycle among Manual, AF-S, AF-C, and AF-A modes (unless you've redefined the Fn2 button to some other behavior). You can also switch to Manual focus using the *i* menu or Photo Shooting/Video Recording menu options. Some lenses, including F-mount lenses attached using an FTZ adapter, may have a dedicated focus mode switch with an M position. There are some advantages and disadvantages to using manual focus. While your batteries will last slightly longer in manual focus mode, it will take you longer to focus the camera for each photo, a process that can be difficult for some types of subjects. I'll tell you more about manual focus later in this chapter.

Choosing an Autofocus Area Mode

If your camera isn't focusing on the correct subject, autofocus speed and activation are pretty much wasted effort. When you select one of the AF-area modes, you're telling your Z5 II *which* areas of the frame should be a *starting point* for the autofocus process. There are three aspects that are commonly overlooked or misunderstood:

- **Point/Counterpoint.** Your Z5 II is said to have 299 different focus points within the frame, of which 273 can be individually selected by the photographer. However, those figures actually refer to 299/273 *groups* of photosites that provide the data used to calculate focus. In reality, the camera collects information from roughly one million individual photosites and organizes them into 299 (in Auto-area AF mode) or 273 (for user-selectable AF-areas) focus points. So, your Z5 II's focus areas can collect data much more precisely than you'd think.

- **Linear sensitivity.** Your camera's sensor has 4032 rows of pixels, each 6048 pixels wide. In every twelfth row, most of the pixels in that row are AF photosites, with effectively no gaps between them. So, the camera is very, very sensitive to vertically oriented subject matter, as I showed you in Figure 3.4. Because the remaining rows of pixels don't collect AF information, the Z5 II is less sensitive to subjects with mostly horizontal lines. Keep in mind you can always rotate the camera 90 degrees for such subjects, lock focus, and then rotate the camera back 90 degrees to compose your image.

- **Not locked in.** The third often-misunderstood aspect of autofocus is that even though you can specify a particular AF-area mode and location within the frame—and move that location using the directional controls—the Z5 II is smart enough to override your setting. Indeed, the camera will start to calculate focus centered on the area you specify. It's indicated by a box on the screen, surrounded by smaller square dots that indicate additional available focus points (as seen in the examples shown in Figure 3.7). But if contrast is too low the camera may switch from that central box to an area of higher contrast if located near one of the auxiliary dots arranged around the periphery of that center square. Or, if you have enabled AF subject detection (described shortly), the camera will favor elements like heads or eyes, even if located outside that central box.

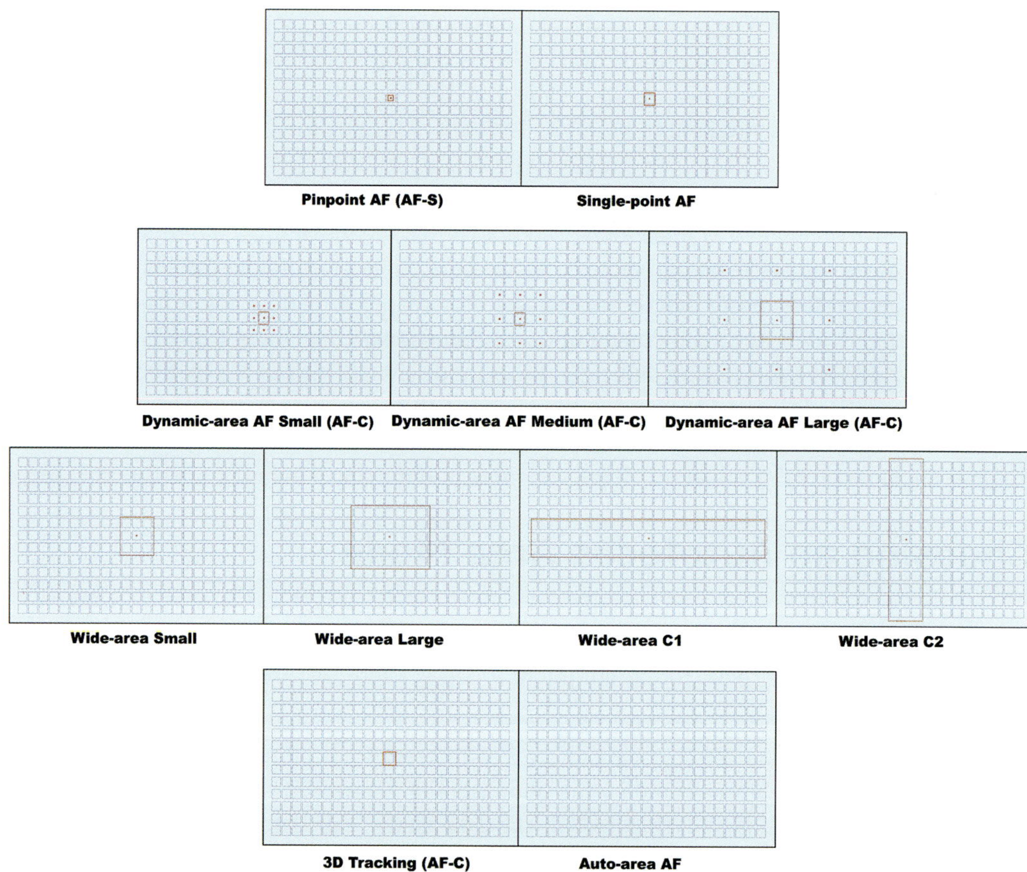

Figure 3.7 AF-area mode focus point patterns.

As with Focus mode, you can select the AF-area mode from the *i* menu or use the entry in the Photo Shooting or Video Recording menus. The *i* menu is your best choice, as it also allows you to choose AF subject detection options, as I'll describe shortly. The Z5 II has six main AF-area modes for focus point selection, with several variations for two of them (plus Subject-tracking AF mode, available when shooting video). I'm going to describe each of the modes and explain how to use them. The locations with the frame used to calculate focus are arranged in the patterns shown in Figure 3.7. You can use the multi selector and sub-selector directional controls to move the focus points around within the frame in each of these AF-area modes, except for Auto-area AF, in which the Z5 II chooses the active focus points for you.

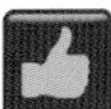 **NOTE** With all AF-area modes (except for Auto-area AF and 3D-tracking), a dot appears in the middle of the focus point when it is located in the center of the frame. It disappears when the focus area is moved from the center. You can return the focus point to the center of the frame by pressing the OK button.

Pinpoint AF (AF-S Only)

This mode is available only in Single AF (AF-S) focus mode. In this mode, you always select the focus point manually, using the multi selector or sub-selector "joystick" (which, helpfully, will respond to your thumb presses not only in the left/right and up/down directions, but diagonally, as well). As I mentioned, you can return the focus point to the center at any time by pressing the OK button.

The focus point is represented by the tiny red box shown at upper left in Figure 3.7. You have an extraordinary amount of freedom in placing the focus area, which is roughly one-quarter the size of that used for Single-point AF (described next). Pinpoint AF uses phase detection first and then confirms focus using contrast detection within the selected area; it's not limited by the positions represented by the larger gray boxes.

Obviously, selecting an AF point so precisely can be time-consuming, as it takes a tedious number of presses of the left/right buttons to move from one side of the frame to the other. (The focus point will wrap around to the other side if you've enabled that behavior using Custom Setting a9.) Pinpoint AF is best suited for subjects that don't move or, at least, are temporarily stationary, such as a bird hidden among leaves. Although slow, it's very accurate, and is especially good for macro work and any photography undertaken with the Z5 II mounted on a tripod.

Single-Point AF

As with the other user-selectable area modes, you can select the focus point manually, using the multi selector directional buttons. The Z5 II evaluates focus based solely on the point you select from among the 273 available focus points, making this another good choice for subjects that don't move much. Single-Point AF is excellent for achieving focus on a subject that might otherwise blend in with its background. This mode is available with both AF-S and AF-C focus modes, but because the focus box is so small it's not ideal for moving subjects and AF-C autofocus.

SOME TIPS

Visibility: Increase the visibility of the focus point using the Focus Point Border Width option in Custom Setting a10: Focus Point Display. Select 3 as the width to see the focus point much more clearly, say, in bright lighting conditions.

Faster Adjustments: You can speed up the AF point's traverse by limiting the number of selectable points using Custom Setting a4: Focus Points Used Alternating Points, which allows much faster positioning of your focus zone. However, the Alternating Points setting does not affect the number of focus points used with Pinpoint AF or with Wide-area AF (Small or Large), which I'll describe shortly.

Dynamic-Area AF

In this mode, available only when AF-C is active, you still select the *primary* focus point yourself from among those available using the multi selector. The Z5 II will focus on that point in most cases, but if the subject departs from the selected area, the camera uses information from the surrounding areas. As I noted earlier, if the user-selected primary focus point isn't suitable for focusing, the camera will use one of the secondary focus points instead. That might be the case if the selected focus point is on an area of low contrast, such as the sky, or the subject is too small (perhaps a distant object).

You can choose from three different Dynamic-area sizes: Small, Medium, and Large, shown in the second row in Figure 3.7. The red-highlighted points surrounding the main focus box show the active focus points. You can dispense with viewing the additional points on the display by setting Custom Setting a10: Focus Point Display > Dynamic-area AF Assist to Off. You can move the grouping to any of the 273 points, but when the grouping reaches the top border or corners, some of the potential points are outside the array, effectively giving you fewer points to work with.

Dynamic-area AF is a more sophisticated version of Single-point AF. You can select the *initial* focus point and then trust the Z5 II's smarts to continue focusing on a moving subject as long as that subject remains within the Dynamic-area's autofocus frame pattern. That frees you to concentrate on framing your composition rather than worrying about whether your subject remains in focus.

This setting is excellent for slow-moving subjects, as seen in Figure 3.8, left, but flexible enough to follow subjects that move erratically from side to side (say, a child at play or a basketball player moving around the court on defense), because the Z5 II can use the distance information to differentiate the original subject from objects that are closer or farther away, especially human subjects (see Figure 3.8, right). However, many photographers also use this setting for birds in flight. Very rapid motion may call for the camera's tracking feature, described shortly.

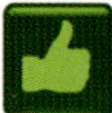

TIP In Pinpoint AF, Single-point AF, or Dynamic-area AF, if you want to lock the focus distance you've selected for a series of shots, you can temporarily lock the focus point by partially depressing and holding the shutter release or pressing and holding the AF-ON button. Press the OK button to move the single focus point back to the center of the frame quickly.

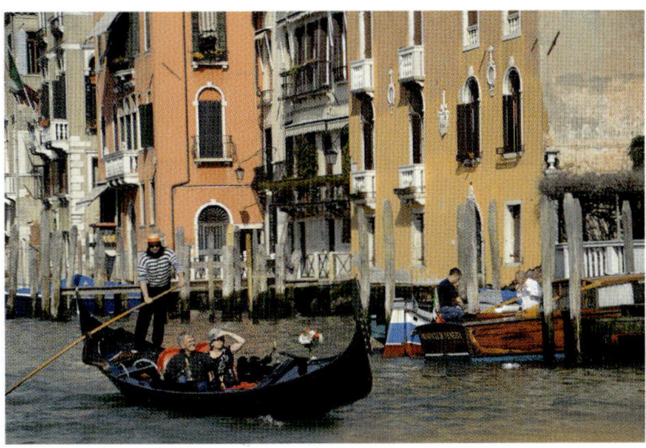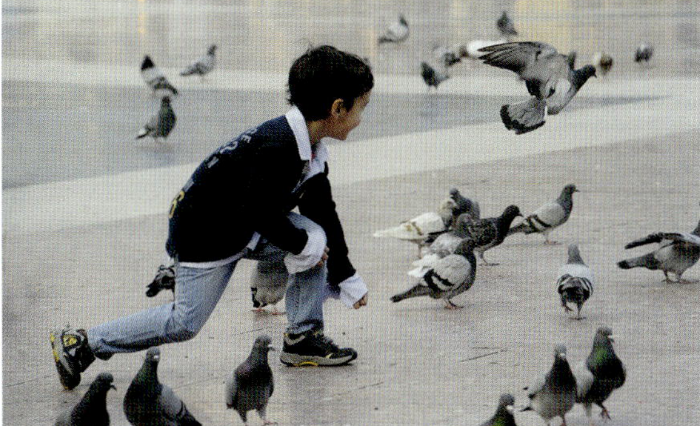

Figure 3.8 Focus on slow-moving subjects with Dynamic-area AF (left). It can work with more erratic subjects, too (right), but may require using the Z5 II's tracking feature.

Wide-Area AF (Small and Large; C1, C2)

With the Wide-area AF modes, you choose the location of *zones* containing focus points, rather than a specific initial focus point. The Z5 II will use the focus points within the zones, which you can move around the display. Two zones are defined for you. Choose either the smaller of the wide-area zones or an even larger zone, like the two outlined in red at left in the third row in Figure 3.7. Two additional customizable modes are available and shown at right in the same row. They are labeled C1 and C2, each with 77 combinations with dimensions from 1×1 to 21×13 in FX still photo mode and 66 different combinations from 1×1 to 21×11 in video mode.

I use the customizable zones C1 and C2 a lot, as they are especially good for subjects that occupy a predictable region of the frame. Although I was shooting the basketball game shown in Figure 3.9 with a 14mm lens, I hoped to capture some exciting action under the hoop. I set my Wide-area AF (C1) zone to a tall rectangle that encompassed the area around the basket, and my Z5 II tended to ignore players at the periphery, even if they ventured close to the baseline.

If you're using subject detection, you should activate Custom Setting a10: Focus Point Display > AF-C In-Focus Display. When you've done that, the Wide-area box will appear in red and a smaller

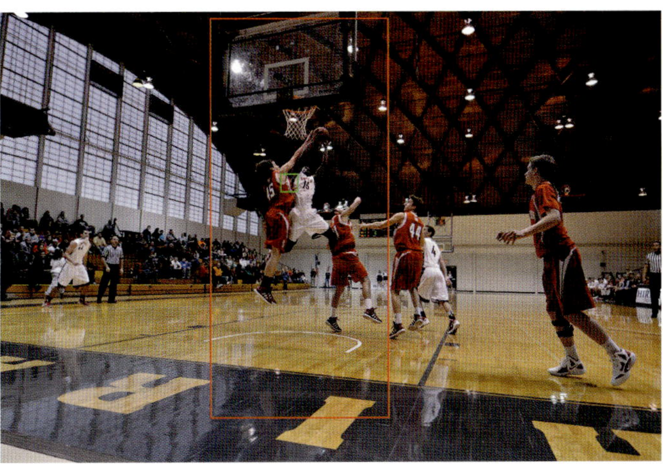

Figure 3.9 A custom Wide-area AF zone can be tailored to concentrate on a specific area of the frame.

green box will indicate subject-detection focus. When the camera does not detect a subject, the Wide-area box will appear in green instead, and the camera will focus (generally) on the closest object (until a detected subject appears). It's a handy way to keep track of what your Z5 II is doing.

3D-Tracking

This AF option, available only in AF-C mode, tells the Z5 II to lock in focus on a subject you specify, and then follow it as that subject moves within the frame (or you move the camera). The Z5 II identifies the subject using several qualities, such as color, the pattern of the subject (including shape and size), and, if active and appropriate, subject detection. It works best when these aspects are clearly distinct from the subject's surroundings. By default, the tracking box is displayed in white (instead of red), to remind you that you're using 3D-tracking. However, you can change it to red using Custom Setting a10: Focus Point Display > 3D tracking Focus Point Color, which I did for the illustration at bottom left in Figure 3.7.

The 3D-tracking mode might do a great job following a rooster around a chicken coop but might get easily confused if you tried to track a single chick scuttling around within a flock. If your target happens to be one included in the Z5 II's subject-detection algorithms, tracking performance can be further enhanced. Keep in mind, though, that in this mode, subject detection may not be given top priority. One advantage of 3D-tracking is that it works with *all kinds* of moving objects, and it isn't limited to the defined subject-tracking categories (people, animals, birds, vehicles, or airplanes).

When in 3D-tracking mode, you can activate tracking by placing the displayed focus point over your subject and pressing the shutter-release button down halfway. The Z5 II will then focus on the subject and continue to track/focus as it moves within the frame. Release the shutter button if you want to recompose with a different subject. If your subject moves too quickly, leaves the frame or is blocked by other objects, is too similar to other subjects in the frame, or changes in appearance, tracking may fail. **Note:** A similar function, Subject-tracking AF, is available in video mode, using the OK button or shutter release as the trigger to begin following a selected subject.

Automatic-Area AF

With Auto-area AF, autofocus point selection is out of your hands; the Z5 II performs the task for you using its own intelligence. It will work with the distance information supplied by the lens and, if enabled, its subject-detection technology to distinguish humans, animals, vehicles, etc., from their background. In that case, a prioritized subject at the side of the frame will be detected and used to evaluate focus, while the camera ignores the background area in the frame.

In AF-S mode, the active focus points, bounded by the blue boxes shown at bottom right Figure 3.7, are highlighted with green boxes that illuminate as you hold the shutter release down halfway; until that happens, you have no idea where in the frame the Z5 II will be focusing. In AF-C mode, red boxes appear around the focused area, highlighted in that color to indicate that the current focus point is only tentative and won't be locked in until you press the shutter release down all the way. If you'd rather see which points are being used for focus in green, use Custom Setting a10: Focus Point Display > AF-C In-Focus Display, as described earlier.

Birds in flight—one of the most difficult of all autofocus targets—can often be grabbed using Automatic-area AF in combination with the Z5 II's avian-oriented subject-detection option. Subject detection and tracking features merit a more detailed discussion of their own, which I'll provide in an upcoming section.

> **REDUCING YOUR OPTIONS**
>
> If you find yourself using only certain AF-area modes, you can tell the Z5 II to "hide" the modes you do not work with. Custom Setting a8: Limit AF-Area Mode Selection allows you to enable or disable any of the AF-area modes (except Single-point AF, which is mandatory). If you need more help activating this option, I'll explain it in Chapter 7.

Reach Out and Touch Something

I described the powerful touch-screen features of the Z5 II in Chapter 1. They are especially useful when applied to achieving focus and (optionally) taking a picture with little more effort than a gesture. You can activate touch options using the Touch Controls entry in the Setup menu, enabling them for playback only (if you want to avoid unintentional activation), or for both playback and shooting functions. A Touch icon appears at the left edge of the LCD monitor screen. Tap it to cycle among these behaviors:

- **Touch AF.** The Z5 II positions the focus point where you touch the screen. If you are using Auto-area AF or Subject-tracking AF in video mode, when you lift your finger, the camera will track your subject as it or the camera moves. Press OK to cancel tracking, or when you want to reposition the focus point. This option is most useful in AF-C mode, because it allows you to select a focus point and focus with one tap.

- **Move Focus Point.** The Z5 II will position the focus point you indicate on the screen but will not *focus or take a picture*. However, like Touch AF, if you are using Auto-area AF or Subject-tracking AF in video mode, when you lift your finger, the Z5 II will track your subject as it or the camera moves. Use this mode when you want to decide when to initiate focus in both AF-C and AF-S focus modes.

- **Touch Shutter/Touch AF.** Tap the screen, and the Z5 II will *immediately* focus on that point and take a picture when you lift your finger. It works in both AF-C and AF-S modes. This is a great option. For example, if you unexpectedly see some action taking place, you can tap the touch screen to take a photo right away and then continue to shoot (if you like) with the camera continuing to track the subject you just shot.

- **Off.** Touch focus/shutter is disabled.

Subject Detection

Improvements in subject detection have gone a long way toward fixing one of the most significant limitations of autofocus: the camera doesn't really know which of the many objects within the frame you want to focus on. Previous systems tended to lock onto the closest objects or use information from the Matrix metering system to identify likely subjects (usually humans, due to the tell-tale coloring of their faces). Adding patterns and textures to the features provided some improvements. Things really became interesting when Nikon (as well as other vendors) added enough intelligence to their image-processing algorithms to allow cameras to discern human bodies, individual faces, then eyes.

As Nikon's subject-detection technology has improved, it has added the ability to identify people, animals, birds, vehicles, and even airplanes. It can locate torsos and limbs, differentiate between race cars and passenger vehicles, and tell the difference between large birds and aircraft. This technology is possible because mirrorless cameras collect their autofocus information directly from the sensor at higher resolutions than were possible with the AF components embedded in the floor of the mirror box of dSLR cameras.

As I noted earlier, the *i* menu AF-area option lets you choose an AF-area mode and subject-detection type (or turn subject detection off) from a single screen (see Figure 3.10, left). You can also choose your subject from the AF Subject Detection Options entry of the Photo Shooting menu—but then you'll need to use the separate AF-area mode to specify area. (See Figure 3.10, right.)

Subject detection can be used to assign focus-priority with any of the Wide-area AF or Auto-area AF modes and may also be used with 3D-tracking AF (but may be overridden by the camera). When active, the Z5 II will first look for large identifiable components, such as the shape of vehicles or airplanes, or the bodies of humans, animals, and birds. If the subject is large enough within the frame, the system will next zero in on a major component, such as the front end of vehicles or the face or head of a living creature. When enough detail is available, focus can use the eyes or other small components. Once locked in on a likely subject, the AF system can ignore the background or other objects in the scene.

The appearance of the AF indicator boxes provides a clue to how the Z5 II is calculating focus. A single large, medium, or small square box indicates the Z5 II has detected a torso, face, or eye of a living creature, respectively (or the equivalent-size part of a non-animate subject). A triangle next to

Figure 3.10 Choose both AF-area mode and subject-detection options from the *i* menu (left). Subject-detection options can also be specified in the Photo Shooting menu (right).

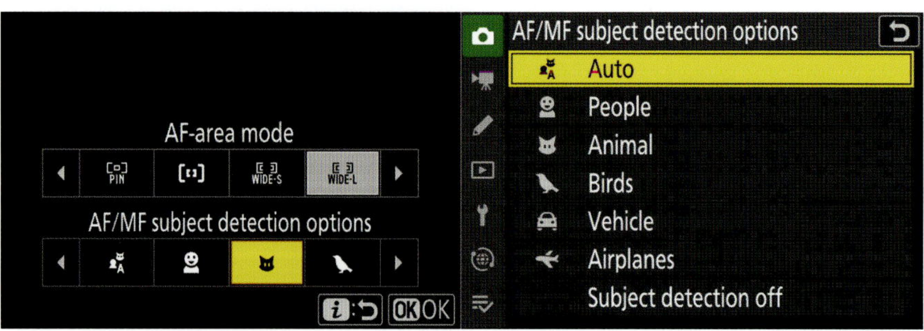

a box indicates more than one face or eye has been found, and you can use the left/right directional controls to move to the next face or eye. When AF-A switches to AF-C mode, a dancing array of tiny boxes shows that subject detection is not being used and the camera will search subjects that are close, large, and/or high in contrast.

You'll get the best results when your subjects are facing the Z5 II directly; the features become less accurate as the face turns away from the camera toward a profile view. The camera will look for both human faces and eyes and attempt to focus on the nearest eye. If the camera cannot positively identify an eye, it will switch to Face-detection mode automatically. This mode is the most versatile when your subjects are relatively close to the camera, as eyes will be relatively larger and easier to detect. Face detection alone will work well for groups, or when your subject is farther away from the camera.

If you're shooting animals or birds, the Z5 II will try to detect animal bodies, faces, and eyes and focus on them. Remember to turn this option off if no animals are present, as the feature sometimes "finds" the face of a dog or cat in unlikely places, such as shrubbery that happens to resemble a furry friend.

You can't directly select the subject-detection focus zone yourself (although you can narrow it down considerably by defining a very small zone using Wide-area AF [C1 or C2]). Instead, a box will be displayed when the camera detects a likely subject. You don't need to press the shutter release to activate this behavior—in this mode, the Z5 II starts looking for faces immediately. Several faces may be detected, with a box aligned with the selected face (usually, the face that is closest to the camera) or the selected eye (if eye detection is active). When a human or animal face or eye is detected, you have several options at your disposal:

- **Face or eye detected.** If at least one face or eye is found, a box will appear around the detected feature.
- **Multiple faces/eyes.** If more than one face or eye is present, the box will include one or two triangles indicating that you can use the left or right directional controls to move the highlighting to the next face or eye. Figure 3.11 shows what the screen looks like when two eyes are detected (left), or when multiple faces are found (right).
- **Select different face/eye.** Use the directional controls to switch to a different face or eye. If touch operation is enabled, you can tap a face with your finger and the Z5 II will focus on that face (and take a picture immediately when you remove your finger from the screen if you've activated Touch Shutter/Touch AF).
- **Tracking.** If the subject with the highlighted face moves or you reframe the image, the Z5 II will track and follow the selected face or eye.
- **Locking focus.** In AF-S mode, when you press down the shutter release halfway, the Z5 II attempts to focus the face or eye. As sharp focus is achieved, the border turns green. If the camera is unable to focus, the border blinks red. Focus may also be lost if the subject turns away from the camera and is no longer detectable. In AF-C mode, the focus continues to concentrate on the selected face/eye until the shutter release is pressed down all the way to take the picture.

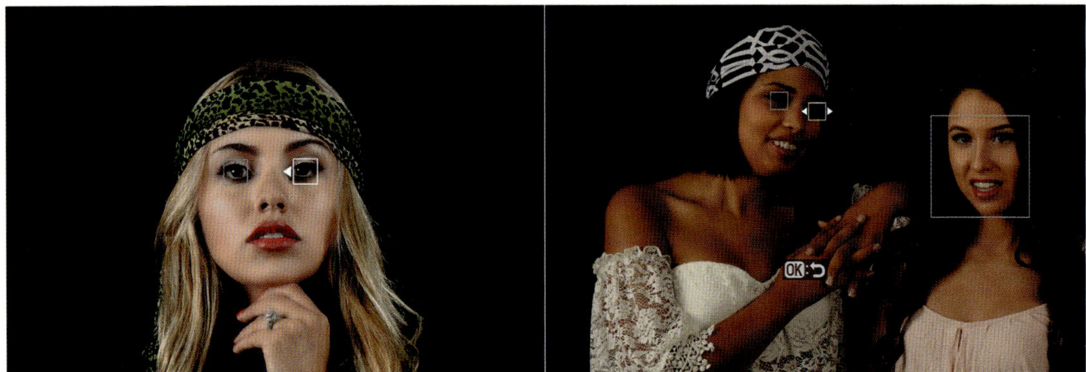

Figure 3.11 When an eye or face is detected, a box appears around the eye or face.

3D-Tracking

The useful 3D-tracking autofocus feature is one of those capabilities that can be confusing at first, but once you get the hang of it, it's remarkably easy to use. This feature is available only when you're using AF-C focus mode and the Photo/Video selector switch is set to the Photo position. (The video equivalent is Subject-tracking AF, described in Chapter 10.)

The Z5 II intelligently uses the color, shape, size, and patterns found within your subject to track its movement within the frame and does the best job when these features are distinct from other objects in view. If subject detection is turned on, the camera will use that information, too. Here are my recommended steps for using this feature:

1. **Choose refocus delay.** Navigate to Custom Setting a3: Focus Tracking with Lock-on. Choose the Blocked Shot AF Response value from 1 (Quick) to 5 (Delayed). This determines how quickly the Z5 II refocuses when an intervening object passes in front of the subject you have chosen to track. With Quick, the camera will wait only a short moment, then refocus on the new object. With the maximum Delayed setting, the interrupting subject matter will be ignored for a period of time.

   You'll want to use a delay setting when shooting sports in which players or officials are likely to pass in front of the camera unexpectedly. A Quick setting will work well when shooting continuously, allowing the camera to refocus rapidly.

2. **Specify focus point display.** A focus point box is displayed on the screen in this mode. You have two settings to make using Custom Setting a10: Focus Point Display:

   - **Activate AF-C Point Display.** Select AF-C In-focus Display and set to On. The Z5 II will then change the active focus points to green when they are in focus. This setting applies to all focus modes, not just 3D-Tracking.

   - **3D-Tracking Focus Point Color.** You can select an appropriate contrasting color (red or white) for the focus box as you move it around the screen using the multi selector.

3. **Select your subject.** Move the red or white focus box within the frame to "aim" the Z5 II until the subject you want to focus on and track is located within the border. Because you can select at any time, if, say, you're shooting sports, you can wait until just before some action is going to begin, and then choose your subject. To specify a subject for tracking, press the shutter release down halfway. (See Figure 3.12.)

4. **Change subject.** If your subject leaves the frame or you decide to track a different subject, release the shutter-release button, and resume at Step 3.

5. **Focus.** When the tracked subject is brought into focus, the active focus points turn green, seemingly take on a life of their own, and will "follow" your subject around on the LCD as you reframe your image. (In other words, the subject being tracked doesn't have to be in the center of the frame for the actual photo.) Best of all, if your subject moves, the camera will follow it as required. You can reframe as desired.

6. **Tracking continues.** The only glitches that may pop up might occur if your subject is small and difficult to track, is too close in tonal value to its background, or if the subject approaches the camera or recedes sufficiently to change its relative size on the LCD significantly. The camera may also be unable to track subjects that leave the frame, are moving too fast, are too large/small, or too bright/dark. Because tracking uses subject distance, color, any patterns present, and brightness, it works best when used with subject matter that differs in colors/patterns and brightness from its surroundings.

7. **Take your picture.** Press the shutter release down all the way.

8. **Or exit.** To cancel focus tracking, release the shutter-release button.

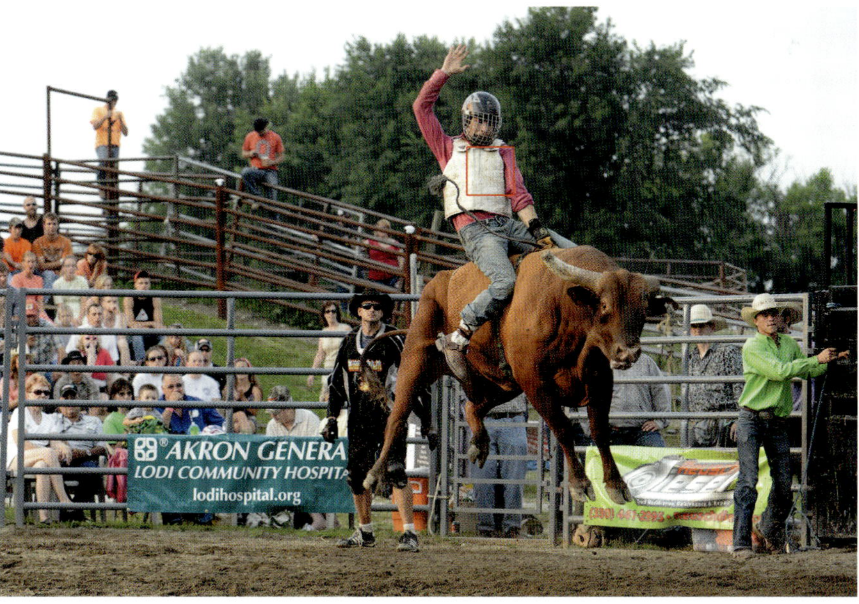

Figure 3.12 Position the frame on the subject and half-press the shutter button to begin tracking it.

Store by Orientation

Some types of shooting call for different ways of choosing a focus point's orientation. For example, say you're shooting a sport like basketball that lends itself to both horizontal and vertical framing. You may rotate your camera constantly as the action unfolds but want the focus point to remain in the upper portion of your horizontal or vertical frame. That won't happen if you are shooting with a camera in its default mode. Your chosen focus point will stay fixed relative to the other points and "rotate" along with the camera.

The same focus point in the Z5 II's array is used regardless of the camera's orientation. If you've set your focus point for the basket or net when the camera is rotated in one direction vertically (that is, the top of the vertical frame), the focus point will encompass the right side of the frame when the camera is in the horizontal position and evaluate the floor if you happen to rotate it vertically in the other direction.

However, you have another option, tucked away in Custom Setting a5: Store Points by Orientation. When either Focus Point or Focus Point and AF-area Mode are selected, the focus point does not shift as the Z5 II is rotated. This feature allows *different* focus points to be selected for each of the three likely camera orientations (ignoring the possible, but less likely, upside-down horizontal position, which simply inverts the normal position in which you hold the camera). If you've chosen Focus Point and AF-area Mode, you may specify a different AF-area mode for each orientation in addition to the focus point position.

When Store Points by Orientation is activated, simply rotate the Z5 II to any of the three configurations, and select the focus point you want. Repeat, if you like, for the other two. Then, as you shoot, you'll notice the focus point shifting in the viewfinder as you rotate the camera. You don't need to keep the point in the same relative position in the frame (as I just described). You can select any focus point for any of the three orientations if, for example, you're shooting architecture and want to focus on a different position in the frame as you vary camera orientation.

Manual Focus

The Nikon Z5 II supplies you with powerful manual focusing aids. You can zoom in to your subject to manually focus on an enlarged image, view color-coded cues that show you which parts of the image actually *are* in focus, or check an electronic "rangefinder" that alerts you when a given subject is in focus. There is even a split-screen display zoom option that allows you to evaluate focus on two different areas of the frame. These manual focus aids are great features. Indeed, the switch to mirrorless technology has actually revived interest in old-school manual focus.

Some subjects lend themselves to manual focus, especially close-up or *macro* photography, in which AF can be a creative hindrance. If you're photographing a flower, why let the camera decide which leaf or petal should be sharpest—particularly if you are using a relatively large aperture and selective focus as an effect? A mirrorless camera's live view is especially useful when focusing manually because you have extra tools at your disposal to focus precisely and quickly.

Here are the basic steps for quick and convenient setting of focus manually with the camera:

- **Activate manual focus.** Switch to manual focus by sliding the switch on the lens to the M position, or by selecting Manual focus using the *i* menu.

- **Aim at your subject and turn the control/focusing ring on the lens.** Turn the control/focusing ring until your subject appears to be in the sharpest possible focus. While you can redefine the focus/control ring's function (as described in Chapter 7), in Manual focus mode it can *only* be used to adjust focus. Note that some lenses, such as the Z 24-70mm f/4 S optic, lack a control ring and have only a focus ring.

- **If you have difficulty focusing.** If you are unable to focus precisely, you have three options: magnification (press the Zoom In button to magnify your view), focus peaking (which provides a colored array around the edges within your image that are sharply focused), and using the electronic rangefinder to provide focus indicators in the display.

  - **Magnification.** To magnify a portion of the image and enhance your ability to focus, press the Zoom In button located at lower right of the LCD monitor. As you press the button repeatedly, to enlarge the view to eight different levels of magnification, a navigation window, seen at top in Figure 3.13, appears with a yellow box at the approximate location within the overall frame of the magnified view. You can relocate the zoomed area using the multi selector. Press the OK button at any time to restore the zoom window to the center of the frame. **Note:** If you're using a power zoom lens like the Nikkor Z 28-135mm f/4 PZ, the Zoom In button may be set to activate the optical zoom feature instead of using Custom Setting f13.

  - **Focus peaking.** Activate this feature using the instructions for Custom Setting a12: Focus Peaking in Chapter 7. As the colored edges change during focus, it becomes easier to determine when your subject is precisely focused. (See Figure 3.13, center.) Choose Peak 1 (low sensitivity), Peak 2 (standard sensitivity), or Peak 3 (high sensitivity), depending on the contrast of your subject. You can change the peaking from the default red to yellow, blue, or white. The alternate hues may be needed to provide a strong contrast between the peaking highlights and the color of your subject.

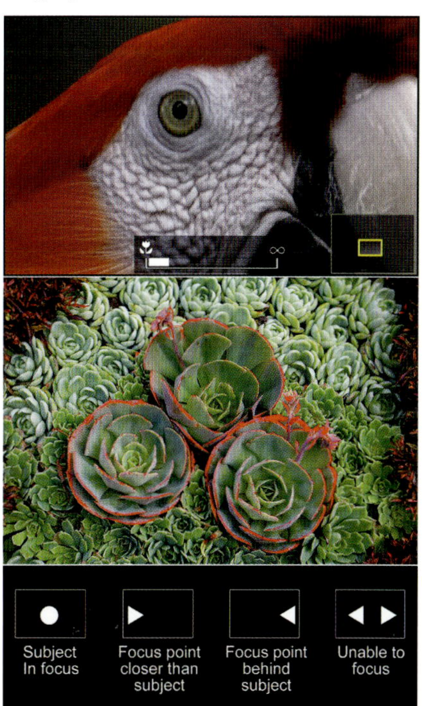

Figure 3.13 You can magnify the image to make manual focusing easier (top). With Peaking Highlights activated, in-focus areas are highlighted in color (center). The electronic rangefinder in the lower-left corner of the display shows manual focus status (bottom).

- **Use the electronic rangefinder.** Position the focus point over the subject and rotate the focus ring until sharp focus is achieved using the electronic rangefinder feature. The focus point will change to green and the in-focus indicator at lower left in the display will change according to the symbols shown at bottom in Figure 3.13. Note that while the electronic rangefinder appears when in manual focus or manual focus override, it shows the direction in which you should rotate the ring, with *most* lenses. Some lenses, especially those from third parties, rotate in the opposite direction, however.

- **Preview depth-of-field.** Your Z5 II doesn't have a Pv (Preview) button by default, but you can define one, say, the Fn1 button, using Custom Setting f2: Custom Controls. Then, when you press the defined Pv button, the lens will stop down to the aperture selected by you (in Manual mode) or by the camera (in Aperture-priority mode). (This doesn't work in Program or Shutter-priority mode, because the aperture isn't determined in either mode until you lock exposure or take a photo.) To open the aperture to maximum again, release the button.

- **Split-screen display zoom.** Like depth-of-field preview, this feature isn't available by default. You must add it to the *i* menu, using Custom Setting f1: Customize *i* Menu. I'll describe this capability next.

Split-Screen Display Zoom

Split-screen Display Zoom is most useful when the camera is mounted on a tripod. To use it, you must assign the Split-screen Display Zoom behavior to the *i* menu, using Custom Setting f1: Customize *i* Menu, as described in Chapter 7. When you activate this feature, the live view LCD display is divided into two boxes, each showing a separate area of the frame side-by-side. To use this capability, just follow these steps:

1. **Split the screen.** Press the *i* button and scroll to the icon representing the Split-screen Display Zoom function that you have added to the customized *i* menu. Press OK to activate.

2. **Areas are indicated by a navigation window.** The screen will split into two areas, shown next to each other. The relative positions of the two areas are shown in a magnification window, seen at lower right in Figure 3.14.

3. **Zoom in or out of the split display.** Use the Zoom In and Zoom Out buttons to magnify or reduce magnification of both portions of the image.

4. **Choose one of the two sides of the frame.** Press the OK button to select one of the two sides of the frame.

5. **Move selected area horizontally.** You can use the left/right buttons to scroll that box's selected area from side to side.

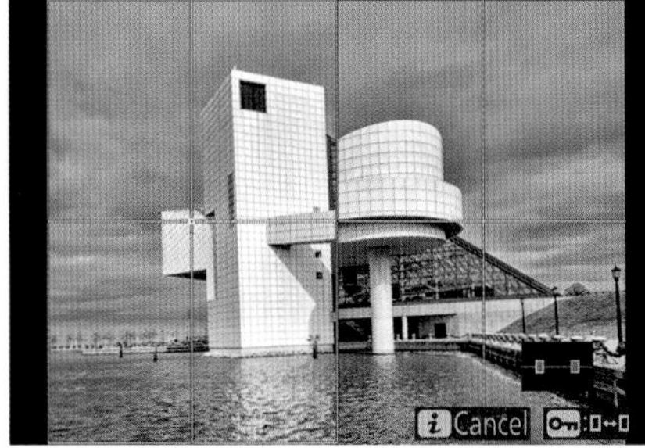

Figure 3.14 Split-screen display in live view.

6. **Move both areas vertically.** Press the up or down buttons to scroll *both* areas up or down simultaneously. In other words, the split-screen images will always match horizontally, but you can adjust either of their positions left or right. Landscape photographers have already noted that they'd like the ability to change the locations in both horizontal and vertical directions.

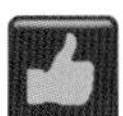 **NOTE** Because the split screen shows areas on opposite sides of the frame, you can also use it to horizontally align the image, so that the horizon or any buildings that span the image are oriented at the same angle. I'll describe additional applications next.

7. **Focus on selected area.** When either box is selected, you can focus the image on *that* area by pressing the shutter-release button halfway.

8. **Exit.** Press the *i* button again to exit the split-screen display.

You're probably wondering what else this feature is useful for—unless you're way ahead of me. Here are some typical applications. These are all fairly technical in nature, and likely to be needed only for specialized types of photography, particularly in the architectural and landscape fields. But if you do need the split-screen feature, you'll really need it.

- **Check horizontal alignment.** Some subjects lend themselves to symmetrical compositions (or, *demand* such treatment, in the case of buildings or other bi-laterally symmetrical scenes that look weird if the camera has been placed slightly to one side or the other). Use the split screen to view comparable parts of the same image simultaneously to see if the camera is aligned appropriately.

- **Check front/back tilt.** Sometimes you unintentionally lean the camera forward or back slightly, which can produce fall-back or fall-forward distortion effects when shooting very tall or very deep subjects (*pitch*) or rotate the camera around its base (imagine a line running vertically through, say, the tripod socket; that's *yaw*). You might also *roll* the camera by rotating it along the axis that runs through the center of the lens. You can use the split-screen feature in conjunction with the live view virtual horizon (discussed earlier in this chapter) to ensure the camera is completely level by comparing the two magnified sides of the image.

- **Control perspective and focus.** The split screen allows you to check the focus of different parts of a scene, which landscape photographers and those using shift-tilt lenses will like. The split screen can be used to select either side of the image and focus on the side that you want to be rendered most sharply.

Using the Focus/Control Ring

One innovation found on certain lenses is the addition of a *control ring* to replace the familiar single *focus ring* used on traditional lenses and some Z-mount lenses, while the second involves the Z-series' dependence on a technology called *focus-by-wire* to perform the actual focus adjustments.

When focusing manually, the control ring can function like a traditional focus ring in many ways, providing manual override of autofocus and fully manual focusing. However, you can *redefine* the behavior of the control to apply other customizable functions, including step-less aperture control, exposure compensation, and ISO sensitivity adjustment. The most popular of these options is probably the step-less (no-click) aperture setting for video capture, which allows changing the f/stop silently while capturing video. Some like the ability to add/subtract exposure compensation quickly, or the option to change ISO sensitivity on the fly with a single twist of the control ring. Just remember that when you're using an F-mount lens on the camera with an FTZ adapter, any control ring behaviors you've specified don't apply.

A second innovation comes from the focus-by-wire functions. Conventional lenses have a mechanical linkage between the traditional focusing ring and the lens elements that move during focus adjustment. Focus override, which allows fine-tuning focus during the AF process, requires a special arrangement within the lens to allow the focus ring to assume control when the photographer wants to make adjustments without exiting to manual focus. Thanks to focus-by-wire, all Z-mount lenses deliver an electrical signal directly to the built-in motors, bypassing the mechanical linkage. So, overriding the AF system is as simple as rotating the ring any time you want.

Focus-by-wire also enables the camera to adjust the "throw" of the lens during manual focus to match the speed with which you turn it. In ancient times, it was common to require a *lot* of rotation of a focusing ring to focus from the minimum focus distance to infinity, providing precise manual focus. Once autofocus became the norm, lens designers began to produce lenses that required a *reduced* amount of throw to focus, so that each degree of rotation covered a larger portion of the focus distance from minimum to infinity. That led to faster focus, while making accurate manual focus more difficult.

Focus-by-wire, however, allows the AF operation to *adapt* to the rotational speed of the focus/control ring. Rotate rapidly, and the throw is relatively short—you may need to turn the ring only one-third of the way around to make a focus adjustment. Slow down your focusing motion, though, and each movement becomes more precise. You may have to rotate the ring all the way around to make the same adjustment that required only a one-third turn when done rapidly. You can easily see how this feature makes manual focus both more convenient and more precise. Your options, described in more detail in Chapter 7, include the ability to adjust rotation range, how dramatically focus changes with a given twist of the focus ring, and swapping the functions of the control ring and focus ring with lenses that have both. I'll show you how to implement these using Custom Settings f10, f11, and f12 in Chapter 7.

Trap (Auto) Focus

This technique comes in handy when you know where the action is going to take place (such as at the finish line of a horse race), but you don't know exactly *when*. The solution is to prefocus on the point where the action will occur and then tell your camera not to take the photo until something moves into the prefocus spot (see Figure 3.15). It's a good technique for sports action when you know that, say, a runner is going to pass by a certain position. You can also use trap focus for hand-held macro shots—set focus for a particular distance and then move the camera toward your subject. The shutter will trip automatically when your subject comes into focus.

Trap focus in Viewfinder mode isn't as difficult as you might think. The key is to decouple the focusing operation from the shutter-release function.

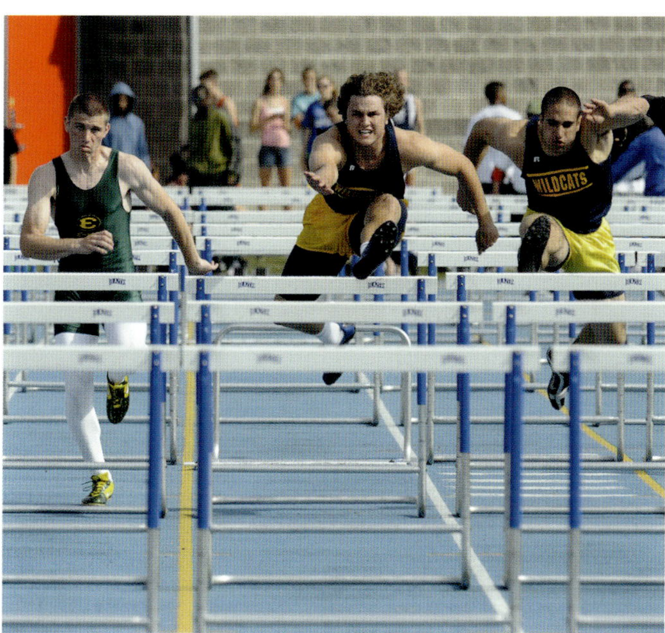

Figure 3.15 By pre-focusing on a point between two of the hurdles, trap focus captured this athlete the instant he moved into the point of focus.

Just follow these steps:

1. **Confirm AF-ON button.** First, access Custom Setting f2 and make sure the AF-ON button (or another button you have assigned to the AF-ON behavior) is set to AF-ON, and not some other function. You want the AF-ON button to activate autofocus.

2. **Confirm AF-S Focus Priority.** Make sure Custom Setting a2 is set to Focus. The shutter will trip only when your subject is in focus when using AF-S.

3. **Disable Out-of-Focus Release.** By default, Custom Setting a6: AF Activation is set to Shutter/AF ON, which means the shutter-release button initiates exposure metering *and* autofocus. You want to start autofocus separately, using the AF-ON button only. Highlight AF-ON Only and press the right button to reveal the Out-of-Focus Release option and choose Disable. Press OK.

   Henceforth, pressing the shutter release halfway down does *not* activate autofocus. That happens *only* when you press the AF-ON button and focus lock will occur *only* when something occupies the preset plane you specify in Step 7.

4. **Set focus mode to AF-S.**

5. **Set your point selection mode to Single-point AF.**

6. **Make sure your lens is set to autofocus (either A or M/A).**

7. **Prefocus on the spot where the action will occur or an equivalent distance.** Use the focus ring on your lens. I like to manually focus on that point to make sure it is the exact position I want to capture. For Figure 3.15, I focused on a plane between the third and fourth hurdles, which were located 30 feet apart (the standard for men's hurdle events). You can also press the AF-ON button to focus on that point and then release the button. In either case, further AF activity will cease. The prefocused distance is the "trap" you've set for your pending subject.

8. **Reframe your picture, if necessary, so that nothing is at the prefocused distance.** If an object occupies that spot, the camera will take the photo immediately when you press the shutter release.

9. **Press and hold down the shutter release all the way.** The camera will not refocus, because you've disconnected the autofocus function from the shutter release.

10. **Trap sprung!** The picture will be taken when a subject moves into the prefocused area. Note that trap focus may not work well with some subjects, particularly when using small f/stops. Increased depth-of-field may cause the camera to take the photo when your subject has barely entered the trap and not yet perfectly in the preselected focus plane.

11. **Don't forget to right!** When you've finished using trap focus, you'll need to return your focus behavior to its "natural" state, most specifically, by returning Custom Setting a6 to Shutter/AF ON.

Back-Button Focus

Back-button focus (often just referred to as BBF) is a tool you can use to separate two functions that are commonly locked together—exposure and autofocus—so that you can lock in exposure while allowing focus to be attained at a later point, or vice versa. It's a *good* thing, although using back-button focus effectively may require you to unlearn some habits and acquire new ways of coordinating the action of your fingers.

As you have learned, the default behavior of your Nikon camera is to set both exposure and focus (when AF is active) when you press the shutter release down halfway. When using AF-S mode, that's that: both exposure and focus are locked and will not change until you release the shutter button or press it all the way down to take a picture and then release it for the next shot. In AF-C mode, exposure is locked and focus set when you press the shutter release halfway, but the camera will *continue to refocus* if your subject moves for as long as you hold down the shutter button halfway. Focus isn't locked until you press the button down all the way to take the picture.

What back-button focus does is *decouple* or separate the two actions, as you did with trap focus, described above. You can retain the exposure lock feature when the shutter is pressed halfway but assign autofocus *start* and/or autofocus *lock* to a different button. So, in practice, you can press the shutter button halfway, locking exposure, and reframe the image if you like (perhaps you're photographing a backlit subject and want to lock in exposure on the foreground, and then reframe to include a very bright background as well).

But, in this same scenario, you *don't* want autofocus locked at the same time. Indeed, you may not want to start AF until you're good and ready, say, at a sports venue as you wait for a ballplayer to streak into view in your viewfinder, or when you're photographing a garden and expect a butterfly to alight somewhere nearby. With back-button focus, you can lock exposure on the spot where you expect the athlete or insect to be and activate AF at the moment your subject appears. Your camera gives you a great deal of flexibility, both in the choice of which button to use for AF, and the behavior of that button. That's where the learning of new habits and mind-finger coordination comes in. You need to learn which back-button focus techniques work for you, and when to use them.

Back-button focus lets you avoid the need to switch from AF-S to AF-C when your subject begins moving unexpectedly. You retain complete control. It's great for sports photography when you want

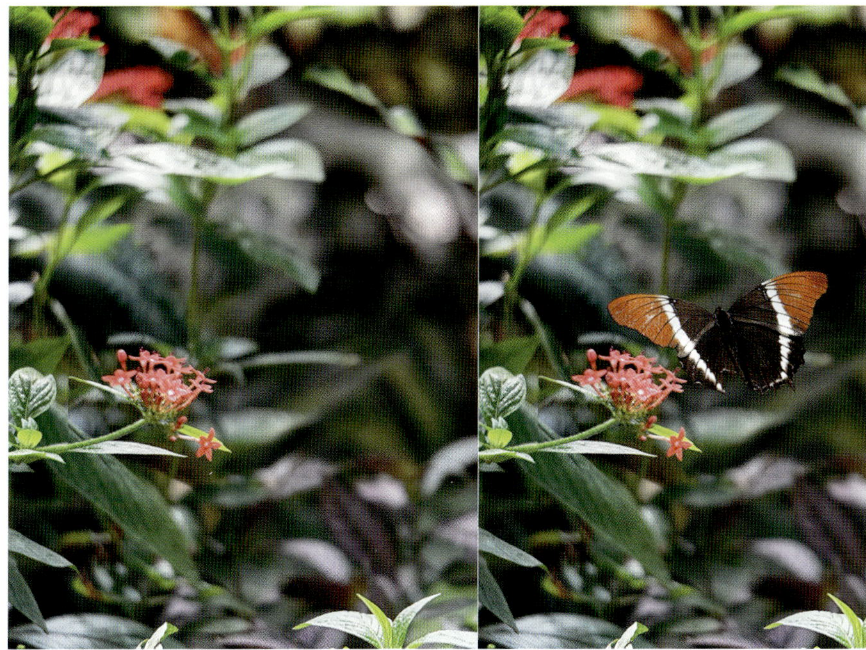

Figure 3.16 Lock your exposure for the garden by pressing the shutter release halfway; then activate autofocus when the butterfly decides where to land.

to activate autofocus precisely based on the action in front of you. It also works for static shots. You can press and release your designated focus button and then take a series of shots using the same focus point. Focus will not change until you once again press your defined back button. (See Figure 3.16.)

Want to focus on a spot without moving the focus point within your frame? Use back-button focus to zero in focus with the current focus area—no need to move it—then reframe. Focus will not change. Don't want to miss an important shot at a wedding on a photojournalism assignment? If you're set to *focus-priority* there may be a delay in taking a picture until the focus is optimum; in *release-priority* there may still be a slight delay. With back-button focus you can focus first and wait until the decisive moment to press the shutter release and take your picture. The camera will respond immediately and not bother with focusing at all. Back-button focus can also save battery power. Constantly refocusing in AF-C mode can consume a lot of power.

Activating Back-Button Focus

Here's how to set up back-button focus. Just follow these steps:

1. **Align AF activation to AF-ON function only.** As with trap focus, you want to initiate autofocus only with the AF-ON behavior, using the AF-ON button (or another button assigned the AF-ON behavior). Navigate to Custom Setting a6: AF Activation. There, the options are Shutter/AF-ON or AF-ON only. With the former option, pressing the shutter release halfway *or* the AF-ON control will enable *both* autoexposure and autofocus. Instead, select AF-ON Only to decouple the two functions, so that AF activation starts *only* when you press your designated AF-ON button. However, for back-button focus, you'll want to press the right directional button and *enable* Out-of-Focus Release.

2. **Assign AF-ON function.** Most users of BBF prefer to use the AF-ON button to initiate autofocus. However, if you'd rather use a different button, Custom Setting f2: Custom Controls can assign the AF-ON function to the button of your choice. In all cases, if you've followed these steps, the defined button is used to *initiate* autofocus. The shutter-release button cannot be used to initiate autofocus.

3. **Set Focus Mode to AF-C.**

4. **Confirm Release Priority.** Make sure Custom Setting a1 is set to Release.

5. **Activate Focus.** As you frame your subject, wait until you want to initiate focus, then press the AF-ON button and your AF-C focus mode will kick into action. You then have two options:

   - **Release the AF-ON button.** When you release the button, focus will be locked and the plane of focus will not change, so you can reframe as needed (just as with AF-S).

   - **Track focus.** Continue to press the AF-ON button and AF-C mode will continue to operate as necessary to keep your subject in focus. With the button held down, you can take pictures by pressing the shutter release fully.

Focus Shift Shooting

Focus stacking—which Nikon calls Focus Shift shooting—is used as a way of increasing the narrow depth-of-field commonly encountered when doing macro (close-up) photography of flowers or other small objects at short distances. In some cases, depth-of-field will be so narrow that it's impossible to keep the entire subject in focus. Although having part of the image out of focus can be a pleasing effect for a portrait of a person, it is likely to be a hindrance when you are trying to make an accurate photographic record of a flower or small piece of precision equipment.

Focus Shift shooting provides enhanced depth-of-field by taking multiple shots at different focus distances, and, using software, combining the in-focus areas of each image. The technique requires a non-moving object, so some subjects, such as flowers, are best photographed in a breezeless environment. With the Z5 II's Focus Shift shooting feature, the camera takes a series of pictures starting at a focus point you specify. The camera then adjusts the focus slightly between each image, refocusing from closest to your subject to infinity. You end up with a series of images that can be combined using two simple Photoshop commands, which I will describe shortly. Figure 3.17 can help you visualize what's going on. At top in the figure is a still life close-up captured at f/2.8 and focused on the nearest objects. The center image shows the scene, but with the focus on the back rows. Focus Shift takes as many as 300 separate exposures at different focus points in-between (although only 45 shots were needed for this example) and then merges them in a way that uses only the *sharpest* pixels in each individual image, as seen at bottom in the figure.

It's a shame, but most of the discussions you see about focus stacking don't really explain the full potential and advantages of this powerful technique. Here's a summary:

- **Focus stacking increases depth-of-field.** Everybody knows this; it's the first thing associated with the technique. The second thing they think of is macro photography. But the process can be used for many other types of static subjects, including landscape and architectural photography.

- **Focus stacking makes the best use of your lens' sharpness.** Yes, you can increase DOF without focus stacking just by stopping down your lens to a smaller aperture. However, every lens has an optimum, sharpest, aperture. If you use a smaller f/stop you will lose sharpness due to *diffraction effects,* as I explain in Chapter 5. So, the increased *range* of sharpness comes at the cost of some definition. Apertures *wider* than a given lens' best f/stop will be less sharp due to uncorrected aberrations and other effects that are reduced at the optimum aperture.

  But with focus stacking, each and every exposure in the stack can be made using the *sharpest* aperture setting available with that lens.

- **Focus stacking can alleviate image noise effects.** You don't always have absolute control over the lighting you use, especially if you're working with electronic flash. So, if you shoot at f/32 to get maximum depth-of-field you may have to boost your Z5 II's ISO sensitivity to compensate, potentially to the point of increasing noise levels in your image. A single image shot at f/32 and ISO 1000 might have depth-of-field similar to a stack-focus image exposed at f/5.6 and ISO 100, but pixel-peepers may find the sharpness and noise qualities to be very different.

- **Focus stacking provides unprecedented control over focus range.** You can choose exactly what areas of your image are in sharp focus, including some ways I discovered that are impossible to achieve under normal conditions.

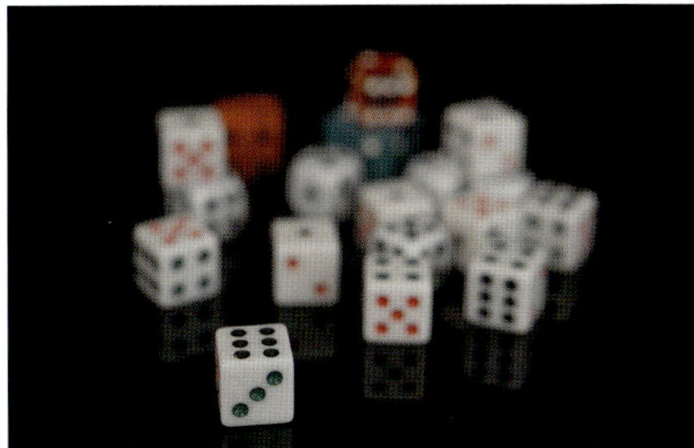
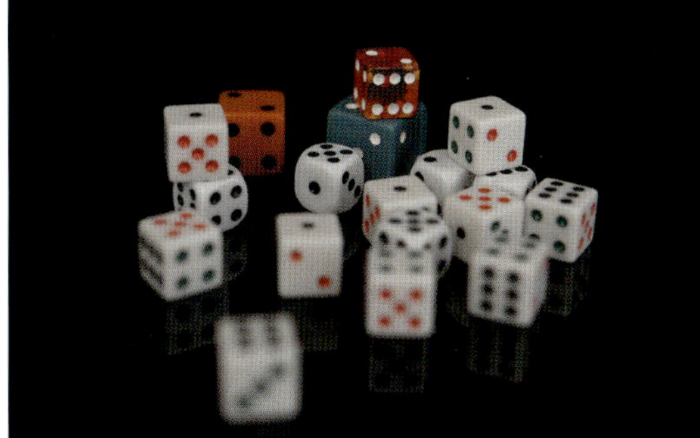
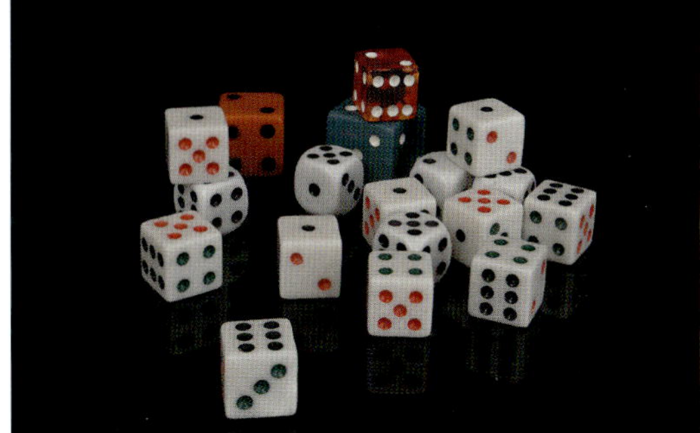

Figure 3.17 Images focused at the nearest focus planes (top) are combined with others at increasing distances, to a most distant point (center), and then merged to produce an image with extreme depth-of-field (bottom).

With focus shift shooting, you have dozens or hundreds of individual images to work with, each with a narrow plane of focus. You can, then, pick and choose exactly where your depth-of-field begins and ends with remarkable precision. If, for creative reasons, you want everything a millimeter in front of your main subject to be blurry, and everything a millimeter or more behind it to blur, you can do that, while keeping your subject tack sharp. When stacking your final image, all you have to do is not merge any of the frames in the area you want to be out of focus. You even can achieve the seemingly impossible effect of having the planes of sharpest focus at the front and rear of a scene, with the *middle* portion weirdly out of focus.

Focus Shift How-To

Fortunately, producing a conventional focus-stacked image doesn't require my variety of unhinged thinking if all you want is enhanced depth-of-field. Here are the detailed steps you can take to use Focus Shift shooting for your own deep-focus images:

1. **Set the camera firmly on a solid tripod.** A tripod or other equally firm support is absolutely essential for this procedure. You don't want the camera (or the subject) to move at all during the exposures.

2. **Use a remote release, if desired.** It's probably best if you trigger the camera without moving it. However, the procedure does pause for a short period of time once you activate it, perhaps giving your tripod/camera time to settle down even if you begin by poking the OK button with your finger.

3. **Attach a lens with an appropriate focus range.** Focus Shift shooting uses the lens's built-in autofocus motor, and so will not work with lenses that do not autofocus on the Z5 II.

4. **Set the focus modes.** Use the *i* menu to choose AF-S (single focus) and Single-point AF.

5. **Set the quality of the images to JPEG FINE.** Use the Photo Shooting or *i* menu to make this adjustment. Your final files will be quite large, particularly if you are capturing more than a few dozen individual images, so JPEG Fine * or RAW files can be unwieldy to work with.

6. **Set the exposure, ISO, and white balance manually.** Use test shots, if necessary, to determine the best values.

   - **Maintain exposure.** Indoors, when lighting conditions are stable, turn off autoexposure, Auto ISO, and Auto White Balance to prevent visible variations from arising among the multiple shots that you'll be taking. When shooting indoors, you don't want the camera to change exposure, the ISO setting, or white balance between shots. However, if you're *outdoors* where lighting may change, you may need to use Aperture-priority to keep a constant exposure.

   - **Avoid wide apertures, too.** As I said above, even though you'll be effectively increasing depth-of-field through focus stacking, you should still avoid the *widest* apertures of your lens, as well as the smallest, as they are rarely the sharpest f/stops. In addition, because wide apertures do have less DOF, if you shoot at f/2.8, say, instead of f/5.6, the camera will need to capture more shots.

   - **Close down a few stops.** I always close down at least 1.5 f/stops. Shutter speed is not as important (and less so if you're using flash). Since the camera is on a tripod, ambient-light exposures won't add any blur from camera movement, but I tend to avoid very slow speeds anyway to keep the process speedy and efficient. You can manually set a slightly higher ISO sensitivity, if needed, to obtain the shutter speed/aperture combination you want to use.

7. **Avoid conflicting features.** Disable vibration reduction, even with lenses that can detect being mounted on a tripod; if your lens has VR and an on/off switch, slide the VR switch to Off. Make sure Photo Flicker Reduction and High Frequency Flicker Reduction are turned off. The self-timer cannot be used to start the sequence. If Picture Control is set to Auto, change it to Standard. You may also use one of the other "original" Picture Controls (as described in Chapter 5) if you want to apply that control's effect to your stack.

8. **Set focus point to nearest point.** Use the directional buttons to position the red focus box on the subject nearest the camera lens that you want to include. The less of the foreground you include in your set, the fewer shots you'll need to complete your sequence. Focus *slightly in front of that subject.* It's safer to include some of the out-of-focus foreground and discard those images.

9. **Access the Focus Shift shooting menu.** It's shown in Figure 3.18. Select an appropriate setting for each of the following parameters, using my guidelines:

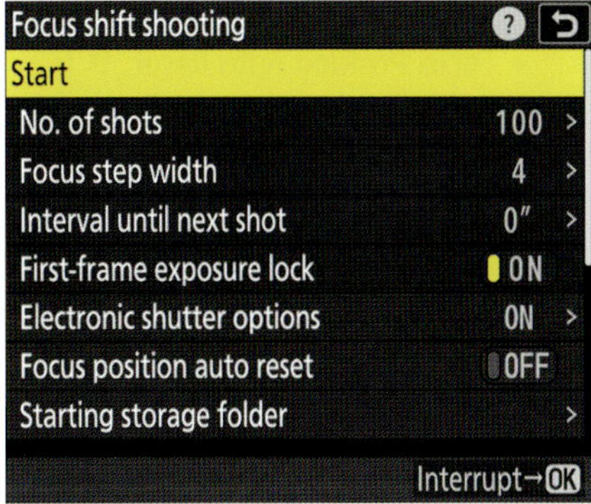

Figure 3.18 Focus Shift Shooting options.

- **No. of Shots.** You can choose from 1 to 300 individually refocused shots. The number of images captured will depend on how finely you want to have the camera change focus between shots (and you'll combine this with the step width option described next). For a subject with a lot of fine detail and depth (such as a macro shot of an insect), you'll want lots of images, a hundred or more, to record focus at many different planes. For architectural or landscape scenes taken with a wide-angle lens, you'll need fewer.

- **Focus Step Width.** You can specify values from 1 (a narrow slice per adjustment) to 10 (a much wider focus change). Nikon does not specify how much each increment changes the focus, for a very good reason: it *can't.* Depending on the focal length of your lens and your f/stop, the effective plane of apparent focus may vary from narrow, to very narrow, to super-narrow in macro shooting environments.

  You may need some trial-and-error to choose the correct number of shots and focus step width. For example, with 50 shots and a wide focus step, the first 10 may encompass your entire subject and the last 40 may be wasted on completely out-of-focus images. It's often worthwhile to take a test shot, view a slide show of all your images, and decide whether to increase/decrease the number of shots and/or focus step width.

  As a guideline, you should consider using a step width of 4 or 5 for distant subjects (e.g., landscapes) and smaller steps (1 or 2) for macro photos, because the changes in focus are large between steps with close-ups.

- **Interval Until Next Shot.** You can select 00 seconds to 30 seconds. At 00 seconds, the camera will take all the photos consecutively at a rate of up to 5 frames per second in Single Shot or Continuous mode. (You can't use the self-timer release mode.) The 00-second setting works well when shooting by ambient light that doesn't change. However, you can use flash, too. Just specify an interval that is greater than the maximum recycle rate of your flash. **Note:** Also consider how much your flash heats up when fired at brief intervals, particularly when the full power of the flash is needed for each shot. Multiple shots at close-range in macro mode can work fine, because only a fraction of the flash's power is used for each exposure.

- **First-Frame Exposure Lock.** Choose On and the camera will lock exposure at the settings calculated for the first shot. You'll use this most of the time, as you will get the best results if the illumination does not change between shots. Select Off to tell the camera to recalculate exposure for each frame. You might do that when shooting landscapes on a day with intermittent clouds. Your results may not be as good as if the lighting was kept consistent, however.

- **Electronic shutter options.** You can turn the Z5 II's electronic shutter on or off and choose a volume level from 0 (silent) to 3 (loudest). These options can make the shooting process quieter or totally silent. You might want to specify a value of 1 to make it easier to discern when the process begins and ends. The e-shutter also reduces internal camera movement (from shutter curtain "bounce") and saves wear and tear on your mechanical shutter.

- **Focus Position Auto Reset.** When set to On, after the Focus Shift sequence is finished, the Z5 II will refocus at the specified starting position. If you're shooting tests or simply want to try again after making some other adjustment, this allows you to repeat your previous focus settings. It can be a time-saver. If set to Off, focus remains at the position of the final shot. I haven't been able to think of a reason why you'd want this, but Nikon, in their wisdom, probably came up with something.

- **Starting Storage Folder.** Choose New Folder, and each time you shoot a sequence, the camera will create a fresh folder. I can't think of a reason you would not want to do that. Select Reset File Numbering, and the file numbering is reset each time a new folder is created, which makes it easier to differentiate between the first, last, and in-between images of your set.

The next step is to process the images you've taken in Photoshop. Transfer the images to your computer, and then follow these steps:

1. In Photoshop, select File > Scripts > Load Files into Stack. In the dialog box that then appears, navigate on your computer to find the files for the photographs you have taken, and highlight them all.

2. At the bottom of the next dialog box that appears, check the box that says, "Attempt to Automatically Align Source Images," then click OK. The images will load; it may take several minutes for the program to load the images and attempt to arrange them into layers that are aligned based on their content.

3. Once the program has finished processing the images, go to the Layers panel and select all the layers. You can do this by clicking on the top layer and then Shift-clicking on the bottom one.

4. While the layers are all selected, in Photoshop go to Edit > Auto-Blend Layers. In the dialog box that appears, select the two options, Stack Images and Seamless Tones and Colors, then click OK. The program will process the images, possibly for a considerable length of time.

5. If the procedure worked well, the result will be a single image made up of numerous layers that have been processed to produce a sharply focused rendering of your subject. (See Figure 3.17, bottom.) If it did not work well, you may have to take additional images the next time, focusing very carefully on small slices of the subject as you move progressively farther away from the lens.

6. You'll want to flatten the final image before saving it. The stack of individual shots will easily be more than 2GB, which exceeds the maximum file size of some older storage media and/or OS file systems.

Although this procedure can work very well in Photoshop, you also may want to try it with programs that were developed more specifically for focus stacking and related procedures, such as Helicon Focus (www.heliconsoft.com), PhotoAcute (www.photoacute.com), or CombineZM (https://combinezm.informer.com).

Electronic Flash

4

Some consider electronic flash a necessary evil, providing supplementary illumination that is often harsh or less natural looking, as well as difficult to use. However, what they are deriding is *bad* flash photography, as applied by photographers who don't understand how to use strobes properly or are too lazy to fully apply the creative versatility flash offers. In practice, when you need extra illumination or want more control over light, a Nikon SB-series Speedlight or a compatible external flash offered by third parties can be a lifesaver.

Fortunately, it's easy to become adept at using electronic flash. With many flash units you can select either TTL (through-the-lens) fully automatic flash metering or manual flash output ranging from full power (1/1) to 1/32 power, in whole-stop increments. You can also choose a *flash mode* (such as fill flash), and dial in *flash compensation,* which is much like exposure compensation as explained in Chapter 3. If you decide to use one external flash mounted on the accessory shoe on top of the Z5 II, making these adjustments is easier than ever, thanks to Nikon's *unified flash control* for its SB-300, SB-400, and SB-500 units. (While the flagship—and expensive—SB-5000 is unified flash control-compatible, that mode is not supported by the Z5 II.) The SB-5000 and many older Nikon flash units can still be used with your Z5 II, but you will need to use controls on the flash themselves. This chapter will introduce you to what you need to know to use your external electronic flash.

FLASH IN THE PAN?

Since the mirrorless Z-series cameras were introduced, Nikon has been downplaying its participation in the flash photography arena dramatically. Indeed, the company has not introduced a new electronic flash unit for a decade and has turned over the reins to third-party manufacturers. As is the case with lenses, there are suppliers eager to support Nikon's burgeoning mirrorless product line, including Nissin, Godox, ProFoto, and others. They offer too many different models to evaluate and explain in this book. In addition, the churn rate for the units that are available is quite rapid. I will describe the current Nikon SB-series flash units and the most popular discontinued models later in this chapter for those who own or may buy them. For information on third-party offerings and how to use them—particularly for radio and optical wireless photography with multiple units—you'll need to consult the manuals provided with the Nikon TTL-compatible electronic flash. Nikon provides a remote flash overview, beginning on page 400 of the Z5 II manual.

Electronic Flash Basics

While the latest generation of LED-based studio lights are increasing in popularity, electronic flash has remained the studio light source of choice for many pro photographers. It's more intense (and its intensity can be varied to order by the photographer using the strobe's power adjustment features) and freezes action reliably. Flash frees you from the need for a tripod (unless you want to use one to lock down a composition), and has a snappy, consistent light quality that matches daylight.

Electronic flash illumination is produced by photons generated by an electrical charge that is accumulated in a component called a *capacitor* and then directed through a glass tube containing xenon gas, which absorbs the energy and emits the burst of light. In automatic mode (which Nikon calls *iTTL*), the main flash is preceded by one or more mini-bursts, which Nikon dubs "monitor preflash," that allow gauging how much light is bouncing back from your subject and background, and to communicate with other external flash units linked wirelessly. In practice, external strobes can be linked to the camera in several different ways: mounted on the camera in dedicated flash/CLS mode, triggered wirelessly by CLS-compatible units, connected in wired, non-intelligent mode (for example, when using studio flash), through radio/infrared flash units, transmitters and receivers, or through optical connections (old-school "slave" mode). (See Figure 4.1.)

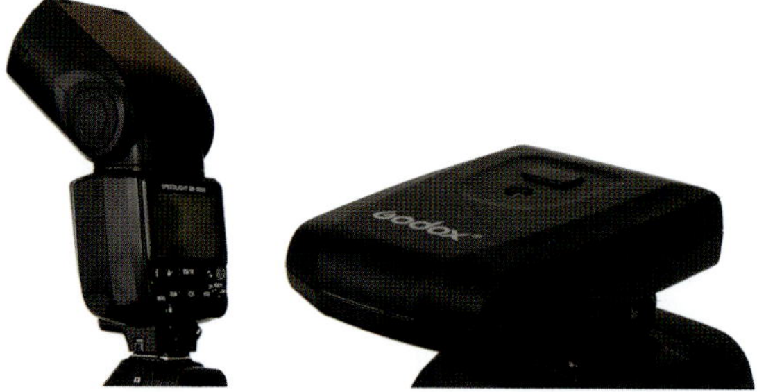

Figure 4.1 The Nikon SB-5000 offers radio control (left). Third-party add-ons also can use radio transmission to trigger electronic flash units (right).

The Moment of Exposure

The Z5 II has a vertically traveling shutter that consists of two curtains. Just before the flash fires, the front curtain opens and moves down to the opposite side of the frame, at which point the shutter is completely open. The flash can be triggered at this point (so-called front-curtain sync), making the flash exposure. Then, after an interval, during which the exposure is made, a rear curtain begins moving down the sensor plane, covering up the sensor again. That delay can vary from 30 seconds to the maximum sync speed, which is the maximum shutter speed you can use when working with flash. Ordinarily, the top sync speed is 1/200th second, but can be faster when using high-speed sync, a feature available, discussed later in this chapter.

When I refer to *sync speed* in this book, I will be talking about the maximum shutter speed you can use, and I will explain how to choose that value shortly. Figure 4.2 illustrates how your Z5 II's shutter works, with a fanciful illustration of a generic unit (your camera's shutter *does not* look like this). Both curtains are tightly closed at upper left. At upper right, the front curtain begins to move downward, starting to expose a narrow slit that reveals the sensor behind the shutter. At lower left, the front curtain moves downward farther until, as you can see at lower right in the figure, the sensor is fully exposed.

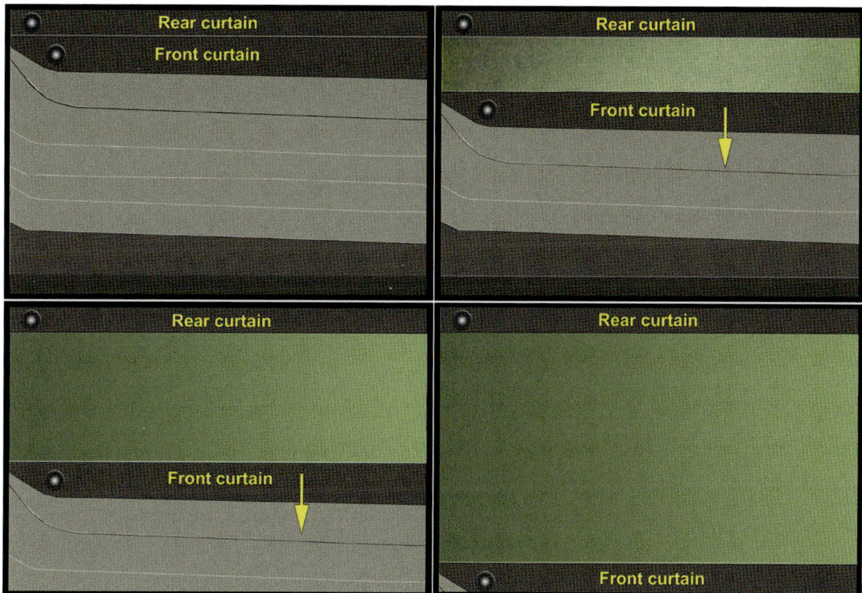

Figure 4.2 A focal plane shutter has two curtains, the lower, or front curtain, and an upper, rear curtain.

Here's a more detailed look at what transpires when you take a photo using electronic flash, all within a few milliseconds of time. The following list assumes you are using iTTL exposure mode:

1. **Flash sync mode.** After you've selected a shooting mode, choose the flash sync option available. You can access the Flash Mode entry in the Photo Shooting menu. If you change flash sync mode frequently, you can also define a button to summon the adjustment using Custom Setting f2: Custom Controls (described in Chapter 7). As I promised, I'll explain your sync options shortly.

2. **Metering method.** Choose the metering method you want, from Matrix, Center-weighted, Spot, or Highlight-weighted metering.

3. **Activate flash.** Mount an external flash (or connect it with a cable) and turn it on. A ready light appears in the viewfinder and on the back of the dedicated flash when the unit is ready to take a picture (although the flash might not be *fully* charged when the indicator first appears).

4. **Check exposure.** Select a shutter speed when using Manual, Program, or Shutter-priority modes; select an aperture when using Aperture-priority and Manual exposure modes.

5. **Lock flash setting (if desired).** Optionally, if the main subject is located significantly off-center, you can frame so the subject is centered, lock the flash at the exposure needed to illuminate that subject, and then reframe using the composition you want. Lock the flash level using the Flash Value (FV) Lock button you designate (many assign the Fn1 or Fn2 button to this function, using Custom Setting f2). Press the FV lock button, and the flash will emit a monitor preflash to determine the correct flash level, and then flash will be locked at that level until you press the FV lock button again to release it. FV lock icons appear in the display.

6. **Take photo.** Press the shutter release down all the way.

7. **Distance data received.** Z-mount lenses, as well as F-mount E-, D-, or G-series lenses attached using an adapter, now supply focus distance to the camera.

8. **Preflash emitted.** The external flash sends out several preflash bursts. One series of bursts can be used to control additional wireless flash units in Commander mode, while another is used to determine exposure. The preflashes happen in such a brief period before the main flash that they are virtually undetectable.

9. **Exposure calculated.** The preflash bounces back and is measured at the sensor. It calculates brightness and contrast of the image to determine exposure. If you're using Matrix metering (more on metering modes shortly), the camera evaluates the scene to determine whether the subject may be backlit (for fill flash); whether a subject requires extra ambient light exposure to balance the scene with the flash exposure; or whether the camera classifies the scene in some other way. The camera-to-subject information as well as the degree of sharp focus of the subject matter is used to locate the subject within the frame. If you've selected Spot metering, only standard i-TTL (without balanced fill flash) is used. (See the sidebar "i-TTL Flash Control".)

10. **Front curtain opens.** The exposure by ambient light begins when the physical shutter curtain is fully open.

11. **Flash fired.** At the correct triggering moment (depending on whether front- or rear-curtain sync is used), the camera sends a signal to one or more flashes to start flash discharge. The flash is quenched as soon as the correct exposure has been achieved.

12. **Shutter closes.** The electronic rear curtain "descends" to conclude the exposure, and the live view from the sensor resumes. You're ready to take another picture. Remember to press the defined FV lock button (if used) again to release the flash exposure if your next shot will use a different composition.

13. **Exposure confirmed.** Ordinarily, the full charge in the flash may not be required. If the flash indicator in the viewfinder blinks for about three seconds after the exposure, that means that the entire flash charge was required, and it *could* mean that the full charge wasn't enough for a proper exposure. Be sure to review your image on the monitor to make sure it's not underexposed, and, if it is, make adjustments (such as increasing the ISO setting) to remedy the situation.

---

i-TTL FLASH CONTROL

CLS-compatible flash units include up to several Flash Control modes, depending on the model. (I'll explain them all later in this chapter.) With the one you'll use most often, TTL mode, the camera calculates and sets flash exposure (but applies any flash exposure compensation you dial in, as explained later). In Manual mode, you adjust the output level of the flash.

In TTL mode, the camera selects one of two variations:

- **i-TTL balanced fill flash (TTL BL).** The camera analyzes the preflash reflection from all areas of the frame and adjusts the output to provide a balance between the main subject of your image and the background lighting.

- **Standard i-TTL fill flash.** The brightness of the background is not considered in setting the flash output. This mode tends to emphasize the main subject, even if some background detail is lost. You can force the camera to select Standard i-TTL fill flash by switching to Spot metering mode. Use flash exposure compensation to adjust the main subject/background balance as required.

A Tale of Two Exposures

Calculating the proper exposure for an electronic flash photograph is a bit more complicated than determining the settings for continuous light. The right exposure isn't simply a function of how far away your subject is (which the camera can figure out based on the autofocus distance that's locked in just prior to taking the picture). Various objects reflect more or less light at the same distance so, obviously, the camera needs to measure the amount of light reflected back and through the lens.

That measurement is complicated by two things: a picture taken using flash is actually *two separate exposures*: the exposure produced by the flash itself, and the exposure that results from the continuous, ambient light that is also illuminating your subject. If the calculations are correct, the plane in which your main subject resides will be properly exposed. However, anything more than slightly in *front of* or *behind* that plane will be overexposed or underexposed (respectively), thanks to the inverse square law: the intensity of the light is inversely proportional to the square of the distance. In practice, that means a light source that is 12 feet away from a subject provides only one-quarter as much illumination as the same source located 6 feet away. In f/stop terms, you need to open up two stops whenever the distance doubles. (See Figure 4.3.)

So, as you shoot, you need to consider "depth-of-light" (the range in which a subject is acceptably illuminated in front of and behind the plane used to calculate the exposure) in addition to depth-of-field. Fortunately, in many flash photography situations, the main subject is the closest thing to the lens, so there often won't be a problem with overexposed foreground objects. Backgrounds, however, are another story. In daylight situations, photographers generally let the daylight provide most of the exposure and use the flash only to fill in shadows.

However, if you're photographing indoors or at night, the background, not illuminated by the flash, will appear darker than the foreground subject. Fortunately, every flash picture consists of *two* exposures, the exposure produced by the flash, and a second exposure that results from the background

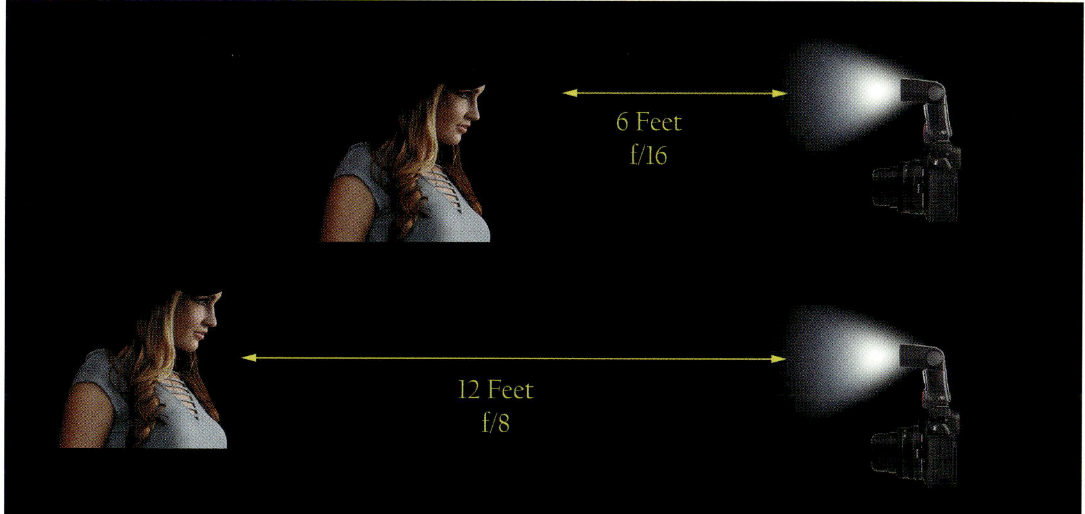

Figure 4.3 A light source that is twice as far away provides only one-quarter as much illumination.

illumination. For the flash exposure, the shutter speed is more-or-less irrelevant, as long as you're using a shutter speed slower than the synchronization speed. The f/stop selected and the power output of the flash determine the exposure.

The ambient light exposure is more "normal," using both the shutter speed and aperture. Slower shutter speeds allow more ambient light to reach the sensor, and higher shutter speeds allow less. If you want to *minimize* the ambient portion of the exposure, use a higher shutter speed, up to the sync speed when not using High-Speed Sync (discussed later in this chapter). To *maximize* the ambient exposure, use a slower shutter speed. The camera has a special Slow Sync shutter setting that automatically uses these slower speeds to balance flash/ambient exposures, but you can also use Custom Setting e2: Flash Shutter Speed to specify the slowest/fastest shutter speed used under normal conditions.

There are several complications involved in balancing flash and ambient light exposures. So-called "mixed" lighting is one of them. Your flash is balanced for daylight, while ambient light is often incandescent or some other "warm" illumination. The second problem that arises stems from the fact that while the flash exposure is concluded in an instant (typically 1/1000th to 1/50000th of a second), the ambient light continues for the entire time the shutter is open. So, you end up with *two* images produced by the *dual* exposures. If the subject is moving, the additional ambient light exposure produces a "ghost" image. The best way of handling that conundrum is to adjust the sync setting, and I'm going to explain how to do that shortly.

Measuring Exposure

By this time, you should be wondering how flash is measured, as the flash burst isn't available for evaluation until it's triggered when you press the shutter release down all the way to take the picture. The solution is to fire the flash multiple times. The first pulse is a *monitor preflash* that can be analyzed, then followed virtually instantaneously by a series of pulses (if required) to communicate wirelessly with any optically triggered remote flash units. Only then is the main flash triggered, which (when shooting in autoflash mode) emits exactly the calculated intensity needed for a correct exposure. (All these pulses happen so quickly that they may appear to you to be a single burst.)

Because of the exposure calculations, the primary flash may be longer in duration for distant objects and shorter in duration for closer subjects, depending on the required intensity for exposure. This default through-the-lens evaluative flash exposure system is called i-TTL BL (for intelligent Through The Lens, Balanced Fill Flash) and can operate whenever you have attached a Nikon-dedicated flash unit. With CLS-compatible flash units, your automatic exposure is calculated by measuring a preflash and determining an appropriate exposure from that.

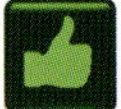

NOTE When using Programmed Auto mode, the *largest* aperture available may be constrained, depending on your ISO setting. For example, The *widest* f/stop available at ISO 100 is f/4, even if your lens is capable of an aperture of f/2.8 or larger. If your flash isn't powerful enough to illuminate your subject at f/4, you'll end up with an underexposure.

The available f/stops at various ISO values are shown in Table 4.1. Since Shutter-priority mode limits which shutter speeds are available, Aperture-priority is almost always your best autoexposure mode for flash.

TABLE 4.1 Available Apertures for Programmed Auto

ISO VALUE	MAXIMUM APERTURE	ISO VALUE	MAXIMUM APERTURE
ISO 64	f/3.5	ISO 800	f/7.1
ISO 100	f/4	ISO 1000	f/7.1
ISO 125	f/4.5	ISO 1250	f/8
ISO 160	f/4.5	ISO 1600	f/8
ISO 200	f/5	ISO 2000	f/9
ISO 250	f/5	ISO 2500	f/9
ISO 320	f/5.6	ISO 3200	f/10
ISO 400	f/5.6	ISO 4000	f/10
ISO 500	f/6.3	ISO 5000	f/11
ISO 600	f/6.3	ISO 6400	f/11

Choosing a Flash Sync Mode

The Z5 II has five *flash sync modes*, plus a sixth (High-Speed Sync, described later) that comes into play in some circumstances. The five main modes, plus Off (which disables the flash) are selected using the Photo Shooting menu's Flash Mode entry. (See Figure 4.4 for the icons.) Those modes (which I've listed in logical order, so the explanation will make more sense, rather than the order in which they appear during the selection cycle) are as follows:

- **Fill flash/Front-curtain sync (available in PSAM and Auto modes).** This setting, available in all exposure modes, should be your default setting. In this mode, the flash fires as soon as the front curtain opens completely. The shutter then remains open for the duration of the exposure, until the rear curtain closes. If the subject is moving and ambient light levels are high enough, the movement will cause that secondary "ghost" exposure that appears in front of the flash exposure.

- **Rear-curtain sync (available in PSAM modes).** With this setting, which can be used with Program, Shutter-priority, Aperture-priority, or Manual exposure modes, the front curtain opens completely and remains open for the duration of the exposure. Then, the flash is fired and the rear curtain closes. If the subject is moving and ambient light levels are high enough, the movement will cause a secondary "ghost" exposure that appears behind the flash exposure (trailing it). You'll find more on "ghost" exposures next. In Program and Aperture-priority modes, this setting tells the camera to combine rear-curtain sync with slow shutter speeds (just like slow sync, discussed below) to balance ambient light with flash illumination. (It's best to use a tripod to avoid blur at these slow shutter speeds.)

Note: Rear-curtain sync may not synchronize with some studio flash equipment.

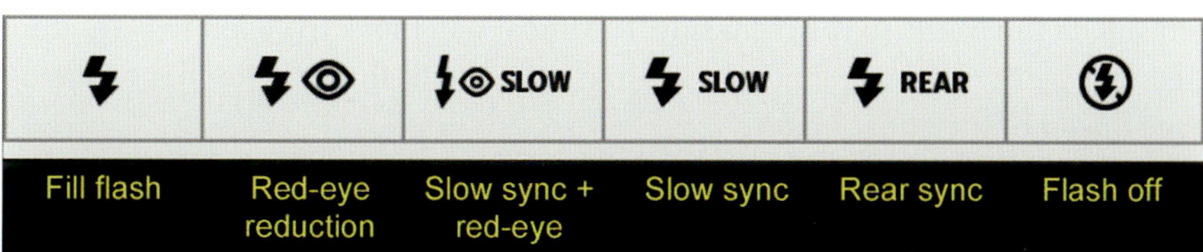

Figure 4.4 Icons for flash sync modes include fill flash/front-curtain sync, red-eye reduction, slow sync + red-eye, slow sync, rear-curtain sync, and flash off.

- **Red-eye reduction (available in Auto and PSAM modes).** In this mode, there is a one-second lag after pressing the shutter release before the picture is actually taken, during which the attached flash unit's red-eye reduction feature is used, causing the subject's pupils to contract (assuming they are looking at the camera), and thus reducing potential red-eye effects. Don't use with moving subjects or when you can't abide the delay.

- **Slow sync (available in P or A modes).** This setting allows Program and Aperture-priority modes to use shutter speeds as slow as 30 seconds with the flash to help balance a background illuminated with ambient light with your main subject, which will be lit by the electronic flash. You'll want to use a tripod at slower shutter speeds, of course.

- **Slow-sync + Red-eye (available in PA modes).** This mode combines slow sync with the external flash's red-eye reduction behavior when using Program or Aperture-priority modes.

- **Flash off (available in Auto and PSAM modes).** The flash does not fire, even if powered on.

Ghost Images

The difference might not seem like much, but whether you use front-curtain sync (the default setting) or rear-curtain sync (an optional setting) can make a significant difference to your photograph *if the ambient light in your scene also contributes to the image.* At faster shutter speeds, particularly the sync speed, there isn't much time for the ambient light to register, unless it is very bright. It's likely that the electronic flash will provide almost all the illumination, so front-curtain sync or rear-curtain sync isn't very important.

However, at slower shutter speeds, or with very bright ambient light levels, there is a significant difference, particularly if your subject is moving, or the camera isn't steady. In any of those situations, the ambient light will register as a second image accompanying the flash exposure, and if there is movement (camera or subject), that additional image will not be in the same place as the flash exposure. It will show as a ghost image and, if the movement is significant enough, as a blurred ghost image trailing in front of or behind your subject in the direction of the movement.

As I mentioned earlier, when you're using front-curtain sync, the flash goes off the instant the shutter opens, producing an image of the subject on the sensor. Then, the shutter remains open for an additional period (which can be from 30 seconds to the sync speed). If your subject is moving, say, toward the right side of the frame, the ghost image produced by the ambient light will produce a blur on the right side of the original subject image. That makes it look as if your sharp (flash-produced) image is chasing the ghost (see Figure 4.5, top), which looks unnatural to those of us who grew up with lightning-fast Justice League-style superheroes who always left a ghost trail *behind them* (see Figure 4.5, bottom).

So, Nikon provides rear-curtain sync to remedy the situation. In that mode, the shutter opens, as before. The shutter remains open for its designated duration, and the ghost image forms. If your subject moves from the left side of the frame to the right side, the ghost will move from left to right, too. *Then*, about 1.3 milliseconds before the rear shutter curtain closes, the flash is triggered, producing a nice, sharp flash image *ahead* of the ghost image.

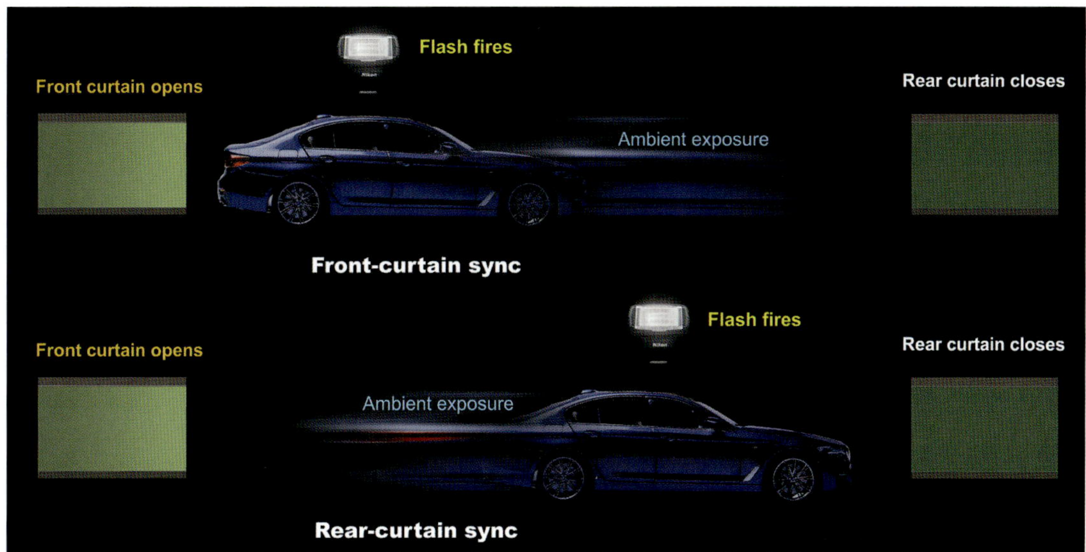

Figure 4.5 Front-curtain sync produces an image that trails in front of the flash exposure (top), while rear-curtain sync creates a more "natural-looking" trail behind the flash image (bottom).

Avoiding Sync Speed Problems

Using a shutter speed faster than the sync speed can cause problems. Triggering the electronic flash only when the shutter is completely open makes a lot of sense if you think about what's going on. To obtain shutter speeds faster than the sync speed, only part of the sensor is exposed at one time, by starting the second curtain on its journey before the first curtain has completely opened. That effectively provides a briefer exposure as a slit of the shutter passes over the surface of the sensor. If the flash were to fire during the time when the front and rear curtains partially obscured the sensor, only the slit that was actually open would be exposed.

You'd end up with only a narrow band, representing the portion of the sensor that was exposed when the picture is taken. For shutter speeds *faster* than the sync speed, the rear curtain begins moving *before* the front curtain reaches the bottom of the frame. As a result, a moving slit, the distance between the front and rear curtains, exposes one portion of the sensor at a time as it moves from the top to the bottom. Figure 4.6 shows three views of our typical (but imaginary) focal plane shutter.

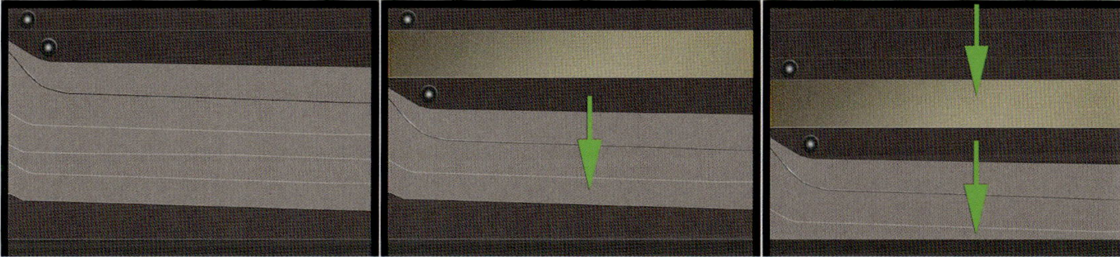

Figure 4.6 A closed shutter (left); partially open shutter as the front curtain begins to move downward (middle); only part of the sensor is exposed as the slit moves (right).

At left is pictured the closed shutter; in the middle version you can see the front curtain has moved down about 1/4 of the distance from the top; and in the right-hand version, the rear curtain has started to "chase" the front curtain across the frame toward the bottom.

If the flash is triggered while this slit is moving, only the exposed portion of the sensor will receive any illumination. You end up with a photo like the one shown in Figure 4.7. Note that a band across the bottom of the image is black. That's a shadow of the rear shutter curtain, which had started to move when the flash was triggered. Sharp-eyed readers will wonder why the black band is at the *bottom* of the frame rather than at the top, where the rear curtain begins its journey. The answer is simple: your lens flips the image upside down and forms it on the sensor in a reversed position. You never notice that, because the camera is smart enough to show you the pixels that make up your photo in their proper orientation during picture review. But this image flip is why, if your sensor gets dirty and you detect a spot of dust in the upper half of a test photo, if cleaning manually, you need to look for the speck in the *bottom* half of the sensor.

I generally end up with sync-speed problems only when shooting in the studio, using studio flash units rather than my Nikon-dedicated Speedlights. That's because if you're using "smart" flash (like one of the Nikon Speedlights), when a strobe is attached any unintentional goof in shutter speed

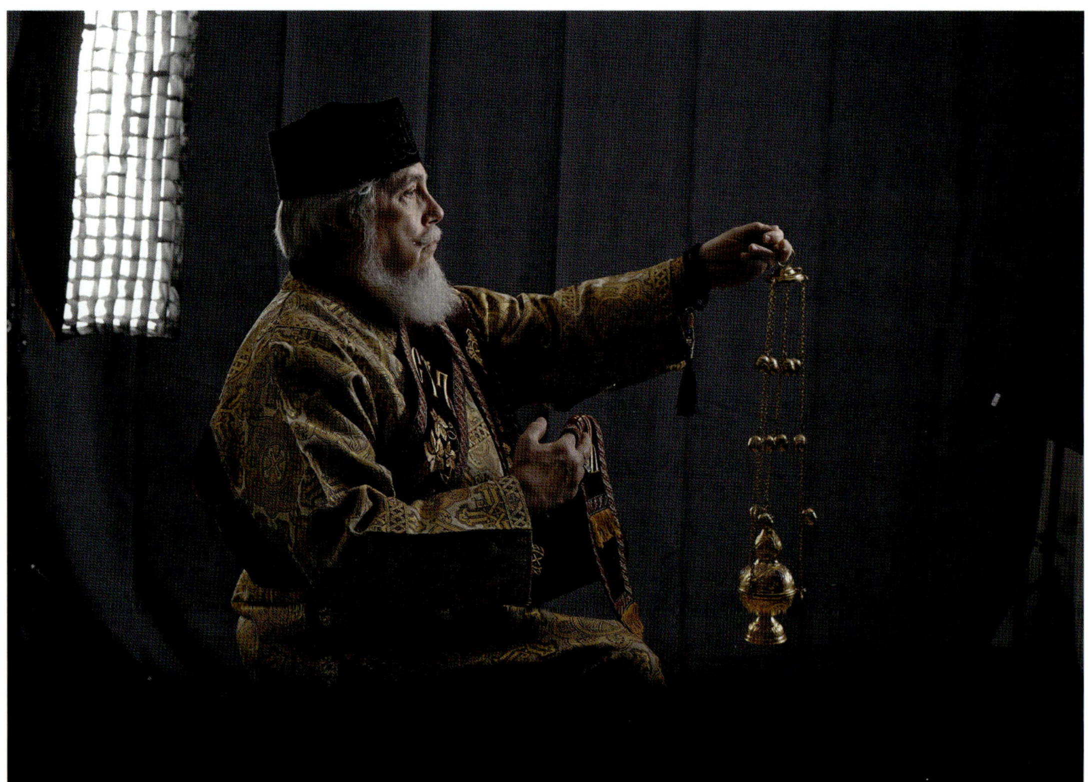

Figure 4.7 If a shutter speed faster than the sync speed is used, you can end up photographing only a portion of the image.

settings is corrected. If you happen to set the shutter to a faster speed in S or M mode, it will automatically be adjusted down to the sync speed as soon as you turn on the flash (or prevent you from choosing a faster speed if the flash is already powered up). In A or P modes, where the camera selects the shutter speed, it will never choose a shutter speed higher than the sync speed when using flash. In P mode, shutter speed is automatically set from 1/60th to the sync speed when using flash.

But when using a non-dedicated flash, such as a studio unit plugged into an adapter mounted on the accessory shoe, the camera has no way of knowing that a flash is connected, so shutter speeds faster than the sync speed can be set inadvertently.

> **SILENCE ISN'T GOLDEN**
>
> One oddity you need to be aware of is that you can't use electronic flash if you've activated the Z5 II's Silent mode in the Setup menu, which uses the electronic shutter. If you want a quieter mode, use the Camera Sounds entry of the Setup menu and set Beep to Off.

High-Speed Sync

Note that the Z5 II can use a feature called *high-speed sync* that allows shutter speeds faster than the sync speed with certain external Nikon flash units. When using Auto FP high-speed sync, the flash fires a continuous series of bursts at reduced power for the entire duration of the exposure, so that the illumination is able to expose the sensor as the slit moves.

As I said earlier, triggering the electronic flash only when the shutter is completely open makes a lot of sense if you think about what's going on. To obtain shutter speeds faster than the sync speed, only part of the sensor is exposed at one time, by starting the rear curtain on its journey before the front curtain has completely opened. That effectively provides a briefer exposure as a slit of the shutter passes over the surface of the sensor. If the flash were to fire during the time when the front and rear curtains partially obscured the sensor, only the area defined by the slit that was actually open would be exposed.

This technique is most useful outdoors when you need fill-in flash but find that the sync speed is way too slow for the f/stop you want to use. For example, at ISO 200, an outdoors exposure is likely to have a sync speed of, say, f/14, which is perfectly fine for an ambient/balanced fill-flash exposure if you don't mind the extreme depth-of-field offered by the small f/stop. But, what if you'd rather shoot at 1/1600th second at f/5.6? High-speed sync will let you do that, and you probably won't mind the reduced flash power, because you're looking for fill flash, anyway. This sync mode offers more flexibility than, say, dropping down to ISO 100.

High-speed sync is also useful when you want to use a larger f/stop to limit the amount of depth-of-field for selective focus techniques. Select a shutter speed higher than the sync speed, and the faster sync speed automatically reduces the effective light of the flash, without other intervention from you.

To use Auto FP sync with units like the Nikon SB-5000, SB-910/SB-900, SB-700, SB-500, SB-R200, and a few discontinued Speedlights like the SB-800 and SB-600, there is no setting to make on the flash itself. You need to use Custom Setting e1 to specify 1/200 s (Auto FP). When using P or A exposure modes, the shutter speed will be set to the sync speed when a compatible external flash is attached. Higher shutter speeds than the sync speed—all the way up to 1/8000th second—can then be used with full synchronization, at reduced flash output. There are also situations in which you might want to set flash sync speed to *less* than the sync speed, say, because you *want* ambient light to produce secondary ghost images in your frame. You can choose the following settings:

- **1/200 s (Auto FP).** This setting allows using the compatible external flash units with high-speed synchronization at 1/200th second. When enabled, the camera activates auto FP sync when the camera selects a shutter speed of 1/200th second or faster in Programmed and Aperture-priority modes. In Shutter-priority and Manual exposure modes, you can select the faster speed yourself up to 1/8000th second (or 1/2000th second can be used if Electronic Front-Curtain Shutter is specified as Shutter Type in Custom Setting d6). Non-compatible flash units will be used at speeds no faster than 1/200th second.

- **1/200 s.** At this default setting, only shutter speeds up to 1/200th second can be used with flash.

- **1/200 s–1/60 s.** You can also specify a specific shutter speed from the range of speeds 1/200th second to 1/60th second to be used as the synchronization speed for external flash units. Forcing a slower shutter speed produces a "slow-sync" effect. For example, when 1/60th second has been set as the maximum flash shutter speed, ambient light is more likely to contribute to the exposure. (See Figure 4.8.) That can help balance the flash exposure with available light falling on the background (use a tripod or VR to minimize ghost images). Or, that slow shutter speed can help generate ghost images when you intentionally want them to appear in your image, say, to create a feeling of motion.

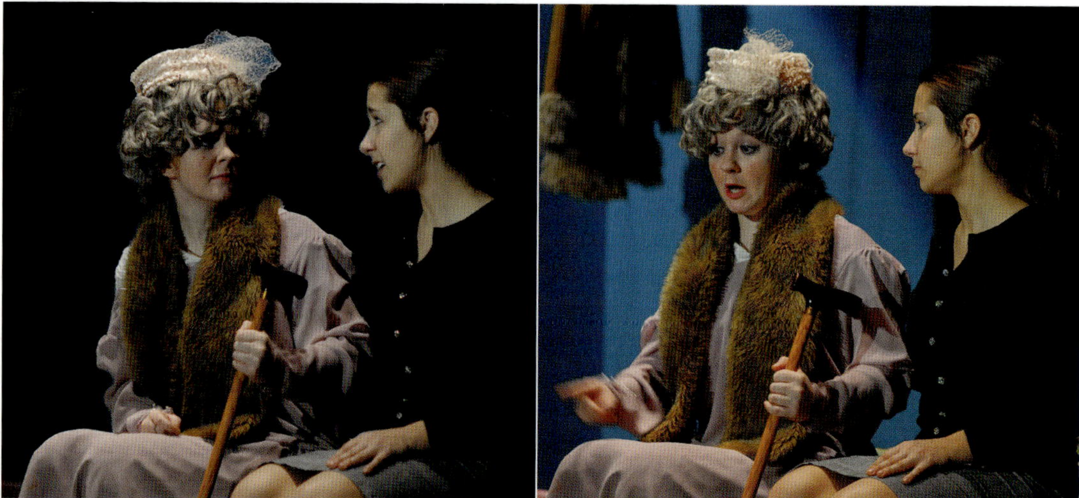

Figure 4.8 With a shutter speed of the sync speed, the background is dark (left). At 1/60th second, the ambient light behind the actors provided detail in the background (right).

Using External Flash

Using an external flash provides you with more power, access to high-speed sync, and can provide more pleasing lighting, if only because an external on-camera flash is elevated enough to cause shadows to fall behind many subjects and can be tilted to provide softer bounce lighting. Multiple external flash units can be used to provide a variety of advanced lighting setups. In this section, we'll deal with the Nikon Creative Lighting System (CLS), which was introduced in July 2003, when the company unveiled the SB-800 Speedlight, a flash unit compatible with early professional digital SLRs, such as the Nikon D2h/D2hs, and, within a few months, more affordable models like 2004's Nikon D70 and all subsequent digital cameras from the company. CLS has the following features, although not all of these are supported by every Nikon camera:

- **i-TTL.** Compatible external units can use intelligent through-the-lens (iTTL) exposure control to calculate exposure based on a monitor preflash that is fired a fraction of a second before the main burst and then evaluated by the same RGB exposure technology used for continuous light measurements. The system's intelligence allows sophisticated adjustments, such as balancing the flash exposure with the ambient light exposure, say, when you shoot in full daylight to fill in the shadows.

- **Advanced wireless lighting.** AWL is a system that uses the same preflash concept to communicate triggering and exposure information to external flash units that aren't physically linked to the camera and located within a reasonable distance (say, about 30 feet). You may be able to divide multiple flash units into up to three different "groups," and communicate with them using your choice of any of four "channels" (to avoid having your flash units triggered by the master flash of another Nikon photographer in the vicinity).

- **FV Lock.** A *flash value* locking system allows you to fix in place the current flash exposure so that you can, for example, measure flash exposure for a subject that is not in the center of the frame and then reframe while using that value for subsequent exposures. You can define an Fn button to perform this function, as described in Chapter 7. When FV lock is activated, the camera meters only a center area of the frame even if Matrix metering has been selected, when the flash is mounted in the hot shoe. In wireless modes, metering is done using the average of the entire frame.

- **Auto FP high-speed sync.** Focal plane HS sync allows synchronizing an external flash while using shutter speeds faster than the sync speed. With a compatible flash and camera, higher shutter speeds can be set, although only a part of the flash's illumination is used, and flash range is reduced (sometimes to as little as a few feet).

- **Zoom coverage.** Some CLS-compatible flash units have a powered zoom head built in to allow changing the area covered by the flash to match the focal length of the lens in use, as communicated by the camera to the flash itself. Zooming can also be done manually.

- **Flash color information communication.** The exact color temperature of the light emitted by a CLS-compatible flash can vary, based on the duration of the flash burst. The flash is initially rather blue in color and becomes redder as the burst continues. The Speedlight is able to send information to the camera to allow adjusting white balance in AWB mode based on the true color information of the flash exposure.

If you want to temporarily disable a flash that's attached and powered up, a handy way to do this is to assign the Flash Disable/Enable function to the Fn1 or Fn2 buttons, using Custom Setting f2, as described in Chapter 7. Then, when you press the button, any external flash attached and powered up will not fire while the button is held down. This is useful if you want to temporarily disable the flash, say, to take a picture or two by available light, and then return to normal flash operation.

> **ADVANCED FLASH FEATURES**
>
> As I noted at the beginning of this chapter, Nikon has begun scaling back its support for its own electronic flash units, and multiple third-party vendors, including Godox, Nissin, Profoto, and others have been quick to fill the vacuum with innovative and versatile flash units of their own that are compatible with Nikon's Advanced Wireless Lighting and Creative Lighting System technology.
>
> Flash accessories, including triggers, are available from PocketWizard, RadioPopper, Godox, and others. There are too many options to cover in this book, so if you're planning on using off-camera flash, multiple flash units, optical or radio wireless operation, repeating flash, modeling lights, and other advanced features, you'll want to check the documentation furnished with your particular device.

Using Flash Exposure Compensation

Of course, flash exposure compensation is also available with the Z5 II's external flash units. If the exposure produced by your flash isn't satisfactory, you can manually add or subtract exposure to the flash exposure calculated by the camera. You can use the Flash Compensation entry in the Photo Shooting menu or assign Flash Mode/Flash Compensation to a button, such as Fn1, using Custom Setting f2: Custom Controls, as explained in Chapter 7. When assigned to a button, you can adjust Flash Mode by pressing the button and rotating the main command dial, and Flash Compensation by holding the button and rotating the sub-command dial. You can make adjustments from –3 EV to +1 EV in 1/3 EV increments.

As with ordinary exposure compensation, the adjustment you make remains in effect until you zero it out by pressing the button assigned to flash mode/flash compensation and rotating the sub-command dial until 0 appears on the display. To view the current flash exposure compensation setting, press the defined button. When compensation is being used, an icon will be shown in the display.

As also described in Chapter 7, you can use Custom Setting e3: Exposure Compensation for Flash to balance ambient light and flash exposure over the entire frame or just take into account the background. The option specifies how the flash level is modified when you apply exposure compensation. (The camera has separate ambient light exposure compensation and flash exposure compensation settings.) You can adjust one or the other, or both if you are using flash. Custom Setting e3 affects only *exposure compensation* (the ambient kind) when you are also using flash. It determines how ambient exposure compensation is applied when some of the illumination will also come from a flash unit.

- **Entire frame.** When you apply ambient exposure compensation (press the exposure compensation (EV) button on the top panel to the right of the ISO button and rotate the main command dial), both ambient *and* flash exposure compensation are adjusted over the entire frame. That balances the exposure for the two elements.

- **Background only.** When this option is selected, *only* ambient exposure compensation is changed when you apply it; flash exposure compensation is unaffected. So, exposure compensation is applied only to the background areas of your image, which are typically illuminated by ambient light. Flash exposure compensation is not affected but can be set separately if you've assigned Flash Mode/Compensation to a button using Custom Setting f2, as described earlier. If that's the case, just rotate the sub-command dial to adjust flash compensation.

> ### EXPOSURE COMPENSATION COMBINES
>
> An important thing to remember is that any ambient light and flash exposure compensation you specify *are combined*. So, if you select +2 EV using the Exposure Compensation button on the top panel (to the right of the ISO button), and then choose +2 flash exposure compensation, you end up with +4 EV added and, probably, an overexposed image.

Specifying Flash Shutter Speed

This is another way of specifying the shutter speed used when working with flash. Unlike Custom Setting e1: Flash Sync Speed described earlier, this setting determines the *slowest* shutter speed that is available for electronic flash synchronization when you're not using a "slow-sync" mode. When you want to avoid ghost images from a secondary exposure, you should use the highest shutter speed that will synchronize with your flash. This setting prevents Programmed or Aperture-priority modes from selecting a shutter speed that captures ambient light along with the flash.

With Custom Setting e2: Flash Shutter Speed, select a value from 30 s to 1/60 s, and the camera will avoid using speeds slower than the one you specify with electronic flash if you don't override that decision by deliberately choosing slow sync, slow rear-curtain sync, or red-eye reduction with slow sync. If you think you can hold the camera steady, a value of 1/30 s is a good compromise; if you have shaky hands, use 1/60 s or higher. Those with extraordinarily steady grips or who are using vibration reduction can try the 1/15 s setting. Remember that this setting only determines the slowest shutter speed that will be used, not the default shutter speed, which is set with Custom Setting e1.

Flash Control

As I noted earlier, some newer Nikon electronic flash units, such as the SB-500, SB-400, or SB-300 Speedlights are compatible with the unified flash control system and can be adjusted by the Flash Control setting in the Photo Shooting menu. All other Nikon electronic flash units, including the SB-5000, SB-600, SB-700, SB-800, SB-900, and SB-910 must be adjusted using the controls *on the flash itself*. Not all of the options can be accessed by every one of the Speedlights listed. For example, with the SB-400, you can only choose between TTL and Manual exposure, plus manual output levels. Unavailable options will be grayed out. To use the Flash Control menu entry, the flash must be mounted on the hot shoe, powered up, and not set in a Remote mode.

The exact options available from the Flash Control screen will vary, depending on the capabilities of the flash unit you are using. I'll discuss each of the adjustments available, whether they are chosen from the Flash Control menu or using the flash unit's own controls, in the sections that follow. Consult your flash unit's manual for the exact procedures used to make the adjustments described.

Working with Nikon Flash External Units

Nikon offers several external flash units that are compatible with CLS, ranging from the top-of-the-line SB-5000 to the entry-level SB-300. Nikon seems to be increasingly relying on third-party manufacturers like Nissin and Profoto for flash compatibility with their newer cameras. There are a number of older units that have been officially or unofficially discontinued, such as the SB-500, SB-600, SB-400, SB-800, and SB-910/SB-900, which are still available, in both new and used condition. Unfortunately, it's not possible to cover available third-party flash units, although Nissin, Profoto, and Godox provide excellent options. However, for those of you who already have or may consider buying one of Nikon's SB-series units—even the discontinued models that are still readily available—I'm going to describe the most recent ones in this section.

Nikon SB-300

This entry-level Speedlight is the smallest and most basic of the Nikon series of Speedlights. The SB-300 has a limited, easy-to-use feature set suited for point-and-shoot photography and some slightly more advanced techniques. Do note however that it does not support wireless off-camera flash. The SB-300 has a moderate guide number of 18/59 (meters/feet) at ISO 100. Its main advantage, then, is to provide some additional elevation of the flash above the camera to provide an improved coverage angle and less chance of red-eye effects. Its flash head tilts up to 120 degrees, with click stops at 120, 90, 75, and 60 degrees when the flash is pointed directly ahead. It has a zoom flash head. The SB-300 is lighter in weight at 3.4 ounces than the SB-400 it replaces and uses two AAA batteries.

Nikon SB-400

Discontinued, but still widely available new from many retailers, this entry-level Speedlight was, until the SB-300 was unveiled, the smallest and most basic of the series. The SB-400 has a limited, easy-to-use feature set suited for point-and-shoot photography and some slightly more advanced techniques. Do note however, that, like the SB-300, it does not support wireless off-camera flash. The 4.5-ounce SB-400 has a moderate guide number of 21/69 at ISO 100 when the zooming head (which can be set to either 18mm or 27mm) is at the 18mm position. It tilts up to 90 degrees, allowing you to bounce the light off of a ceiling, but it cannot be rotated to the side.

Nikon SB-500

This Nikon flash unit has a permanent place in my bag, because it's small enough to justify carrying it around even when I have no expectation of needing a flash unit. It has a guide number of 24/79 at ISO 100, a speedy recycle time of about 3.5 seconds, and runs on 2 AA batteries for up to 140 flashes. It includes a built-in LED video light with three output levels and can also be used for still photography as fill light, especially

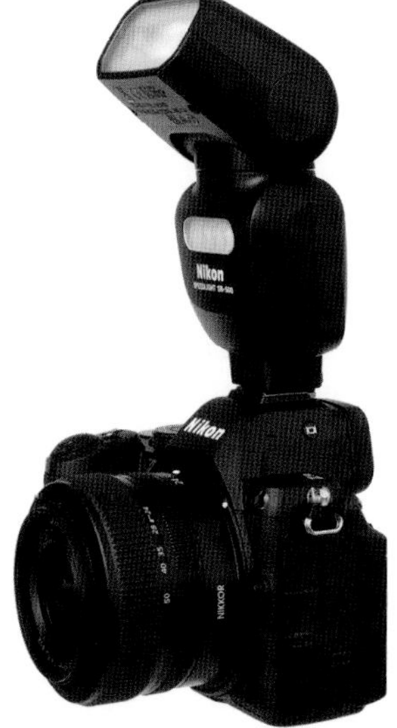

Figure 4.9 The Nikon SB-500 offers a tilting and rotating head, plus a video light.

at the brightest setting. It's perfect for wireless mode, with four wireless channels and two groups available in Commander mode. The SB-500's head tilts up to 90 degrees, with click-stops at 0, 60, 75, and 90. It rotates horizontally 180 degrees to the left and right, for flexible bounce-flash lighting. (See Figure 4.9.) If you need a zoom head to adjust flash output to better distribute light at various focal lengths, you're better off with the SB-700 even with its limited zoom range (described next); this unit lacks zooming capabilities.

Nikon SB-700

This affordable unit has a guide number of 28/92 (meters/feet) at ISO 100 when set to the 35mm zoom position. It has many of the top-model SB-910's features, including zoomable flash coverage equal to the field of view of 24-120mm settings with a full-frame camera, and extra-wide 14mm coverage with a built-in diffuser panel. It has a built-in modeling flash feature, and a wireless Commander mode.

But the SB-700 lacks some important features found in the SB-910 and SB-5000. Depending on how you use your Speedlight, these differences may or may not be important to you. They include:

- **No repeating flash mode.** You can't shoot interesting stroboscopic effects with the SB-700 as you can with the SB-5000 or older SB-910/900 units.
- **No port for external power pack.** Using an external battery pack, like those available from Quantum and others, can be important for wedding and event photographers who want to fire off a bunch of shots quickly, while avoiding frequent changes of the AA batteries the SB-700 uses. An external pack has another benefit: more exposures before the Speedlight slows down to prevent overheating. External batteries don't generate heat inside the flash as internal batteries do.
- **No external PC/X sync socket.** This option, not found on the SB-700, is of limited use for those who want to attach an off-camera flash to any camera which does have a PC/X contact.
- **Limited zoom range.** The SB-700's zoom head is limited to 24-120mm, plus 14mm with the diffuser panel. The ability to match the zoom head to the focal length you're using can match the coverage to the field of view, so the flash's output isn't wasted illuminating areas that aren't within the actual frame.

Nikon SB-910

The Nikon SB-910 was the flagship of the Nikon flash lineup until the SB-5000 model was unveiled. However, the SB-910 remains one of the most-used Nikon flash units (along with its predecessor, the SB-900), so I'll continue to include it in my coverage of Speedlights for the foreseeable future. It's still widely available used and has a guide number of 34/111.5 (meters/feet) when the "zooming" flash head (which can be set to adjust to the coverage angle of the lens) is set to the 35mm position. It includes Commander mode, repeating flash, modeling light, and selectable power output, along with some extra capabilities.

The SB-910 was basically a slight reboot of the older SB-900, which gained a bad reputation for overheating and then shutting down after a relatively small number of consecutive exposures (as few as a dozen or so shots). The SB-910 also can overheat but features a different thermal protection system.

Instead of disabling the flash as it begins warming up, the SB-910 increases the recycle time between flashes, giving the unit additional time to cool a bit before the next shot. While this "improvement" is not a real fix, it does encourage you to slow your shooting pace a bit to stretch out the number of flashes this Speedlight produces before it must be shut down for additional cooling.

Nikon estimates that you should be able to get 190 flashes from the SB-910 when using AA 2600 mAh rechargeable batteries, if firing the Speedlight at full output once every 30 seconds, with a minimum recycling time of 2.3 seconds (which gradually becomes longer as the flash heats up and the thermal protection kicks in). To get the maximum number of shots from your batteries, Nikon figures that AF-assist illumination, power zoom, and the LCD panel illumination are switched off.

There are some improvements, such as illuminated buttons and a restyled soft case, but, in general, the SB-910 is very similar to the SB-900 that we Nikon photographers have learned to know and fear. For example, you can angle the flash and rotate it to provide bounce flash. It includes additional, non-through-the-lens exposure modes, thanks to its built-in light sensor, and can "zoom" and diffuse its coverage angle to illuminate the field of view of lenses from 8mm to 200mm.

The SB-910 and SB-900 reduce red-eye effects simply because the units, even when attached to the hot shoe and not used off-camera, are mounted in a higher position that tends to eliminate reflections from the eye back to the lens.

Nikon SB-5000

This Speedlight is currently the flagship of the Nikon flash lineup and is likely to remain so for a while; as I noted earlier, there are rumors that Nikon has ceased developing new Speedlights and has handed the reins over to a third-party manufacturer. Since we've already seen the company selling Nikon-branded lenses made by Tamron, that move is entirely plausible.

While it resembles the SB-910 and has a virtually identical guide number (34.5/113 meters/feet), it more or less solves the overheating problem that plagued its top-line predecessors. A novel internal cooling system purportedly allows up to 90 consecutive shots, or 120 shots at five-second intervals without overheating. (Wedding photographers will love this.)

However, the big news is the addition of radio control to the optical triggering available with previous Nikon flash units that could be operated wirelessly. Radio control allows triggering the flash from a distance of nearly 100 feet—without requiring a line-of-sight connection. The SB-5000 retains compatibility with Nikon's earlier optical wireless system, so your current flash units can be used with it in non-radio mode.

Note that the SB-5000 and many other Nikon flash units contain firmware that can be updated. The Custom Settings readouts on the flash itself will tell you what firmware version you currently have. If an update is required, you'll need to download the firmware module from the Nikon website. Load it onto a memory card and then mount the flash on your camera and power it up. You'll find a fourth entry in the Firmware section of the Setup menu, marked S (for Speedlight or Strobe). The SB-910's firmware can be updated through the camera/flash connection just like the camera's own firmware.

Photo Shooting Menu

Many adjustments and settings require a trip to the camera's extensive menu system, which has dozens of individual top-level entries and many additional options tucked away in sub-menus. But under that thicket of choices is the kind of versatility that makes the Z5 II a highly tweakable and fine-tunable camera. If your Z5 II doesn't behave in exactly the way you'd like, chances are you can make a small change in the menus that will tailor it to your exact needs.

However, just telling you what your options are and what they do doesn't really give you the information you need to use your camera to its fullest. What you really want to know is *why* you would want to choose a particular option, and *how* making a particular change will help improve your photographs in a given situation. That's a big job, and I'm going to devote a large portion of this book to demystifying the menu choices for you. In this chapter, I'll devote no more than a paragraph or two to the blatantly obvious settings and concentrate on the more confusing aspects of the camera setup. If you need a refresher on menu navigation, you'll find it in Chapter 1.

Photo Shooting Menu Options

Here are the entries found in the Photo Shooting menu:

- Reset Photo Shooting Menu
- Storage Folder
- File Naming
- Role Played by Card in Slot 2
- Image Area
- Tone Mode
- Image Quality
- Image Size Settings
- RAW Recording
- ISO Sensitivity Settings
- White Balance
- Set Picture Control
- Manage Picture Control
- Set Picture Control (HLG)
- Color Space

- Active D-Lighting
- Long Exposure NR
- High ISO NR
- Vignette Control
- Diffraction Compensation
- Auto Distortion Control
- Skin Softening
- Portrait Impression Balance
- Photo Flicker Reduction
- High-Frequency Flicker Reduction
- Metering
- Flash Control
- Flash Mode
- Flash Compensation

- Release Mode
- Focus Mode
- AF-Area Mode
- AF/MF Subject Detection Options
- MF Subject Detection Area
- Vibration Reduction
- Link VR to Focus Point
- Auto Bracketing
- Multiple Exposure
- HDR Overlay
- Interval Timer Shooting
- Time-lapse Video
- Focus Shift Shooting
- Pixel Shift Shooting

Reset Photo Shooting Menu

Options: Yes, No

My preference: N/A

This setting is the first entry of the Photo Shooting menu, shown in Figure 5.1. The camera has, in effect, *four* different kinds of resets. This is one of them.

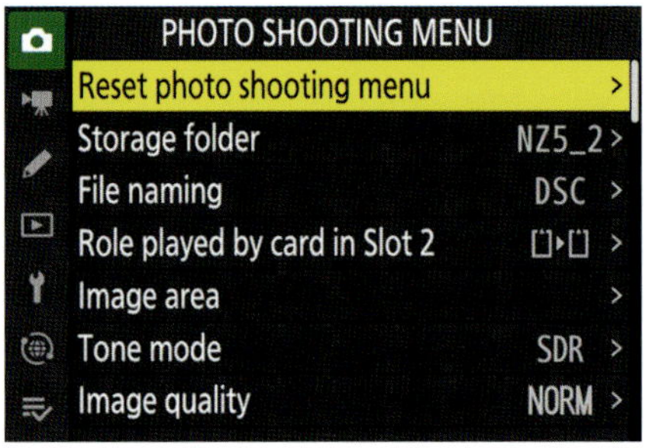

- **Photo Shooting menu reset.** Use this option to reset the values of the current Photo Shooting menu to the values shown in Table 5.1.

- **Video Recording menu reset.** The Video Recording menu has its own settings, which are reset separately, as described later in this chapter.

- **Custom Settings menu reset.** This option, which I'll describe in Chapter 7, is used to reset the Custom Settings entries. It has no effect on camera settings or Photo Shooting menu banks.

- **Setup menu reset.** This option resets all settings except for Language and Time Zone/Date to their default values. Use this option with caution, as it even erases copyright information and your user settings (described in Chapter 9). In that chapter, I'll also show you how to save/load settings so you can retrieve settings you saved, even after you've used the Setup menu reset.

Figure 5.1 Common shooting settings can be changed in the Photo Shooting menu.

Table 5.1 shows the default values that are set using Reset Photo Shooting Menu. If you don't know what some of these settings are, I'll explain them later in this section.

TABLE 5.1 Reset Photo Shooting Menu Default Settings

FUNCTION	VALUE	FUNCTION	VALUE
Storage Folder		ISO Sensitivity Settings	
Rename	NZ5_2	ISO Sensitivity	100
Select Folder by Number	100	Auto ISO Sensitivity Control	On
Select Folder From List	--	Maximum Sensitivity	64000
File Naming	DSC	Maximum Sensitivity Flash	Same as without flash
Role Played by Card in Slot 2	Overflow	Minimum Shutter Speed	Auto
Image Area		White Balance	Auto$_1$ Keep overall atmosphere
Choose Image Area	FX (36 × 24)	Set Picture Control	Auto
DX Crop Alert	Off	Manage Picture Control	--
Tone Mode	SDR	Set Picture Control (HLG)	Standard
Image Quality	JPEG/HEIF normal	Color Space	sRGB
Image Size Settings		Active D-Lighting	Off
Image Size	Large	Long Exp. NR	Off
Enable DX Image Sizes	Off	High ISO NR	Normal
Image Size (DX)	Large	Vignette Control	Normal
RAW Recording	High Efficiency*		

TABLE 5.1 Reset Photo Shooting Menu Default Settings *(continued)*

FUNCTION	VALUE
Diffraction Compensation	On
Auto Distortion Control	On
Skin Softening	Off
Portrait Impression Balance	Off
Photo Flicker Reduction	Off
High-Frequency Flicker Reduction	Off
Metering	Matrix Metering
Flash Control	
Flash Control Mode	TTL
Wireless Flash Options	Off
Remote Flash Control	Group flash
Flash Mode	Fill flash
Flash Compensation	0.0
Release Mode	Single Frame
Focus Mode	AF Mode Auto-switch
AF-Area Mode	Auto-area AF
AF/MF Subject Detection Options	Auto
MF Subject Detection Area	Off
Vibration Reduction	Normal
Link VR to Focus Point	On
Auto Bracketing	
Auto Bracketing On/Off	Off
Auto Bracketing Set	AE & flash
Number of Shots	3F
Increment	1.0
Multiple Exposure	
Multiple Exposure Mode	Off
Number of Shots	3
Overlay Mode	Average
Save Individual Pictures (RAW)	On
Overlay Shooting	On
Select First Exposure (RAW)	--
HDR Overlay	
HDR Mode	Off
HDR Strength	Auto
Save Individual Images (RAW)	Off

FUNCTION	VALUE
Interval Timer Shooting	Off
Choose Start Day/Time	Now
Interval	1 min.
No. Intervals × Shots/Interval	0001x1
Exposure Smoothing	On
Electronic Shutter Options	
Electronic Shutter	On
Volume	0
Interval Priority	Off
Focus Before Each Shot	Off
Options	Off
Starting Storage Folder	
New Folder	No
Reset File Numbering	No
Time-Lapse Video	Off
Interval	5 sec.
Shooting Time	25 min.
Exposure Smoothing	On
Electronic Shutter Options	
Electronic Shutter	On
Volume	0
Choose Image Area	FX
Video file Type	H.265 8-bit MOV
Frame Size/Frame Rate	3840 × 2160; 30p
Interval Priority	Off
Focus Before Each Shot	Off
Destination	Slot 1
Focus Shift Shooting	
Number of Shots	100
Focus Step Width	5
Interval Until Next Shot	0
First-Frame Exposure Lock	On
Electronic Shutter Options	
Electronic Shutter	On
Volume	0
Focus Position Auto Reset	Off
Starting Storage Folder	
New Folder	No
Reset File Numbering	No
Pixel Shift Shooting	
Pixel Shift Shooting Mode	Off
Number of Shots	16
Delay	2 sec.
Interval until next shot	0 sec.

Storage Folder

Options: Rename: NZ5_2 (default); Select Folder by Number: 100 (default); Select Folder from List
My preference: I use the Select Folder by Number option frequently to organize images by topic or time frame.

If you want to store images in a folder other than the one most recently created and selected by the camera, you can switch among available folders on your memory card or create your own folder. Remember that any folders you create will be deleted when you reformat your memory card.

Storage folders are always created within the top-level DCIM (Digital Camera Images) folder on your memory card. If you happen to use the same memory card in more than one camera, even if it is from a manufacturer other than Nikon, the other camera's image folders will reside amicably in the same DCIM folder. The "foreign" folders will use their own nomenclature; if you spot one named 100MSDCF, for example, it might have been created there by, say, a Sony camera. You generally won't need to access or use any other top-level folders, such as NIKON (which stores saved user settings, Picture Controls, and IPTC [International Press Telecommunications Council] information). The MISC folder and a top-level file with a name like NIKON001.DSC are used for housekeeping and not typically accessed.

Why create your own folders? Perhaps you're traveling and have a high-capacity memory card and want to store the images for each day (or for each city that you visit) in a separate folder. Maybe you'd like to separate those wedding photos you snapped at the ceremony from those taken at the reception. As I mentioned earlier, the camera automatically creates a folder on a newly formatted memory card with a name like 100NZ5_2, and when it fills with 5,000 images (an increase from the limitation of 999 images in most previous Nikon cameras) or a picture numbered 9999, it will automatically create a new folder with a number incremented by one (such as 101NZ5_2).

Folders are always identified using a three-digit number, followed by a five-character folder name. Although the default characters are NZ5_2, you can specify a name of your choice. To create your own folder or select an existing folder:

1. **Access active folder entry.** Choose Storage Folder in the Photo Shooting menu and press the right multi selector button.

2. **Choose function.** Three options are listed: Rename, Select Folder by Number, and Select Folder from List.

   - **Rename.** Highlight and select Rename (see Figure 5.2, left), and you'll be taken to a screen similar to the one shown at right in Figure 5.2, with five spaces to enter information for the naming scheme. Only numbers from 0 to 9, uppercase alpha characters, and an underline can be selected. Note that you can only change the name of your folder scheme—existing folders cannot be renamed. See the section, "Entering Text" for a primer on using the on-screen keyboard.

   - **Select Folder by Number.** If you've chosen this option, a screen appears with three digits representing the possible folder numbers from 100 to 999. Use the left/right multi selector buttons to move between the digits, and the up/down buttons to increase or decrease the value of the digit. If a folder already exists with the number you dial in, an icon appears showing the folder is empty, partially full, or it has 5,000 images or a picture numbered 9999 (and can contain no more images).

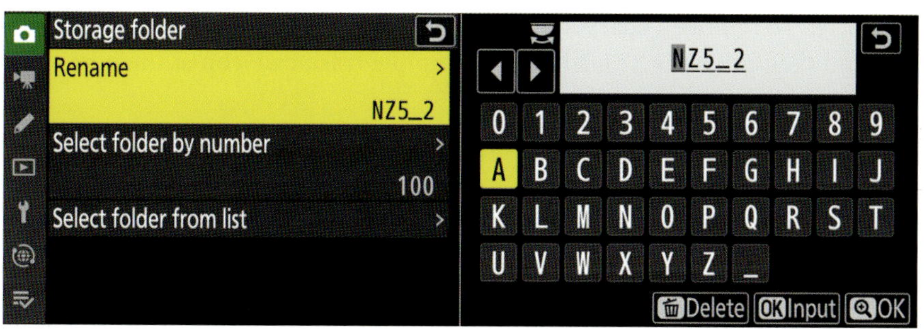

Figure 5.2 Entering a default storage folder name.

Press OK to create the new folder and make it the active folder. You'd want to use this option to create a new folder *or* when you don't know whether a folder by a particular number already exists. If a folder with that number already resides on the memory card, you can use it (if it is not full); if it doesn't exist, you can create it.

- **Select Folder from List.** From among the available folders shown, scroll to the one that you want to become active for image storage and playback. I sometimes do this to "sort" my images in the camera when traveling. I could enable a particular folder when I am taking photos of landscapes, and switch to a different folder when shooting urban scenes. This feature is handy when you want to display a slide show located in a particular folder. Use this option if you know that the folder you want to use already resides on the memory card. Press OK to confirm your choice and make the folder active.

3. **Exit menus.** Press the MENU button or tap the shutter release to exit.

Entering Text

As mentioned, the Z5 II offers several opportunities to enter text, so you can change folder names, insert your name as "Artist," or provide copyright information. The camera uses a fairly standardized text-entry screen to name files, rename Picture Controls, create new folder names, and enter image comments and other text. You'll be using text entry with other functions that I'll describe later in this book. The screen looks like the one shown in Figure 5.2, right, with some variations (for example, some functions have a less diverse character set or offer more or fewer spaces for your entries). To enter text, just use the touch screen to "type" your characters or, alternatively, use the multi selector navigational buttons to scroll around within the array of alphanumerics. (I invariably use the touch screen for this, unless I am outdoors, wearing gloves, and really, really need to enter text.)

- **Highlight a character.** Use the touch screen or multi selector keys to scroll around within the array of characters.

- **Insert highlighted character.** Tap the character or press the multi selector OK button to insert the highlighted character. The cursor will move one place to the right to accept the next character.

- **Non-destructively move forward/backspace.** Use the main command dial to move the cursor within the line of characters you've entered. This allows you to skip ahead or backspace and replace a character without disturbing the others you've entered. Although it's a bit more difficult for the ham-handed, you can also tap the left/right triangles on the screen located to the immediate left of the text-entry area to move the cursor.

- **Erase a highlighted character.** To remove a character you've already input, move the cursor to high-light that character, and then press the Trash button or tap the trash can icon at the bottom of the screen.
- **Confirm your entry.** When you're finished entering text, press the Zoom In button to confirm your entry, then press the MENU button to return to the Photo Shooting menu, or press the MENU button a second time (or just tap the shutter release) to exit the menu system entirely.

File Naming

Options: Choose three-letter prefix, DSC (default)

My preference: Z52

The camera automatically applies a name like _DSC0001.jpg or DSC_0001.nef to your image files as they are created. You can use this menu option to change the names applied to your photos, but only within certain strict limitations. In practice, you can change only three of the eight characters, the *DSC* portion of the filename. The other five are mandated either by the Design Rule for Camera File System (DCF) specification that all digital camera makers adhere to or to industry conventions.

DCF limits filenames created by conforming digital cameras to a maximum of eight characters, plus a three-character extension (such as .jpg, .nef, or, in the case of audio files, .wav) that represents the format of the file. The eight-plus-three (usually called 8.3) length limitation dates back to an evil and frustrating computer operating system that we older photographers would like to forget (its initials are D.O.S.), but which, unhappily, lives on as the wraith of a file-naming convention.

Of the eight available characters, four are used to represent, in a general sense, the type of camera used to create the image. By convention, one of those characters is an underline, placed in the first position (as in _DSCxxxx.xxx) when the image uses the Adobe RGB color space (more on color spaces later), and in the fourth position (as in DSC_xxxx.xxx) for sRGB/BT.2100 and RAW (NEF) files. That leaves just three characters for the manufacturer (and you) to use. Nikon, Sony, and some other vendors use DSC (which may or may not stand for Digital Still Camera, depending on who you ask), while Canon prefers IMG. The remaining four characters are used for numbers from 0000 to 9999, which is why your camera "rolls over" to DSC_0000 again when the 9999-number limitation is reached.

When you select File Naming in the Photo Shooting menu, you'll be shown the current settings for both sRGB and Adobe RGB. Press the right multi selector button, and you'll be taken to the (mostly) standard Nikon text-entry screen described above and allowed to change the DSC value to something else. In this version of the text-entry screen, however, only the numbers from 0 to 9 and characters A to Z are available; the filename cannot contain other characters. As always, press the Zoom In button to confirm your new setting.

Because the default DSC characters don't tell you much, don't hesitate to change them to something else. I use Z52. However, if you don't need or want to differentiate between different camera models, you can change the three characters to anything else that suits your purposes, including your initials (DDB_ or JFK_, for example), or even customize for particular shooting sessions (EUR_, GER_, FRA_, and JAP_ when taking vacation trips). You can also use the filename flexibility to partially overcome the 9999-numbering limitation. You could, for example, use the template 501_ to represent the first 10,000 pictures you take with a Z5 II camera, and then 502_ for the next 10,000, and 503_ for the 10,000 after that. That scheme would let you account for 990,000 different images without repeats.

All this assumes you don't rename your image files in your computer. In a way, filenaming verges on a moot consideration, because they apply *only* to the images as they exist in your camera. After (or during) transfer to your computer, you can change the names to anything you want, completely disregarding the 8.3 limitations (although it's a good idea to retain the default extensions). If you shot an image file named DSC_4832.jpg in your camera, you could change it to Paris_EiffelTower_32.jpg later. Indeed, virtually all photo-transfer programs allow you to specify a template and rename your photos as they are moved or copied to your computer from your camera or memory card.

I usually don't go to that bother (I generally don't use transfer software; I just drag and drop images from my memory card to folders I have set up) but renaming can be useful for those willing to take the time to do it.

Role Played by Card in Slot 2

Options: Overflow (default), Backup, RAW Slot 1—JPEG/HEIF Slot 2, JPEG/HEIF Slot 1—JPEG/HEIF Slot 2

My preference: Overflow for everyday shooting; Backup when traveling

This entry allows you to specify the function of the second memory card slot, choosing to use the secondary slot to accept overflow images when the primary card fills up, create a backup of all the files stored on the primary card, or to split your RAW+JPEG/HEIF files between primary and secondary slots. The Video Recording menu's Destination entry offers a fourth option: you can select which slot is used to store your video clips (and can therefore choose the largest memory card or fastest memory card for your videos). Keep in mind that if you have only one card inserted, the camera will ignore the options you specify here. The Slot 2 functions are these:

Overflow

In this case, when the memory card in the primary slot fills up, the camera automatically switches over to the card in the secondary slot (Slot 2). The changeover happens quickly, and you're not even likely to notice, unless you have your eye on the "slot" indicators on the display, as the camera provides no notification of the switchover. There are many ways to use this capability:

- **"Limitless" capacity.** My standard operating procedure is to put one 128GB or 256GB memory card in each slot. As a practical matter, that means I can shoot all day (or, sometimes all week) without changing memory cards, even if I am shooting landscapes and bracketing everything (either to optimize exposure, or, when the camera is mounted on a tripod, to capture files for later HDR processing). Or, I might be shooting sports/photojournalism, where the common practice is to change memory cards when your media is 80 percent full to eliminate the possibility of missing anything important due to a card change at an inopportune time. To be honest, I have yet to encounter a shoot (or even a single *trip*) in which I have filled up two 128GB or larger cards in a single session. But if you're using smaller cards and doing a lot of shooting, this capability can be a lifesaver.

- **Small/fast—with backup.** For some sports, if you are shooting continuously, you will want your fastest memory card in the primary slot to maximize write speed out of the camera's buffer, but the real speed demons in the memory card world can be expensive. So, instead of an affordable 64GB medium-speed card, you may put a (per gigabyte) more expensive 64GB high-speed card in the primary slot, and back it up with a slower (and cheaper) 128GB card in the secondary slot. You can capture images with the fastest card you've got, yet not have to worry about missing shots, because you have a backup card installed in the secondary slot.

- **Put smaller cards to use.** If you don't think you'll need the overflow capacity, but still want to have it just in case, put a smaller card that you don't use much anymore in the secondary slot. Z5 II users may run into that situation with their collection of old 32GB (or even smaller!) SD cards.

  If your large card that you didn't think would fill *does* come up short, you won't lose any shots. They'll be directed to that 32GB SD card you put in the secondary slot for insurance. I sometimes do this when I am using several cameras and have a limited number of large cards at my disposal. For example, I often shoot with two cameras in the same session. I'll save the biggest cards for primary use and use smaller SD cards in the secondary slot, knowing that any overflow shots will be stored on the small backup cards if necessary.

- **Stretch your budget.** After spending an arm and a leg for your Z5 II, you'd like to avoid replacing your limited-capacity 32GB SD memory cards for a little while. With one card in each slot, you can double your shooting before it's time to swap cards.

Backup

In this case, each photograph you take is recorded on the memory cards in both the primary and secondary slot. The write process takes longer, so it may not be your best option when shooting sports. Keep in mind that for best results, both cards should have the same write speed. Saving to the secondary slot with a less speedy card can be considerably slower than writing to a fast card in the primary slot. If speed is not important, the backup function is otherwise a seamless way to create a backup copy of every image you take. If you're shooting RAW+JPEG/HEIF, both files associated with each image are recorded on both slots. Here are some of my favorite applications:

- **Critical shots backed up instantly.** When I was a photojournalist, a lot of the images I took, particularly of news events, were literally once-in-a-lifetime shots that couldn't be duplicated under any circumstances. I also shot weddings, and while it was sometimes possible to restage a particular setup or pose, that was never a satisfactory option, even if done on the day of the nuptials. So, there was always a degree of trepidation until the film was processed or digital files backed up. With dual-slot backup capabilities, backup files can be made instantly, as you shoot. What a relief!

- **Great when there's No-Fi.** Many pros (and more than a few amateurs) rely on in-camera Wi-Fi or Bluetooth connectivity to beam backups to a nearby laptop computer for safekeeping, or, at events, so that an assistant can process some images while photography continues. But, sometimes that's not possible, or, perhaps, you don't own the necessary equipment. Making a backup in your camera is a great alternative when wireless capabilities are unavailable or impractical. You can even shuttle the secondary slot card to an assistant at intervals while retaining the "main" copy of your images in the camera.

- **Leave your personal storage device or computer at home.** When I travel overseas, I like to pack light, with only a carry-on bag that holds my shooting gear and some of my clothing, with the rest of my apparel relegated to the second tote that qualifies as a "personal" item. But I've always carried a laptop so I can make backup copies of my images while I travel. I've found that my dual-card Nikon cameras can easily replace the external backup options if I want to travel *extra* light on shorter trips. I can back up each image as it's shot automatically.

  If you would prefer that your shooting not be slowed down using this backup feature, you can also shoot on one card (to allow faster capture) and make a duplicate with a card-to-card copy when you're finished shooting. Or you can use the Playback menu's Copy Image(s) feature to make an extra copy of only the images you want. On a recent cross-country trip along the old Route 66, I copied each day's shooting to a spare memory card before turning in for the night.

- **Instant copy to share.** Want to give a traveling companion copies of all the images you shoot? Create a backup as you take the photos and hand over the copy on the spot. (Again, if you want to share only *some* of your pictures, you can use the Copy Image(s) feature instead.) If you're using a Z5 II, this procedure can make good use of a large collection of old, cheap SD cards.

- **Segregate your images.** I've managed to accumulate a collection of 16GB and 32GB SD memory cards that I use in my Z5 II. I sometimes put these to work in travel photography applications on long trips. Each day I put one of these cards in my camera, specify Backup mode, and shoot the images for that day. The next day, I insert a different SD card for backup. I've got copies of each day's shots and have segregated them onto separate memory cards for simple day-by-day organization.

RAW Slot 1—JPEG (or HEIF) Slot 2

In this mode, if you've used the Image Quality setting (discussed shortly) to specify RAW+JPEG, the RAW files are saved to the card in the primary slot, and the JPEG files are saved to the card in the secondary card in Slot 2. If you've selected RAW or JPEG only (rather than both), the images are stored in the primary slot, until that card fills; then the photos overflow to the secondary slot. (This is effectively the same as the Overflow option.) You'll find this mode useful under the following conditions:

HEIF NOTE

The Z5 II has a Tone mode entry in the Photo Shooting menu that allows substituting the HEIF (High Efficiency Image File) format for JPEG. I'll explain the Tone mode entry and HEIF in more detail later in this chapter, but confine most descriptions to JPEG, which will be used almost exclusively by the vast majority of readers of this book.

- **Separate RAW and JPEG.** Perhaps you like to store your RAW and JPEG files in separate locations. This mode makes it easy to do that. Copy the card containing the RAW files to one destination on your computer, and the JPEG files from the other card to a second destination. The only complication is that the memory card in the primary slot is likely to fill up more quickly than the card with the smaller JPEG files in the secondary slot, so if you shoot to the capacity of the card in the primary slot, you'll need to replace it more often than you will the card with the JPEG files. Or, if you want the two cards to be mirror images of each other (but in different formats), you can swap them both out at the same time, with the secondary slot card only partially full. If you're short on memory cards, you could alternatively temporarily switch the Slot 2 function to Overflow, and continue shooting with both RAW and JPEG images recorded on the same card until it, too, fills up.

- **Faster backup of RAW+JPEG.** If you shoot RAW+JPEG, using the Backup option means that you're saving *four* files each time you press the shutter release. That can slow you down in some situations if you're rapid-firing a sequence of images. Storing RAW files on one card and JPEG files on the other is a faster way of capturing a backup, because only two files are saved per click. If you have a problem with one of your JPEG files, you can easily produce a new JPEG from the RAW file. The reverse is not true, however. If your NEF file gets munged, your RAW information is lost forever, even though you still have the JPEG version. So, use this option carefully if your RAW files are especially important for a particular shooting session.

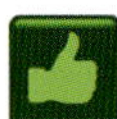

NOTE If you're using the Multiple Exposure or HDR Overlay options (described later in this chapter) and have selected Save Individual Pictures (RAW) for either, the camera will save RAW images even in a JPEG-only mode. The RAW files will be stored on both memory cards *in addition to* the combined JPEG multiple exposure or HDR version.

JPEG (or HEIF) Slot 1—JPEG (or HEIF) Slot 2

This is an interesting pair of options that allows you to save *two* JPEG (or HEIF) versions. (The HEIF choice is available only if you've selected HLG as your Tone mode.) The image stored in the primary slot will have the compression and size characteristics you specify in the Image Quality and Image Size entries, while an additional version will be saved in the other slot using the same Quality/Size settings, *or at your option* in a space-saving Basic compression and an image size you specify here.

In other words, you can specify a "main" image stored in the primary slot in JPEG (or HEIF) Fine, Normal, or Basic (or their extra-quality variations marked with an asterisk) in Large, Medium, or Small sizes. Then, you can choose to save a second copy of the JPEG (or HEIF) in Large, Medium, or Small size or Medium or Small size, but using *only* Basic compression. This entry operates only when using JPEG-only or HEIF-only mode. If you're shooting in RAW (only) or RAW+JPEG/HEIF, the camera defaults to Backup mode, as described above.

This capability might come in handy if you wanted to capture a reduced-size or lower-resolution version, say to transfer to your smartphone or tablet for posting on social media or for emails.

Image Area

Options: Image Area: FX (36 × 24) (default); DX (24 × 16); 1:1 (24 × 24); 16:9 (36 × 20); DX Crop Alert: On, Off (default)

My preference: FX (36 × 24), On

Using Image Area, you can manually specify the image area to be used, which the camera will apply regardless of what type of lens is mounted. Use this option to force the image area issue (as when you're using a DX-format lens that the camera can't detect automatically), or to use a particular image area for all your shots in a session.

Your choices include:

- **FX (36 × 24).** This is the full FX image-format area, roughly 36mm × 24mm, producing a 24.4MP image when Large is selected using the Image Size entry described shortly.
- **DX (24 × 16).** This fills the image frame with the image in the center 24mm × 16mm of the sensor, creating a 1.5X *crop factor.* Your final image will be about 10.6MP in Large size.
- **1:1 (24 × 24).** An image cropped to a square may be useful to emphasize a centered image, such as a close-up of a flower, when you want to direct the eye to the middle of the frame, rather than have it roam around within your image. The resulting 16.3MP photo still has outstanding resolution even though you're discarding pixels at left and right of the frame.
- **16:9 (36 × 20).** This is a useful cropping that allows you to take still photos using the same 16:9 proportions as a high-definition video frame. I like this crop when I'm producing storyboards for video productions, as my still image compositions will match the aspect ratio of the videos.

If you activate DX Crop Alert, a DX icon will flash in the upper-right corner of the display when DX mode is active. I always enable this warning. Unlike dSLR cameras, which maintain the same image in the optical viewfinder with crop mark overlays, your Z5 II enlarges the cropped image to fill the display. It's easy to overlook the difference in the image area and capture a large number of images with a crop you really didn't intend to use. You may have specified the DX crop to get a little extra "reach" when shooting sports.

Tone Mode

Options: SDR (default), HLG

My preference: Use as needed

This entry allows you to depart from the familiar standard dynamic range (SDR) world to the tonal realm of hybrid log gamma (HLG). An additional Tone mode, Nikon-log (N-Log), can be chosen within the Video File Type entry of the Video Recording menu. Still photographers will be concerned primarily with the choice between SDR and HLG; if you specify SDR here, the camera will save its non-RAW images in JPEG format. Choose HLG and HEIF images will be saved instead. You'll find more information about HEIF in the next section.

Image Quality

Options: RAW+JPEG/HEIF (Fine*, Fine, Normal*, Normal, Basic*, Basic), RAW, JPEG/HEIF (Fine*, Fine, Normal*, Normal [default], Basic*, Basic)

My preference: RAW+JPEG Fine* for everyday shooting; JPEG Fine* for sports

This setting allows you to choose to capture images in RAW format, in JPEG format, or both simultaneously. The entry also allows you to choose the amount of image compression applied to images. You can use this menu entry or opt for the quickest way by pressing the *i* button, selecting the Image Quality entry, and either rotating the command dial or pressing the OK button to select quality from a screen of choices.

When selecting a file format, you can choose RAW only, RAW+ six different JPEG quality levels (Fine*, Fine, Normal*, Normal, Basic*, and Basic), or any of those six JPEG (or HEIF) quality levels alone (with no RAW captured). When you elect to store only JPEG/HEIF versions of the images you shoot, you can save memory card space as you bypass the larger RAW files. Or, you can save your photos as RAW files, which consume more than twice as much space on your memory card. Or, you can store both at once as you shoot.

Many photographers choose to save *both* JPEG and a RAW, so they'll have a JPEG version that might be usable as is, as well as the original "digital negative" RAW file in case they want to do some processing of the image later. You'll end up with two different versions of the same file: one with a .jpg extension, and one with the .nef extension that signifies a Nikon RAW file.

To choose the combination you want using the menu system, access the Photo Shooting menu, scroll to Image Quality, and select it. Screens similar to the one shown in Figure 5.3 (left and right) will appear. Scroll to highlight the setting you want, and either press OK or push the multi selector right button to confirm your selection.

In practice, you'll probably use the JPEG Fine* and RAW+JPEG Fine* (with the "extra quality" star) selections most often. Why so many choices, then? There are some limited advantages to using some of the higher compression and lower resolution options. Settings that are less than max allow stretching the capacity of your memory card so you can shoehorn quite a few more pictures onto a single memory card. That can come in useful when on vacation and you're running out of storage, or when you're shooting non-critical work that doesn't require 24 megapixels of resolution (such as photos taken for real-estate listings, web page display, photo ID cards, or similar applications). Some photographers like to record RAW+JPEG Basic so they'll have a moderate-quality JPEG file for review only and no intention of using for editing purposes, while retaining access to the original full-resolution/uncompressed RAW file for serious editing.

For most work, using lower resolution and extra compression is false economy. You never know when you might need that extra bit of picture detail. Your best bet is to have enough memory cards to handle all the shooting you want to do until you have the chance to transfer your photos to your computer or a personal storage device.

Figure 5.3 You can choose RAW, JPEG, or RAW+JPEG formats here. Nikon is adding the ability to substitute HEIF for JPEG.

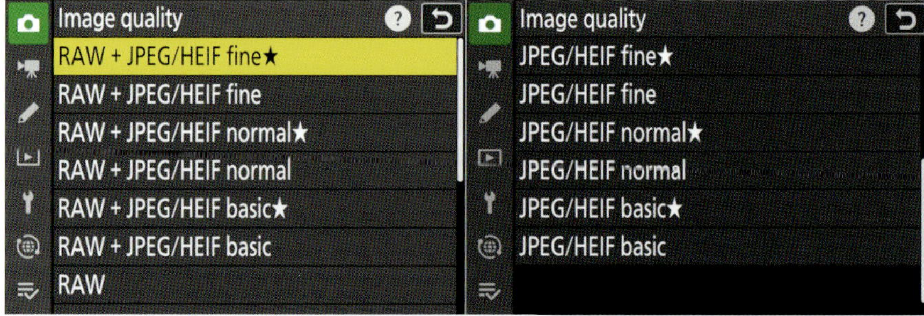

Optimal Quality or Optimal Size?

Nikon has merged the JPEG-oriented Optimal Quality and Optimum Size options offered with previous cameras into the Image Quality entry. The difference:

- **Optimal Quality (marked with a star).** Choose this option if you want to maintain the best image quality possible at a particular JPEG setting and don't care if the file size varies. Because the camera will use only the minimum amount of compression required at each JPEG setting, file size will vary depending on scene content, and your buffer may hold fewer images during continuous shooting. If you're not shooting continuously, this setting will provide optimum image quality.

  At the Fine * setting, the camera will apply a 4:1 compression ratio; use 8:1 at the Normal * setting, and a rigorous 16:1 compression ratio at Basic *. Figure 5.4 shows a cropped portion of an image recorded with Optimal Quality (top) and one in which Size Priority was used to provide extra compression (bottom).

- **Size Priority (no star).** When this option is selected, the camera will create files that are fairly uniformly sized JPEG images. The camera will first compress the images according to the ratios I described above for Optimal Quality images. It will then apply whatever *additional* compression is required to reduce the size of the image file to the target size. Because some photos have content that is more easily compressible (for example, plain areas of sky can be squeezed down more than areas filled with detail), to maintain the standard file size more compression must be applied to some images, and less to others.

  As a result, there may be a barely noticeable loss of detail in the more heavily compressed images. The uniform file size also means that the camera's buffer will hold the maximum number of shots during continuous shooting, allowing you to shoot longer sequences without the need to pause and wait for some images to be written to the memory card. In practice, you may find you can shoot continuously until the memory card fills.

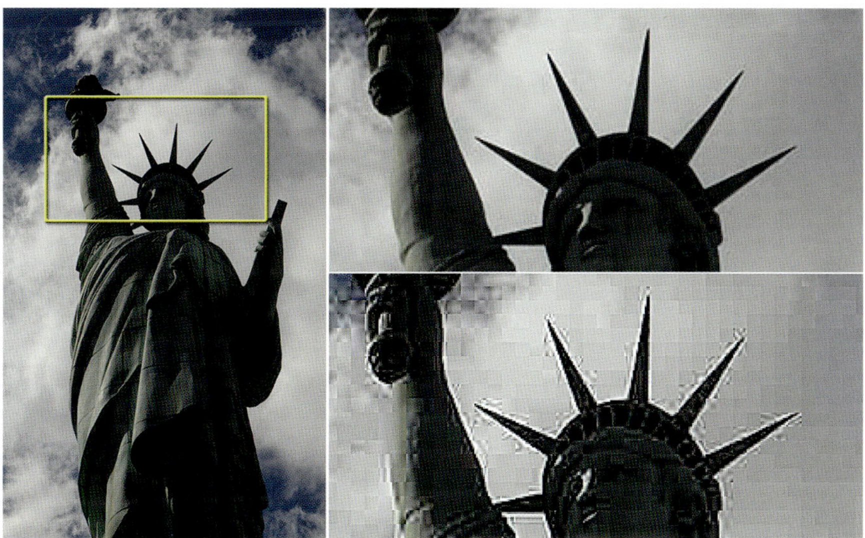

Figure 5.4 At low levels of JPEG compression, the image looks sharp even when you enlarge it enough to see the actual pixels (top); when using extreme JPEG compression (bottom), an image obviously loses quality.

HEIF vs. JPEG

The discussion above applies to the Nikon Z5 II when you're using the RAW format alone, RAW+ JPEG/HEIF, or JPEG or HEIF formats alone. As I mentioned earlier, since your camera supports the HEIF format, you can choose to capture images in that format instead of JPEG when working with virtually all commands that manipulate a JPEG image.

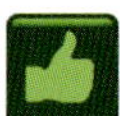

NOTE The Image Quality menu options appear to be the same in either case; the format (JPEG or HEIF) is enabled using a separate entry, Tone Mode, described earlier. When Tone Mode is set to SDR (Standard Dynamic Range), the JPG format will be used; if HLG (Hybrid Log Gamma) is selected instead, the still images will be saved in HEIF format, with a .HIF extension.

Unless you're using an iPhone and are deep into its features, you probably don't know much about the relatively recent HEIF format. The Apple's iOS 11 operating system for its smart devices was the first consumer product to use the HEIF format. Canon was the first digital camera company to support it, with Sony following thereafter.

In a nutshell, HEIF images use an advanced compression scheme to produce files with higher image quality that may be only half the size of JPEGs, and have more features, including transparency and 16-bit color. The downside is that, as I write this, no browser supports it natively, and many software applications as well as operating systems like Windows 10 and Android need updates to accommodate HEIF. Macs need macOS High Sierra or later to interpret HEIF images. If you're using a recent iPhone with HEIF, it can convert your images to JPEG automatically when you export them but will use the format to deploy special features internally (say, for Live images). So, while HEIF may eventually replace JPEG (last updated in 1994), the transition will take many years.

> **JPEG DEFAULT**
>
> As I noted earlier, because HEIF is such a new format that has yet to build a solid following, I expect most of you will work with JPEGs for nearly all of your work when not using RAW. So, for the most part, I will use JPEG as an example for many functions. You can assume that in nearly all cases HEIF can be substituted even if I don't use "JPEG/HEIF" terminology every time. If JPEG or HEIF *only* apply, I will point that out.

JPEG vs. RAW

You'll sometimes be told that RAW files are the "unprocessed" image information your camera produces before it's been modified. That's nonsense. RAW files are no more unprocessed than film is after it's been through the chemicals to produce a negative or transparency. A lot can happen in the developer that can affect the quality of a film image—positively and negatively—and, similarly, your digital image undergoes a significant amount of processing before it is saved as a RAW file. Nikon even applies a name (EXPEED 7) to the digital image processing (DIP) chips used to perform this magic.

A RAW file is more similar to a film camera's processed negative. It contains all the information obtained from the Z5 II's photosites *after* it has been run through the camera's analog-to-digital converter algorithm, which makes several adjustments, including white balance and suppression of hot pixels in longer exposures. The data, captured in 14-bit channels per color (and stored in a 16-bit space), has no sharpening or application of any special filters or other settings you might have speci-fied when you took the picture. Those settings are *stored* with the RAW file so they can be applied when the image is converted to a form compatible with your favorite image editor. However, using RAW conversion software such as Adobe Camera Raw or Nikon NX Studio, you can override those settings and apply settings of your own. You can select essentially the same changes there that you might have specified in your picture-taking options.

RAW exists because sometimes we want to have access to all the information captured by the camera before the camera's internal logic has processed it and converted the image to a standard file format like JPEG. Having that data available can provide slightly more resolution (especially if you're apply-ing noise reduction to your JPEG images), and the ability to tweak things like white balance and exposure settings.

So, why don't we always use RAW? Some photographers avoid using Nikon's RAW NEF files on the misguided conviction that they don't want to spend time in post-processing, forgetting that, if the camera settings you would have used for JPEG are correct, each RAW image's default attributes will use those settings and the RAW image will not need much manipulation. Post-processing in such cases is *optional*, and overwhelmingly helpful when an image needs to be fine-tuned.

Although some photographers do save *only* in RAW format, it's more common (and frequently more convenient) to use RAW plus one of the JPEG options, or, if you're confident about your settings, just shoot JPEG and eschew RAW altogether. In some situations, working with a RAW file can slow you down a little. RAW images take longer to store on the memory card and must be converted from RAW to a format your image editor can handle, whether you elect to go with the default settings in force when the picture was taken or make minor adjustments to the settings you specified in the camera.

As a result, those who depend on speedy access to images or who shoot large numbers of photos at once may prefer JPEG over RAW. Wedding photographers, for example, might expose several thousand photos during a bridal affair and offer hundreds to clients as electronic proofs for inclusion in an album. Wedding shooters take the time to make sure that their in-camera settings are correct, minimizing the need to post-process photos after the event. Given that their JPEGs are so good, there is little need to get bogged down shooting RAW.

Sports photographers also avoid RAW files. I recently photographed an air show that was an all-day affair, and, to make sure I didn't miss any peak moments as the aircraft flyovers, military sky-divers, and other action unfolded, I set my camera at the maximum rate and fired away. I managed to shoot 7,200 photos in a single day. I certainly didn't have any plans to do post-processing on very many of those shots, so carefully exposed and precisely focused JPEG images were my file format of choice that day.

JPEG was invented as a more compact file format that can store most of the information in a digital image, but in a much smaller size. JPEG predates most digital SLRs and was initially used to squeeze down files for transmission over slow dial-up connections. Even if you were using an early dSLR with 1.3MP files for news photography, you didn't want to send them back to the office over the telephone line communications that were common before high-speed Internet links became dominant.

But, as I noted, JPEG provides smaller files by compressing the information in a way that loses some image data. JPEG remains a viable alternative because it offers several different quality levels. At the highest quality Fine level, you might not be able to tell the difference between the original RAW file and the JPEG version.

In my case, I shoot virtually everything at RAW+JPEG Fine*. Most of the time, I'm not concerned about filling up my memory cards as I usually have multiple 128GB and 256GB cards with me. I also use a MacBook Air with an external 4TB hard drive. When shooting sports, I'll shift to JPEG Fine (with no RAW file) to squeeze a little extra speed out of my camera's continuous shooting mode, and to reduce the need to wade through eight-photo bursts taken in RAW format.

HIDDEN JPEGS

You may not be aware that your RAW file contains an embedded JPEG file, hidden inside in the JPEG Basic format. It's used to provide thumbnail previews of JPEG files, which is why you may notice an interesting phenomenon when loading a RAW image into a program like Adobe Lightroom. When the software first starts interpreting the RAW image, it may immediately display this hidden JPEG view which has, as you might expect, all the settings applied that you dialed into the camera. Then, as it finishes loading the RAW file, the application (Lightroom in particular) uses its own intelligence to fine-tune the image and display what it thinks is a decent version of the image, replacing the embedded JPEG. That's why you may see complaints that Lightroom or another program is behaving oddly: the initial embedded JPEG may look better than the final version, so it looks as if the application is degrading the image quality as the file loads. Of course, in all cases, once the RAW file is available, you can make your own changes to optimize it to your taste.

There is a second use for these hidden JPEG files. If you shoot RAW without creating JPEG files and later decide you want a JPEG version, there are dozens of utility programs that will extract the embedded JPEG and save it as a separate file. (Google "JPEG extractor" to locate a freeware program that will perform this step for your Mac, PC, or other computer.)

Image Size Settings

Options: JPEG: Large (default), Medium, Small; Enable DX Image Sizes: Off (default), On; Image Size (DX): Large (default)

My preference: Large

The next menu command in the Photo Shooting menu (see Figure 5.5) lets you select the resolution, or number of pixels captured in JPEG (Large, Medium, and Small) in full frame or any of the crop modes when using a single-frame release mode or continuous-shooting release mode of 15 frames per second or slower.

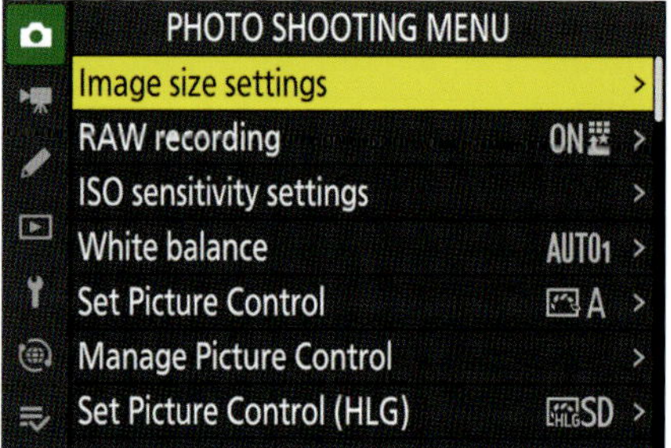

Figure 5.5 The next seven entries in the Photo Shooting menu.

This entry has one option that can be a bit confusing, so read the following clarification carefully:

- **Image Size.** By default, this entry allows you to specify the image size for *all* of the camera's image area modes. That is, when you specify Large, Medium, or Small here, that size is applied to FX (full frame), DX, 1:1, and 16.9 crops. This is the behavior we are all used to. The resolutions of each are shown in Table 5.2.

- **Enable DX Image Sizes.** On first glance, this seems like an entry that could be used to disable selecting the DX crop mode entirely. Not so! What it actually does is activate the ability to specify a *separate* image size when using DX mode, as described next.

- **Image Size (DX).** If, and *only if,* the option above is set to ON, you can choose to specify Large, Medium, or Small image sizes that will be applied *only* in DX mode. That size will override the setting you made above under Image Size that will continue to be used with FX, 1:1, and 16:9 sizes. This gives you the ability to mix and match image sizes and crops. You could, for example, automatically capture DX images in a space-saving Small format each time you selected the DX crop (or the camera switched to DX mode automatically when a mounted DX lens is detected), while using Large format with any other mode.

Select image sizes using this menu entry or by pressing the *i* button and accessing the Image Size Settings option. Rotate either command dial or press OK to select size from a screen. **Note:** You may find this menu entry grayed out completely if you've set your camera to shoot continuously at 15 or 30 frames per second (C15/C30). All images are shot at Large Image Size, but you can choose either FX (36 × 24) or DX (24 × 16) Image Areas. JPEG/HEIF Normal compression is used. Shutter speeds are limited to 1/8000–1/60th second.

TABLE 5.2 Image Size Settings Options

IMAGE AREA	SIZE	RESOLUTION	MEGAPIXELS
FX (36mm × 24mm)	Large	6048 × 4032	24.4MP
	Medium	4528 × 3024	13.7MP
	Small	3024 × 2016	6.1MP
DX (24mm × 16mm)	Large	3984 × 2656	10.6MP
	Medium	2976 × 1992	5.9MP
	Small	1984 × 1328	2.6MP
1:1 (24mm × 24mm)	Large	4032 × 4032	16.3MP
	Medium	3024 × 3024	9.1MP
	Small	2016 × 2016	4.1MP
16:9 (36mm × 20mm)	Large	6048 × 3400	20.6MP
	Medium	4528 × 2544	11.5MP
	Small	3024 × 1696	5.1MP

RAW Recording

Options: Lossless Compression, High Efficiency* (default), High Efficiency
My preference: High Efficiency*

When you've selected any RAW setting for Image Quality, you can choose the type (amount) of compression applied to RAW files as they are stored on your memory card. The default value (High Efficiency*) and its slightly less aggressive counterpart, High Efficiency, work best for most situations and actually discard some of the information deemed to be redundant from a visual standpoint, so that, theoretically, you won't *notice* that details are missing, and the file can be made more compact. Nikon calls them "visually" or "virtually" lossless. The Lossless Compression choice is available if you want to preserve all the information in the original image, but in most cases it's very difficult to tell the difference. You can select from:

- **Lossless Compression.** This setting uses what you might think of as reversible algorithms that discard no image information and provide significantly smaller RAW files. The size varies depending on the particular image but will average around 28.6MB. That's still almost 2.5X the size of the typical 11.3MB Large JPEG Fine file.

- **High Efficiency*.** Use this default setting if you want to store more images on your memory card and are willing to accept a tiny potential loss in image quality in the highlights, after significant editing. The resulting RAW files can be 33 percent or more smaller than Lossless Compressed images, typically producing an 18.1MB file. The difference may show up only if you perform certain types of extensive post-processing on an image, such as heavy image sharpening or some types of tonal corrections.

- **High Efficiency.** This is the most highly compressed setting, producing files that are around 60 percent smaller than Lossless Compression: roughly 12.3MB—about the same as a Large JPEG Fine image. You may see a noise increase in shadows with underexposed images, and some color changes at higher ISO settings.

As a practical matter, you will probably want to use Lossless Compression nearly 100 percent of the time, even when you are shooting a lot of long continuous sequences. The only real reason to use the other options is when you have only limited memory card storage available for some reason. (Shame on you!) That's because the generous buffer of the Nikon Z5 II can easily handle 166–200 frames *in any of the Image Quality settings,* RAW (NEF) included, as long as you're using an SDR as your Tone mode and a relatively fast memory card.

ISO Sensitivity Settings

Options: ISO sensitivity: Auto (Auto mode only), 100–64000, plus Hi 0.3 to Hi 1.7; Auto ISO Sensitivity Control: On, Off; Maximum Sensitivity: 200–64000, plus Hi 0.3 to Hi 1.7; Maximum Sensitivity with Flash: 200–64000, plus Hi 0.3 to Hi 1.7 and Same as Without Flash; Minimum Shutter Speed: Auto, 1/8000–30 seconds
My preference: Varies by subject type

You can make direct ISO settings without resorting to this menu entry. Just press the ISO button, located just south of the shutter release, and then rotate the sub-command dial to switch between Auto ISO and fixed ISO settings, and the main command dial to select specific fixed ISO values.

This menu entry has two parts, which give you more flexibility through its ISO Sensitivity and Auto ISO Sensitivity Control adjustments. The top line, ISO Sensitivity, produces a screen that allows you to specify a fixed ISO setting. The available settings range from ISO 100 through ISO 64000, and thence up to Hi 1.7 (ISO 204800 equivalent) and down to Lo 1.0 (ISO 50 equivalent). The available settings are determined by the size of the increment you've specified in Custom Setting b1: 1/3- or 1-step values. Use this ISO Sensitivity menu when you find it more convenient to set ISO using the color LCD monitor or viewfinder. Note that when the mode dial is set to the Auto position, an additional Auto setting is available in the fixed ISO list. It is separate from the Auto ISO Sensitivity option described next.

The Auto ISO Sensitivity Control menu entries at the bottom half of the screen let you specify how and when the camera will adjust the ISO value for you automatically under certain conditions. This capability can be potentially useful, although experienced photographers tend to shy away from any feature that allows the camera to change basic settings like ISO that have been carefully selected. But you needn't fear Auto ISO. You can set some firm boundaries so the camera will use this adjustment in a fairly intelligent way.

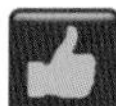

NOTE When mode dial is set to the green-labeled Auto position, all of the four Auto ISO Sensitivity Control options described next are grayed out and unavailable. Instead, the default ISO setting is Auto, but you can select any of the fixed ISO values from Lo 1.0 to Hi 1.7. When Auto ISO is activated in PASM modes, the camera can bump up the ISO sensitivity, if necessary, whenever an optimal exposure cannot be achieved at the current ISO setting. Of course, it can be disconcerting to think you're shooting at ISO 400 and then see a grainier ISO 6400 shot during LCD review. While the camera provides a flashing ISO-Auto alert in the display, the warning is easy to miss.

As you choose one of the Auto ISO options, you'll want to keep in mind how Auto ISO makes its adjustments. In Program and Aperture-priority modes, the camera will first attempt to set an exposure using a shutter speed of 1/8000th second down to the Minimum Shutter Speed value you specify below. It will then begin increasing the ISO rather than use a slower speed. In Shutter-priority mode, the shutter speed you select will always be used, but if the smallest or largest apertures aren't sufficient, the camera will raise or lower the ISO setting. In Manual exposure mode, your selected shutter speed and aperture are always used, and the camera will increase or decrease ISO sensitivity as needed to produce the correct exposure. In effect, Auto ISO gives you automatic exposure in Manual exposure mode. Here are the important considerations to keep in mind when using the options available for Auto ISO:

- **Off.** Set Auto ISO Sensitivity Control to Off, and the ISO setting will not budge from whatever value you have specified, and the entries below will be grayed out and unavailable. Use this setting when you don't want any ISO surprises, or when ISO increases are not needed to counter slow shutter speeds. For example, if the camera is mounted on a tripod, you can safely use slower shutter speeds at a relatively low ISO setting, so there is no need for a speed bump. On the other hand, if you're shooting hand-held and the camera, set for Program (P) or Aperture-priority (A) mode, wants to use a shutter speed slower than, say, 1/30th second, it's probably a good idea to increase the ISO to avoid the effects of camera shake. If you're using a longer lens, a shutter speed of 1/125th second or higher might be the point where an ISO bump would be a good idea. In that case, you can turn the automatic ISO sensitivity control on or remember to boost the ISO setting yourself.

- **Maximum Sensitivity/Maximum Sensitivity with Flash.** Use these parameters to indicate the highest ISO setting you're comfortable having the camera set on its own. You can choose the max ISO setting the camera will use from ISO 200 up to ISO 64000, plus the four "expanded" settings all the way up to Hi 1.7. Use a low number if you'd rather not take any photos at a high ISO without manually setting that value yourself. Dial in a higher ISO number if getting the photo at any sensitivity setting is more important than worrying about noise. When using the Maximum Sensitivity with Flash setting, you can specify Same As Without Flash, so the camera will perform similarly both with and without an optional flash.

  I've gotten surprisingly good results at ISO 25600; you should try it out yourself before ruling out this seemingly extreme ISO setting. Note that if you've selected an ISO setting that is *higher* than the Maximum Sensitivity you specify here, the camera will use the higher ISO value instead.

- **Minimum Shutter Speed.** This setting allows you to tell the camera how slow the shutter speed must be before the ISO boost kicks in, within the range of 30 seconds to 1/8000th second. The default value is Auto. When Auto is highlighted, press the right multi selector button, and a screen appears allowing you to fine-tune Auto to respond Slower or Faster.

  If you set a value manually, 1/30th second is a good choice, because for most shooters in most situations, any shutter speed longer than 1/30th is to be avoided, unless you're using a tripod, monopod, or looking for a special effect. That shutter speed, coupled with the available vibration reduction features, will generally produce images with minimal blur from camera/photographer shake.

  If you have a great deal of confidence in vibration reduction, steady hands, or the camera is partially braced against movement (say, you're using that monopod), a slower shutter speed, down to 1 full second, can be specified. Similarly, if you're working with a telephoto lens and find even a relatively brief shutter speed "dangerous," you can set a minimum shutter speed threshold of 1/250th second. When the shutter speed is faster than the minimum you enter, Auto ISO will not take effect.

  Your camera is smart in Auto ISO mode. For example, if you accidentally set a minimum shutter speed that is faster or slower than you've specified in Custom Setting e1: Flash Sync Speed or Custom Setting e2: Flash Shutter Speed, the camera will instead use a minimum shutter speed that is within the range set by e1 and e2. (You'll find more on these Custom Settings in Chapter 7.)

  You'll recall that Program and Aperture-priority modes can adjust the shutter speed. When Auto ISO is active, the camera will adjust the ISO setting *only* if the minimum shutter speed specified here would produce underexposure. In all other cases, the camera will simply adjust the shutter speed to produce an appropriate exposure and not touch the ISO setting.

  In addition, when Minimum Shutter Speed is set to Auto, the exposure system is clever enough to try to use faster shutter speeds with telephoto lenses (which are more subject to camera-motion blur). It will use the traditional 1/focal length rule of thumb. This feature works only with autofocus lenses; older manual focus lenses not equipped with a CPU chip are not compatible with this extra function. If you wish to tweak this Auto minimum shutter speed setting, press right when selecting Auto, and adjust the Auto setting to be faster or slower, which tells the camera to use a faster or slower shutter speed than the 1/focal length rule.

White Balance

Options: Auto: $AUTO_0$ Keep White; $AUTO_1$ Keep Overall Atmosphere (default); $AUTO_2$ Keep Warm Lighting Colors; Presets: Natural Light Auto, Direct Sunlight, Cloudy, Shade, Incandescent, Fluorescent (three types), Flash, Choose Color Temperature, Preset Manual

My preference: $AUTO_0$ (Keep White)

This setting lets you tweak the white balance setting applied to JPEG images, and which is embedded in the RAW image for interpretation by your image editor when the RAW file is imported. Your camera has a bewildering array of white balance settings, including three Auto modes, and, in practice, all of them are, at best, a little bit wrong. However, many are close enough that you may not notice the difference; all the presets can be adjusted by you using white balance fine-tuning and, when importing RAW files, you have even greater flexibility.

In addition to three varieties of full Auto white balance, this menu entry allows you to choose Natural Light Auto, Direct Sunlight, Cloudy, Shade, Incandescent, three types of Fluorescent illumination, Flash, a specific color temperature of your choice, a preset value taken from an existing photograph, or a measurement you make. Some of the settings you make here can be duplicated using the WB button (by default the Fn1 button), using the main and sub-command dials, but this menu entry can often be easier to use until you become familiar with your camera. Your white balance settings can have a significant impact on the color rendition of your images, as you can see in Figure 5.6, a shot of an obscure Liverpool drummer named Pete Best.

As I noted, the fastest way to change white balance settings is to use direct setting controls. Hold down the Fn1 (WB button), then rotate the main command dial to choose one of the main settings. Your choices appear on the LCD monitor as you dial. When Auto, Fluorescent, K (Choose Color Temperature), or PRE (Preset Manual) are shown, you can also select a sub-option by holding down the WB button while rotating the sub-command dial. You can also press the *i* button, select the White Balance icon (by default the second entry from the left of the top row), and rotate the main command dial and sub-command dial, as described above. I'll explain your options next.

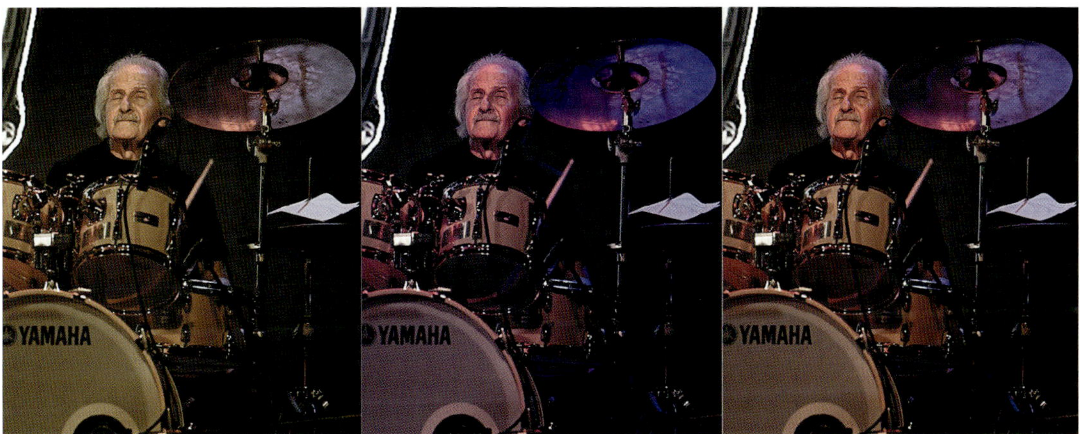

Figure 5.6 Adjusting color temperature can provide different results of the same subject at settings of 3400K (left), 5000K (middle), and 6500K (right).

Figure 5.7 The White Balance menu has pre-defined values, plus the option of setting color temperature and presets you measure yourself.

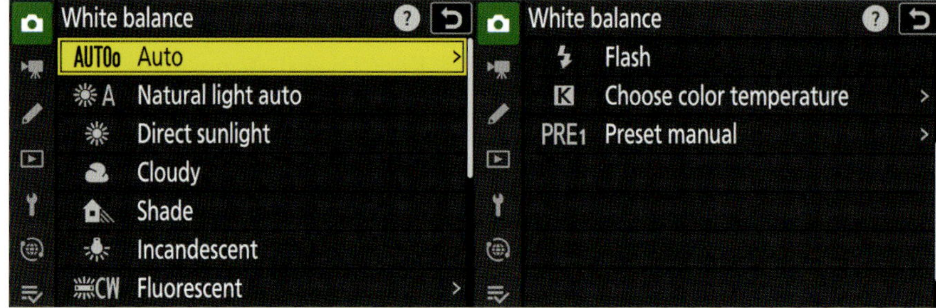

This menu entry offers additional options, including fine-tuning presets and the ability to capture and store custom preset color temperatures. Select the White Balance entry on the Photo Shooting menu, and you'll see an array of choices like those shown in Figure 5.7. If you choose Fluorescent, you'll be taken to another screen that presents three different types of lamps: Cool-White, Day White, and Daylight fluorescent. If you know the exact type of non-incandescent lighting being used, you can select it or settle on a likely compromise.

The K Choose Color Temperature selection allows you to select from an array of color temperatures in degrees Kelvin from 2500K to 10000K, and then further fine-tune the color bias using the fine-tuning feature described below. Select Preset Manual to record or recall custom white balance settings suitable for environments with unusual lighting or mixed lighting, as described later in this section.

For all other settings, highlight the white balance option you want, then press the multi selector right button to view the fine-tuning screen shown in Figure 5.8. The screen shows a grid with two axes, an amber-blue axis extending left/right, and a green-magenta axis extending up and down the grid. By default, the grid's cursor is positioned in the middle, and a readout to the right of the grid shows the cursor's coordinates on the A-B axis (yes, I know the display has the end points reversed) and G-M axis at 0,0.

You can use the multi selector's up/down and right/left buttons to move the cursor to any coordinate in the grid, thereby biasing the white balance in the direction(s) you choose. The amber-blue axis makes the image warmer or colder (but not actually yellow or blue). Similarly, the green-magenta axis preserves all the colors in the original image but gives them a tinge biased toward green or magenta. When you've fine-tuned white balance, either using the Photo Shooting menu options or the WB (Fn1) button, an asterisk appears in the white balance section of the display to remind you that this tweaking has taken place.

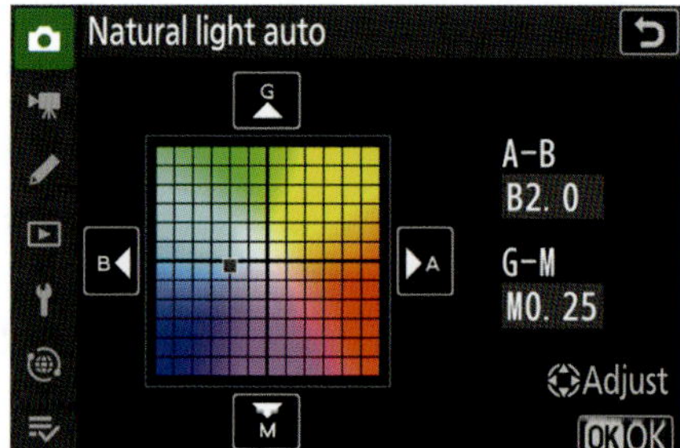

Figure 5.8 Specific white balance settings can be fine-tuned by changing their bias in the amber-blue, magenta-green directions—or along both axes simultaneously.

Why Color Varies

Color temperature—how "bluish" or how "reddish" the light appears to be to the digital camera's sensor—is the main factor you'll have to contend with. Indoor illumination is quite warm, comparatively, while daylight, in contrast, seems much bluer to the sensor. Our eyes (our brains, actually) are quite adaptable to these variations, so white objects don't appear to have an orange tinge when viewed indoors, nor do they seem excessively blue outdoors in full daylight. Yet, these color temperature variations are real, and the sensor is not fooled.

Fortunately, the only time you need to think in terms of *actual* color temperature is when you're making adjustments using the Choose Color Temperature setting in the White Balance entry within the Photo Shooting menu, which allows you to dial in exact color temperatures, if known, as described earlier. You can also shift and bias color balance along the blue/amber and magenta/green axes, and bracket white balance.

So-called "white" light is produced by a spectrum of colors that, when added together, provide the neutral color needed for accuracy. Artificial light sources don't necessarily offer the same balanced spectrum found in sunlight. Some portions of the spectrum may be deficient or truncated or include gaps with certain wavelengths missing entirely. As a result, all artificial light sources are assigned a color rendering index (CRI), which compares the source with a perfect "reference" light source at a particular color temperature.

With the decline in use of traditional incandescent and halogen bulbs, CRI has become more important. A CRI of 80-plus is considered acceptable; for critical applications like photography, a CRI higher than 93 is best. Daylight fluorescents and deluxe cool white fluorescents suitable for photography might have a CRI of about 79 to 95, which is perfectly acceptable for most photographic applications. Less desirable are warm white fluorescents, which may have a CRI of 55. White deluxe mercury vapor lights are even less suitable with a CRI of 45, while low-pressure sodium lamps can vary from CRI 0-18. If you're using such a source not intended for photography, it may be worth your while to determine its color rendering index before you shoot. The figure is often supplied on the packaging of the light source.

To recap, your chief tools for getting correct color in your images are these:

- **"Canned" presets.** Nikon does give you a wide range of pre-defined adjustment types to choose from when you need a quickie solution. You can choose from four kinds of Auto white balance settings, and six illumination categories (with three fluorescent variations). Strictly speaking, in any given situation, all of them are likely to be wrong to some extent. All versions of Nikon's Auto settings lose accuracy with light sources cooler than 3500K. Even "daylight" can vary widely, depending on local conditions or even how far you are from the equator.

- **Visual evaluation.** If you've set Custom Setting d10 to Show Effects of Settings, your camera will display the scene using the current white balance parameters. An image on the display may look too blue or too red if your WB specs are way off. Unfortunately, this is not a precise tool, as neither the LCD monitor nor viewfinder are able to reproduce colors with 100 percent accuracy, and our eyes tend to adapt to color variations so that colors look "right" to us, even when they are not.

- **White balance bracketing.** I included white balance bracketing, which is not available when you're shooting a RAW file, in my explanation of bracketing in Chapter 2, and won't repeat that discussion here. The bracketing adjustments are made only on the amber/blue axis (no bracketing in the magenta/green bias is possible), but you can select whether the bracketed shots are spread in the blue *or* amber directions (that is, each one bluer/less blue or yellower/less yellow) or balanced to provide both blue- and amber-oriented brackets.

- **Specific color temperatures.** If you know or have an estimate of the scene's color temperature, you can enter that directly, as described earlier.

- **Manual Presets.** You can tell the camera to measure the color temperature of a given scene, and then store that value in one of the six PRE slots, as described next.

To capture a white balance setting, just follow these steps:

1. **Use gray or white reference.** Place the neutral reference, such as a white piece of paper or a gray card, under the lighting you want to measure. You can also use one of those white balance caps that fit on the front of your lens like a lens cap.

2. **Choose Preset Manual.** Press the *i* button, choose White Balance, and rotate the main command dial until Preset Manual (PRE) is selected.

3. **Select "slot."** Rotate the sub-command dial until the slot (d-1 to d-6) you want to use as your white balance register is shown. Press OK twice. The screen shown in Figure 5.9, left, appears.

4. **Activate Measure mode.** Press and hold the OK button until the screen shown at right in Figure 5.9 appears. In my illustration, I've set up a gray card with a green border. You will see the PRE text flashing at the upper-right of the screen.

5. **Measure White Balance.** Tap the touch screen at the point where your gray or white reference appears or use the multi selector to move the target frame over that area. (Note that you can't relocate the frame if a flash is attached.) Then press OK again *or* press the shutter release down all the way.

6. **Success?** If the white balance information was captured, a message Data Acquired appears. Press the *i* button or icon on the screen to exit. If the camera was unable to measure white balance, you'll be asked to try again. (Try using a different target if you fail on successive attempts.)

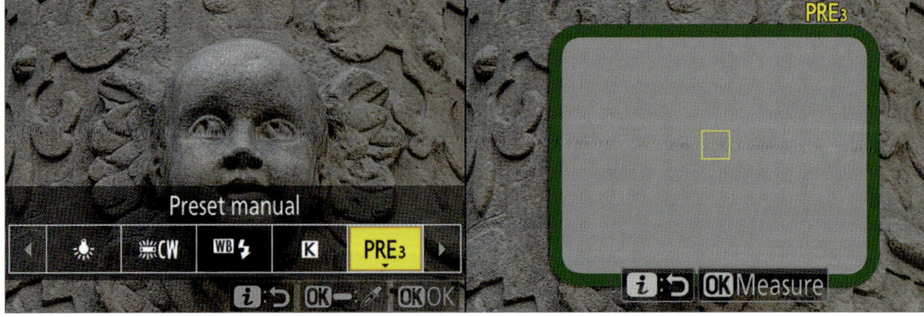

Figure 5.9 To define a new preset, highlight the PRE, left, and rotate the sub-command dial to choose a slot (d1 to d6). Then capture a neutral white or gray target (right).

The preset value you've captured will remain in the slot until you replace that white balance with a new captured value. It can be summoned at any time (use the *i* button menu or the WB button) and when PRE is chosen with the main command dial, select your preset by rotating the sub-command dial until the desired white balance slot is displayed. You can also choose an existing image or protect a captured white balance from being overwritten:

1. Choose Preset Manual from the White Balance menu, and press the right directional button.

2. A screen of thumbnails appears, showing the six "slots" numbered d-1 to d-6. Use the multi selector buttons to highlight one of the thumbnail slots and press the Zoom In button.

3. The next screen that appears (see Figure 5.10) has four options: Fine-tune, Edit Comment, Select Picture, and Protect.

   - Choose Fine-tune to fine-tune the amber/blue / magenta/green white balance of an image already stored in one of the four user slots.

   - Choose Edit Comment to add or change the comment applied to d-1 to d-6. The comment can be used as a label to better identify the white balance information in the slot, with terms like Gymnasium Daytime or Rumpus Room. (The standard text-editing screen shown earlier in this chapter appears.)

   - Choose Select Picture to view the standard image-selection screen and highlight and choose the existing image you want to use. Press the Zoom In button to confirm your choice and copy the white balance of the selected image to the slot you selected in Step 2. Note that the image must be taken with your current camera—you can't "recycle" the white balance of favorite shots captured with a different model.

   - Choose Protect to lock the white balance setting currently stored in the selected slot. Use this to preserve a captured white balance setting.

4. Press OK to confirm your white balance setting.

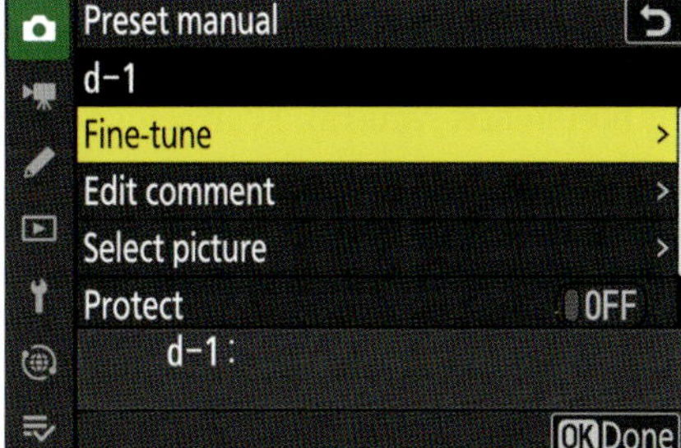

Figure 5.10 The Preset Manual screen lets you fine-tune preset white balance settings, label them with a comment, select an image to use as a white balance reference, and protect captured settings.

To use an existing white balance setting you've already stored, just follow these steps:

1. **Scroll to Preset Manual in the White Balance menu.** Press the right directional button. The screen shown in Figure 5.11 appears.

2. **Select preset.** Use the directional controls to highlight the "slot" containing the value you stored earlier.

3. **Confirm.** Press OK to confirm and exit back to the Photo Shooting menu.

4. **Exit.** Press MENU twice to exit the Photo Shooting menu.

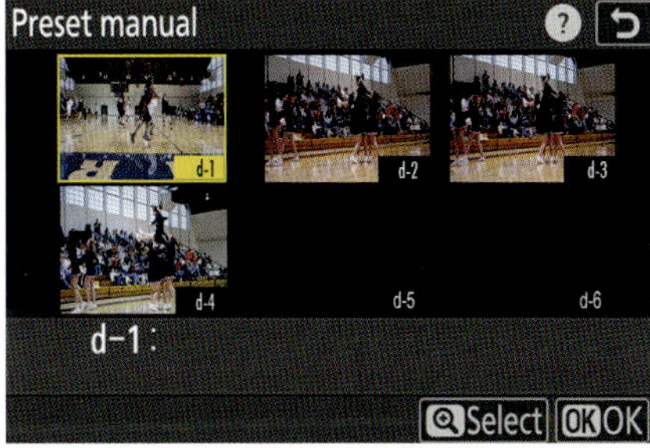

Figure 5.11 When you capture a scene's white balance, it will be stored in the selected slot.

You can also select an existing preset using the *i* menu:

1. **Press the *i* button.** Highlight the White Balance option in the top row.
2. **Select Preset.** Rotate the command dial until the Preset option (PRE) appears.
3. **Choose your preset.** Rotate the sub-command dial until the preset (numbered 1 to 6) appears.
4. **Exit.** Press the *i* button twice to confirm and exit.

Set Picture Control

Options: Auto (default), Standard, Neutral, Vivid, Monochrome, Flat Monochrome, Deep Tone Monochrome, Portrait, Rich Tone Portrait, Landscape, Flat; Creative Picture Controls (01–20): Dream, Morning, Pop, Sunday, Somber, Dramatic, Silence, Bleached, Melancholic, Pure, Denim, Toy, Sepia, Blue, Red, Pink, Charcoal, Graphite, Binary, and Carbon

My preference: Neutral: I can select other styles during RAW processing; Flat when extended dynamic range without HDR processing is needed.

Nikon has considerably expanded its Picture Control roster in recent years, adding 20 Creative Picture Controls that add special effects to your images as you shoot. Most recently, Nikon added the ability to download Picture Controls from Nikon Imaging Cloud (when enabled using the Nikon Imaging Cloud command in the Network menu, as described in Chapter 9).

The Picture Control styles allow you to choose your own sharpness (in three different ways, as I'll explain shortly), plus adjust contrast, brightness, color saturation, and hue settings applied to your images when using P, S, A, and M modes.

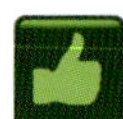

NOTE When Tone Mode, described earlier, is set to HLG, this Set Picture Control entry is grayed out; use the Set Picture Control (HLG) entry that follows instead. In video mode, use the HLG Quality setting in the Video Recording menu.

The three types of Picture Controls available:

- **Original Picture Controls.** Your camera has predefined styles, which it calls Original Picture Controls: Standard, Neutral, Vivid, Monochrome, Flat Monochrome, Deep Tone Monochrome, Portrait, Rich Tone Portrait, Landscape, and Flat. There is also an Auto setting, which examines your image and applies one of these controls as appropriate. Flat Monochrome, Deep Tone Monochrome, and Flat are relatively new options, with extended, dynamic ranges that lend themselves itself to fine-tuning in an image editor. Video shooters who plan to process their clips also love the versatility of the Flat setting, which allows preserving detail in highlights and shadows when correcting (or "grading") video in advanced video-editing software.

  Note that each of the predefined styles has its own default settings for Sharpening (with four variations), along with Contrast, Brightness, Saturation, and Hue. (Monochrome does not have Saturation or Hue settings.) For example, the default Sharpening is +4 for Vivid and Landscape; +3 for Standard and Monochrome; +2 for Neutral and Portrait; and +1 for Flat. Even more interesting, the effects of each increment aren't consistent between Picture Controls.

A +1 sharpening applied to the Standard control isn't the same as the +1 applied to the Neutral control. Each of the other parameters available for the preset styles have their own defaults. Any changes you make are *edits* of the default values defined for that particular style.

- **Creative Picture Controls.** These are 20 new special-effects styles, each assigned a number from 1 to 20. Nikon has given a fanciful name to each Creative Picture Control that more or less provides a hint to how the effect modifies your image. The available creative styles include Dream, Morning, Pop, Sunday, Somber, Dramatic, Silence, Bleached, Melancholic, Pure, Denim, Toy, Sepia, Blue, Red, Pink, Charcoal, Graphite, Binary, and Carbon. These 20 additional Creative Picture Controls offer the same parameter adjustments as Original Picture Controls, plus an Effect Level slider for specifying the *amount* of the special effects provided, on a scale from 0 to 100 in increments of 10 steps. You can edit the parameters of these Picture Controls, too. I'll explain Creative Picture Controls shortly.

  Note: If you're using Nikon Imaging Cloud, you can download Picture Controls wirelessly using the "Add Cloud Picture Control Files" option that appears at the very end of the Creative Picture Controls list (after 20: Carbon). The new controls can be loaded, saved, edited, renamed, or deleted using the Manage Picture Control entry, discussed next.

- **User Controls.** You can define up to nine Picture Controls of your own, numbered C-1 to C-9. Each User Control is based on one of the predefined styles (any of the Original or Creative Controls). You'll use the Manage Picture Control entry, described in the next section.

While all the canned Original and Creative Picture Controls have their preset parameters, their most valuable trait is your ability to *edit* the settings of any of those styles, so they better suit your taste. You can adjust the existing styles, in which case an asterisk appears next to their name in the menus or save your adjustments as a User Control. But wait, there's more! You can *copy* these styles to a memory card, edit them on your computer, and reload them into your camera at any time. So, effectively, you can have several sets of custom Picture Control styles available: those currently in your camera, as well as a virtually unlimited library of user-defined styles that you have stored on memory cards.

As I've noted, using and fully managing Picture Control styles is accomplished using two different menu entries. This entry, Set Picture Control, has two functions: it allows you to *choose* an existing Original or Creative style and to *edit* any of those predefined styles that Nikon provides. The Photo Shooting menu entry that follows this one, Manage Picture Control, gives you the capability of creating and editing user-defined styles, using one of the canned Original or Creative Picture Controls as a foundation.

PHOTO/VIDEO PICTURE CONTROLS OVERLAP

As you'll learn in Chapter 6, the Video Recording menu has its own Set Picture Controls entry with the same styles available. However, you have the choice of editing and saving a separate version of each individual control, or selecting the Same As Photo Settings option, which will mean the settings you make here will be automatically applied to its Video Recording counterpart.

Choosing a Picture Control Style

To choose from one of the predefined Original or Creative styles or to select a user-defined style you've created (numbered C-1 to C-9), follow these steps:

1. Choose Set Picture Control from the Photo Shooting menu. The screen shown in Figure 5.12 appears. Remember that Picture Controls that have been modified from their standard settings have an asterisk next to their name.

2. Scroll down to the Picture Control you'd like to use. The ones shown in the figure are followed by the last Original Control, Flat, and then the Creative Controls, and, at the tail end of several screens, any User Controls you have created.

3. Press OK to activate the highlighted style. (Although you can usually select a menu item by pressing the multi selector right button, in this case, that button activates editing instead.)

4. Press the MENU button or tap the shutter release to exit the menu system.

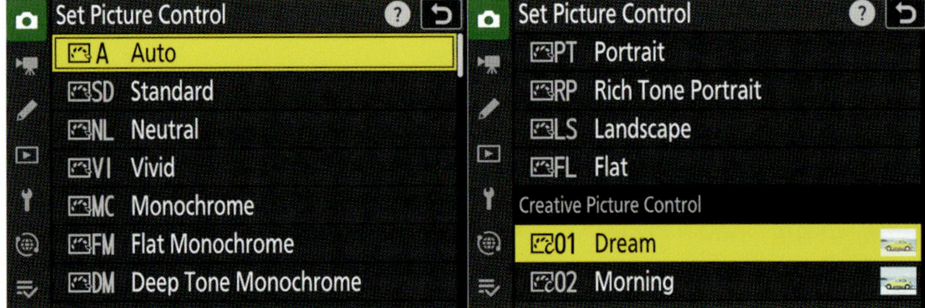

Figure 5.12 You can choose from Auto or the predefined Picture Controls shown here, the Creative Picture Controls, or the User Controls located farther down the scrolling list.

Editing a Picture Control Style

You can change the parameters of any of Nikon's predefined Original Picture Controls (including Auto), Creative Picture Controls, or any of the (up to) nine user-defined styles you create. You are given the choice of using the quick-adjust/fine-tune facility to modify a Picture Control with a few sliders. You can edit these controls using this Set Picture Control entry in the Photo Shooting menu, and you can also edit them when you access a style from the *i* menu.

To make quick adjustments to any Picture Control except the Monochrome style and Creative Picture Controls 13 to 20, follow these steps:

1. Choose Set Picture Control from the Photo Shooting menu.

2. Scroll down to the Picture Control you'd like to edit.

3. Press the multi selector right button to produce an adjustment screen similar to the one shown in Figure 5.13.

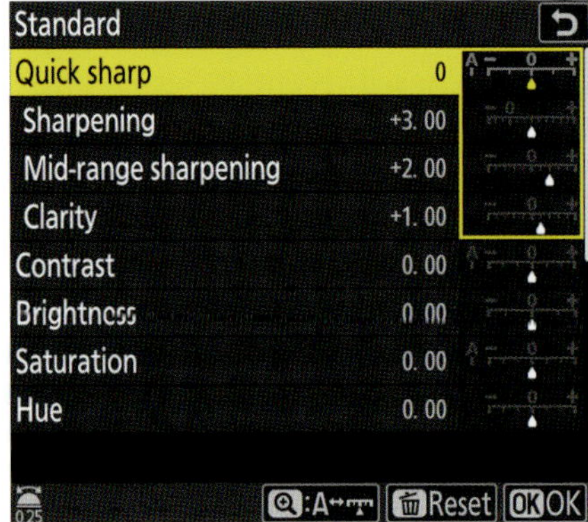

Figure 5.13 Sliders can be used to make quick adjustments to your Picture Control styles.

4. Use the Quick Sharp slider and the left/right directional controls to change the three individual Sharpening adjustments (Sharpening, Mid-Range Sharpening, and Clarity) simultaneously. Alternatively, scroll down to each of those three adjustments and tweak Sharpening, Mid-Range Sharpening, or Clarity independently. (See the next section, "Super Sharpness," for an explanation of the latter parameter.)

5. Next, scroll down to the Contrast, Brightness, Saturation, and Hue sliders with the up/down directional controls, then use the left/right directional controls to adjust the parameter by one or rotate the sub-command dial to make adjustments in finer 0.25 increments. A gray triangle will appear under the original setting in the slider as you make a change. (Saturation and Hue cannot be adjusted for Monochrome, Flat Monochrome, Deep Tone Monochrome, or Creative Picture Controls 13 to 20.)

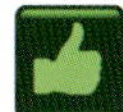 **TIP** You can adjust the Auto Picture Control, but each of your modifications are applied *on top of* the Auto adjustments. That is, in Auto Picture Control mode, the camera will automatically adjust, say, Contrast, and then apply any contrast adjustments you have specified, in the range Auto-2 to Auto+2. Because the Auto Picture Control's adjustments may vary depending on what your camera "decides" the image needs, you should edit with caution.

6. Instead of making changes with the slider's scale, when you're working with the Contrast and Saturation adjustments, you can move the cursor to the far left and choose A (for Auto—just press the Zoom-in button) and the camera will adjust these parameters automatically, depending on the type of scene it detects.

7. Press OK to save your adjustments or press the Trash button to reset the values to their defaults.

PICTURE CONTROLS WITH THE *i* MENU

You can also access the exact same functions just described by pressing the Picture Control button on top of the camera, or by using the *i* menu. When working with the *i* menu, navigate to the Set Picture Control icon (located by default as the first icon on the left in the top row in Figure 5.14, left), and rotate the main command dial if all you want to do is select a Picture Control from a scrolling list. If you'd like to *edit* the control, press OK. When you've highlighted the control you want to edit, press the down button to produce a screen like the one seen in Figure 5.14, right. The column at the far right contains all the parameters listed in Steps 4 and 5 above, while the adjustment slider for the currently highlighted parameter appears at the bottom. Once you've made your edits, press OK to confirm and exit, or the *i* button to exit without making changes.

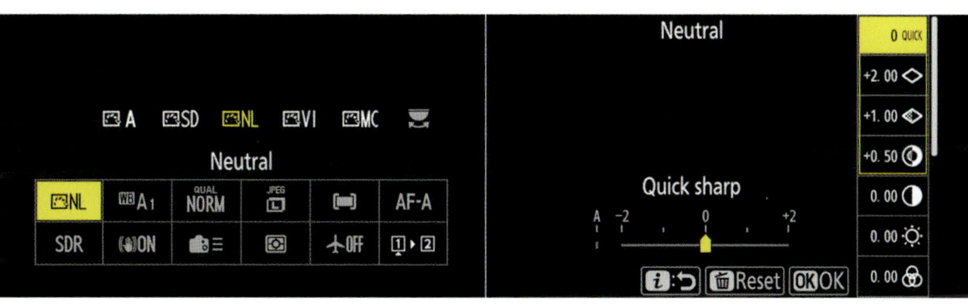

Figure 5.14 Picture Controls can be accessed and edited from the *i* menu.

Editing Picture Controls in the camera is fairly easy, but if you intend to make a lot of changes or want to get creative and build a roster of custom controls, you may find the free downloadable Picture Control Utility 2 useful. The interface (shown in Figure 5.15) is fast and straightforward to use and offers the option to save your edited controls to a file (for storage/archiving); to a memory card for transfer to your camera; or launch Nikon NX Studio, Capture NX-D, or View NXi, and apply it immediately to an image.

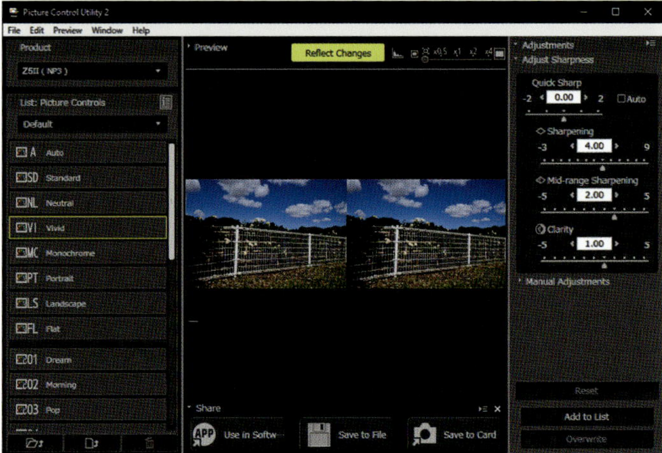

Figure 5.15 The Picture Control Utility 2.

If you plan to use a Picture Control in a camera other than your Nikon Z5 II, you should know that Nikon has used three different file structures over the years, reducing the seamless compatibility previously available. The Edit > Add Product entry on the utility allows you to add dSLR, mirrorless, and Coolpix cameras, or specify which of the three file types (with .NCP, .NP2, or .NP3 extensions) is appropriate for your camera.

CUSTOM CURVES

Nikon has thrown you a curve ball by adding an additional customizable parameter that you *can't* edit in the camera. You can add a Photoshop- or Lightroom-like Curve/Tone Curve (respectively) to a User-created Picture Control concocted on your computer with the Picture Control Utility. When creating/editing a User control in the utility, you can select Manual Adjustments, click the Use Custom Curve box, and adjust the tone curve exactly as you would in your image editor. Once saved as a User setting and copied to your camera using the Manage Picture Controls entry discussed shortly, that curve will be applied to your images when the custom User setting is active. Should you try to edit that control in-camera, you'll see the Contrast and Brightness parameters are grayed out, and their values labeled USER.

SUPER SHARPNESS

Amateur photographers like to be told that their pictures will be "clear and sharp," a simplification of picture quality that is likely to satisfy most of them. As an enthusiast, you know that many other factors also are part of image quality, including color, tonal range, and contrast. Indeed, sharpness itself is more complex than you might expect. Other parameters, such as Contrast, Brightness, Saturation, and Hue are virtually self-explanatory, because you've probably worked with them many times in Photoshop or another image editor.

When it comes to the adjustments you can make in terms of sharpness, there are three different parameters, and multiple ways of controlling them. The Picture Controls have separate sliders for all three, plus a fourth slider, Quick Sharp, which adjusts all of the three simultaneously.

Here's a breakdown:

- **Sharpening.** This control affects the appearance of fine details and patterns because it modifies the sharpness of the contours (edges) of your subjects. The lower the number, the softer those outlines will be; higher numbers produce more distinct details.
- **Mid-range sharpening.** Adjusts overall sharpness according to the fineness of patterns and lines in the mid-tones adjusted by the Sharpening and Clarity controls. In Video mode, this parameter works only when Video Quality has been set to High in the Video Recording menu. Keep in mind that increasing sharpness also increases contrast, so you'll want to use this control judiciously when capturing high-contrast scenes.
- **Clarity.** This adjusts the overall sharpness of the image and the sharpness of thicker outlines without affecting brightness or dynamic range. Think of Clarity as a type of sharpening/enhancing effect applied to the mid-tones of an image. While sharpening generally adjusts only the contours of your subject matter, Clarity makes details sharper while maintaining the gradation of highlight and shadow areas. High values produce contrasty and vivid images with darkened colors and improved detail in the midtones. Low values reduce midtone detail and flatten colors. You might want to apply Clarity to make hazy or fog-clouded subjects look clearer without losing details, or when you want to soften hard-edge subjects. Conversely, if your scene already is contrasty, use Clarity with caution, just as I advised for Mid-range Sharpening. Your best bet is to play with the control to see how you like the results. The camera applies +1 Clarity by default to Standard, Vivid, Landscape, and Monochrome Picture Controls.

Editing the Monochrome Picture Controls

Editing the three Monochrome styles or the Creative Picture Controls 13 to 20 is similar to customizing the other styles, except that the parameters differ slightly. Sharpening, Contrast, and Brightness are available, but, instead of Saturation and Hue, you can choose a filter effect (Yellow, Orange, Red, Green, or none) and a toning effect (black-and-white, plus seven levels of Sepia, Cyanotype, Red, Yellow, Green, Blue Green, Blue, Purple Blue, and Red Purple). (Keep in mind that once you've taken a JPEG photo using one of these styles, you can't convert the image back to full color.) To adjust Filters or Toning:

1. Choose Set Picture Control from the Photo Shooting menu.
2. Scroll down to any of the three Monochrome Picture Controls or to one of the Creative Picture Controls that have Filter and Toning options, numbered 13 through 20.
3. Press the multi selector right button to produce an adjustment screen similar to the one shown in Figure 5.16.
4. Set Sharpening, Contrast, and Brightness exactly as you would with the other Picture Controls.
5. Optionally, scroll down to Filter Effects or Toning (which appears after Filter Effects in the scrolling list and is shown at the bottom of the figure).

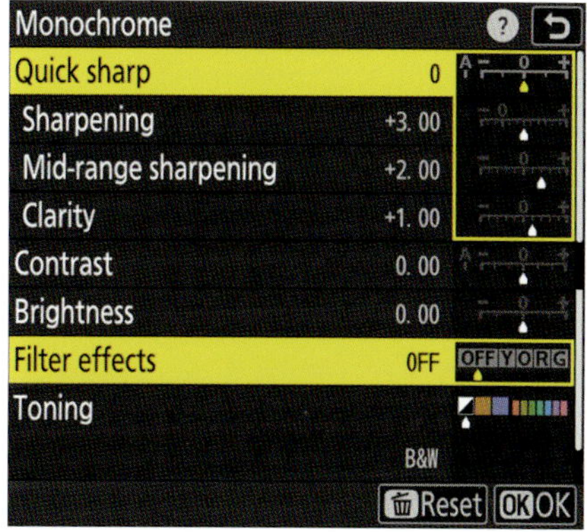

Figure 5.16 Editing Monochrome Picture Style parameters.

6. When Filter Effects is highlighted, you can choose Off, Yellow, Orange, Red, or Green. Press OK to finish or Trash to reset to the original values.

7. When Toning is highlighted, you can press the left/right directional controls to choose a tone: Black/White, Sepia, Cyanotype, Red, Yellow, Green, Blue Green, Blue, Purple Blue, or Red Purple. Once you've selected a tone (other than Black/White), press the down button to move to the intensity control, then use the left/right buttons to set a toning strength from +1 to +7. Press OK to confirm, or Trash to reset.

FILTERS VS. TONING

Although some of the color choices seem to overlap, you'll get very different looks when choosing between Filter Effects and Toning. Filter Effects add no color to the monochrome image. Instead, they reproduce the look of black-and-white film that has been shot through a color filter. That is, Yellow will make the sky darker, and the clouds will stand out more, while Orange makes the sky even darker and sunsets more full of detail. The Red filter produces the darkest sky of all and darkens green objects, such as leaves. Human skin may appear lighter than normal. The Green filter has the opposite effect on leaves, making them appear lighter in tone. Figure 5.17 at left shows the same scene shot with no filter, then Yellow, Green, and Red filters. The Sepia, Blue, Green, and other toning effects, on the other hand, all add a color cast to your monochrome image. Use these when you want an old-time look or a special effect, without bothering to recolor your shots in an image editor. Toning is shown at right in Figure 5.17.

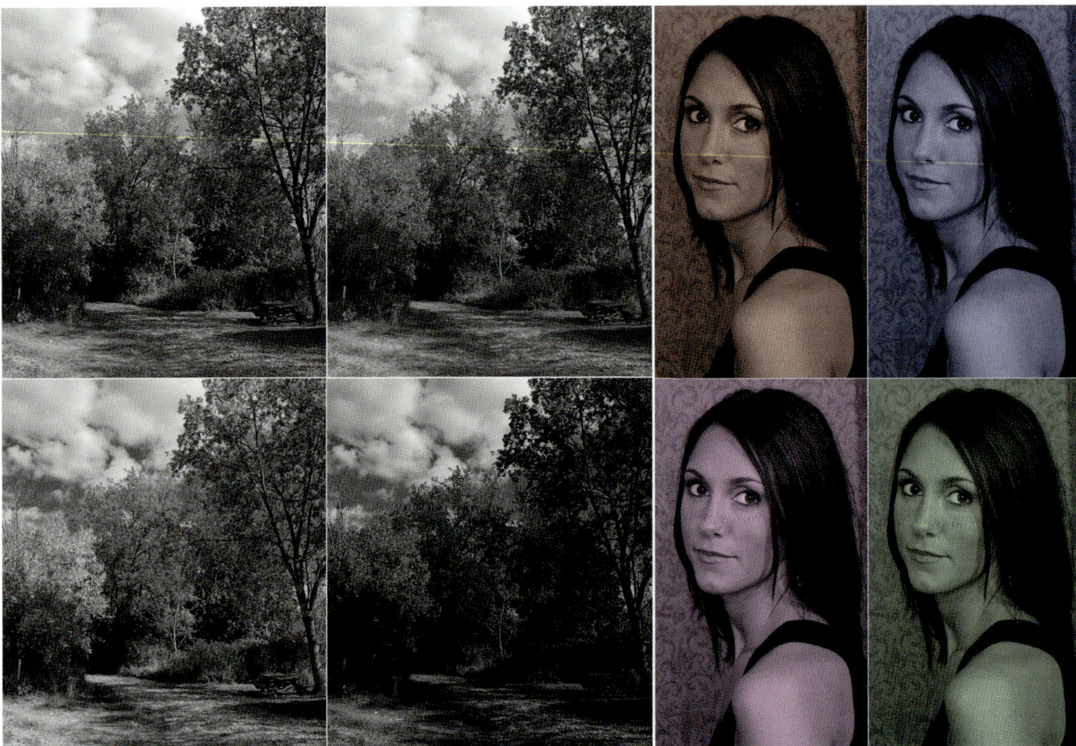

Figure 5.17 Left: Color filter effects: No filter (upper left); yellow filter (upper right); green filter (lower left); and red filter (lower right). Right: Toning effects: Sepia (upper left); Purple Blue (upper right); Red Purple (lower left); and Green (lower right).

Editing Creative Picture Controls

The Creative Picture Controls are located farther down the scrolling list after the predefined controls (see Figure 5.18, left). They have approximately the same adjustments found in the Original Picture Controls. However, you'll probably find adjusting them to be trickier, because it can be difficult to see how a particular parameter applies to a particular special effect. For example, you know that the Vivid original style emphasizes color saturation but what, exactly, goes into making, say, the Dream creative style? Simply looking at samples with a particular effect applied may not help, as you can see in Figure 5.18, right. The differences between many of the controls is subtle. Charcoal, Graphite, Binary, and Carbon may differ primarily in amount of contrast, for example.

Nikon provides some simplified descriptions, which may seem a little vague, like a New Age song title, forcing us poor users to evoke our own mental images with only fuzzy visual references. Nikon's summaries are along these lines (for what it's worth):

- **Dream.** Lightness, warmth, pale sepia-like orange, brightening darker areas with smooth edges and a soft appearance.
- **Morning.** Atmosphere of fresh morning air, dark areas brightened, with bluish/cyan tones with a sense of transparency. Refreshing image.
- **Pop.** Highest degree of saturation for more colorful tones and textures, even with brighter images.
- **Sunday.** Open atmosphere as if the image were captured on a Sunday afternoon. Increased contrast, blown highlights, for a stronger impression.
- **Somber.** Melancholic, calm atmosphere, like after a rain, with increased saturation and suppressing brightness with compressed tones.
- **Dramatic.** Profound expression emphasizing light and shade at high contrast (like the bleach filter in some image editing plug-ins), suitable for dramatic expression of light.
- **Silence.** Transient and lonely contemplative feeling; tranquil, soft images with reduced saturation.
- **Bleached.** Serious impression with greenish, low-saturation images and metallic feel. Minutely rendered details with tasteful silvery tone.

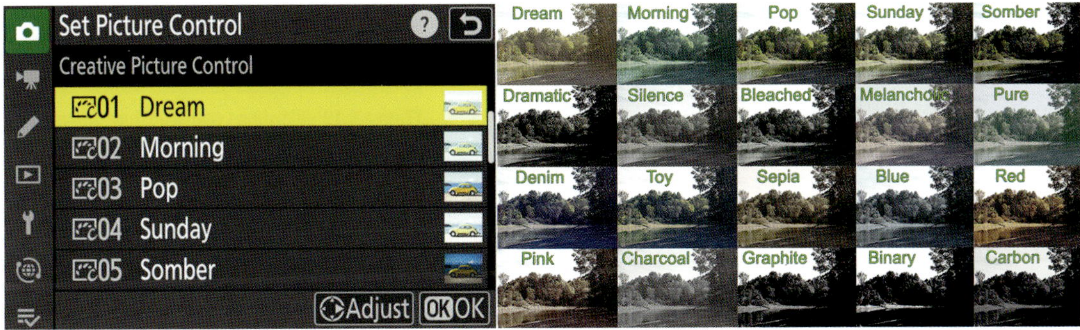

Figure 5.18 The Creative Picture Controls are numbered for easy reference (left). Effect sample thumbnails (right).

- **Melancholic.** Retro expression with slightly melancholic atmosphere, magenta tinged, restrained sharpness and reduced saturation.
- **Pure.** Soft image, as if viewed through a veil, with soft blue-green tone, tranquil ambience.
- **Denim.** Deep tone, strong blue shifted toward cyan, high saturation.
- **Toy.** Inspired by toy cameras, but deeper and calmer impression, with high saturation, blue shifted toward indigo.
- **Sepia.** First of the true "color-influenced" Creative Picture Controls, provides sepia images with faded colors, similar to a colorized monochrome picture. This control and the next seven all have Filter Effects and Toning options, as described above.
- **Blue.** Yet more melancholy, this time with a quiet, bluish tone, similar to cyanotypes.
- **Red.** Retro images with heavy amber-red tone.
- **Pink.** No relation to Alecia Beth Moore (P!nk), but still able to deliver a soft, gentle romantic tone with a pinkish atmosphere.
- **Charcoal.** Gentle, monochrome images resembling black-and-white drawings with minimal loss of detail in shadows and highlights, but softer edge sharpness.
- **Graphite.** Sharpened edges and lustrous blacks with crisp, accentuated contrast.
- **Binary.** Two-tone images for crisp black-and-white.
- **Carbon.** Stable, deep, dignified images with less contrast than Graphite, producing strong, black-based gradation.

As the names and descriptions of each of these 20 Creative Picture Controls don't adequately describe their effects, my recommendation is to evaluate each individually and use the controls to tweak them to your preferences. If you use the *i* menu to select a Picture Control, you can preview the effect in the display. You'll notice an additional slider, Effect Level, which simply specifies how strongly the effect is applied to the image, on a scale of 0 (zero effect) to 100 (maximum effect). This allows you to attenuate the amount of the effect, or to mix an Original control with a Creative control. For example, if you set the Creative control to 80, the camera will apply the default Original control using the remaining amount. The Dream style controls are shown in Figure 5.19, as an example. You can always adjust these styles and save them under a new name as a User Control, as I'll describe in the Manage Picture Control section that follows.

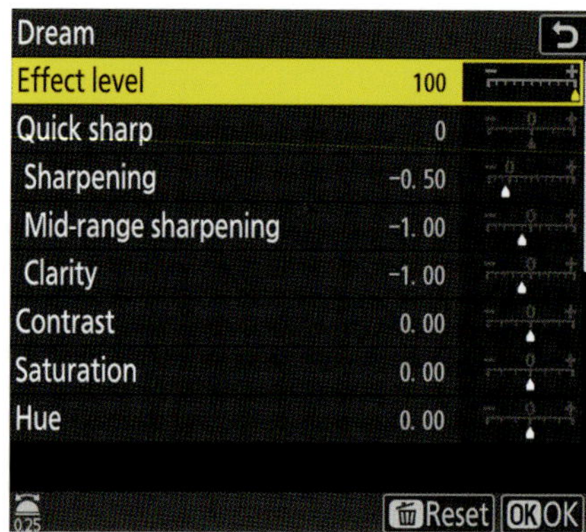

Figure 5.19 Adjusting Creative Picture Controls.

Manage Picture Control

Options: Save/Edit, Rename, Delete, Load/Save
My preference: N/A

The Manage Picture Control menu entry can be used to create new styles, edit existing styles, rename or delete them, and store/retrieve them from the memory card. Here are the basic functions of this menu item, which can be found on the Photo Shooting menu directly below the Set Picture Control entry:

- **Make a copy.** Choose Save/Edit (see Figure 5.20, left), select from the list of available Picture Controls, and press OK to store that style in one of the user-defined slots C-1 to C-9 (with slots C-1 and C-2 shown already occupied in Figure 5.20, right).

- **Save an edited copy.** Choose Save/Edit, select from the list of available Picture Controls, and then press the multi selector right button to edit the style, as described in the previous section. Press OK when finished editing and then save the modified style in one of the user-defined slots C-1 to C-9.

- **Rename a style.** Choose Rename, select from the list of user-defined Picture Controls (you cannot rename the default styles), and then enter the text used as the new label for the style, using the standard text-entry screen shown earlier in this chapter in Figure 5.2. You may use up to 19 characters for the name.

- **Remove a style.** Select Delete, choose from the list of user-defined Picture Controls (you can't remove one of the default styles), press the multi selector right button, highlight Yes in the screen that follows, and press OK to remove that Picture Control.

- **Store/retrieve style on card.** Choose Load/Save, then select Copy to Camera to locate a Picture Control on your memory card and copy it to the camera, Delete from Card to select a Picture Control on your memory card and remove it, or Copy to Card to duplicate a style currently in your camera onto the memory card. This last option allows you to create and save on your card Picture Controls in excess of the nine that can be loaded into the camera at one time, for a maximum of 99 custom Picture Controls. Once you've copied a style to your memory card, you can modify the version in the camera, give it a new name, and, in effect, create a whole new Picture Control.

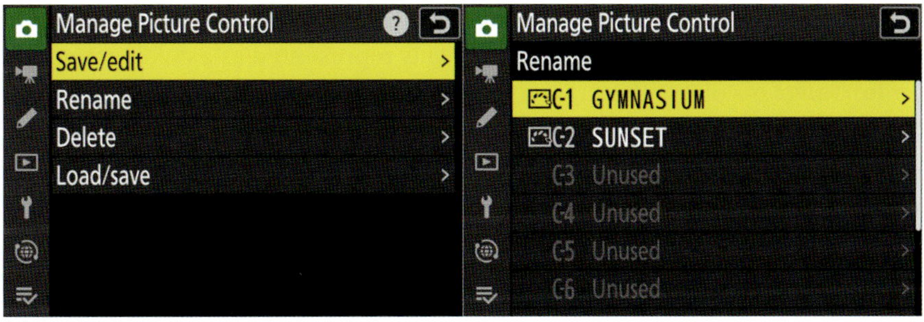

Figure 5.20 You can save, edit, rename, delete, or load and save Picture Controls (left). Picture Controls that you define can be stored in your camera's settings (right).

Set Picture Control (HLG)

Options: Standard (default), Monochrome, Flat
My preference: N/A

As noted, when Tone Mode, described earlier, is set to HLG to enable creating HEIF files and HLG video, the conventional Picture Control entry is grayed out. Only Standard, Monochrome, and Flat HLG Picture Controls can be selected from this menu entry. You can adjust the parameters as with the conventional controls described earlier, with the exception that new Highlights and Shadows sliders are available. The extended dynamic range of HEIF files allows making adjustments to bring out or preserve detail in the highlights and shadows to a greater extent than would have been available with JPEG images.

Color Space

Options: sRGB (default), Adobe RGB
My preference: Adobe RGB

This is the first entry in the next section of the Photo Shooting menu (see Figure 5.21). The Color Space option gives you two different color spaces (also called *color gamuts*), named Adobe RGB (because it was developed by Adobe Systems in 1998) and sRGB (supposedly because it is the *standard* RGB color space). These two color gamuts define a specific set of colors that can be applied to captured images.

Unfortunately, it's impossible to capture *all* the colors we see because of the limitations of the sensor and the filters used to capture the fundamental red, green, and blue colors, as well as that of the phosphors used to display those colors on the LEDs in your camera and computer monitors. Nor is it possible to *print* every color our eyes detect, because the inks or pigments used don't absorb and reflect colors perfectly. On the other hand, the camera does capture quite a few more colors than we need: a 14-bit RAW image can include up to 16,384 per color channel, or 4.4 *trillion* hues.

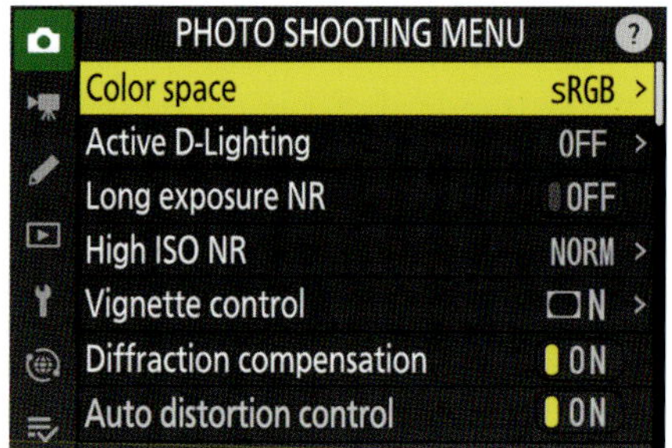

Figure 5.21 The next section of the Photo Shooting menu.

The set of colors, or gamut, that can be reproduced or captured by a given device (scanner, digital camera, monitor, printer, or some other piece of equipment) is represented as a color space that exists within the larger full range of colors. That full range is represented by the odd-shaped splotch of color shown in 5.22, as defined by scientists at an international organization back in 1931. The colors possible with Adobe RGB are represented by the black triangle in the figure, while the sRGB gamut is represented by the smaller white triangle. The location of the corners of each triangle represent the position of the primary red, green, and blue colors in the gamut.

A third color space, ProPhoto RGB, represented by the yellow triangle in the figure, has become more popular among professional photographers as more and more color printing labs support it. While you cannot *save* images using the ProPhoto gamut with your camera, you can convert your

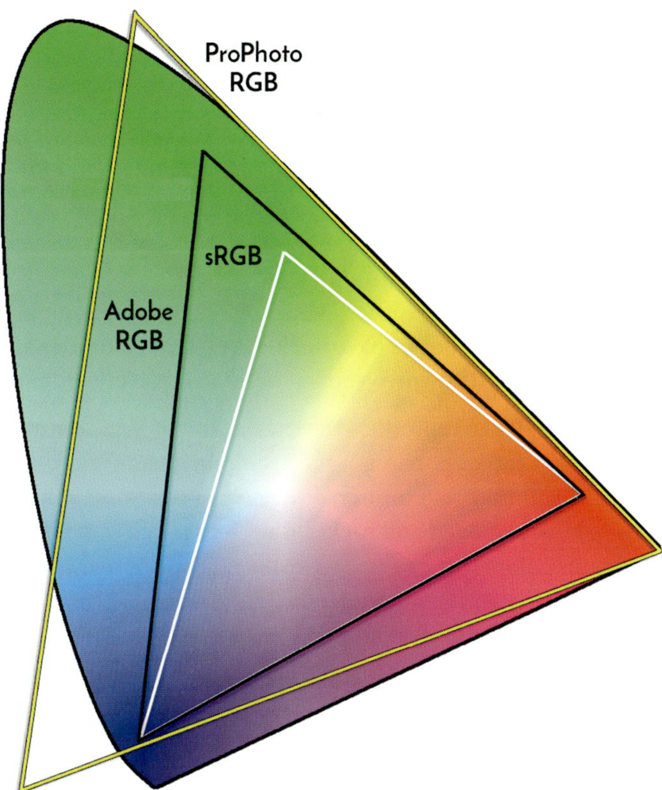

Figure 5.22 The outer curved figure shows all the colors we can see; the outlines show the boundaries of Adobe RGB (black triangle), sRGB (white triangle), and ProPhoto RGB (yellow triangle).

photos to 16-bit ProPhoto format using Adobe Camera RAW when you import RAW photos into an image editor. Converting your files won't actually provide you with a larger color gamut, however, even though ProPhoto encompasses virtually all the colors we can see (and some we can't), giving advanced photographers better tools to work with in processing their photos. It potentially has richer reds, greens, and blues, although, as you can see from the figure, its green and blue primaries are imaginary (they extend outside the visible color gamut). Those with exacting standards need not use a commercial printing service if they want to explore ProPhoto RGB: many inkjet printers can handle cyans, magentas, and yellows that extend outside the Adobe RGB gamut.

Regardless of which triangle—or color space—is used, you end up with some combination of 16.8 million different colors that can be used in your photograph. (No one image will contain all 16.8 million!) But, as you can see from the figure, the colors available will be *different*.

Adobe RGB, like ProPhoto RGB, is an expanded color space useful for commercial and professional printing, and it can reproduce a wider range of colors. It can also come in useful if an image is going to be extensively retouched, especially within an advanced image editor, like Adobe Photoshop, which has sophisticated color management capabilities that can be tailored to specific color spaces.

The downside is that Adobe RGB images tend to look less saturated on your Z5 II's display and your computer monitor, and when viewed on those devices, is likely to be significantly different from what you will get if you output the photo to a printer. The best solution is to *profile* your monitor for the Adobe RGB color space to improve your on-screen rendition using widely available color-calibrating hardware and software. Your camera display can't be profiled but is not ideal for evaluating color while shooting anyway.

Of course, because Adobe RGB has that wider color gamut than sRGB, it can be your best choice if you will be printing JPEG images on an inkjet printer or a high-end digital printer. You should use the same color space setting in your image-editing software, typically using a color management profile. To that end, you'll need to investigate the wonderful world of *color management*, which uses hardware and software tools to match or *calibrate* all your devices, as closely as possible, so that what you see more closely resembles what you capture, what you see on your computer display, and what ends up on a printed hardcopy. Entire books have been devoted to color management, and most of what you need to know doesn't directly involve your camera, so I won't detail the nuts and bolts here.

While both Adobe RGB and sRGB can reproduce the exact same 16.8 million absolute colors, Adobe RGB spreads those colors over a larger portion of the visible spectrum, as you can see in the figure. Think of a box of crayons (the jumbo 16.8 million crayon variety). Some of the basic crayons from the original sRGB set have been removed and replaced with new hues not contained in the original box. Your "new" box contains colors that can't be reproduced by your computer monitor, but which work just fine with a commercial printing press. For example, Adobe RGB has more "crayons" available in the cyan-green portion of the box, compared to sRGB, which is unlikely to be an advantage unless your image's final destination are the cyan, magenta, yellow, and black inks of a printing press.

You might actually prefer sRGB as it is well suited for the range of colors that can be displayed on a computer screen and viewed over the Internet. If you plan to take your image file to a retailer's kiosk for printing, sRGB is your best choice, because those automated output devices are calibrated for the sRGB color space that consumers use.

If you plan to use RAW+JPEG for most of your photos, go ahead and set sRGB as your color space. You'll end up with JPEGs suitable for output on your own printer, but you can still extract an Adobe RGB version from the RAW file at any time. It's like shooting two different color spaces at once—sRGB and Adobe RGB—and getting the best of both worlds.

Active D-Lighting

Options: Auto, Extra High, High, Normal, Low, Off (default)

My preference: Off

Active D-Lighting is a feature that improves the rendition of detail in highlights and shadows when you're photographing high-contrast scenes. It's closely related to, and should not be confused with, *D-Lighting*, which is a "non-active" internal retouching option located in the Retouch options in the Playback version of the *i* menu (and described in Chapter 8). (Retouch was a top-level menu tab in earlier Nikon Z-series cameras, up through the Z7 II and Z6 II.)

Active D-Lighting, unlike Retouch menu D-Lighting post-processing, applies its tonal improvements *while you are actually taking the photo.* That's good news and bad news. It means that, if you're taking photos in a contrasty environment, Active D-Lighting can automatically improve the apparent dynamic range of your image as you shoot, without additional effort on your part. However, the process does take some time, and you'll need to disable the feature once you leave the high-contrast lighting behind. You wouldn't want to use Active D-Lighting for continuous shooting of sports subjects, for example.

This entry gives you six choices: Auto, Extra High, High, Normal, Low, and the default, Off. (**Note:** The Retouch version has only Extra High 1, Extra High 2, High, Normal, and Low options.) You may need to experiment with the feature a little to discover how much D-Lighting you can apply to a high-contrast image before the shadows start to darken objectionably. Figure 5.23 shows a "before-and-after" example of Active D-Lighting applied to improve shadow detail. By the time the sample images shown have been half-toned and rendered to the printed page, the differences may be fairly subtle.

For best results, use the Matrix metering mode, so the Active D-Lighting feature can work with a full range of exposure information from multiple points in the image. Active D-Lighting works its magic by subtly *underexposing* your image so that details in the highlights (which would normally be overexposed and become featureless white pixels) are not lost. At the same time, it adjusts the values of pixels located in midtone and shadow areas, so they don't become too dark because of the underexposure. Highlight tones will be preserved, while shadows will eventually be allowed to go

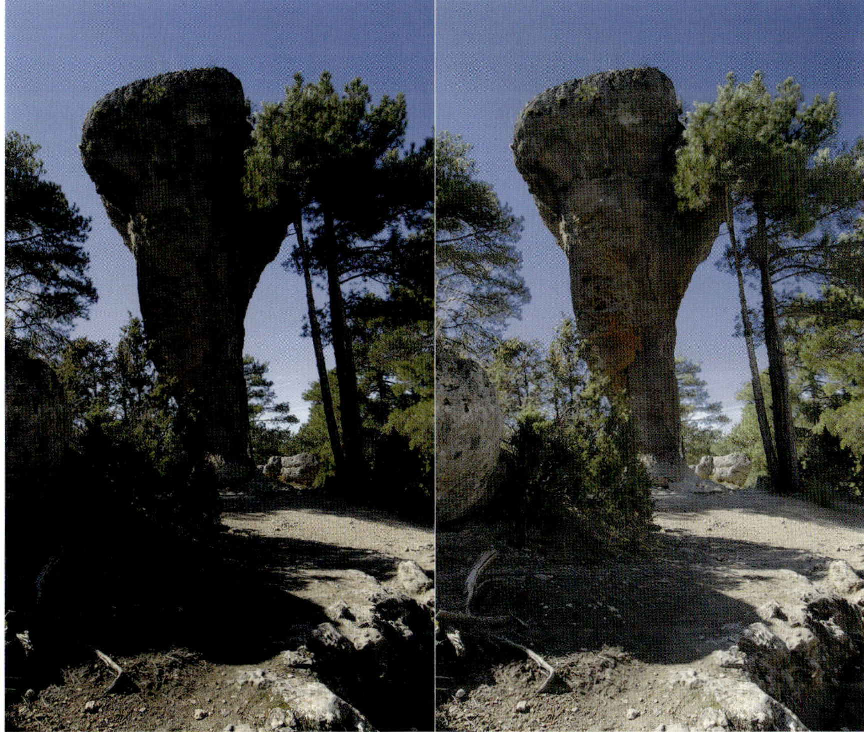

Figure 5.23 No Active D-Lighting (left); and Extra High (right).

dark more readily. Bright beach or snow scenes, especially those with few shadows (think high noon, when the shadows are smaller) can benefit from using Active D-Lighting.

It's important to *always* keep in mind that Active D-Lighting not only adjusts the contrast automatically of your image, it modifies exposure for both existing light and flash as well, as I've noted. The amount of exposure adjustment varies, depending on the level you select, as shown in Table 5.3.

TABLE 5.3 Active D-Lighting Adjustments

SETTING	AMBIENT EXPOSURE ADJUSTMENT	FLASH EXPOSURE ADJUSTMENT
Auto	Exposure calculated based on Matrix metering	Exposure calculated based on Matrix metering
Extra High	−1 stop	−1 stop (or more)
High	−2/3 stop	−1 stop
Normal	−1/3 stop	−2/3 stop
Low	No adjustment	−1/3 stop

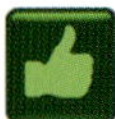

TIP Active D-Lighting cannot be used at ISO Hi 0.3 to Hi 1.7. Nikon warns that its use may create noise as random bright pixels, fog, or lines, with uneven shading sometimes visible. In Manual exposure mode, the Auto mode just applies −1/3 and −2/3 stop adjustments to ambient light and flash (respectively).

Nikon gives you a lot of flexibility in using Active D-Lighting. You can choose the setting yourself, or let the camera *vary* the amount of tweaking by using Active D-Lighting Bracketing, as described in Chapter 2. You'll find this is a useful feature, if used with caution.

Long Exposure NR

Options: Off (default), On

My preference: Off. I prefer to apply noise reduction when processing the RAW file.

Visual noise is that awful graininess caused by long exposures and high ISO settings, and which shows up as multicolored specks in images. This setting helps you manage the kind of noise caused by lengthy exposure times. In some ways, noise is like the excessive grain found in some high-speed photographic films. However, while photographic grain is sometimes used as a special effect, it's rarely desirable in a digital photograph. There are easier ways to add texture to your photos.

Some noise is created when you're using shutter speeds longer than one second to create a longer exposure. Extended exposure times allow more photons to reach the sensor but increase the likelihood that some photosites will react randomly even though not struck by a particle of light. Moreover, as the sensor remains switched on for the longer exposure, it heats up, and this heat can be mistakenly recorded as if it were a barrage of photons. This menu setting can be used to activate the long exposure noise-canceling operation performed by the EXPEED 7 digital signal processors.

Here are your options:

- **Off.** This default setting disables long exposure noise reduction. Use it when you want the maximum amount of detail present in your photograph, even though higher noise levels will result. This setting also eliminates the extra time needed to take a picture caused by the noise-reduction process. If you plan to use only lower ISO settings (thereby reducing the noise caused by ISO amplification), the noise levels produced by longer exposures may be acceptable. For example, you might be shooting a waterfall at ISO 100 with the camera mounted on a tripod, using a neutral-density filter and a long exposure to cause the water to blur. (Try exposures of 2 to 16 seconds, depending on the intensity of the light and how much blur you want.) To maximize detail in the non-moving portions of your photos for the exposures that are one second or longer, you can switch off long exposure noise reduction.

- **On.** When exposures are longer than one second, the camera takes a second, blank exposure to compare that to the first image. Noise (pixels that are bright in a frame that *should* be completely black) in the "dark frame" image is subtracted from your original picture, and only the noise-corrected image is saved to your memory card. Because the noise-reduction process effectively doubles the time required to take a picture, you won't want to use this setting when you're rushed. A message [Performing Noise Reduction] appears on the display during the process. **Reminder:** If you're using Interval Timer Shooting, make sure your interval between shots is longer than your exposure time to avoid interrupting the noise reduction. Moreover, if you turn off the camera before processing is finished, noise reduction will be canceled and only the unprocessed image will be saved.

High ISO NR

Options: High, Normal (default), Low, Off

My preference: Normal

Noise can also be caused by higher ISO sensitivity settings. The camera offers direct settings up to ISO 64000 and extended settings that go even higher, up to Hi 1.7 (the equivalent of ISO 204800). Although it costs you some detail, High ISO noise reduction, which can be set with this menu option, may be a good option in many cases. You can choose Off when you want to preserve detail at the cost of some noise graininess, and the camera will apply High ISO NR only at the highest settings. Or, you can select Low, Normal, and High noise reduction.

The effects of high ISO noise are something like listening to a CD in your car and then rolling down all the windows. You're adding sonic noise to the audio signal, and while increasing the CD player's volume may help a bit, you're still contending with an unfavorable signal-to-noise ratio that probably mutes tones (especially higher treble notes) that you really want to hear.

The same thing happens when the analog image signal is amplified: you're increasing the image information in the signal but boosting the background fuzziness at the same time. Tune in a very faint or distant AM radio station on your car stereo. Then turn up the volume. After a certain point, turning up the volume further no longer helps you hear better. There's a similar point of diminishing returns for digital sensor ISO increases and signal amplification as well.

As the captured information is amplified to produce higher ISO sensitivities, some random noise in the signal is amplified along with the photon information. Increasing the ISO setting of your camera raises the threshold of sensitivity so that fewer and fewer photons are needed to register as an exposed pixel. Yet, that also increases the chances of one of those phantom photons being counted among the real-life light particles, too.

Fortunately, the stacked CMOS sensor and its dual EXPEED 7 digital-processing chips are optimized to produce low noise levels, so ratings as high as ISO 6400 can be used routinely (although there will be some noise, of course), and even ISO 12800 can generate good results. I regularly shoot concerts at ISO 3200, and indoor sports at ISO 6400. I've even been impressed with results I get at ISO 25600 when High ISO NR is applied. Some kinds of subjects may not require this kind of noise cancellation, particularly with images that have a texture of their own that tends to hide or mask the noise.

Vignette Control

Options: High, Normal (default), Low, Off

My preference: Normal

Some lenses may not be up to the challenge of covering the frame evenly, producing darkening in the corners of your images at certain focal lengths, which is called *vignetting*. If you consistently encounter vignetting, this option may help. You can choose from High, Normal, Low, and Off. It's difficult to quantify exactly how much corner-brightening each setting provides. Your best bet is to shoot some blank walls of a single color with lenses that seem to have this problem and try a few at each of the settings. Then select the value that best seems to counter vignetting with your particular lenses. Results with zoom lenses will vary depending on your focal length setting. Only JPEG images are automatically corrected, but the adjustments can also be applied to RAW files during import.

Diffraction Compensation

Options: On (default), Off

My preference: On

Diffraction is a phenomenon that reduces the sharpness of your image when working at smaller f/stops, especially f/22 or f/32 (if your lens has those apertures available). This feature attempts to counteract that effect and works well enough that I leave it enabled by default. Unfortunately, Nikon doesn't deign to tell you what diffraction actually is, or how much it affects your photographs.

Introductory photo courses hammer into budding photographers the idea that smaller f/stops increase sharpness by extending depth-of-field and optimizing the optical effects of particular lenses. In practice, while few lenses are their sharpest wide open, most achieve their maximum sharpness stopped down two or more f/stops; beyond that, diffraction kicks in, and can actually *reduce* apparent sharpness, due to scattering and interference of individual photons as they pass through smaller lens openings. In effect, the edges of your lens aperture affect proportionately more photons as the f/stop grows smaller. The relative amount of space available to pass freely decreases, and the number of collisions of photons with the edges of the aperture increases.

Typically, this happens at a particular f/stop with a particular pixel size, and that f/stop is said to be the diffraction limit for that camera/sensor. Point-and-shoot cameras, with their tiny sensors, may begin to show diffraction effects at f/5.6. The photons striking the edges of the diaphragm are disrupted from their paths and begin to interfere with those passing through the center of the lens. While this phenomenon takes place at all apertures, it is most pronounced at smaller f/stops.

The best analogy I can think of is a pond with two floating docks sticking out into the water, as shown in Figure 5.24. Throw a big rock in the pond, and the ripples pass between the docks relatively smoothly if the structures are relatively far apart (top). Move them closer together (bottom), and some ripples rebound off each dock to interfere with the incoming wavelets. In a lens, smaller apertures produce the same effect.

Other than the Diffraction Compensation algorithms Nikon has included in the camera, there's no "cure" for diffraction-limited images, other than to use larger f/stops, or to apply some sharpening of the image in your editor (which is likely to be a losing cause). It is important, then, to be aware of the effects of diffraction on images captured with the camera and take them into account before choosing a small aperture.

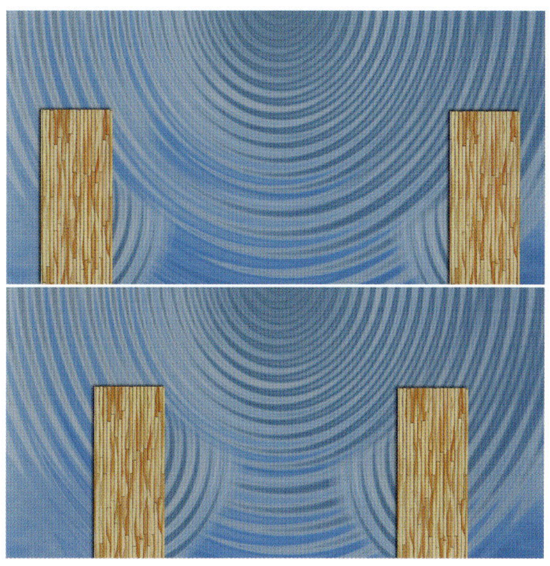

Figure 5.24 Diffraction interference can be visualized as ripples on a lake.

Auto Distortion Control

Options: On (default), Off

My preference: On

Wide-angle lenses are prone to barrel distortion, in which straight lines appear to bow outward, especially near the edges of the frame. Telephoto lenses often have the opposite problem: lines may bend inward, producing pincushion distortion. Both of these types of distortion can be easily corrected in your image editor, but your camera's digital image processing chip has similar algorithms built in and can do the job for you. Your choices are easy: just select On or Off to enable or disable this feature. Note that if you have a Z-mount lens attached, On is chosen by default and this menu entry is grayed out and unavailable; it is used primarily with the FTZ adapters.

For the process to work, the lenses must be of a type that can communicate electronically with the camera to let the camera know what type of lens it is working with. All Z-mount lenses can supply the needed information (so turning the feature off is disabled), but if you're using a non-Z-mount lens with an FTZ adapter, you should be working with a G- or D-type optic. The camera will warp the photo before saving it to your memory card, cropping a bit if necessary, to exclude some areas of the image.

Skin Softening

Options: High, Normal, Low, Off (default)

My preference: N/A

This is the first entry on the next page of the Photo Shooting menu. (See Figure 5.25.) Nikon is putting your camera's face recognition prowess to work with an optional complexion-flattering feature that removes texture from portrait shots of humans. The camera can detect and process up to three subjects, using High, Normal, or Low levels of softening. You can also disable the feature by selecting Off. You can specify one level here for stills, and a different level in the Video Recording menu for videos.

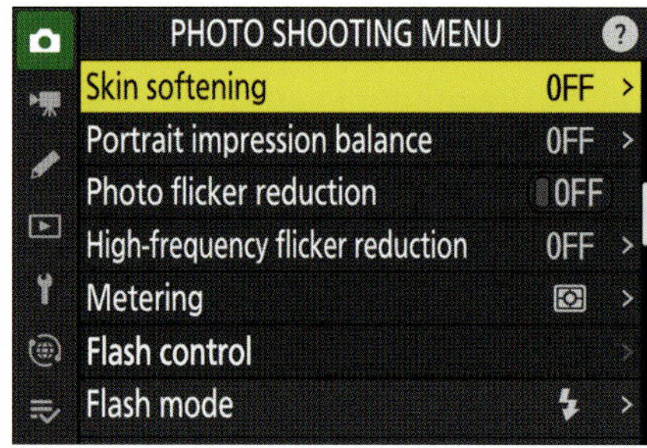

Figure 5.25 The next screen of the Photo Shooting menu.

You don't need to select People or Auto under the AF Subject Detection options entry (discussed later in this chapter). If you let the camera choose the focus point by selecting Auto-area AF as your AF-area mode, left and right triangles will flank the focus point chosen. The left/right directional controls can be used to move from one subject to another.

Portrait Impression Balance

Options: Mode 1, Mode 2, Mode 3, Off (default)

My preference: Use as needed

This entry allows you to create up to three separate profiles that specify magenta/amber-yellow color bias (greens and blues are not affected) and set a brightness level to be used when shooting portraits. To create a specific balance, just follow these steps:

1. **Access this entry.** Navigate to the Portrait Impression Balance entry in the Photo Shooting menu.

2. **Select Mode 1, 2, or 3.** Highlight the mode you want to use/define and press the right directional button. (See Figure 5.26, left.)

Figure 5.26 Customizing a Portrait Impression Balance.

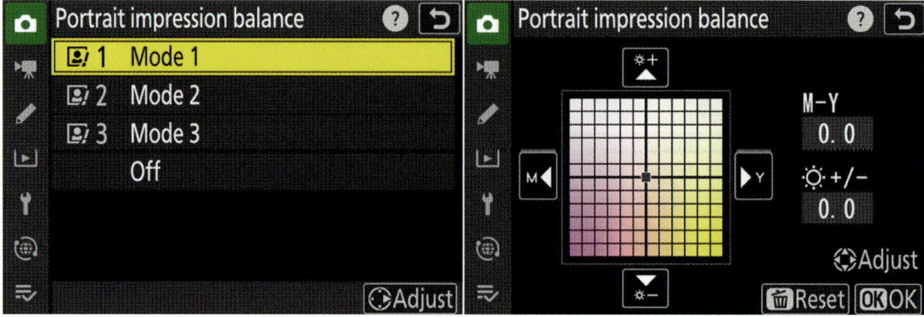

3. **Adjust color bias and/or brightness.** When the screen shown in Figure 5.26, right, appears, use the directional controls to move the setting point from the center. Up/down adjusts brightness, while left/right moves the point along the magenta/amber-yellow axis.

4. **Exit.** Press OK to confirm and exit, or the Trash button to cancel your adjustments. Modes that have been changed from the default value will be marked with an asterisk on the display.

This feature is not available when Monochrome, Flat Monochrome, Deep Monochrome, or Creative Picture Controls are active, nor when Monochrome is selected for Set Picture Control (HLG), as described earlier.

Photo Flicker Reduction

Options: On, Off (default)

My preference: Use as needed

You've been living with flickering artificial illumination all your life and never noticed it. Old-fashioned incandescent lights using 60 Hz (Hertz) circuits flicker at 100 to 120 cycles per second but change their intensity only by a few percent. That's generally not enough to cause discomfort or affect photography. Other types, such as fluorescent and mercury-vapor sources, however, can produce banding, flickering, or alternate light/dark exposures.

Novice sports photographers often ask me why shots they take in certain gymnasiums or arenas have inconsistent exposure, wildly varying color, or banding. The answer is that certain types of artificial lighting have a much more pronounced blinking cycle at 120 Hz in the US and 100 Hz in most other countries. That more extreme flickering is still virtually imperceptible to the eye but can be captured by the camera if you take a picture using a shutter speed faster than 1/125th second.

This setting, when enabled, detects the light source's blinking frequency (it's optimized for 100 Hz to 120 Hz), and takes the picture the moment when the flicker has the least effect on the final image. If you've been using digital cameras for a long time, you may remember there was a nagging problem called *shutter lag,* the delay between when the shutter release was pressed all the way down and when the picture was actually taken. Flicker reduction brings shutter lag back, but for a positive reason.

This flicker reduction feature uses the exposure meter to detect light flicker in the 100 Hz and 120 Hz frequencies. When enabled, the camera delays shutter release timing a tiny bit to avoid the "dim" cycle of the light source and giving you a frame that's evenly lit and fully illuminated. If you're taking photos continuously (a common mode when capturing sports), the camera adjusts both the release timing and frame rate so you can capture each shot during the light source's maximum output. You may experience that slight shutter release time lag as the camera "waits" for the proper instant, and your continuous shooting rate may be reduced, which makes this setting a necessary evil for sports and other activities involving action.

When flicker is detected, a green dot will appear next to the Flicker icon in the shooting display, which will briefly go dark when the shutter is triggered. There is an exception for Continuous

High-Speed+ mode; the display will darken only after the first shot in a sequence, and the frame rate will be prioritized.

The feature may not work well for scenes with dark backgrounds, decorative or especially bright lighting, and is not effective when making Bulb or Time exposures.

High-Frequency Flicker Reduction

Options: On (Shutter speed fine tuning), Off (default)

My preference: Off

While the Photo Flicker Reduction entry described above does a good job with most light sources, some newer types of lighting, including higher-quality LED lamps, flicker with lower intensities and much higher frequencies, and require more advanced correction. This setting allows fine-tuning the shutter speed in Shutter-priority or Manual exposure modes so that it syncs up with the cycle of flickering light sources to reduce or eliminate those undesirable banding effects. Shutter speeds between 1/30th and 1/8000th second can be fine-tuned when Auto or Mechanical shutter Type is specified using Custom Setting d6; when electronic front-curtain shutter is used, the top adjustable speed is 1/2000th second. **Note:** This adjustment produces "odd" fractional shutter speeds, like 1/250.3 second that confound those who don't use this feature, or don't use it frequently enough to realize why they are suddenly seeing these speeds when they accidentally (or even intentionally) invoke high-frequency flicker reduction. Most online forums feature at least a few posts a week about this from panicked photographers who prefer trial-and-error (or error-and-error) to actually reading the manual.

Here's how to use High-Frequency Flicker Reduction:

1. **Enable High-Frequency Flicker Reduction.** If you suspect your scene has LED illumination and want to use S or M exposure modes, navigate to this entry and turn this feature on.
2. **Take sample image.** Capture a sample image and review it in magnified Playback mode and look for banding.
3. **Fine-tune shutter speed.** Examine your scene through the viewfinder, pressing the Magnify button to zoom in.
4. **Adjust shutter speed.** Rotate the command dial until the banding disappears. The shutter speed display will change in smaller 1/96th-stop increments. For example, instead of switching from 1/250th to 1/320th second, successive clicks will take you to 1/250.5 to 1/252.3 to 1/254.2 to 1/256th second, and so on. You can fine-tune your shutter speed in the range between 1/8000th and 1/30th second.
5. **Take new sample image.** Confirm that your adjustment has worked by taking and examining a new sample image of your scene.
6. **Adjustment is "sticky."** Your new shutter speed will remain if you turn the camera off and on again. Should you switch to an exposure mode other than M or S, normal shutter speed increments will return in those modes, but your fine-tuned setting will be restored when you switch back to M or S. Turn High-Frequency Flicker Reduction off to revert to normal speed selection in those modes.

Metering

Options: Matrix (default), Center-weighted, Spot, Highlight-weighted metering

My preference: Matrix

This menu entry is a slower alternative to setting the metering mode using the Z5 II's *i* menu. It exists primarily so you can assign this menu entry to a custom key using the Custom Setting f2: Custom Controls menu entry (explained in Chapter 7).

For example, if you tend to change metering mode frequently, even a visit to the *i* menu can be bothersome. Define, say, a button to Metering, and each time you press that button you'll be able to rotate the command dial to flip among the four choices. Note that you can also define a button to immediately switch to a specific metering mode, so you can, for example, set Matrix metering as your default mode, then toggle to Spot metering while holding down the defined button.

I explained how to use each of these metering modes in Chapter 2 and won't repeat that information here.

Flash Control

Options: Flash control mode: TTL (default), Manual; Wireless flash options; Group flash options

My preference: N/A

Compatible flashes include the Nikon SB-500, SB-400, or SB-300 Speedlights, but *not* the SB-5000, which *is* compatible with unified flash control on some other Z-series models. I explained how to use the available options in Chapter 4 and will not duplicate that information here. You must make adjustments for the SB-5000, as well as all other Nikon electronic flash units, including the SB-600, SB-700, SB-800, SB-900, and SB-910 using the controls on the flash itself.

Before you howl "planned obsolescence!" you should know that *all* Nikon pro bodies that lacked an external flash have *always* required making most settings on the optional flash. The Flash Control feature is a relatively recent addition to the Nikon line, made possible by features built into the (fairly) recent flash units cited, so you're actually gaining capability. If you connect any of the other Speedlights (I own all of them, and I tried), the Flash Control entry is grayed out.

Flash Mode

Options: Fill Flash (default), Red-eye Reduction, Slow Sync, Slow Sync+Red-eye, Rear-curtain Sync, Flash Off

My preference: N/A

This setting specifies whether the camera uses fill flash, red-eye reduction, rear-curtain sync, or disables the flash entirely. I explained when and why to use each of these in Chapter 4 and won't repeat that information here.

Flash Compensation

Options: −3.0 to +1.0 stops of exposure (default: 0.0)

My preference: N/A

The Z5 II has this separate entry for setting flash exposure compensation, the first entry on the next page of the Photo Shooting menu (see Figure 5.27). You can use flash exposure compensation to adjust the flash output to balance the brightness of the main subject illuminated by the flash, compared to the background. Don't confuse this entry with Custom Setting e3: Exposure Compensation for Flash (described in Chapter 7), which tells the camera to apply flash exposure compensation to the background only, or to the entire frame. The two options work together to let you effectively balance your flash output between the two.

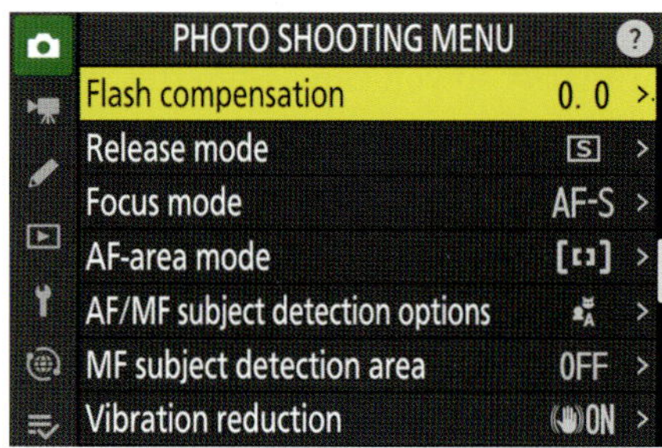

Figure 5.27 The next page of the Photo Shooting menu.

Release Mode

Options: Single Frame (default), Continuous L, Continuous H, Continuous H (extended), C15, C30, Self-timer

My preference: N/A

This entry is a slower alternative to using the Release mode button on the upper-left corner of the back of the camera to switch from one release mode to another, as described in Chapter 1.

Focus Mode

Options: AF-A (default), AF-S, AF-C, MF

My preference: N/A

This entry is a slower alternative to using the *i* menu to switch from one focus mode to another, as explained in Chapter 3. It can be assigned to a custom key if you need fast access to this setting.

AF-Area Mode

Options: Pinpoint AF, Single-point AF, Dynamic-area AF (Small, Medium, Large), Wide-area AF (Small, Large, C1, C2), 3D-tracking, Auto-area AF (default)

My preference: N/A

You can choose the AF-area mode to be used. I described AF-area selection in Chapter 3 and won't repeat my advice here. Like several entries discussed above, it duplicates its *i* menu counterpart and by default is assigned to the Fn2 button for direct access. This menu entry is a slower alternative to using the *i* menu to switch from one focus mode to another.

AF/MF Subject Detection Options

Options: Auto (default), People, Animal, Birds, Vehicle, Airplanes, Subject Detection Off

My preference: Auto

You can set the priority for the type of subject the camera will look for during autofocus, using an amazing range of types. Subject detection is possible when any of the Wide-area AF modes (Small, Large, Custom 1, Custom 2), 3D-tracking, or Auto-area AF are active. You can set separate priorities for detection in the Photo Shooting and Video Recording menus. I explained subject detection in detail in Chapter 3 and won't duplicate that information here.

MF Subject Detection Area

Options: All, Wide (Large), Wide (Small), Manual Focus Subject Detection Off (default)

My preference: N/A

Choose All to allow subject detection in all areas of the frame during manual focus operations. If more than one subject is found, the initial target will have a gray box around it. You can move to a different subject by pressing the left/right directional controls. Choose Wide (Large) or Wide (Small) to confine subject detection to the current focus area.

Vibration Reduction

Options: On (or Normal) (default), Spt (Sport), Off

My preference: N/A

Use this setting to enable vibration reduction built into some lenses, a great feature that counters camera/photographer shake. The VR options may vary depending on which lens you are using. When VR is enabled, an indicator appears at the left side of the viewfinder or LCD monitor when using the main shooting screen. Use On (or Normal; the nomenclature varies depending on the lens) for subjects that are not moving to counter camera shake or photographer jitteriness. The Sport setting is recommended for fast and unpredictably moving subjects, especially if you're panning the camera to follow their movements. In that case, in Sport mode, the camera's vibration reduction ignores side-to-side movement and corrects only camera shake in other directions. It's a good choice if your Z5 II is mounted on a monopod. Sport mode also doesn't re-center the VR elements between shots, allowing for faster response.

Use Off if the camera is locked down on a tripod, or if you don't need it and want to conserve the small percent reduction in battery life that VR produces. If you will be swiveling the camera on the tripod or using a monopod, then turning VR off is not required (use Sport mode, as I suggested). You can also use F-mount lenses with an FTZ adapter, which may include their own vibration reduction. The switches on the adapted lens overrides any setting you make here.

Link VR to Focus Point

Options: On (default), Off

My preference: N/A

This entry is the first on the last page of the Photo Shoot-ing menu. (See Figure 5.28.) Your Z5 II is smart enough to know how to adjust its vibration reduction to optimize image blur (from camera movement) at the current focus point. The VR can't be previewed on the display before the picture is taken; it's applied only when the shutter release is pressed down all the way. That's because, prior to that action, the focus point may change (especially in AF-C focus mode). It's enabled by default, but you can turn it off here.

Note: Although enabled, blur minimalization will be applied to the center of the frame instead of the current focus point if you are using a Z-mount lens that has its own built-in VR. Synchro VR overrides this entry. The center of the frame will also be used during video recording or in Auto-area AF mode if multiple focus points are displayed.

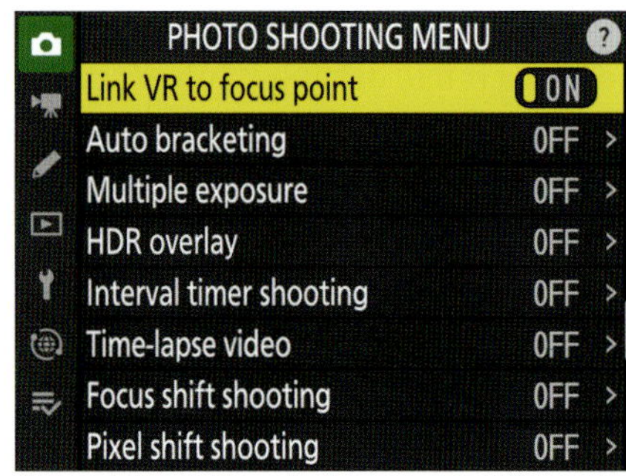

Figure 5.28 The last page of the Photo Shooting menu.

Auto Bracketing

Options: Auto Bracketing: Off (default), On; Auto Bracketing Set (default: AE & Flash Bracketing), Number of Shots (default: 3), Increment (default: 1.0), Amount (ADL bracketing only)

My preference: N/A

This setting allows you to set up bracketing, a useful technique explained in detail in Chapter 3. I won't repeat the step-by-step instructions here. To recap, your options are as follows:

- **Auto Bracketing On/Off.** Enable or disable bracketing.
- **Auto Bracketing Set.** Autoexposure and Flash bracketing, Autoexposure Bracketing (only), Flash bracketing (only), White balance bracketing, Active D-Lighting bracketing.
- **Number of Shots.** Use the left/right directional controls or the touch screen to specify the number of shots in your bracket set: 3, 5, 7, or 9.
- **Increment.** The size of the increments specified in Custom Setting b2: EV Steps for Exposure Control (1/3, 1/2, 1 stop) apply here.
- **Amount (ADL bracketing only).** If you're doing Active D-Lighting bracketing, you can select up to five shots, which will determine the amount of ADL applied to each in the range Off, Low, Normal, High, and High*.

Multiple Exposure

Options: Multiple Exposure Mode: On (Series), On (Single Photo), Off; Number of Shots: 2 to 10; Overlay Mode: Add, Average, Lighten, Darken; Save Individual Pictures (RAW): On, Off; Overlay Shooting: On, Off; Select First Exposure (RAW)

My preference: Multiple Exposure Mode: On (Series); Number of Shots/Overlay Mode, varies

This option lets you combine from 2 to 10 exposures into one image without the need for an image editor such as Photoshop, and it can be an entertaining way to return to those thrilling days of yesteryear, when complex photos were created in the camera itself. In truth, prior to the digital age, multiple exposures were a cool, groovy, far-out, hep/hip, phat, sick, fabulous way of producing composite images. Today, it's more common to take the lazy way out, snap two or more pictures, and then assemble them in an image editor like Photoshop.

Your Nikon Z5 II's Retouch features, available from the Playback version of the *i* menu, can serve as an in-camera replacement for Photoshop, allowing you to combine two images using the Overlay mode (Add) option. As many as 10 shots can be combined using the Motion Blend option of the Retouch entry in the Playback *i* menu. The advantage of post-processing in the camera is that you can preview your effect before creating a final image. However, the "live" features of the Multiple Exposure entry are more versatile.

You can turn the Multiple Exposure feature off, direct the camera to continue taking multiple exposures until you turn it off (Series), or revert to non-multiple exposure mode after taking one picture (Single Photo). You can elect to keep all exposures, or discard all but the combined multiple exposure, and use a RAW image on your memory card as the base photo on which subsequent pictures are overlaid.

You should keep in mind that some of Nikon's previous implementations of multiple exposure allowed you to choose between combining the exposures of each image to produce the final shot or dividing the exposures equally among the shots. The Z5 II has additional options and calls the array of choices "Overlay mode," described below.

Once you've selected an Overlay mode, you can turn the use of overlays on or off using the Overlay Shooting option in the sub-menu. The camera has one additional feature, Save Individual Pictures (RAW), which, as you might expect, tells the camera to save the individual photos used to create the multiple exposure in separate RAW files.

This capability can be useful in several ways. First, you may find that one specific frame of your multiple exposure might have made an excellent stand-alone image in its own right. When Save Individual Pictures (RAW) is active, you can retrieve that frame and use it as you like. In addition, having all the shots of the multiple exposure available means you can use them to create your own multi-shot image in Photoshop or your favorite image editor. I do this most often when I discover that one frame doesn't "work" for a given multiple exposure image, but the others meld together well. I can create my own version manually, adjusting brightness, contrast, or other parameters as I go, to "fine-tune" what started out as an automated multiple exposure.

Also useful is the Select First Exposure (RAW) option. If you want to overlay all your subsequent multiple exposures on top of an existing image already on your memory card (say, a background that you'd like to merge with your sequence), you can choose this setting. You'll be taken to the camera's standard image selection screen and offered the choice of any RAW image available on your card. This is a cool way of replacing boring one-color backgrounds with something more interesting.

To take your own multiple exposures, just follow these steps (although it's probably a good idea to do a little planning and maybe even some sketching of a layout on paper first, if that's possible):

1. **Choose capture sequence.** There are two ways to capture multiple exposure images in sequence:
   - **Individual frames.** Each image in the sequence is taken one at a time when you specify, either by pressing the shutter release in Single shot mode, or by using the self-timer. You'd want to use this mode to combine subjects precisely as you frame them individually.
   - **With one press of shutter release.** Use Continuous Low or Continuous High release modes and the camera will expose all images in the sequence one after another. You'd use this mode to track a moving subject.

2. **Activate the feature.** Choose Multiple Exposure from the Photo Shooting menu. (See Figure 5.29.)

3. **Choose Multiple Exposure mode.** Select Multiple Exposure mode. A submenu appears with three choices:

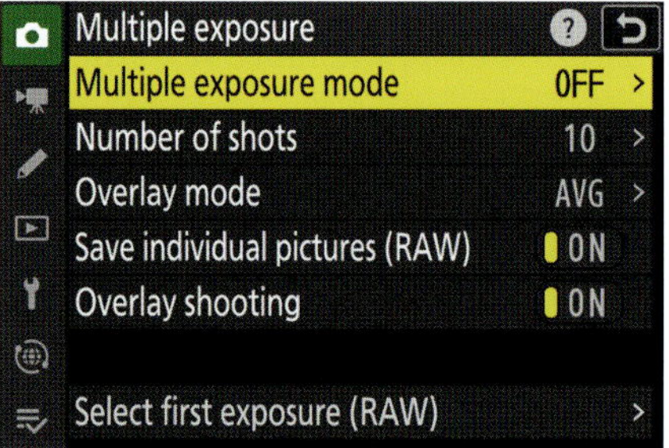

Figure 5.29 The Multiple Exposure menu.

   - **On (series).** The Multiple Exposure feature remains active even after you've taken a complete set of exposures for the number of shots you specified. Use this if you want to shoot several multiple exposures in a row. Remember to turn it off when you're done.
   - **On (single photo).** Once you've taken a single set of multiple exposures, the feature turns itself off. In this mode, when using Continuous Low or Continuous High, the camera will capture one sequence and then return to non-multiple exposure mode.
   - **Off.** Use this option to cancel multiple exposures.

4. **Choose exposures per frame.** Select Number of Shots, choose a value from 2 to 10 with the directional controls, and press OK.

5. **Specify ratio of exposure between frames.** Choose Overlay Mode and select Add, Average, Lighten, or Darken:
   - **Add.** In this mode, each new exposure is added to the previous shots. I use this when photographing a subject that is moving against a dark background. A series of renditions, each fully exposed, appears in the overlaid image to track the subject's movement.
   - **Average.** In this mode, the camera divides the overall exposure by the number of shots in the series and gives each shot that fraction of the overall exposure. That is, for a four-shot multiple series, the specified exposure for each is set at 1/4 of the total amount. I use this when shooting subjects with a great deal of overlap. (See Figure 5.30, left.)

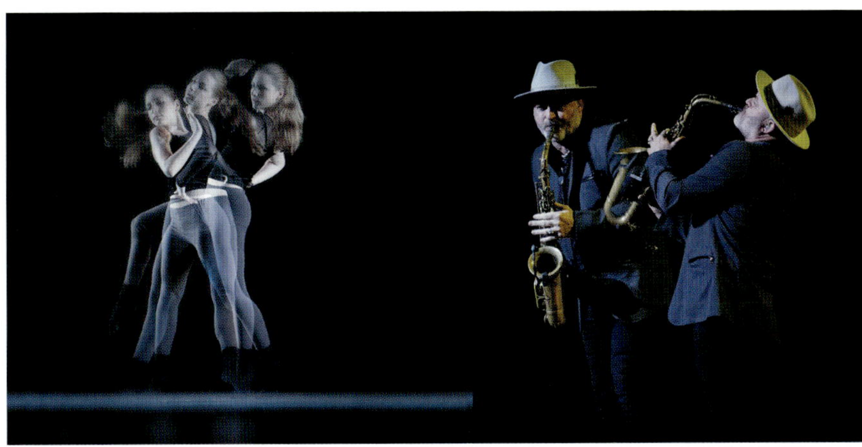

Figure 5.30 Average overlay mode (left) and Add overlay shooting mode (right).

- **Lighten.** The camera compares pixels in the same position in each exposure and uses only the brightest. This effect is similar to the Lighten blending mode in Photoshop, Lightroom, and other image-editing software. Use this to allow the lightest tones of each shot in the series to show through, such as multiple bursts in a fireworks show. The sky will remain dark, but the pyrotechnics will be captured perfectly. You may have to experiment with this setting until you become familiar with what it does to your images.

- **Darken.** Similar to the Lighten blending mode, only just the darkest pixels are saved. You'd use this in situations that are the opposite of those typical of the Add selection. That is, if the background is light, and a darker subject is moving across that background, Darken would provide separate images.

6. **Confirm setting.** Press OK to set the Overlay mode exposure ratio.

7. **Save Individual Pictures (RAW).** Ordinarily, the camera combines all the shots into a single exposure. However, you can ask the camera to save *all* the individual images in the series as RAW files by choosing On in the Save Individual Pictures (RAW) entry. **Note:** The camera is smart enough to save RAW images as requested *even if Image Quality is currently at a JPEG-only setting.* You'll end up with a combined JPEG image, plus the desired RAW versions.

8. **Overlay Shooting.** This setting shouldn't be confused with Overlay mode, described above. If you select On, then each subsequent exposure is superimposed in the previous images on the LCD display as you shoot. That's particularly useful when you're capturing each image individually. For Figure 5.30, right, I shot two images of saxophonist Todd Cooper of the Alan Parsons Project individually, moving the camera slightly between shots to create a collage of sorts. It was easy to do in Live View mode using this overlay feature.

9. **Select First Exposure (RAW).** This is a great feature! You can select an existing RAW image on your memory card and use that as the background for your subsequent multiple exposures. As you capture the individual shots, they will be blended with the background image using the Overlay mode you've selected.

10. **Shoot your multiple exposure set.** In Single shot mode, capture the photo by pressing the shutter-release button multiple times until all the exposures in the series have been taken. When using Continuous Low or Continuous High, the entire series will be shot in a single burst as you hold down the shutter-release button. As each exposure is made, the remaining exposures indicator in the lower-right corner of the frame will indicate which frame is being captured, counting down from r10 to r00, for example. A blinking multiple exposure icon at the right edge of the display vanishes when the series is finished. **Reminder:** You'll need to deactivate the Multiple Exposure feature once you've finished taking a set in On (series) mode, as the setting remains even after the camera has been powered off.

Keep in mind if you wait longer than 30 seconds between any two photos in the series, the sequence will terminate and combine the images taken so far. If you want a longer elapsed time between exposures, go to the Playback menu and make sure On has been specified for Picture Review, and then extend the Standby Timer using Custom Setting c3: Power Off Delay to an appropriate maximum interval. The camera will grant you an additional 30 seconds beyond that. The Multiple Exposure feature will then use the monitor-off delay as its maximum interval between shots.

HDR Overlay

Options: HDR mode: On (Series), On (Single Photo), Off (default); HDR Strength: Auto (default), Extra High, High, Normal, Low; Save Individual Pictures (RAW)

My preference: HDR mode: On (Series); HDR Strength: Auto

I was surprised at how well Nikon has solved the hand-held auto HDR problem, because there are two stumbling blocks that, at least theoretically, should lead to less-than-awesome results. First, when your camera can perform HDR for you on the fly, there is the tendency to put the feature to work under non-optimal conditions; specifically, impromptu hand-held situations. If you've done any traditional HDR, you know that the technique works best when the camera is mounted on a tripod, so that the bracketed exposures are virtually identical except for the exposure itself. Although all HDR software can correct for slight camera movement and align images that are slightly out of register, the results I've gotten have not been great. I expected hand-held HDR to be comparable. However, Nikon's implementation does an excellent job.

The second theoretical weakness of the HDR feature is the limitation of combining just two shots to arrive at the final image. The best traditional HDR photos I've produced have involved at least three shots, and more frequently five or more, each separated by a stop of exposure. The camera takes two shots, total, and combines them. Despite these speed bumps, I've been pleased with my results. I outlined the steps for using HDR Overlay in Chapter 2 and won't repeat them here.

Interval Timer Shooting

Options: Start; Start Options: Choose Start Day and Start Time; Interval; Intervals × Shots/Interval; Exposure Smoothing: On/Off; Electronic Shutter Options: On/Off, Volume; Interval Priority: On/Off; Focus Before Each Shot: On/Off; Options: AE Bracketing, Time-lapse Video, Off; Starting Storage Folder: New Folder, Reset File Numbering

My preference: N/A

The Z5 II's built-in time-lapse photography feature allows you to take pictures for up to 999 intervals in bursts of as many as nine shots, with a delay of up to 24 hours between shots/bursts, and an initial start-up time of as long as 24 hours from the time you activate the feature. That means that if you want to photograph a rosebud opening and would like to photograph the flower once every two minutes over the next 16 hours, you can do that easily. If you like, you can delay the first photo taken by a couple hours, so you don't have to stand there by the camera waiting for the right moment.

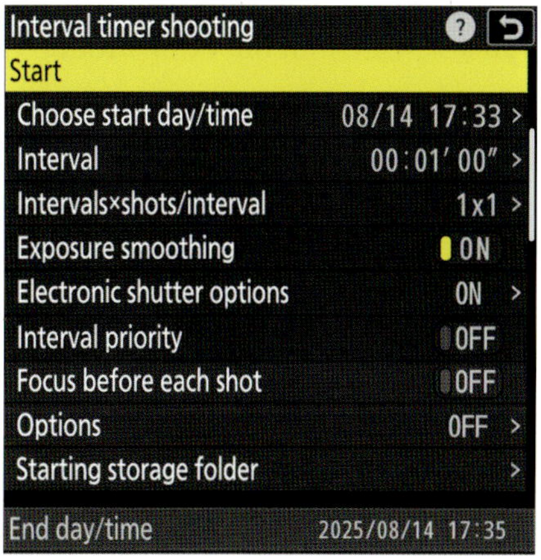

Or you might want to photograph a particular scene every hour for 24 hours to capture, say, a landscape from sunrise to sunset to the following day's sunrise again. I will offer two practical tips right now, in case you want to run out and try interval timer shooting immediately: *use a tripod, and for best results over longer time periods, plan on connecting your camera to an external power source!*

As you can see from the Options listing above and Figure 5.31, the available parameters are numerous, with many additional settings nested in submenus. I described them in detail in Chapter 2 and won't recap here.

Figure 5.31 Interval timer shooting options.

Time-Lapse Video

Options: Start, Interval, Shooting Time, Exposure Smoothing, Electronic Shutter Options, Choose Image Area, Video File Type, Frame Size/Frame Rate, Interval Priority, Focus Before Each Shot, Destination

My preference: None

As I said in Chapter 2, time-lapse videos correspond to interval timer shooting, described previously, but allow shooting video clips instead of still photographs (or a series of still photographs). The camera automatically creates a silent time-lapse video at the frame resolution and rate you specify. Nikon recommends using a white balance other than Auto and covering the eyepiece opening to prevent light from entering the viewfinder and affecting exposure. And, of course, you'll want to use a tripod and either a fully charged battery or optional AC adapter or other power source. I provided instructions for shooting time-lapse videos in Chapter 2 and won't repeat that information here.

Focus Shift Shooting

Options: Start, Number of Shots, Focus Step Width, Interval Until Next Shot, First-Frame Exposure Lock, Electronic Shutter Options, Focus Position Auto Reset, Starting Storage Folder

My preference: N/A

Focus shift/stacking is a great technique that allows combining a series of photos, each taken using a different plane of focus, so that they can be combined in an image editor to produce a single image with greatly enhanced depth-of-field. Macro photographers (in particular) have long used focus stacking in their work. The Focus Shift Shooting feature greatly simplifies capture of the individual shots, which can include up to 300 different images. I covered this feature in detail in Chapter 3 and will not repeat that information here.

Pixel Shift Shooting

Options: Pixel Shift Shooting Mode, Number of Shots, Delay, Interval Until Next Shot
My preference: N/A

If your camera's 24.5MP resolution isn't enough, the Z5 II offers an amazing Pixel Shift shooting capability that can mimic the amount of detail you might expect from a sensor with a whopping 96 megapixels! The limitations: the camera takes 8, 16, or 32 separate pictures that are merged in the free Nikon Studio NX software, and they must be captured with the Z5 II rock-steady on a tripod, and I strongly recommend using a remote release.

The secret behind the pixel-shift process is that your Z5 II doesn't actually have 24MP of resolution in the first place. It does have 24MP worth of pixels, but each pixel can only detect one color—red, green, or blue. When you capture a conventional picture, about 6MP are sensitive *only* to blue light, another 6MP detect only red light, and 12MP are sensitive to green light. Even though each pixel captures only one of the three RGB colors, by examining the values of surrounding pixels, the Z5 II can make a pretty good guess as to the actual color of a particular pixel through an interpolation process called *demosaicing*. The algorithms may tell the camera that a pixel captured by a green-sensitive photosite is probably red or blue instead. This works fairly well, but, as you might think, isn't perfect.

Figure 5.32 shows a small section of a Bayer array, named after Kodak scientist Dr. Bryce Bayer, who patented the technology in 1976. He specified using twice as many green elements as red or blue to simulate human vision, which, in daylight, combines two different types of cells in the retina that are most sensitive to green light. At left, I've superimposed the array's red, green, and blue microfilters over a representation of the photosensitive layer beneath, which is colored gray for the illustration. At right in the figure, I show how the pixels are arranged: every other pixel is green, and the remaining pixels are red or blue, alternating rows.

While each pixel detects only one of the primary colors in ordinary shooting, the pixel-shift process fixes this deficiency by capturing *multiple* images, shifting the sensor slightly between shots so that each photosite has the opportunity to read each of the primary colors in turn. You can choose whether to take 4, 8, 16, or 32 different shots; with the larger number of shots determining the

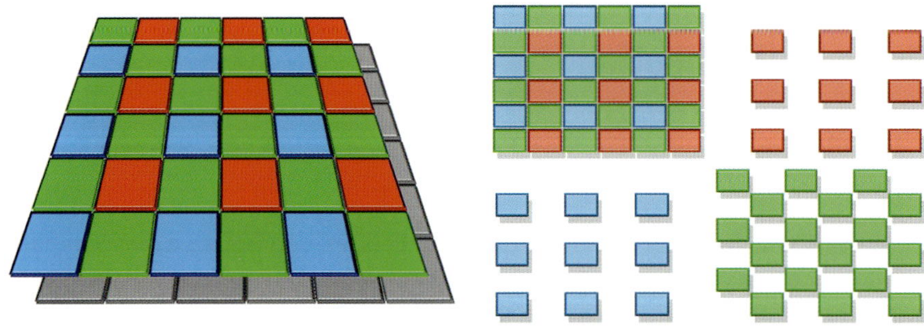

Figure 5.32 A section of a Bayer array (left) and relative distribution of the red, green, and blue filters (right).

amount of shift between individual images and type of image processing performed using Nikon NX Studio:

- **4 shots.** The Z5 II captures four separate exposures which can be processed using Nikon NX Studio to produce a picture with improved color reproduction.
- **8 shots.** A total of 8 shots are taken and processed by NX Studio to produce a photo with improved color and reduced noise.
- **16 shots.** The Z5 II captures 16 images that can be processed to create a higher resolution version with improved color reproduction.
- **32 shots.** Combining the 32 shots captured in this mode gives you a higher resolution image with improved color and reduced noise.

In practice, the Z5 II starts with the first shot, which produces the standard image that results from non-shift mode. Then, the sensor shifts to grab additional images to capture information such that all colors are captured by every photosite. The result is a higher degree of detail without the need to "guess" which colors each pixel represents. With up to 32 shots captured, that's a huge amount of information, prodigious enough that the camera cannot process it internally (and you wouldn't want to wait that long between shots even if it could). So, the NX Studio's software interprets these multiple shots for you, to produce a single image in which every pixel reflects the actual color of your subject. You get more detail and potentially more accurate color at the cost of a little post-processing.

Capturing Your Images

Pixel shift works *only* with non-moving, static subjects, and neither the camera nor subject matter can move *at all* during the sequence of exposures. For that reason, you'll get the best results shooting indoors, as there are many factors outdoors that can cause subject/camera movement, even when a tripod is used. For example, you'd need to pay special attention to foliage; if there is any breeze at all, the leaves on trees will move. Using a high shutter speed may help somewhat, but, like MPG, your actual results may vary considerably between different sets of shots when working outdoors.

The plane of focus must not change, either, so you should use manual focus. The exposure itself should be constant, so I recommend manual exposure when using ambient lighting, as long as the illumination itself remains constant. Outdoors, swiftly moving clouds can cause changes in lighting, and indoors you'll find that fluorescent and other non-incandescent sources flicker slightly. I've found that Nikon's electronic flash units work well, even in automatic exposure mode, and can provide consistent illumination between shots (if you set the interval between them appropriately, as described below).

To capture a pixel-shift image, just follow these steps:

1. **Steady your camera.** Mount your Z5 II on a rock-solid tripod. If possible, use only the legs of the tripod to achieve the shooting elevation you want, and avoid raising the center column. Lock all the tripod's positional controls. If you're using a lightweight tripod, suspend your camera bag or another weight from the center column to steady it. In my tests, I discovered that even almost imperceptible movement (which can be produced simply by pressing the Z5 II's shutter release too vigorously) can ruin a series. The tip-off: a slight amount of blurring in the first shot of a series, or a "ghost" image from ambient light when using flash, compared to the additional exposures, taken after a short delay.

2. **Connect the Z5 II to a remote release device or cable.** You'll want to eliminate any camera shake caused by pressing the shutter release manually.

3. **Update pixel map.** Nikon recommends using the Pixel Mapping feature (described in Chapter 9) to disable any defective pixels before using Pixel Shift.

4. **Power.** Make sure you have a fully charged battery or have connected the camera to an external power source.

5. **Shoot RAW.** NX Studio processes RAW files.

6. **Set exposure and focus manually.** Manually focus to get the sharpest possible image. Your extra resolution is wasted if you haven't focused properly. (Take a test shot, if you want.)

7. **Check your lighting.** Indoors, I use incandescent light or flash instead of fluorescent illumination; the flickering fluorescent lighting causes can produce banding in your image. Keep in mind that softer lighting (such as that produced by umbrellas, soft boxes, diffusers, or bounce lighting) reduces glare but may mask that extra detail you're looking for. More contrasty illumination (generally, direct lighting) can emphasize detail—and also any defects in your subject matter.

8. **Access Pixel Shift feature.** Navigate to the Pixel Shift Shooting entry of the Photo Shooting menu (see Figure 5.33, upper left). Select Pixel Shift Shooting Mode and specify On (Series) or On (Single Photo). (See Figure 5.33, upper right.)

9. **Number of shots.** Choose 4, 8, 16, or 32 shots, as shown center left in the figure. I recommend starting with four-shot sequences to help you master the pixel-shift feature. The exposures are made quickly, and the files are smaller and are combined faster in Nikon NX Studio. You'll rapidly see how and where your technique can be improved.

10. **Delay.** You can select an optional delay of 1 to 10 seconds before capture begins. Select a longer pause if you plan to use flash. Just set the time for the amount of time it takes for your flash to recycle; you can err on the side of caution if using battery-powered units, which may have varying recycle times. (See Figure 5.33, center right.)

11. **Interval between shots.** Use the up/down controls to choose the amount of delay between shots, from 0 to 30 seconds. This default setting of zero will capture all the images continuously, one after another. This is usually your best choice, because it minimizes the chance of even slight movement of your subject between shots. (See Figure 5.33, lower left.)

12. **Trigger the shutter to take your images.** When you've finished making settings, the message shown at lower right in Figure 5.33 appears. Don't touch the camera between shots.

Processing Your Pixel-Shift Exposures

Once you've captured your images, transfer them to your computer and launch the Nikon NX Studio software (which you can download from the Nikon website in your country). Then, just follow these steps:

1. **Navigate to image folder.** In the Folders panel (seen at lower left in Figure 5.34), browse to your images using the directory/folder tree.

2. **Click Picture Shift Merge icon.** I've highlighted it with a green box at upper right in the figure. (The green box does *not* appear on your screen.)

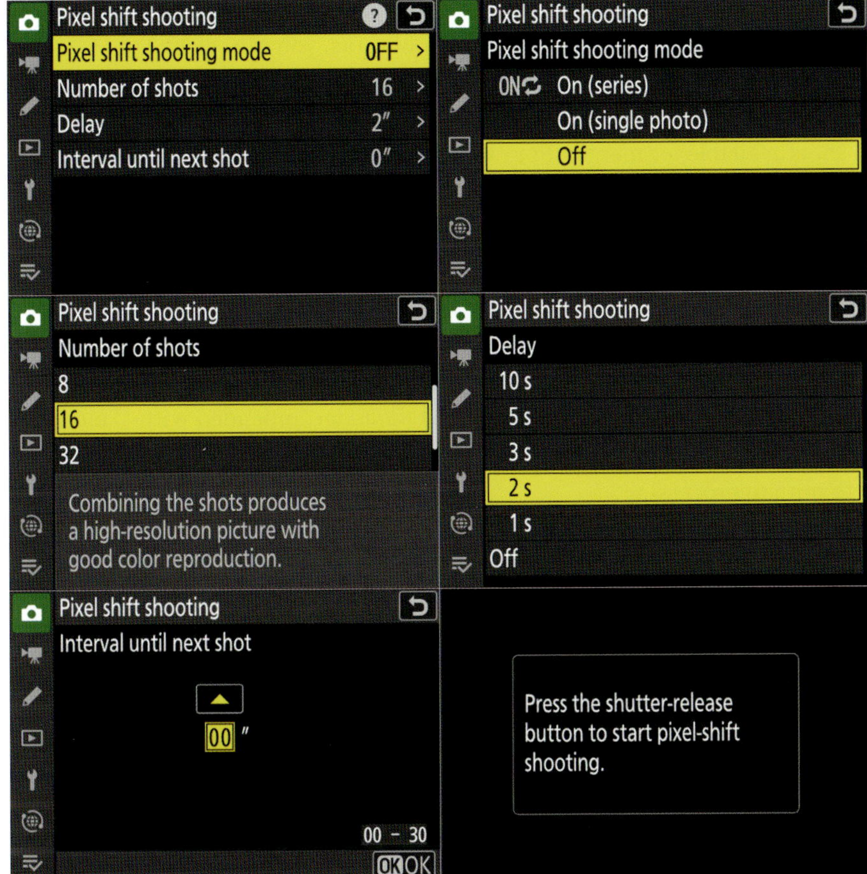

Figure 5.33 Choose Pixel Shift parameters.

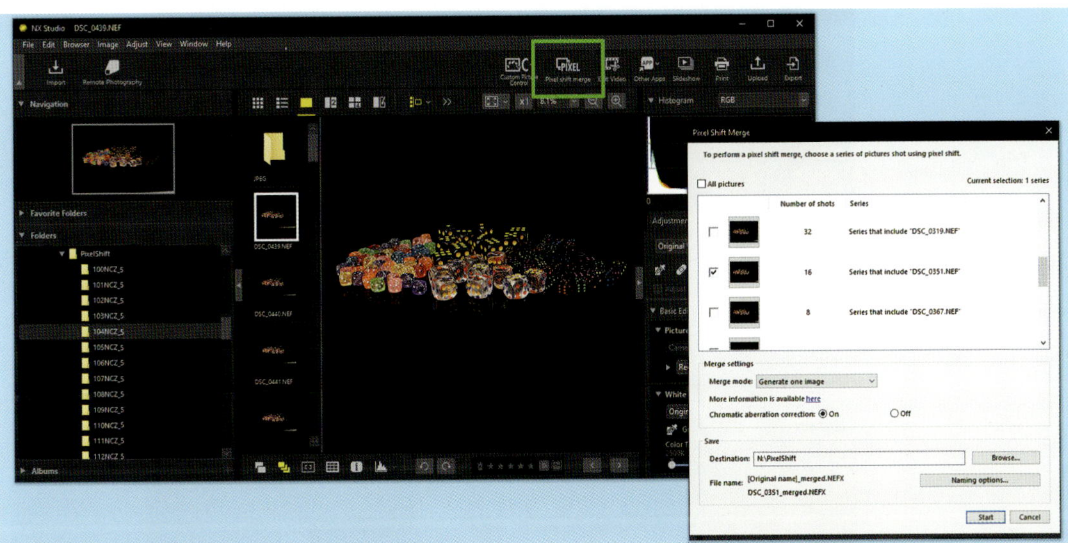

Figure 5.34 Processing the RAW files in Nikon NX Studio.

3. **Choose sequence.** A dialog box, shown at right in the figure, will appear showing the sequences available. For example, if you selected 32 as your number of shots, you can select 32-, 16-, 8-, or 4-shot sequences. If you choose more than one, all will be merged when you proceed.

4. **Select Merge Mode.** Here you choose the number of images to be generated. The number depends on the number of shots available for merger. For example, if you chose 32 Shots you can generate two images from 16 shots each; four images from 8 shots each; or eight images from 4 shots apiece.

5. **Enable/Disable Chromatic Aberration Correction.** You can specify additional processing to reduce chromatic aberration effects if you want.

6. **Destination.** Specify or browse to a destination folder for your merged images.

7. **File Name.** NX Studio will create an .NEFX file (which can be later opened and modified using NX Studio) and give it a name that incorporates the original file name appended with "_merged." You can select a different name structure here.

8. **Begin.** Click Start to initiate processing.

You'll end up with a 96-megapixel image like the one shown at top in Figure 5.35. It's difficult to show the difference on the printed page, but at the bottom of the figure you can see the original image at left and the increased resolution version at right.

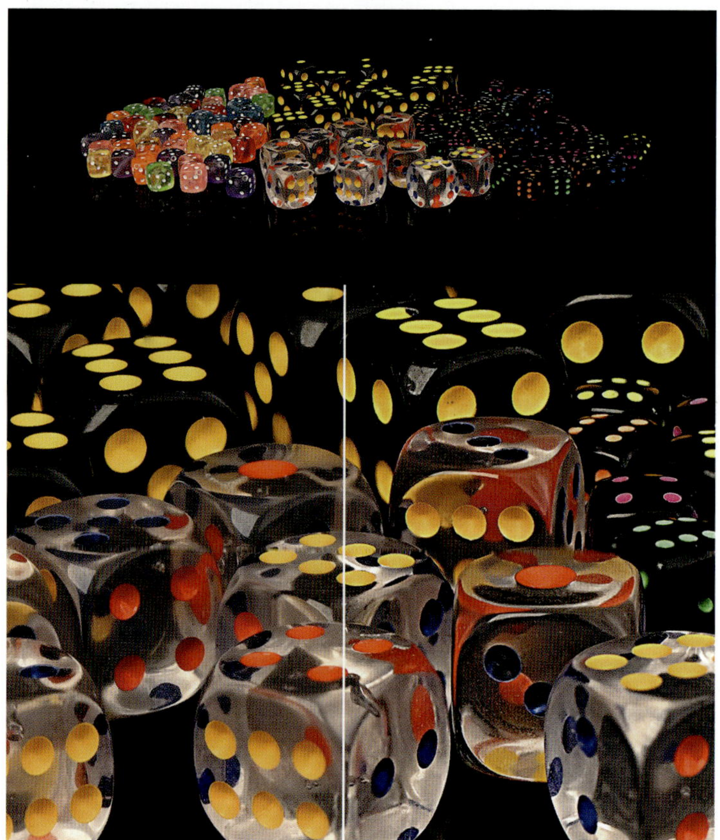

Figure 5.35 The final composite image (top); an enlargement of the original image (lower left); and the pixel-shift version (lower right).

Video Recording Menu 6

Although the main focus of this book is mirrorless still photography, your Z5 II has awesome video capabilities that truly deserve a full book of their own. I'm going to provide an introduction to video recording in Chapter 10, which will have longer explanations of the key options described in this Video Recording menu overview.

Video Recording Menu

Some of the Video Recording menu's entries duplicate the entries in the Photo Shooting menu but apply specifically to video shooting. Others are unique to movie making. For entries that overlap those used for still photography, I'll simply refer to the relevant description that I included in Chapter 5 and won't repeat that information here.

- Reset Video Recording Menu
- Storage Folder
- File Naming
- Destination
- Video File Type
- Frame Size/Frame Rate
- Image Area
- ISO Sensitivity Settings
- White Balance
- Set Picture Control
- Manage Picture Control
- HLG Quality
- Active D-Lighting
- High ISO NR
- Vignette Control
- Diffraction Compensation
- Auto Distortion Control
- Skin Softening
- Portrait Impression Balance
- Video Flicker Reduction
- High-frequency Flicker Reduction
- Metering
- Focus Mode
- AF-Area Mode
- AF/MF Subject Detection Options
- Product Review Mode
- MF Subject Detection Area
- Video Self-Timer
- Vibration Reduction
- Electronic VR
- Microphone Sensitivity
- Attenuator
- Frequency Response
- Wind Noise Reduction
- Mic Jack Plug-in Power
- Headphone Volume
- Timecode
- External Recording Control (HDMI)
- Hi-Res Zoom

Reset Video Recording Menu

Options: Yes, No

My preference: N/A

This setting restores Video Recording menu options (only) to their default values (see Table 6.1). This is the first entry in the Video Recording menu (see Figure 6.1).

Storage Folder

Options: Rename: NZ5_2 (default); Select Folder by Number: 100 (default); Select Folder from List

My preference: I use the Select Folder by Number option frequently to organize files by topic or time frame.

You can specify the name used for folders on your memory card. This entry functions exactly as described in Chapter 5, and changes here will be reflected in the Photo Shooting menu. Basically, this is a duplicate of the still photo shooting version.

File Naming

Options: Choose three-letter prefix; DSC (default)

My preference: Z52

The prefix used for video files (only) can be specified here. This entry functions exactly as described in Chapter 5, but in this case, the prefix you create here will be used only for video files. Any filename you've entered in the Photo Shooting menu will not be affected.

Destination

Options: Slot 1 (default), Slot 2

My preference: N/A

You can select which card slot will be used to store your videos. When you access this entry, the camera will display the length of the video that can be recorded on each card using the current frame size and frame rate settings. The Z5 II does not offer the additional behavior options (such as overflow or backup) available in the Photo Shooting menu.

Video File Type

Options: N-RAW 12-bit (NEV), H.265 10-bit (MOV), H.265 8-bit (MOV) (default), H.264 8-bit (MP4); Choice of SDR/N-Log tone modes for N-RAW and H.265 10-bit file types, plus HLG for H.265

My preference: N/A

Here you can choose from among an array of video file types, color depths, tone modes, and file formats. There's a lot of alphabet soup here, but I'll explain the differences among Nikon's RAW (NEV), MOV, and MP4, explain the three tone modes, and discuss the other video file type parameters in more detail in Chapter 10.

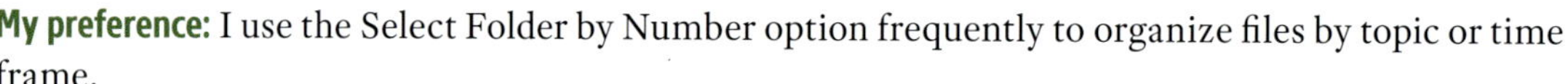

Figure 6.1 The first page of Video Recording menu entries.

TABLE 6.1 Default Video Recording Menu Values

OPTION	DEFAULT	OPTION	DEFAULT
Reset Video Recording Menu	--	Video Flicker Reduction	Auto
Storage Folder		High-Frequency Flicker Reduction	Off
Rename	NZ5_2		
Select Folder by Number	100	Metering	Matrix metering
Select Folder from List	--	Focus Mode	Full-time AF
File Naming	DSC	AF-Area Mode	Auto-area AF
Destination	Slot 1	AF/MF Subject Detection Options	
Video File Type	H.265 8-bit MOV	Subject Detection	Auto
Frame Size/Frame Rate	3840 × 2160; 30p	AF When Subject Not Detected	On
Image Area		Product Review Mode	Off
Choose Image Area	FX	MF Subject Detection Area	MF Subject Detection Off
DX Crop Alert	Off		
ISO Sensitivity Settings		Video self-timer	Off
Maximum Sensitivity	51200	Vibration Reduction	Same as photo settings
Auto ISO Control (Mode M)	On	Electronic VR	Off
ISO Sensitivity (Mode M)	100	Microphone Sensitivity	Auto
White Balance	Same as photo settings	Attenuator	Off
Set Picture Control	Same as photo settings	Frequency Response	Wide range
Manage Picture Control	--	Wind Noise Reduction	Off
HLG Quality		Mic Jack Plug-in Power	On
Quick Sharp	0	Headphone Volume	15
Contrast	0	Timecode	
Saturation	0	Record Timecodes	Off
Hue	0	Count-up Method	Record run
Active D-Lighting	Off	Timecode Origin	--
High ISO NR	Normal	Drop Frame	On
Vignette Control	Normal	External Recording Control (HDMI)	Off
Diffraction Compensation	On		
Auto Distortion Control	On	Hi-Res Zoom	Off
Skin Softening	Same as photo settings		
Portrait Impression Balance	Off		

Frame Size/Frame Rate

Options: 4K (3840 × 2160): 60/50p, 30/25p (default), 24p; Full HD (1920 × 1080): 120/100p, 60/50p, 30/25p, 24p; Slow Motion (1920 × 1080): 30/25p (4X slow motion), 24p (5X slow motion)

Options (Raw Video Only): [FX] 4K (4032 × 2268): 30/25p, 24p; [DX] 4K (3984 × 2240): 30/25p, 24p

My preference: N/A

The options listed are the frame resolutions and frame rates available with the various video file types shown under the Video File Type entry above. The particular sizes and rates available vary, depending on the file type. You'll find more information on selecting these in Chapter 10.

Image Area

Options: Choose Image Area: FX (default); DX; DX Crop Alert: On, Off (default)

My preference: FX, On

Although high-definition video has been traditionally shot using a 16:9 aspect ratio, you can tell the Z5 II to either shoot using the full-frame area or use a 1.5X (DX) crop. The DX crop is *automatically* applied when the camera detects a DX-type lens has been mounted. These crops produce the apparent "magnification" or "lens multiplier" effect, providing, say, a 100mm lens with the same field of view as a 150mm. If you activate DX Crop Alert, an icon will appear in the display whenever a cropped image area has been selected.

Exceptions:

- **With RAW video:** The crops you choose here will be ignored when the video file type is N-RAW 12-bit (NEV). The actual image area is determined by the Frame Size/Frame Rate you select for your RAW video.

- **With an FX lens mounted:** When shooting 1920 × 1080, 120/100p (fast motion) or 1920 × 1080, 30/15p 4X or 24p 5X (slow motion), the image area is fixed at FX and DX mode cannot be selected.

- **With a DX lens mounted:** The image area is fixed at DX and fast-motion and slow-motion shooting are not available. If you have selected 1920 × 1080, 120/100p (fast motion), the camera will switch to 1920 × 1080 60/50p instead. If you have selected 1920 × 1080, 30/15p 4X or 24p 5X (slow motion), the camera will switch to 1920 × 1080 60/50/60p, respectively.

- **When Electronic VR is activated:** An additional slight crop is applied to allow the camera to shift the image around within the frame to account for camera movement. (I'll explain this feature in Chapter 10.)

ISO Sensitivity Settings

Options: Maximum sensitivity: 200–51200, Hi 0.3 to Hi 2.0; Auto ISO Control (Mode M); ISO Sensitivity (Mode M): 100–51200, plus Lo 1.0 to Lo 0.3 and Hi 0.3 to Hi 2.0

My preference: Varies by subject type

This entry (the first shown in Figure 6.2) operates much like its Photo Shooting menu counterpart, except that you cannot make direct ISO settings here for Programmed Auto, Aperture-priority, or Shutter-priority exposure modes, for which Auto ISO is *always* enabled. (Auto ISO can be turned off only in Manual exposure mode.)

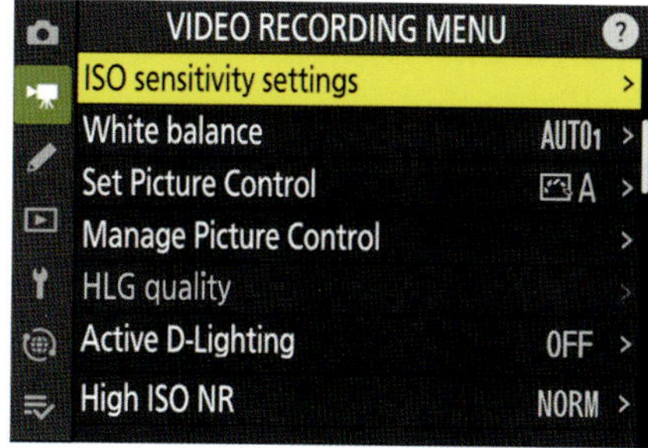

Figure 6.2 The next page of Video Recording menu entries.

- **Maximum sensitivity.** Use this parameter to indicate the highest ISO setting you're comfortable having the camera set on its own. You can choose the max ISO setting the camera will use from ISO 200 up to ISO 51200, plus the four "expanded" settings all the way up to Hi 2.0. Use a low number if you'd rather not take any photos at a high ISO without manually setting that value yourself. Dial in a higher ISO number if getting the video at any sensitivity setting is more important than worrying about noise.

- **Auto ISO control (Mode M).** As I noted above, Auto ISO can be disabled *only* in Manual exposure mode. It is on by default, but you can turn it off, here.

- **ISO sensitivity (Mode M).** You can specify a particular ISO Sensitivity setting for Manual exposure in the range ISO 100–Hi 2.0.

White Balance

Options: Same as Photo Settings (default); Auto: $AUTO_0$ Keep White; $AUTO_1$ Keep Overall Atmosphere; $AUTO_2$ Keep Warm Lighting Colors; Presets: Natural Light Auto, Direct Sunlight, Cloudy, Shade, Incandescent, Fluorescent (three types), Choose Color Temperature, Preset Manual

My preference: N/A

As with many of the Video Recording menu entries in this chapter, you can choose to share settings with the entry's Photo Shooting menu counterpart by choosing Same as Photo Settings here. However, if, as is likely for serious video work, you need to use different white balance parameters when shooting video, you can specify your settings here. When Same as Photo Settings is *not* chosen, this entry's white balance adjustments stand alone and do not affect those in the Photo Shooting menu.

Making the adjustments is done as described in Chapter 5; I won't repeat that information here.

Set Picture Control

Options: Same as Photo Settings (default), Auto, Standard, Neutral, Vivid, Monochrome, Flat Monochrome, Deep Tone Monochrome, Portrait, Rich Tone Portrait, Landscape, Flat; Creative Picture Controls (01–20): Dream, Morning, Pop, Sunday, Somber, Dramatic, Silence, Bleached, Melancholic, Pure, Denim, Toy, Sepia, Blue, Red, Pink, Charcoal, Graphite, Binary, and Carbon

My preference: Neutral works well for video, too, if you don't need the extended dynamic range of the Flat setting.

Choose Same as Photo Settings to share Picture Controls between still photo and video shooting. Or specify Picture Controls here to be used only when shooting video. The settings can be adjusted as described in Chapter 5. **Note:** The Set Picture Control menu item will be grayed out and unavailable when HLG Tone mode is selected under Video File Type, described above. The only "Picture Control" available for HLG video capture is the HLG Quality setting, as described in the section after next.

Manage Picture Control

Options: Save/Edit, Rename, Delete, Load/Save

My preference: N/A

The Manage Picture Control menu entry can be used to create new styles, edit existing styles, rename or delete styles, and store/retrieve them from the memory card. The adjustments will be applied to the Picture Controls used by the Video Recording menu—either the same controls as the Photo Shooting menu or the specific controls specified for video use. The functions are the same as described in Chapter 5.

HLG Quality

Options: Quick Sharp, Sharpening, Mid-Range Sharpening, Clarity, Contrast, Saturation, Hue

My preference: N/A

This entry gives you control over the only Picture Control that can be used for HLG video. It is grayed out until you change the Video File Type to H.265 10-bit (MOV), as described above, and specify the HLG Tone mode. (See Figure 6.3, left and center.) You can then navigate to this entry to view the screen seen at right in the figure.

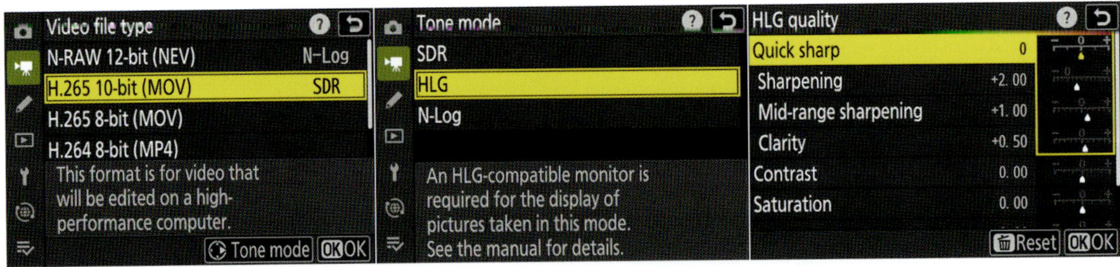

Figure 6.3 When HLG video is enabled (left, center), the HLG Quality Picture Control can be modified (right).

Then, make your adjustments:

1. Use the Quick Sharp slider and the left/right directional controls to change the three individual Sharpening adjustments (Sharpening, Mid-Range Sharpening, and Clarity) simultaneously. Alternatively, scroll down to each of those three adjustments and tweak Sharpening, Mid-Range Sharpening, or Clarity independently.

2. Next, scroll down to the Contrast, Saturation, and Hue sliders with the up/down directional controls, then use the left/right directional controls or the sub-command dial to decrease or increase the effects. A yellow triangle will appear under the original setting in the slider as you make a change.

3. Press the Trash button to reset the values to their defaults.

4. Press OK when you're finished making adjustments.

Active D-Lighting

Options: Extra High, High, Normal, Low, Off (default)

My preference: Off

Use this entry to specify the Active D-Lighting parameters used for video (only). Adjustments you make here are not reflected in the Photo Shooting menu counterpart; the two entries are separate. The settings function as described in Chapter 5, except that Auto is not available for video.

High ISO NR

Options: High, Normal (default), Low, Off

My preference: Normal

Use this entry to specify the High ISO noise reduction applied when shooting video; these settings correspond to those in the Photo Shooting menu but are separate and do not affect the other menu's parameters.

Vignette Control

Options: High, Normal (default), Low, Off

My preference: Normal

This is the first entry on the next page of the Video Recording menu settings (see Figure 6.4). The Video Recording and Photo Shooting menus share a single Vignette Control setting, so any changes made in either are reflected in the other. I explained this feature in detail in Chapter 5.

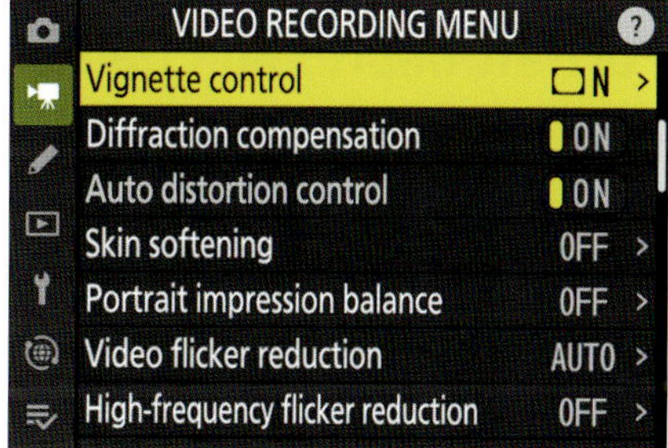

Figure 6.4 The next page of the Video Recording menu.

Diffraction Compensation

Options: On (default), Off

My preference: On

As described in Chapter 5, diffraction is a phenomenon that reduces the sharpness of your image when working at smaller f/stops, especially f/22 or f/32 (if your lens has those apertures available). Settings made here are carried over to this entry's counterpart in the Photo Shooting menu.

Auto Distortion Control

Options: On (default), Off

My preference: On

This is another entry that adjusts a single set of parameters shared by the Video Recording menu and Photo Shooting menu. You can read more information about Auto Distortion Control in Chapter 5.

Skin Softening

Options: Same as Photo Settings (default), High, Normal, Low, Off

My preference: N/A

Nikon is putting your camera's face recognition prowess to work with an optional complexion-flattering feature that removes texture from portrait shots of humans. The camera can detect and process up to three subjects, using High, Normal, or Low levels of softening. You can also disable the feature by selecting Off. You can specify one level here for Video Recording, and a different level in the Photo Shooting menu for stills.

If you let the camera choose the focus point by selecting Auto-area AF as your AF-area mode, left and right triangles will flank the focus point chosen. The left/right directional controls can be used to move from one subject to another.

This feature is disabled when N-RAW 12-bit (NEV) is selected for the Video File Type, or H.265 10-bit (MOV) is the Video File Type and N-Log is chosen as the tone mode.

Portrait Impression Balance

Options: Mode 1, Mode 2, Mode 3, Off (default)

My preference: Use as needed

This entry, like its Photo Shooting menu counterpart, allows you to create up to three separate profiles that specify magenta/amber color bias (greens and blues are not affected) and set a brightness level to be used when shooting portraits. **Note:** Your setting here applied to video can be different from the one used for stills in the Photo Shooting menu.

To create a specific balance, just follow these steps:

1. **Access this entry.** Navigate to the Portrait Impression Balance entry in the Video Recording menu.
2. **Select Mode 1, 2, or 3.** Highlight the mode you want to use/define and press the right directional button.
3. **Adjust color bias and/or brightness.** Using the directional controls to move the setting point from the center, set the desired color bias and brightness. Up/down adjusts brightness, while left right moves the point along the magenta/amber-yellow axis.
4. **Exit.** Press OK to confirm and exit, or the Trash button to cancel your adjustments. Modes that have been changed from the default value will be marked with an asterisk on the display.

Video Flicker Reduction

Options: Frequency: Auto (default), 50 Hz, 60 Hz

My preference: Use as needed

This is similar to the Photo Flicker Reduction option in the Photo Shooting menu described in Chapter 5. Like its counterpart, this setting, when enabled, detects the light source's blinking frequency (it's optimized for 100 Hz to 120 Hz), and captures a frame at the moment when the flicker has the least effect on the final image. You can select 50 Hz or 60 Hz (depending on the frequency used in your particular area) if the Auto setting fails to reduce flicker. **Note:** Nikon warns that the Z5 II's video flicker reduction may not be effective with very bright subjects; choose a smaller aperture to see if that helps.

High-Frequency Flicker Reduction

Options: On (Shutter speed fine-tuning), Off (default)

My preference: Off

As I noted in Chapter 5, while the Video/Photo Flicker Shooting entries do a good job with most light sources, some newer types of lighting, including higher-quality LED lamps, flicker with lower intensities and much higher frequencies, and require more advanced correction. This setting allows fine-tuning the shutter speed in Shutter-priority or Manual exposure modes so that it syncs up with the cycle of flickering light sources to reduce or eliminate those undesirable banding effects. **Note:** The setting you make here is separate from its counterpart in the Photo Shooting menu.

Metering

Options: Matrix (default), Center-weighted, Highlight-weighted metering

My preference: Matrix

This is the first entry in the next page of the Video Recording menu (see Figure 6.5). This menu entry, also described in Chapter 5, exists primarily so you can assign this menu entry to a custom key using the Custom Setting g2: Custom Controls menu entry. Note that Spot metering is not available in video mode.

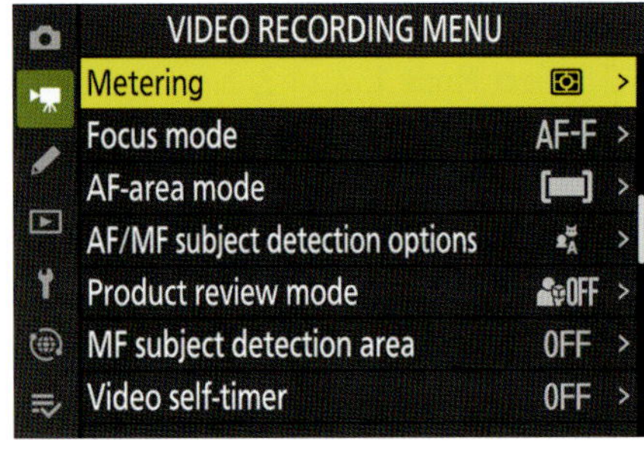

Figure 6.5 The next page of the Video Recording menu.

Focus Mode

Options: AF-S, AF-C, AF-F (default), Manual Focus

My preference: N/A

This entry is separate from its Photo Shooting menu counterpart, and includes AF-F (Full-time AF), which tells the Z5 II to focus continually during video shooting and is not available in still photography mode. I'll explain focus modes for video in more detail in Chapter 10.

AF-Area Mode

Options: Single-point AF, Wide-area AF (Small, Large, C1, C2), Subject-tracking AF, Auto-area AF (default)

My preference: N/A

AF-area modes for video can be specified in exactly the same way as described in Chapter 5, but settings you make here are independent of the ones selected in the Photo Shooting menu for still photography. This entry's chief difference between its Photo Shooting menu counterpart is that Pin-point, 3D-tracking, and Dynamic-area AF are not available for video shooting, but Subject-tracking AF can be used to lock in on a subject and continue focusing on it as it moves within the frame.

AF/MF Subject Detection Options

Options: Subject Detection: Auto (default), People, Animal, Birds, Vehicle, Airplanes, Subject detection off; AF when subject not detected: On (default), Off

My preference: Auto

You can set the priority for the type of subject the camera will look for during autofocus, using an amazing range of types. Subject detection is possible when any of the Wide-area AF modes (Small, Large, Custom 1, Custom 2), Subject-tracking AF, or Auto-area AF are active. You can set separate priorities for detection in the Photo Shooting and Video Recording menus. I explained subject detection in detail in Chapter 3 and won't duplicate that information here.

Product Review Mode

Options: On, On (Customize focus area), Off (default)

My preference: N/A

Those who do product reviews for YouTube and social media will love this new feature. It forces the Z5 II to prioritize focus on objects close to the camera, typically the product being reviewed. You can begin your sequence with the focus on yourself and the LCD reversed to face you for reference. Then, as the product is moved into the frame, focus will change to zero in on your subject. When enabled, this entry makes all the focus mode and AF-area mode settings for you.

There are three options:

- **On.** Your product can be anywhere in the frame, and the camera will focus on it as it is brought in front of the camera as the closest object.

- **On (Customize focus area).** Select this option, then press the right directional button to produce the screen shown in Figure 6.6. Use the up/down (height) and left/right (width) directional buttons to change the size of the desired focus area.

- **Off.** Disables the feature.

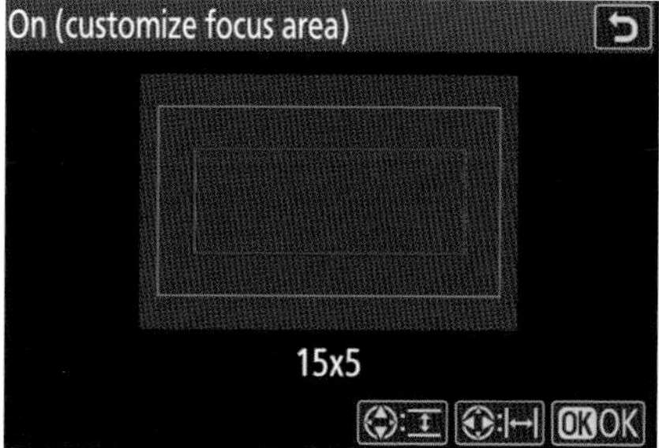

Figure 6.6 Customize the focus area for product reviews.

MF Subject Detection Area

Options: Auto-area (All), Wide-area AF (Large), Wide-area AF (Small), Manual Focus Subject Detection Off (default)

My preference: Auto-area (All)

Guess what? You can tell your camera to detect subjects for you *even when you are focusing manually.* Choose Auto-area (All), and the camera will search for subjects within the entire frame. If multiple subjects are present, the first one detected will be shown with a gray focus point indicator and left/right triangle-shaped pointers that show you can switch to one of the other subjects using the left/right directional buttons. You can also choose Wide-area AF (Large or Small) to limit subject recognition to the current focus area.

Video Self-Timer

Options: Off (default), 2 seconds, 10 seconds

My preference: N/A

This handy feature allows setting a 2-second or 10-second delay before video filming starts. Perhaps you want to eliminate any possibility of camera shake being visible from vibration caused when you start recording by pressing the video-recording button. While a remote release might be your best choice, you can use this self-timer instead. The 10-second delay is particularly useful for content creators who want the video to start capture/live streaming after they've raced back to their desk/presentation area after manually activating the recording. The self-timer lamp stops flashing and glows steadily for two seconds before the timer expires, giving you plenty of warning that it's time to smile.

Vibration Reduction

Options: Same as Photo Settings (default), On (or Normal), Spt (Sport), Off

My preference: N/A

Use this setting (the first on the next screen, shown in Figure 6.7) to enable/disable vibration reduction, a great feature found in some lenses that counters camera/photographer shake. The VR options may vary depending on which lens you are using.

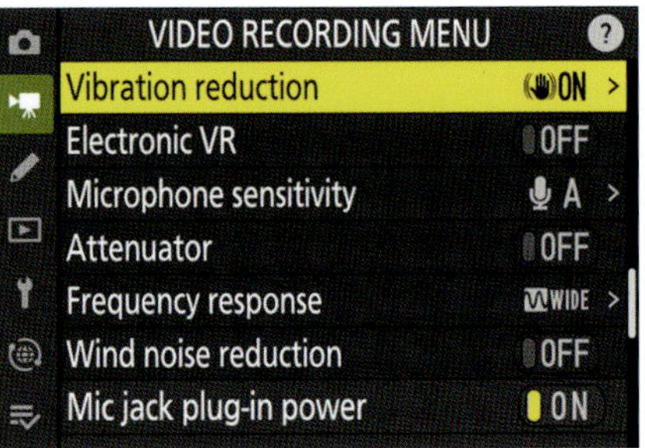

Figure 6.7 The next page of the Video Recording menu.

Electronic VR

Options: On, Off (default)

My preference: Off

As I noted in Chapter 5, electronic VR is a type of anti-shake technology that has long been provided in pro and amateur camcorders. Hi-Res Zoom must be disabled in the Video Recording menu, and N-RAW 12-bit (NEV) and 120/100p frame rates and slow-motion capture are disabled. You'll find a detailed discussion of electronic VR in Chapter 10.

Microphone Sensitivity

Options: Auto (default), Manual, Microphone Off

My preference: Varies

This entry has three options that control your camera's built-in microphone or any external microphone you attach. You can choose Auto, Manual (to set recording levels yourself [with a handy volume meter on screen showing the current ambient sound levels]), or turn the microphone off entirely if you're planning to record silent video, use another sound recording source, or add sound in post-production. (See Figure 6.8.)

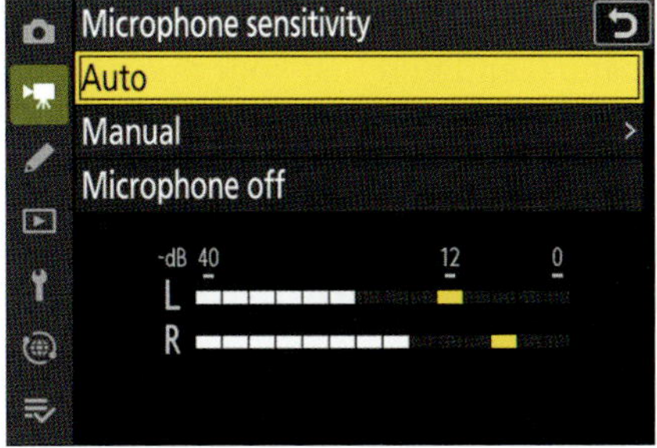

Figure 6.8 Adjust the sensitivity of your audio input.

Attenuator

Options: On, Off (default)

My preference: Varies

When working in noisy environments, choose Enable to reduce the microphone gain and minimize audio distortion from background sounds.

Frequency Response

Options: Wide Range (default), Vocal Range

My preference: Varies

Select from Wide Range frequency response to record a broad range of sounds, or Vocal Range to optimize audio recording for vocals. You'll find an entire section on recording sound in Chapter 10.

Wind Noise Reduction

Options: On, Off (default)

My preference: Varies

Wind blowing across your microphone can be distracting. This setting reduces wind noise (and may also affect other sounds, so use it carefully) for the built-in microphones *only*. Your external microphone, like the Nikon ME-1, may have its own wind noise reduction filter on/off switch.

Mic Jack Plug-in Power

Options: On (default), Off

My preference: Varies by microphone

Some microphones require power from the camera to operate; some do not. If you consult your manual and find that your mic does not require power from the camera, you should set this option to Off. That will avoid possible noise from the power supply that can occur. The plug-in Nikon ME-1 microphone does draw power from the camera, but many third-party mics do not.

Headphone Volume

Options: 15 (default); Values 0–30

My preference: N/A

Use this entry, the first in the last page of the Video Recording menu (see Figure 6.9), to adjust the volume of headphones you've plugged into the camera's headphones jack.

Timecode

Options: Record Timecodes: On, On with HDMI Output, Off; Count-up Method: Record Run, Free Run; Timecode Origin: Reset, Enter Manually, Current Time; Drop Frame: On, Off

My preference: N/A

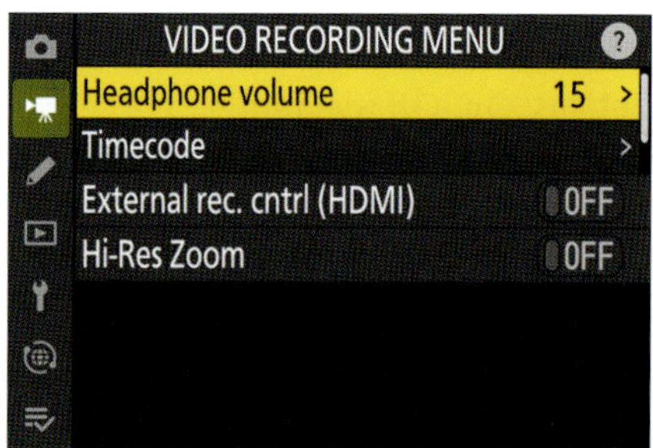

Figure 6.9 The last page of the Video Recording menu.

Advanced video shooters find SMPTE (Society of Motion Picture and Television Engineers)-compatible time codes embedded in the video files to be an invaluable reference during editing. To oversimplify a bit, the time system provides precise *hour:minute:second:frame* markers that allow identifying and synchronizing frames and audio. The timecode system includes a provision for "dropping" frames to ensure that the fractional frame rate of captured video (remember that a 24 fps setting actually yields 23.976 frames per second while 30 fps capture gives you 29.97 actual "frames" per second) can be matched up with actual time spans.

As I noted, I won't be covering the most technical aspects of movie shooting in great detail (including detailed use of time codes, raw HDMI streaming, etc.). If you're at the stage where you're using time codes, you don't need a primer, anyway.

However, the Time Code submenu does include the following options:

- **Record Timecodes.** Turn timecodes off or on. You can select On; On with HDMI Output to append the time code to the HDMI video output; or Off to not use timecodes.
- **Count-Up Method.** Choose Rec Run, in which the time code counts up only when you are actually capturing video, or Free Run (also known as Time of Day), which allows the time code to run up even between shooting clips. The latter is useful when you want to synchronize clips between multiple cameras that are shooting the same event. When using Free Run, even if the cameras record at different times, you'll be able to match the video that was captured at the exact same moment during editing. When Free Run is selected, the time code will always be recorded to the movie file, except for high frame rate (240/200 or 120/100 fps) clips.
- **Timecode Origin.** Normally, the camera uses its internal clock to specify the hours:minutes:seconds, with frames set to :00 when you begin shooting. This entry allows you to manually enter any hour:minute:second:frame of your choice, or to Reset the start time to 00:00:00:00 manually or by pressing the shutter-release button on the optional WR-T10 remote controller. You can also use the current time specified by your camera's clock.
- **Drop Frame.** The 30 fps setting yields 29.97 actual frames per second, 60 fps gives you 59.95 frames per second, and 120 fps provides 119.9 fps, causing a discrepancy between the actual time and the time code that's recorded. Enable and the camera will skip some time code numbers in drop-frame mode at intervals to eliminate the discrepancy. When disabled (non-drop frame mode), you may notice a difference of several seconds per hour.

External Recorder Control (HDMI)

Options: On, Off (default)

My preference: N/A

Use this entry to allow your camera's controls to stop and start recording on a compatible external recorder.

Hi-Res Zoom

Options: On, Off (default)

My preference: N/A

This is a cool setting that uses your camera's extra resolution to provide a high-quality digital zoom effect—even to prime lenses, which have a fixed focal length, of course. When active, you can zoom in and out by pressing the Fn1 or Fn2 buttons, or by rotating the lens control ring.

To start zooming, just follow these steps:

1. **Assign zooming controls**. By default, you can use the left/right directional buttons to zoom in or out. If you prefer, you can go to Custom Setting g2: Custom Controls (*not Custom Controls f2: Shooting!*) and assign Hi-Res Zoom + to the Fn1 button, and Hi-Res Zoom – to the Fn2 button. (You cannot assign these controls to any other button.) Alternatively, you can delegate zooming to the lens control ring (if your lens has one) with a separate Custom Control definition.

2. **Enable Hi-Res Zoom.** Set this entry to On.

3. **Select zoom speed.** Visit Custom Setting g7: High-Res Zoom Speed, and select a slower, faster, or standard zooming speed.

4. **Choose Video File type.** You must be shooting 1920 × 1080 30p/25p/24p.

5. **Switch to Video mode.** This zoom is not available in Photo mode. Your AF-area mode is automatically set to Wide-are AF (Large) and Electronic VR is turned off.

6. **Zoom, zoom.** As you zoom in and out, a zoom display bar appears at the bottom of the screen showing the amount of zoom from 1X to 2X.

Custom Settings Menu 7

Unlike the Photo Shooting and Video Recording menu options, which you are likely to modify frequently as your picture-taking environment changes, Custom Settings are slightly more stable sets of preferences that let you tailor the behavior of your camera in a variety of different ways for longer-term use.

Some options are minor tweaks useful for specific shooting situations or convenience. Perhaps you'd like to assign a frequently used feature to one of the Fn buttons or turn on the grid display to make it easier to align vertical or horizontal shapes.

Best of all are the settings that improve the way your camera operates. Custom Setting b6, for example, provides a way to fine-tune the exposures your camera calculates for each of the metering modes: Matrix, Center-weighted, Spot, and Highlight-weighted. If you find that one consistently over- or underexposes more than you like, it's easy to dial in a permanent correction. Should you feel that the camera is taking a few pictures that are out of focus, Custom Settings a1 and a2 can be used to tell it not to fire until optimum focus is achieved.

This chapter concentrates on explaining all the options of the Custom Settings menu and, most importantly, when and why you might want to use each setting.

Custom Settings Menu Layout

The Custom Settings entries are arranged in seven different categories, as shown in Figure 7.1: Focus, Metering/Exposure, Timers/AE Lock, Shooting/Display, Bracketing/Flash, Controls, and Video. Some of those may seem to be an odd match. What does bracketing have to do with flash? Oh, wait! You can *bracket* flash (as well as non-flash) exposures. The category system does have an advantage. Once you're familiar with what settings are available within each category, you can select the Custom Settings menu, scroll down to the specific category you want, press the multi selector right button, and enter the Custom Settings system at that point, skipping the other entries.

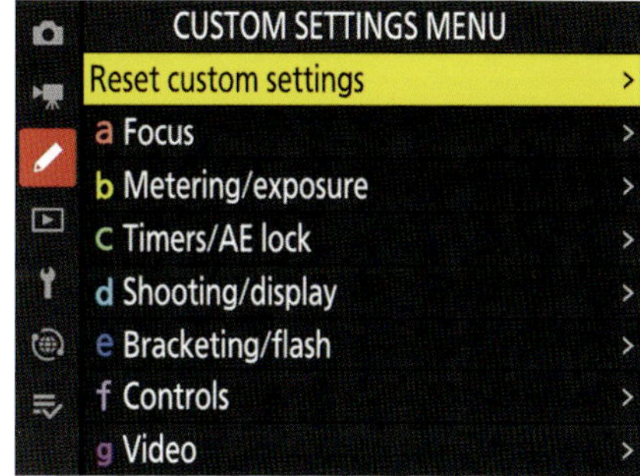

Figure 7.1 Entries are allocated among seven categories in the Custom Settings menu.

However, once you get past the main Custom Settings screen, the entries are one long scrolling list, so if you've guessed wrong about where you want to start, you can enter the list at any point and then scroll up or down until you find the entry you want. Or, press the multi selector left button to get back to the main screen, then move down to another entry point and re-enter. The Custom Settings menu items are all color- and letter-coded: **a** (red) for focus functions; **b** (yellow) for metering/exposure; **c** (green) for timers and AE lock features; **d** (light blue/cyan) for shooting/display functions; **e** (dark blue) for bracketing/flash; **f** (purple) for adjustments to the controls; and **g** (magenta) to adjust Video mode functions.

For simplicity, in this book I consistently refer to the Custom Settings menu entries by their letter/names, so that you always know that when I mention Custom Setting a5, I am describing the fifth entry in the Focus menu: Store Points by Orientation. That terminology makes it easy to jump quickly to the specific entry. Note that in the figures that illustrate each of the separate Custom Settings categories in this chapter, that category's entries are shown on as few screens as possible. In practice, as you scroll through the listings, the entries for a category may be spread over several different screens.

You can select a Custom Settings function as you do any menu entry, by pressing the multi selector right button, and navigating through the screen that appears with the up/down (and sometimes left/right) buttons. Confirming an option is usually done by pressing the OK button, pushing the multi selector right button, or sometimes by choosing Done when a series of related options have been chosen.

At the top level, you'll see these entries:

- Reset Custom Settings
- a. Focus
- b. Metering/Exposure
- c. Timers/AE Lock
- d. Shooting/Display
- e. Bracketing/Flash
- f. Controls
- g. Video

Reset Custom Settings

Options: Reset: Yes, No

My preference: N/A

You can restore the settings of the Custom Settings banks to their default values. If you don't know what some of these settings are, I'll explain them later in this chapter. Be careful when changing any of your carefully tailored customized settings back to the defaults.

a. Focus

The red-coded Focus options deal with some of the potentially most vexing settings. After all, incorrect focus is one of the most damaging picture killers of all the attributes in an image. You may be able to compensate for bad exposure, partially fix errant color balance, and perhaps even incorporate motion blur into an image as a creative element. But if focus is wrong, the photograph doesn't look right, and no amount of "I meant to do that!" pleas are likely to work. The focus options enable you to choose how and when autofocus is applied (using the AF-S or AF-C focus mode), the controls used to activate the feature, and the way focus points are selected from the available zones. Figure 7.2 shows the first seven entries in the Custom Settings: Focus section.

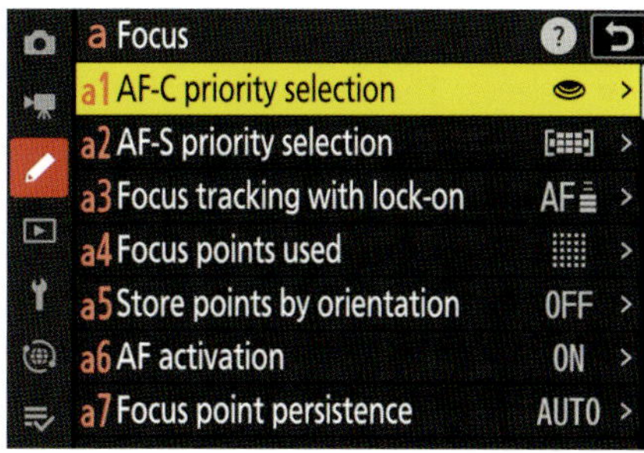

Figure 7.2 The first seven Focus options.

a1 AF-C Priority Selection

Options: Release (default), Focus+Release, Focus

My preference: Release

As you learned in Chapter 3, when not shooting movies, the Z5 II has two primary autofocus modes, continuous autofocus (AF-C) and single autofocus (AF-S), plus AF-A, which switches between the two modes depending on whether the subject is moving or stationary. (Video mode adds a third: Full-time autofocus [AF-F].) This menu entry allows you to specify what takes precedence in AF-C mode when you press the shutter release all the way down to take a picture: focus-priority or release-priority. You can choose from:

- **Release.** When this option is selected (the default), the shutter is activated when the release button is pushed down all the way, even if sharp focus has not yet been achieved. Because AF-C focuses and refocuses constantly when autofocus is active, you may find that an image is not quite in sharpest focus. Use this option when taking a picture is more important than absolute best focus, such as fast action or photojournalism applications. (You don't want to miss that record-setting home run, or the protestor's pie smashing into the Governor's face.) Using this setting doesn't mean that your image won't be sharply focused; it just means that you'll get a picture even if autofocusing isn't quite complete. If you've been poised with the shutter release pressed halfway, the camera probably has been tracking the focus of your image.

- **Focus+Release.** Choose this option when you want an intermediate priority setting between release-priority and focus-priority (discussed next). It's a good choice for continuous shooting, as the slight pause before focus is locked in gives the camera a little extra time to achieve sharp focus for the first frame of a sequence, while retaining that focus setting for subsequent shots.

- **Focus.** The shutter is not activated until sharp focus is achieved. This is best for subjects that are not moving rapidly. AF-C will continue to track your subjects' movement, as long as it remains within the active focus area, but the camera won't take a picture until focus is locked in. You might miss a few shots, but you will have fewer out-of-focus images.

a2 AF-S Priority Selection

Options: Release, Focus (default)

My preference: Focus

This is the counterpart setting for single autofocus mode.

- **Release.** The shutter is activated when the button is depressed all the way, even if sharp focus is not quite achieved. Keep in mind that, unlike AF-C, the camera focuses only *once* when AF-S mode is used. So, if you've partially depressed the shutter release, paused, and then pressed the button down all the way, it's possible that the subject has moved, and release-priority will yield more out-of-focus shots than release-priority with AF-C.
- **Focus.** This default prevents the camera from taking a picture until focus is achieved and the in-focus indicator in the viewfinder glows steadily. If you're using single autofocus mode, this is probably the best setting. Moving subjects really call for AF-C mode in most cases.

a3 Focus Tracking with Lock-on

Options: Blocked Shot AF Response: 5 (Delayed), 4, 3 (default), 2, 1 (Quick)

My preference: 3

Sometimes new subjects interject themselves in the frame temporarily. The classic example used is a football game, when a referee dashes in front of your camera briefly just as a receiver is about to make a catch. This setting lets you specify how quickly the camera reacts to these transient interruptions that would cause relatively large changes in focus before refocusing on the "new" subject matter. Fickle focus can be especially vexing when relying on AF-C to preserve focus while shooting continuously. At other times, you *want* the camera to identify and lock onto a new subject that enters the frame. You were tracking that receiver, but the ball is intercepted and capturing the cornerback's run is now your goal. This entry gives you two tools to help you tame both sluggardly and fidgety autofocus.

Using the Blocked Shot AF Response slider shown in Figure 7.3, you can specify a long delay, so that the interloper is ignored, or a shorter delay, so that the camera immediately refocuses when a new subject moves into the frame. A setting of 5 (Delayed) causes the camera to ignore the intervening subject matter for a significant period of time. Use this setting when shooting subjects, such as sports, in which focus interruptions are likely to be frequent and significant. You can also choose a setting of 1 (Quick) which tells the camera to wait only a moment before refocusing.

Very high continuous frame rates may work better when you allow refocusing to take place rapidly, without a lock-on delay. Intermediate settings from 2 to 4 provide different amounts of delay. The middle value, 3, offers an intermediate delay before the camera refocuses on the new subject. It's often the best choice when shooting sports in either of the continuous shooting modes, as the long delay can throw off autofocus accuracy at higher frames-per-second

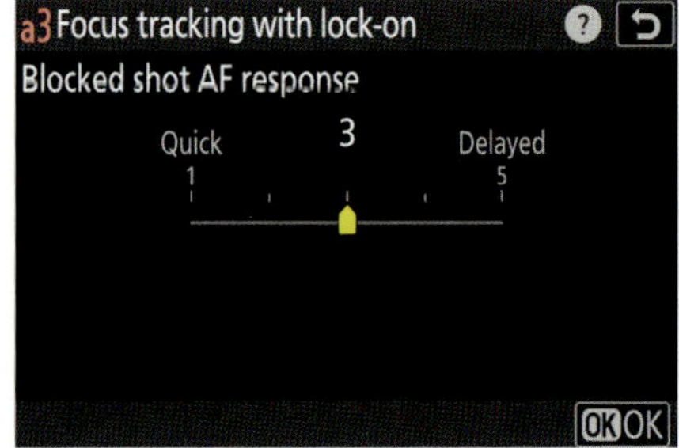

Figure 7.3 Options for Focus Tracking with Lock-on.

settings. The Nikon Z5 II *always* uses the value of 3 when the AF-area mode is set to 3D-tracking. If the AF-area mode is set to Auto-area AF, the camera will ignore "Quick" settings of 1 or 2 you may have made (and use 3 instead) but will happily respond to the delayed settings of 4 or 5 if you've selected them here.

a4 Focus Points Used

Options: All Points (default), Alternating Points

My preference: Depends on subject

You can choose the number of focus points available when you manually select a zone using the multi selector up/down and left/right buttons. You have two choices:

- **All.** This is the default. Up to 273 positions are available for manual selection when your AF-area mode is not Auto-area AF (which uses up to 299 points). The exact number used varies by the active AF-area mode.
- **Alternating Points.** This option does *not* disable 75 percent of the AF sensors; they remain active and functional. What it does do is limit the number of positions you can *select* to alternating points and rows, allowing you to move the position of the selected focus point more quickly. This can be the best choice for faster focus point selection when taking pictures of relatively large, evenly illuminated subject matter such that manually choosing the precise initial focus point/zone is not particularly beneficial.

  I often use Single-point AF and enable the Alternating Points option—the available focus areas are plenty and can be set quickly as action moves around the floor when photographing basketball games. The exceptions? When using Pinpoint AF, the available focus points remain exactly the same when single-pressing the directional control even though you have selected this option.

a5 Store Points by Orientation

Options: Focus Point, Focus Point and AF-area mode, Off (default)

My preference: Focus Point and AF-area mode

Here you can choose whether separate focus points can be selected for landscape and portrait orientations of the camera, and whether you can select a different AF-area mode for each orientation, as explained in detail in Chapter 3.

When you choose Off, the focus point will maintain the same relative position as you rotate the camera, and the AF-area mode will remain the same. Select Focus Point, and you can choose a different focus point when the camera is set to horizontal orientation, rotated 90 degrees clockwise from horizontal, or rotated 90 degrees counterclockwise from horizontal. With focus point and AF-area mode enabled, your AF-area setting will be preserved as well. In all cases, an upside-down orientation is not supported.

If you're shooting birds in flight or other wildlife or scenic vistas (it's called landscape mode for a reason), you can stick with the default value, Off. The focus point and AF-area mode choices are especially useful for portraits, fashion, sports, photojournalism, and street photography.

a6 AF Activation

Options: Shutter/AF-ON (default), AF-ON Only: Out-of-focus Release, Enable (default), Disable

My preference: AF-ON Only, Out-of-focus Release Disable. Recommended for anyone proficient in back-button focus, described in Chapter 3

You can specify whether the camera focuses when the shutter release is pressed halfway or disable that behavior. You'd want to disable shutter-release AF activation if you elect to use *back-button focus*. Your choices are as follows:

- **Shutter/AF-ON.** Pressing the shutter release halfway, *or* either the AF-ON button or a different button you have defined for AF activation (as described under Custom Controls later in this chapter) always activates autofocus.

- **AF-ON Only.** Pressing the shutter release halfway does not activate autofocus. Instead, you can activate AF by pressing the AF-ON button or another button you've defined for the AF-ON behavior with the Custom Controls commands described later, and in Chapter 3 under the back-button focus section. **Note:** You can bypass the AF-ON button by tapping the screen when Touch Focus is enabled.

  The camera allows additional fine-tuning of your AF-ON Only setting. When this option is highlighted, you can press the multi selector right button and choose from two Out-of-Focus Release options:

  - **Enable.** The camera can take photos when the shutter release is pressed all the way down, even if you have not pressed the AF-ON button and focus has therefore *not* taken place. Effectively, this is release-priority. You might find this useful to enable grab shots that take place without warning, and you want a photo even if it may not be in perfect focus. You still have the option of activating AF by pressing the AF-ON button before you press the shutter release all the way, but if you do not, the photo will still be captured.

    Warning: This is a dangerous setting, and when you choose AF-ON Only, Enable is the *default* behavior. It works well if you are using back-button focus and gotten into the habit of pressing the AF-ON button to initiate autofocus. However, if you are *not* using back-button focus and choose AF-ON Only *be sure to select disable* (described next) to avoid unwanted out-of-focus photos that may result if you forget to press the AF-ON button before pushing the shutter release down all the way.

  - **Disable.** If the image is not in focus, pressing the shutter release down all the way *will not* take a picture (effectively focus-priority). You *must* activate AF by pressing the AF-ON button before using the shutter release to take a picture. It keeps the camera from taking a picture until after autofocus has been activated. This option applies only when focus-priority has been specified for AF-C or AF-S using Custom Setting a1 or a2 and you are using an AF-area selection mode that allows the user to select the focus area or zones (in other words, [almost] all AF-area modes other than Auto-area AF). **Exception:** If your AF-area mode is Pinpoint AF, this setting is ignored and the shutter *can be released even if the subject is not in focus.*

    This option will prevent you from accidentally taking out-of-focus pictures if you forget you are using AF-ON to activate autofocus and press the shutter release without remembering to initiate AF.

a7 Focus Point Persistence

Options: Auto (default), Off

My preference: Auto

This is an esoteric setting that some will find useful. Choose Auto, and the focus point selected by the camera in Auto-area AF or Wide-area AF modes remains in effect when you change to one of the modes in which the focus point is selected by the user. Select Off, and the focus point last chosen by you is restored. This setting comes into play when you:

- **Press a button that changes AF-area mode.** You've assigned AF-area mode, AF-area mode+AF ON, Recall Shooting Functions, or Recall Shooting Functions (Hold) behavior to that button.
- **Press shutter release halfway.** You are changing AF-area mode while focusing with the shutter button half-pressed.
- **Change from auto point selection to manual point selection.** You are switching from an AF-area mode in which the camera chooses the focus point to one that is selected manually. It would apply, for example, if you're switching from Auto-area AF or one of the Wide-area AF modes to Single-point AF or any other mode in which the user chooses the focus point.

Make sure Auto is enabled when you want to let the camera choose the focus point, then lock in that point because you want to switch to 3D-tracking to follow an erratic or fast-moving subject. If set to Off, the camera will change to your last focus point instead.

a8 Limit AF-Area Mode Selection

Options: Pinpoint, Single-point AF, Dynamic-area AF (Small, Medium, Large), Wide-area AF (Small, Large, C1, C2), 3D-tracking, Auto-area AF (default is all available)

My preference: N/A

This is the first entry in the next group of AF settings. (See Figure 7.4.) If there are certain AF-area modes that you don't use, you can disable them using this menu item. That will enable you to switch AF-area modes more quickly, especially when making adjustments when the Focus mode/AF-area mode is assigned to a function button/dial combination, such as the Fn2 button (the default), or another button using Custom Setting f2: Custom Controls (Shooting), as described later in this chapter.

Indeed, some shooters use only two or three modes and can dispense with the others. **Note:** The AF-area modes available from the *i* menu are not changed and remain available should you decide you need to use one of them.

Single-point AF-area mode is always available and cannot be disabled. However, you can highlight any of the others and press the multi selector right button to remove the check box next to that mode's label to disable it. You can thus enable Single-point AF, plus any combination of the other AF-area modes. I explained this feature in Chapter 3.

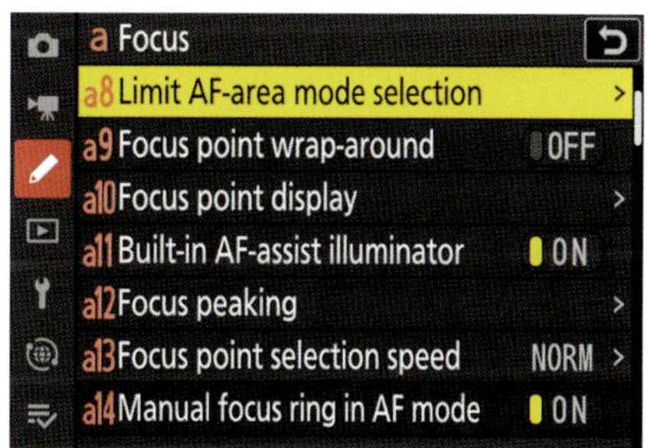

Figure 7.4 The next page of the Focus menu.

a9 Focus Point Wrap-Around

Options: Off (default), On

My preference: Off

This setting is purely a personal preference parameter. When you press the directional controls to choose a focus point, the camera can be told to stop when the selection reaches the edge of the array, or, it can continue, wrapping around to the opposite edge, like Pac-Man leaving the playing area on one side or top/bottom to re-emerge on the other. (I hope I'm not revealing my age, here.) Your choices are simple; decide which behavior you prefer:

- **On (Wrap).** Pressing the left/right or up/down buttons when you've reached the edge of the focus point display wraps the selection to the opposite side, still moving in the same direction. If you find yourself frequently needing to scoot from one side of the frame to the other, this setting can save you a lot of button presses. You need to train yourself to be aware of and use the wrap-around feature.

- **Off (No Wrap).** The focus point selection stops at the edge of the focus zone array. If you're set in your ways or don't often need to zip from one side to the other, the default setting will cater to your habits.

a10 Focus Point Display

Options: Manual Focus mode: On (default), Off; Dynamic-area AF Assist: On (default), Off; AF-C In-focus display: On (default), Off; 3D-tracking Focus Point Color: White (default), Red; Focus Point Border Width: 1 (default), 2–3

My preference: Manual Focus mode: On, Dynamic-area AF assist: On, AF-C In-focus Display: On, 3D-tracking Focus Point Color: White, Focus Point Border Width: 2

How do you want the focus points displayed in the viewfinder? This entry gives you three toggle controls and a color choice during 3D-tracking. Your focus point options include:

- **Manual Focus mode.** When you're using manual focus instead of autofocus, the camera still monitors how well your image is in focus, using the active focus point. Here, you can choose how it is displayed.
  - **On.** Active point illumination is always shown when using manual focus. Select this option if you like to know what focus point is being used.
  - **Off.** Active point illumination is enabled during manual focus only during focus point selection as you move the point around the frame with the multi selector directional buttons.
- **Dynamic-area AF assist.** Can provide optional position information when using Dynamic-area AF.
  - **On.** Shows both the focus point selected *and* the surrounding focus points when using Dynamic-area AF. You might want to choose On as a reminder that the cluster of points around the main focus point are active. This setting has an important benefit: it clearly reminds you that you are using Dynamic-area AF, and displays the coverage of the Small, Medium, and Large variations.

- **Off.** Only the selected focus point is shown. Once you become accustomed to using that AF-area mode and think you don't need to know how large the focus area is, you can turn the display Off and slightly declutter your screen.
- **AF-C In-focus Display.** The camera can let you know when focus is achieved when using AF-C focus.
  - **On.** The focus point will be displayed in green when the subject is in focus. Seeing focus points turn green can be a comforting confirmation.
  - **Off.** The focus point is always displayed in red or yellow, whether the subject is in focus or not. Because focus can change rapidly and repeatedly when working with AF-C, the default setting is Off, which many prefer to keep visual distractions to a minimum when shooting fast-moving subjects.
- **3D-tracking Focus Point Color.** You can specify whether a white or red box will be shown around the tracked subject when using 3D-tracking. If you've chosen On for AF-C in-focus display (above), the indicator will switch to green when focus is achieved.
- **Focus point border width.** You can choose the size of the focus point border in the range of 1 to 3. A setting of 2 makes it much easier to locate the focus point when shooting in bright daylight.

a11 Built-in AF-Assist Illuminator

Options: On (default), Off

My preference: Off

There is a green LED on the left front panel (as you hold the camera). It can illuminate to provide additional lighting to improve autofocus when using the AF-S focus mode. The illuminator is effective over a very narrow range (Nikon says 3'4" to 9'10") and its anemic burst of light can be obstructed by any lens hood you have mounted, or even a stray finger. I usually disable this feature, because I shoot so many photos at concerts and other events where the AF-assist light is distracting (or even forbidden—choreographers have told me dancers may orient their twirling moves on theater lights they perceive during a spin).

Nikon says the Profoto A10 electronic flash (a high-end $1,000-plus strobe) can optionally be used as an AF-assist illuminator when mounted on the Z5 II's accessory shoe. If you've enabled that mode, it will ignore the Off setting and override your camera's built-in illuminator. If you disable the function on the flash, the Z5 II's built-in illuminator will function normally.

a12 Focus Peaking

Options: Focus Peaking Display: On, Off (default); Focus Peaking Sensitivity: 3 (High Sensitivity), 2 (Standard) (default), 1 (Low Sensitivity); Focus Peaking Highlight Color: Red (default), Yellow, Blue, White

My preference: N/A

Focus peaking is a focusing aid available to provide colored highlights around the edges of objects as they come into sharp focus. The most important parameter is Focus Peaking Sensitivity, which you can set to Low Sensitivity, Standard, or High Sensitivity. The Low setting is the most precise; only a narrow focus plane is used, while at the High setting, the "depth of focus" is deeper, so that more of the subject is considered to be in focus. Standard uses a value somewhere in between. You'd want to use Low Sensitivity and a magnified view for critical focus, and High Sensitivity for speed, especially if you're using a smaller f/stop that is more forgiving of slight focus errors.

You can choose from among red, yellow, blue, or white as your contrasting color. If your subject has a predominant color, you should select a peaking color that contrasts. For example, you might want to use yellow as your peaking tone when photographing red roses. I explained how to use focus peaking and showed you what it looks like in action in Chapter 3.

a13 Focus Point Selection Speed

Options: Low, Normal (default), High

My preference: Normal

You can select how quickly you can manually move the selected focus point around the frame. With up to 273 selectable focus points, changing your current point's position can be cumbersome, and you'll rarely, if ever, want to use the Low speed option. Normal actually works quite well in most situations. The High speed option can be useful when you're working with AF-area modes that use the largest number of individual points, such as Single-point AF.

a14 Manual Focus Ring in AF Mode

Options: On (default), Off

My preference: On

Autofocus generally kicks in when you press the shutter release halfway. Many lenses allow you to press the shutter release halfway down to autofocus (or press your designated AF-ON button) and then fine-tune focus by rotating the lens's focus ring. If at any time you want to refocus automatically, release the shutter button or designated AF-ON button, and press again. Override AF by rotating the focus ring, then press the shutter release down all the way to take the picture. Or, you can lift your finger from the release button and then half-press it again to reactivate AF.

Normally, that's a good thing. However, sometimes you might want to turn off the manual refocus option to avoid accidentally disturbing focus set by the AF system. This setting adds that capability to compatible lenses that have a control ring in addition to a focusing ring. When set to Off with such lenses, the lens focus ring can't be used to manually focus in AF mode. Of course, you can disable the control ring on lenses that have only one or two rings by choosing Control Ring in Custom Setting f2: Custom Controls, and selecting None as its behavior, instead. But if a lens has three rings, this entry is the only way to disable the manual focus function. **Note:** This entry appears *only* when a compatible lens is mounted on the camera. Nikon does not provide a list of these optics, but I can confirm it does work with most lenses, including my favorite 24-120mm f/4 walk-around zoom.

b. Metering/Exposure

The yellow-coded Metering/Exposure Custom Settings (see Figure 7.5) let you define six different parameters that affect exposure metering.

b1 ISO Sensitivity Step Value

Options: 1/3 Step (default), 1 Step
My preference: 1/3 Step

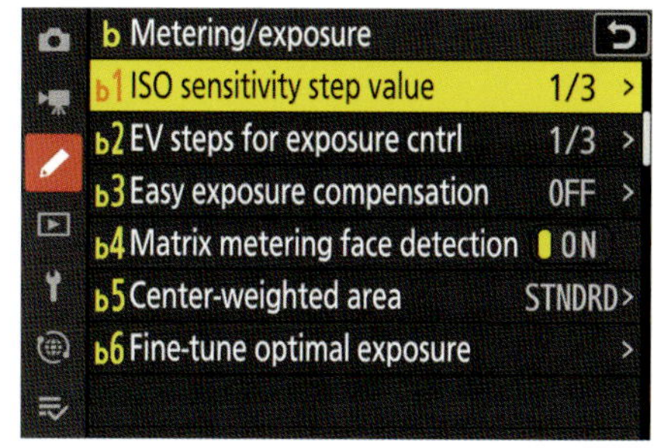

Figure 7.5 The Metering/Exposure menu.

This is the first setting in the Metering/Exposure section (see Figure 7.5). This setting tells the camera the size of the "jumps" it should use when making ISO sensitivity adjustments—either one-third (the default) or one stop. Choose the 1/3-stop setting when you want the finest increments between ISO settings. For example, the camera will use values such as 100, 125, 160, 200, 250, 320, and so forth, giving you (and the autoexposure system) maximum flexibility.

With full-stop increments, you will have larger and more noticeable changes between settings. The camera will offer ISO settings such as 100, 200, 400, and 800, instead. These coarser adjustments are useful when you want more dramatic changes between different exposures.

b2 EV Steps for Exposure Control

Options: 1/3 EV Steps (default), 1/2 EV Steps, 1 EV Steps
My preference: 1/3 EV Steps

This setting tells the camera the size of the "jumps" it should use when making exposure adjustments—either one-third stop, one-half stop, or one full stop. The increment you specify here applies to f/stops, shutter speeds, autoexposure bracketing, and EV changes—with one exception. If you specify the 1 EV option, exposure compensation will use 1/3 stop instead.

Choose the 1/3-stop setting when you want the finest increments between shutter speeds and/or f/stops. For example, the camera will use shutter speeds such as 1/60th, 1/80th, 1/100th, 1/125th, and 1/160th second, and f/stops such as f/5.6, f/6.3, f/7.1, and f/8, giving you (and the autoexposure system) corresponding flexibility.

As with ISO settings, using 1/2-stop or full-stop increments, you will have larger and more noticeable changes between settings. Using the full-stop settings as an example, the camera will apply shutter speeds such as 1/60th, 1/125th, 1/250th, and 1/500th second, and f/stops including f/5.6, f/8, f/11, and f/16. These coarser adjustments are useful when you want more dramatic changes between different exposures. I sometimes use the 1 EV setting when I am experimenting with manual HDR exposures and want large jumps between shots.

> **WAIT, WHAT?**
>
> Remember that, as I noted above, when the 1 EV setting is chosen, changes to *shutter speed, aperture, and bracketing* exposure settings will be made in 1 EV steps, but *exposure compensation and flash exposure compensation* adjustments will still be made in 1/3 EV increments. Nikon apparently feels that large exposure compensation jumps should be avoided, resulting in this confusing exception.

b3 Easy Exposure Compensation

Options: On (Auto Reset), On, Off (default)

My preference: Off

This setting potentially simplifies dialing in EV (exposure value compensation) adjustments by specifying whether the Exposure Compensation button must be pressed while adding or extracting EV compensation. Because of the possibility of confusion or error, I tend to leave this setting turned off, which is the default. Your choices are as follows:

- **On (Auto Reset).** This setting allows you to add or subtract exposure by rotating the sub-command dial when in Program (P) or Shutter-priority (S) exposure modes, or by rotating the main command dial when using Aperture-priority (A) mode. Rotating either dial has no effect in Manual (M) exposure mode. (If you've reversed the behavior of the command dials using Custom Setting f6, the "opposite" command dial must be used to make the changes.) Any adjustments you've made are canceled when the camera is shut off, or the standby timer expires, and the exposure meters go back to sleep. **Note:** However, if you've activated an EV change *not* using the command dials, but by pressing the EV button located to the southeast of the shutter release, or a dial defined to perform exposure compensation, the reset *does not occur* when you power off and on again.

  That's a useful mode, because most of us have made an EV adjustment and then forgotten about it, only to expose a whole series of improperly exposed photos. You can still have "sticky" EV settings when Easy Exposure Compensation is turned on: just hold down the Exposure Compensation button when you make your changes. You can also increase the Power Off Delay interval (using Custom Setting c3, described shortly) to a longer period so your adjustment will remain in force for a longer period of time.

- **On.** This setting brings the Easy Compensation mode into conformance with the camera's behavior when the Exposure Compensation button is pressed: in either case, any EV modifications you make will remain until you countermand them. As I have mentioned several times, forgetting to "turn off" EV changes after you've moved on to a different shooting environment is a primary cause of over- and underexposure among those of us who are forgetful or who ignore the flashing EV warnings.

- **Off.** With this default setting, you must always press the Exposure Compensation button while rotating the main command dial to add or subtract exposure. Use this choice when you don't want any EV changes unless you deliberately make them by pressing the button.

b4 Matrix Metering Face Detection

Options: On (default), Off

My preference: Off

Face detection has become so accurate and useful that the ability to adjust exposure expressly to take into account faces contained within the frame is a highly desirable *optional* feature. This entry allows you to enable such adjustments when you are using Matrix metering. The ability of Matrix metering to calculate exposure from a detailed array of segments within the frame allows the Z5 II to measure the light reflected from faces and optimize exposure based on them.

This setting is especially useful when shooting portrait-type images or other people pictures in which humans fill most of the frame. However, scenes in which people make up a smaller component of the image area can end up being improperly exposed when exposure priority is given to humans. I leave this setting Off most of the time, because Matrix metering generally does an excellent job with a wide variety of scenes. I turn it on primarily when shooting candid portraits under varying lighting conditions.

b5 Center-Weighted Area

Options: Small, Standard (default), Average

My preference: Standard

In many ways, Center-weighted metering is a hold-over from the early days of through-the-lens (TTL) exposure metering. The earliest cameras with this feature calculated exposure using the average of the entire frame. Center-weighting was developed to give additional priority to the area of the image where the most important subject matter was likely to appear. In the Z5 II, a "fuzzy" central circle is used to calculate 75 percent of the total exposure, with the remainder of the frame used to account for the rest. Nikon recommends using Center-weighted metering for bright, contrasty scenes and when using circular polarizers.

Your choices with this entry include Small (with an 8mm circle); Standard (the default), with a 12mm circle, and Average, which is the same as the old-time full-frame averaging systems. I've found that changing the size really has very little effect most of the time. By default, the camera will show a translucent gray circle in the display that represents the size of the center-weighted area in display configurations 1–3 (which cycle through when you press the DISP button). You can disable/enable the circle using the Custom Monitor/Viewfinder Shooting Display entries (d19/d20), as described later in this chapter.

b6 Fine-Tune Optimal Exposure

Options: Default (none), Plus or minus one stop in 1/6-stop increments for: Matrix metering, Center-weighted metering, Spot metering, Highlight-weighted metering

My preference: N/A

This setting is a powerful adjustment that allows you to dial in a specific amount of exposure compensation that will be applied, invisibly, to every photo you take using each of the four metering modes. No more can you complain, "My camera always underexposes by 1/3 stop!" If that is actually the case, and the phenomenon is consistent, you can use this custom menu adjustment to compensate.

Exposure compensation is usually a better idea (does your camera *really* underexpose that consistently?), but this setting does allow you to "recalibrate" your camera yourself. However, you have no indication that fine-tuning has been made: any exposure compensation you add/subtract here is not reflected in the Z5 II's live view display. You'll need to remember what you've done. After all, you someday might discover that your camera is consistently *over*exposing images by 1/3 stop, not realizing that your Custom Setting b6 adjustment is the culprit.

In practice, it's rare that the camera will *consistently* provide the wrong exposure in any of the four metering modes, especially Matrix metering, which can alter exposure dramatically based on an internal database of typical scenes. Fine-tune optimal exposure may be most useful for Spot metering, if you always take a reading off the same type of subject, such as a human face or 18 percent gray card. Should you find that the gray card readings, for example, always differ from what you would prefer, go ahead and fine-tune optimal exposure for Spot metering, and use that to read your gray cards. To use this feature:

1. **Select fine-tuning.** Choose Custom Setting b6: Fine-tune Optimal Exposure from the Custom Settings menu.

2. **Consider yourself warned.** In the screen that appears, choose Yes after carefully reading the warning that Nikon insists on showing you every time this option is activated.

3. **Select metering mode to correct.** Choose Matrix, Center-weighted, Spot, or Highlight-weighted metering in the screen that follows by highlighting your choice and pressing the multi selector right button. (See Figure 7.6, left.)

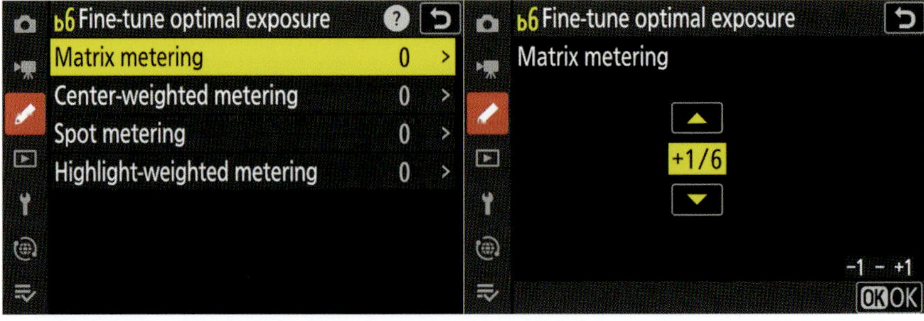

Figure 7.6 You can fine-tune any of four metering modes (left). Increments of 1/6 stop are available (right).

4. **Specify amount of correction.** Press the up/down buttons to dial in the exposure compensation you want to apply. You can specify compensation up to +/− one stop, in increments of 1/6 stop, half as large a change as conventional exposure compensation. This is truly *fine-tuning*. (See Figure 7.6, right.)

5. **Confirm your change.** Press OK when finished. You can repeat the action to fine-tune the other exposure modes if necessary.

c. Timers/AE Lock

This category (see Figure 7.7) is a mixed bag of settings, covering how the shutter release and AE-L buttons interact (c1) and entries that adjust delay times (c2 and c3).

c1 Shutter-Release Button AE-L

Options: Off (default), On (half press), On (burst mode)

My preference: On when using back-button focus, as described in Chapter 5

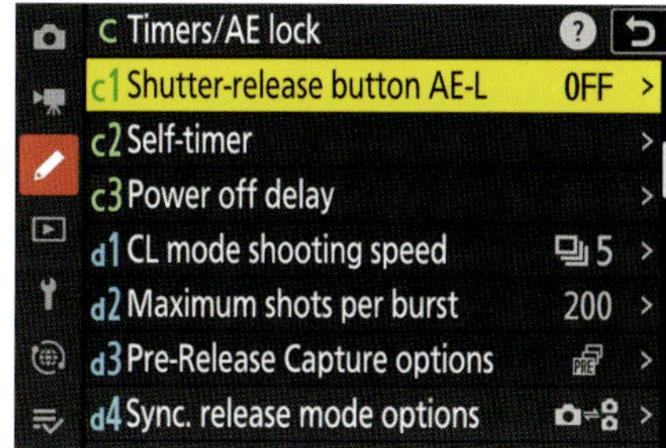

Figure 7.7 The Timers/AE Lock settings.

This is another of Nikon's easily confusing options for controlling how and when autofocus and exposure are activated and locked. The intent is to allow you to separate autofocus and autoexposure activation and locking.

- **Off.** Exposure is locked *only* when the sub-selector (AE-L/AF-L) button (or another button assigned to that function) is pressed. This is the default. The shutter release does not lock exposure.

- **On (half press).** Exposure locks when either the shutter-release button is depressed *halfway* or the sub-selector (AE-L/AF-L) button is held down. If you always want exposure locked when the shutter release is pressed halfway, use this option.

- **On (burst mode).** Exposure locks when the shutter-release button is pressed down all the way. You'd do this during continuous shooting, when you press the shutter release and hold it down while your series of shots is captured. This option locks the exposure for the first image, ensuring that all the other images in the sequence are given the same exposure.

LOCKED EXPOSURE VS LOCKED SETTINGS

Locking the amount of exposure does not mean you are locking the *settings* your camera uses. When using Shutter-priority, Aperture-priority, or Programmed Auto modes, exposure is locked, but you can still rotate the main command dial to change to a different shutter speed (in S mode) or sub-command dial to switch to a different aperture (in A mode). In P mode, the main dial will provide different combinations of both shutter speed and aperture. The camera will adjust the other setting to provide the same overall exposure.

c2 Self-Timer

Options: Self-timer Delay (default: 10 sec.), Number of Shots (default: 1), Interval Between Shots (default: 0.5 sec.)

My preference: N/A

This setting lets you choose the length of the self-timer shutter-release delay when Release mode is set to Self-Timer. Your options include:

- **Self-timer Delay.** The default value is 10 seconds. You can also choose 2, 5, or 20 seconds. If I have the camera mounted on a tripod or other support and am too lazy to attach the MC-30A cable release (I have three, one for each camera bag, so I *always* have one available), I can set a 2-second delay that is sufficient to let the camera stop vibrating after I've pressed the shutter release. I use a longer delay time if I am racing to get into the picture myself and am not sure I can make it in 10 seconds. The lamp on the front of the camera will blink when the countdown begins and then illuminate steadily for the final two seconds.

- **Number of Shots.** After the timer finishes counting down, you can take from 1 to 9 different shots. This is a godsend when shooting photos of groups, especially if you want to appear in the photo itself. You'll always want to shoot several pictures to ensure that everyone's eyes are open and there are smiling expressions on each face. Instead of racing back and forth to trigger the self-timer multiple times, you can select the number of shots taken after a single countdown. For small groups, I always take at least as many shots as there are people in the group—plus one. That gives everybody a chance to close their eyes.

- **Interval Between Shots.** If you've selected 2 to 9 as your number of shots to be snapped off, you can use this option to space out the different exposures. Your choices are 0.5, 1, 2, or 3 seconds. Use a short interval when you want to capture everyone saying "Cheese!" The 3-second option is helpful if you're using flash, as 3 seconds is generally long enough to allow the flash to recycle and have enough juice for the next photo.

c3 Power Off Delay

Options: Separate settings for Playback, Menus, Picture Review, Standby Timer

My preference: Playback (20 seconds); Menus (1 minute); Picture Review (4 seconds); Standby Timer (10 minutes for sports, weddings, other events with frequent shooting)

You can adjust the amount of time the viewfinder or LCD monitor displays remain on when no other operations are being performed. The delays you can adjust include:

- **Playback.** This parameter controls how long until the displays are turned off after the Playback button is pressed. The default is 10 seconds. This setting is *not* the same as the Picture Review that occurs when you press the Playback button.

- **Menus.** Menus will display for up to 1 minute by default, then disappear if there is no user activity. The default value is usually fine.

- **Picture Review.** Determines how long an image is displayed automatically because Picture Review in the Playback menu is set to On. The default is four seconds.

- **Standby Timer.** The camera displays, sensor, and exposure meters will remain active until this timer expires. The default is 30 seconds, and the display will warn you by dimming a few seconds before putting the camera to sleep. This is generally the most critical of the four; keep in mind that your sensor remains energized the whole time and uses a lot more juice than cameras that rely on an optical viewfinder. **Note:** If you've selected 10 seconds, the Z5 II will keep the camera active for an *additional* 10 seconds while the *i* menu is displayed.

You'll rarely need or want to have playback, menus, or picture review active for long periods. But sports shooters, wildlife photographers, and some others prefer a longer delay because they can keep their camera always "at the ready" with no delay to interfere with taking an action shot that unexpectedly presents itself. Extra battery consumption is just part of the price paid.

For example, when I am shooting football, a standby timer of 20 seconds is plenty, because the players lining up for the snap is my signal to get ready to shoot. But for basketball or soccer, I typically set the standby timer for 30 minutes, because action is virtually continuous. My camera has plenty of power, and I carry two sets of spare batteries. I rarely shoot much more than 1,000 to 1,200 shots at any sports event, so that's often sufficient juice even with the standby timer set for 30 minutes or No Limit.

Some exceptions to be aware of:

- **Resetting the Standby Timer.** Tapping the shutter release (or another button) will extend the Standby Timer's active period. You'll receive a warning when the display dims just before the Standby Timer expires.
- ***i* menu extension.** If you happen to set the Standby Timer to 10 seconds, the Z5 II will extend the active display to 20 seconds if the *i* menu is in use.
- **Picture Review override.** The camera will always override the review display when the shutter button is partially or fully depressed, so you'll never miss a shot because a previous image was on the screen.
- **Self-timer extension.** All four timers extend by 60 seconds when you're using the self-timer.
- **Video recording.** You should set the Standby Timer to Unlimited when using your camera as a Web cam or when recording to an external device through the Z5 II's HDMI port.

d. Shooting/Display

This menu section offers a variety of sometimes unrelated shooting and display options not found elsewhere, but which are not frequently changed, making them suitable for a Custom Settings entry. Figure 7.8 shows the first seven entries of the Z5 II's Shooting/Display menu.

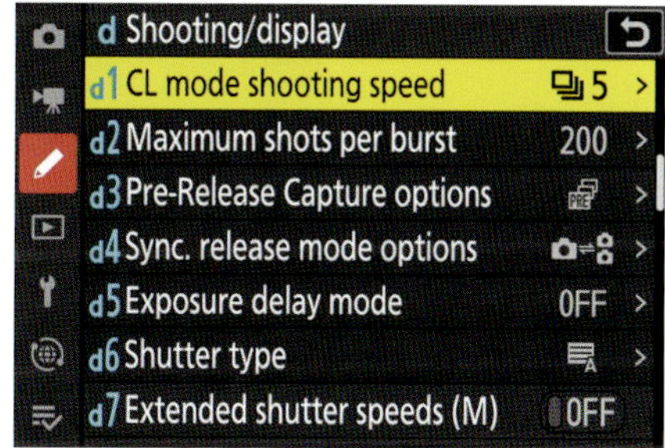

Figure 7.8 A mixed bag of entries is found in the Shooting/Display submenu.

d1 CL Mode Shooting Speed

Options: 1–7 fps (default: 5 fps)

My preference: Varies

You can specify the frames-per-second shooting rate for Continuous (Low) speed mode from 1 frame per second to 7 frames per second. Faster rates are better for sports action, such as the image shown in Figure 7.9, and can be effectively coupled with the Z5 II's Pre-Capture options (described shortly) to help snag a picture at a decisive moment.

Choose one of these firing speed ranges for Continuous (Low) from among those available that is suitable for the kind of shooting environment you're in:

- **Normal continuous shooting.** I set my camera to the 1 fps rate most of the time, so that I can take multiple shots quickly without needing to press the shutter release repeatedly. A one-second rate isn't so fast that I end up taking a bunch of shots that I don't want, but it is fast enough that I can shoot a series.

- **Bracketing.** When I'm using bracketing, I generally have the camera set to shoot a bracketed set of three pictures: under, normal, and overexposure. With the camera set to 3 fps, I can press the shutter once and take all three bracketed shots, with basically the same framing, within about one second.

- **HDR bracketing.** On the other hand, if you're bracketing to combine individual images in an image editor to produce a high dynamic range photo, you'll want the exposures to be captured as quickly as possible. That will minimize any differences between the images, so they can be more easily aligned as they are merged.

Figure 7.9 High frame rates can capture a critical moment when shooting sports action.

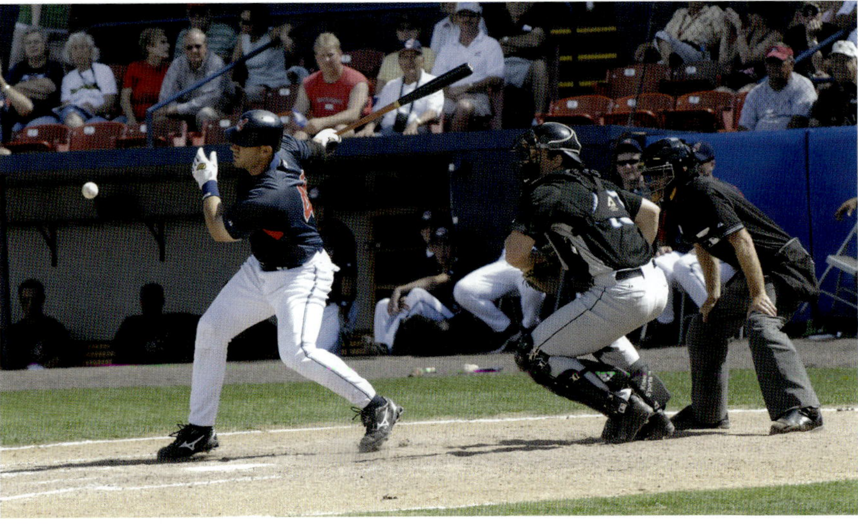

- **Slower action sequences.** For some types of action, such as long-distance running, golf, swimming, or routine baseball plays, a rate of 2 fps might be sufficient. You can make this more reasonable speed available by defining it here as the continuous low-speed frame rate.
- **Faster action sequences.** You can specify higher frame rates, up to 7 fps when you want to grab more images in a brief burst. However, in most cases, you'll use Continuous High or Continuous High (Extended) mode for this type of photography. Dialing in a slightly slower speed here makes it easy to switch back and forth just by changing the release mode setting from Continuous Low to Continuous High or Continuous High (Extended).

d2 Maximum Shots Per Burst

Options: 1–200 shots, 200 (default)

My preference: 200

When you have a camera with fast continuous shooting speeds, it's easy to get carried away. I've taken as many as 7,200 shots in a single day at an airshow, which was a thrilling experience (both from a photographic and observer viewpoint), but it was less exciting to spend hours wading through so many images to find the keepers among the near-misses.

At all Image Size/Quality settings, your Z5 II can shoot continuously for hundreds of shots without filling its buffer or even producing a slow-down of the shooting rate. If you'd rather put an upper limit on the number of images in a continuous burst, you can do that here. The default value is 200. I generally leave this setting at the default, but in addition to laziness and dwindling memory card space, there are other reasons why a lower value would be useful. Say you wanted to illustrate an event sequence—such as a golfer's swing over a period of two seconds—and wanted to end up with a 4 × 4 array of 16 individual images. Theoretically, you could set the maximum burst to 16 shots, choose a frame rate of 8 frames per second, and end up with exactly that. In practice, however, it would be smarter to apply a fudge factor and capture 18–20 frames (or more) and use 16 shots from the middle of the sequence. Why? Because the action you are illustrating is unlikely to take exactly two seconds.

d3 Pre-Release Capture Options

Options: Pre-release Burst: Off (default), 0.3, 0.5, 1.0 seconds; Post-release Burst: 1, 2, 3 seconds, Max (default)

My preference: Pre-release Burst: 1 second; Post-release Burst: Max

Your Nikon's pre-release capture feature is one capability for which the term "game-changer" is not hyperbole. It gives you the ability to capture images that took place up to a full second *before* you pressed the shutter release. In effect, you can partially nullify the limitations of human reaction times and capture bursts of lighting and other spontaneous events without a specialized light/sound trigger, and capture decisive sports action or unpredictable wildlife movement with ease. If you're like me, you've spent a lot of time waiting for a butterfly to alight, only to end up with photos of blossoms where a rare specimen *used to be*. Or, you've tried, without success, to capture an osprey at the moment it dives and snares a fish.

Your Nikon's pre-release capture options make such pictures easy. When the shutter release is pressed halfway, the camera will immediately begin capturing images in its buffer, just as if you were taking a picture. However, this stream of images remains in the buffer and is not written to your memory card. The images cycle through the buffer, which retains up to the most recent one second's worth. You can keep half-pressing the shutter release for up to 90 seconds. When you press the shutter button down all the way during that span, the camera transports the most recent one second's worth of images (or just 1/3 or 1/2 second's worth as you specify) to the memory card. It continues to grab images for a few additional seconds.

This feature works only when the Z5 II is set to the C15 or C30 release modes, which can capture from roughly 5 to 30 frames *before* the shutter release is pressed down all the way, along with additional action that happens up to around four seconds *after* you trigger the sequence. You can set your pre-release options ahead of time; the Z5 II's time-travel features remain dormant until you specifically switch to C15/C30 release modes. Note that high-speed images are always captured in JPEG (or HEIF) Normal format. Here's how to get set up:

1. **Access the d3 Pre-release Capture Options entry.** When you navigate to this entry, you'll be shown two sets of options: Pre-release burst and Post-release burst.

2. **Choose pre-release duration.** The Pre-release burst screen, shown at left in Figure 7.10, is Off by default. To enable pre-release capture, choose 0.3 seconds (actually, about a third of a second), 0.5 seconds, or 1.0 seconds. That will determine both the duration of your pre-buffering, as well as the number of images captured before the shutter release is pressed down all the way.

3. **Choose post-release burst.** The camera can continue to capture moments that occur after the shutter release is pressed. Depending on how important the post-shot sequence is, you can choose 1, 2, or 3 seconds, or Max (in which case capture will continue until the buffer fills, which is usually about four seconds, or you release the shutter button). For events that happen in a split second, such as a lightning burst, you sometimes won't care much about post-event images (but keep in mind that multiple bolts of lightning can happen in rapid succession).

4. **Choose capture speed.** Hold down the release mode button and rotate the main command dial to select C15 or C30 high-speed frame capture modes, as seen at left in Figure 7.11.

5. **Confirm pre-release mode.** Check the upper-right edge of the LCD monitor, as shown in Figure 7.11, right, or at the bottom of the viewfinder to see the PRE icon displayed. You have activated pre-release capture.

Figure 7.10 Set Pre-release burst (left) and Post-release burst (right).

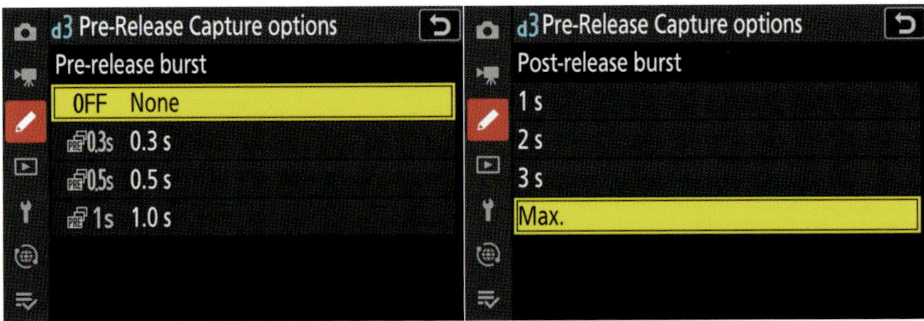

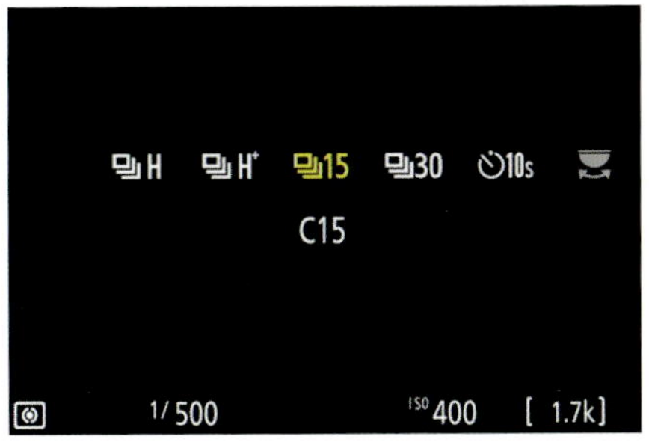
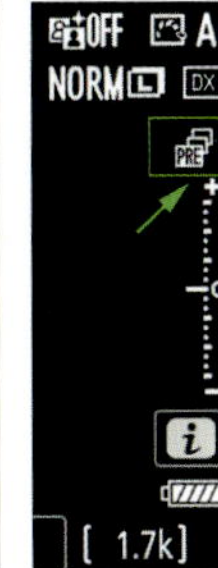

Figure 7.11 Choose capture speed (left). Pre-release indicator (right).

6. **Capture images.** Press and hold the shutter release halfway to begin capturing images to the buffer. A green dot will appear in the PRE icon to show that images are being buffered. If you hold down the shutter release halfway for more than roughly 60 seconds, the PRE icon begins blinking, and at 90 seconds a ! warning appears and pre-release capture is cancelled. To resume, lift your finger from the shutter release and press it halfway again.

Note: If the time between when you press the shutter halfway and then all the way down to direct images to the memory card is less than the specified pre-release burst, you won't get a full set of images. In other words, if you have set a 1-second pre-release burst but press the shutter release all the way less than one second after buffering begins, you'll save only the frames already accumulated, plus any captured during the post-release burst.

7. **Select image.** You can review the burst you've captured in the camera or in your image editor to select the version that captures the decisive moment in your sequence. (See Figure 7.12.)

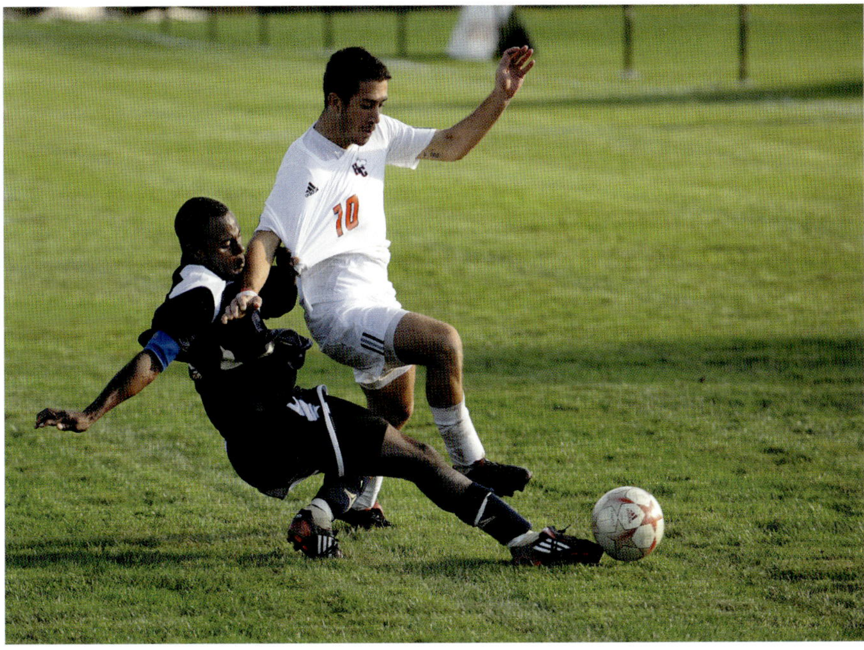

Figure 7.12 You'll improve your chances of getting a great action shot with the Z5 II's Pre-release Capture feature.

> **TIPS**
>
> - For moving subjects (rather than lightning, for example) you might want to use a focal length slightly wider than necessary to frame your image tightly. Give yourself some extra room to account for sudden, erratic movement when your subject takes flight or performs some other action.
> - Choose your AF-area mode carefully. You will probably want to use Wide-area AF (L) with subject detection appropriate for your subject matter.
> - You're going to capture many images even if you don't buffer a lot of extra frames. Take advantage of the Series Playback options (described in Chapter 8). You can set your camera to display the burst in real time for a few seconds, and specify that only the first image in a burst appears in thumbnail views. These will help you review and access your bursts more efficiently.

d4 Sync. Release Mode Options

Options: Sync (default), No Sync

My preference: Sync

If you own multiple compatible Nikon cameras that can be linked over a Wi-Fi network, you can configure them such that they all fire at the same time. One camera acts as a master that controls the shutter release of the additional cameras. Sports photographers love this capability, because they can install remote cameras, say, above a basketball rim, and then position themselves along the baseline to shoot action in the paint. One click of the master camera produces shots from both angles simultaneously. (This is basically how I cover basketball games, except for the part about having a second, remote-controlled camera mounted high above the rim.)

d5 Exposure Delay Mode

Options: 3, 2, 1, 0.5, 0.2 seconds, Off (default)

My preference: Off

This is a marginally useful feature. (It can actually be mildly annoying if you forget to turn it off.) With the Z5 II, it's used to force the camera to snap a picture about 0.2, 0.5, 1, 2, or 3 seconds (your choice) after you've pressed the shutter-release button all the way, like a limited-delay self-timer.

It's useful when you are using shutter speeds of about 1/8th to 1/60th second hand-held and want to minimize the effects of the vibration that results when you depress the shutter button. It can also be used when the camera is mounted on a tripod, although the self-timer function, set to a two-second delay, is more useful in that scenario. When switched On, the camera will pause while you steady your steely grip, taking the picture about one second later. When turned Off, the picture is taken when the shutter release is pressed, as normal.

One interesting side-effect of this mode is that it separates the normally invisible pre-flash produced by any camera's external flash that's connected with the delay. That can have an unwanted side-effect. For example, if you're shooting living subjects (human or animal), and set the delay for one second, your subject may be startled by the initial flash and close their eyes just before the main flash fires 1,000 milliseconds later. Longer delays can produce incorrect exposures if you happen to accidentally (or intentionally) reframe or pan during the interval between when the pre-flash fires (and the camera calculates exposure) and the moment when the shutter opens/flash fires to take the actual picture.

Z5 II users can substitute the self-timer's 2- or 5-second delays and use the longer 10- or 20-second timers if needed.

d6 Shutter Type

Options: Auto (default), Mechanical Shutter, Electronic Front-Curtain Shutter
My preference: Auto

Your camera has an electronic front-curtain shutter that can be used to commence an exposure without the need for the (potentially) vibration-causing physical shutter curtain, or from other camera movement at slow shutter speeds. This setting allows you to specify whether the mechanical shutter or electronic front-curtain shutter are always used (with several exceptions), or Auto if you want the camera to choose the shutter type depending on shutter speed. In Auto mode, the e-front curtain shutter is used at slow shutter speeds (only) to reduce blur from camera shake induced by the mechanical shutter's movement. At faster shutter speeds, Auto mode will use the mechanical shutter to both start and end exposure. That's because with fast lenses and brief shutter speeds, the electronic first-curtain shutter can distort the bokeh effect (the out-of-focus disc produced by highlights).

Other exceptions: If you've specified Silent mode in the Photo Shooting menu (see Chapter 5), the electronic shutter is always used, regardless of the setting here. In addition, the electronic front-curtain shutter is available only when you're using a shutter speed of 1/2000th second or slower. In use, the camera "dumps" the current image display on the EVF or LCD monitor, then begins exposure. The mechanical rear-curtain shutter terminates the exposure. So, while the electronic front-curtain shutter is quieter, this mode isn't totally silent. Its chief benefit is avoiding a tiny amount of vibration that can occur from "shutter bounce." (The mechanical front curtain isn't totally damped after it descends.) If you really want to avoid any possibility of shutter vibration, choose the 0.2-second setting in Custom Setting d5: Exposure Delay mode, described above.

For quieter operation, choose the Silent mode setting in the Setup menu, described in Chapter 5. With Silent mode you can use any shutter speed—but you cannot use flash (or long exposure noise reduction). In addition, the beep speaker is automatically turned off and your continuous-shooting frame rate will change. With the electronic front-curtain shutter, you *can* use flash, but you have that 1/200th second top shutter speed limitation, and your beeper will sound if enabled. I explained front- and rear-curtain shutter components in more detail in Chapter 3.

d7 Extended Shutter Speeds (M)

Options: Off (default), On (Allows exposures of 60, 90, 120, 180, 240, 300, 480, 600, 720, and 900 seconds)

My preference: Off

Extra-long shutter speeds, up to 900 seconds, are available in Manual exposure mode if you activate the feature here. Once you've done that, the next shutter speed shown after 30 seconds is 60 seconds, followed by 90 seconds and up to 900 seconds (15 minutes). The Bulb and Time settings are still available, but moved to the very end, which can be inconvenient if you need to access one of them while this setting is enabled. At the (conventional) shutter speeds between 1 second and 30 seconds, the actual exposure time will differ slightly (a 30-second exposure will last 32 seconds) but will match again if you set a speed between 60 and 900 seconds.

d8 Limit Selectable Image Area

Options: All Available (default), Individually Disable DX, 1:1, or 16:9 Formats

My preference: FX, DX, and 16:9 only enabled

This is the first entry on the next group of menu entries (see Figure 7.13). Your camera may provide you with more image area formats than you ever need—but it also gives you the ability to make any of them (except the full-frame FX choice) invisible.

Disabling or enabling one or more image area options is easy. Highlight any format (except FX, which cannot be disabled) and press the right multi selector button or press OK to mark or unmark your choice. You must press MENU to confirm. I don't use the 1:1 image area much, so I disable it. I sometimes shoot in DX mode for sports to capture more compact 10.6MP images with the DX format's 1.5X field-of-view crop. When I am taking stills to use for movie storyboards, I prefer to shoot them using the same high-definition 16:9 proportions that the movie will be captured in, so I keep that available.

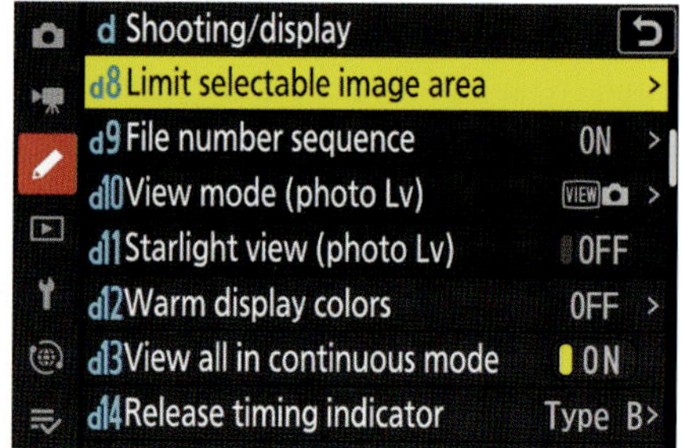

Figure 7.13 The next group of Shooting/Display entries.

The image areas you specify can be selected using the Image Area entry of the Photo Shooting and Video Record menus. If you mount a Nikon F-mount DX (APS-C type) lens on the Z5 II using an FTZ adapter, the camera *automatically* switches to DX mode; indeed, the Image Area options are not available. Unfortunately, that means you can't manually change to FX mode for those lenses (some of them do cover the full frame at certain focal lengths). But when working with both Z-mount and F-mount full-frame lenses, you can choose one of the cropped image areas; the camera will enlarge the DX crop to fill the display and add black bars at top, bottom, or sides (as appropriate) to provide a visual reference for the other crops. (That's a distinct advantage this mirrorless model has over its dSLR siblings, which must use a mask to show the image area when using the optical viewfinder.)

d9 File Number Sequence

Options: On (default), Off, Reset

My preference: On

The camera will automatically apply a file number to each picture you take, using consecutive numbering for all your photos over a long period of time, spanning many different memory cards, starting over from scratch when you insert a new card or when you manually reset the numbers. Numbers are applied from 0001 to 9999, at which time the camera "rolls over" to 0001 again.

The camera keeps track of the last number used in its internal memory and, if File Number Sequence is turned On, will apply a number that's one higher, or a number that's one higher than the largest number in the current folder on the inserted memory card. You can also start over each time a new folder has been created on the memory card or reset the current counter back to 0001 at any time. Here's how it works:

- **On.** At this default setting, the camera will use the number stored in its internal memory any time a new folder is created, a new memory card is inserted, or an existing memory card is formatted. If the card is not blank and contains images, then the next number will be one greater than the highest number on the card *or* in internal memory (whichever is higher).
- **Off.** If you're using a blank/reformatted memory card, or a new folder is created, the next photo taken will be numbered 0001. File number sequences will be reset every time you use or format a card, or a new folder is created (which happens when an existing folder on the card contains 5,000 shots).
- **Reset.** The camera assigns a file number that's one larger than the largest file number in the current folder, unless the folder is empty, in which case numbering is reset to 0001. At this setting, new or reformatted memory cards will always have 0001 as the first file number.

HOW MANY SHOTS, REALLY?

The file numbers produced by the camera don't provide information about the actual number of times the shutter has been tripped—called *actuations*. For that data, you'll need a third-party software solution, such as the free Opanda iExif (www.opanda.com) for Windows or the non-free ($39.95) GraphicConverter for Macintosh (www.lemkesoft.com). These utilities can be used to extract the true number of actuations from the Exif information embedded in a JPEG file.

---

d10 View Mode (Photo Live View)

Options: Show effects of settings: Always, Only when flash not used (default); Adjust for ease of viewing: Auto, Custom

My preference: Always, except when using studio flash

This entry provides control over when the display reflects how your current settings of white balance, Picture Controls, and exposure compensation will affect your image when the photo is actually taken. It's a good way to preview the "look" of your image as it is adjusted by your selected settings. In Manual exposure mode, you will even be able to preview how your *exposure* will change the image; the displays will actually lighten or darken to reflect exposure changes. Sounds like a good idea, right?

However, there are times when you *don't* want to see the effects of the settings you've made in the display. For example, when you are using flash in Manual exposure mode, the camera has no way of knowing exactly how much light will be illuminating your scene. You'll especially want to change this setting to Off when working with "dumb" studio strobes connected using an old-school PC/X connector, when connected to a Nikon AS-15 Sync Terminal adapter attached to the hot shoe.

After all, that f/16 aperture you've selected may be ideal for a shot exposed by your studio strobes, but the camera will show you a preview based on the ambient light, rather than the flash. The result? Your display image is very, very dim.

However, in all other cases, at the Show Effects of Settings > Always setting, the display reflects the *relative* effects of any white balance, Picture Control, or exposure compensation settings you've made. In that mode, this allows for a reasonable representation of what the photo will look like and enables you to evaluate whether the current settings will provide the effects you want.

> **STILLS ONLY**
>
> This setting has no effect in video mode; the effects of your camera settings *always* are reflected in what you see in the display when capturing movies.

The Always option can be especially helpful when you're using any of the Picture Controls, because you can preview the exact rendition that the selected effect and its overrides will provide. It's also very useful when you're setting some exposure compensation, as you can visually determine how much lighter or darker each adjustment makes the image. And when you're trying to achieve correct color balance, it's useful to be able to preview the effect of your white balance setting.

If you'd like to preview the image *without* the effect of settings visible, you can disable the feature, and the display will no longer accurately depict what your photo will look like when it's taken. So, for most users, Always is the most suitable option. Unfortunately, this setting has caused more than a few minutes of head-scratching among new users who switch to Manual exposure mode and find themselves with a completely black (or utterly white) screen. The black screen, especially, may fool you into thinking your camera has malfunctioned. Here is an overview of your options for this setting:

- **Always.** The camera always adjusts the display. A VIEW indicator with a camera icon next to it appears when adjustments are active. The exact behavior differs, depending on your shooting mode:
    - **Manual exposure mode.** As you make manual adjustments to shutter speed, f/stop, or ISO, the screen will darken or brighten to reflect your exposure fine-tuning. White balance and the effects of any Picture Controls you select will also be reflected in the display.
    - **Note:** Even when using Manual exposure, the camera will continue to calculate what the correct exposure *should* be, and if it decides an appropriate exposure is not possible at the current settings, the aperture or shutter speed readouts or the plus/minus exposure bar will blink. When that happens, the display no longer represents the final image.

- **Manual exposure mode + ISO Auto.** You'll recall that in Manual exposure mode, when ISO Auto is enabled, two things happen. First, if your manual settings don't allow an appropriate exposure, the camera will increase or decrease the ISO sensitivity to produce a correct exposure. In that case, the screen won't darken/brighten until you exceed the ability to make an adjustment (based on your current ISO Auto parameters, set as described in Chapter 6). When those limits are reached, the display will adjust to account for the over- or underexposure.

  Second, when ISO Auto is active in Manual exposure mode, you can apply exposure compensation, and the display will brighten or darken to reflect your EV changes. If ISO Auto is disabled, exposure compensation has no effect in Manual exposure mode.

- **Auto exposure modes.** Exposure changes you apply using exposure compensation will be reflected in the display image, along with White Balance and Picture Control effects. The exposure changes resulting from automatic adjustments made in Aperture-priority, Shutter-priority, or Programmed Auto modes won't result in any changes in the display. However, if any of the automatic modes are unable to provide an appropriate exposure (as shown by blinking indicators), the display may not represent the actual image you'll capture.

- **Only When Flash is not Used.** The alternative to Always is to tell the camera to adjust the display for ease of viewing *only* when a compatible Speedlight is not attached and powered up. Ease of Viewing overrides the adjustments the Z5 II would ordinarily make as described above, so if you choose this option, the display will *not* reflect exposure, exposure compensation, White Balance, or Picture Control effects *when a compatible flash is in use.*

- **Adjust for ease of viewing.** You can disable the on-screen adjustments when needed, say, when you're using a studio flash connected to your camera through the PC/X terminal. A VIEW indicator with an icon representing the profile of an eyeball (VIEW ▷) is visible when adjustments are active. Unfortunately, using this option disables the useful live histogram display. There are two options for this setting:

  - **Auto.** The display adjustments make it easier to view the scene even if that doesn't actually represent the brightness or darkness that will be produced by the actual exposure.

  - **Custom.** You can individually adjust which of your camera settings are applied to the preview image, while leaving the others disabled:

    - **White Balance.** Select either Preview Current Setting, Auto, or Choose Color Temperature. The latter allows you to specify a specific Kelvin value to use.

    - **Set Picture Control.** Choose Preview Current Setting or Adjust for Ease of Viewing (which *does not* apply the Picture Control to the preview image).

    - **Brighten Shadows.** Select Off (shadows reflect the effects of your settings) or Brighten shadows by factors of +1 to +3 stops.

d11 Starlight View (Photo Live View)

Options: Off (default), On

My preference: Off

Under many circumstances, your Z5 II may be able to see better at night than you can, especially if your eyes have not yet adjusted to the darkness. This entry can make viewing under low-light conditions easier, by reducing the frame rate of the display and increasing the exposure. The display will be noisier and slower, but easier to view, and the autofocus system will always use contrast detection confirmation. Unfortunately, because the brightness is boosted, you must use the exposure metering bar to judge exposure, as the visual representation will no longer be accurate.

d12 Warm Display Colors

Options: Warm Display Color Options: Mode 1, Mode 2, Off; Warm Color Display Brightness: +/– 3

My preference: N/A

Many devices—probably including your smartphone or e-reader—have an option or setting that switches to a warmer illumination for the screen at night or under darker conditions, offering comfortable viewing with your night-adapted vision and, perhaps, making it easier to fall asleep. Your camera offers a similar feature (although much more pronounced), especially useful for astrophotography and other night shooting. Your options include:

- **Warm Display Color Options.** Choose from:
    - **Mode 1.** The menu display information changes to red on black (as shown in Figure 7.14) and the viewfinder and rear LCD monitor display overlays are reduced in intensity and tinted red.
    - **Mode 2.** The menu display information takes on the red/black color scheme, along with the icons and overlays. The live view image of your subject and playback views are not affected other than the icons on those screens.
    - **Off.** Warm colors are not applied.

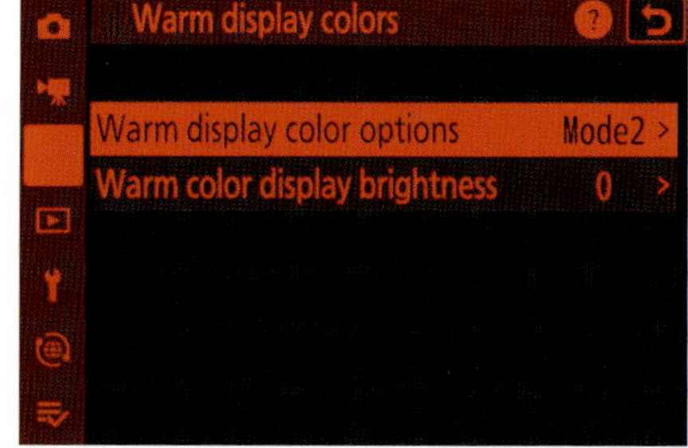

Figure 7.14 The warm display options help preserve your night vision.

- **Warm Color Display Brightness.** As you can see from the figure, the display is quite dim. This option lets you increase or decrease brightness using the up/down directional controls.

d13 View All in Continuous Mode

Options: On (default), Off

My preference: On

This setting lets you specify whether the viewfinder displays the scene at all times during burst shooting with all continuous release modes. If you select Off, the viewfinder turns black during continuous exposures.

d14 Release Timing Indicator

Options: Indicator Type: Type A, Type B (default), Type C, Off

My preference: Type B

This entry allows you to enable a visual indicator in the viewfinder that shows you that the Z5 II is taking pictures. It's a useful solution to a "feature has become a bug" problem: the nifty silent photography features of your camera's electronic shutter mean that it's not always easy to see whether you're actually capturing images.

I always use the Camera Sounds entry in the Setup menu (as described in Chapter 9) to silence my Z5 II when doing street photography, shooting performances, meetings and religious services, and in other situations where noises can be undesirable. While there are various indicators in the display that demonstrate your camera is capturing images, it's nice to have a prominent visual cue as a constant reminder. You can choose any of three Types, plus Off if you want no visual prompt (see Figure 7.15). They are as follows:

- **Type A.** The display goes black for a moment, taking you back to the thrilling days of SLR yesteryear.

- **Type B.** A line appears at the top, bottom, left, and right edges of the display. This is the default.

- **Type C.** Lines appear only at the left and right of the display. This is a least-intrusive indicator, and also the easiest to miss if you're not alert.

- **Off.** No indicator appears.

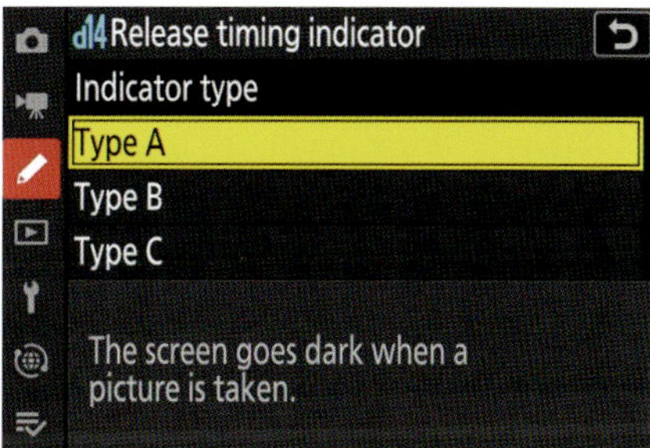

Figure 7.15 Choose indicator type.

d15 Image Frame

Options: On (default), Off

My preference: On

This is the first entry in the final page of the Shooting/Display options (shown in Figure 7.16). This feature tells the camera to display a faint line around the edge of the image area. It's an essential tool for framing your image when shooting in very dark areas, such as outdoors at night or in dark theaters or auditoriums. Under these conditions, you may not be able to discern the edge of the image frame from the surrounding dark area of the display. In addition, the Z5 II has a Viewfinder Display Size entry in the Setup menu that allows reducing the size of the viewfinder display to make it more easily seen by those wearing glasses. When enabled, you'll clearly see where your scene ends and the non-image area begins.

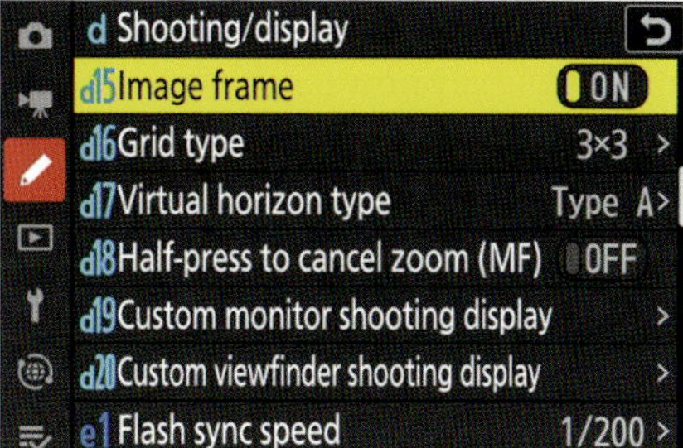

Figure 7.16 The next group of Shooting/Display entries.

d16 Grid Type

Options: 3 × 3 (default), 4 × 4, 5:4, 1:1, 16:9

My preference: 3 × 3

The camera can display five different types of guidelines that can be overlaid on the viewfinder and rear LCD monitor image as you cycle through the available displays with the DISP button. The guides offer some help when you want to align vertical or horizontal lines, particularly for architectural or scenic photography, and in visually arranging your compositions in the frame to allow cropping in post-production. The latter offers extra flexibility compared to choosing a fixed aspect ratio using the Image Area option in the Photo Shooting menu (which also crops any RAW files you capture). You're not locked into the composition you worked with when the image was captured. You can select a Rule of Thirds grid, or Nikon's traditional Rule of Quarters layout, plus centered 5:4, 1:1, and 16:9 overlays. (See Figure 7.17.) You might want the 5:4 guide when you plan to produce a lot of 8 × 10 prints or the 16:9 overlay for storyboard images that will be used to plan your next video shoot.

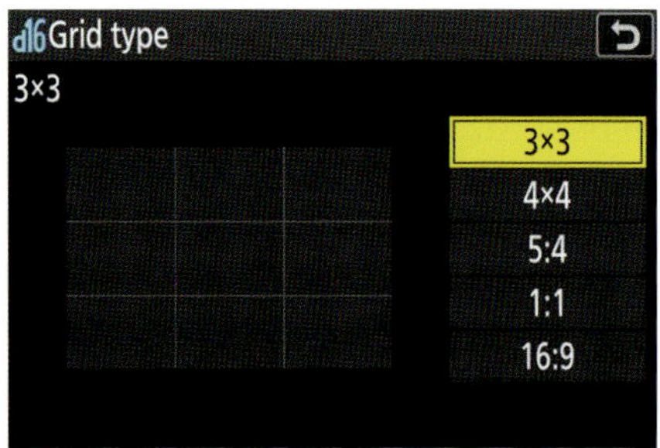

Figure 7.17 Grid types.

Note: This setting does not enable/disable grid display; it only specifies what type of overlay will be used. To activate a grid, you have to include that as an option in one of your display layouts using the Custom Monitor Shooting Display and Custom Viewfinder Shooting Display entries discussed in the d19 and d20 sections.

d17 Virtual Horizon Type

Options: Type A (default), Type B

My preference: Type B

Your Z5 II can overlay a virtual "horizon" guide on the viewfinder and rear LCD monitor to show approximately how far the camera's position varies from level, in terms of rotation around the axis of the lens and upward/downward tilt. There are two types of indicators, Type A and Type B, shown at left in Figure 7.18. Neither are 100 percent accurate, but can provide a useful guide, especially when shooting scenics and architecture.

Type A features pairs of lines, with the inner lines showing the degree of pitch, and the outer lines representing rotation. When the camera is level, the lines will turn green and line up at the horizontal center of the screen (see Figure 7.18, top center). When the camera is tilted up, the inner indicators sink below the longer rotational indicators and rise above it when the camera is tilted down (see Figure 7.18, top right).

The Type B guides consist of indicators at the bottom of the display (for rotation) and right side (for pitch/tilt), as seen in Figure 7.18, bottom center. The indicators show the current orientation when the camera is rotated or tilted (Figure 7.18, bottom right).

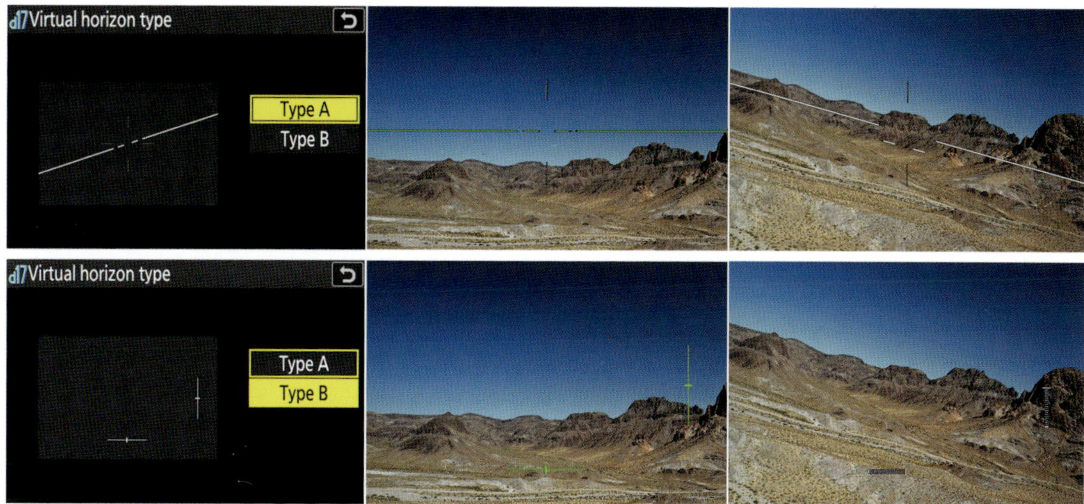

Figure 7.18 Two types of virtual horizons (left). Display when the camera is level (center) and rotated/tilted (right).

Note: As with gridlines, choosing a virtual horizon *type* does not enable *display* of the indicator. You'll need to specify Virtual Horizon as one of your active custom monitor/viewfinder displays, as described shortly, and then activate that display using the DISP button when you want to use the feature.

d18 Half-press to Cancel Zoom (MF)

Options: Off (default), On

My preference: Off

As mentioned in Chapter 3, when the Z5 II is set to manual focus, you can press the Zoom In button to enlarge the image on your display to make focusing easier. By default, you need to press the Zoom Out button to restore normal view. If you set this entry to On, you can quickly return to full-image view by pressing the shutter-release button halfway. If you do a lot of manual focusing, say, for macro photography, activating this quick cancel feature can be a time-saver. Keep in mind that if you're using a power zoom lens, the Zoom In button may be set to provide optical zooming instead.

d19 Custom Monitor Shooting Display

Options: Display 1, Display 2, Display 3, Display 4, Display 5

My preference: Varies

The preview image seen in the optical viewfinder of conventional dSLR cameras can display only a limited amount of information that can be shown, and it differs significantly from what you see on the same camera's rear LCD live view. Mirrorless cameras like the Nikon Z5 II, in contrast, can show virtually identical views on both displays; the amount and types of information available is virtually unlimited.

The bad news is that your display can easily become too cluttered for easy viewing and composition. Fortunately, Nikon has given you the ability to create up to five different customized screens for *each* type of display, so you can tailor your view to show only and exactly what you want to see. This entry is used to set up configurations for your rear LCD monitor. There are sets of information to choose from, which you can enable by placing a checkmark next to the label/icon representing that information:

- **Minimum.** If none of the label/icons are checked, the display will show only the focus point, shutter speed, aperture, ISO, and exposure bar as appropriate.
- **Simple.** P, A, S, or M shooting modes, metering mode, battery status, and the shots remaining indicator are added to the minimum display.
- **Detailed Shooting Info.** In addition to the minimum display, you'll see release mode, focus mode, focus area, white balance information, Active D-Lighting, Picture Controls, Image Quality/Size indicators, and the current Image Area.
- **Touch Controls.** An icon for enabling/disabling touch AF controls and the *i* menu icon are added to the minimum display.
- **Virtual Horizon.** Only the minimum information and the virtual horizon indicators are shown.
- **Histogram.** A live histogram is added to the minimum.
- **Framing grid.** The grid you specified using the Grid Type entry will be shown along with the minimum information.
- **Center indicator.** A cross-hair appears in the exact center of the frame, added to the minimum display.
- **Center-weighted area.** The part of the frame emphasized by center-weighted metering is shown as a faint circle of the size you have chosen.

To customize your LCD display, you just need to follow a few simple steps:

1. **Access this menu entry.** The screen shown at left in Figure 7.19 appears.
2. **Apply customization.** Highlight the numbered Display choice you want to customize and press the multi selector right button. The screen shown in Figure 7.19, right, pops up.
3. **Enable/disable sets.** Highlight any of the information sets and press the multi selector right button to enable or disable that set. When finished, press MENU to confirm and exit to the previous screen.

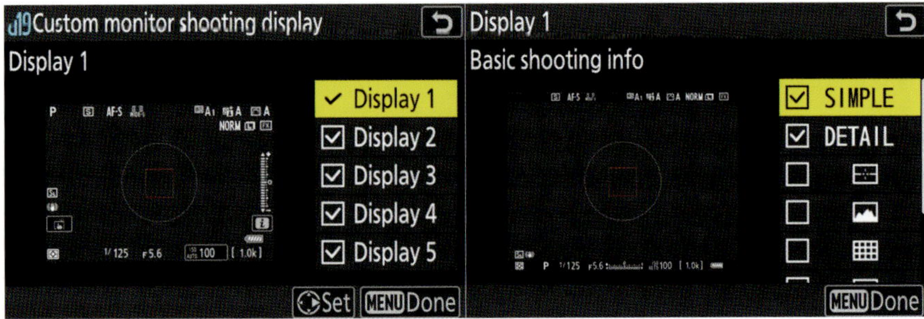

Figure 7.19 Choose which displays to enable (left) and specify the types of information shown (right).

4. **Enable/display displays.** The camera will cycle among the available displays when you press the DISP button. You can have as few as one or as many as five displays enabled at one time. Highlight a particular display 2–5 and press the OK button to enable or disable it. Display 1 cannot be disabled and will always be available.

5. **Exit.** Press MENU to confirm and exit.

d20 Custom Viewfinder Shooting Display

Options: Display 1, Display 2, Display 3, Display 4

My preference: Varies

Use this entry to customize your viewfinder displays. It operates similarly to the Custom Monitor Shooting Display entry, but Touch Controls are not one of the available sets, and it offers only four different Display variations.

e. Bracketing/Flash

There are lots of useful settings in this submenu (see Figure 7.20) that deal with bracketing and electronic flash (hence the cleverly concocted name). I provided a thorough description of using bracketing in Chapter 2, and a complete rundown of flash options in Chapter 4. In this section, I'll offer a recap of the settings at your disposal.

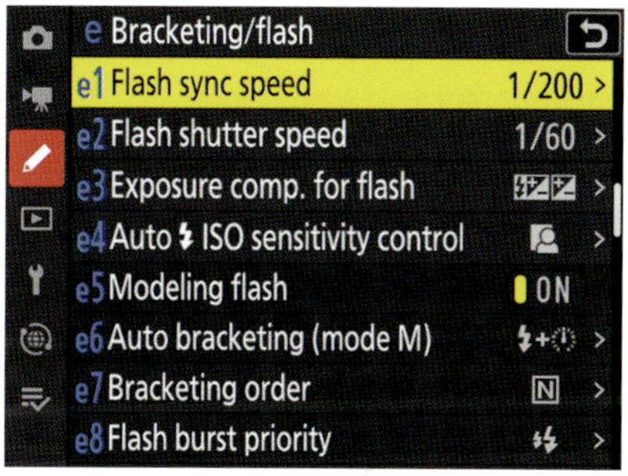

e1 Flash Sync Speed

Options: 1/200 s (Auto FP), 1/200 s–1/60 s (default: 1/200 s)

My preference: 1/200 s (Auto FP)

Figure 7.20 Bracketing and flash options are available in this menu.

As you learned in Chapter 4, the sensor must be fully energized when the external flash fires; otherwise, you'll capture an image of one edge or the other of the mechanical shutter or the electronic first-curtain shutter's virtual "curtain" in your photo. Ordinarily, the fastest shutter speed during which the sensor is completely energized for an instant is 1/200th second. However, there are exceptions when you can use faster shutter speeds with certain flash units (such as the Nikon SB-5000, SB-910, SB-700, and SB-R200) for automatic FP (focal plane) synchronization. This is called Auto FP *high-speed sync* (usually abbreviated HSS). The HSS feature allows you to use higher shutter speeds to supply fill flash, say, outdoors, where a shutter speed of 1/500th second might be needed to enable a wider aperture for reduced depth-of-field.

There are also situations in which you might want to set flash sync speed to *less* than 1/200th second, say, because you *want* ambient light to produce secondary ghost images in your frame. (I described all these sync issues in Chapter 4.)

To address your choice of flash sync speeds, you can choose from the following settings:

- **1/200 s (Auto FP).** At these two settings, you may use individual shutter speeds up to 1/200th second with any Nikon flash and compatible third-party units. However, you can also use *faster* shutter speeds with flash units compatible with high-speed sync (such as those mentioned above, plus some third-party flashes). If one of those units is mounted and powered up:
  - **P or A mode:** The camera selects the shutter speed in both Program and Aperture-priority modes. With an HSS-compatible flash attached, the camera is free to select a shutter speed as fast as 1/8000th second (or 1/2000th second if the electronic front-curtain shutter is used).
  - **S or M mode:** In these modes, *you* select the shutter speed, and you can select one as fast as 1/8000th second (or 1/2000th second with the electronic front-curtain shutter) in high-speed sync mode.
- **1/200 s–1/60 s.** You can specify a shutter speed from 1/200th second to 1/60th second to be used as the synchronization speed for flash units.

e2 Flash Shutter Speed

Options: 1/60 second (default) to 30 seconds

My preference: 1/30 second

This setting determines the *slowest* shutter speed that is available for electronic flash synchronization in the PASM exposure modes when you're not using a "slow-sync" mode (described in Chapter 4). As you may know, when you're using flash, the flash itself typically provides virtually all of the illumination that makes the main exposure, and the shutter speed determines how much, if any, of the ambient light contributes to that second, non-flash exposure. Indeed, if the camera or subject is moving, you can end up with two distinct exposures in the same frame: the sharply defined flash exposure and a second, blurry "ghost" picture created by the ambient light.

If you *don't* want that second exposure, you should use the highest shutter speed that will synchronize with your flash. This setting prevents Program or Aperture-priority modes (which both select the shutter speed for you) from inadvertently selecting a "too-slow" shutter speed. You can select a value from 30 s to 1/60 s, and the camera will *avoid* using speeds slower than the one you specify with electronic flash (unless you've selected slow sync, slow rear-curtain sync, or red-eye reduction with slow sync, as described in Chapter 4). The "slow-sync" modes do permit the ambient light to contribute to the exposure (say, to allow the background to register in night shots, or to use the ghost image as a special effect). For brighter backgrounds, you'll need to put the camera on a tripod or other support to avoid the blurry ghosts that can occur from camera shake, even if the subject is stationary.

If you are able to hold the camera steady, a value of 1/30 s is a good compromise; if you have shaky hands, use 1/60 s. Those with extraordinarily solid grips, a tripod, or a lens with vibration reduction can try the 1/15 s setting (or slower when using a tripod). Remember that this setting only determines the *slowest* shutter speed that will be chosen by the camera, not the default shutter speed.

e3 Exposure Compensation for Flash

Options: Entire Frame (default), Background Only

My preference: Background Only

Use this to specify how the camera modifies the flash level when you apply exposure compensation. Keep in mind that your camera has separate ambient light exposure compensation and flash exposure compensation settings. They enable you to adjust one or the other, or both if you are using flash. The camera will attempt to balance ambient and flash exposure compensation, but when you add or subtract compensation when the flash is attached and powered up, *both* change. This setting affects only *exposure compensation* (the ambient kind) when you are also using flash. It determines how ambient exposure compensation is applied when some of the illumination will also come from a flash unit:

- **Entire Frame.** When you apply ambient exposure compensation (press the EV button on top of the camera to the right of the ISO button and rotate the main command dial), both ambient *and* flash exposure compensation are adjusted over the entire frame. That balances the exposure for the two elements. While this works in many situations, you may find that with backgrounds and subject matter that differ widely in brightness, your results may be less than optimum.

- **Background Only.** When this option is selected, *only* ambient exposure compensation is changed when you apply it; flash exposure compensation is unaffected. So, exposure compensation is applied only to the background areas of your image, which are typically illuminated by ambient light. Flash exposure compensation is not affected but can be set separately. I prefer to use this setting and control each type of exposure compensation myself.

e4 Auto Flash ISO Sensitivity Control

Options: Subject and Background (default), Subject Only

My preference: Subject and Background

This setting allows you to customize how Auto ISO sensitivity control makes its adjustments. If you choose Subject and Background, the exposure meter will take into account both your subject matter and the background—the entire scene, in other words—when automatically changing ISO sensitivity. Choose Subject Only and the Z5 II will adjust automatic ISO sensitivity based only on what it deems to be the primary subject, as determined by the focus plane and metering data.

e5 Modeling Flash

Options: On (default), Off

My preference: On

Certain compatible external flash units (like the SB-5000, SB-500, SB-700, SB-800, and SB-910/SB-900) have the capability of simulating a modeling lamp, which gives you the limited capability of previewing how your flash illumination is going to look in the finished photo. The modeling flash is not a perfect substitute for a real incandescent or fluorescent modeling lamp, but it does help you see how your subject is illuminated and spot any potential problems with shadows.

While your flash may have a button that can trigger the modeling light, this option uses a button on the camera, which is usually more convenient. When this feature is activated, pressing the button you have defined as the Preview (depth-of-field) button on the camera briefly triggers the modeling flash for your preview. (You can define a Preview button using Custom Setting f2: Custom Controls, as described later in this chapter.)

Selecting Off disables the feature. You'll generally want to leave it On, except when you anticipate using the depth-of-field preview button for depth-of-field purposes (imagine that) and do *not* want the modeling flash to fire when the flash unit is charged and ready. Some external flash units, such as the SB-5000 and SB-910, have their own modeling flash buttons.

e6 Auto Bracketing (Mode M)

Options: Flash/Speed (default), Flash/Speed/Aperture, Flash/Aperture, Flash/ISO Sensitivity, Flash Only

My preference: Flash/Speed

When you are using Manual exposure mode and Auto ISO Sensitivity Control is set to Off in the Photo Shooting menu, the camera allows you to specify what exposure parameters—flash output, shutter speed, ISO, and aperture—are used to create the bracketed images. Here are your options and reasons to select each of them. Remember that these apply *only* when you are bracketing in Manual exposure mode and Auto ISO sensitivity is disabled. If Auto ISO is active, this entry is ignored.

- **Flash/Speed.** If you've selected AE Bracketing in Auto Bracketing Set in the Photo Shooting menu, the camera will adjust only the shutter speed during bracketed exposures. If you selected AE & Flash Bracketing, instead, the camera will also adjust the flash output level when flash is used. The aperture will remain the same, making this a good choice for HDR photos or other subjects where you want to keep the same amount of depth-of-field in successive shots.

- **Flash/Speed/Aperture.** The camera can use both shutter speed and aperture when AE Bracketing is selected, plus flash output level if AE & Flash Bracketing was selected and flash is used. This gives the camera the maximum amount of flexibility in choosing exposure parameter combinations. That's especially helpful when shooting bracket sequences of 7 or 9 shots (and/or with large increments, say, 3 stops, between shots). That's because such extreme adjustments in exposure may be difficult to achieve with only one or two parameters available—particularly when ambient light only is being bracketed. (The flash is able to adjust its output over a very wide range.)

- **Flash/Aperture.** The camera varies aperture only if AE Bracketing is specified, or aperture and flash output if AE & Flash Bracketing is selected in the Photo Shooting menu. Your selected shutter speed remains the same, so you would want to use this if retaining the same shutter speed is important (say, when shooting sports).

- **Flash/ISO Sensitivity.** The camera will adjust ISO sensitivity alone if AE Bracketing has been specified. If AE & Flash Bracketing are enabled, both ISO sensitivity and flash level will be adjusted.

- **Flash Only.** The camera varies the flash output only when AE & Flash Bracketing is active. No ambient light bracketing is done.

e7 Bracketing Order

Options: MTR > Under > Over (default), Under > MTR > Over

My preference: Under > MTR > Over, which orders frames by increasing exposure

Use this setting to define the sequence in which bracketing is carried out. Your choices are the default: MTR > Under > Over (metered exposure, followed by the version receiving less exposure, and finishing with the picture receiving the most exposure) and Under > MTR > Over, which orders the exposures from least exposed to most exposed (for both ambient and flash exposures). The same order is applied to white balance bracketing, too, but the values are Normal > More Yellow > More Blue and More Yellow > Normal > More Blue. (Nikon actually calls "yellow" by the term "amber," but I've found "yellow" easier to understand.)

This order works well if you are shooting at least three images in your sequence. If you set bracketing to just two exposures, the specified order is used, but one of the three is omitted. You'll find lots more about bracketing in Chapter 2. When doing ADL bracketing, this setting has no effect.

e8 Flash Burst Priority

Options: Prioritize Frame Advance Rate, Prioritize Precise Flash Control (default)

My preference: Prioritize Frame Advance Rate

Now that some flash units can recycle quickly enough to allow using strobes during continuous shooting, this option has become necessary. It allows you lock flash exposure to the value calculated for the *first frame* in a continuous burst, rather than calculate exposure for each individual frame (which is the default). The problem with the more precise flash exposure mode is that the Speedlight will need to issue a monitor pre-flash before each shot, potentially slowing the frame rate.

I recommend doing some tests and evaluating whether your flash is able to recycle fast enough at the distances and frame rates you use most frequently. When you're satisfied that locking exposure at the first calculated value won't produce a string of underexposed images, you can safely select Prioritize Frame Advance Rate.

f. Controls

You can modify the way various control buttons and dials perform when shooting still photos by using the options in this submenu. You can even modify the twelve adjustments that appear in the *i* menu. The first seven Controls entries are shown in Figure 7.21. Note that you can also make some control adjustments for Video mode, and I'll cover those in the section that follows this one.

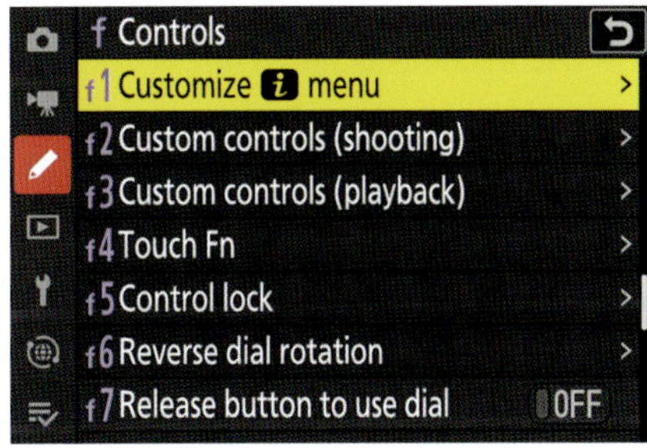

Figure 7.21 Modify the behavior of the camera's controls with these menu options.

f1 Customize *i* Menu

Options: Allows defining functions available from the *i* menu. Includes different functions that you can use to replace or add to those provided in the default version of the *i* menu.

My preference: Varies

The quick-access *i* menu can be a valuable tool for jumping directly to the controls that make frequently used adjustments. The bad news is that the 12 default entries on the *i* menu may not be ones you use often. The good news is that if you would rather have some other tools available in the *i* menu, there's a good chance you can replace your own "useless" *i* menu entries with those that are more to your liking. These 12 entries occupy the *i* menu by default. You can choose to keep these, move them, or replace them with other functions:

Set Picture Control	White Balance	Image Quality	Image Size	AF-area Mode/ Subject Detection	Focus Mode
Tone Mode	Vibration Reduction	Custom Controls (Shooting)	Metering	Airplane Mode	View Memory Card Information

Depending on your shooting habits, many of these are likely candidates for replacement with other functions. Indeed, many of the default entries in the bottom row of the *i* menu may have you wondering why Nikon put them there in the first place. No less than seven of the 12 default *i* menu functions can easily be replaced by other commands that you may use more often. Here are my suggestions:

- **White Balance.** The default behavior of the Fn1 button is White Balance, so the White Balance entry in the *i* menu can be replaced without losing quick access to that function.
- **Focus mode/AF-area mode/Subject detection.** Nikon has a confusing overlap, with the Fn2 button and *i* menu focus default dial behaviors being different:
    - **Fn2 button.** Main command dial: Focus mode; Sub-command dial: AF-area mode
    - ***i* menu.** Either command dial: Focus mode

    So, you could replace the *i* menu option and just use the Fn2 button to adjust focus mode.
- **Tone mode.** This function in the *i* menu switches between SDR (standard dynamic range), and HLG (for high dynamic range video). Changes here have no effect on Tone settings in video mode. If you don't use the non-standard tone modes, you can replace this *i* menu entry with a more useful function of your choice.
- **Vibration Reduction.** Unless you frequently fiddle with your VR settings, you can do without this function in the *i* menu, as well.
- **Custom Controls.** This setting does nothing but provide a shortcut to the Custom Settings f2 screen.
- **Airplane mode.** Use of your camera's Airplane mode isn't necessarily limited to when you're airborne. Turning it on is a quick way of disabling your camera's power-sucking Wi-Fi features. However, few of us need to use this feature often enough to justify a slot in the *i* menu.
- **View Memory Card Information.** This *i* menu choice doesn't let you switch between memory cards; it only shows you the current card functions. Replace it with something else.

Below is a list of functions you can assign to the 12 *i* menu slots. The default *i* menu functions are in boldface:

- Choose Image Area
- **Tone Mode (*i* menu default)**
- **Image Quality (*i* menu default)**
- **Image Size (*i* menu default)**
- **View Memory Card Information (*i* menu default)**
- Exposure Compensation
- ISO Sensitivity Settings
- **White Balance (*i* menu default)**
- **Set Picture Control (*i* menu default)**
- Set Picture Control (HLG)
- Color Space
- Active D-Lighting
- Long Exposure NR
- High ISO NR
- Skin Softening
- Portrait Impression Balance

- **Metering (*i* menu default)**
- Flash Mode
- Flash Compensation
- **Focus Mode (*i* menu default)**
- **AF-area Mode/Subject Detection (*i* menu default)**
- **Vibration Reduction (*i* menu default)**
- Auto Bracketing
- Multiple Exposure
- HDR Overlay
- Interval Timer Shooting
- Time-lapse Video
- Focus Shift Shooting
- Pixel Shift Shooting
- Focus Tracking with Lock-on
- Silent Mode
- Pre-release Capture Options

- Release Mode
- Shutter Type
- **Custom Controls (Shooting) (*i* menu default)**
- Exposure Delay Mode
- View Mode (Photo Lv)
- Split-screen Display Zoom
- Focus Peaking
- Monitor/Viewfinder Brightness
- Warm Display Colors
- **Airplane Mode (*i* menu default)**
- Wireless Remote Connection (ML-L7)
- Bluetooth Remote Control Connection
- Power Battery Pack Information

I don't use the Airplane mode function very often, so I replaced it with Multiple Exposure. It was easy to do:

1. Choose Custom Setting f1: Customize *i* menu.
2. Highlight the Airplane mode icon in the bottom row and press OK. (See Figure 7.22, left.)
3. Choose replacement. From the screen that appears, scroll to Multiple Exposure. Press OK to select and confirm. (See Figure 7.22, center.)
4. You'll be returned to the Customize *i* menu screen, with your changes made in the menu, as shown in Figure 7.22, right.

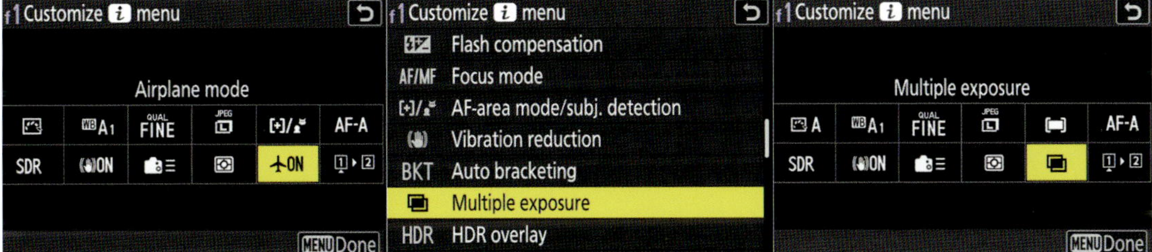

Figure 7.22 Replacing Airplane mode with Multiple Exposure in the *i* menu.

f2 Custom Controls (Shooting)

Options: Allows defining functions for camera/lens controls
My preference: Varies

Your Nikon Z5 II has a large number of controls that can be programmed to perform various functions in still photography shooting mode. (Different behaviors can be assigned for use when the camera is in Video Recording mode or Playback mode.) The number and location of the controls and their default behaviors are shown in Table 7.1. The programmable controls include function buttons and a few others that are only available if you own a certain piece of gear, such as a lens that has the M-Set (Memory Set), Lens Fn, or Lens Fn2 buttons. Keep in mind that command dials and lens control rings can also be assigned functions.

There are a total of more than six dozen *different* still photography actions that can be programmed (plus None—no action), augmenting or *replacing* the button's original function. When redefining your camera's operating features, you should always consider the side-effects of choosing your own non-standard control configuration. Your custom settings can be a boon, or if you don't remember the assignments you've made as you work, a hindrance.

TABLE 7.1 Programmable Controls

Z5 II CONTROLS	CAMERA LOCATION	DEFAULT BEHAVIOR
Fn1 button	Front	White balance
Fn2 button	Front	Focus mode/AF-area mode
Fn button (vertical)	Top	Exposure Compensation
AF-ON button	Back upper right	AF-ON
Release mode/Protect button	Back left	Release mode
DISP button	Back upper right	Cycle live view information
Sub-selector center button	Back upper right	AE/AF lock
OK button	Direction pad center	Select center focus point
Playback button	Back lower right	Playback
AF-ON (Vertical)	Back upper right of grip	Same as AF-ON button
Multi-selector center (Vertical)	Lower back of grip	AE/AF lock
Video Record button	Top right	Live view display on/off
ISO sensitivity button	Top right	ISO sensitivity
Exposure compensation	Top right	Exposure Compensation
Picture Control button	Top right	Set Picture Control
Command dials	Front/Back	--
L-Fn	Lens	AE/AF lock
L-Fn2	Lens	AF-ON
Lens Fn ring (Counterclockwise)	On lens	Recall focus position
Lens Fn ring (Clockwise)	On lens	Recall focus position
Lens memory set button	Lens	Save focus position
Lens control ring	On lens	Manual/Auto focus

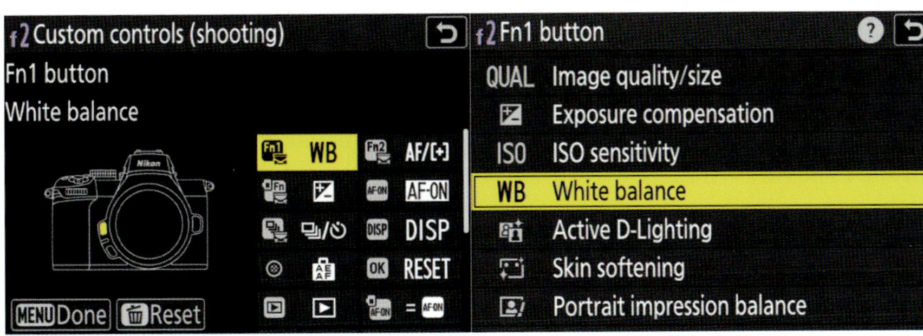

Figure 7.23 Highlight a control (left) and press OK to summon a list of possible definitions (right).

To apply a definition, highlight the button name on the screen shown at left in Figure 7.23.

Then scroll through the list of available options, as shown at right in Figure 7.23. Some choices in the scrolling list are behaviors that require nothing more than a button press to activate. Nikon inserts a "Press" header at the start of the listing for those behaviors. For example, if a button is defined as Preview or Matrix Metering, you simply press and hold the button to activate the depth-of-field preview, or to switch from your current mode to Matrix Metering. When you release the defined button, the preview stops or the camera returns to your previous metering mode.

The other behaviors follow a header that reads "Press+Command Dials." Those options include those listed from "Choose Image Area" to "Choose Non-CPU Lens Number." Behaviors that do use the command dials produce a screen that displays the options for that behavior, plus an icon prompt representing a main or sub-command dial (or both). For instance, you'd press and hold the defined button and rotate the main command dial to change the flash sync mode, and the sub-command dial to add/subtract flash exposure compensation.

The definitions you assign to your controls are highly personal and should be implemented to reflect the features you will most need to have available at the press of a button or spin of a dial. Remember that once you re-assign a control from its default value, you must remember it in order to avoid becoming hopelessly confused. You'll no longer be able to loan your camera to someone else without risking confusing *them* as well.

- **Quickly switch to an alternate focus mode or AF-area mode.** You might use Auto-area AF most of the time to let the camera select a focus point for you, yet quickly switch to Single-point AF while you hold down the defined button. You can then move the focus point around within the frame with the directional controls. The Focus mode/AF-area mode behavior allows you to press a defined button and then rotate the main command dial to choose a focus mode and change the AF-area mode by rotating the sub-command dial.

- **Switch metering modes.** If you use Matrix metering mode most of the time and want to be able to use Spot metering when appropriate, just assign a button to that function.

- **Disable/enable flash.** You can leave your external flash attached and powered up yet disable it quickly at the press of a defined button. That would allow you to intermingle photos taken by ambient light, and those in which flash illumination is added, on the fly.

- **Bracketing burst.** This option adds some versatility to exposure, flash, or ADL bracketing by telling the camera to take all the exposures in a bracketed set in one burst. You must have activated a bracketing program, as described in Chapter 2. Perhaps you've been shooting bracketed sequences in Single-shot mode (rather than continuous mode) and decide you want to capture an entire set at once. Define a key for the Bracketing Burst function and hold it down. Then, each time you press the shutter release an entire burst will be captured. If the release mode has already been set for a continuous mode or white balance bracketing has been selected, the camera will capture all the exposures in the set while the shutter release is held down.

- **Add a RAW image while shooting only JPEGs.** When the +RAW behavior is specified, pressing the defined key tells the camera to shoot an additional RAW image even if the current Image Quality setting is JPEG (only) while the button is held down. That will allow you to capture a RAW image if you think you might need one later, say, to adjust color balance for a picture taken under tricky illumination.

- **Activate the framing grid.** Even if you don't use the alignment grid often, you can define a key to produce it at the press of a button.

- **FAQs (Frequently Accessed Quickly).** Have a menu entry you need to access quickly—and often? A button can be defined to jump to the top item in your My Menu list (as described in Chapter 9), which can be that most-used entry. Or, you can define a button to produce the My Menu list, which you can populate with your own personal most-used items.

- **Choose Image Area.** If you're shooting in FX mode and decide you want to switch to one of the crop modes, a defined button+command dial definition can invoke the image area of your choice. Note that you can enable/disable any of the crop modes (but not FX mode) so that rotating the command dial switches among as many or as few modes as you want.

- **Other frequently used settings.** Other button+command dial definitions can let you switch exposure modes, change white balance, access multiple exposure options, or control HDR settings quickly, too.

f3 Custom Controls (Playback)

Options: Allows defining functions for Playback mode.

My preference: Varies

You can define a set of functions that will be enabled in Playback mode different from the ones summoned in Photo Shooting or Video Recording modes. These include:

- Protect
- Delete
- Zoom On/Off
- Filtered Playback
- Filtered Playback (Select Criteria)
- Start Series Playback
- Voice Memo

- Select for Upload to Computer
- Select for Upload (FTP)
- Thumbnail On/Off
- View Histograms
- Choose Slot and Folder
- Cycle Info Display (DISP)
- Resume Shooting

- Rating
- None
- Additional functions combined with command dials, such as RAW Processing, Trim, Resize, and retouching commands

Selection of a control to re-define and specification of the preferred function can be done as described under Custom Controls (Shooting).

f4 Touch Functions

Options: Enable/Disable Touch Functions: On, Off (default); Assign Touch Function: Move Focus Point (default), Switch Eyes, Framing Grid, Zoom On/Off (50%, 100% (1:1), 200%, 400%), Virtual Horizon; Touch Fn Area: Wide Orientation, Tall Orientation

My preference: Enable, Move Focus Point

This setting allows you to specify one of several different functions you can perform using the LCD screen's touch controls while composing your images in the viewfinder or turn touch functions off completely. Here are your options:

- **Enable/Disable Touch Functions.** This simply activates or deactivates the behavior you choose below.
- **Assign Touch Function.** Here you can select which function you want to apply when you are using the viewfinder but want to invoke a feature by touching the LCD screen.
  - **Move Focus point.** If you find moving the focus point using the directional buttons is awkward (perhaps you have small hands), you can specify a location using your thumb instead by selecting this option. If moving the point with the camera up to your eye, specifying the top-right quadrant or right half of the active focus area would be a better choice ergonomically. Make sure that Custom Setting f5: Control Lock > Focus-point Lock (described next) is turned off.
  - **Switch eyes.** This option allows you to tap the LCD to jump from one eye to another during subject detection.
  - **Framing grid.** If you want quick access to the framing grid, choose this behavior.
  - **Zoom on/off.** This option zooms the display in or out when activated. You can choose 50%, 100% (1:1), 200%, or 400%. Tap a second time to cancel zooming.
  - **Virtual Horizon.** Tapping enables or disables display of the Virtual Horizon feature discussed earlier.
- **Touch Function Area.** You can choose which area of the LCD screen responds to your touch. Choose a portion of the screen that is most comfortable for you. For example, a right-eyed person might want to desensitize any area outside the upper-right quadrant. You have nine different areas for both horizontal and vertical camera orientations:
  - **"Wide" orientation.** With the camera held horizontally, you can specify the "sensitive" areas:
    - **Entire Screen.** You can touch anywhere within the LCD screen.
    - **Top or Bottom Right or Left Quadrants.** Select any of the four corners of the screen.
    - **Left or Right or Top or Bottom Half.** Choose left or right sides of the screen, or top or bottom.
  - **"Tall" orientation.** With the camera rotated to portrait orientation, you can choose any of the areas listed for Wide, plus Same As Wide Orientation to keep the same setting.

f5 Control Lock

Options: Shutter Speed Lock, Aperture Lock, Focus-point lock (default: Off for all three)
My preference: Varies

There are times when you'll want to lock the shutter speed at a particular value when using Shutter-priority or Manual exposure modes and times when you want to lock down a particular f/stop when using Aperture-priority or Manual exposure modes. Or, you may wish to lock in a particular focus plane, perhaps for a macro series. You can use this entry to lock the shutter speed, aperture, or focus point (or a combination of the three) so it can't be changed. I use this most in the studio when I use Manual exposure and studio lights. Once I've set the exposure for a series of shots, I lock my Shutter Speed/Aperture Lock button and freeze the settings, so I don't have to worry about accidentally rotating a command dial.

If you think accessing this menu entry to lock in a setting is needlessly complex, you're right. It makes a lot more sense to define a physical button to provide this function, as described earlier under f2: Custom Controls (Shooting). I assigned the function to the Fn1 button. To lock the shutter speed and/or aperture, I first set either or both to the value I want. Then, I press the Fn1 button and rotate the main command dial to lock/unlock shutter speed and the sub-command dial to lock/unlock aperture. An L symbol appears next to the locked setting in the viewfinder/LCD monitor displays. Hold the assigned button and press any direction on the multi selector to lock and unlock the focus point.

Note that when the camera is set to Shutter-priority, you are able to enable/disable only the Shutter Speed Lock and focus-point functions. When set to Aperture-priority, only aperture lock and focus point are accessible. In Manual exposure mode, you can adjust all three, and in Program mode, only focus point can be locked. **Note:** Focus-point lock does not keep the 3D-tracking autofocus-area mode from adjusting focus. Only the starting position of the focus point is locked.

f6 Reverse Dial Rotation

Options: Reverse Rotation Direction of Main and Sub-command Dials: Exposure Compensation: Checked, Unchecked (default); Shutter Speed/Aperture: Checked, Unchecked (default)
My preference: Varies

This menu entry can swap the rotational direction of the command dials. This is most useful if you're coming to the Nikon world from another vendor's product that uses the opposite operational scheme. Keep in mind that redefining basic controls in this way can prove confusing if someone other than yourself uses your camera, or if you find yourself working with other Nikon cameras that have retained the normal command dial behavior. The reason that the dials are set for their default directions is to match the direction of rotation of the aperture ring/sub-command dial (when changing the aperture). Turning any of them to the left decreases exposure, while rotating to the right increases exposure. You can reverse dial direction for Exposure Compensation, Shutter Speed/Aperture settings, or both.

f7 Release Button to Use Dial

Options: On, Off (default)

My preference: Off

Normally, any button used in conjunction with a command dial, such as the Exposure Compensation or ISO buttons, must be held down while the command dial or sub-command dial is rotated. That is the behavior when this entry is set to Off, the default, and is usually the best choice for most of us. However, there are times—especially when you are hand-holding a camera with a large lens—that it can be challenging to hold down a button while simultaneously rotating a dial. That's where this option comes in handy.

If you choose On, you just need to press the button once. You can then release it and rotate a command dial to make your setting and continue to make adjustments until you press the button a second time—or until the Standby timer expires or you press the shutter release. I recommend leaving this option set to Off, instead. Holding down a button is not inconvenient, and it's too easy to forget to make that second button press when you're in a hurry to capture the decisive moment. The button/command dial combinations affected by this entry include the Exposure Compensation, ISO, Release mode, and Fn1 and Fn2 buttons.

f8 Reverse Indicators

Options: Direction of exposure indicators: +0–, –0+ (default)

My preference: –0+

This is the first of the next eight entries of the Controls menu. (See Figure 7.24.) By default, the exposure indicators at the bottom of the display have the negative values shown at the left of the zero point, and positive values to the right (–0+). That's the orientation used by vendors of other cameras, such as Canon, and by Nikon since the introduction of the Nikon D4 dSLR. This setting allows you to reverse the direction (+0–). You might want to do this if you're coming to a system that uses the reverse orientation, have been using older Nikon cameras for a loooong time, or, for some reason, you own and use quite a few old manual focus AI and AI-S Nikkor lenses. (Older Nikon

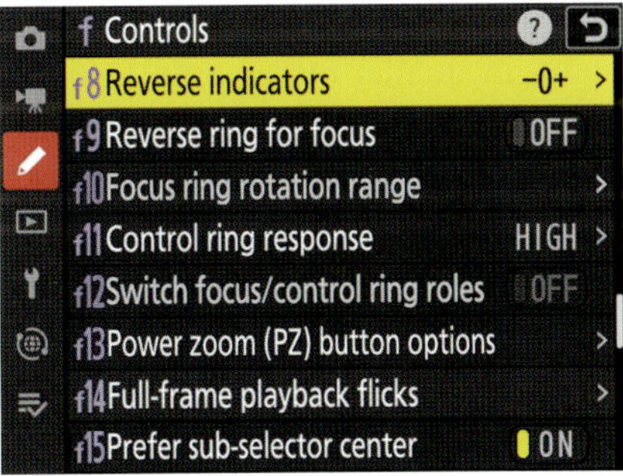

Figure 7.24 The next entries in the Controls menu.

lenses have the smallest aperture on the ring to the left, and the largest to the right, so rotating the aperture ring to the right increases exposure; to the left decreases exposure.) My oldest camera still in frequent use is a Nikon D3200, and it uses the current scheme, so I've gone with the flow.

f9 Reverse Ring for Focus

Options: On, Off (default)

My preference: Off

This is another setting for grizzled veterans who refuse to update to the 21st century, or those coming to Nikon from some other platforms. You can reverse the direction of rotation for the focus or control rings on Z-mount lenses during manual focus to match the direction of older Nikon optics. This setting does not affect non-autofocus Z-mount lenses, such as the S Nikkor 58mm f/0.95 Noct lens, or F-mount lenses attached using an FTZ adapter. In addition, the left/right pointing triangles that appear in the viewfinder as a manual focus aid do not switch directions to match.

f10 Focus Ring Rotation Range

Options: Non-linear (default), 90, 120, 150, 180, 210, 240, 270, 300, 330, 360, 540, 720 degrees, Max

My preference: Non-linear for still photography

One of the perks of the focus-by-wire electronics of the typical Z-mount lens is that you can adjust how dramatically focus changes with a given twist of the focus ring. Tweaking the manual focus response can be useful for sports photography, for example, and an absolute necessity for some types of videography. It's possible only because compatible lenses use an electronic system to transfer focus ring rotation to a variable-speed motor that actually does the focusing, rather than a fixed mechanical linkage used in traditional lenses.

At the default setting, rotating the focus mechanism responds in a non-linear manner. If you rotate the ring quickly, the focus plane is adjusted by a large amount. Slower rotation produces adjustments in smaller increments. Ordinarily, that's exactly what you'd want for still photography; if a major focus change is needed (something that can be frequent with action shooting), you want it to happen quickly. But fine-tuning, say, for macro photography, is better suited to smaller changes to the focus plane.

In some circumstances, non-linear focus is less desirable, and this entry allows you to define exactly how you'd like the focus ring to respond. A fixed speed can be specified over a particular rotational range with compatible lenses. The "fastest" focus parameter is 90 degrees; a lens will adjust focus from the minimum distance to maximum (or vice versa) with a mere 90 degrees of rotation. If you start with the lens focused at some midpoint, the amount of rotation will be even less.

You can choose fixed arcs from 90 to 360 degrees in 30-degree increments, plus 540 and 720 degrees, and a setting labeled Max (which requires focusing from the minimum to infinity over the maximum distance available at the current lens settings).

This linear focus characteristic is particularly useful for movie-making, since any manual focus changes you make *while capturing video* can be seen in the footage. It's essential if you're using pull- or push-focus techniques, which use selective focus with a wide aperture to draw the viewer's attention from, say, an object in the foreground to something in the background. The change can be subtle if done slowly, or dramatic, if performed quickly, but in either case the focus adjustment needs to be smooth rather than jerky.

This setting may not work with all lenses, although Nikon has periodically issued firmware updates to bring additional optics into the fold. If your lens is not compatible, this entry will be grayed out and focus will be fixed at non-linear.

f11 Control Ring Response

Options: High (default), Low

My preference: Low

Adjusting the responsiveness of a lens ring isn't exclusively the province of manual focus adjustments. The "bonus" control ring introduced with Nikon's Z-mount optics, and available on selected lenses, can be assigned roles such as aperture and power aperture setting, exposure compensation, and ISO sensitivity adjustments using Custom Setting f2: Custom Controls (Shooting) as described earlier in this chapter. The response isn't quite as granular as focus ring rotation range: you can choose the default, High (for fast response), or Low to make the ring less sensitive to smaller rotations. I happen to like the more measured response and set my cameras to Low. **Note:** This setting does not apply if the control ring behavior is set to focus.

f12 Switch Focus/Control Ring Roles

Options: On, Off (default)

My preference: Off

If your lens includes both a focus ring and control ring, you may find it more convenient to use the innermost or outermost rings for either focus or the custom behavior. This setting allows you to reverse the functions with compatible lenses. Set to Off, the focus ring focuses, and the control ring performs its defined function. Select On, and the two rings trade functions.

f13 Power Zoom (PZ) Button Options

Options: Use Zoom In/Zoom Out buttons: On, Off (default); Power zoom speed: –3 (slower) to +3 (faster)

My preference: N/A

The good news is that Nikon is making power zoom (PZ) lenses available in Z mount, including the Nikkor Z 28-135mm f/4 PZ full-frame lens and the Nikkor Z DX 12-28mm f/3.5-5.6 PZ VR optic. They are targeted at videographers, vloggers, and content creators.

These lenses can be used for both video capture and stills, and, as you might guess, it would be most useful for video shooting that can best take advantage of their power zoom features. This entry allows you to assign the zoom in/zoom out functions to the Zoom In and Zoom Out buttons and specify a power zooming speed. The lenses' internal linear motor is used to adjust focal lengths, and zooming can be controlled via the camera buttons, plus additional options, including the optional ML-L7 Bluetooth Remote, the SnapBridge app, or when using NX Tether Software.

f14 Full-Frame Playback Flicks

Options: Flick Up; Flick Down; Flick Advance Direction

My preference: N/A

This setting lets you customize how your Z5 II behaves when you use a finger to flick up, down, or side to side on the rear LCD screen during Playback. When Touch Controls is enabled in the Setup menu, the screen can be used to perform a variety of functions. They include initiating focus and specifying a focus spot, navigating menus, entering text, and performing functions during image review playback. The flick features for Playback, shown in Figure 7.25, include:

- **Flick Up.** An upward motion on the screen can be assigned different functions:
  - **Rating.** One specific rating will be given to the currently displayed image. You'll need to decide which rating will be given when you activate this option. Select from zero to five stars, or a mark that indicates the image is a candidate for deletion. This is a convenient choice if you have a large number of images to which you want to assign a particular star rating or, more commonly, to mark some for deletion.
  - **Select for Upload to Computer.** The current image will be assigned for transfer using all methods.
  - **Select for Upload (FTP).** The current image will be assigned for transfer using FTP.
  - **Protect.** The flicked image will be marked as Protected. A second flick will unprotect it.
  - **Voice memo.** Recording will begin for a voice memo; if a voice memo has already been recorded for the displayed image using the Record Voice Memo option of the Playback version of the *i* menu, it will be played back.
  - **None.** Upward flicks are ignored.
- **Flick Down.** Downward flicks on the screen can be assigned one of the exact same functions available for the Flick Up gesture. In general, you'll want to choose a complementary behavior, say, to assign one rating using a flick up, and a different rating for a flick down. I set my cameras so that an upward swipe protects that image, while a downward swipe marks it for later deletion, as sort of a thumbs up/thumbs down procedure.
- **Flick Advance Direction.** Use this option to change from the default left/right gesture to advance to the next image during playback to the reverse (right to left). **Note:** The *labels* in the menu entry both read Left-Right; it is only the *arrows* separating the two words that flip direction.

Figure 7.25 Playback flick options, left. Choices for Flick Up (and Down), right.

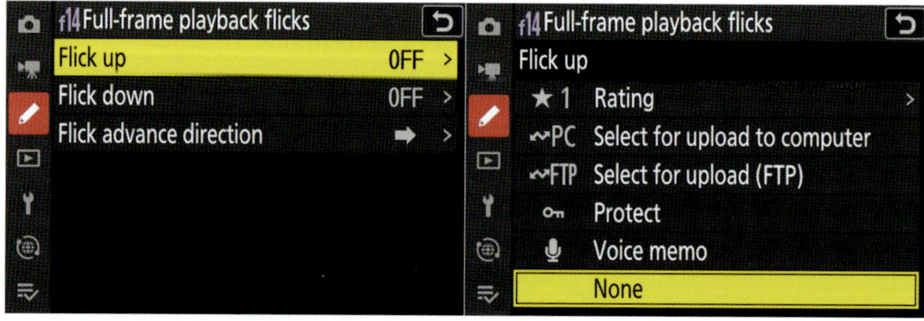

f15 Prefer Sub-Selector Center

Options: On (default), Off

My preference: Off

I've been guilty of not using the sub-selector joystick/button as often as I could, because, as a clumsy person, I found I was often unintentionally moving the focus point when I meant to be pressing the selector perpendicularly inward to summon its button behavior (the default is AE/AF lock). Nikon provided a kind of fix for that problem by adding this entry. At the new default setting, On, pressing the sub-selector inward disables focus point movement, so you don't have to worry that accidental slight shifts of your thumb off-center will cause the focus point to stray.

You can choose Off to restore the original behavior if you're coordinated enough to be able to press (to invoke the button function) while adroitly (and intentionally) moving the focus point simultaneously. Nikon even has some advice for those with finger skills: assign AF-area mode to the sub-selector button, and you'll be able to temporarily switch AF-area modes and reposition the focus point at the same time.

g. Video

Here you can set separately for movie shooting some of the options available for still shooting. The first seven entries in this menu are shown in Figure 7.26.

g1 Customize *i* Menu

Options: Allows defining functions available from the Video Recording version of the *i* menu. Includes different functions that you can use to replace or add to those provided in the default version of the *i* menu.

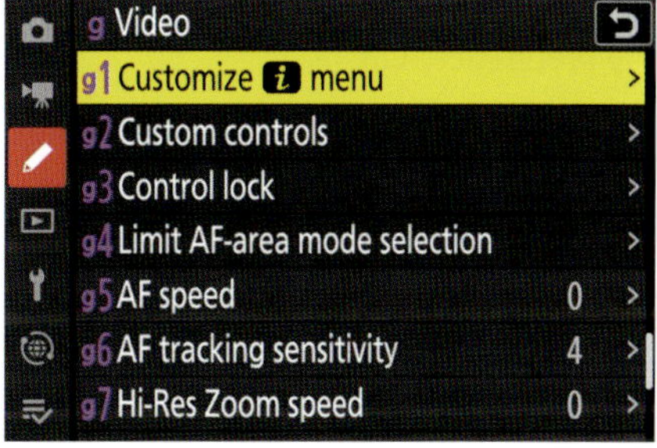

Figure 7.26 The first seven entries of the Custom Settings Video options.

My preference: Varies

The Video Recording version of the Customize *i* menu entry can be a valuable tool for quick access to video-oriented commands. That's especially true since there are several entries, including Set Picture Control, Airplane mode, and Destination that are ripe for replacement with functions you use more often. These 12 entries occupy the *i* menu by default. You can choose to keep these, move them, or replace them with other functions:

Set Picture Control	White Balance	Frame Size/ Rate	Microphone Sensitivity	AF-area mode/ Subject Detection	Focus Mode
Electronic VR	Vibration Reduction	Custom Controls	Product Review Mode	Airplane Mode	Destination

As I noted earlier, several of the default *i* menu functions are already available using other direct controls that duplicate their behavior or can be replaced with other behaviors such as White Balance.

g2 Custom Controls

Options: Allows defining functions for camera/lens controls

My preference: Varies

The programmable controls available for defining functions used when in Video Recording mode are more or less the same as those for still photography, with a few exceptions. For example, the OK button cannot be defined for button+dial functions. The actual behaviors you can assign to those controls include some that are different from those available in Photo Shooting mode or are used in different ways. Among the video-oriented options available for assignment are Hi-Res Zoom, Power Zoom, Pattern Tone Range, Microphone Sensitivity, and Power Aperture.

The latter comes in two varieties: Power Aperture (Open) and Power Aperture (Closed). The function can be assigned to open/close the aperture when the Fn1 and Fn2 buttons are pressed, or to perform that function when the Lens Fn Ring is rotated clockwise or counterclockwise. Note that the ability to change frame size and frame rate cannot be assigned to one of these controls; fast access is available only from the *i* menu.

g3 Control Lock

Options: Shutter Speed Lock, Aperture Lock, Focus-point lock (default: Off for all three)

My preference: Varies

As I noted earlier, you may want to lock the shutter speed at a particular value when using Shutter-priority or Manual exposure modes. That's especially true for video shooting, as faster shutter speeds (those more than twice the frame rate) can produce unwanted visual effects, such as "judder" (explained in Chapter 12). You may also want to lock down a particular f/stop when using Aperture-priority or Manual exposure modes, as unwanted changes in aperture cause changes in depth-of-field, which can be visibly jarring in video. You can use this entry to lock the shutter speed, aperture, or focus point (or a combination of the three) so they can't be changed.

Note that when the camera is set to Shutter-priority, you are able to enable/disable the Shutter speed lock and the Focus-point lock functions. When set to Aperture-priority, only aperture lock and focus point are accessible. In Manual exposure mode, you can adjust all three, and in Program mode, only focus point can be locked. **Note:** Focus-point lock does not keep the 3D-tracking autofocus-area mode from adjusting focus. Only the starting position of the focus point is locked.

g4 Limit AF-Area Mode Selection

Options: Single-point AF, Wide-area AF (Small, Large, C1, C2), Subject-tracking AF, Auto-area AF (Default is all available)

My preference: N/A

This entry is the equivalent of Custom Setting a8, used for still photography. It functions exactly as its counterpart described earlier, except, in Video Recording mode, Pinpoint AF and Dynamic-area AF options aren't available and 3D-tracking AF is replaced by Subject-tracking AF for video.

Single-point AF-area mode is always available and cannot be disabled. However, you can highlight any of the others and press the multi selector right button to remove the checkbox next to that mode's label to disable it. You can thus enable Single-point AF, plus any combination of the other AF-area modes. I explained this feature in Chapter 3.

g5 AF Speed

Options: Autofocusing speed (+/–5) (default: 0); When to Apply: Always (default), Only While Recording

My preference: Varies

The speed with which the camera autofocuses takes on a different significance when you're shooting movies, because any AF changes are recorded within the movie itself. You may want focus to change slowly as a scene unfolds and people or objects move within the frame, or the frame itself is recomposed. Or, during action sequences, you might prefer to have AF keep pace with subject and camera changes and focus rapidly. This entry lets you speed up or slow down focus speed in Movie mode, using a slider moved via the touch screen or multi selector directional buttons. The When to Apply option can be set to Always (in which case

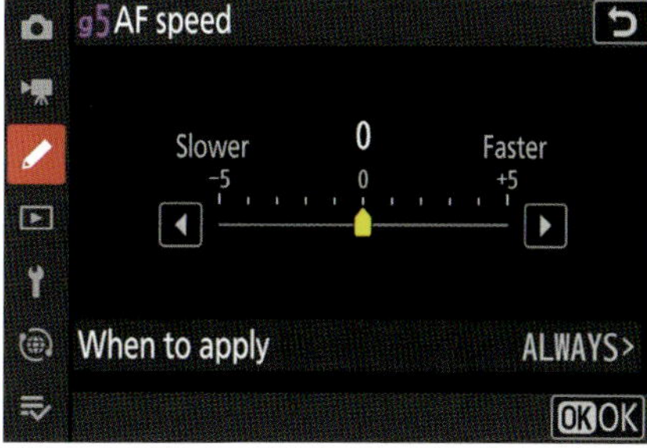

Figure 7.27 Setting AF Speed.

the camera's autofocus will refocus constantly at the speed you select) or Only While Recording (so the focus speed is changed only when you're actually capturing video). When using AF-F (full-time autofocus) you might prefer normal focusing speed (which is equivalent to +5—as fast as possible) as you compose your shot and then have the camera switch automatically to a preferred slower speed once you start recording. (See Figure 7.27.)

g6 AF Tracking Sensitivity

Options: 7 (Low) to 1 (High); 4 (default)

My preference: Varies

This is roughly the movie equivalent of Custom Setting a3: Focus Tracking with Lock-on for still photography. It specifies how quickly the AF system responds when the subject either exits the frame or something else intervenes—the referee at a football game is the classic example.

A setting of 7 (Low) causes the camera to ignore the intervening subject matter for a significant period of time. Use this setting when shooting subjects, such as sports, in which focus interruptions are likely to be frequent and significant. You can also choose a setting of 1 (High), which tells the camera to wait only a moment before refocusing. The middle value, 4, the default, offers an intermediate delay before the camera refocuses on the new subject.

g7 Hi-Res Zoom Speed

Options: −5 (Slower) to +5 (Faster)

My preference: Depends on speed of subject

This entry is available, but its setting is activated only if you've used Custom Setting g2: Custom Controls to assign the Hi-Res Zoom function to the Fn1 button, Fn2 button, or Lens Fn ring (in both clockwise or counterclockwise directions). Once enabled, you can use this entry to specify how quickly zooming occurs, from −5 (Slower) to +5 (Faster). You'll want to experiment to see just how rapid zooming takes place and adjust this entry to account for the speed of movement of your subject.

g8 Power Zoom (PZ) Button Options

Options: Use Zoom In/Zoom Out buttons: On, Off (default); Power zoom speed: Pre/post recording: −5 (slower) to +5 (faster) (default: 3), During recording: −5 (slower) to +5 (faster) (default: 0)

My preference: N/A

This function is the first in the next group of video settings (see Figure 7.28). It provides options for using power zoom lenses, as described earlier.

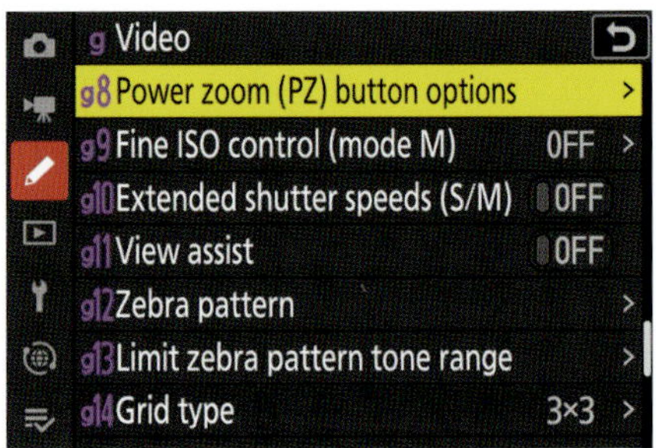
Figure 7.28 The next group of video settings.

g9 Fine ISO Control (Mode M)

Options: On (1/6 EV), Off

My preference: Off

If you need very fine control over ISO sensitivity, you can change this setting from the camera's default value of 1/3 stop to a more granular 1/6 stop.

g10 Extended Shutter Speeds (S/M)

Options: Off (default), On

My preference: Off

As I've already mentioned, the optimum shutter speeds for video recording can vary, depending on the frame rate you're using; anything *shorter* than about twice the frame rate produces an undesirable look. In addition, *longer* shutter speeds are locked out to prevent blurring/distortion that I'll describe shortly. Your Z5 II automatically limits the available slow shutter speeds whenever you are in Video Recording mode. This setting allows a partial override of those limits.

- **Off (default).** At this setting, the slowest shutter speed you can use roughly corresponds to the frame rate, from 1/125th second at 120p down to 1/25th second at 24p.

■ **On.** The slowest shutter speed available for 60/50p, 30/25p, and 24p changes to 1/4 second. At those speeds, the camera will include repeated copies of the same frame to fill out a full-second's worth of video. That is, at 60p and a shutter speed of 1/60th second you'd end up with 60 individual images for each second to elapsed time. But at 60p and a 1/4-second exposure time, the camera would fill out each second with 14 copies of the original frame (15 in all).

Keep in mind that slow shutter speeds may also produce blurring from subject movement as well as camera movement. Mounting the Z5 II on a tripod and/or VR/electronic VR can counter *camera* shake but will have no effect on the movement of your *subject*. Nikon says that the main reason for using these slow shutter speeds is to reduce the need to increase the ISO setting to capture very dark subjects.

g11 View Assist

Options: On, Off (default)

My preference: Off

This setting provides a more natural-looking live preview of your video when you're using the high dynamic range video options HLG or N-log. The colors are simplified and increased from the flat recorded appearance to a high contrast representation. You'll need to activate this *only* when you are using HLG or N-log *and* review your videos on your Z5 II's display.

g12 Zebra Pattern

Options: Pattern Tone Range: Highlights, Mid-tones, Off (default); Pattern: Pattern 1 (forward diagonal lines), Pattern 2 (back-leaning diagonal lines); Highlight Threshold: 255, 250 (default), 245, 240, 235, 230, 225, 220, 215, 210, 205, 200, 195, 190, 185, 180, 175, 170, 165, 160, 155, 150, 145, 140, 135, 130, 125, 120; Mid-tone Value: 0 to 255; Mid-tone Range: +5 to +20

My preference: N/A

Video has its own version of the still photography's Highlights display ("blinkies"), commonly known as Zebra display, because it uses contrasting stripes to represent blown highlights. It warns you when the brightest areas of your image may be overexposed when capturing video—but does so *before* you begin capture. Instead of solid flashing indicators, the camera displays one of two striped "zebra" patterns in the affected areas. The zebra stripes jump out at you and make it easy to identify exactly which highlights may be overexposed. You can then adjust exposure or lighting to bring the highlights under control.

This menu entry allows you to specify a number of parameters:

■ **Pattern tone range:** Here you choose whether you want the Zebra display to indicate high values for either highlights or mid-tones. Or you can choose Off to disable the Zebra display. The Highlights choice is useful for checking for overexposure. Use mid-tones instead to ensure that the middle tonal values of your scene are within the range you specify. If they are "off" you can adjust the lighting. The actual limits for highlights or mid-tones are set below.

Note: I used Custom Setting g2: Custom Controls to assign the Pattern Tone Range function to a function button. I can then turn the Zebra display on or off by pressing that button while shooting video.

- **Pattern:** Choose from Zebra pattern 1 (forward-tilting diagonal lines) or Pattern 2 (back-leaning lines).

- **Highlight threshold:** Set a brightness value above which the Zebra pattern will appear. You can choose 28 values from 255 to 120. The default is 250, but a more common setting is 235 for average facial tones. (More on that shortly.)

- **Mid-tone range:** You can choose brightness values from 0 (black) to 255 (white) to specify the tone you want to reside in the middle of your selected range. Then, choose an acceptable range deviation, between +5 to +20 of your value setting.

So, exactly how bright *is* too bright? A value of 255 indicates pure white, so any Zebra pattern visible when using this setting indicates that your image is extremely overexposed. Any details in the highlights are gone and cannot be retrieved. Settings from 213 to 235 can be used to make sure facial tones are not overexposed. As a general rule of thumb, Caucasian skin generally falls in the 235 range, with darker skin tones registering as low as 213, and very fair skin or lighter areas of your subject edging closer to 248. Once you've decided the approximate range of tones that you want to make sure do *not* blow out, you can set the Zebra pattern sensitivity appropriately and receive the flashing striped warning on the LCD. (See Figure 7.29.) The pattern does not appear in your final image, of course—it's just an aid to keep you from blowing it, so to speak.

Zebra patterns are a much more useful tool than "blinkies," because you are given an alert *before* you take the picture and can actually specify exactly how bright *too bright* is. The feature is not new: it has long been used in video equipment, dating back before the digital age. Veteran videographers will note that Nikon uses a section of the 0–255 brightness value scale, rather than the traditional IRE measure of a video signal level, in which numbers from 70 to 100/100+ are used. The Zebra feature has been a staple of professional video shooting for a long time, as you might guess from the moniker assigned to the unit used to specify brightness: IRE, a measure of video signal level, which stands for *Institute of Radio Engineers.*

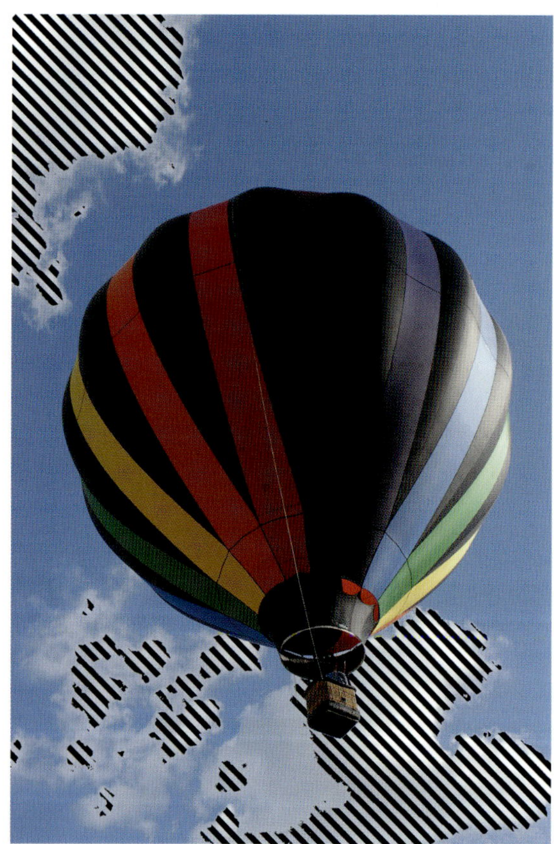

Figure 7.29 The stripes show an area is overexposed.

g13 Limit Zebra Pattern Tone Range

Options: Highlights, Mid-tones, No Restrictions (default)

My preference: N/A

This setting provides a way to limit activation of Pattern Tone Range, although it's only useful when you've defined a custom button to turn the Zebra display on or off, as I recommended above. If you select Highlights or Mid-tones, the Zebra display is enabled *only* if you've selected Highlights or Mid-tones (respectively) under the Pattern Tone Range option of Custom Setting g12. Choose No Restrictions (the default), and the Zebra display will always be turned on or off when the button is pressed.

g14 Grid Type

Options: 3 × 3 (default), 4 × 4, 2:35:1, 1:85:1, 4:3, 1:1, 90%

My preference: N/A

The display grids available for video recording have an additional function beyond simple compositional aspects. Movies can be shot or edited to produce specific aspect ratios, depending on the intent of the production. Your Nikon Z5 II's grids can be used as *marker frames* to remind you of those proportions while you're recording, so you can keep the important subject matter within those boundaries.

They are a popular tool for videographers because they allow viewing the area outside the actual frame that will be captured (the "look-around area") so you can monitor moving subjects before they enter the frame. In professional productions, it's useful to look at the region outside the captured frame to detect when boom microphones, careless crew members, or other objects threaten to intrude on the frame. It's common to shoot movies knowing in advance that they will be cropped down eventually for display in a slightly different format. The director simply makes sure that the important parts of the frame are included in the "safety zone" that will never be cropped out. For example, you wouldn't want to put two characters who are talking to each other at opposite ends of the entire frame but would instead locate them in the safety zone so both would be visible.

The marker frames available with the Z5 II are shown in Figure 7.30. Here's an overview of how they are used:

- **No grids.** Keep in mind that when grids are not displayed, the image you see in the viewfinder and rear LCD *is already cropped* for you when the camera is in Video Recording mode. You will view the area captured when shooting Full HD and 4K video in 16:9 format, at 1920 × 1080 and 3840 × 2160 resolutions. This is a popular widescreen format and is used for movies and television. Its panoramic view is excellent for documentaries, sports action, or any scenes with lots of detail, and was used in some *Avengers* movies.

  It was established by the Society of Motion Picture and Television Engineers. **Note:** The Digital Cinema Initiatives standards organization has defined additional resolution/aspect ratio specifications that you don't need to worry about, in general.

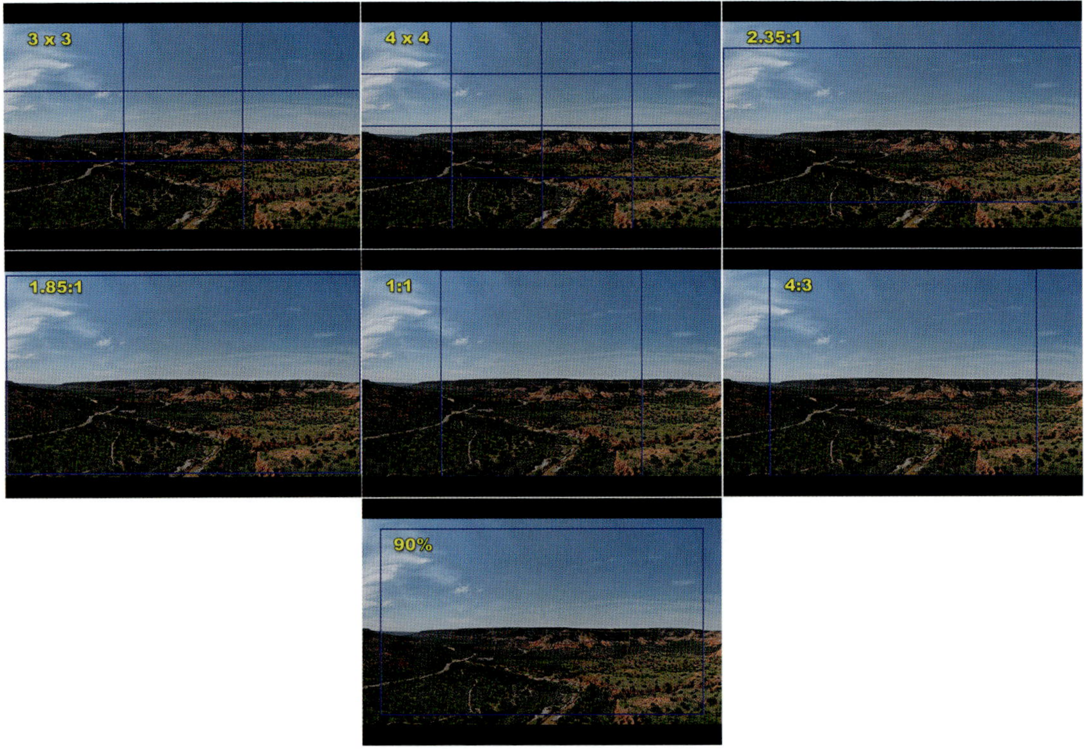

Figure 7.30 The seven grids available for video recording.

- **3 × 3, 4 × 4, 1:1, and 4:3.** The first two are most often used to help you determine whether horizontal and vertical lines are skewed and can also be used as a Rule of Thirds or Rule of Quarters guide for composition. The latter two are specific aspect ratios you might want to incorporate into your compositions. Some filmmakers, like Wes Anderson, still use the 4:3 aspect ratio to provide an "old-timey" look.

- **1:85:1.** This aspect ratio, wider than 4:3 but not as panoramic as 16:9, is often used for drama, romantic comedies, and other films where the emphasis is on the actors rather than their surroundings, like *Forrest Gump* and *The Godfather* trilogy.

- **2:35:1.** These proportions, along with the more common 2:39:1, are called CinemaScope format (or, often, just "Scope"), an extremely wide aspect ratio used in *Star Wars*.

- **90 Percent.** Your camera provides a 90 percent safety zone to represent the area that will always be shown when the movie is viewed on a standard HDTV.

Note: This setting does not enable/disable grid display; it only specifies what type of overlay will be used. To activate a grid, you have to include that as an option in one of your display layouts using the Custom Monitor Shooting Display and Custom Viewfinder Shooting Display entries discussed shortly.

g15 Brightness Information Display

Options: Histogram (default), Waveform Monitor, Waveform Monitor (Large)

My preference: N/A

This is the first entry in the final batch of Video settings (see Figure 7.31). This is a super-techie option for serious videographers who want to replace the histogram with a waveform monitor display (small or large), as shown in Figure 7.32. You'll need to learn how to interpret the information shown for it to be of any use. The waveform display provides luminance information showing how bright areas are, with horizontal grid lines at the 25, 50, and 75 percent levels, rather than IRE values. Total black is represented at the bottom of the graph and total white at the top, something like a histogram turned on its side.

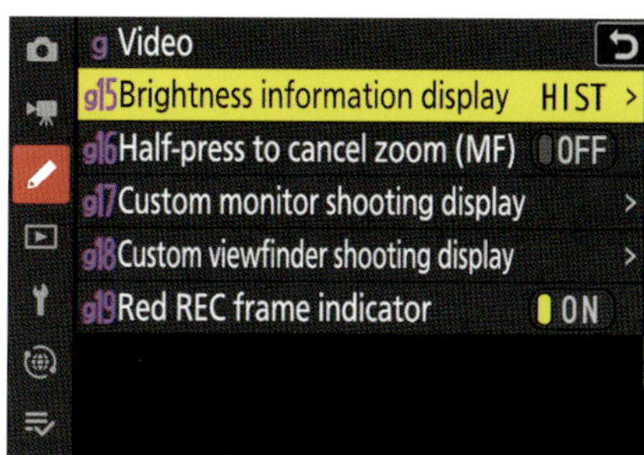

Figure 7.31 The final entries.

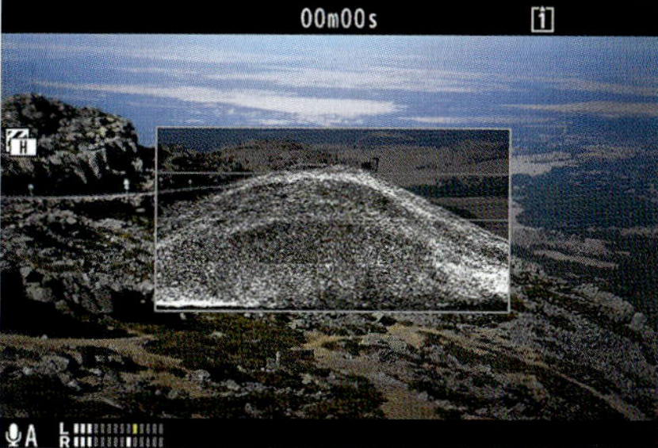

Figure 7.32 Waveform monitor display (Large).

g16 Half-press to Cancel Zoom (MF)

Options: Off (default), On

My preference: Off

This is the video version of Custom Setting d18, described above.

g17 Custom Monitor Shooting Display

Options: Display 1, Display 2, Display 3, Display 4

My preference: Varies

This is the video counterpart of the still photo Custom Monitor Shooting Display (d19) entry. It differs in providing only four different displays (instead of five); the Histogram option is labeled Brightness Information, instead (with the two Waveform options mentioned above); and there is no Center-weighted display available. You can set up your displays as described earlier.

g18 Custom Viewfinder Shooting Display

Options: Display 1, Display 2, Display 3

My preference: Varies

This is the video version of the still photo Custom Viewfinder Shooting Display. It offers three display options, rather than four, and the same entries as its g17 counterpart just described.

g19 Red REC Frame Indicator

Options: On (default), Off

My preference: On

By default, your Z5 II displays a transparent red frame around the edge of the display while video recording is underway. This indicator is more noticeable than the solid red circle that is shown at the upper-left corner of the frame. It serves to remind you that your camera is "live" and recording, much like the tally light found on professional video cameras and monitors. An important difference is that actual tally lights are visible to those in front of the camera, too, so that subjects are aware they are being recorded. Nikon's Recording Frame Indicator is not intrusive, so I keep it enabled at all times.

Playback Menu

8

The blue-coded Playback menu has 13 entries where you select options related to the display, review, transfer, and printing of the photos you've taken. Figure 8.1 shows the first seven entries. Note that some entries, such as Delete, are *functions*, rather than settings, and do not have a default value, as such.

- Delete
- Playback Folder
- Playback Display Options
- Delete Pictures from Both Slots
- Dual-format Recording PB Slot
- Filtered Playback Criteria
- Series Playback
- Picture Review
- After Delete
- After Burst, Show
- Record Camera Orientation
- Auto-Rotate Pictures
- Copy Image(s)

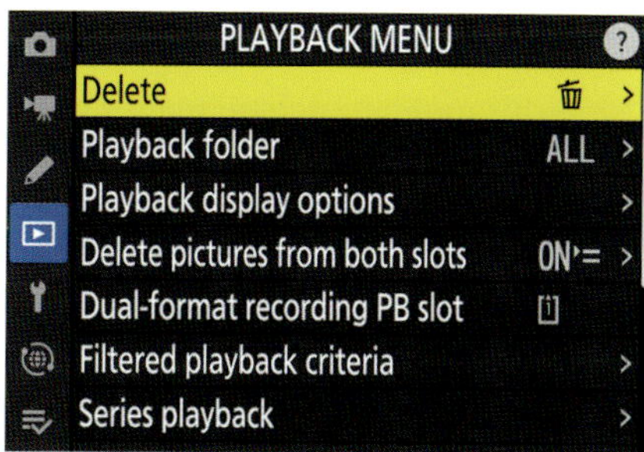

Figure 8.1 The first seven Playback menu entries.

Delete

Options: Selected Pictures, Candidates for Deletion, Pictures Shot on Selected Dates, All Pictures
My preference: N/A

Choose this menu entry and you'll be given four choices, shown in Figure 8.2, upper left: Selected Pictures (to choose individual images to delete); Candidates for Deletion (to remove images rated using the Delete option); Pictures Shot on Selected Dates (to remove all photos taken on a particular day); or All Pictures (to remove all images in the folder currently selected for playback). To select images, use one of these options:

- **Selected Pictures.** A selection screen, like the one shown at upper right in Figure 8.2, appears. Scroll through the thumbnails of the images displayed using the multi selector's directional buttons. Hold down the Zoom In button to enlarge the highlighted thumbnail to full-screen view. Press the Zoom Out button to mark a highlighted image for deletion, or to unmark one that has already been marked. A yellow checkmark is overlaid on the upper-right corner of a thumbnail when an image is marked for removal. When finished marking, press OK to delete. Choose Yes from the screen that appears, or No to cancel.

- **Candidates for Deletion.** This option deletes images that you have already marked for deletion using the Rating feature of the Playback version of the *i* menu. You cannot select images here. Instead, in Playback mode, press the *i* button and choose Rating from the screen that appears (see Figure 8.2, lower left). Then rotate the main command dial and select the Trash can icon (see Figure 8.2, lower right). If you change your mind at this point and want to retain one of your "candidates," press the Zoom Out button to deselect it.

- **Pictures Shot on Selected Dates.** A list of dates on which pictures were taken appears. Press the right multi selector button to checkmark a date, or to unmark a date that has been selected. Once you've highlighted one or more dates, if you're sure you want to delete all those images, press the Zoom Out button to confirm those dates. You'll be taken to a View Pictures screen that displays thumbnails of the images you have specified for deletion, giving you one last chance to change your mind. Once you've reviewed them, you can press OK to delete all those pictures or press the Zoom Out button to return to the Select Date screen.

- **All Pictures.** Choose your Slot and press OK, then select Yes or No to delete the images.

Using this menu to delete images will have no effect on images that have been marked with an overlaid Protect key icon applied using the Playback *i* menu's Protect option. Keep in mind that deleting images in this way is slower than just wiping out the whole card with the Format command, so using Format is generally much faster than choosing Delete: All Pictures, and also is a safer way of returning your memory card to a fresh, blank state.

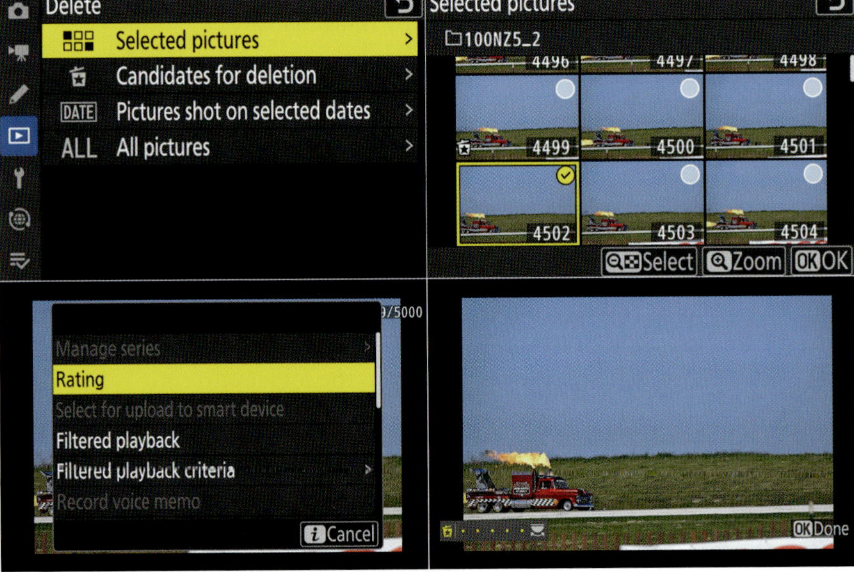

Figure 8.2 Select pictures to delete (top). Assign Delete rating using the Playback version of the *i* menu (bottom).

Playback Folder

Options: NZ5_2, All (default), Current
My preference: N/A

Your camera will create folders on your memory card to store the images that it creates. It assigns the first folder a number, like 100NZ5_2, and when that folder is filled, a new folder is automatically created numbered one higher, such as 101NZ5_2. A folder is completely full when it contains 5,000 images, or a picture numbered 9999. If you use the same memory card in another camera, that camera will also create its own folder. Thus, you can end up with several folders on the same memory card, until you eventually reformat the card and folder creation starts anew.

This menu item allows you to choose which folders are accessed when displaying images using the Playback facility. Your choices are as follows:

- **NZ5_2.** Only the folders on your memory card created by the camera will be used, and those created by other cameras ignored. Images in all the camera's folders will be displayed. This is the default folder name. You can rename these folders using the Storage Folder > Rename entry in the Photo Shooting menu.

- **All (default).** All folders containing images that the camera can read will be accessed, regardless of which camera created them. You might want to use this setting if you swap memory cards among several cameras and want to be able to review all the photos (especially when considering reformatting the memory card). You will be able to view—and avoid unintentionally deleting—images even if they were created by a non-Nikon camera if those images conform to the Design Rule for Camera File system (DCF) specifications.

- **Current.** The camera will display only images in the current folder. For example, if you have been shooting heavily at an event and have already accumulated more than 5,000 shots in one folder (or an image has been stored that's numbered 9999) and the camera has created a new folder for the overflow, you'd use this setting to view only the most recent photos, which reside in the current folder. You can change the current folder to any other folder on your memory card using the Storage Folder option in the Photo Shooting menu, described in Chapter 5.

Playback Display Options

Options: Basic photo info: Focus Point, Mark First Shot in Series; Additional photo info: Exposure Info, Highlights, RGB Histogram, Shooting Data, Overview, None (Picture only), File Info; Detailed photo info: Basic Shooting Data, Flash Data, Picture Control/HLG Data, Other Shooting Data, Copyright Info, Location Data, IPTC Data
My preference: N/A

You'll recall from Chapter 7 that a great deal of information, available on multiple screens, can be cycled through by pressing the DISP button when previewing images, and that you could select which items are shown. This menu item helps you reduce/increase the Playback screen clutter by specifying which information and screens will be available. To activate or deactivate an info option, scroll to that option and press the right multi selector button to add a checkmark to the box next to that item. Press the right button to unmark an item that has previously been checked. If no boxes are checked, only the default view—the image with basic information shown at the bottom of the frame—is displayed. Shooting data may require multiple pages, which you can scroll through using the multi selector up and down buttons. Your additional info options include:

- **Focus Point.** Activate this option to use red highlighting to display the focus point(s) that were active when the image was captured.
- **Mark First Shot in Series.** You can have a marker inserted for the first image captured during a continuous shooting sequence. An icon representing a stack of images and the number of shots in the sequence will appear in the upper-right corner of the first image when played back.
- **Exposure Info.** Shows only frame number and basic exposure information, including release mode, shutter speed, aperture, exposure compensation, and ISO sensitivity.
- **Highlights.** When enabled, overexposed highlight areas in your image will blink with a black border during picture review. That's your cue to consider using exposure compensation to reduce exposure, unless a minus EV setting will cause loss of shadow detail that you want to preserve. You can read more about correcting exposure in Chapter 2.
- **RGB Histogram.** Displays both luminance (brightness) and RGB histograms on a screen that can be displayed using the up/down multi selector buttons. I explained the use of histograms in Chapter 2.
- **Shooting Data.** Activates the pages of detailed shooting data listed in this menu and described just below (starting with Basic Shooting Data).
- **Overview.** Activates the overview screen. You must scroll down the list to access this option.
- **None (Picture Only).** A screen with the image only and no photo information will be displayed.
- **File Info.** Displays information about the image file, including file and folder name.
- **Basic Shooting Data.** Shows a screen with the full range of information, including exposure data, lens settings, white balance settings, focus/autofocus modes, etc.
- **Flash Data.** Displays flash type, modes, and flash compensation information.
- **Picture Control/HLG Data.** Shows any Picture Control settings in effect for the image, and HLG Quality settings for video.
- **Other Shooting Data.** Includes noise reduction, Active D-Lighting, HDR strength, Vignette control, any retouching that has been done, and image comments.
- **Copyright Info.** Displays copyright data, if recorded.
- **Location Data.** If location data supplied by GPS, including latitude, longitude, altitude, and Universal Coordinated Time (UTC), are embedded in the file, it will be shown on this screen.
- **IPTC Data.** If you've enabled and specified IPTC information, it will be displayed here.

Delete Pictures From Both Slots

Options: Yes (Confirmation Required) (default), Yes, No

My preference: Yes (Confirmation Required)

This entry lets you choose whether to retain additional copies of an image when deleting pictures using the Playback menu entry described above. As you learned in Chapter 5, your camera is able to store multiple copies of the same image in different locations, depending on the role you've selected for the second card slot. If you've set the second slot to function as an Overflow destination when your first card fills up, only one copy of each picture will exist, so this entry has no bearing.

However, if you've specified a function for the secondary slot other than Overflow (that is, Backup, RAW Slot 1—JPEG/HEIF Slot 2, JPEG Slot 1—JPEG/HEIF Slot 2), then you'll end up with duplicates of the same image. I recommend sticking with the default setting, so that when you decide to trash a particular image, the camera will remind you that a copy is stored on the other card and ask for confirmation. Choose Yes, and the copy will always be removed forthwith; No, and it will be retained as a backup in case you change your mind or have made an error.

Dual-Format Recording PB Slot

Options: Slot 1/Slot 2

My preference: Slot containing JPEG images

Your camera has two memory card slots. You can specify how the memory card in each slot is used. You can tell the camera to use the second slot for *overflow* once the first slot card fills; copy each shot to *both* for backup; or to save RAW images on one card and the JPEG versions on the other card.

This entry comes into play only when you are shooting in RAW+JPEG mode and have chosen RAW Slot 1—JPEG Slot 2 or JPEG Slot 1–JPEG Slot 2 in the Slot 2 Function entry for the Z5 II instead. That specifies which of the two versions of your dual-format images should be displayed during Playback. You can elect to have the version stored in Slot 1 displayed, or the version stored in Slot 2.

Filtered Playback Criteria

Options: Protect; Picture Type (Photos, Videos); Rating (Zero to Five Stars, Not Rated, Candidate for Deletion); Select for Upload to The Cloud/Computer/FTP; Voice Memo; Retouched Pictures

My preference: N/A

Ordinarily, your camera will show you all the available images in the active folder during Playback. You can choose several types of filters to weed through your images so that only the ones meeting your criteria are shown. A white border appears around the image to remind you that only the filtered images are being displayed. In addition to this menu entry, filtered playback and setting filtered playback parameters are also available from the Playback version of the *i* menu. This entry is used to specify which filters will be used when you initiate filtered playback using the Playback *i* menu.

The filters available include:

- **Protected images.** You must Protect images individually or in groups.
- **Picture Type.** Choose Photos or Videos.
- **Rating.** You can select any combination of zero to five stars, unrated images, or pictures marked as candidates for deletion.
- **Uploads.** You can view those selected for upload to the cloud or to your computer. You can select pictures for transfer in the Playback version of the *i* menu. You can view only photos that have previously been uploaded to a cloud, your computer, or FTP server, those that have not yet been uploaded, or both types.
- **Voice memo.** View images that have been tagged with a recorded voice memo using the Playback version of the *i* menu. Voice memos can be listened to using the *i* menu during review.
- **Retouched pictures.** Review all images that have been retouched using the Playback version of the *i* menu.

Because you can select any combination of the listed parameters, you can do things like review only protected still photos with four or five star ratings, if that's what you want. This is a handy way of sorting through a lot of images quickly, if you've taken the time to protect them or assign a rating. To search for images using the filters you've specified, just follow these steps:

1. Press the Playback button to display an image.
2. Press the *i* button to display the *i* menu.
3. Select Filtered Playback from the menu.
4. Press OK to display the filtered images.

Series Playback

Options: Sub-selector Displays First Shot, On (default), Off; Auto Series Playback, On, Off (default); Auto Series Playback Options: Loop playback, Wait before playback, Auto Series Playback Speed; List series as Single Thumbnails, On, Off (default)

My preference: All On

This entry provides some shortcuts that can be helpful when reviewing images during playback. There are three options:

- **Sub-selector Displays First Shot.** When enabled (the default), only the first shot in each burst is displayed when using the sub-selector to scroll left or right through images during picture review. To see the individual images in the burst, tilt the sub-selector up or down. Photos not part of a continuous burst will be displayed normally, and not skipped. Choose Off, and the sub-selector functions the same as the multi selector directional controls.
- **Auto Series Playback.** This setting is Off by default, and after you've finished capturing a continuous sequence, you can start reviewing your images manually. If you'd rather have the camera display the individual pictures in sequence automatically, turn this option On. When you press Playback to view the first image in a series, after about three seconds the camera will begin showing the remaining images one after another.

- **Auto Series Playback Options.** When Auto Series Playback is enabled, you can choose:
  - **Loop playback.** The burst of images will be played repeatedly.
  - **Wait before playback.** Select Long, Normal, Short, and Start Immediately to specify a delay time before playback starts.
  - **Auto series playback speed.** Choose to display the series of images at 5, 15, or 30 frames per second, or at the current release mode speed. If the current release mode is Single or Self-timer, the playback speed will be 3 frames per second.
- **List Series as a Single Thumbnail.** Do yourself a favor and activate this option. It will save time when trying to find an individual scene or sequence using thumbnails. When enabled, only the first shot in a continuous sequence will be displayed as a thumbnail with a "stack" overlay indicating there are other images in the series.

Picture Review

Options: On, On (Monitor Only), Off (default)
My preference: N/A

This is the first of the remaining entries in the Playback menu. (See Figure 8.3.) There are certain shooting situations in which it's useful to have the picture you've just shot pop up on the monitor automatically for review. Perhaps you're fine-tuning exposure or autofocus and want to be able to see whether your most recent image is acceptable. Or maybe you're the nervous type and just want confirmation that you actually took a picture. Picture review has saved my bacon a few times when I accidentally made an inappropriate setting (such as specifying ISO 25600 when it really wasn't needed or desirable).

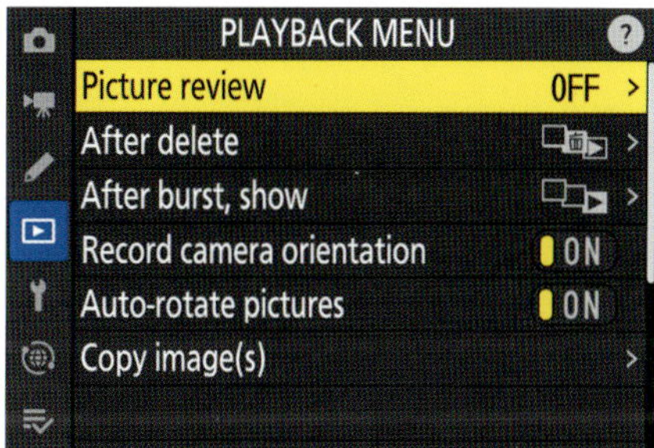

Figure 8.3 The remaining entries in the Playback menu.

A lot of the time, however, it's a better idea to *not* automatically review your shots to conserve battery power (the LCD monitor and EVF are two of the major juice drains) or to speed up or simplify operations. For example, if you've just fired off a burst of eight shots during a football game, do you *really* need to have every frame display as the camera clears its buffer and stores the photos on your memory card? This menu operation allows you to choose which mode to use. You can elect to have the review image always appear, appear on the LCD monitor only, or never appear. Unfortunately, Nikon neglected to give us an On (Viewfinder Only) option for image review, but I'm going to give you several workarounds.

- **On.** Picture review is automatic after every shot is taken, and your image will appear in the viewfinder or on the LCD monitor (depending on which you are using).
- **On (Monitor Only).** Picture review is displayed *only* on the rear-panel LCD monitor, and then only if you are *not* currently looking through the viewfinder; to see Picture review, move the camera away from your eye.
- **Off.** Picture are displayed only when you press the Playback button. Nikon, in its wisdom, has made this the default setting.

QUENCH THAT MONITOR!

When I am shooting concerts and performances where the audience area is darkened, I don't want the LCD monitor lighting up after every shot and annoying people. Even so, I may want to review my images and would like them to appear immediately—just not on the monitor. There are several ways to activate that behavior:

- If you select ON with this menu entry, if your Limit Monitor Mode Selection option (in the Setup menu and described in Chapter 9) is set to activate Automatic Display Switch, as long as you keep your eye up to the viewfinder, the image preview will not appear on the monitor.
- A better choice is to disable Automatic Display Switch and enable just Viewfinder Only or Monitor Only options. Then you can manually toggle between the viewfinder and monitor using the VF/Monitor button located on the left side of the viewfinder hump. Your image review will appear *only* on the currently selected screen.
- If you absolutely want to prevent having your image review appear on the monitor, visit the Limit Monitor Mode Selection entry and disable everything but Viewfinder Only.
- A compromise is to use the Monitor Brightness entry in the Setup menu and set it to −5. This produces a very dark screen, which is unlikely to annoy those around you. It also makes it difficult to judge exposure from the monitor alone. (*That's what the histogram is for!*)

After Delete

Options: Show Next (default), Show Previous, Continue as Before

My preference: Show Next

When you've deleted an image, you probably will want to do one of three things: display the next picture (in the order shot); show the *previous* picture; or show either the next *or* previous picture, depending on which way you were scrolling during picture review. You can select which action to take:

- **Show Next.** It's likely that you'll want to look at the picture taken after the one you just deleted, so Nikon makes this the default action.
- **Show Previous.** I use this setting a lot when shooting sports with a continuous shooting setting. After the sequence is taken, I press the Playback button to see the last picture in the series and sometimes discover that the whole sequence missed the boat. I sometimes go ahead and press the Trash button twice to delete the offending image, then continue moving backward to delete the five or six or eleven other pictures in the wasted sequence. You'll often find yourself with time on your hands at football games and feel the urge to delete a stinker series of shots to save you time reviewing back at the computer (plus freeing up a little space on your card).
- **Continue as Before.** This setting makes a lot of sense: if you were scrolling backward or forward and deleting photos as you go, you might want to continue in the same direction weeding out bad shots. Use this setting to set your camera to behave that way.

After Burst, Show

Options: First Picture in Burst, Last Picture in Burst (default)

My preference: Last Picture in Burst

This menu choice allows you to determine which image is shown after a continuous series of shots are captured, when Image Review is turned off. In practice, the camera will *not* display any images on the LCD monitor while you are shooting a burst, allowing the camera to capture frames and store them on your memory card at maximum speed. However, when the burst is complete, one image will then be shown on the screen—either the first image of the series or the last image captured. I prefer to view the final image; if it's okay in terms of exposure and focus, I can assume the others in the series are similar and move on to initiate another burst immediately if I want. Select First Picture in Burst, instead, if you want to see the initial shot and then, perhaps, continue checking subsequent photos.

Record Camera Orientation

Options: On (default), Off

My preference: On

With the default setting, the camera orientation (horizontal or vertical) will be recorded and stored with images as they are captured. That enables your computer and its software as well as the Z5 II to automatically rotate the images to the correct orientation when displayed.

Auto-Rotate Pictures

Options: On (default), Off

My preference: Off

When you rotate the camera to photograph vertical subjects in portrait (tall), rather than landscape (wide) orientation, you probably don't want to view them tilted onto their sides later, either on the monitor and viewfinder or within your image viewing/editing application on your computer. The camera has a directional sensor built in that can detect whether it was rotated when the photo was taken and hide this information in the image file itself.

The orientation data is applied in two different ways. It can be used by the camera to automatically rotate images when they are displayed on the monitor and viewfinder (when On is enabled), or you can ignore the data and let the images display in non-rotated fashion when Off is selected (so you have to rotate the camera to view them in their proper orientation). As mentioned earlier, your image-editing application can also use the embedded file data to automatically rotate images on your computer screen.

This menu choice deals only with whether the image should be rotated when displayed on the *camera LCD monitor* or *in the electronic viewfinder.* If you de-activate this option, your image-editing software can still read the embedded rotation data if stored (because Record Camera Orientation was enabled) and properly display your images. When Auto-Rotate Pictures is turned off, the camera does not rotate pictures taken in vertical orientation. The image is large on your display, but you must rotate the camera to view it upright. When Auto-Rotate Pictures is turned on, the camera rotates pictures taken in vertical orientation on the monitor screen so you don't have to turn the camera to view them comfortably. However, this orientation also means that the longest dimension of the image is shown using the shortest dimension of the monitor, so the picture displayed (but not the image itself) is reduced in size.

So, turn this feature On if you'd rather not turn your camera to view vertical shots in their natural orientation, and don't mind the smaller image. Turn the feature Off if, as I do, you'd rather see a larger image and are willing to rotate the camera to do so. Rotating the camera is no big deal, and worth the trouble to see the largest possible review image on the display.

Copy Image(s)

Options: Select Source, Select Picture(s), Select Destination Folder, Copy Picture(s)?
My preference: N/A

The ability to work with two memory cards simultaneously ranks as one of my favorite features in any camera that offers dual slots. One of the best uses for two cards is to make back-up images while traveling, or at any other time that your computer isn't easily accessible. Here are some examples of what I do:

- **Shoot to two cards simultaneously.** This gives you an instant backup in case pictures on your primary card become corrupt or erased. Ideally, your two cards should be equal in storage size.
- **Make a copy.** Use this Copy Image(s) facility to make a copy of images you shot on one card to your second card. Instead of shooting on two cards at once (which does slow down the camera a bit), use only one card when you take photos, then make a backup onto a second card at the end of the day. You can copy all or only some of the photos you've shot.
- **Make copies to distribute.** Z5 II owners, because their cameras can work with cheap SD cards, have an option. I bought a bunch of 16GB SD memory cards for $4 each, and I find it's quick and easy to make multiple copies of photos, not for backup, but for distribution either on the spot, say, to provide models I've hired with some raw (not RAW) images or to send by snail mail to colleagues, friends, or family. Such small cards won't hold many images, but in many cases, that's enough space. No computer required!
- **Leave your laptop or external storage at home.** Since I've begun using Nikon cameras with dual memory card slots, I leave my hard disk/personal storage device with its built-in reader or my laptop at home more often. If I am going to be gone for only a day or two, it's easier to just make copies in the camera, and not bother with another external device.

To copy images from one card to another, just follow these steps (which are available only when two memory cards are present in the camera):

1. **Access copy menus.** Choose Copy Images(s) from the Playback menu. There are four choices that may be available to you: Select Source, Select Picture(s), Select Destination Folder, and Copy Picture(s)?. They are shown at upper left in Figure 8.4.

   - If you have images on only one card, all other choices will be grayed out, and the card containing images will be selected automatically.

   - If there are images on both cards already, you can choose Select Source to specify which card slot as the source to copy from.

   - If you have already marked some images previously, then all four choices will be available.

2. **Select Source.** If you have images on both cards and want to choose images from the non-default slot that is pre-selected, highlight Select Source and press the right button on the multi selector. Choose the desired slot and press the right button again to return to the previous menu. (See Figure 8.4 right.)

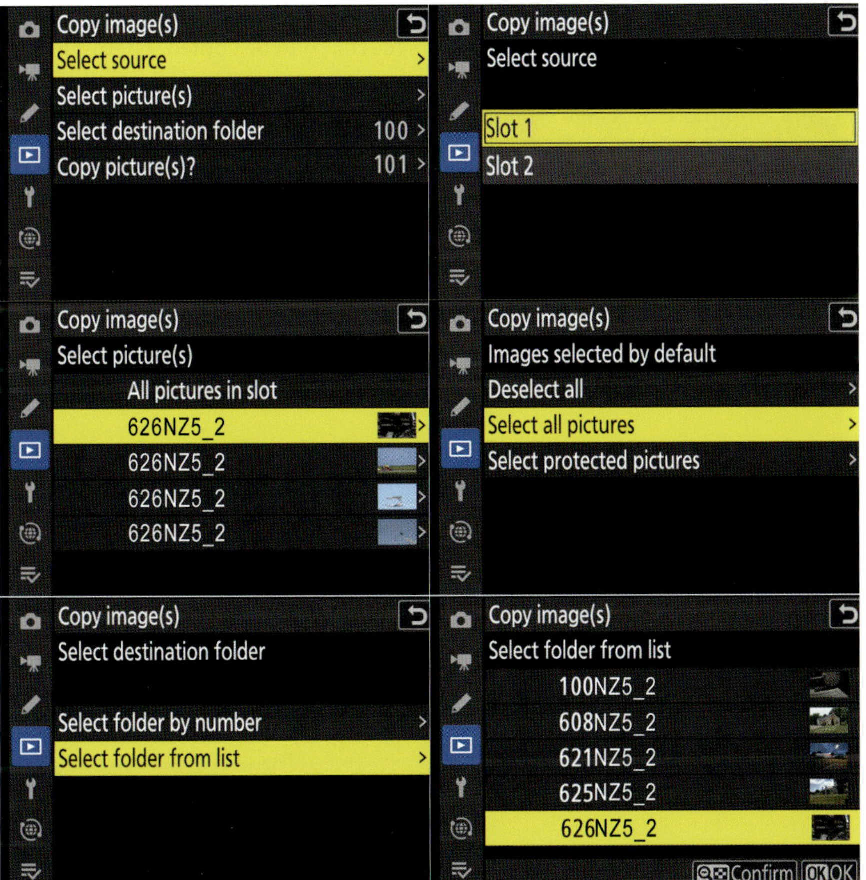

Figure 8.4 These six screens allow you to select a source slot, specific images, destination folder, and initiate copying.

3. **Select Pictures.** Highlight Select Picture(s) and press the right button. The screen shown at left center in Figure 8.4 appears. You can now choose from:

   - **All Pictures in Slot.** If you select this, all the images on the card will be selected and you'll be returned to the previous menu.

   - **Images in a folder in that slot.** If more than one folder resides on that card, all will be shown. Select a folder and press the right button, and the screen shown at center right in Figure 8.4 appears. You can again choose Select All Pictures or Select Protected Pictures (which you have previously marked). The top choice in the list, Deselect All, automatically unselects previously selected images (if any) and takes you to the Deselect All/Select screen that allows you to highlight individual images and checkmark them with the OK button.

4. **Select destination folder.** When finished selecting images, press OK to return to the Copy Image(s) screen. There, you can optionally choose Select Destination Folder and select a folder by number, or from a list of existing folders on the target card. If you do not specify a destination folder the camera will create one for you on the destination memory card. (See Figure 8.4, lower left and right.)

5. **Start copying.** If you do not want to choose a specific destination, select Copy Pictures(s)?. You'll see a confirmation screen that displays the number of images that will be copied. Highlight Yes, press OK, and a progress screen with a green progress bar appears while the copying is underway. You'll see a Copy Complete message when the task is finished. Press OK, and then the MENU button twice to back out of the menus; or just tap the shutter-release button.

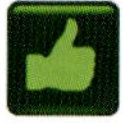

TIP The Copy command will ask for confirmation before overwriting images on the destination card that have the same name as the source images. You can choose Replace Existing Image, Replace All, Skip, or Cancel the rest of the copying operation.

The Setup, Network, Retouch, and My Menus

9

We're not done covering the menu options yet. There are four more menus to deal with. These include the Setup menu, which deals with adjustments that are generally outside the actual shooting experience, such as formatting a memory card, adjusting the time, or specifying touch controls; the Network menu, used to connect your camera to smart devices and computers; the Retouch menu, which contains the post-processing options you can apply to your images after you've taken a photo; and the My Menu system, which can help you set up a customized menu that contains only the entries you want, or your most recently accessed entries.

Setup Menu Options

There is a long list of entries in the orange-brown coded Setup menu. The first page of entries is shown in Figure 9.1. All the Setup menu options let you make additional adjustments on how your camera *behaves* before or during your shooting session, as differentiated from the Photo Shooting menu, which adjusts how the pictures are actually taken. Your choices include:

- Format Memory Card
- Save User Settings
- Reset User Settings
- Language
- Time Zone and Date
- Monitor Brightness
- Monitor Color Balance
- Viewfinder Brightness
- Viewfinder Color Balance
- Viewfinder Display Size
- Limit Monitor Mode Selection
- Auto Rotate Info Display
- AF Fine-Tuning Options
- Non-CPU Lens Data
- Distance Units
- Save Focus Position
- Save Zoom Position (PZ lenses)
- Auto Temperature Cutout

- Clean Image Sensor
- Image Dust Off Reference Photo
- Pixel Mapping
- Image Comment
- Copyright Information
- IPTC
- Headphone/Remote Cord Connector Function
- Voice Memo Options
- Camera Sounds
- Silent Mode
- Touch Controls
- Self-portrait Mode
- HDMI
- USB Connection Priority
- Conformity Marking

- Battery Info
- USB Power Delivery
- Energy Saving (Photo Mode)
- Slot Empty Release Lock
- Save/Load Menu Settings
- Reset All Settings
- Firmware Version

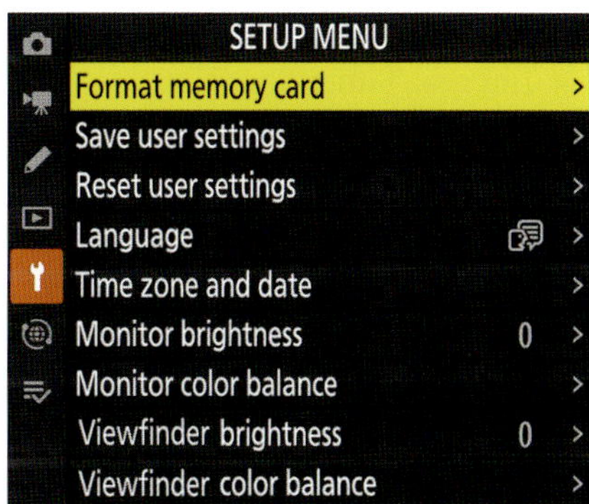

Figure 9.1 The Setup menu allows you to adjust how the camera behaves.

Format Memory Card

Options: Slot 1 (default), Slot 2; All Pictures On Memory Card Will Be Deleted. OK: Yes, No
My preference: N/A

I recommend using this menu entry to reformat your memory card after each shoot, choosing Slot 1 or Slot 2, as appropriate. Although you can move files from the memory card to your computer, creating a blank card, or delete files using the Playback menu's Delete feature, both of those options can leave behind stray files (such as those that have been marked as Protected). Format removes those files completely and beyond retrieval (unless you use a special utility program) and establishes a spanking-new fresh file system on the card. **Note:** Formatting in a computer with the memory card inserted in a card reader *will not* produce the kind of file system your camera requires.

Save User Settings

Options: Save to U1, Save to U2, Save to U3
My preference: N/A

User settings are groups of camera shooting settings that the camera stores in one of three memory "slots," labeled U1, U2, and U3. Set up your camera with the settings you want to be able to recall and save them using this menu entry. Then rotate the mode dial to the U1, U2, or U3 position when you want to access them.

Available settings include:

- Shutter speed in S and M modes
- Aperture in A and M modes
- Flexible Program settings in P mode
- Exposure and flash compensation
- Metering, Autofocus, and AF-area modes
- Flash mode
- Bracketing settings
- Most adjustments in Photo Shooting, Video Recording, and Custom Settings menus, except for those listed next

The settings you *cannot* save include:

Photo Shooting Menu:

- Storage Folder
- Manage Picture Control
- Multiple Exposure
- Interval Timer Shooting
- Time-lapse Video
- Focus Shift Shooting
- Pixel Shift Shooting

Video Recording Menu:

- Storage Folder
- Manage Picture Control

Follow these steps to store your settings:

1. **Choose mode.** Rotate the mode dial to the shooting mode you'd like to store, such as P, A, S, or M.
2. **Adjust settings.** Enter the settings you want to store on the camera, using the camera controls, Photo Shooting, Video Recording, and Custom Settings menus. (Setup menu entries cannot be saved.)
3. **Select Save User Settings.** Navigate to this entry in the Setup menu.
4. **Choose memory register.** Choose Save to U1, Save to U2, or Save to U3 and press the right directional button.
5. **Save.** Choose Save Settings on the confirmation screen or Cancel to abort.

Reset User Settings

Options: Reset U1, Reset U2, Reset U3
My preference: N/A

You can return the settings stored in the U1, U2, or U3 registers to their factory default values using this menu entry. Simply select the entry, choose Reset U1, Reset U2, or Reset U3, and press the right directional button. Press OK to confirm.

Language

Options: In the Americas: English, Español, Français, Português (PT)
My preference: English, of course, pero estoy mejorando constantemente en español.

Nikon's thrown us a curveball in the language option department. Instead of the couple dozen languages offered in many previous Nikon cameras, camera bodies sold in North and South America now offer only the official languages commonly used on those continents. And their endonyms are listed in their own language in the menu (rather than Spanish, French, or Portuguese). The changes were either done "for user convenience" (which is rarely true) or to prevent gray market imports from one area of the world to another. **Fun Fact:** Português (PT) indicates that traditional Portuguese (which has 10 million speakers in Portugal) is used, rather than Português (BR), which is less formal and is spoken worldwide (by 200 million in Brazil alone). Go figure.

If you'd like to see your menus and prompts in German, Japanese, or some other language, you'll need to buy a camera built for Europe or Asia, respectively. As far as I know, Nikon does not offer the ability to install firmware updates from other areas to a camera intended for a different locale. Fortunately, I haven't heard any reports of anyone trying this and munging their camera. This change won't impact a large number of us, but for expats who want to use their native tongue, it's an inconvenience, at best.

Time Zone and Date

Options: Time Zone, Date and Time, Date Format, Daylight Saving Time (default: Off)

My preference: N/A

Use this menu entry to adjust the internal clock. Your options include:

- **Time Zone.** You can choose your local time zone. I sometimes forget to change the time zone when I travel (especially when going to Europe), so my pictures are all time-stamped incorrectly. I like to use the time stamp to recall exactly when a photo was taken, so keeping this setting correct is important.
- **Date and Time.** Use this setting to enter the exact year, month, day, hour, minute, and second.
- **Date Format.** Choose from Y/M/D (year/month/day), M/D/Y (month/day/year), or D/M/Y (day/month/year) formats.
- **Daylight Saving Time.** Use this to turn daylight saving time On or Off. Because the date on which DST goes into effect each year has been changed from time to time, if you turn this feature on you may need to monitor your camera to make sure DST has been implemented correctly.

Monitor Brightness

Options: Lo 2, Lo 1, –5 to +5 (default: 0), Hi 1, Hi 2

My preference: N/A

Choose this menu option and a screen appears allowing you to specify brightness (see Figure 9.2, left). Use the multi selector up/down keys to adjust the brightness to a comfortable viewing level. Under the lighting conditions that exist when you make this adjustment, you should be able to see all 10 swatches from black to white. If the two left-end swatches blend together, the brightness has been set too low. If the two whitest swatches on the right end of the strip blend together, the brightness is too high. Brighter settings use more battery power but can allow you to view an image on the monitor outdoors in bright sunlight. You can adjust brightness plus/minus 5, with additional Lo 1, Lo 2, Hi 1, and Hi 2 settings available if you happen to need an extremely dim or bright screen.

When you have the brightness you want, press OK to lock it in and return to the menu. Although the Z5 II has a great viewfinder, you'll still find yourself using the monitor for both preview and review functions. I often tilt the LCD upward when shooting from low perspectives, so I don't have to crouch or kneel or tilt it forward when I am holding the camera overhead for a periscope view.

Figure 9.2 Choose to adjust monitor brightness (left) or monitor color balance (right).

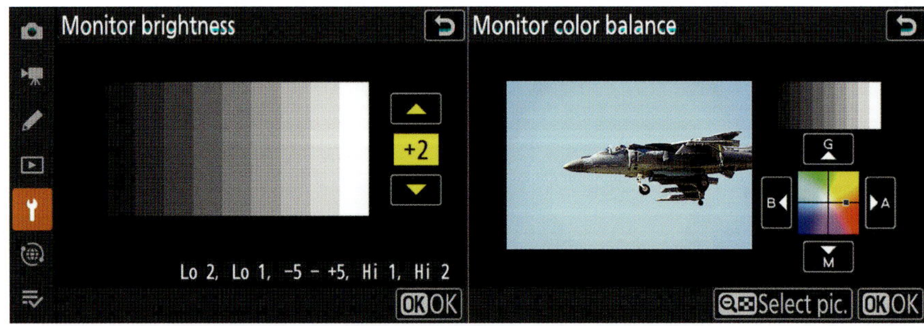

Note: This feature cannot be used if Viewfinder Only is selected for monitor mode, or when your eye is placed next to the viewfinder. In addition, if you've specified HLG as the Tone Mode in the Photo Shooting menu, the rendition of highlights, in particular, declines as the brightness of the monitor is increased.

Monitor Color Balance

Options: Choose reference picture; Adjust color balance (default: A-B:0, G-M:0)

My preference: N/A

This entry allows you to adjust the color balance of the LCD monitor using an image residing on your memory card as a reference. (See Figure 9.2, right.) By default, the large thumbnail image will be the last photograph taken, or, if you are using Playback mode, the last photograph viewed. You can also press the Zoom Out button to select a different reference image on your memory card from a thumbnail list.

Use the multi selector directional buttons to bias the monitor hue along the blue/amber (left/right buttons) and/or green/magenta (up/down buttons) axes. The grayscale tone strip above helps you judge the neutrality of your selected balance settings. Press OK to confirm your adjustment. Changing the monitor color balance has *no* effect on the color balance of the photos you take, but will affect how you evaluate images, as the colors will be different. **Note:** This feature cannot be used if Viewfinder Only is selected for monitor mode, or when your eye is placed next to the viewfinder.

Viewfinder Brightness

Options: Auto (default); Manual: Lo 2, Lo 1, −5 to +8 (default: 0), Hi 1, Hi 2

My preference: N/A

You can also adjust the brightness for the electronic viewfinder. Although the settings screens are similar, the Viewfinder option includes an Auto setting that will modify brightness based on ambient-light conditions. In Manual mode, while peering through the viewfinder at the grayscale patches, you can brighten/darken the display using a −5 to +8 range, plus Lo 2, Lo 1, Hi 1, and Hi 2. Use the multi selector up/down keys to adjust the brightness to a comfortable viewing level. When you have the brightness you want, press OK to lock it in and return to the menu. **Note:** This feature cannot be used if Monitor Only is selected for monitor mode.

Viewfinder Color Balance

Options: Adjust color balance (default: A-B:0, G-M:0)

My preference: N/A

Viewfinder color balance is adjusted using the same procedure described above for Monitor Color Balance, while looking through the viewfinder window. **Note:** This feature cannot be used if Monitor Only is selected for monitor mode, and changing from the default color balance will affect your evaluation of your images.

Viewfinder Display Size

Options: Standard (default), Small

My preference: Standard

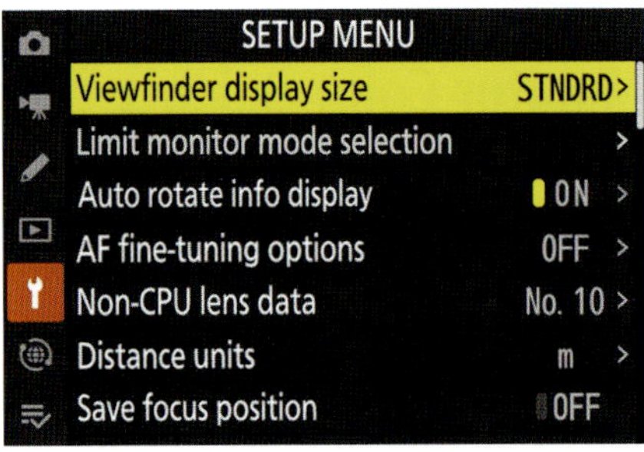

Figure 9.3 The second group of Setup menu options.

This is the first entry in the next group of Setup menu options. (See Figure 9.3.) The distance your eye can be from the viewfinder and still see the entire frame is called the *eyepoint* and is 21mm for the Nikon Z5 II. Most users will be able to view the whole frame comfortably using the Standard setting with the factory eyecup, but may have problems if they wear glasses or use one of those fancy third-party flexible eyecups. You can use this entry to slightly decrease the size of the viewfinder display, which may make it easier to view the corners of the frame.

I was a sports photographer for many years, and Nikon had a "high-eyepoint" sports finder prism replacement for my film cameras that extended the eyepoint to 25mm. Nevertheless, I've spent my whole career shooting without my glasses and relying on the diopter adjustment knob and prefer to stick with that.

Limit Monitor Mode Selection

Options: Automatic Display Switch, Viewfinder Only, Monitor Only, Prioritize Viewfinder 1, Prioritize Viewfinder 2; (default: All enabled)

My preference: Enable All

One of my favorite features is the ability to use the electronic viewfinder for tasks that, on a digital SLR, require looking at the LCD monitor. For example, I can keep the camera up to my eye and make menu adjustments and review images I've shot in Playback mode—even under the brightest daylight conditions.

This menu item lets you choose which monitor viewing modes are available when you press the monitor mode button (located on the left side of the viewfinder hump). Pressing the button repeatedly cycles among the options you've enabled. At least one *must* be enabled (you cannot disable all of them). Your options are as follows:

- **Automatic Display Switch.** The active display always switches from the monitor to the viewfinder when you place your eye up to the viewfinder (or when anything else comes in proximity to the sensor located above the viewfinder window). When you remove your eye from the EVF, the display switches to the LCD monitor. This is often the most convenient mode. However, you may encounter unwanted switching if something other than your eye comes within roughly two inches of the viewfinder sensor. For example, if you've swiveled the monitor and are using the touch screen, a finger may switch the display. Artifacts on the eye sensor, including dirt and moisture, and swiveling the display can disable monitor switching.

- **Viewfinder Only.** The monitor is disabled, and the viewfinder is used exclusively for shooting, navigating menus, or image playback. This is my preferred mode in dark venues—especially concerts—where an illuminated LCD can distract or annoy others. I can access most camera features with the menus and viewfinder, so, for example, I don't need to fumble with my fingers to use the exposure compensation dial. I also use Viewfinder Only outdoors when the monitor washes out or is difficult to view. **Note:** Nikon doesn't document this, but if you connect the Z5 II to an external monitor using an HDMI cable, the Limit Monitor Mode Selection entry is grayed out, and you *can't* eliminate monitor display, so this option, if set, is ignored (fortunately).
- **Monitor Only.** The viewfinder is disabled, and display is directed to the LCD monitor only. This is my choice when I'm composing and shooting using the monitor—say, for macro photography or other scenes shot with the camera at waist level or lower or mounted on a tripod. I don't want the eye sensor to switch to the EVF as I work, so I switch to the Monitor Only setting.
- **Prioritize Viewfinder 1/2.** With these options, when you're shooting pictures, the display is directed to the viewfinder exclusively; it turns on when you move your eye to the EVF and turns off when you remove your eye. Versions 1 and 2 behave slightly differently:
  - **Prioritize Viewfinder 1.** The viewfinder is active only when your eye is up to the viewfinder. You can toggle the rear LCD on or off by pressing the MENU or Playback buttons.
  - **Prioritize Viewfinder 2.** The viewfinder is active when your eye is detected at the viewfinder. In addition, the viewfinder will become active for a few seconds when the camera is first turned on, or when the shutter release is pressed halfway. It will turn off again after a few seconds if your eye is not at the viewfinder. You can toggle the rear LCD on or off by pressing the MENU or Playback buttons.

The two Prioritize modes save more than a little power, especially if there are intervals when you are not taking photos at all, but don't want to turn off the camera. (The image sensor and the electronic viewfinder can always be active when the camera is powered up, in contrast to digital SLRs that are, effectively, in a low-power mode until you start using the exposure meters, autofocus mechanism, or LCD monitor.)

When you're reviewing images in Playback mode, while capturing movies, or when menus are displayed, the monitor *will* turn on when you remove your eye from the viewfinder.

Auto Rotate Information Display

Options: On (default), Off

My preference: On

Your camera's viewfinder and rear LCD shooting displays can rotate 90 degrees automatically when you change from a landscape to a portrait shooting stance. All the indicators and text labels will rotate, too, making it easier to view your readouts. Unfortunately, only the shooting displays (including the *i* menu) rotate. The conventional menus remain in their fixed landscape mode, because their layout doesn't lend itself to a portrait configuration.

AF Fine-Tuning Options

Options: AF Fine-Tune On/Off (default: Off), Fine-tune and Save Lens, Default, List Saved Values, Choose Value for Current Lens

My preference: N/A

Troubled by lenses that don't focus exactly where they should, producing back-focus or front-focus problems? If your problems are *consistent* and not periodic, there is no need to send your lens and/or camera into Nikon for servicing. The camera allows you to fine-tune focus for up to 40 different lenses and adjust focus for both wide and telephoto ends of the zoom range for zoom lenses. Best of all, it works perfectly with both Z-mount and F-mount lenses (using an FTZ adapter).

You may never need to use this feature, particularly with Z-mount S-series lenses, which use fast stepper motors that are extremely accurate, and because the Z5 II uses the sensor image to focus, misalignment is not frequently a problem when using Z-mount lenses. However, if you are working with older F-mount lenses and an FTZ adapter, slight focus errors are more common, often stemming from sensor/mount alignment variations.

To fine-tune your lenses, first perform some tests to see just how much fine-tuning is required, using one of the many available third-party alignment charts. The only problem I've run into is that with some lenses, particularly short focal length lenses, using large negative values (0 to –20) to move the focal point closer to the camera sometimes results in being unable to focus to infinity. If you run into that, you may be better off sending the lens to Nikon so they can recalibrate the focus for you. As you commence the tuning process, the camera will automatically recognize any CPU-equipped Nikon lens, both F-mount and Z-mount, and report the serial number of the Z lens. It may or may not be able to identify non-Nikon lenses, and I recommend using the third-party vendor's focus adjustment system (using their proprietary USB dock) to make changes.

I'll provide you with detailed, step-by-step instructions on using this feature in Chapter 11. Meanwhile, this overview describes the five choices found in this menu option, shown at upper left in Figure 9.4:

- **AF Fine-Tune (On/Off).** Enable/disable application of your AF fine-tuning changes.
- **Fine-tune and Save Lens.** View or enter an adjustment for the lens currently mounted on your camera. You can select values from 0 to +20 to move the focal point farther from the lens, and 0 to –20 to move the focal point closer to the sensor. If a zoom lens is mounted, you can set a value for both the wide-angle and tele ends of its range. (See Figure 9.4, upper right.) Both the original values and new settings are shown, so you can quickly return to the default if you want.

  Press OK to save your new values. You can elect to overwrite the value already in place for the lens, or save your settings under a new name, as shown in Figure 9.4, center left and right. Although the settings are called "Lens Number," you can actually apply a more detailed alphanumeric description.

- **Default.** Set the default value to be applied to lenses that haven't been recalibrated. You'd use this if your camera has a certain amount of front- or back-focus problems with *all* lenses. Use with caution, as it affects every CPU lens that you use.

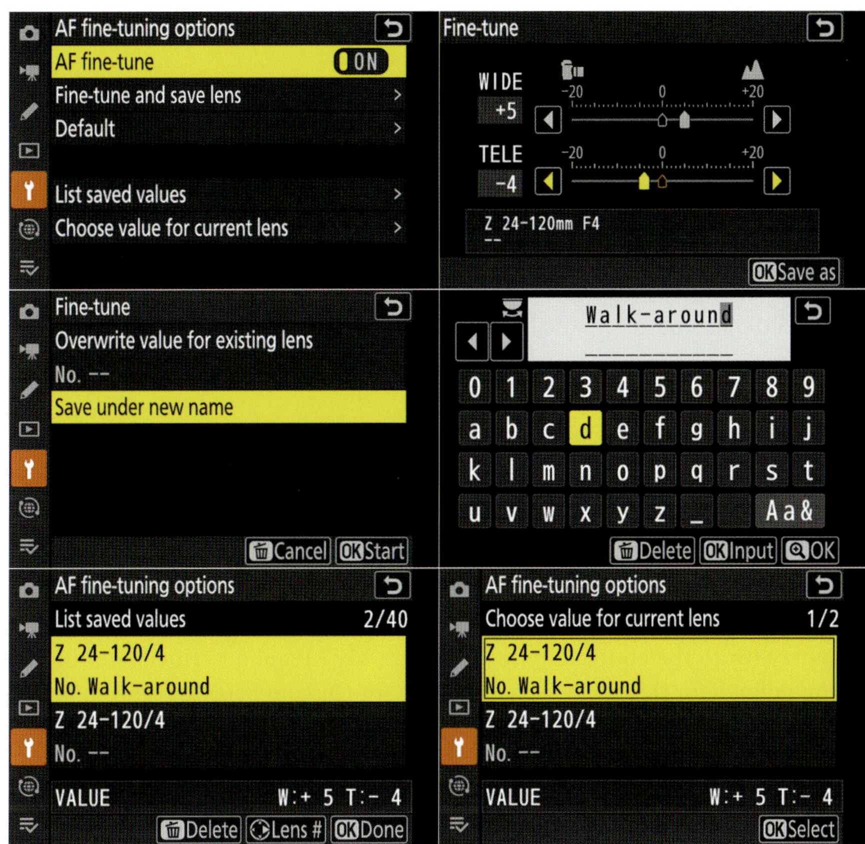

Figure 9.4 The autofocus of lenses can be adjusted here.

- **List Saved Values.** View, label, and delete tuning values you've saved. (See Figure 9.4, lower left.) Highlight a value and press the right directional button to view more information (including the serial number of a Z-mount lens) and press the right button a second time if you want to rename the setting. You can delete a value by highlighting it and pressing the Trash button.

- **Choose Value for Current Lens.** If more than one value setting is available for a current lens you can choose which to apply. (See Figure 9.4, lower right.)

Non-CPU Lens Data

Options: Lens Number, Focal Length (mm), Maximum Aperture, Lens Name

My preference: N/A

This is an odd entry, as it contributes absolutely nothing to the operation of your camera, other than enabling it to embed the focal length and maximum aperture available of some older manual focus lenses in the EXIF data embedded in your image file. I use this option more than most, because I own some 15 older manual focus lenses I picked up in the '60s and early '70s and still use for their unique characteristics. (My old Nikkor-P 105mm f/2.5 looks really cool on a retro-styled Nikon Df, Z fc or Zf.)

One of the best accessories is an FTZ adapter, which makes it easy to mount Nikon F-mount lenses to the camera. It gives you four types of functionality in PSAM modes:

- **AF-S, AF-P, and AF-I lenses, plus AF-S/AF-I teleconverters.** These retain all their features, including autofocus and autoexposure.
- **AF and AF-D lenses.** You must focus these optics manually, but with AF-D lenses the electronic rangefinder will assist in determining correct focus. Focus Peaking (described in Chapter 7) works with either type. You can adjust the aperture electronically and use Aperture-priority autoexposure.
- **AI-P and all lenses with a CPU chip.** You get manual focus only (with Focus Peaking) and Aperture-priority exposure.
- **AI, AI-S, and Series-E lenses.** These lenses offer manual focus and manual exposure only, but you can still use this menu entry to specify the maximum aperture and focal length of the lens (zoom focal length ranges are not supported). That information will be included in the EXIF metadata but *not* the actual aperture used to take the photo. You may also be able to mount and use non-AI F-mount lenses (pre-1977) but may have mechanical interference problems.

For AI, AI-S, and Series-E lenses, you'll need to specify lens focal length data and maximum aperture. The camera allows defining up to 20 different lenses, and you can choose any of them with a quick trip to this menu entry (or to the equivalent menu item in My Menu, described later in this chapter), or using a button defined for this feature, as described for Custom Setting f2 in Chapter 7.

To enter this information, follow these steps. Note that you can configure the lens's information even if the lens is not mounted on the camera. (The camera has no way of knowing which of these lenses are attached.)

1. Choose Non-CPU lens data from the Setup menu.
2. Highlight Lens Number and press the multi selector left/right buttons to choose a number. If you are defining several lenses, I recommend numbering them in order of increasing focal length, or, if you prefer, in order of frequency of use.
3. Scroll down to Focal Length (mm), press right, and choose a focal length between 0.1mm and 9000mm.
4. Scroll down to Maximum Aperture, press right, and choose a maximum f/stop.
5. Scroll down to Lens Name, press right, and use the text-entry screen to enter a name for the lens.
6. Exit. Press OK to save the lens data, or MENU to cancel. You can now select a registered lens number from this menu entry, or by choosing the lens number with a button you define for the function.

Distance Units

Options: Meters, Feet (default)

My preference: N/A

This entry defines the distance units (meters or feet) used by the camera for certain distance display functions, including the focus distance indicator for manual focus.

Save Focus Position

Options: On, Off (default)

My preference: Off

The current focus point position is, by default, not a "sticky" setting. That is, when you turn the camera off, the user-specified placement of the focus point within the frame may be discarded and return to the default location when the camera is powered up again. That can be inconvenient if you're shooting the same or similar subject matter over and over, particularly if the camera is mounted on a tripod. It's common to turn the camera off if you won't be taking any photos for several minutes, for example, when you're photographing wildlife and have the focus point centered, say, over a bird's nest in a nearby tree. Activate this feature and you can turn the camera off to save battery power as needed and have the selected focus point restored when you turn the camera on again. If some conditions change, such as zoom setting, the focus point may be different when the camera is powered up again.

Save Zoom Position (PZ Lenses)

Options: On, Off (default)

My preference: N/A

This is the first entry in the next group of Setup menu settings (see Figure 9.5). As you learned in Chapter 7, Custom Settings f13 and g8 allow choosing to use the Zoom In and Zoom Out buttons to control a Nikon lens equipped with power zoom. Other buttons can be defined instead using Custom Setting f2 and g2. This entry tells the camera whether the current zoom position is saved when the camera is turned off and then restored when powered up again.

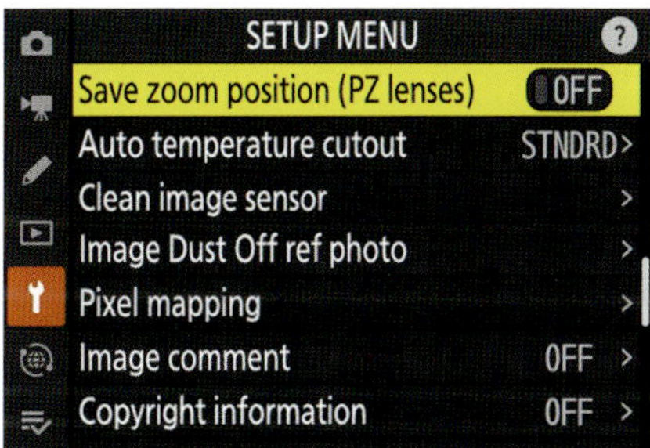

Figure 9.5 The next page of Setup menu entries.

Auto Temperature Cutout

Options: Standard (default), High

My preference: Standard

This entry helps you manage your camera's behavior as it begins to heat up during heavy use. Mirrorless cameras like the Nikon Z5 II tend to run quite a bit hotter than your grandfather's dSLR, generally because their image sensors are energized continually as you make settings and preview your image on the display. The viewfinder and rear LCD themselves produce additional heat, and some activities, particularly 4K video captured at higher frame rates, generate even higher temperatures. Ambient temperature needs to be taken into account, too, even if you're not shooting in Death Valley.

To avoid damaging the sensor and other components (including your fingers), the camera will turn off automatically when its internal temperature rises beyond recommended levels. High temperatures tend to increase visual noise, too, so you have an additional reason for avoiding running hot.

You have your choice of two settings:

- **Standard.** At this default setting, you'll get plenty of warning when the Z5 II reaches significant heat thresholds. A thermometer icon appears on the display, followed by a more urgent warning with an exclamation point, and then a countdown timer indicating when the camera will shut off.
- **High.** This setting gives you an additional amount of time, adding a HIGH thermometer before the countdown begins. Be aware that the camera can become hot to the touch; if you're shooting video, it's likely that the Z5 II will be mounted on a tripod. That's a good thing, as long as you know that touching the camera body can be painful or dangerous.

Clean Image Sensor

Options: Start; Automatic Cleaning: Clean at Shutdown (default), Cleaning Off

My preference: Automatic Cleaning (Clean at Shutdown)

This entry gives you some control over the automatic sensor cleaning feature, which removes dust through a vibration cycle that shakes the sensor until dust, presumably, falls off. If you happen to take a picture and notice an artifact in an area that contains little detail (such as the sky or a blank wall), you can access this menu choice, place the camera with its base downward, and choose Clean Now. A Cleaning Sensor message now appears, and the dust you noticed has probably been shaken off.

You can also tell the camera when you'd like it to perform automatic cleaning without specific instructions from you. Select from:

- **Start.** Triggers the dust-shaking cycle immediately. For best results, remove the lens and point the camera downward so the dust can fall outside the camera body.
- **Automatic Cleaning: Clean at Shutdown.** This removes any dust that may have accumulated since the camera has been turned on, say, from dust infiltration while changing lenses.
- **Automatic Cleaning: Cleaning Off.** No automatic dust removal will be performed. Use this to preserve battery power, or if you prefer to use automatic dust removal only when you explicitly want to apply it.

Image Dust Off Ref Photo

Options: Start, Clean Sensor and Then Start

My preference: N/A

This menu choice, available only when the Z5 II is set to Photo (rather than Video) mode, lets you "take a picture" of any dust or other particles that may be adhering to your sensor. The camera will then append information about the location of this dust to your photos, so that the Image Dust Off option in NX Studio can be used to mask the dust in the RAW image.

To use this feature, select Image Dust Off Ref Photo, choose either of the two Start options, and then press OK. A screen will appear asking you to take a photo of a bright featureless white object 10cm (about four inches) from the lens. Nikon recommends using a lens with a focal length of at least 50mm. If you're using a zoom lens, zoom to the longest focal length. If autofocus is enabled, focus will be set to infinity automatically; you should manually focus to infinity if AF is not active. Note that the dust-off information can be applied to *all* your images, not just those taken with the lens used to capture the reference photo.

Point the camera at a solid-white card and press the shutter release. If the reference object is too dark or light, you may be asked to try again with a different object. An image with the extension .ndf will be created and can be used by Nikon NX Studio as a reference photo if the "dust-off" picture is placed in the same folder as an image to be processed for dust removal.

Pixel Mapping

Options: Start

My preference: N/A

Even with the most sophisticated manufacturing techniques and quality control measures, producing a sensor with absolutely no defects among 24.5 million individual photosites is quite a challenge. Sometimes a pixel "dies" and becomes permanently dark or, worse, becomes stuck or "hot" so that it will be displayed as a bright spot in areas that should be dark or even black. Pixel mapping provides a way to detect those defective pixels and automatically map them, so they no longer contribute to your images. Instead, information from surrounding pixels will be used to determine how that photosite appears in your image.

If you notice what appears to be a bad pixel, compare several different shots to see if it appears in the same place. Keep in mind that some "bad" pixels can be caused by overheating and will return to normal once your camera has been powered down for a short period. If you need to permanently correct for a bad pixel, just follow these steps:

1. Select Pixel Mapping from the Setup menu. This entry may not be available if the camera is already overheated or its battery is not fully charged.
2. Press the right directional button and choose Start.
3. Do not operate the camera, turn it off, or disconnect from external power while pixel mapping is underway!
4. When the operation is complete, you can turn off the camera.

Image Comment

Options: Attach Comment, Input Comment

My preference: N/A

The Image Comment is your opportunity to add a copyright notice, personal information about yourself (including contact info), or even a description of where the image was taken (e.g., Browns Super Bowl 2028), although text entry is a bit too clumsy (even when using the touch screen) for doing a lot of individual annotation of your photos. (But you still might want to change the comment each time, say, you change cities during your travels.) The embedded comments can be read by many software programs, including Nikon NX Studio.

The standard text-entry screen can be used to enter your comment, with up to 36 characters available. For the copyright symbol, embed a lowercase "c" within opening and closing parentheses: (c). You can input the comment, turn attachment of the comment On or Off using the Attach Comment entry, and press the Zoom In button or tap OK on the LCD monitor when you're finished working with comments. If your fingers are too fat for typing on the touch screen or you find typing with a cursor too tedious, you can enter your comment in Nikon NX Studio and upload it to the camera through a USB cable.

Copyright Information

Options: Attach Copyright Information, Artist, Copyright

My preference: N/A

This is an expansion of the Image Comment capability, allowing you to specify the name of the "artist" (photographer), and enter copyright information. Use the standard Nikon text-entry screen. Highlight the Attach Copyright Information option and press the right multi selector button, which toggles it On or Off to control whether your copyright data is embedded in each photo as taken. The touch screen comes in useful for this input, as well.

IPTC

Options: Edit/Save, Delete, Auto Embed During Shooting, Load/Save

My preference: N/A

This is the first entry within the next group of Setup menu options. (See Figure 9.6.) Photojournalists, especially, will want to create IPTC (International Press Telecommunications Council) entries, a standardized metadata format that can be embedded in each image you take automatically. You can include caption, event ID, headline, object name, city, state, country, category, supplemental categories, byline, byline title, writer/editor, credit, and source for each available slot. The information from a given slot can be copied to your memory card, and you can select one of the listings to be automatically embedded into your image files during a particular shoot. Many major publications and news agencies require including IPTC data with submissions, so you should become familiar with the process.

You can create your IPTC entries ahead of time, or on the fly as you begin your shoot. The data can be added directly from your camera's text-entry screens (which can be tedious even with a touch screen) or typed up on your computer. Nikon's NX Mobile Air software for iOS and Android can speed things up by filling in IPTC fields using your device's voice-to-text capabilities. The app also allows you to add voice memos. Creating an IPTC dataset ahead of time is often your best option. Nikon offers a free downloadable Windows/macOS program IPTC Preset Manager.

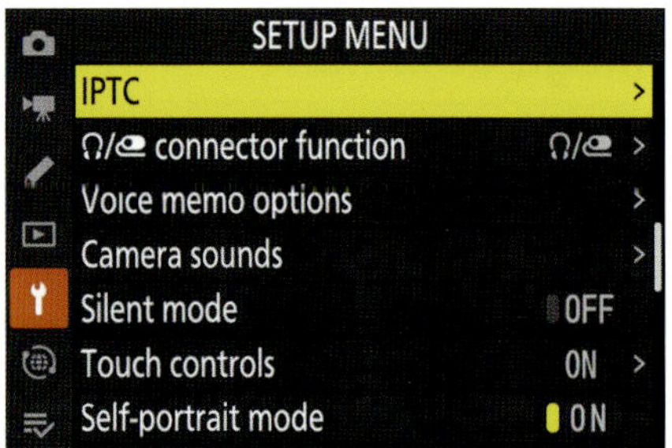

Figure 9.6 More Setup menu entries.

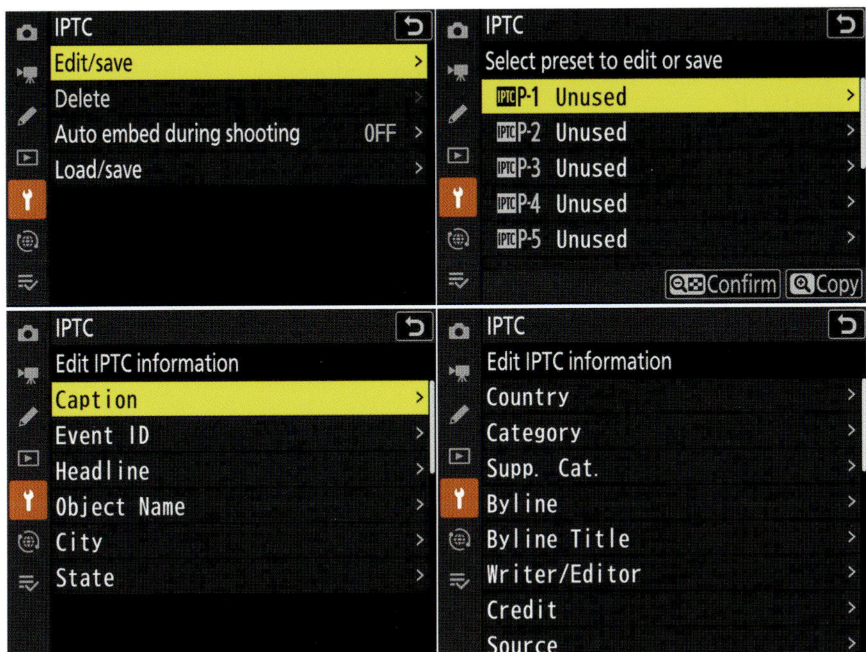

Figure 9.7 Adding IPTC datasets to your images' EXIF metadata.

When you access this entry in the camera, you'll first see a screen similar to the one shown in Figure 9.7, upper left, with options for editing/saving IPTC data, deleting existing datasets, enabling/disabling automatic embedding of IPTC data as you shoot, and loading/saving data with a memory card. There are ten slots available, numbered IPTC-P-1 to IPTC-P-10. (See Figure 9.7, upper right.) Select a slot, use the Rename item to give it a name, then select the Edit IPTC Information option to view a scrollable list of available fields (see Figure 9.7, lower left and right). You can enter the information using the standard Z5 II text-entry screen and then save it on your memory card.

The Caption field can contain up to 2,000 characters, Event ID can have 64. The other 12 fields have a maximum length of 256. To embed one of the ten entries in each image's EXIF metadata, choose Auto Embed During Shooting and select the entry you want to apply. All the data fields you have populated will be added, along with copyright information you may have specified as described above.

Headphone/Remote Cord Connector Function

Options: Auto Switch (default), Headphone

My preference: Auto Switch

Nikon has dispensed with the remote/accessory terminal found on some earlier Nikon dSLR and mirrorless models and combined the wired remote control function with the same terminal that accepts a headphone connector. The Z5 II will recognize whether the MC-DC3 wired remote or most headphones are connected and respond appropriately, so the default Auto Switch setting will do the job most of the time. However, if you find your camera does not "see" your particular headphone, you can change this setting to Headphone, instead, as needed. You'll then need to remember to revert to Auto Switch when you want to use the MC-DC3 (or compatible) remote.

Voice Memo Options

Options: Voice memo control: Press and hold, Press to Start/Stop; Audio output (playback): Speaker/
headphones volume, HDMI, Off

My preference: N/A

Voice memos are an annotation feature. You can use it to optionally accompany each image you
shoot with a voice recording of up to 60 seconds in length, which is stored as a separate WAV (waveform audio file format) file on your memory card. The memo will have the same name (other than
extension) as the image file.

Before you start recording voice memos, you'll want to set up the available options using the two
options available with this entry.

Voice Memo Control

This setting determines what happens when you activate voice memo recording. To begin a voice
memo, in Playback mode with the image you want to annotate visible, press the *i* button and select
Record Voice Memo from the list of options that pops up. Recording begins immediately; press
OK to stop. This sub-entry lets you specify how the voice recording is performed if you've assigned
a button to the function so you can bypass the *i* menu entry. If you choose Press and Hold, the OK
button must be held down; recording ceases when the button is released. Select Press to Start/Stop
instead, and the relevant button can be pressed once to begin and a second time to stop recording.

Once recording has commenced, you can speak for up to 60 seconds. A microphone icon appears
in the display as an indicator. Only one memo is allowed per image; if a picture already has a voice
memo, it must be deleted before a new one can be recorded.

Audio Output (Playback)

This choice routes the audio output, enabling you to play back your voice memos using the speaker
on the camera (located on the top-left shoulder of the camera, just above the Z5 II logo), or to the
HDMI or audio-video output ports:

- **Speaker/headphones volume.** If you choose this option, you can use the up/down multi selector
  directional buttons to increase or decrease the playback volume.
- **HDMI.** Select this choice if you've connected your camera to an HDTV through the HDMI port.
  The sound will be played back through the external device's speakers.
- **Off.** Voice memos are not played back at all.

Recording a Voice Memo

Basic voice memo recording is fairly easy. You cannot add memos to video clips or Image Dust Off
exposures, nor to still images that have already been assigned a voice memo (you must delete the
original memo first).

Once you've set up all the options, the basic steps are these:

- **Initiate voice memo recording.** There are three ways to record a voice memo:
  - *i* **menu.** You can access the feature from the Playback version of the *i* menu whenever the image you want to annotate is visible on the display.
  - **Assigned button.** If you record a lot of voice memos, you can assign the function to a button. Use Custom Setting f3: Custom Controls Playback, as described in Chapter 7, and designate Voice Memo to the button of your choice.
  - **Flick.** Use Custom Setting f14: Full Frame Playback Flicks (also explained in Chapter 7), and assign Voice Memo to either Flick Up or Flick Down. You can then initiate a recording with a simple flick to the LCD screen.
- **Interrupt a recording.** Don't worry about missing a shot if an opportunity comes up while you're recording a voice memo. Pressing the shutter release halfway ends a recording automatically. So does pressing the MENU button, Playback button, or turning the camera off.
- **Play back a memo.** Review the image in playback mode, either as a full-frame image or a highlighted thumbnail. Images with voice memos available have a musical note icon superimposed in the upper-left corner of the full-frame image. Press the *i* menu button and choose Play Voice Memo. Playback will stop when the entire voice memo has been played or the Voice Memo button is pressed a second time.
- **Delete a memo.** Press the Trash button. A screen will pop up offering the choice of deleting both the picture and voice memo, or of deleting only the voice memo. Use the up/down buttons to choose, then press the Trash button a second time to delete. Press the Play button to exit without deleting either. When you delete a memo, you can then record a new one for that image if you like.

Camera Sounds

Options: Beep: On/Off; Volume, 1–3; Pitch, High, Low
My preference: Beep Off

Your Z5 II has two options that let you take pictures quietly and unobtrusively. Those of us who shoot concerts, events, street work, or stealth photography tend to prize the sounds of silence. The internal beeper provides a (usually) superfluous chirp to signify various functions, such as the countdown of the self-timer, the termination of interval-timer/time-lapse recording, when touch functions are used, or when autofocus is confirmed in AF-S mode (unless you've selected release-priority in Custom Setting a2). You can (and probably should) switch it off if you want to avoid the beep because it's annoying, impolite, distracting (at a concert or museum), or undesired for any other reason. Note that the beeper is automatically squelched if you've activated Silent Mode, discussed next. Choose this menu entry, and select one of the following:

- **Beep On/Off.** Enable or disable the beeper.
- **Volume.** Select values of 1 (soft) through 3 (loud). A quarter-note icon appears in the shooting information display.
- **Pitch.** Select High for a high-pitched beep, or Low for a deeper tone.

Silent Mode

Options: On, Off (default)

My preference: Off

This is an additional quiet mode which enables the electronic shutter (regardless of how Custom Setting d6: Shutter Type is set). It also disables the beep and reduces some additional sounds even further. The Z5 II's built-in speaker is muted, and the camera enters a slightly crippled mode in which your continuous shooting rate may drop, and aperture and focus may be slower as they operate more quietly. Electronic flash, photo flicker reduction, and long exposure noise reduction are disabled. You'll still hear a click when the standby timer expires and the sensor vibration reduction locks in its present position. To completely mute the standby timer, change Custom Setting c3: Power Off Delay > Standby Timer to No Limit. I rarely have need of near-silent operation (which is virtually impossible to achieve, anyway), so I generally leave this setting turned off.

Touch Controls

Options: Enable (default), Disable, Playback Only; Glove Mode: On /Off (default)

My preference: N/A

This entry allows you to specify when touch controls are available. Your choices include:

- **Enable.** Touch control is available for both menu functions and image review/playback, plus for specifying a focus point and taking a picture using the Touch Shutter/Touch AF feature.
- **Playback Only.** Touch control is not available for navigating menus but can be used when reviewing images.
- **Disable.** No touch controls are available.
- **Glove Mode.** Select On or Off.

Self-Portrait Mode

Options: Off (default), On

My preference: N/A

Self-portrait mode is a cool feature useful for taking selfies and recording product reviews. When enabled, and the LCD monitor is reversed to face forward, the image on the display becomes a mirror image, so the subject being captured is shown in the same orientation they are accustomed to when viewing themselves in a mirror. However, the actual still photo or video is captured from the normal perspective. In addition, three icons appear in the upper-right corner of the screen that can be tapped to activate several self-portrait mode features:

- **Self-timer icon.** You can activate a delay before capture begins in both Photo and Video modes and specify the number of still images taken after the timer elapses.
- **Exposure compensation icon.** Tap this icon to produce a screen allowing you to brighten or darken the scene.

- **Product review icon.** In Video mode, a third icon appears which you can tap to cycle through the Product Review mode options: Off, On, or On (Customize Focus Area), explained in Chapter 6.

- **Touch AF/Touch Shutter.** In addition to the three icon-oriented functions listed above, you can use the Touch AF and Touch Shutter features that are available when the LCD monitor is in other orientations.

HDMI

Options: Output Resolution (default: Auto); Output Range (default: Auto), Output Shooting Information (default: On), Mirror Camera Information Display, (default: On)

My preference: N/A

This entry is the first in the last group of Setup menu entries. (See Figure 9.8.) It deals with the High-Definition Multimedia Interface (HDMI) video connection. The port allows you to play back your images on HDTV and HD monitors using an HDMI cable, and direct video output to external video recorders, such as the Atomos Ninja V and Ninja Ultra. I use HDMI playback for slide shows, too, and captured most of the screenshot images in this book using the HDMI output and a $25 4K video capture device with OBS (Open Broadcaster Software) Studio.

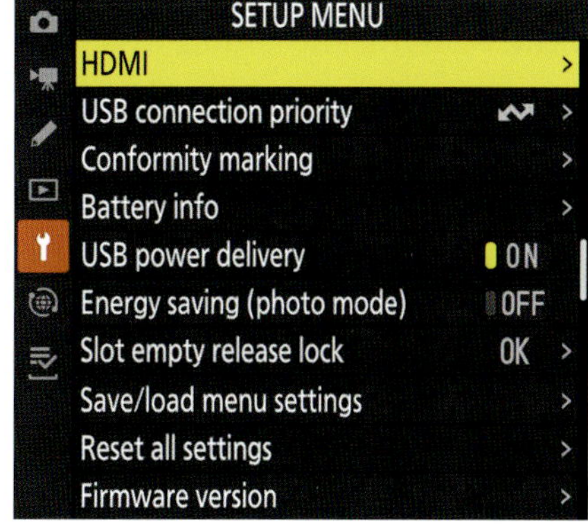

Figure 9.8 The last group of Setup menu entries.

Before you link up your equipment, you'll want to choose from the following options:

- **Output Resolution.** Select Auto and the camera will sense the correct output resolution to use. It will try to determine whether the external device supports the frame size/rate currently enabled in the camera. If not, it will try lower resolutions and slower frame rates. Auto will be applied (even if you select another resolution) when the HDMI port is used to display the image during video capture and video playback. The available resolutions all use progressive scanning; 1080i is not available in Auto mode.

  You can also choose specific resolutions, including 2160p (4K), 1080p (Full HD), and 720p (Standard HD). These are all progressive scan. You can also select 1080i if your device accepts only interlaced scanning. However, in that case, footage captured at 120p, 60p, 30p, or 24p is output at 60i, and 100p, 50p, or 25p are output at 50i. Note that 10-bit video is output at 10 bits only to HDMI recorders that support it.

- **Output Range.** Choose Auto (the default, and the best choice under most circumstances); Limited Range; or Full Range. In most cases, the camera will be able to determine the output range of your HDMI device. If not, you can choose a range:

  - **Limited Range.** This setting uses values of 16 to 235, clipping off the darkest (0–16) and brightest (235–255) portions of the image. Use Limited Range if you're plagued with reduced detail in the shadows of your image.

  - **Full Range.** This may be your choice if shadows are washed out or excessively bright. It accepts video signals with the full range from 0 to 255.

- **Output Shooting Information.** Choose On, and the icons and shooting information shown on the electronic viewfinder or LCD monitor will be included in the output to the external device. Select Off and the information will be stripped out.
- **Mirror Camera Information Display.** When directing output to an external device, you may want to also have it shown on the rear LCD monitor (the default), especially if the external device is a monitor not physically attached to the camera. If you're using a recorder/display mounted on the camera or its cage, you can save some battery power by choosing Off for this item.

Additional HDMI settings are available in the Video Recording menu, described in Chapter 6. They include External Recording Control (HDMI) for devices that support control from the camera.

USB Connection Priority

Options: Upload (default), Shooting

My preference: Upload

This setting determines the mode the Z5 II enters when the camera is connected to a computer over a USB cable. Ostensibly, it seemingly determines whether the rear LCD monitor display is effectively blanked while the camera is connected to a computer with a USB cable. (Tethering software may override this, however.) In practice, this setting can affect upload speeds. With the default Upload setting, the LCD screen displays only a message "The camera is in upload priority mode," and the transfer speed will be optimized. Pressing the shutter release halfway reactivates the screen. If you choose Shooting instead, the LCD display functions normally but transfer speeds slow down.

Conformity Marking

Options: Display only. No selections.

My preference: N/A

This entry does nothing but display the various international standards with which the camera complies. It's included here because Nikon can easily update the listing during a firmware upgrade. The alternative might be to print new labels (like the one with the serial number of the camera located behind the tilting/swiveling LCD monitor on the camera) each time a change is made.

Battery Info

Options: None. This screen is purely informational.

My preference: N/A

When invoked, you can see the following information (if the MB-N12 is mounted and contains two batteries, the data for both will be displayed):

- **Charge.** The current battery level, shown as a percentage from 100 to 0 percent.
- **No. of shots.** This shows the number of actuations with the current battery since it was last recharged. This number can be larger than the number of photos taken, because other functions, such as white balance presetting, can cause the shutter to be tripped.

- **Battery Age.** Eventually, a battery will no longer accept a charge as well as it did when it was new and must be replaced. This indicator shows when a battery is considered new (0); has begun to degrade slightly (1,2,3); or has reached the end of its charging life and is ready for replacement (4). Batteries charged at temperatures lower than 41 degrees F may display an impaired charging life temporarily, but return to their true "health" when recharged above 68 degrees F.

USB Power Delivery

Options: On (default), Off

My preference: N/A

This setting allows you to specify whether power supplied by external sources through the USB Type-C port on the Z5 II can be used to power the camera, thereby limiting the drain on the camera's battery. A USB Power Delivery icon appears at the lower right of the shooting display when the camera is being powered from an external source. The power sources can be Power Delivery-compatible chargers and power banks, the optional Nikon EH-8P AC adapter, or a computer with a USB Type-C port supplying sufficient juice. A battery must be installed in the camera even if the external power is being used to operate it. Your options are as follows:

- **On.** The camera can be operated through a power source connected via the USB port. Power will be drawn *only* while the camera is on, except if a Bluetooth upload is in progress or the camera is storing an image on a memory card when the camera is turned off.
- **Off.** When power is supplied to the USB port, charging of the battery will take place, but the camera cannot be operated using the external source's juice.

Energy Saving (Photo Mode)

Options: Off (default), On

My preference: N/A

This is an additional power-saving option that sets the shooting displays to a slower refresh rate and turns off the display roughly 15 seconds before the Standby Timer that you set using Custom Setting c3: Power Off Delay elapses. This setting is overridden if your Standby Timer has been set for No Limit or a delay of less than 30 seconds. It also does not take effect if the camera is connected to another device using the HDMI port, when attached to an AC adapter or power from the USB Type-C port, in self-portrait mode, during zoom, or if the camera is connected to a computer and exchanging data.

When enabled, energy is saved and your battery life is extended, but the display refresh rate may be reduced. Disable this setting, and battery life will not be extended. The display screen may still dim a few seconds before the standby timer expires.

Slot Empty Release Lock

Options: Release Locked (LOCK), Enable Release (OK)(default)

My preference: Release Locked

This option gives you the ability to snap off "pictures" without a memory card installed—or to lock the shutter release if that is the case. It is sometimes called play mode, because you can experiment with your camera's features or even hand your camera to a friend to let them fool around, without any danger of pictures actually being taken.

Back in our film days, we'd sometimes finish a roll, rewind the film back into its cassette surreptitiously, and then hand the camera to a child to take a few pictures—without actually wasting any film. It's hard to waste digital film, but "shoot without card" mode is still appreciated by some, especially camera vendors who want to be able to demo a camera at a store or trade show, but don't want to have to equip each and every demonstrator model with a memory card. Choose Enable Release to activate "play" mode or Release Locked to disable it.

The pictures you actually "take" are displayed on the LCD monitor with the legend "Demo" superimposed on the screen, and they are, of course, not saved. Note that if you are using the optional Camera Control Pro 2 software to record photos from a USB-tethered camera directly to a computer, no memory card is required to unlock the shutter even if Release Locked has been selected.

Save/Load Menu Settings

Options: Save Menu Settings, Load Menu Settings

My preference: N/A

You can store many camera settings to your memory card in a file named NCSETxxx.bin, with the xxx representing the camera model (you can't load settings for your Nikon Z5 II into a non-Z5 II model, for example). Settings can be reloaded to the same model later using this menu item. This is a good way to archive your favorite camera settings for the Playback menu, all Photo/Video Recording Shooting menus, Custom Settings menu, the Setup menu settings, and all My Menu items. You can restore your settings if you've messed them up or save multiple sets of settings to multiple memory cards. If you own more than one Z5 II camera, this is a handy way to share settings between them. You can save only one group of settings at a time to a particular card. If you want to save multiple settings, simply use multiple memory cards. Note that storing/restoration is an all-or-nothing proposition. When you select Save Menu Settings, all your current settings are stored on the memory card; choose Load Menu Settings, and the current settings are replaced with the values stored on the memory card. The following settings are *not* saved, with a few exceptions noted:

- **Playback menu.** Playback Folder and Slide Show.
- **Photo Shooting menu.** Storage Folder, HDR Overlay, Multiple Exposure, Interval Timer Shooting, Time-lapse Movie, and Focus Shift Shooting settings.
- **Video Recording menu.** Storage Folder.

- **Custom Settings menu.** All saved.
- **Setup menu.** Date and Time, Monitor Brightness, Monitor Color Balance, Viewfinder Brightness, Viewfinder Color Balance, AF Fine-tuning.
- **My Menu/Recent Settings.** All My Menu entries, All recent settings, Active tab are all saved.

Reset All Settings

Options: Reset, Do Not Reset
My preference: N/A

This entry resets all settings, including Copyright Information and other user-generated settings, except Language and Time Zone and Date. You should save your current settings to a memory card before using this entry, just to be safe. This command requires use of a confirmation screen to make sure you don't remove your settings accidentally. After the reset, you'll be instructed to turn the camera off. The next time the camera is powered up, the default settings will be in place.

Firmware Version

Options: Display Current Settings, Update, Auto Update, Remove Firmware Files
My preference: N/A

You can see the current firmware release in use in the menu listing. If a new firmware update is in the top-level of a memory card, additional options appear allowing you to proceed with an update, and, after the update, to erase the firmware file from the memory card. You can find instructions for updating firmware in Chapter 12. Note that you now have the option of updating your firmware from Nikon Imaging Cloud, described later in this chapter.

Network Menu

Given that the focus of this book is on still photography and not Information Technology, this section is for reference only, and is not intended to serve as an extended connectivity how-to. We won't be going down the IT rabbit hole in this book. It's unlikely that the majority of you will be using the most advanced connection technology Nikon has to offer, including connections to FTP servers.

At the time I write this, some capabilities, particularly FTP connectivity, need some (ahem) fine-tuning. But others, such as wireless connections through the camera and SnapBridge, have overcome most of the previous obstacles and can now be accessed more easily by following the instructions Nikon provides in the connection guide section of its Z5 II Reference Guide. Your wireless options alone are these:

- **Camera to smart device using Bluetooth LE.** In this mode, you'll use SnapBridge and the Bluetooth LE capabilities built into both the smart device and the camera. Bluetooth LE is a more efficient low-energy protocol that allows wireless connectivity to remain active even when the camera is technically powered off.

- **Camera to smart device using the camera's built-in Wi-Fi hot spot.** SnapBridge will link the two devices with your smart device logging in to the Wi-Fi access point built into the camera.

- **Camera to computer using the camera's built-in Wi-Fi hot spot.** Your computer will connect to the camera's built-in Wi-Fi access point directly, without need for an external network.

- **Camera to computer using a wireless router.** Your camera will connect to your computer's access point supplied by your home/office router.

- **Camera to Nikon Imaging Cloud using a wireless router.** This is a new free service that allows uploading images from your camera to Nikon Imaging Cloud storage, saving image shooting data as a "recipe," creating and managing Picture Controls, and downloading new firmware updates directly to your camera from the cloud.

Once you're connected, you can perform a variety of functions, including controlling your camera using SnapBridge when connected to a smart device, and NX Tether, Camera Control 2 (or other tethering software, such as Lightroom) when connected to a computer. I've found that most users end up working with SnapBridge-to-camera links most of the time, because they can do the following:

- **Auto uploads.** You can use SnapBridge to automatically upload JPEG images (but not RAW files) from your camera to your smart device. However, that restriction does not force you to shoot only JPEG images. The Z5 II can be set to automatically generate a 2MP or 8MP JPEG version when shooting RAW, and transfer that without the need for you to manually create a JPEG file. It will use the image settings you've specified for JPEG.

- **Upload selected photos.** During image review, you can press the *i* button and choose Select to Upload to Smart Device to choose specific images to transfer to your smart device. Up to 1,000 photos can be marked for upload in one session.

- **Resize images.** Obviously, uploading full-resolution images to your smart device would be slow and use a lot of storage space on your device. SnapBridge defaults to low-resolution, 2-megapixel images (which should be fine for smart device display or sharing on social media), and the app lets you specify a larger 8MP upload size.

- **Add credits.** The app also lets you choose to embed comments and copyright information entered in the Setup menu (as described earlier in this chapter) or entered using the SnapBridge app itself.

- **Multiple devices.** If you own multiple phones and tablets, you can pair the camera with as many as five different devices. However, the camera can connect to only one at a time. You can manually switch between devices using the connection options described shortly.

- **Remote control.** You can trigger the shutter using your smart device (as long as the camera is on), giving you wireless remote control without the need of purchasing an accessory.

- **Imprint photos.** You can overlay comments or the time the photo was taken.

The complete Network menu is shown in Figure 9.9.

- Airplane Mode
- Nikon Imaging Cloud
- Connect to Smart Device
- Wireless Remote (ML-L7) Options
- Bluetooth Remote Control Options
- Connect to Computer
- Connect to FTP Server
- Connect to Other Cameras
- ATOMOS AirGlu BT Options
- USB
- Router Frequency Band
- MAC Address

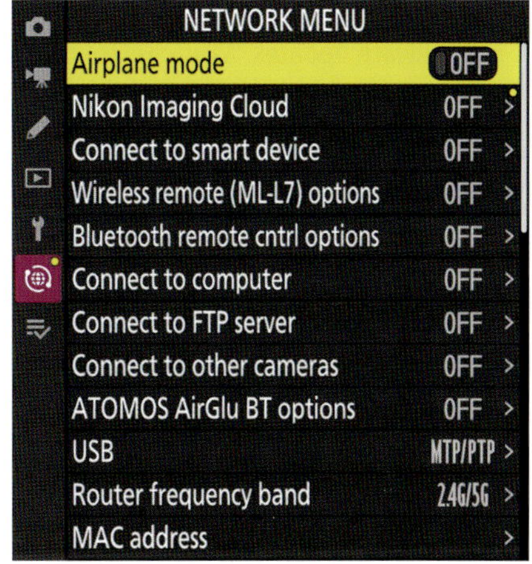

Figure 9.9 The Network menu.

Airplane Mode

Options: Off (default), On

My preference: On

Like the Airplane mode on your smartphone or tablet, this option turns off Wi-Fi and Bluetooth capabilities. I enable the feature any time I am not planning to use Bluetooth or Wi-Fi, because it saves a lot of power.

Nikon Imaging Cloud

Options: Connect to Nikon Imaging Cloud, Wi-Fi Settings, Connection Options, Photo Upload, Photo Upload Options: Auto Select for Upload, Upload RAW+JPEG As, Upload RAW+HEIF As, JPEG+JPEG Slot Selection, HEIF+HEIF Slot Selection, Upload Folder, Deselect All?; View Errors, About Nikon Imaging Cloud, Unlink Nikon Imaging Cloud

My preference: N/A

This free service was originally introduced for the Nikon Z6 III, and has since been added to other cameras, including the Z5 II. The currently available features can be accessed from the website (see Figure 9.10, upper left) and using entries in the camera's Nikon Imaging Cloud menu. Here's an overview of the web features:

- **Image Transfer.** You can tell the Z5 II to push images to the Image Cloud, where they can be transferred to Adobe's Creative Cloud, Google Drive and Google Photos, One Drive, Dropbox, and Nikon Image Space. Note that the images don't remain in Image Cloud; they are deleted automatically after 30 days, so you'll want to transfer them to a more permanent home before that. (See Figure 9.10, upper right.)
- **Imaging Recipes.** These are effects, looks, and techniques, including Cloud Picture Control presets you can download to your camera. As this is written, there are nearly four dozen contributors with recipes from well-known creatives including portrait recipes from Brandon Woelfel,

Takahiro Sakai, and Luiz Claudio (Luizclas), as well as modules from Emilie Hill (travel); Aparupa Day (nature and wildlife); and Danny Gevirtz (video). (See Figure 9.10, lower left.)

- **Firmware updates.** You can install firmware updates for your Z5 II from Nikon Imaging Cloud, using the Firmware Version entry of the Setup menu, described earlier in this chapter, and in more detail in Chapter 12. (See Figure 9.10, lower right.)

- **Nikon Image Space.** This free sharing service has been around for a while in various iterations, and Nikon Imaging Cloud can be integrated with it. It's one of the options you have available for more permanent storage of the images you upload from your Z5 II.

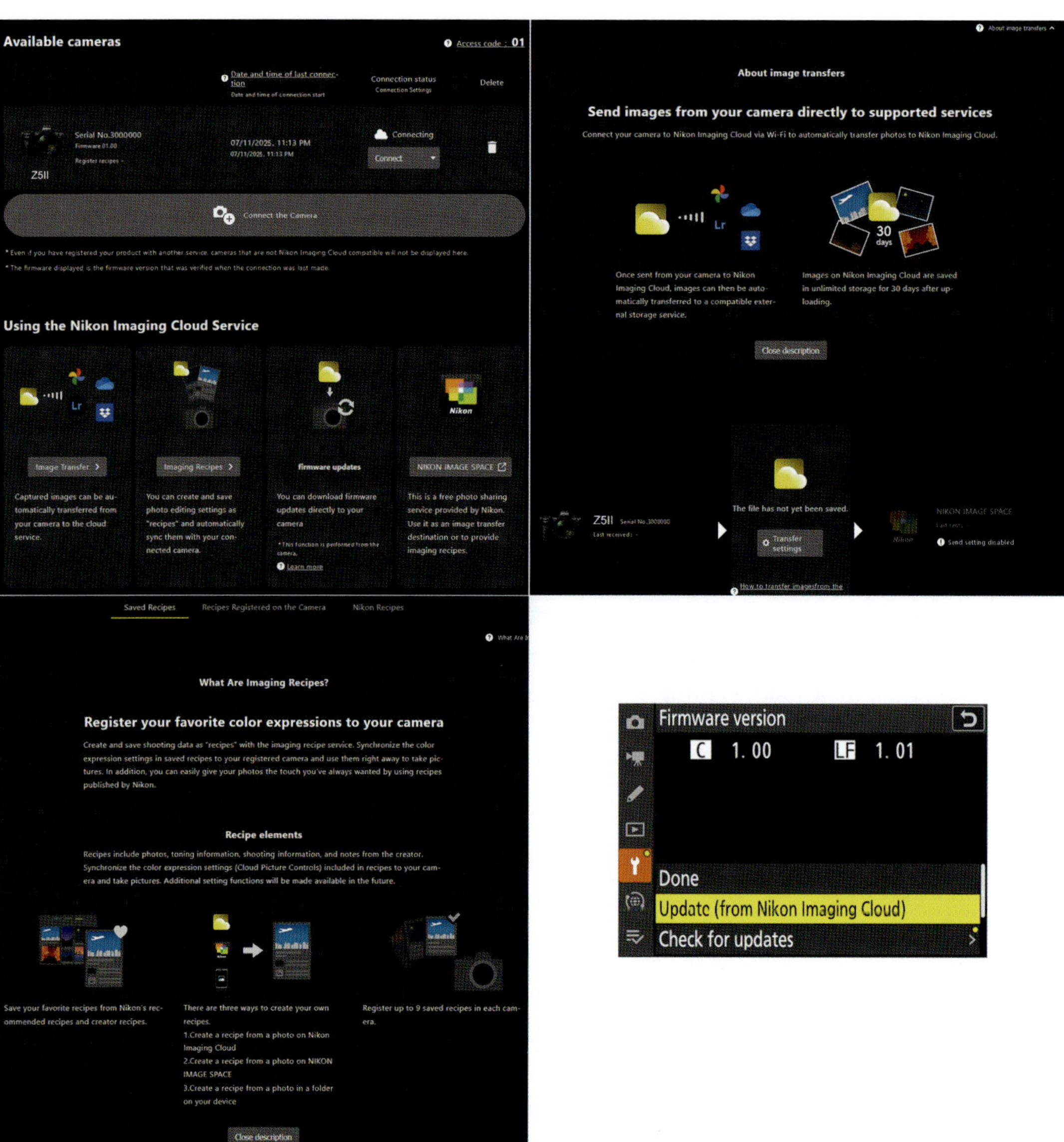

Figure 9.10 Nikon Imaging Cloud web features.

Nikon Imaging Cloud features are also available from the camera's menu, shown in Figure 9.11. They include:

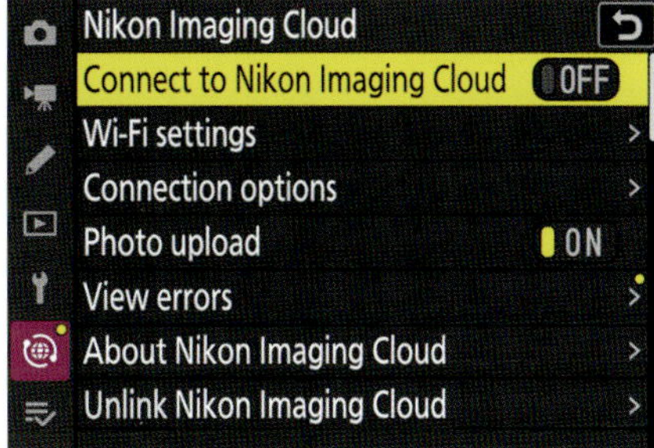

Figure 9.11 Nikon Imaging Cloud settings.

- **Wi-Fi Settings.** This entry includes the Wi-Fi connection settings you already used to set up Imaging Cloud. You can return here to create new connections.

- **Connection Options.** If your camera is connected to Nikon Imaging Cloud, the connection will remain active. To save power, you can enter some parameters here, telling the camera to connect only when powered externally over USB, whether to connect when powered down, and whether to disconnect when the connection is inactive for a time. (See Figure 9.12, left.)

- **Photo Upload.** You can turn the automatic photo upload feature on or off here.

- **Photo Upload Options.** Here you can enable/disable auto selection of images for upload, specify how RAW and JPEG/HEIF images are transferred, select an upload folder, or deselect all options. (See Figure 9.12, right.) Note that you can also use the Playback *i* menu to upload images to Nikon Imaging Cloud.

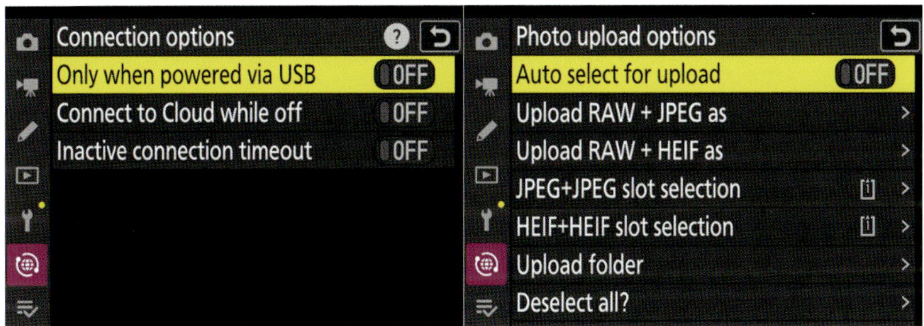

Figure 9.12 Connection Options (left); Photo Upload Options (right).

- **View Errors.** Provides a QR code you can access to view an error log, if compiled.

- **About Nikon Imaging Cloud.** This is the entry you used to begin setup of Imaging Cloud.

- **Unlink Nikon Imaging Cloud.** This entry unlinks your camera from your Imaging Cloud account. You would definitely want to do this if you sell or otherwise dispose of your camera to prevent others from accessing your account. The Reset All Settings entry in the Setup menu (described earlier in this chapter) should also be used.

Setting Up Nikon Imaging Cloud

To begin using Nikon Imaging Cloud, just follow these steps:

1. **Access the Nikon Imaging Cloud entry of the Network menu.** The screen shown at left in Figure 9.13 appears. If your camera has not been registered for Imaging Cloud, you'll see a notification at the bottom of the screen.

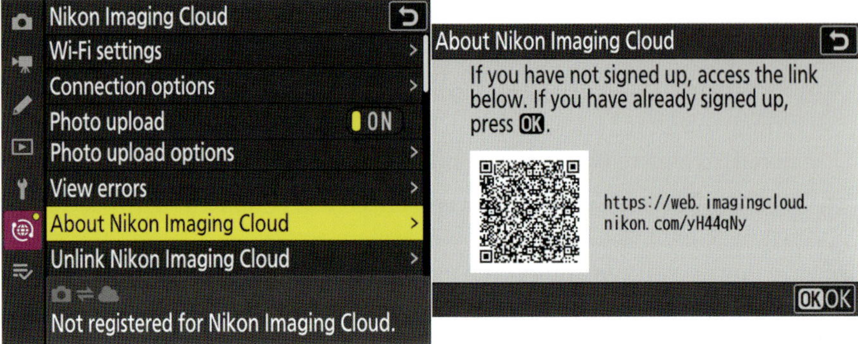

Figure 9.13 Choose About Nikon Imaging Cloud to begin setup (left). Use the QR code or URL to sign up/sign in (right).

2. **Begin registration.** Highlight About Nikon Imaging Cloud and press the right directional button. The screen shown at right in Figure 9.13 appears. You can register using your smart device by photographing the QR code shown on the camera and pressing OK. If you prefer to do the registration on your computer, type in the URL displayed instead.

3. **Visit the Nikon Imaging Cloud website.** Figure 9.14, left, shows what the website looks like on a computer; it will be similar if you are accessing it using your smart device. You can view a video offered at the bottom of the screen and/or go directly to Sign In/Sign Up.

4. **Sign In/Sign Up.** If you already have a Nikon ID, click Sign In and enter your Nikon ID and Password. If you don't have an ID, click Sign Up and the screen shown at right in Figure 9.14 appears. Click Next to proceed.

5. **Connect Camera.** Once you've logged on, the screen shown at left in Figure 9.15 appears. Click Connect Camera to proceed to the screen seen at right in the figure.

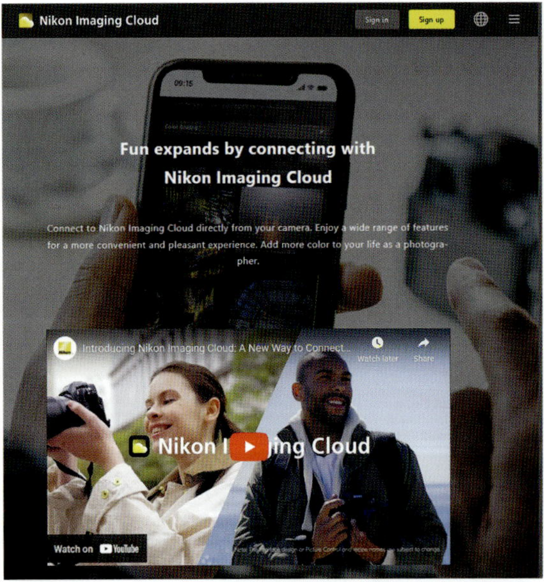

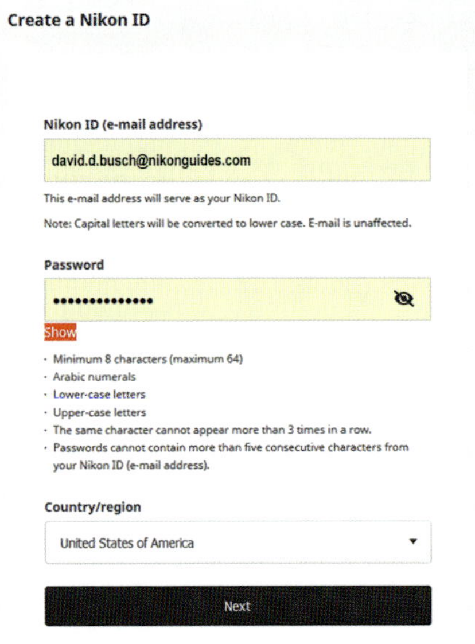

Figure 9.14 View an informational video or sign up/sign in (left). Creating a Nikon ID (right).

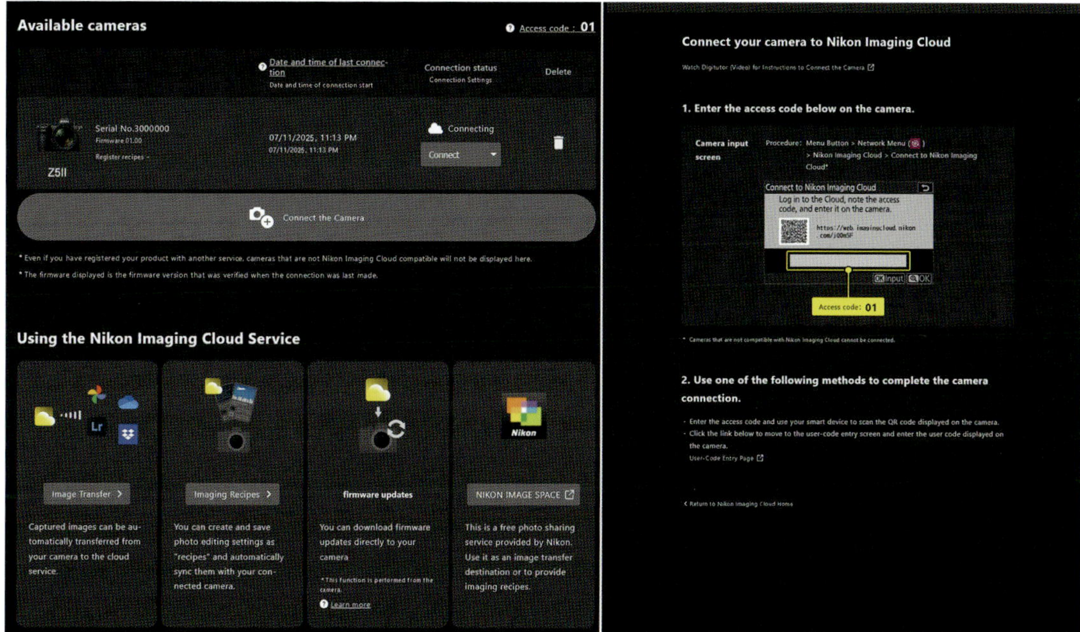

Figure 9.15 Connecting your camera (left and right).

6. **Camera Input.** On the Z5 II, you'll see a screen with a box to enter the access code provided by the website. When you've entered the code, the Connection Wizard will start, suggesting you search automatically for a Wi-Fi network. You can also enter the network manually if you are a masochist or an IT expert (or, as is usual, both). See Figure 9.16, upper left and right.

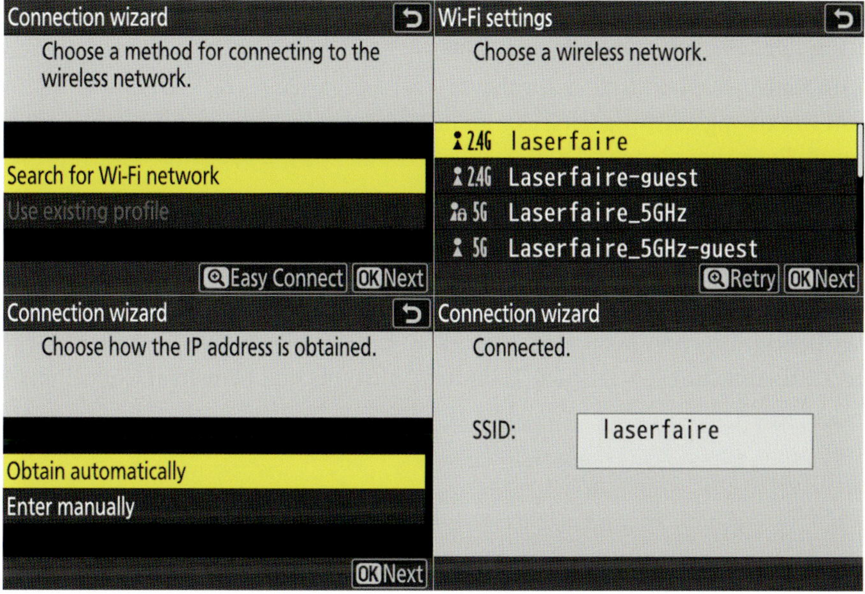

Figure 9.16 Making a Wi-Fi connection.

7. **Choose IP Address.** You can obtain an IP address automatically (recommended), as seen in Figure 9.16, lower left. When you're connected, the screen shown at lower right appears.

8. **Connect to Nikon Imaging Cloud.** Your camera can now connect to Imaging Cloud. Follow any instructions until the Connection Wizard's Setup Complete screen appears.

Connect to Smart Device

Options: Pairing (Bluetooth), Select Pictures for Upload, Wi-Fi Connection (AP Mode), Wi-Fi Connection (STA Mode), Upload While Off, Location Data (Smart Device)

My preference: N/A

Use this entry to set up your SnapBridge or Wi-Fi connection to your smartphone or tablet. Connecting your camera to your smart device (phone or tablet) is generally done using the SnapBridge application on the device (although there are other apps that perform some of the same functions). The Nikon SnapBridge app supports *only* camera-to-smart-device communications. Your first step in using SnapBridge is to download and install the SnapBridge app onto your smart device from the Google Play store or the Apple App store. You'll find step-by-step instructions for making the connection with SnapBridge in Nikon's PDF manual. Here's an overview of the options available within this entry:

- **Pairing (Bluetooth).** You can initiate pairing the Z5 II to your smart device, view a list of devices that have already been paired and select one, and enable/disable Bluetooth.

- **Select Pictures for Upload.** You can enable Auto Select for Upload to transfer pictures to your smart device as they are taken, manually select individual images, or deselect all marked images.

- **Wi-Fi Connection (AP Mode).** In Access Point mode, you can use Wi-Fi to connect your camera to a smart device using the Z5 II's built-in access point. Select the camera's SSID (Service Set Identifier), authentication/encryption method, password, and channel. You can also view your current Wi-Fi settings or reset settings to default values.

- **Wi-Fi Connection (STA Mode).** Station Mode is similar to AP mode, except you are connecting to the smart device on an existing network, such as your home network, using that network's wireless LAN connection. Even though your device is linked to the Z5 II, it can still connect to the Internet while using this mode.

- **Upload While Off.** You can tell your Z5 II to continue uploading images over a wireless connection even if the camera is ostensibly powered down. Obviously, this option can drain the Z5 II's battery if not used carefully.

- **Location Data (Smart Device).** This option appears if a linked smart device is able to share its location data with the Z5 II. You can view latitude, longitude, altitude, and Universal Coordinated Time data.

Wireless Remote (ML-L7) Options

Options: Wireless remote connection (ML-L7), On, Off (default), Save wireless remote controller, Delete wireless remote controller, Assign Fn1 button, Assign Fn2 button

My preference: N/A

This option allows you to make several settings for the ML-L7 Wireless Remote, a Bluetooth device. Once it has been paired with your Z5 II, you can use it to perform the following functions using the controls shown in Figure 9.17:

- Take photos or stop/start movie.
- Zoom in and out of preview/review image.
- Access and navigate camera menus.
- Playback images and movies.

Once you've paired the remote (as described next), just press the remote's power button while the camera is turned on (and Airplane Mode is not active). When the green LED at upper right flashes about once every second, the remote is searching for your camera. It will turn off once the two devices are linked. To set up the ML-L7, just follow these steps:

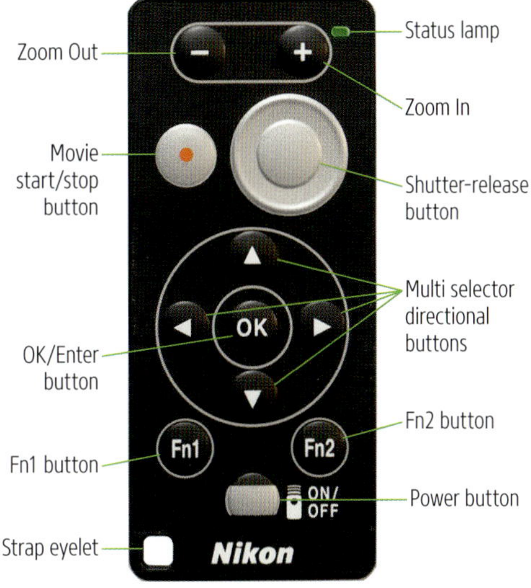

Figure 9.17 The Nikon ML-L7 Bluetooth wireless remote control.

1. **Access Wireless Remote (ML-L7) Options.** A screen similar to the one shown at upper left in Figure 9.18 will appear. Initially, the Wireless Remote Connection option will be grayed out until you've paired with your camera.

2. **Highlight Save Wireless Remote Controller.** Press OK. The green LED at upper right on the remote will begin flashing quickly (about every half-second) and you'll see, in turn, the three update messages on your camera's display. (See Figure 9.18, upper right.)

3. **Connection confirmed.** When the Wireless Remote Controller Saved message appears, the green LED will illuminate steadily for a few seconds, then turn off. Press OK to exit the connection screen.

4. **Connection activated.** The Wireless Remote Connection icon will change to ON, as shown at upper left in the figure. Henceforth, the Z5 II and the remote can connect automatically, at least until you subsequently pair either with a different device (see the caution, below).

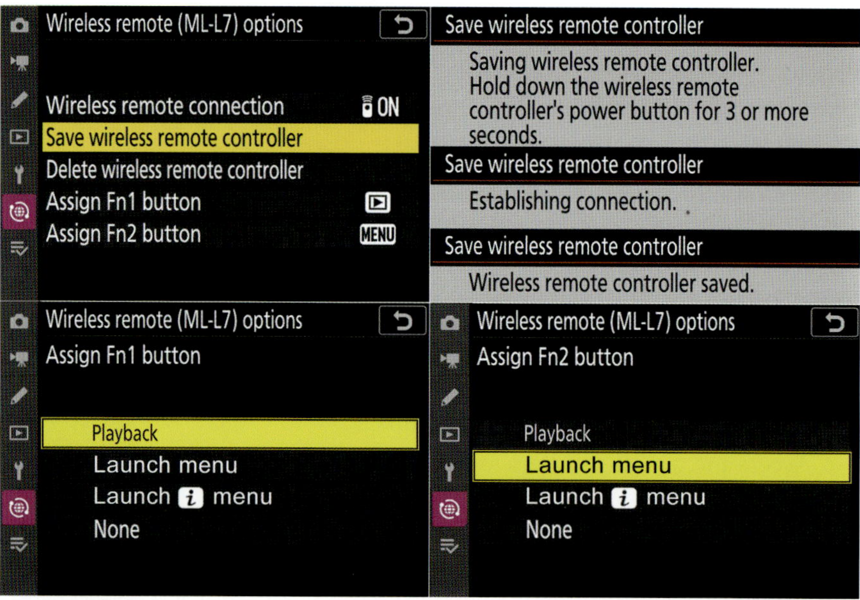

Figure 9.18 Setting up the ML-L7 Bluetooth remote control.

5. **Assign function keys.** You can now assign a function to the Fn1 and Fn2 buttons *on the remote control*. Note that their functions are different from those of the Fn1 and Fn2 buttons *on the camera*. You can define the functions from the screens shown at bottom in Figure 9.18. Your choices are:

- **Playback (Fn1 default).** This option assigns the Playback function to the Fn1 button by default.

- **Launch menu (Fn2 default).** With this definition, pressing the function button will produce the Z5 II's menu system, which you can then navigate using the directional buttons and OK button on the remote.

- **Launch *i* menu.** Calls up the Z5 II's *i* menu. This option is probably more useful than the MENU button choice. It's more likely you'll want to make settings adjustments available with the *i* menu, which is there, of course, to give you fast access to the most common shooting settings.

- **None.** Deactivates a particular function button. Use this if you have some fear you'll accidentally call up Playback or *i* menu functions.

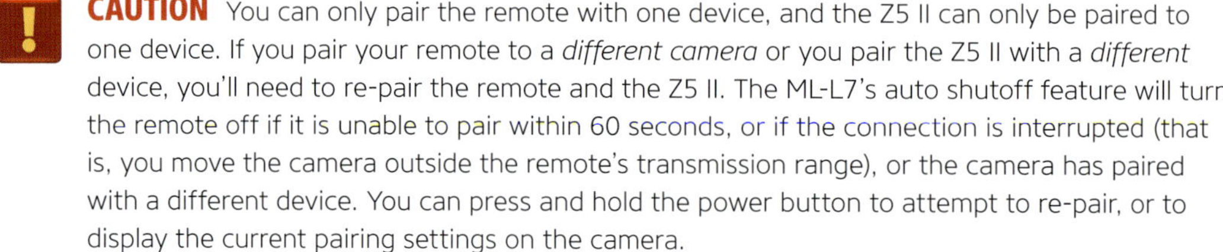

CAUTION You can only pair the remote with one device, and the Z5 II can only be paired to one device. If you pair your remote to a *different camera* or you pair the Z5 II with a *different* device, you'll need to re-pair the remote and the Z5 II. The ML-L7's auto shutoff feature will turn the remote off if it is unable to pair within 60 seconds, or if the connection is interrupted (that is, you move the camera outside the remote's transmission range), or the camera has paired with a different device. You can press and hold the power button to attempt to re-pair, or to display the current pairing settings on the camera.

The LED that flashed green during setup also indicates shooting status. One orange or red flash indicates that still photography or movie recording, respectively, have started. Two orange or red flashes indicate still photography or movie recording have ended (respectively). **Note:** Once you've set Wireless Remote Connection (ML-L7) to On, the Z5 II will look for the remote each time it is powered up. If you don't plan on using the remote every time you operate the camera, turning the feature Off until you're ready to work with it again will save some battery power.

Bluetooth Remote Control Options

Options: On, Off (default); Save Wireless Remote Controller; Delete Wireless Remote Controller

My preference: N/A

Nikon allows additional Bluetooth remote controls provided by third parties to link to your Nikon Z5 II. At the time this was written, the SmallRig SR-RG2 Wireless Shooting Grip was compatible. As with all Bluetooth devices, it must be paired with your camera the first time it is used, and, as with the ML-L7, only one remote can be paired to a particular camera. The Z5 II will use the last paired device by default. Choose this menu entry to start/end a connection with a device you have already paired, following the instructions provided by the third party. You can save a connected controller, or delete it.

Connect to Computer

Options: Network Settings: Create Profile, Copy to/from Card, End Current Connection; Connection Type: Picture Transfer, Camera Control; Options: Adjust upload settings

My preference: N/A

You have a choice of how you connect your Z5 II to your computer (instead of to your smart device). You can link your camera to your computer with a wireless link to your local area network with a direct wireless connection from the camera to the computer (Access-point or AP mode) or by linking to your home/office network's wireless router (Station or STA mode).

In most cases, your Nikon camera's Bluetooth and Wi-Fi capabilities, coupled with SnapBridge, will supply all the connectivity you'll ever need. You may never want to connect to your computer. However, some photographers, particularly those who shoot in a studio or at events, like to take the next step and shoot tethered, in which images captured by the camera show up almost instantaneously on a computer. Such transfers are most useful for quick edits, demonstrations, client previews, and evaluating images as they are taken. In most cases, *wireless* tethering is not especially practical, because the transfer takes too long.

Instead, photographers who need this capability generally use cables to link their cameras to the computer, and work with software specifically designed for tethering, such as Adobe Lightroom, NX Tether, Nikon Camera Control 2, Capture One Pro, or Helicon Remote.

In (only slightly) less technical terms, it can use the camera's built-in Wi-Fi to connect wirelessly to a computer in "Access Point Mode" with the camera serving as an ad hoc wireless LAN access point. When connected in this way, the camera's Wi-Fi hot spot substitutes for an Internet connection. As such, it's an option when working outdoors or in other locations that don't have a stand-alone router/wireless network. Connecting to a computer using existing LAN infrastructure can also be used, and Nikon dubs this "Station Mode."

As I noted earlier, I'm devoting all the available space in this book to photography topics and tips, rather than diverting pages to IT topics. That's because if you need these advanced capabilities, you probably already know all about IP and MAC addresses, SSIDs, and other stuff and don't need an explanation from me. Here's a quick overview of how to connect to your computer:

1. **Choose Connection Type.** At the screen that appears, shown at upper left in Figure 9.19, press the right button and choose Picture Transfer or Camera Control (say, if you're using NX Tether), as shown in Figure 9.19, upper center, and press OK.

2. **Select Create Profile.** The Connection Wizard will allow you to choose a name for this network profile. Highlight Network Settings and press the right directional button to produce the screen shown at upper right in Figure 9.19. Press OK to enter one using the standard text-entry screen or press the Zoom In button to accept the default name supplied. (See Figure 9.19, lower left.)

3. **Select Wireless Type.** Next, select the type of wireless connection you want. (See Figure 9.19, lower center.)

   - **Direct connection.** If you choose Direct Connection to Computer, you'll be shown the SSID of your camera and asked to connect your computer to that access point. (See Figure 9.19, lower right.)

   - **Wi-Fi Connection.** Instead of using your computer to connect to the camera's built-in access point, you can do the reverse and have the camera log into your *computer's* Wi-Fi network. The camera will then search and present a list of available networks (see Figure 9.20, upper left). In most cases, you can allow the camera to obtain an IP address automatically (see Figure 9.20, upper right). You'll be notified when the IP address has been set and asked to start the Wireless Transmitter Utility on your computer and then select your own Z5 II (see Figure 9.20, lower left and right). Station mode allows the computer to continue to connect to the Internet while communicating with your camera. Follow the instructions provided to pair the computer with your Z5 II.

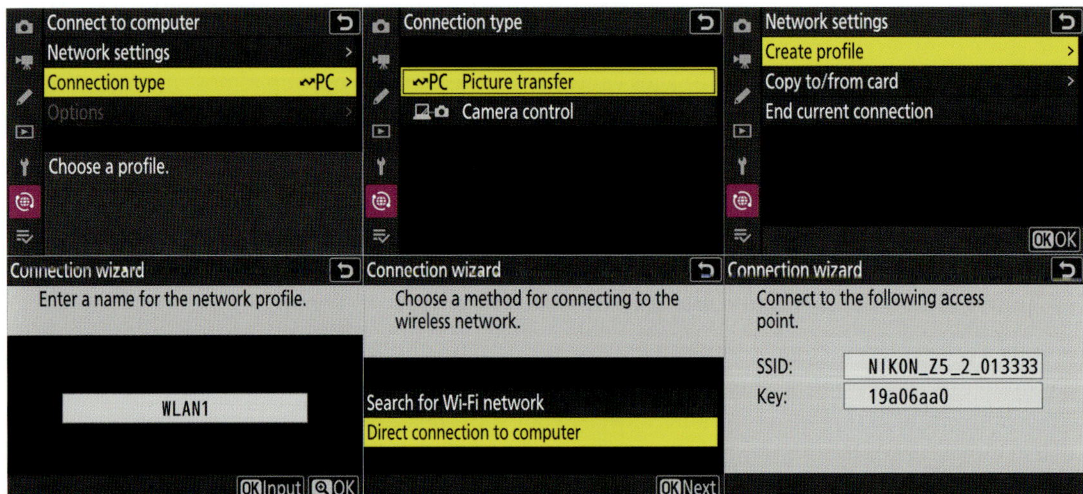

Figure 9.19 Connecting using Access-Point mode.

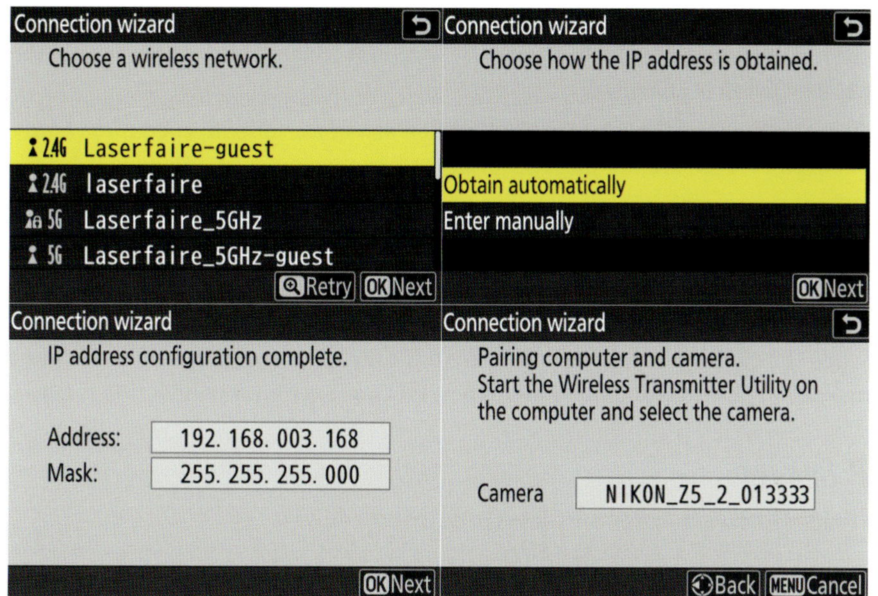

Figure 9.20 Making a Wi-Fi connection using Station mode.

Here's a summary of the options available with this entry:

- **Create Profile.** Runs a connection wizard, which will search for an existing Wi-Fi network or allow you to connect directly to the computer using your camera's built-in network.
- **Copy to/from Card.** You can copy network settings you've previously stored on a memory card, or copy your current network settings to a card, if it is not password-protected.
- **End Current Connection.** This disconnects the current camera-to-computer connection.
- **Connection Type.** You can choose Picture Transfer, which allows uploading photos to your computer, either as they are taken or as you select them for transfer. Alternatively, you can opt for Camera Control to allow you to operate your camera and take photos using either Camera Control Pro 2 (an extra-cost option), or the free NX Tether software.
- **Options.** Here you can specify upload options:
  - **Auto Upload.** Choose On to mark each new still photo for upload. (Videos cannot be auto uploaded.)
  - **Delete After Upload.** Select On to delete photos from the memory card once the upload is completed. Files already marked for transfer will not be deleted. This is a dangerous option. Use it with care.
  - **Upload RAW+ JPEG (or RAW+HEIF) As.** Here you can choose to upload only the JPEG/HEIF, only RAW, or both RAW and JPEG/HEIF if you are shooting both types of still photographs.
  - **JPEG+JPEG Slot Selection (or HEIF+HEIF Slot Selection) > Slot 1, Slot 2.** Select the source slot for auto upload when JPEG/HEIF Slot 1—JPEG/HEIF Slot 2 is specified for the role played by the card in Slot 2 in the Photo Shooting menu.

- **Upload RAW Video As > RAW video + MP4, MP4 only.** You can specify whether both the N-RAW video and its MP4 proxy version are uploaded, or, if you want to save time, whether only the more compact MP4 version is uploaded.
- **Upload Folder.** This marks all still photos in a folder you select for upload, *even if they have already been uploaded.* Videos are not marked for upload, as they must be uploaded from the playback display.
- **Deselect All?** This removes the upload marker from all images, including those currently being uploaded.

You can instruct your camera to automatically upload new still photos (but not videos) to your smart device or computer when the camera and device are linked. If they are not connected, the camera will mark a maximum of 1,000 photos and upload them the next time a wireless connection is made.

Connect to FTP Server

Options: Network Settings, Options, Choose a Profile (Information only)

My preference: N/A

As I mentioned earlier, I'm not going to try and explain infrequently used FTP options in this book, so this section is just an overview for the IT-savvy. Any previous FTP connection profiles you've created will be shown here, or you can create a new one and specify the options. You can connect to an FTP server using access points or station mode, using options described earlier (Auto Upload, Delete After Upload, Upload RAW+JPEG/HEIF As, JPEG+JPEG Slot Selection (or HEIF+HEIF Slot Selection), Upload RAW Video As, Upload Folder, and Deselect All?). Additional options appropriate for FTP uploads are also available:

- **Overwrite If Same Name.** Duplicate files will be overwritten if you choose On. Select Off, and the camera will add numbers to the names of the new files if necessary to prevent overwriting existing files.
- **Protect If Marked for Upload.** Choose On to protect files marked for upload. Protection is removed once the files are uploaded.
- **Upload Marking.** Adds a time stamp noting the upload time/date to the images on the memory card.
- **Keep connection.** Preserves FTP connections on errors.
- **Manage root certificate.** Loads or manages FTP root certificates.

If you want to avoid manually entering SSID, encryption keys, IP addresses, etc., the Connection Wizard and Easy Connect option (which uses either Push-Button WPS or PIN-entry WPS) are available to help you create a profile and establish a connection.

Connect to Other Cameras

Options: Synchronized Release (On, Off), Network Settings, Master/Remote, Group Settings, Group Name, Synchronize Date and Time, Overwrite Copyright Info

My preference: N/A

Some features that professional photojournalists need boggle the mind of those of us with more modest requirements. Nikon is not out to disappoint its most demanding customers and offers considerably advanced features. One of these is this capability to connect multiple compatible cameras in order to synchronize their clocks (for applications when matching the date and time a picture was taken is essential). The other is the ability to synchronize up to 10 remote cameras in the same group simultaneously.

Synchronized release is done by creating host profiles for each camera using a Network Settings screen similar to the ones shown earlier. The cameras are ordinarily connected using a wireless LAN, whereupon each camera captures images when triggered by the master camera, then saves them to their own memory cards. The Standby timer does not expire automatically in synchronized release mode.

The master camera will display a Remote Camera List which shows each of the group's cameras and their IP addresses, along with status, such as Connected, Busy (controlled by a different master camera), Off, or Error. The time for the most recent shot will be shown. The master camera can also edit the settings of each remote camera and temporarily suspend connections.

ATOMOS AirGlu BT Options

Options: Connect to Atomos AirGlu BT, Save Atomos AirGlu BT Pairing Info, Delete Atomos AirGlu BT Pairing Info, Camera

My preference: N/A

As discussed in Chapter 10, professional video editing uses time codes to synchronize footage captured from multiple sources or sessions. Atomos uses its own time code synchronization with its UltraSync accessory to share the data between devices, including its Ninja V monitor, cameras, audio recorders, and smartphones over Bluetooth. This entry allows pairing your Z5 II with these devices using Bluetooth. Using this entry you can:

- Make a Bluetooth connection to a paired UltraSync Blue device.
- Create and save the initial pairing of the camera with the UltraSync Blue device.
- End the connection and remove pairing information.
- Specify a name the UltraSync Blue device will apply to your camera.

USB

Options: MTP/PTP, iPhone, USB Streaming (UVC/UAC)

My preference: N/A

This setting allows you to choose the protocol used for image transfer when your camera is connected to your computer using a USB cable. If you want to transfer images directly from the Z5 II to your computer over USB, you'll first need to set USB Connection Priority in the Setup menu, as described earlier in this chapter. That entry determines whether the camera disables shooting information and switches to upload mode when a USB connection is live.

Then, you'll need to use this entry to determine the protocol used for transfer. Your choices are as follows:

- **MTP/PTP.** The acronyms stand for Media Transfer Protocol (in which the connected device appears as a mass storage/disk drive on the computer) and Picture Transfer Protocol (in which the device *does not* appear as a disk drive). This choice actually enables only PTP; if you connect your camera to your computer and use the File Manager, you'll *see* the Z5 II shown with a drive icon, but clicking on it shows no files. To transfer your pictures, you'll need to use a software application that works with PTP. You can also use connection applications like Nikon Camera Control Pro to operate your camera over the USB connection. The free Nikon NX Tether can be used to take photos remotely and transfer them to an application such as NX Studio.
- **iPhone.** This option allows you to connect your iPhone to your camera using the Nikon application NX MobilAir and a Lightning-to-USB cable needed for iPhones introduced before the iPhone 15. Later models can use the USB-C cable supplied with the Z5 II. **Note:** When this option is selected, the Z5 II's built-in camera network functions are disabled, and you will *not* be able to power the camera or charge the battery using the USB connection. If you need those features, select MTP/PTP instead.
- **USB Streaming (UVC/UAC).** Third-party USB-to-Ethernet adapters are available that allow you to connect your Z5 II (or another compatible camera) to a computer for streaming purposes using an Ethernet cable when this option is enabled.

Router Frequency Band

Options: 2.4 GHz/5 GHz, 2.4 GHz, 5 GHz

My preference: N/A

If you have a home network, you're probably familiar with the two frequency bands used by your wireless router and access point. Most routers have both 2.4 GHz and a faster 5 GHz band which can be used individually or combined for access by devices that can take advantage of dual band operation. This entry lets you specify which band your camera uses—or both, if that is your preference.

MAC Address

Options: N/A

My preference: N/A

This option displays the MAC address of your camera. This is the Media Access Control identifier (it has nothing to do with Mac computers), which is a unique serial number that only your device—such as your Z5 II camera—uses when connected to a network.

Retouch Menu

The Retouch menu contains the post-processing options you can apply to your images after you've taken a photo. When reviewing an image in Playback mode, press the *i* button and *i* menu choices available during playback appear, as seen at left in Figure 9.21. (Like the other menus in this book, I've edited the figure to show more entries than can actually appear on your screen at once, for clarity.) Highlight Retouch and press the multi selector right button to view your options, shown in expanded mode at right in Figure 9.21. They include:

- RAW Processing (current picture)
- RAW Processing (multiple pictures)
- Trim
- Resize (current picture)
- Resize (multiple pictures)
- D-Lighting
- Straighten
- Distortion Control
- Perspective Control
- Monochrome
- Overlay (add)
- Lighten
- Darken
- Motion Blend

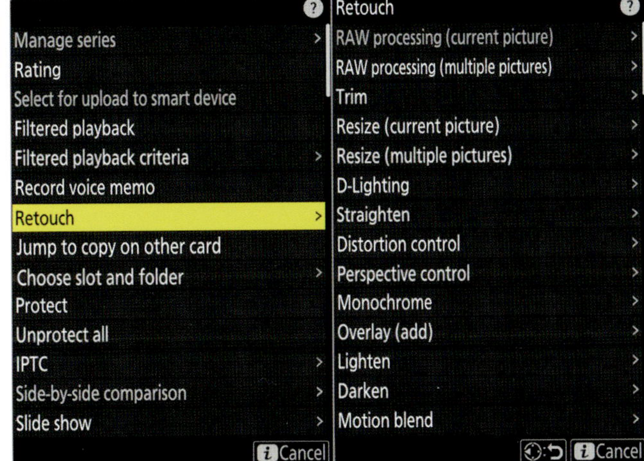

Figure 9.21 The Retouch menu allows simple in-camera editing.

The Retouch menu is most useful when you want to create a modified copy of an image on the spot, for immediate printing or e-mailing without first importing into your computer for more extensive editing. You can also use it to create a JPEG version of an image in the camera when you are shooting RAW-only photos. You can retouch images that have already been processed by the Retouch menu, except for copies created with the Image Overlay option. You may notice some quality loss when applying more than one retouch option.

Follow these steps:

1. **Choose image retouching option.** From the Retouch menu, select the option you want from those available and press the multi selector right button. **Note:** If you elect to work on an image that has been captured in dual RAW+JPEG (or HEIF) format, *only* the RAW image will be retouched. If you have an image on your memory card that was recorded by a different model, your camera may not be able to display or retouch the image.

2. **Manipulate image.** Work with the options available from that particular Retouch menu feature and press OK to create the modified copy, or Playback to cancel your changes. Keep in mind that if the delay for Menus that you've specified in Custom Setting c3: Power Off Delay expires, the camera will exit the menu screen and any unsaved changes will be canceled. You may want to select a longer power-off delay for Menus.

3. **View copy.** A retouched JPEG image will be the same size and quality as the original, except for copies created using the RAW Processing, Trim, and Resize options. Resized or Cropped copies created from NEF and TIFF images are always saved as JPEG Fine images. During review, retouched copies are overlaid with a paint brush icon in their upper-left corner.

DOUBLE DUTY

Once you've retouched an image using one of the Retouch menu's entries, you can apply most of the remaining options to the manipulated copy (except for those produced by Trim Movie). Any that are not available will be grayed out. That said, it's probably not a good idea to retouch a retouched copy, as you'll lose some image quality each time.

RAW Processing (Current Picture)/(Multiple Pictures)

Options: Image Quality, Image Size, Exposure Compensation, White Balance, Picture Control, Color Space, Active D-Lighting, High ISO NR, Vignette Control, Diffraction Compensation, Portrait Impression Balance; (Multiple Pictures Only): Select Picture(s), Select Date, Select Folder, Choose Destination

My preference: N/A

The RAW Processing feature creates a JPEG version of any image saved in RAW. When I am out of my office, I sometimes need a reduced-resolution JPEG to transfer to my iPhone to send or upload. This entry not only lets you create that JPEG from any RAW file in your camera, but it also allows you to adjust the image quality and size and apply many useful corrections, including white balance adjustments, exposure compensation, and noise reduction. Nikon gives you two versions of the tool, one is labeled (Current Picture), which lets you quickly create the JPEG from any one image. The other is labeled (Multiple Pictures) and can be used to apply the same settings to a group of RAW files as you create your JPEG version. (See Figure 9.22.)

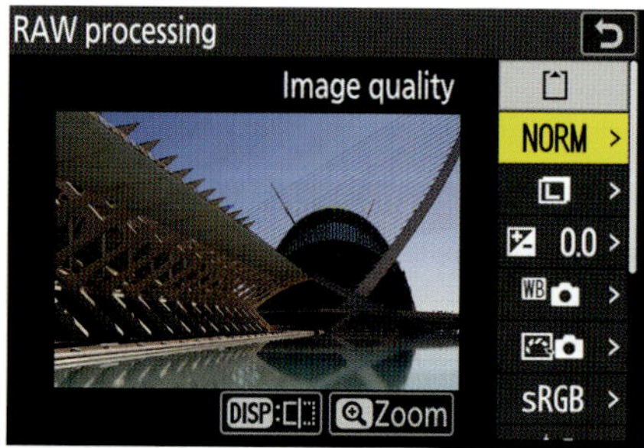

Figure 9.22 Adjust the parameters and then save your JPEG copy from a RAW original file.

Just follow these steps:

1. **Choose RAW image(s).** If you choose the (Current Picture) version, you can begin processing the image immediately. With the (Multiple Pictures) version, you'll be taken to the standard Z5 II image selection routine, which allows you to:

   - **Select Pictures** by viewing thumbnails and pressing the Zoom In button to view individual thumbnails of NEF files full screen, or the Zoom Out button to select/unselect a thumbnail. Press OK to confirm and exit.
   - **Select Date** by selecting from a list showing all dates on which you took photos with that card. Press OK to confirm and exit.
   - **Select Folder** by a folder name and OK to confirm and exit.

2. **Select attributes.** In the RAW processing screen, you can use the multi selector up/down keys to select from these attributes of the RAW image information to apply to the JPEG copies made of your selected image(s). Choose Image Quality (Fine, Normal, or Basic, plus * versions of each), Image Size (Large, Medium, or Small), Exposure Compensation, White Balance, Picture Control, Color Space, Active D-Lighting, High ISO Noise Reduction, Vignette Control, Diffraction Compensation, and Portrait Impression Balance.

3. **Examine image.** Press the Zoom In button to magnify the image temporarily while the button is held down. Press the DISP button to toggle between views of the original and processed image.

4. **Change your mind?** Press the Playback button if you change your mind, to exit from the processing screen.

5. **Execute.** When all parameters are set, highlight EXE (for Execute) at the top of the settings list and press OK. The camera will create a JPEG file for each of the selected images with the settings you've specified, and show an Image Saved message on the monitor when finished.

Trim

Options: Various sizes

My preference: N/A

This option creates copies in specific sizes based on the final size you select, chosen from among 1:1, 3:2, 4:3, 5:4, 16:9, 4:5, 3:4, 2:3, and 9:16 aspect ratios (proportions). You can use this feature to create smaller versions of a picture for e-mailing without the need to first transfer the image to your own computer. Just follow these steps:

1. **Select your photo.** In Playback mode, choose Trim from the Retouch menu.

2. **Choose your aspect ratio.** Rotate the main command dial to change from 3:2, 4:3, 5:4, 16:9 (and their inverses), plus 1:1 aspect ratios. These proportions happen to correspond to the proportions of common print sizes, including the two most popular sizes: 4 × 6 inches (3:2) and 8 × 10 inches (5:4).

3. **Crop in on your photo.** Press the Zoom In/Zoom Out buttons to choose a crop for your picture. The pixel dimensions of the cropped image at the selected proportions will be displayed in the upper-left corner (see Figure 9.23) as you zoom. The trim sizes vary depending on the Image Size and Aspect Ratio selected. The current framed size is outlined in yellow.

4. **Move cropped area within the image.** Use the multi selector left/right and up/down buttons to relocate the yellow cropping border within the frame.

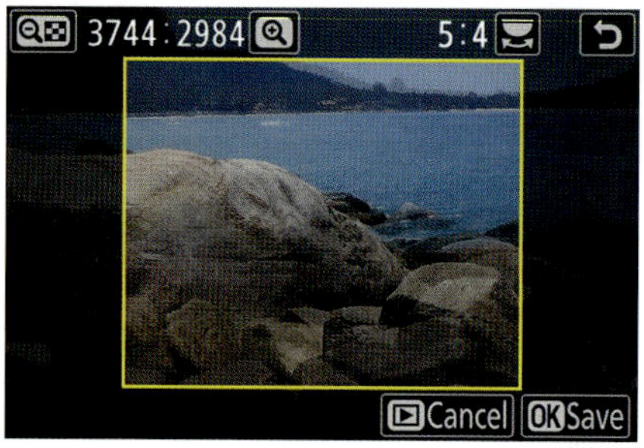

Figure 9.23 The Trim feature of the Retouch menu allows in-camera cropping.

5. **Save the cropped image.** Press OK to save a copy of the image using the current crop and size or press the Playback button to exit without creating a copy. Copies created from JPEG Fine, Normal, or Standard have the same Image Quality setting as the original; copies made from RAW files or any RAW+JPEG setting will use JPEG Fine compression. Note that you may not be able to zoom in on a cropped image during Playback once it has been saved.

Resize (Current Picture)/(Multiple Pictures)

Options: Choose Size; Select Image (Multiple Pictures): Select Picture(s), Select Date, Select Folder, Choose Destination, Choose Size

My preference: N/A

This is another pair of options for resizing the current photo or multiple photos that you select. It can be applied while viewing a single image in full-size mode (just press the *i* button while viewing a photo). You might want smaller images to post on a website or send by e-mail.

1. **Select Pictures.** Choose one or multiple images from the Retouch menu.

2. **Choose size.** Next, select the destination (either Slot 1 or Slot 2), then select the size for the finished copy, from 2304 × 1536 (3.5MB), 1920 × 1280 (2.5MB), 1280 × 856 (1.1MB), or 960 × 640 (0.6MB).

3. **Confirm.** Press OK to create your copy, the *i* button to cancel, or the left directional button to back out of the Size screen. Note that, as with Trim, you may not be able to zoom in on a resized image during Playback once it has been saved.

D-Lighting

Options: High, Normal, Low
My preference: N/A

D-Lighting is the term for Nikon's shadow enhancement processing applied after an image has already been captured, as opposed to Active D-Lighting, which is performed at the time the picture is captured. Thus, this option brightens the shadows of pictures during picture review. Once you've selected your photo for modification, press the multi selector's up/down directional controls to choose from High, Normal, or Low corrections. (See Figure 9.24.) Press the Zoom In button to magnify the image. Press the DISP button to toggle between the unaltered version and your adjusted version. When you're happy with the corrected image compared to the original, press OK to save the copy to your memory card.

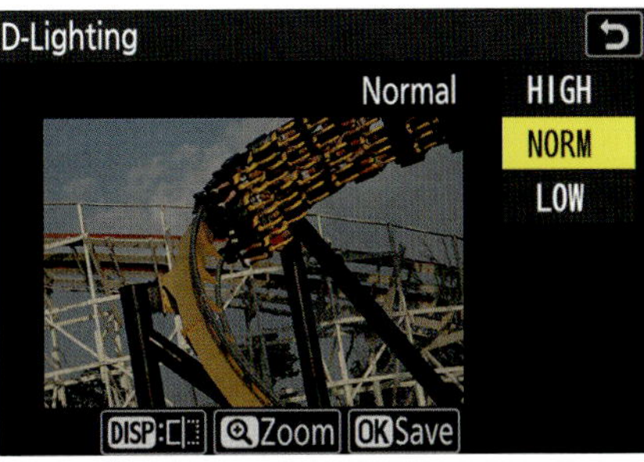

Figure 9.24 An image with dark shadows can be improved with post-shot D-Lighting.

Straighten

Options: Rotation
My preference: N/A

Use this to create a corrected copy of a crooked image, rotated by up to five degrees in either direction, in increments of one-quarter of a degree (–20 to +20). Use the down directional button to rotate clockwise, and the up directional button to rotate counterclockwise. The amount of your correction will be visible on the display. You can zoom in on the image or press the DISP button to toggle between the original and corrected versions. Press OK to make a corrected copy, or the Playback button to exit without saving a copy. Note that you will lose some picture information during this process, as the camera must trim the edges of the rotated image to produce the rectangular final image.

Distortion Control

Options: Auto, Manual
My preference: N/A

This option produces a copy with reduced barrel distortion (a bowing out effect) or pincushion distortion (an inward-bending effect). Both of these forms of *peripheral distortion* are most noticeable at the edges of a photo. If the camera detects distortion, an Auto option appears that allows the camera to make this correction. You can use Manual to make the fix yourself visually. Use the down directional button to reduce barrel distortion (bowing outward of lines at the edges) and the up directional button to reduce pincushion distortion (which produces lines bowing inward). In both cases, some of the edges of the photo will be cropped out of your image. The DISP button toggles between original and corrected versions. Press OK to make a corrected copy, or the Playback button to exit without saving a copy. Note that Auto cannot be used with images exposed using the Auto Distortion Control feature in the Photo Shooting menu.

Perspective Control

Options: Adjust tilt

My preference: N/A

This option lets you adjust the perspective of an image, reducing the falling-back effect produced when the camera is tilted to take in the top of a tall subject, such as a building, or to one side to include a longer structure or object. Choose which orientation you want to correct for (see Figure 9.25, left). Use the multi selector buttons up/down to "tilt" the image in various directions and visually correct the distortion (see Figure 9.25, right). You can zoom in on the image or press the DISP button to toggle between the original image and the corrected image.

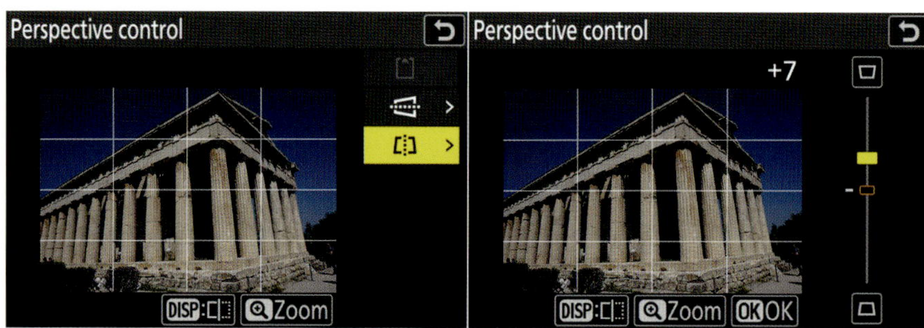

Figure 9.25 Perspective Control lets you fix "falling-back" distortion when photographing tall subjects.

Monochrome

Options: Black-and-white, Sepia, Cyanotype

My preference: N/A

This Retouch choice allows you to produce a copy of the selected photo as a black-and-white image, sepia-toned image, or cyanotype (blue-and-white). You can fine-tune the color saturation of the previewed Sepia or Cyanotype version by scrolling to the right to produce a secondary screen and pressing the multi selector up button to increase color richness, and the down button to decrease saturation. When satisfied, press OK to create the monochrome duplicate, which will be assigned its own filename. Cancel by pressing the Playback button. As always, the DISP button toggles between original image and processed version.

Overlay (Add)

Options: Combine two RAW photos, Add, Lighten, Darken

My preference: N/A

This feature allows you to combine two RAW photos (only RAW files can be used) in a composite image that Nikon claims is better than a "double exposure" created in an image-editing application, because the overlays are made using RAW data. To produce this composite image, follow these steps:

1. **Choose images.** Select the two images from the standard selection screen, pressing the Zoom Out button to mark/unmark thumbnails. Press OK to continue.

2. **Adjust balance.** Press the multi selector up and down buttons to adjust the percentage of each image to be used in the final version, starting from the default 50/50 to your desired proportions. The up button increases the strength of the first picture selected, while the down button increases the strength of the second photo.

3. **Press the OK button** when you're ready to store your composite copy. The combined image is stored in JPEG * format on the memory card and displayed full frame for your review.

Lighten/Darken

Options: Select Individual Pictures, Select Consecutive Pictures, or Select Folder

My preference: N/A

This pair of options aren't used to darken or lighten an individual picture. Instead, they are used to perform a Photoshop-style merger in which the camera compares the pixels in each photo and uses only the brightest or darkest for the final version.

Motion Blend

Options: Select Slot, Select Pictures

My preference: N/A

This option allows you to select a series of RAW (NEF) pictures in a continuous burst, locate moving subjects, and overlay them in a single JPEG image. From 5 pictures (the minimum) to 20 (the maximum) can be selected. Press OK to execute processing. This feature only works if the background of each image is substantially the same and the subject is actually moving in some way.

Using My Menu

The last menu in the main menu screen has two versions: Recent Settings, which simply shows an ever-changing roster of the 20 menu items you used most recently, and My Menu (the default). You'll probably find it more useful to work with the My Menu option most of the time, as it contains only those menu items that you deposit there extracted from the Playback, Photo Shooting, Video Recording, Custom Settings, Setup, and Network menus, based on your own decisions on which you use most. Remember that the camera always returns to the last menu and menu entry accessed when you press the MENU button. So, you can set up My Menu (see Figure 9.26) to include just the items accessed most frequently, and (as long as you haven't used another menu) jump to those items instantly by pressing the MENU button.

Switching back and forth is easy. The My Menu and Recent Settings menus have a menu choice called Choose Tab. Highlight that entry and press the right multi selector button to view a screen that allows you to activate either the My Menu or Recent Settings menu. Press OK to confirm.

I tend to include frequently used functions that aren't available using direct-access buttons in My Menu. For example, I include High ISO NR and Long Exp. NR there, because I may want to turn noise reduction on or off during shooting. I *don't* include ISO or WB changes in My Menu, even though they are available in the menu system, because I can quickly change those values by pressing dedicated buttons and rotating the main and sub-command dials.

Figure 9.26 You can include your favorite menu items in the fast-access My Menu.

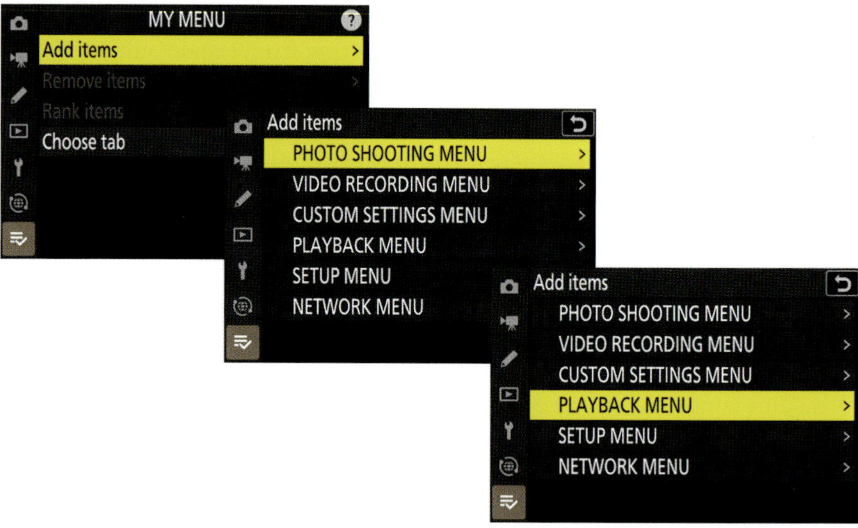

You can add or subtract entries on My Menu at any time, and re-order (or rank) the entries so the ones you access most often are shown at the top of the list. Here's all you need to know to work with My Menu. To add entries to My Menu:

1. Select My Menu and choose Add Items.
2. A list of the available menus will appear (Photo Shooting, Video Recording, Custom Settings, Playback, Setup, and Network menus). Highlight one and press the multi selector's right button.
3. Within the selected menu, choose the menu item you want to add and press OK.
4. The label Choose Position appears at the top of the My Menu screen. Use the up/down buttons to select a rank among the entries and press OK to confirm and add the new item.
5. Repeat steps 1–4 if you want to add more entries to My Menu.

To reorder the menu listings:

1. Within the My Menu screen, choose Rank Items.
2. Use the up/down buttons to select the item to be moved and press OK.
3. Use the up/down buttons to relocate the selected item and press OK.
4. Repeat steps 2–3 to move additional entries.

To remove entries from the list, you can simply press the Trash button while an item is highlighted in the My Menu screen. To remove multiple items, follow these steps:

1. Within the My Menu screen, choose Remove Items.
2. A list with checkboxes next to the menu items appears. Scroll down to an item you want to remove and press the multi selector right button to mark its box. If you change your mind, highlight the item and press the right button again to unmark the box.
3. When finished, press the Trash button or tap the Delete icon on the screen.
4. Press OK to confirm the deletion.

Introduction to Video

Your Nikon Z5 II is bristling with professional-level video features capable of interfacing with equally high-end recorders and other accessories. Pro videographers are actually capturing footage for feature films with mirrorless cameras. Fortunately, for the rest of us, shooting movies with the Nikon Z5 II can be as easy as flipping a switch—the Photo/Video mode switch located to the right of the viewfinder. If you're looking for no-fuss, casual video, after you've selected Video mode, rotate the mode dial to the Auto position, and press the red Video-record button located on top of the camera, just southwest of the shutter-release button. Capture will start; press the Video button again to stop recording. That's all there is to grabbing good video clips.

So, although explaining how to use the full range of sophisticated movie-making features is beyond the scope of this book, I am going to introduce the basics so you'll know what you need to master if you want to go beyond "good" to "excellent." I listed and described the options in the Video Recording menu in Chapter 6.

Quick-Start Checklist

The following is a list of things to keep in mind as you improve your video-capture skills and take your video work to the next level. Some of these items are recaps of information you learned about still photo shooting; others are of special concern for video capture. Even if you decide to just skim through this chapter for now and come back for more after you've explored video capture, you should at least read this section before you begin your epic documentary or feature production.

- **Stills photos in Video mode?** Unfortunately, when the Photo/Video switch is set to capture movies, you cannot press the shutter release down all the way to take a still photo, whether the camera is actively capturing video or in standby mode. You can, however, pause a video during playback and extract an individual frame or consecutive frames from H.265 8-bit (MOV) and H.264 8-bit (MP4) videos, as I'll describe shortly.

- **No flash.** You cannot use flash when the selector switch is set to the Video position.

- **Exposure compensation.** When shooting movies, exposure compensation is available in plus/minus 3 EV steps in 1/3 EV increments. (Remember that still photos offer plus/minus 5 EV steps.)

- **ISO fine-tuning and limitations.** Custom Setting g9: Fine ISO Control (Mode M) allows using 1/6 EV increments when setting ISO sensitivity in Manual exposure mode. The Z5 II uses the base ISO of 100 in Standard Dynamic Range (SDR) video modes. When shooting non-log HDR video in HLG mode, the lowest ISO available is the sensor's dual-gain second base ISO of 400. In addition, ISO Auto is enabled at all times, except in manual exposure mode.

- **Use the right card.** You'll want to use a fast memory card if possible, and be aware of other card restrictions and specifications, as described in the section that follows this one.

- **Length restrictions.** Single video shots can be up to 125 minutes in length, but that mark is likely to be available only if you're using an external power source. With a single fully charged EN-EL15c battery, Nikon estimates that video capture can continue for roughly 85 minutes before the battery poops out. Low and high ambient temperatures, slow shutter speeds, frequent zooming, use of Wi-Fi or Bluetooth, and other factors potentially reduce recording time.

- **Add an external mic.** For the best sound quality, and to avoid picking up the sound of the autofocus or zoom motor, get an external stereo mic. I'll have more advice about capturing sound and describe specific types of microphones later in this chapter.

- **Minimize zooming.** While it's great to be able to use the zoom for filling the frame with a distant subject, think twice before zooming. Unless you are using an external mic, the sound of the zoom ring rotating will be picked up and it will be audible when you play a movie. Any more than the occasional minor zoom will be very distracting to those who watch your videos.

- **Disable Standby Timer.** Be sure to set Custom Setting c3: Power Off Delay > Standby Timer to No Limit, so your camera doesn't power down while you are shooting when you are recording a video via an HDMI connection to an external device.

- **Just press the Video-record button.** You don't have to hold it down. Press it again to stop recording.

Choosing the Right Memory Card

Because video shooting involves capturing multiple frames per second for extended periods of time, video shooting imposes some extra demands on memory cards, especially in terms of size and speed. With still photography, just about any memory card will do, unless you're firing off shots at video-like high continuous shooting rates. Videography is not so forgiving, so you'll want to use a fast memory card, if possible, for conventional Full HD and 4K video. Very fast cards are absolutely essential for RAW Video (discussed later in this chapter), because of the high sustained write speeds required. If you insist on using a slower card, the recording may stop after a minute or two.

Heat builds up from the camera's sensor being energized constantly during continuous shooting and can be increased by high ambient temperatures (i.e., outdoors on a hot day). It's well known that some cards run hotter than others, based on their physical design and electronics. Card characteristics vary sharply by vendor, card model, and capacity, so your best bet is to haunt forums or use Google searches to see which current memory cards produce the least amount of overheating.

Video quality can suffer terribly when the imaging sensor gets hot, so keep the camera in a cool place. When shooting on hot days especially, the sensor can get hot quicker than usual; when there's a risk of overheating, the camera will stop recording and it will shut down about five seconds later. Give it time to cool down before using it again.

Fortunately, by default, the Z5 II will display two warning icons in the upper-left corner of the display, each representing an increasing temperature level. Once the second level has been reached, a countdown timer will appear that indicates when the camera will be powered down automatically.

Capturing Video

Many of the settings in the Video Recording menus (shown in Figure 10.1) are similar to their still photography counterparts in the Photo Shooting menu. In this overview, I'm going to concentrate on the options that are different, and how you can apply them to capturing great video. I described every entry and setting in Chapter 6, and won't repeat the information detailed in that chapter here.

- **Reset Video Recording menu.** You can return the Video Recording menu to its defaults.

- **Storage folder.** Rename, select, or choose a folder from the list of available folders, just as originally described in Chapter 5.

- **File naming.** I recommend using a different substitution in Video mode for the default DSC characters in filenames created for movie files. The limitations and instructions are the same as for the File Naming entry in the Photo Shooting menu, as described in Chapter 5.

- **Destination.** You can select which of the two memory card slots will be used to store video. You can select a different card to be used for video than the one specified with the slot function entries of the Photo Shooting menu. The amount of time available for storing video is displayed when you choose the destination.

- **Video file type.** Here you can select different video formats and resolutions for conventional movies, with additional settings for slow-motion video. The "container" type is MOV for all video file types except H.264 8-bit, which uses MP4. I'll explain the difference between the two later; video-editing software can convert back and forth between either one.

- **Frame size/Frame rate.** Choose from among 4K and Full HD frame sizes and frame rates up to 120/100p, plus Slow-Motion options (all listed in Chapter 6).

- **Image Area.** This parameter determines image area used when capturing video. Your Z5 II provides two variations, which crop 16:9 (HDTV) proportioned areas from the full-frame still photography view: FX and DX. Fortunately, the Z5 II doesn't use a mask to mark off the cropped area. Instead, it helpfully enlarges the captured portion to fill the frame.

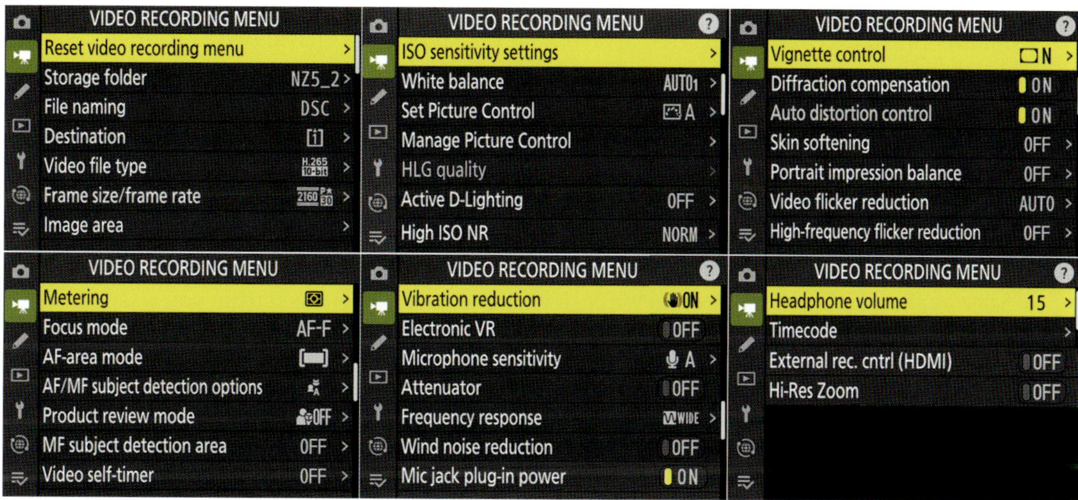

Figure 10.1 Video Recording menus.

WHAT FRAME RATE?

Even intermediate movie shooters can be confused by the choice of 24 fps or 30/25, 60/50, and 120/100 fps, especially since those are only nominal figures (with the camera, the 24 fps setting yields 23.976 frames per second; 30 fps gives you 29.97 actual "frames" per second; 60 fps yields 59.94; while 120p yields 119.88 fps). The difference lies in the two "worlds" of motion images—film and video. The standard frame rate for motion picture film is 24 fps, while the video rate, at least in the United States, Japan, and other places using the NTSC standard, is 30 fps (60 interlaced *fields* per second). Most computer video-editing software can handle either type and convert between them. The choice between 24 fps and 30 fps is determined by what you plan to do with your video. Your camera can also shoot at 25/50/100 fps for use with PAL systems, which don't use NTSC standards.

The short explanation is that, for technical reasons I won't go into here, shooting at 24 fps gives your movie a "film" look, excellent for showing fine detail. (I'll have more to say about that later in this chapter.)

However, if your clip has moving subjects, or you pan the camera, 24 fps can produce a jerky effect called "judder." A 30/60/120 fps rate produces a home-video look that some feel is less desirable, but which is smoother and less jittery when displayed on an electronic monitor. I suggest you try both and use the frame rate that best suits your tastes and video-editing software.

USING DX LENSES

If you use an FTZ adapter (either the original or Mark II model) to mount a lens that the camera recognizes as a DX/APS-C lens, the camera will switch to DX-based movie format automatically (without the need to specify FX or DX with the Image Area entry, which is grayed out, in any case). (Reminder: Image sizes are determined by the frame size/rate with the RAW file types.)

As in still photo mode, you cannot force the camera to use the DX lens as if it were a full-frame optic. Remember that the camera may or may not detect APS-C (DX) lenses from third-party manufacturers.

When Electronic VR is selected using the *i* button menu or Video Recording menu, the camera provides a slight additional crop (to allow adjusting the frame to compensate for camera movement).

- **ISO Sensitivity Settings (for videos).** Like the ISO settings in the Photo Shooting menu, as explained in Chapter 5, this setting allows you to select a fixed ISO setting for Manual exposure mode, from ISO 100 to ISO 51200, plus Hi 0.3, Hi 0.7, Hi 1.0, and Hi 2.0. That allows you greater control over the ISO used. If you've enabled Custom Setting g9: Fine ISO Control (Mode M), increments of 1/6 EV are used instead of the default 1/3 EV.

  When shooting movies in P, A, or S exposure modes, Auto ISO sensitivity is always used. However, in Manual exposure mode Auto ISO can be turned off, or assigned a *maximum* ISO that can be selected automatically, from ISO 200 to Hi 2.0.

- **White balance.** Here you can select the white balance used to shoot movies. You can choose:
  - **Same as photo settings.** The camera will use whatever white balance setting you've specified in the Photo Shooting menu.
  - **Any of the other white balance options.** The selection will apply *only* to video. The white balance of movie clips isn't easy to adjust, so you will usually want to set a specific white balance in this menu entry or opt for Auto white balance. I usually keep this setting the same as selected for still photos.

- **Set Picture Control.** You can specify Same as Photo Settings or independently specify a Picture Control to be used only when shooting movies. The procedures for selecting and modifying a Picture Control in this menu entry are otherwise the same as described in Chapter 7.

  However, of special note here is the Flat Picture Control (available in both still and movie modes), which produces a dull, washed-out rendition. Why would you want that? Flat captures a wider dynamic range than other Picture Control modes, including Standard, giving you a better "raw" video image to fine-tune in your video-editing software, using your program's video color-grading functions. Grading is used to adjust contrast, color, saturation, detail, black level, and white point, and is especially powerful when used with relatively flat images, like those produced by the Flat Picture Control, or with N-log gamma. As I've mentioned, I'll explain N-log in more detail later.

- **Manage Picture Control.** This entry includes the Save/Edit, Rename, Delete, and Load/Save options that operate the same as the corresponding control in the Photo Shooting menu, described in Chapter 5. You can make a copy of a Picture Control, save an edited copy, rename or remove a style, or retrieve a Picture Control from a memory card.

- **HLG quality.** This entry is available when Video File Type is set to H.265 10-bit (MOV), and HLG Tone mode has been selected. You can then make adjustments to the only Picture Control available for HLG video (all others are grayed out and unavailable). You'll find step-by-step instructions for fine-tuning the HLG quality options in Chapter 6.

- **Active D-Lighting.** You can choose Extra High, High, Normal, Low, or Off.

- **High ISO NR.** Video Recording doesn't involve *long* exposures, so the Video Recording menu includes only a High ISO Noise Reduction entry. You can set it to High, Normal, Low, or Off. See the entry for this feature under the Photo Shooting menu, in Chapter 5.

- **Vignette control/Diffraction compensation/Auto distortion control.** These three all operate the same as for still photo shooting and were described in Chapter 5.

- **Skin softening.** You can choose Same as Photo Settings, High, Normal, Low, or Off, which is the default. The camera can detect and process up to three subjects to produce a more flattering look.

- **Portrait impression balance.** Three separate profiles that specify magenta/amber color bias (greens and blues are not affected) and set a brightness level to be used when shooting portraits can be created.

- **Video flicker reduction/High-frequency flicker reduction.** For the former, choose Auto, or select either 50 Hz or 60 Hz, as described in Chapter 5. The High-Frequency version for shutter speed fine-tuning can be turned on or off.

- **Metering.** Only Matrix, Center-weighted, and Highlight-weighted metering, as described in Chapter 4, are available. Spot metering is not available in Video mode.

- **Focus mode.** In addition to AF-S, AF-C, and Manual focus, Full-time AF (AF-F) is available in Video mode. Unlike AF-S or AF-C, the AF-F autofocus mode doesn't need to be activated by pressing the shutter release or designated AF-ON button; AF-F functions as its name suggests— it is active at all times when you're in Video mode. While power consumption is greater, there is less of a lag in achieving sharp focus once you begin video capture.

- **AF-area mode.** Only Single-point AF, Wide-area AF (Small, Large, C1, C2), Subject-tracking AF, and Auto-area AF are available. Pinpoint AF is not available in Video mode.

- **AF/MF subject-detection options.** You can set the priority for the type of subject the camera will look for during autofocus, including People, Animal, Birds, Vehicle, or Airplanes. Subject detection is possible when Subject-Tracking AF, any of the Wide-Area AF modes (Small, Large, Custom 1, Custom 2), or any of the Auto-area AF modes are active. You can set separate priorities for detection in the Photo Shooting and Video Recording menus or deactivate this feature.

- **Product review mode.** As explained in Chapter 6, this entry can be set to On, so that your product can be anywhere in the frame, and the camera will focus on it as it is brought in front of the camera as the closest object. Alternatively, you can create a customized focus area or disable the mode entirely.

- **MF subject detection area.** This entry is used to enable the Z5 II to detect subjects for you *even when you are focusing manually.* Choose Auto-area (All), and the camera will search for subjects within the entire frame. If multiple subjects are present, the first one detected will be shown with a gray focus point indicator and left/right triangle-shaped pointers that show you can switch to one of the other subjects using the left/right directional buttons. You can also choose Wide-area AF (Large or Small) to limit subject recognition to the current focus area.

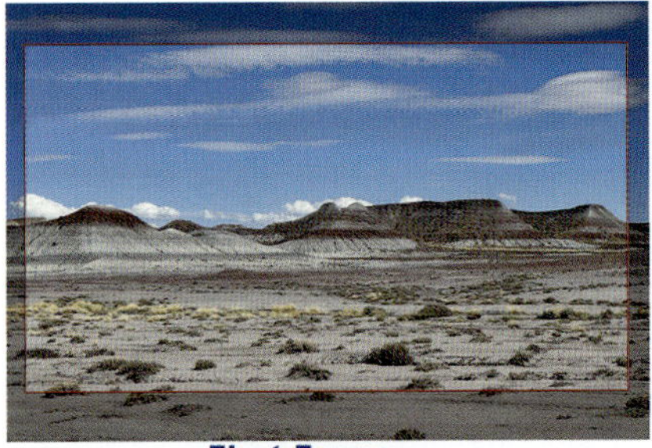

- **Video Self-timer.** You can delay the start of video recording, choosing 2- or 10-second delays, or selecting Off to have capture begin immediately after the Video button is pressed.

- **Vibration reduction.** This menu entry controls the vibration reduction feature built in to some lenses. You can choose Same as Photo Settings, On (Normal), Sport, or Off.

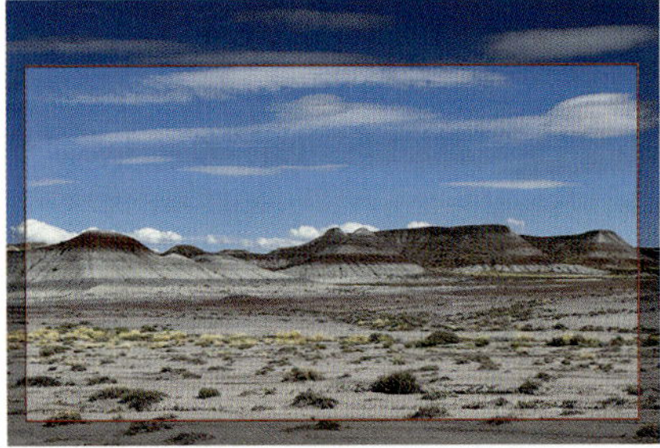

- **Electronic VR.** While the Z5 II has powerful in-body image stabilization, it also features in video mode an electronic version that crops the video frame slightly, and shifts the entire frame up, down, left, right, or diagonally enough to counter some camera movement in those directions. The camera is able to do this because the Z5 II's entire frame isn't used for video; there is always cropping at the top and bottom to provide the HD 16:9 proportions. In Electronic VR mode, some additional cropping is done at the sides to allow adjusting the frame left and right. (See Figure 10.2.)

A "waving hand" indicator appears at the left side of the display when Electronic VR is active. (Nikon adds an "e" to the icon to differentiate it from the conventional VR indicator.) Keep in mind that, because of the cropping, the angle of view is reduced slightly, producing

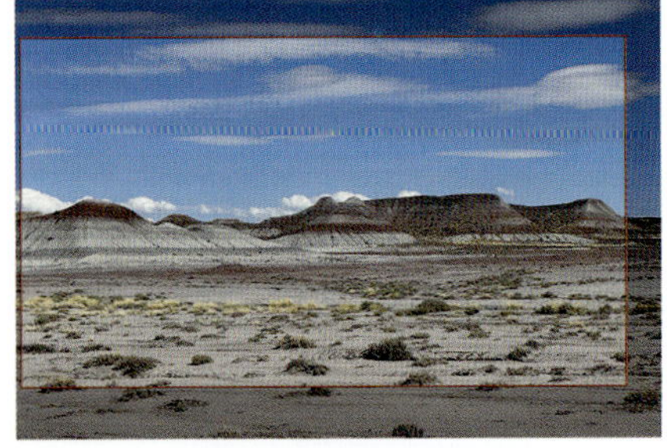

Figure 10.2 How electronic VR works.

a slight focal length "multiplier" effect. This feature is not available with 120/100p frame rates, Hi-Res Zoom or slow-motion video, or when shooting N-RAW 12-bit (NEV) video.

- **Microphone sensitivity.** This entry has three options that control the built-in microphone or any external microphone you attach. You can choose Auto Sensitivity or set recording levels yourself using the Manual Sensitivity option. There's a handy volume meter on the screen showing the current ambient sound levels. You can also turn the microphone off entirely if you're planning to record silent video, use another sound recording source, or add sound in post-production. (See Figure 10.3.)

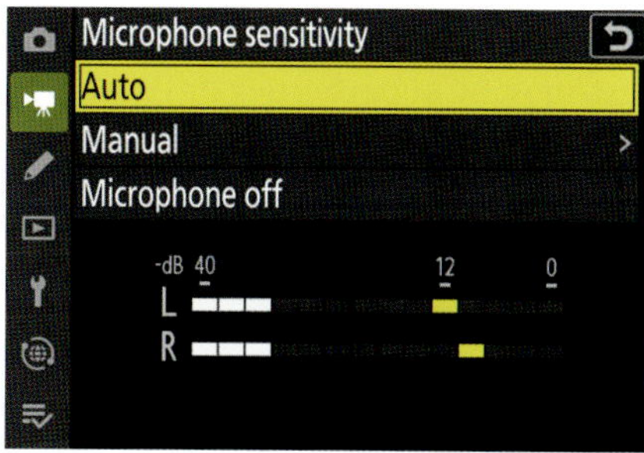

Figure 10.3 Adjusting microphone sensitivity.

- **Attenuator.** Enable this feature to minimize audio distortion from background sounds when capturing video in loud environments.

- **Frequency response.** Select from Wide Range frequency response to record a broad range of sounds, or Vocal Range to optimize audio recording for vocals.

- **Wind noise reduction.** Wind blowing across your microphone can be distracting. This setting reduces wind noise (and may also affect other sounds, so use it carefully) for the built-in microphones *only*. Your external microphone, like the Nikon ME-1, may have its own wind noise reduction filter on/off switch.

- **Mic jack plug-in power.** If your microphone does not need to draw power from the camera, you can set this entry to Off and prevent possible noise produced by the power supply.

- **Headphone volume.** You can set a volume from 0 to 30; the default is 15.

- **Timecode.** As I've noted in several places in this book, including Chapter 6, advanced video editing and other software-oriented topics, such as Photoshop, are generally beyond the scope of this book. In any case, using timecodes is a fairly advanced procedure, and those who use them don't need instruction from me.

  However, the ability to embed timecodes in video is a new and highly useful feature for Nikon interchangeable-lens cameras. As I said in Chapter 6, where all the timecode options are described, they provide precise *hour:minute:second:frame* markers that allow identifying and synchronizing frames and audio. The time code system includes a provision for "dropping" frames to ensure that the fractional frame rate of captured video (remember that a 24 fps setting actually yields 23.976 frames per second while 30 fps capture gives you 29.97 actual "frames" per second) can be matched up with actual time spans.

- **External recording control (HDMI).** Use this setting to allow your camera's controls to stop and start recording on a compatible external recorder.

- **High-res zoom.** This setting uses your camera's extra resolution to provide a high-quality digital zoom effect—even to prime lenses, which have a fixed focal length. When active, you can zoom in and out by pressing the Fn1 or Fn2 buttons, or by rotating the lens control ring. I provided step-by-step instructions for using this feature in Chapter 6.

Slow-Motion Videos

Slow-motion video is a cool feature that allows you to reduce the apparent playback speed of your movies by 4X or 5X, so you can analyze movement, or apply the effect to your next video involving fast-moving superheroes or those intrepid Baywatch lifeguards. It's available only when you have selected H.264 8-bit (MP4) from the Video File Type setting.

In the Frame Size/Frame Rate entry of the Video Recording menu, you have the option of scrolling down to select 1920 × 1080 settings at either 30p × 4 (slow-mo) or 24p × 5 (slow-mo) (both NTSC). Video intended for use in PAL countries can select 25p × 4 or 24p × 5 instead.

In slow-motion mode, the camera records Normal Quality video, at 120/100 frames per second (NTSC/PAL) for up to no more than three minutes. When 120/100 fps video is viewed at 30/25 frames per second, the clip takes four times as long to play back; at 24 fps, the clip requires 5X the normal time. As a result, a three-minute clip will stretch to fill 12 minutes when shot at 30/25 fps, or 15 minutes at 24 fps. You can analyze your golf swing or add a slow-mo effect to your movies. While the three-minute capture rate may seem like a limitation, how often do you really want to watch 12 to 15 minutes of slow-motion "action?"

Shooting Your Video

By this time, you're ready to capture some video. To shoot your movies, follow these steps:

1. **Plug in the microphone (optional).** If you want to use an external monaural or stereo microphone with a 3.5mm stereo mini plug, attach it to the microphone jack on the left side of the camera.

2. **Choose an exposure mode.** Select Program, Shutter-priority, Aperture-priority, or Manual exposure, and Matrix, Center-weighted, or Highlight-weighted metering.

3. **Adjust exposure.** The adjustments you can make depend on the exposure mode you select:

   - **Program.** You can adjust exposure compensation and the screen image will brighten and darken as you make changes. Shutter speed and ISO sensitivity are selected for you by the camera.

   - **Shutter Priority.** You can select the shutter speed.

   - **Aperture-priority.** You can change the f/stop by rotating the sub-command dial or making exposure compensation adjustments. Shutter speed and ISO sensitivity are selected for you by the camera.

   - **Manual exposure.** The main command dial changes the shutter speed, and the sub-command dial adjusts the aperture. You can also change the ISO sensitivity.

4. **Enable movie recording.** Activate movie recording by rotating the Photo/Video switch to the Video position.

5. **Choose a focus and AF-area mode.** Select from autofocus or manual focus using camera settings. Then choose AF-S, AF-C, or AF-F. Select an AF-area mode.

6. **Set audio level.** Use the Microphone Sensitivity entry in the Video Recording menu to specify audio recording level, using Auto Sensitivity to allow the camera to set the volume, or Manual Sensitivity to adjust using an audio meter. You can also turn off audio to record a silent movie, say, if you plan to add a voice-over track, music, or other audio in post-production using your video-editing software.

7. **Start/Stop recording.** Press the red-dotted movie-recording button to begin capture. Press again to stop recording. The LCD monitor display as you're capturing video looks like Figure 10.4, with a rectangular red border indicating that recording is underway. The viewfinder display has the same information, arranged slightly differently, and not overlaid on the image area. You can press the DISP button to increase or decrease the amount of information overlaid on the screen during movie recording.

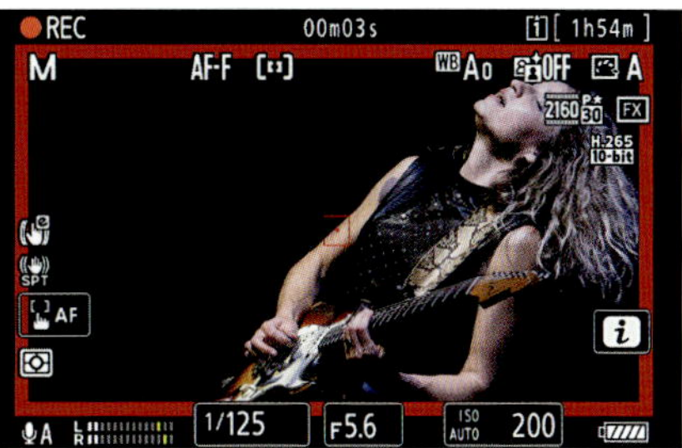

Figure 10.4 The LCD monitor display during movie capture.

8. **No flash.** You can't use electronic flash during movie recording, but you *can* use the built-in LED movie light on the Nikon SB-500 unit.

Using the *i* Button Menu

The *i* button, which is so useful in Photo mode, also offers real-time adjustment of parameters and controls while you capture your video. These are not only important for fine-tuning your movies as you capture them but allow for some special tools that veteran videographers will know and love, but which may be new to still photographers. Here's a description of the useful options that pop up when you press the *i* button. (See Figure 10.5.) Many of these are also available in the Video Recording menu, as explained in Chapter 6.

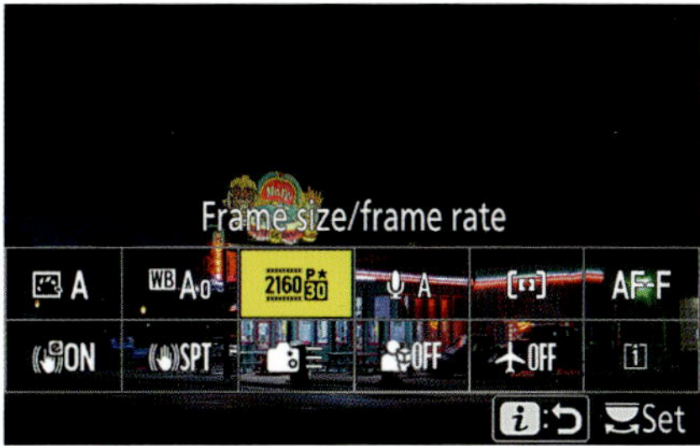

Figure 10.5 *i* button options.

- **Set Picture Control.** You can use any of the Picture Controls described in Chapter 5 in Video mode and specify them here.
- **White balance.** Set your white balance for movie shooting here, using the main command dial for the primary settings and sub-command dial for any options available.
- **Frame size/Frame rate.** Select your frame size and rate here.
- **Microphone sensitivity.** It's useful to be able to use the *i* menu while shooting video to adjust the sensitivity of your microphone on the fly. As this adjustment controls both the built-in and optional external stereo microphones, you might find yourself needing to make your mic more sensitive or less sensitive as the ambient sound conditions change. For example, if you were capturing a clip with only background sound (no vocals) and someone started using a jackhammer a block away, you might want to reduce microphone sensitivity to minimize the clamor.
- **AF-area mode/Subject detection.** Choose from among the available AF-area modes with the main command dial and adjust subject detection with the sub-command dial.
- **Focus mode.** Choose AF-S, AF-C, AF-F, or MF.
- **Electronic VR.** Turn it on or off.
- **Vibration reduction.** You can turn lens-based image stabilization off or choose between Normal and Sport modes.

- **Custom controls.** The command dials do nothing when this setting is highlighted. Press OK to access the Custom Controls setting screen.
- **Product review mode.** Activate this mode quickly when you're ready to record a review.
- **Airplane mode.** Press OK or tap the icon to turn airplane mode on or off. Again, the dials perform no function here.
- **Destination.** Quickly switch from one memory card slot to the other with either command dial, and view how much recording time is available on each card.

As I described in Chapter 7, there is a Custom Setting g1: Customize *i* Menu entry that allows you to swap out and change Video mode *i* menu items. You'll probably want to do so, because Nikon's choice of which features to include in the video *i* menu don't make a lot of sense to me. I think you'll find there are other functions that you need much more. My top candidates for replacement are the Custom Controls and Airplane mode options, which access rarely used features. If you don't frequently use Picture Controls, you can dispense with that one, too.

As in Photo mode, the *i* button has additional features during Playback: you can use available options to trim videos, grab an individual frame as a still photo, apply ratings, and perform other functions. I'll explain these later in this chapter.

Stop That!

You might think that setting your camera to a faster shutter speed will help give you sharper video frames. But the choice of a shutter speed for movie making is a bit more complicated than that. Here's how it works:

- **Program and Shutter-priority modes.** In P mode, the camera selects the shutter speed (such as 1/30th second) and ISO sensitivity appropriate for your lighting conditions. In Shutter-priority mode, you can select a shutter speed from 1/8000th second down to the slowest speed available at your chosen frame rate (e.g., 1/30th second at 30 fps). You can add/subtract exposure compensation.
- **Aperture-priority mode.** This is the mode to use when you want to put selective focus to work by choosing an aperture that will provide more, or less, depth-of-field. In A mode, you can select any f/stop available with your lens, and the camera will choose a shutter speed and ISO setting to suit. Generally, if you choose a large aperture, the camera will lower the ISO sensitivity as much as it can, to allow sticking with a shutter speed of 1/30th second. It will then select shorter shutter speeds, if necessary, under very bright illumination. My camera has jumped up to 1/200th second outdoors under bright daylight when I try to shoot at f/1.8 or f/1.4. In A mode, you can still add or subtract exposure compensation.
- **Manual exposure mode.** In this mode, you have control of aperture, shutter speed (from 1/25th second all the way up to 1/8000th second), and ISO—even if your settings result in video that is completely washed out, or entirely black. Because video capture is in the range of 24 to 120 frames per second, you can't select a shutter speed that is longer than the frame interval. That is, if your video mode is 1920 × 1080 at 30 fps, you can't choose a shutter speed longer than 1/30th second; at 120p, the longest shutter speed available is 1/125th second. Thanks to the Z5 II's ability to activate Auto ISO in manual mode, you can enable semi-manual/semi-automatic exposure, as I'll describe in the "ISO Control in Video Mode" section that follows.

So, how do you select an appropriate shutter speed? As you might guess, it's almost always best to leave the shutter speed at 1/30th second and allow the overall exposure to be adjusted by varying the aperture and/or ISO sensitivity. We don't normally stare at a video frame for longer than 1/30th or 1/24th second, so while the shakiness of the *camera* can be disruptive (and often corrected by VR), if there is a bit of blur in our *subjects* from movement, we tend not to notice. Each frame flashes by in the blink of an eye, so to speak, so a shutter speed of 1/30th second works a lot better in video than it does when shooting stills.

Higher shutter speeds introduce problems of their own. If you shoot a video frame using a shutter speed of 1/200th second, the actual moment in time that's captured represents only about 12 percent of the 1/30th second of elapsed time in that frame. Yet, when played back, that frame occupies the full 1/30th of a second, with 88 percent of that time filled by stretching the original image to fill it. The result is often a choppy/jumpy image, and one that may appear to be *too* sharp.

The reason for that is more social imprinting than scientific: we've all grown up accustomed to seeing the look of Hollywood productions that, by convention, were shot using a shutter speed that's half the reciprocal of the frame rate (that is, 1/48th second for a 24 fps movie). Video cameras use a rotary shutter (achieving that 1/48th-second exposure by using a 180-degree shutter "angle"), but the effect on our visual expectations is the same. For the most "film-like" appearance, use 24 fps and 1/60th-second shutter speed.

Faster shutter speeds do have some specialized uses for motion analysis, especially where individual frames are studied. The rest of the time, 1/30th or 1/60th of a second will suffice. If the reason you needed a higher shutter speed was to obtain the correct exposure, use a slower ISO setting, or a neutral-density filter to cut down on the amount of light passing through the lens.

A good rule of thumb when shooting progressive video (as opposed to interlaced video, which is not offered by the Z5 II) is to use 1/60th second or slower when shooting at 24 fps; 1/60th second or slower at 30 fps; 1/125th second or slower at 60 fps; and 1/250th second or slower at 120 fps.

ISO Control in Video Mode

As I've pointed out several times earlier in the chapter, the Z5 II implements the ISO sensitivity setting slightly differently in video mode. In P, A, and S modes, Auto ISO is mandatory; you can't specify a particular ISO setting. Your exposure adjustment options include only aperture, shutter speed, and exposure compensation through plus/minus EV settings.

If you need or want more control over ISO, say, because you want to avoid high ISO noise, switching to manual exposure is your best bet. You can lock in a specific ISO value if you like or use Auto ISO to provide a sort of semi-manual/semi-automatic exposure mode. *Remember: if you want to set a specific ISO, you must use Manual exposure mode.*

Just navigate to the ISO Sensitivity Settings entry in the Video Recording menu and access the Auto ISO Control (Mode M) option. When enabled, in manual exposure mode the camera will attempt to adjust the ISO setting to provide the correct exposure based on the current shutter speed, aperture, and exposure compensation values you've specified. That means you can select a suitable shutter speed, and an f/stop, and the camera will effectively provide you with autoexposure in Manual exposure mode. The Maximum Sensitivity option within the same entry lets you tell the camera not to use an ISO higher than the value you specify, from ISO 200 to 51200, plus Hi 0.3 to Hi 2.0.

Viewing Your Videos

Once you've finished recording your movies, they are available for review. Film clips show up during picture review the same as still photos, but they are differentiated by a movie camera icon overlay and "Play" prompt. Press the OK button to start playback. During playback, you can perform the following functions:

- **Pause.** Press the multi selector down button to pause the clip during playback. Press the OK button to resume playback.
- **Rewind/Advance.** Press the left/right multi selector buttons to rewind or advance (respectively). Press once for 2X speed, twice for 8X speed, or three times for 16X speed. Hold down the left/right buttons to move to the end or beginning of the clip.
- **Start Slo-mo playback.** Press the down button while the movie is paused to play back in slow motion.
- **Skip 10 seconds.** Rotate the sub-command dial to skip ahead or back in 10-second increments.
- **Change volume.** Press the Zoom In and Zoom Out buttons to increase/decrease volume while a video is being played back. (If the video is paused, Zoom In/Zoom Out will zoom in and out of the current frame.)
- **Trim movie/Save frame.** Press the *i* button and follow the steps in the next section.
- **Exit Playback.** Press the multi selector up button or the Playback button to exit playback.
- **View menus.** Press the MENU button to interrupt playback to access menus.

Trimming Your Videos

In-camera editing is limited to trimming the beginning or end from a clip, and the clip must be at least two seconds long. For more advanced editing, you'll need an application capable of editing movie clips. Google "Movie Editor" to locate any of the hundreds of free video editors available, or use a commercial product like iMovie, Corel Video Studio, Adobe Premiere Elements, or Pinnacle Studio. These will let you combine several clips into one movie, and add titles, special effects, and transitions between scenes.

In-camera trimming can be done using the tools available during Playback. To do in-camera trimming, follow these steps:

1. **Start movie clip.** Use the Playback button to start image review and press the OK button to start playback when you see a clip you want to edit. It will begin playing.
2. **View movie to start point.** To remove video from the beginning of a clip, play the movie until you reach the first frame you want to keep, and then press the down button to pause. The movie progress bar at the bottom left of the screen will show the current position in the movie with

a yellow highlight marker. You can move the marker back and forth frame by frame while the video is paused by pressing the left/right buttons or rotating the main or sub-command dials. (See Figure 10.6, upper left.)

3. **Mark start.** Press the *i* button. The screen shown at upper right in the figure appears. Highlight Trim Video and press the right button. Press the right button again to confirm as the start point. (See Figure 10.6, center left.)

4. **Confirm new start point.** The frame you selected for the new start point should be displayed. If not, you can press the left or right buttons to advance or rewind frame-by-frame. For larger adjustments, rotate the main command left or right one click to skip ahead or back 10 frames, or the sub-command dial one click to skip ahead or back 10 seconds.

5. **Advance to end point.** Press the sub-selector button to switch to selecting the end point. Use the left/right buttons and/or main and sub-command dials to move the end point marker to the desired conclusion of the clip. (See Figure 10.6, center right.) Press the up directional button to lock in the end point.

6. **Save edited clip.** The screen shown at lower left appears. You can save the edited clip as a new file or overwrite the existing file. You can also preview your clip. It's usually a good idea to retain the original in case you want to re-edit the clip later.

7. **File saved.** A progress bar indicates your edited movie is being saved. (See Figure 10.6, lower right.)

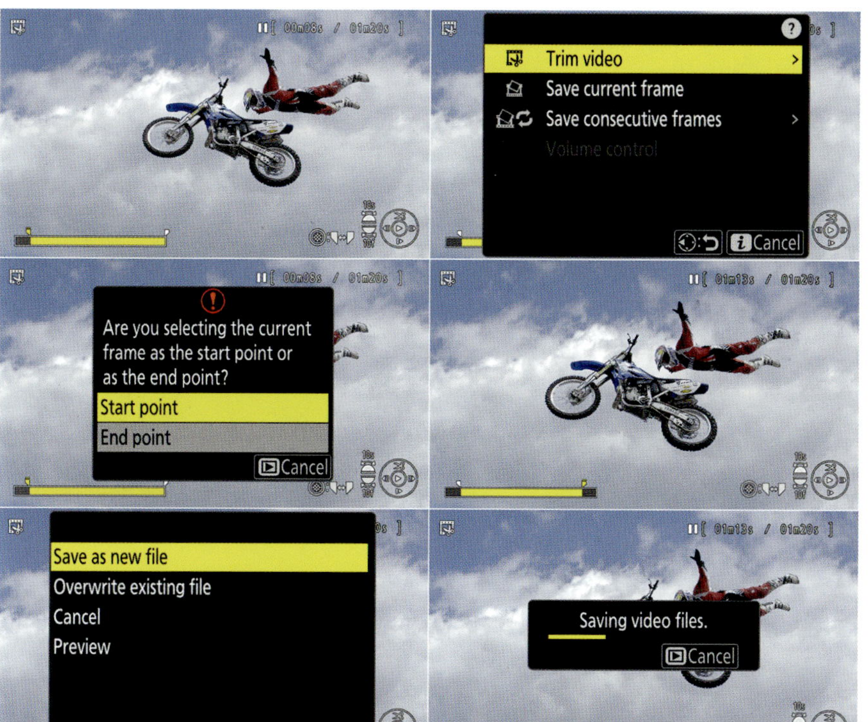

Figure 10.6 Editing a movie clip.

Saving Stills from a Video

You can store any single frame or a series of frames from one of your movies as a JPEG still, using the resolution of the current video format. The feature is available *during Playback* as an *i* menu option, as described above. Just follow these steps (see Figure 10.7):

1. **Pause at desired frame.** As with the video-trimming feature, pause your movie at the frame you want to save by pressing the down button.

2. **Choose single or multiple frames.** Press the *i* button and highlight either Save Current Frame or Save Consecutive Frames.

3. **Save single frame or continue for multiple.** Press the right button to save the current frame and finish, or to move on to choosing how many consecutive frames you want to capture.

4. **Select length of capture.** You can capture all consecutive frames in the next 1, 2, 5, or 10 seconds of your video. Press the right button to first choose a destination (Slot 1 or Slot 2), and then select the number of seconds to be saved.

5. **Frames stored.** Your frames will be saved to the specified memory card.

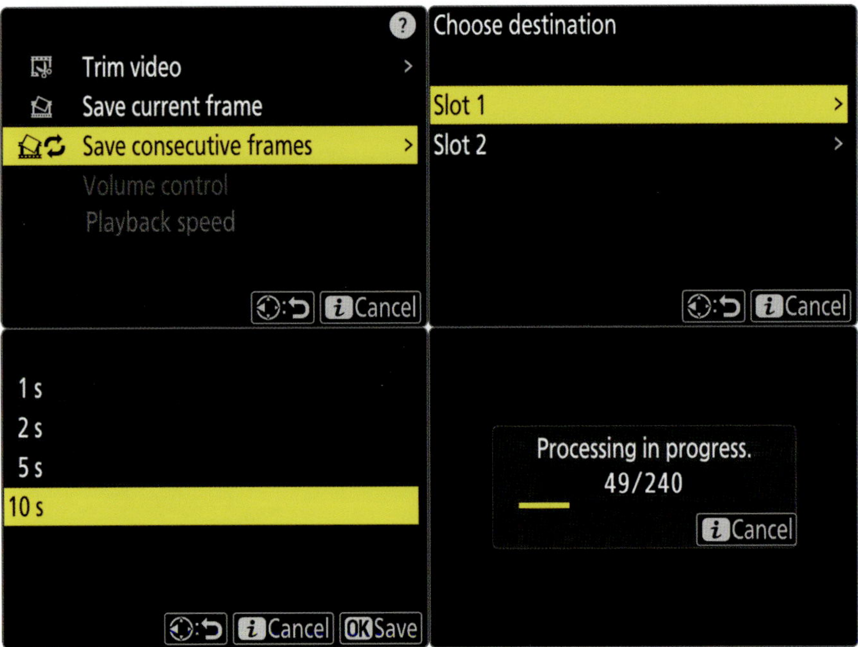

Figure 10.7 Capturing single or multiple frames from video.

Upping Your Video Game

Feature films have been shot entirely or in part using Nikon still cameras. Indeed, the Emmy-winning Showtime television series *Dexter* included many scenes captured with a Nikon camera. The Z5 II really upped the ante by incorporating video capabilities that have been enhanced or simply not available with previous Nikon still cameras. This section will provide a quick overview of some of the available tools.

Using an External Recorder

If you're truly becoming an advanced videographer, you'll probably be working with the camera's ability to output "clean" non-compressed HDMI video to an external monitor or video recorder, including the Atomos Shogun lineup, which includes versions that are quite affordable, at least in terms of professional video gear. You can choose models both with and without an external LCD monitor, and capture to solid-state drives (SSD), a laptop's internal or connected hard drive, or to CFast memory cards (the latter chiefly as a nod to those still using the "fast" version of Compact Flash cards). Such equipment allows very high transfer rates and is certainly your best choice if you're shooting 4K video.

Probably the best of the lot is the Atomos Ninja lineup, which launched with the original Ninja V shown in Figure 10.8 and was followed by the V+ and most recent Ninja and Ninja Ultra models. They are all extremely portable, roughly 13-ounce units with a 5.2-inch screen and price tags that are currently among the lowest for this type of device. Add a battery, HDMI cable, and a 2.5-inch solid-state drive, and you're ready to go.

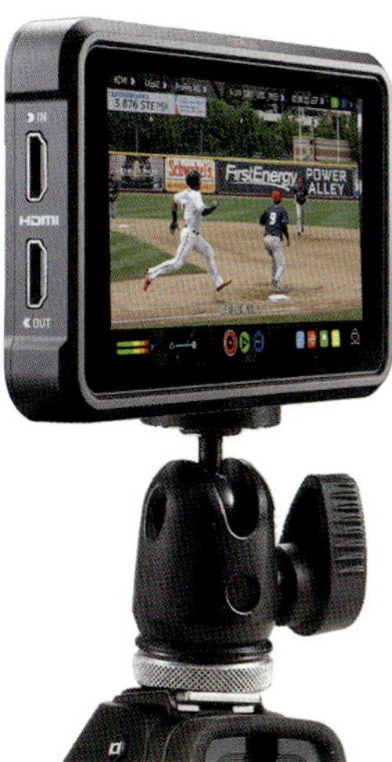

Figure 10.8 The Atomos Ninja V monitor/recorder.

The Ninja monitor-recorders have HDMI input and output jacks on their left edges, as shown in the figure, which allows you to daisy-chain an even larger monitor or other device. A power button, headphone jack, microphone/audio input, and remote jack reside on the other edge. The touch screen enables you to view your video and access the monitor/recorder's menus and controls, which is convenient (except outdoors in cold weather when you're wearing gloves and might wish you had a few buttons to press instead). The only other "defect" of the unit is the noise produced by its fan; even when you're using an external microphone, the fan noise may be picked up in a quiet room.

Why use an external monitor/recorder when your camera has its own nifty monitor and can store quite a lot of video on its memory cards? From a monitor standpoint, an external unit's screen is larger, easier to see, and offers more flexibility in positioning. The screen tilts up or down; mounted on a ballhead like the one in the figure, you can adjust an external screen to any angle, including reversing it to point in the same direction as the lens, so vloggers can monitor themselves as they record or stream their video blog.

External monitor-recorders are especially adept at displaying and storing video captured at high resolutions, fast frame rates, and demanding transfer speeds, using a variety of compression schemes. RAW video isn't actually compressed and is even more demanding. While the Z5 II can capture and store the full range of video types internally, an external recorder can be especially useful for those who do a great deal of videography.

The HDMI port accepts a Type D micro HDMI cable, which can be connected to the monitor, recorder, or other device of your choice. I use HDMI playback for slide shows, too, and captured most of the screenshot images in this book using the HDMI output and a $25 4K video-capture device with OBS (Open Broadcaster Software) Studio. Before you link up your equipment, you'll

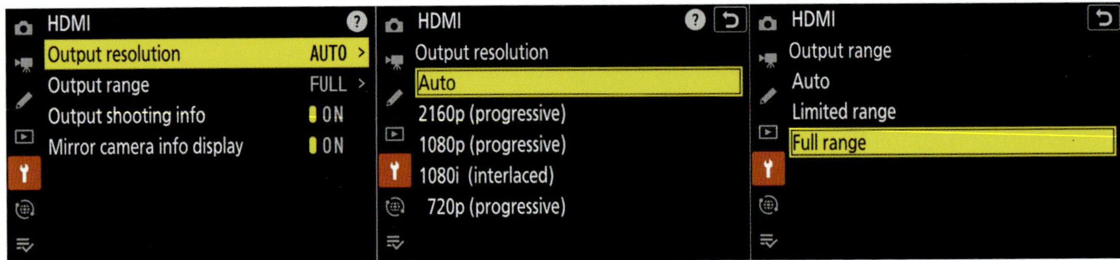

Figure 10.9 Choose output resolution and range.

want to choose from the following options of the HDMI menu entry found in the Setup menu, described in detail in Chapter 9 (see Figure 10.9, left):

- **Output resolution.** Select Auto and the camera will sense the correct output resolution to use. You can also choose specific resolutions, including 2160p (4K), 1080p (Full HD), and 720p (Standard HD), as shown in Figure 10.9, center. These are all progressive scan. You can also select 1080i if your device accepts only interlaced scanning. However, in that case, footage captured at 120p, 60p, 30p, or 24p are output at 60i, and 100p, 50p, or 25p are output at 50i.

  As noted in Chapter 9, 10-bit video is output at 10 bits only to HDMI recorders that support it.

- **Output range.** Choose Auto (the default, and the best choice under most circumstances), Limited Range, or Full Range. In most cases, the camera will be able to determine the output range of your HDMI device. If not, you can choose a range, as described in Chapter 9. (See Figure 10.9, right.)

- **Output shooting information.** Choose On, and the icons and shooting information shown on the electronic viewfinder or LCD monitor will be included in the output to the external device if you want that display included, say, to illustrate operation of the camera. Select Off and the information will be stripped out, leaving you with a clean recording.

- **Mirror camera information display.** When directing output to an external device, you may want to also have it shown on the rear LCD monitor (the default), especially if the external device is a monitor not physically attached to the camera. If you're using a recorder/display mounted on the camera or its cage, you can save some battery power by choosing Off for this item.

Additional HDMI settings are available in the Video Recording menu, described in Chapter 6. They include External Recording Control (HDMI) for devices that support control from the camera.

Tonal Grading

If you've been taking photos for a while, you're probably familiar with all the fixes and tweaks you can do with your still images within image editors like Photoshop. It's relatively easy to adjust color tones, contrast, sharpness, and other parameters prior to displaying or printing your photo. Videos are a little trickier, because any given video typically consists of *thousands* of individual photos, captured at 24 frames per second (or faster), with the possibility that each and every frame within a particular sequence might need fixes or creative adjustments.

Tonal control is one of the key parameters that determine the quality of your video, at least in terms of the dynamic range—the amount of detail in the deepest shadows and brightest highlights. The Z5 II can produce video with an excellent scale of tones, but for more serious productions there are several tools that allow extending the dynamic range using a post-processing tool called color grading.

TECH ALERT #1

Two terms you are likely to encounter, but don't really need to be concerned about (unless you're an advanced videographer) are encoding and bit transfer rate:

- **Encoding.** If you're sending "clean" video output to the HDMI port, while it is not compressed, it is *encoded* using a procedure called *chroma subsampling,* which does reduce the amount of information that needs to be transferred. Chroma subsampling takes advantage of the fact that human beings don't detect changes in color (chroma) as easily as they do for brightness (luma). The designation 4:2:2 simply indicates that the full amount of brightness information is passed along ("4") while the two chroma values are sampled at half that rate ("2:2"). Subsampling in this way reduces the bandwidth of the otherwise uncompressed video signal by as much as one-third with no visual difference.

- **Transfer bit rate.** This is the speed the camera outputs its video to your memory card or external recorder. High transfer rates require fast memory cards; an external recorder should be able to suck up video as quickly as your camera can deliver it.

Other terms will be explained in more detail later on.

TECH ALERT #2

Color grading is a highly technical aspect of video making, at least in terms of the amount of knowledge you need to possess to correctly judge what changing one of the parameters will do to your video. The rest of this section provides an overview with a quick description of the process, so you'll have a starting point when you start to explore advanced video techniques. It's not intended to be a complete guide to using N-log or HLG.

One way of increasing the range of tones in video is to shoot relatively low-contrast footage in order to capture the largest dynamic range possible and then fine-tune the rendition later using editing software. Nikon offers several dynamic range–enhancing features, including an N-log output option that provides low-contrast capture, which can then be manipulated using the *color grading* available in advanced video-processing software.

There are three basic capture modes that affect dynamic range:

- **Standard Dynamic Range.** When choosing a video file type in the Video Recording menu, SDR (Standard Dynamic Range) is one of two options available when shooting N-RAW 12-bit (NEV) video (discussed in the next section). If you select non-RAW H.265 10-bit (MOV) an additional option, HLG is available. SDR mode provides, as its name suggests, the basic "standard" range of tones, unless you modify that range using a Picture Control, most frequently the Flat picture control. Your footage will have relatively low contrast as shot but can be adjusted somewhat with advanced video-editing software.

- **HLG (Hybrid Log Gamma).** This is the second option available for H.265 10-bit (MOV) video file type. It is a high dynamic range recording method developed specifically for television video by a consortium of the British BBC and Japanese NHK broadcast organizations. HLG video, which also makes use of lookup tables, is available only when your video file type is H.265 10-bit (MOV). HLG is not available when using N-RAW.

- **N-Log.** The video file types listed above can also be captured using Nikon's proprietary logarithmic (non-linear) gamma algorithms. I'll explain gamma in more detail shortly. N-Log video can be displayed using something called a lookup table (LUT), which translates a value from one environment to one more suited to another environment. They're used to convert from one color space to another or, in this case, to translate tones captured using N-Log into colors/tones that can be handled by a monitor or other device. I'll describe LUTs in more detail, too.

RAW Truth

The ability to capture RAW video with the Z5 II—Nikon's most affordable Z-series camera—is noteworthy, providing easy access to high-end video editing capabilities to advanced videographers. Although the most sophisticated features of N-RAW are beyond the scope of this book, I'm going to provide a quick overview.

When you select N-RAW 12-bit (NEV) in the Video File Type entry of the Video Recording menu, the camera actually captures *two* video files simultaneously. One is the actual raw video, given an .NEV extension. The RAW video can only be viewed or edited with video software that supports the RAW format. Although you can save N-RAW video internally, you cannot edit it in the camera.

The second format captured at the same time as the N-RAW file is a Full HD 1920 × 1080 H.264 8-bit MP4 *proxy* video. The Z5 II displays the proxy video during playback, and Nikon's own NX Studio software also uses the proxy file instead of the N-RAW clip. Such lower-resolution proxy files are commonly used for editing because they make less demands on the computer system. When the basic editing is complete, the equivalent clips from the N-RAW file replace their proxy counterparts, using the timecodes to synchronize them.

One important difference with N-RAW is that the resolution of 4K video is slightly different. When not shooting RAW, the Z5 II captures 4K video with the standard 3840 × 2160 resolution. In N-Raw, the resolution is 4032 × 2268 pixels in FX video mode and 3984 × 2240 in DX video mode (both 30/25p or 24p).

These other adjustments are needed:

- **Choose SDR or N-Log.** You can select either of these two. HLG, described earlier in this chapter, is not available.

- **HDMI Output resolution limited.** If you're outputting your video to a monitor or recorder through the Z5 II's HDMI port, the maximum resolution available is 1920 × 1080.

- **Disabled features.** Active D-Lighting, High ISO Noise Reduction, Diffraction Compensation, Skin Softening, and Electronic VR are not available.

- **ISO Limitations:** Settings Hi 0.3 to Hi 2.0 cannot be selected.

Gamma, Gamma, Ding Dong

Grading is necessary thanks to our evolutionary heritage: humans don't see differences in tones in a linear manner. An absolutely smooth progression of pixels from absolute black to pure white (with 0 representing black and 256 representing white) would not look like a continuous gradient to our eyes. We'd be unable to detect differences in shadows and highlights that have the same change in tonal values as midtones. So, everything from computer monitors to printers use a correction factor (gamma) to cancel out the differences in the way we see tones.

This correction takes the form of a curve, called a *gamma curve.* If you remember your geometry, the x and y axes on a graph are used to define the shape of a curve, and in the case of gamma curves, the values use logarithmic units (ack!) to define the slope. That's where the term N-log, HLG (hybrid log gamma), and other mind-numbing jargon comes from. The whole shebang is needed to reconcile the ability of sensors to capture, video systems to display, and printers to output a range of tones in a linear way with the actual tones we perceive non-linearly. Gamma correction and gamma compression are used to help make sure that what we get is what we see. While gamma correction between computer platforms (that is, between Macs and PCs) may be different, the actual gamma values defined by video standards like NTSC and PAL are fixed and well-known.

N-log

As I noted above, the digital images we work with are always adjusted using a gamma curve, which changes the relative brightness/darkness of highlights, midtones, and shadows so they more closely resemble how the human eye sees them. You probably have worked with gamma curves if you calibrated your computer monitor or printer. There's really no need to have a deep understanding of the math involved in order to optimize the look of your images or video. And Nikon doesn't ask you to. But it does offer tools like N-log to let you improve their appearance.

TECH ALERT #3

In a camera, changes in sensor sensitivity or exposure are indicated using ISO settings, shutter speeds, or f/stops (for example, f/2 provides twice as much light as f/2.8 which, in turn, provides twice as much light as f/4). Unfortunately, that constant doubling is an inefficient way of storing information; the numbers quickly become too large to fit into the number of bits available to store them.

A much more efficient way to store the same visual information is to use logarithms instead. Those of us who never got much beyond algebra in math class will be happy to know that logarithms can simply be thought of as the flip side of linear visual information. Instead of doubling the number of pixels for each brightness increment, a log scale just increases the same amount for each step. That lets you specify many more brightness levels within the same storage space. Gamma curves/correction are a way of converting captured linear information into a more efficient logarithmic curve.

N-log is a logarithmic gamma curve that is used when the video will be processed after shooting and captures a much larger range of tones (roughly up to 14 stops!) than standard gamma curves. Indeed, the tones captured using N-log can't be displayed in all their glory on a standard TV or monitor, which are generally adjusted for the broadcast television BT-709 standard. Instead, the unprocessed video will look darker and lower in contrast because all those tonal values have been squeezed into the BT-709 (also called REC-709) range. You can enable Custom Setting g11: View Assist to adjust the *appearance* during preview of video recorded using N-Log or HLG (described next); while the colors are simplified and contrast increased, the actual recorded video is not changed.

To enable correcting brightness, saturation, and hue as you work with the expanded dynamic range during editing, you need a lookup table (LUT), as mentioned earlier. The LUT is an array of prese-lected values that map the colors contained in the original captured input to the desired colors of the final video. N-log creates a 3D LUT that assigns each RGB value to a single combined value in the table. You can use this LUT to perform color grading with software including Adobe Premier Pro CC, Apple Final Cut Pro X, and BlackMagic Design DaVinci Resolve 18.

In September 2024, Nikon released five LUTs based on color science developed by RED Digital Cinema, a digital cinematography company acquired by Nikon earlier that year. The downloads include two technical LUTs, which take log format footage and convert it for viewing, and three creative LUTs used to add particular looks to the video.

Video signals normally encompass brightness levels from 0 percent to 110 percent (you read that right: modern video cameras can record detail in highlights that are actually brighter than was possible when the video age began; the old scale was retained, reminiscent of Nigel Tufnel's 11 setting on his amp). However, even the 110 percent provides too much of a limitation; cameras can capture detail in highlights that are even brighter than *that.* So, a log gamma curve (in this case one called N-log) is used to *compress* all that image detail to fit into the space allowed for conventional video signals.

Post-processing and grading in a video editor allows working with all that information and produces a finished video that contains the filmmaker's selection of tonal values in a form that can be displayed comfortably. The full dynamic range can be used to produce the finished movie. You might find that useful when exposing for highlights while avoiding blowing out the sky, or for capturing detail in shadows without losing mid tones and highlights. N-log gives you even better results than using the Flat Picture control, which was also introduced with exactly this application in mind.

RESTRICTIONS

While capturing N-log, Picture Controls, Skin Softening, Portrait Impression Balance, Active D-Lighting, and High ISO NR are disabled. Maximum ISO Sensitivity can only be set in the range ISO 1600–51200, and the lowest recommended value for ISO Sensitivity (Mode M) is ISO 800. (Remember that ISO 800 is the second of the two "base" ISOs available with the Z5 II's dual-gain sensor.) However, you can also choose Lo 0.3 to Lo 2.0 if you can tolerate a decrease in highlight data. You may see some noise or flicker in the LCD monitor. Finally, you'll need to visit the Timecode entry of the Video Recording menu and select On (With HDMI Output) to direct timecodes to the recorder.

HLG/HDR

A new wrinkle in the Nikon toolkit is the addition of HLG (Hybrid-Log Gamma) output, which produces a type of HDR footage used for broadcast video. Note that HDR in video terms is *not* the same thing as HDR for stills (which requires multiple exposures combined into one final image). HLG video is produced by extending the dynamic range of the original captured frames.

One problem with the original implementation of HDR video is that it could only be displayed on an HDR-capable television. So, two of the biggest gorillas in the broadcast industry, BBC and NHK, developed Hybrid-Log Gamma, which produces video that can show HDR content on non-HDR displays. Direct the same video to a 4K television with HLG/HDR support, and it will play back with the increased contrast, brighter highlights, and larger color gamut possible with high dynamic range video.

Refocusing on Focus

Although I explained autofocus and manual focus options in Chapter 5, there are some special considerations for focus when capturing video. The availability of usable AF when capturing movies, thanks to the on-sensor phase-detection autofocus (PDAF), is extremely important. The camera is now able to gauge subject distance and track and refocus on subjects reliably; you really don't want inaccurate focus in video clips, where inconsistent focus is quite obvious when the movie is viewed.

Your three autofocus modes work extremely well. AF-S focuses once and is useful for non-moving subjects; AF-C refocuses only while you're holding down the shutter release or designated AF-ON button. That's particularly useful when you want to retain focus on a particular subject but refocus at your command as needed when the subject moves. AF-F (Full-time AF) is available if you need to refocus constantly as you capture. Use Custom Setting g5: AF Speed to control whether the camera refocuses quickly to follow a moving subject or refocuses more slowly to switch from one subject to another. Custom Setting g6: AF Tracking Sensitivity can enable/disable the ability to switch quickly when a different subject intervenes between the camera and the original subject. Both these fine-tuning behaviors can be used creatively to concentrate/deconcentrate attention on a particular subject or area of the frame.

Manual focus, with help from Custom Setting a12: Focus Peaking, is an option, particularly for those who want to "pull" or "push" focus, a creative technique for redirecting the viewer's attention from one subject to another, located in the foreground or background. The only complication is that the focus isn't particularly linear, so a certain degree of rotation of the focus/control ring doesn't necessarily result in the same amount of adjustment of the focus. I discussed this problem and its solutions in Chapter 3 in the section "Using the Focus/Control Ring."

Shooting Better Video

Producing good-quality video is more complicated than just buying good equipment and learning how to use it. There are techniques that make for gripping storytelling and a visual language the average person is very accustomed to seeing, but also unaware of. After all, by comparison we're used to watching the best productions that television, video, and motion pictures can offer. Whether it's fair or not, our efforts are compared to what we're used to seeing produced by experts. While this book can't make you a professional videographer, there is some advice I can give you that will help you improve your results. There are many different things to consider when planning a video shoot, and when possible, a shooting script and storyboard can help you produce a higher-quality video.

Lens Craft

A discussion of why lens selection is important when shooting movies may be useful at this point. In the video world, not all lenses are created equal. The two most important considerations are depth-of-field, or the beneficial lack thereof, and zooming. I'll address each of these separately.

Depth-of-Field and Video

One thing that makes digital still cameras so attractive for video is that they have relatively large sensors, which provides improved low-light performance and results in the oddly attractive reduced depth-of-field, compared with many professional video cameras.

But wait! you say. No matter what size sensor is used to capture a video frame, isn't the number of pixels in that frame the same? That's true—the final resolution of a Full HD 1080p video image is exactly 1920 × 1080 pixels. For standard HD (720p) the resolution is 1280 × 720 pixels (which the Z5 II does not offer), and for Ultra HD/4K (2160p) the resolution is 3840 × 2160 pixels. The final resolution, at least for the most common 1080p resolution, is the same, whether you're capturing that frame with a point-and-shoot camera, a professional video camera, or a digital SLR. But that's only the *final* resolution. The number of pixels used to *originally* capture each video frame varies by sensor size.

For example, your camera does *not* use only its central 1920 × 1080 pixels to capture a Full HD video frame. If it did that, you'd have to contend with a huge "crop" factor. That doesn't happen! Instead, the camera captures a video frame using an area that stretches across nearly the full width of the sensor, using the *proportions* of a 16:9 area of its sensor. That's true for *all* HD formats: Full HD (1080p), and Ultra HD (4K, 2160p). Your wide-angle and telephoto lenses retain roughly their same fields of view, and you can frame and compose your video through the viewfinder normally, with only the top and bottom of the frame cropped off to account for the wider video aspect ratio. (See Figure 10.10.)

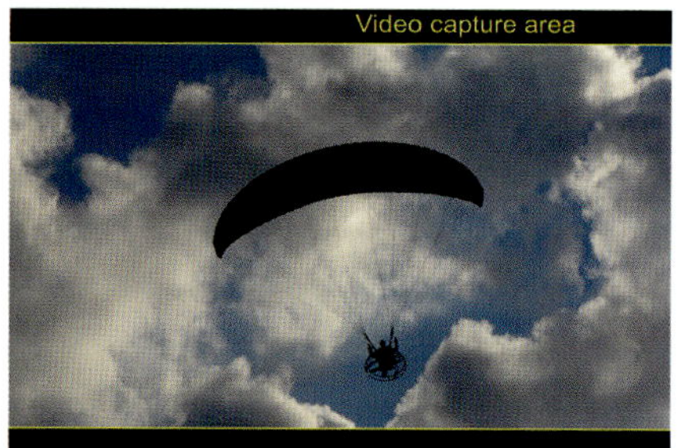

Figure 10.10 The cropped video capture area for HD movies.

A larger sensor calls for the use of longer focal lengths to produce the same field of view, so, in effect, a larger sensor has reduced depth-of-field. And *that's* what makes cameras like the Z5 II attractive from a creative standpoint. Less depth-of-field means greater control over the range of what's in focus. Your camera, with its full-frame sensor, has a distinct advantage over consumer camcorders in this regard, and even does a better job than many professional video cameras. (Some professional video cameras do use large sensors.) Figure 10.11 compares some typical sensor sizes.

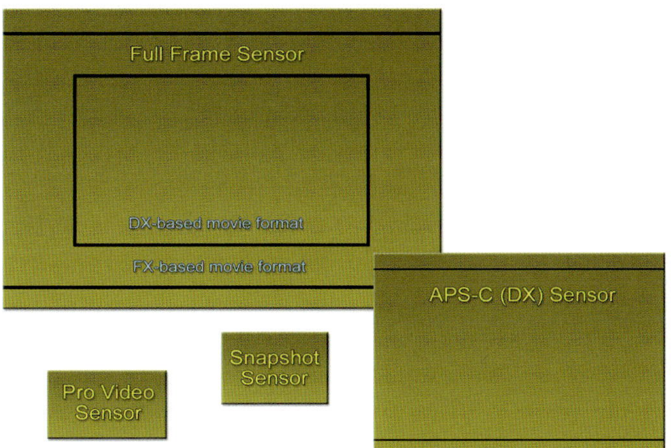

Figure 10.11 Relative size of full frame, DX, snapshot, and pro-video sensors.

Zooming and Video

When shooting still photos, a zoom is a zoom is a zoom. The key considerations for a zoom lens used only for still photography are the maximum aperture available at each focal length ("How *fast* is this lens?"), the zoom range ("How far can I zoom in or out?"), and its sharpness at any given f/stop ("Do I lose sharpness when I shoot wide open?").

When shooting video, the priorities may change, and there are two additional parameters to consider. The first two I listed, lens speed and zoom range, have roughly the same importance in both still and video photography. Zoom range gains a bit of importance in videography, because you can usually move closer to shoot a still photograph, but when you're zooming during a shot most of us don't have that option (or the funds to buy/rent a dolly to smoothly move the camera during capture).

Oddly enough, overall sharpness may have slightly less importance under certain conditions when shooting video. That's because the image changes in some way many times per second (24/30/60/120 times per second), so any given frame doesn't hang around long enough for our eyes to pick out every single detail. You want a sharp image, of course, but your standards don't need to be quite as high when shooting video. Before purchasing any new lens that will be used for video, I recommend checking out discussions in online forums to see what videographers think of those optics. You'll find valuable information about the considerations listed below, as well as the pros and cons of other features, such as the ability to "de-click" the aperture (for silent f/stop changes) or accuracy of the aperture settings (videographers may prefer "T-stops," which represent actual light transmission, over f/stops).

Here are the most important considerations for video shooters:

- **Zoom lens maximum aperture.** The speed of the lens matters in several ways. A zoom with a relatively large maximum aperture lets you shoot in lower light levels, and a big f/stop allows you to minimize depth-of-field for selective focus. Keep in mind that the maximum aperture may change during zooming. A lens that offers an f/3.5 maximum aperture at its widest focal length may provide only f/5.6 worth of light at the telephoto position.

- **Zoom range.** Use of zoom during actual capture should not be an everyday thing unless you're shooting a kung-fu movie. However, there are effective uses for a zoom shot, particularly if it's a "long" one from extreme wide angle to extreme close-up (or vice versa). Most of the time, you'll use the zoom range to adjust the perspective *between* shots, and a longer zoom range can mean less trotting back and forth to adjust the field of view. Zoom range also comes into play when you're working with selective focus (longer focal lengths have less depth-of-field) or want to expand or compress the apparent distance between foreground and background subjects. A longer range gives you more flexibility.

- **Linearity.** Interchangeable lenses may have some drawbacks, as many photographers who have been using the video features of their interchangeable-lens digital cameras have discovered. That's because, unless a lens is optimized for video recording, zooming with a particular lens may not necessarily be linear. Rotating the zoom collar manually at a constant speed doesn't always produce a smooth zoom. There may be "jumps" as the elements of the lens shift around during the zoom.

  Focus may be linear or non-linear, as well. By default, if you rotate the ring of Z-mount lenses quickly, the focus plane is adjusted by a large amount. Slower rotation produces adjustments in smaller increments. As I noted in Chapter 7, because Nikon Z-mount autofocus lenses use focus by wire, it's much easier to design them to focus in a linear manner when that's desirable. Using Custom Setting f10: Focus Ring Rotation Range, you can switch from the default non-linear response to fixed focus behavior over a rotational range from 90 to 720 degrees.

  Linear focus characteristics are useful for movie-making, since any focus changes made *while capturing video* can be seen in the footage. It's essential if you're using selective focus with pull- or push-focus techniques. In either case, the focus adjustment needs to be smooth rather than jerky.

Keeping Things Stable and on the Level

Camera shake's enough of a problem with still photography, but it becomes even more of a nuisance when you're shooting video. The image-stabilization feature found in many Nikon lenses (and some third-party optics) can help minimize this. That's why Nikon's VR-capable zoom lenses (described in Chapter 7) make an excellent choice for video recording if you're planning on going for the hand-held cinema verité look.

The camera also has an *electronic VR* option, which I've described several times in this book. It's not available when capturing N-RAW 12-bit (NEV) video, Full HD 120/100 fps rates, or when shooting slow-motion video. To recap, electronic vibration reduction reduces the frame size by about 10 percent and uses the extra image area to realign the frames to counteract any camera motion.

Just realize that while hand-held camera shots—even image stabilized—may be perfect if you're shooting a documentary or video that intentionally mimics traditional home movie making, in other contexts it can be disconcerting or annoying. And even VR can't work miracles. As I'll point out in the next section, it's the camera movement itself that is distracting—not necessarily any blur in our subject matter.

If you want your video to look professional, putting the camera on a tripod will give you smoother, steadier video clips to work with. It will be easier to intercut shots taken from different angles (or even at different times) if everything was shot on a tripod. Cutting from a tripod shot to a hand-held shot, or even from one hand-held shot to another one that has noticeably more (or less) camera movement can call attention to what otherwise might have been a smooth cut or transition.

Remember that telephoto lenses and telephoto zoom focal lengths magnify any camera shake, even with VR, so when you're using a longer focal length, that tripod becomes an even better idea. Tripods are essential if you want to pan from side to side during a shot, dolly in and out, or track from side to side (say, you want to shoot with the camera in your kid's coaster wagon). A tripod and (for panning) a fluid head built especially for smooth video movements can add a lot of production value to your movies.

ROLL ON, SHUTTER

Another side-effect to watch out for occurs when panning or capturing moving subjects, caused by the *rolling shutter.* Because your camera captures all the horizontal lines one at a time, the last line in a frame is captured a fraction of a second after the first line. So, if the subject or camera is moving from side to side, a vertical subject will appear to lean in the direction opposite the camera's movement, causing what is termed a "Jell-O effect." There's no way to eliminate this defect, but you should be aware of it when shooting. You may be able to edit offending clips out of your finished video.

Shooting Script

A shooting script is nothing more than a coordinated plan that covers both audio and video and provides order and structure for your video when you're in planned, storytelling mode. A detailed script will cover what types of shots you're going after, what dialogue you're going to use, audio effects, transitions, and graphics. A good script needn't constrain you: as the director you are free to make changes on the spot during actual capture. But, before you change the route to your final destination, it's good to know where you were headed, and how you originally planned to get there.

When putting together your shooting script, plan for lots and lots of different shots, even if you don't think you'll need them. Only amateurish videos consist of a bunch of long, tedious shots. You'll want to vary the pace of your production by cutting among lots of different views, angles, and perspectives, so jot down your ideas for these variations when you put together your script.

If you're shooting a documentary rather than telling a story that's already been completely mapped out, the idea of using a shooting script needs to be applied more flexibly. Documentary filmmakers often have no shooting script at all. They go out, do their interviews, capture video of people, places, and events as they find them, and allow the structure of the story to take shape as they learn more about the subject of their documentary. In such cases, the movie is typically "created" during editing, as bits and pieces are assembled into the finished piece.

Storyboards

A storyboard makes a great adjunct to a detailed shooting script. It is a series of panels providing visuals of what each scene should look like. While the ones produced by Hollywood are generally of very high quality, there's nothing that says drawing skills are important for this step. Stick figures work just fine if that's the best you can do. The storyboard just helps you visualize locations, placement of actors, props, and furniture, and helps everyone involved get an idea of what you're trying to show. It also helps show how you want to frame or compose a shot. You can even shoot a series of still photos and transform them into a "storyboard" if you want, such as in Figure 10.12.

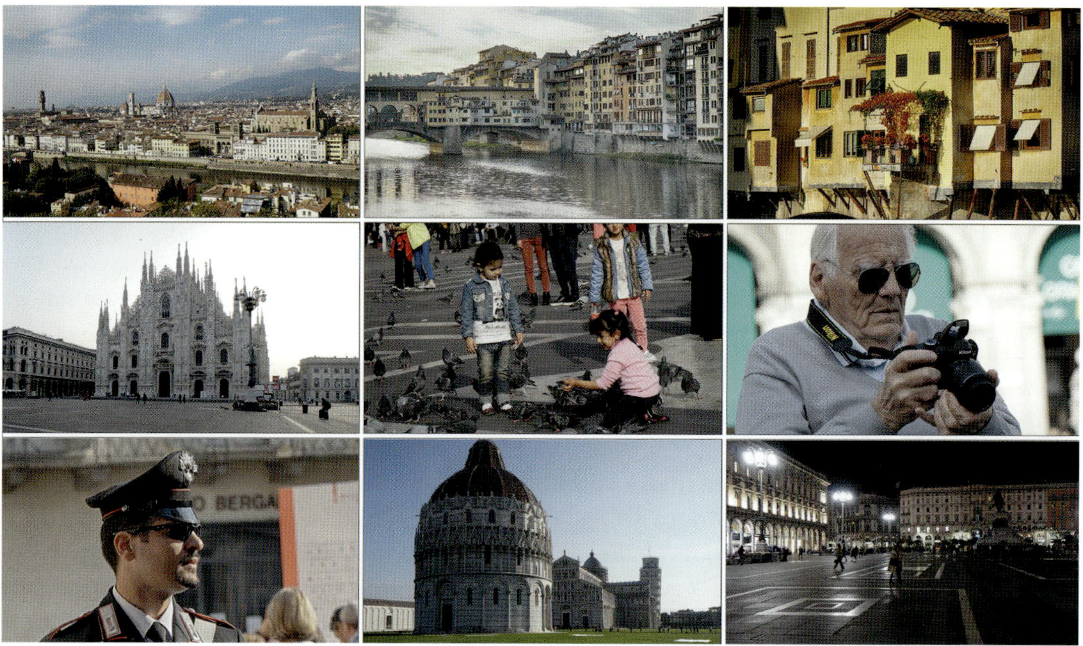

Figure 10.12 A storyboard is a series of simple sketches or photos to help visualize a segment of video.

Storytelling in Video

Today's audience is used to fast-paced, short-scene storytelling. To produce interesting video for such viewers, it's important to view video storytelling as a kind of shorthand code for the more leisurely efforts print media offers. Audio and video should always be advancing the story. While it's okay to let the camera linger from time to time, it should only be for a compelling reason and only briefly. Above all, look for movement in your scene as you shoot. You're not taking still photographs!

It only takes a second or two for an establishing shot to impart the necessary information. For example, many of the scenes for a video documenting a model being photographed in a rock 'n' roll music setting might be close-ups and talking heads, but an establishing shot showing the studio where the video was captured helps set the scene.

Provide variety too. If you put your shooting script together correctly, you'll be changing camera angles and perspectives often and never leave a static scene on the screen for a long period of time. (You can record a static scene for a reasonably long period and then edit in other shots that cut away and back to the longer scene with close-ups that show each person talking.)

When editing, keep transitions basic! I can't stress this one enough. Watch a television program or movie. The action "jumps" from one scene or person to the next. Fancy transitions that involve exotic "wipes," dissolves, or cross fades take too long for the average viewer and make your video ponderous.

Composition

In movie shooting, several factors restrict your composition and impose requirements you just don't always have in still photography (although other rules of good composition do apply). Here are some of the key differences to keep in mind when composing movie frames:

- **Horizontal compositions only.** Some subjects, such as basketball players and tall buildings, just lend themselves to vertical compositions. But movies are shown in horizontal format only. So, if you're interviewing a local basketball star, you can end up with a worst-case situation like the one shown in Figure 10.13. If you want to show how tall your subject is, it's often impractical to move back far enough to show him full-length. You really can't capture a vertical composition. Tricks like getting down on the floor and shooting up at your subject can exaggerate the perspective but aren't a perfect solution.

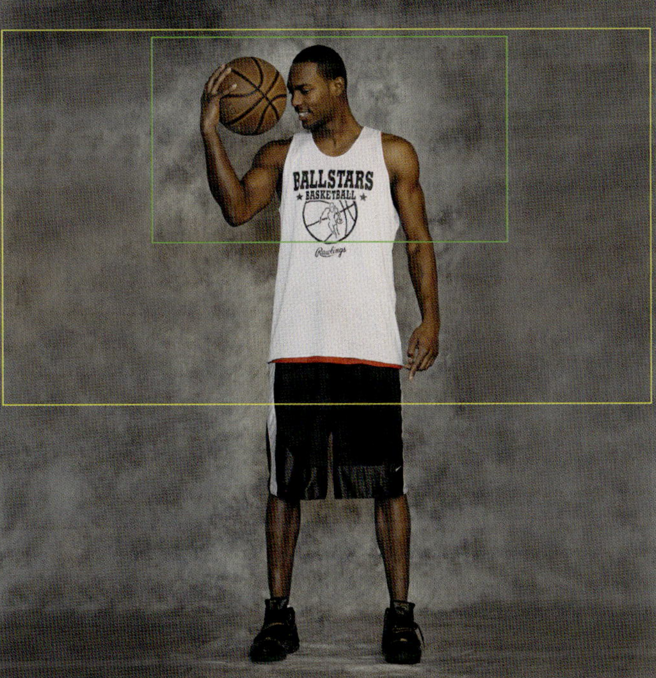

Figure 10.13 Video Recording requires you to fit all your subjects into a horizontally oriented frame.

- **Wasted space at the sides.** Moving in to frame the basketball player as outlined by the yellow box in Figure 10.13 means that you're still forced to leave a lot of empty space on either side. (Of course, you can fill that space with other people and/or interesting stuff, but that defeats your intent of concentrating on your main subject.) So, when faced with some types of subjects in a horizontal frame, you can be creative or move in *really* tight. For example, if I were willing to give up the "height" aspect of my composition, I could have framed the shot as shown by the green box in the figure and wasted less of the image area at either side.

- **Seamless (or seamed) transitions.** Unless you're telling a picture story with a photo essay, still pictures often stand alone. But with movies, each of your compositions must relate to the shot that preceded it, and the one that follows. It can be jarring to jump from a long shot to a tight close-up unless the director—you—is very creative. Another common error is the "jump cut" in which successive shots vary only slightly in camera angle, making it appear that the main subject has "jumped" from one place to another. (Although everyone from French New Wave director Jean-Luc Goddard to Guy Ritchie—Madonna's ex—have used jump cuts effectively in their films.) The rule of thumb is to vary the camera angle by at least 30 degrees between shots to make it appear to be seamless. Unless you prefer that your images flaunt convention and appear to be "seamy."

- **The time dimension.** Unlike still photography, with motion pictures there's a lot more emphasis on using a series of images to build on each other to tell a story. Static shots where the camera is mounted on a tripod and everything is shot from the same distance are a recipe for dull videos. Watch a television program sometime and notice how often camera shots change distances and directions. Viewers are used to this variety and have come to expect it. Professional video productions are often done with multiple cameras shooting from different angles and positions. But many professional productions are shot with just one camera and careful planning, and you can do just fine with your camera.

Here's a look at the different types of commonly used compositional tools:

- **Establishing shot.** Much as it sounds, this type of composition, as shown in Figure 10.14, upper left, establishes the scene and tells the viewer where the action is taking place. Let's say you're shooting a video of your offspring's move to college; the establishing shot could be a wide shot of the campus with a sign welcoming you to the school in the foreground. Another example would be for a child's birthday party; the establishing shot could be the front of the house decorated with birthday signs and streamers or a shot of the dining room table decked out with party favors and a candle-covered birthday cake. In the example, I wanted to show the studio where the video was shot.

- **Medium shot.** This shot is composed from about waist to head room (some space above the subject's head). It's useful for providing variety from a series of close-ups and makes for a useful first look at a speaker. A medium shot is used to bring the viewer into a scene without shocking them. It can be used to introduce a character and provide context via their surroundings. (See Figure 10.14, upper right.)

- **Close-up.** The close-up, usually described as "from shirt pocket to head room," provides a good composition for someone talking directly to the camera. Although it's common to have your talking head centered in the shot, that's not a requirement. In Figure 10.14, center left, the subject was offset to the right. This would allow other images, especially graphics or titles, to be superimposed in the frame in a "real" (professional) production. But the compositional technique can be used with camera videos, too, even if special effects are not going to be added. A close-up generally shows the full face with a little head room at the top and down to the shoulders at the bottom of the frame.

- **Extreme close-up.** When I went through broadcast training, this shot was described as the "big talking face" shot and we were actively discouraged from employing it. Styles and tastes change over the years and now the big talking face is much more commonly used (Maybe people are better looking these days?) and so this view may be appropriate. Just remember, your camera

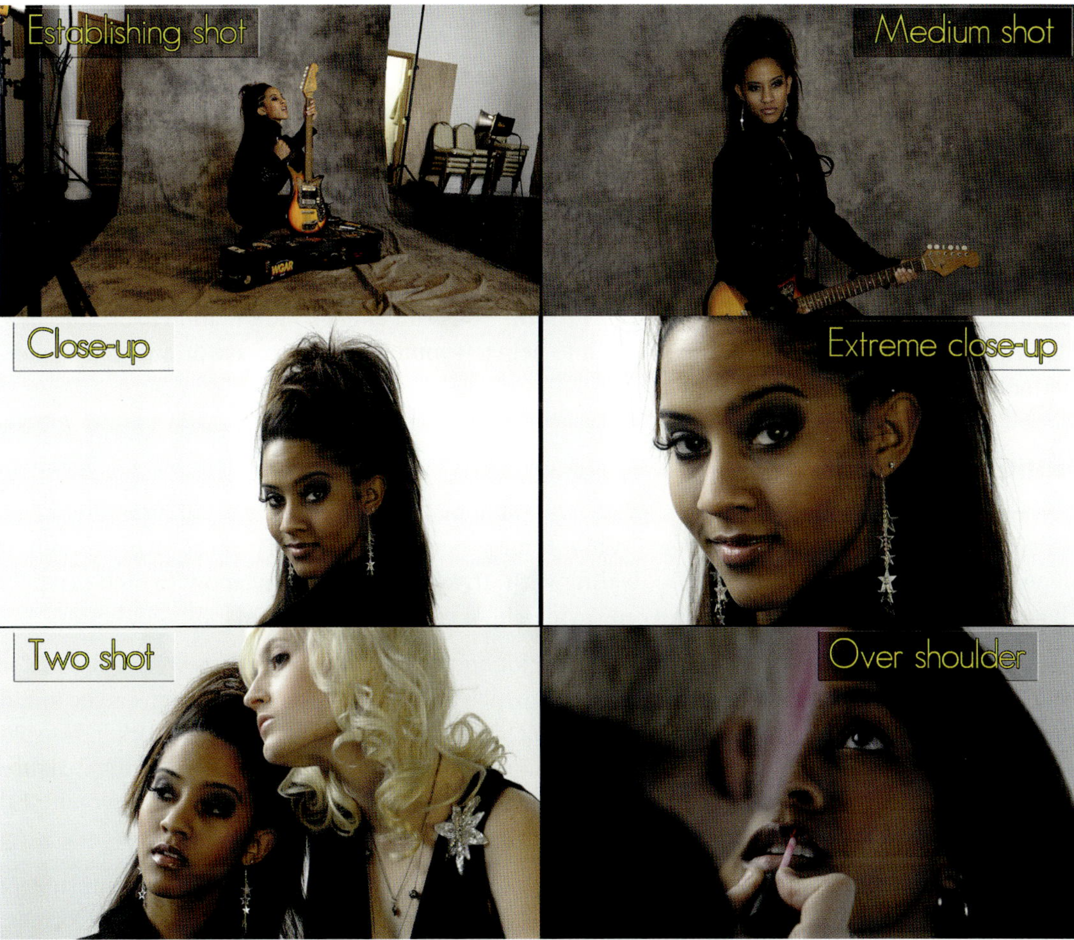

Figure 10.14 Use a full range of shot types.

is capable of shooting in high-definition video, and you may be playing the video on a high-def TV; be careful that you use this composition on a face that can stand up to high definition. (See Figure 10.14, center right.) An extreme close-up is a very tight shot that cuts off everything above the top of the head and below the chin (or even closer!). Be careful using this shot since many of us look better from a distance!

- **Two shot.** A two shot shows a pair of subjects in one frame. They can be side by side or one in the foreground and one in the background. (See Figure 10.14, lower left.) This does not have to be a head-to-ground composition. Subjects can be standing or seated. A "three shot" is the same principle except that three people are in the frame. This version can be framed at various distances such as medium or close-up.

- **Over-shoulder shot.** Long a composition of interview programs, the "over-shoulder shot" uses the rear of one person's head and shoulder to serve as a frame for the other person. This puts the viewer's perspective as that of the person facing away from the camera. (See Figure 10.14, lower right.) An "over-shoulder shot" is a popular shot for interview programs. It helps make the viewers feel like they're the one asking the questions.

Lighting for Video

Much like in still photography, how you handle light pretty much can make or break your videography. Lighting for video can be more complicated than lighting for still photography, since both subject and camera movement are often part of the process.

Lighting for video presents several concerns. First off, you want enough illumination to create a useable video. Beyond that, you want to use light to help tell your story or increase drama. Let's take a better look at both.

Illumination

You can significantly improve the quality of your video by increasing the light falling in the scene. This is true indoors or out, by the way. While it may seem like sunlight is more than enough, it depends on how much contrast you're dealing with. If your subject is in shadow (which can help them from squinting) or wearing a ball cap, a video light can help make them look a lot better.

Lighting choices for amateur videographers are a lot better these days than they were a decade or two ago. An inexpensive incandescent video light, which will easily fit in a camera bag, can be found for $15 or $20. You can even get a good-quality LED video light for less than $100. Work lights sold at many home improvement stores can also serve as video lights since you can set the white balance to correct for any color casts. You'll need to mount these lights on a tripod or other support, or, perhaps, to a bracket that fastens to the tripod socket on the bottom of the camera.

Much of the challenge depends upon whether you're just trying to add some fill-light on your subject versus trying to boost the light on an entire scene. A small video light will do just fine for the former; it won't handle the latter. Fortunately, the versatility of the camera comes in quite handy here. Since the camera shoots video in Auto ISO mode, it can compensate for lower lighting levels and still produce a decent image. For best results though, better lighting is necessary.

Creative Lighting

While ramping up the light intensity will produce better technical quality in your video, it won't necessarily improve the artistic quality of it. Whether we're outdoors or indoors, we're used to seeing light come from above. Videographers need to consider how they position their lights to provide even illumination while up high enough to angle shadows down low and out of sight of the camera.

When lighting for video, there are several factors to consider. One is the quality of the light. It can either be hard (direct) light or soft (diffused) light. Hard light is good for showing detail but can also be very harsh and unforgiving. "Softening" the light, but diffusing it somehow, can reduce the intensity of the light but make for a kinder, gentler light as well.

While mixing light sources isn't always a good idea, one approach is to combine window light with supplemental lighting. Position your subject with the window to one side and bring in either a supplemental light or a reflector to the other side for reasonably even lighting.

Lighting Styles

Some lighting styles are more heavily used than others. Some forms are used for special effects, while others are designed to be invisible. At its most basic, lighting just illuminates the scene, but when used properly it can also create drama. Let's look at some types of lighting styles:

- **Three-point lighting.** This is a basic lighting setup for one person. A main light illuminates the strong side of a person's face, while a fill light lights up the other side. A third light is then positioned above and behind the subject to light the back of the head and shoulders. (See Figure 10.15, left.)

- **Flat lighting.** Use this type of lighting to provide illumination and nothing more. It calls for a variety of lights and diffusers set to raise the light level in a space enough for good video reproduction, but not to create a mood or emphasize a scene or individual. With flat lighting, you're trying to create even lighting levels throughout the video space and minimize any shadows. Generally, the lights are placed up high and angled downward (or possibly pointed straight up to bounce off a white ceiling). (See Figure 10.15, right.)

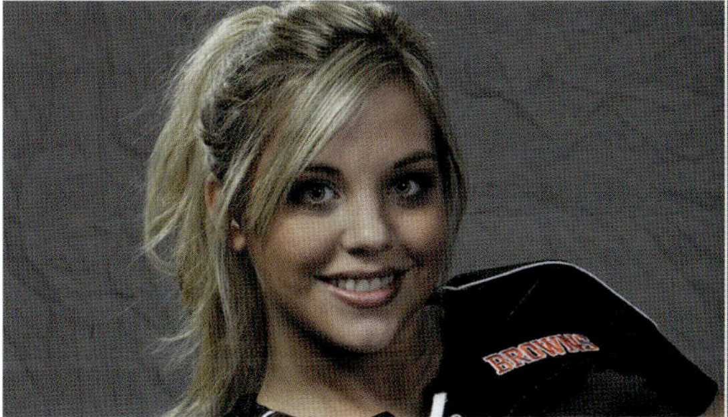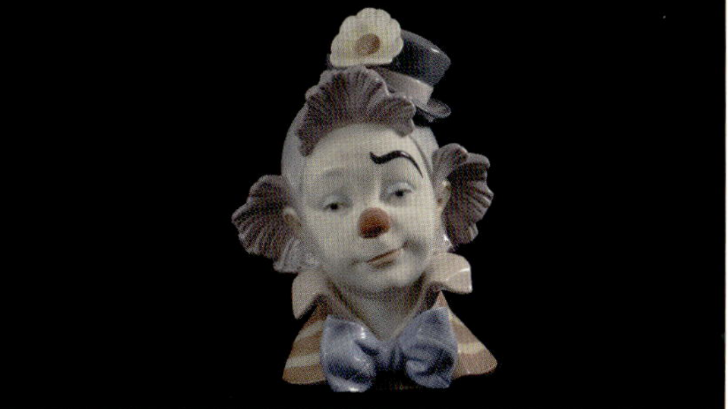

Figure 10.15 With three-point lighting (left) two lights are placed in front and to the side of the subject and another light is directed on the background to provide separation. Flat lighting (right) was bounced off a white ceiling and walls to fill in shadows as much as possible. It is a flexible lighting approach since the subject can change positions without needing a change in light direction.

- **"Ghoul lighting."** This is the style of lighting used for old horror movies. The idea is to position the light down low, pointed upward. It's such an unnatural style of lighting that it makes its targets seem weird and "ghoulish."

- **Outdoor lighting.** While shooting outdoors may seem easier because the sun provides more light, it also presents its own problems. As a rule of thumb, keep the sun behind you when you're shooting video outdoors, except when shooting faces (anything from a medium shot and closer) since the viewer won't want to see a squinting subject. When shooting another human this way, put the sun behind her and use a video light to balance light levels between the foreground and background. If the sun is simply too bright, position the subject in the shade and use the video light for your main illumination. Using reflectors (white board panels or aluminum foil–covered cardboard panels are cheap options) can also help balance light effectively.

Audio

When it comes to making a successful video, audio quality is one of those things that separates the professionals from the amateurs. We're used to watching top-quality productions on television and in the movies, yet the average person has no idea how much effort goes in to producing what seems to be "natural" sound. Much of the sound you hear in such productions is recorded on carefully controlled sound stages and "sweetened" with a variety of sound effects and other recordings of "natural" sound. Google "Foley artist" some time and you'll discover this part of a production is, indeed, a rich and complex art form.

Tips for Better Audio

Since recording high-quality audio is such a challenge, it's a good idea to do everything possible to maximize recording quality. Your Z5 II has a stereo microphone located on each side of the viewfinder housing (what we called a pentaprism in the SLR days). Audio is recorded in 16-bit stereo with a 48 kHz sampling rate, with the sound quality basically limited by the quality of your microphone. While the Z5 II's microphone is good, you'll get better quality from a dedicated external mic. Here are some specific ideas for improving the quality of the audio your camera records:

- **Get the camera and its microphone close to the speaker.** The farther the microphone is from the audio source, the less effective it will be in picking up that sound. While having to position the camera and its built-in microphone closer to the subject affects your lens choices and lens perspective options, it will make the most of your audio source. Of course, if you're using a very wide-angle lens, getting too close to your subject can have unflattering results, so don't take this advice too far. It's important to think carefully about what sounds you want to capture. If you're shooting video of an acoustic combo that's not using a PA system, you'll want the microphone close to them, but not so close that, say, only the lead singer or instrumentalist is picked up, while the players at either side fade off into the background.

- **Use an external microphone.** You'll recall the description of the external microphone port in Chapter 1. As noted, this port accepts a stereo mini-plug from a standard external microphone, allowing you to achieve considerably higher audio quality for your movies than is possible with the built-in microphones (which are disabled when an external mic is plugged in). An external microphone reduces the amount of camera-induced noise that is picked up and recorded on your audio track. (The action of the lens as it focuses can be audible when the built-in microphones are active.)

The external microphone port can provide plug-in power for microphones that can take their power from this sort of outlet rather than from a battery in the microphone. Nikon provides optional compatible microphones such as the ME-1 (see Figure 10.16); you also may find suitable microphones from companies such as Shure and Audio-Technica. If you are on a quest for superior audio quality, you can even obtain a portable mixer that can plug into this jack, such as the affordable Rolls MX401, letting you use multiple high-quality microphones (up to four) to record your soundtrack.

An exciting option designed specifically for still cameras is the Beachtek DXA-MAX 2 audio adapter. It's more expensive but has even more professional sound options and clips right onto the bottom of your camera using the tripod-mounting socket.

One advantage that a sound-mixing device offers over the stock camera is that it adds an additional headphone output jack to your camera, so you can monitor the sound actually being captured by the recorder (you can also listen to your soundtrack through the headphones during playback, which is *way* better than using the built-in speaker). The adapter has two balanced XLR microphone inputs and can also accept line input (from another audio source) and provides cool features like AGC (automatic gain control), built-in limiting, and VU meters you can use to monitor sound input.

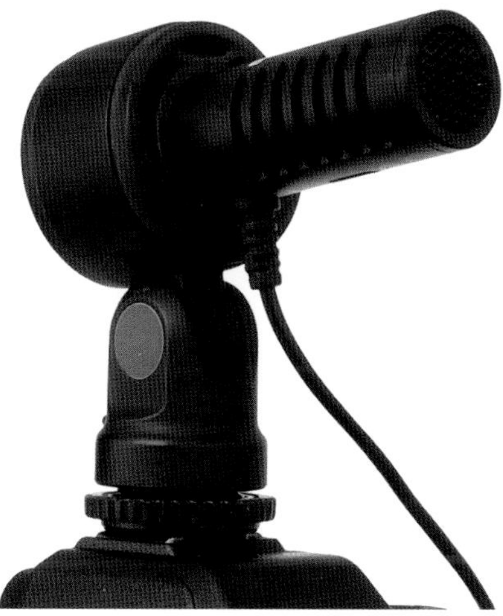

Figure 10.16 Nikon ME-1 external stereo microphone.

- **Hide the microphone.** Combine the first few tips by using an external mic and getting it as close to your subject as possible. If you're capturing a single person, you can always use a lapel microphone (described in the next section). But if you want a single mic to capture sound from multiple sources, your best bet may be to hide it somewhere in the shot. Put it behind a vase, using duct tape to fasten the microphone, and fix the mic cable out of sight (if you're not using a wireless microphone).

- **Turn off any sound makers you can.** Little things like fans and air handling units aren't obvious to the human ear but will be picked up by the microphone. Turn off any machinery or devices that you can, plus make sure cell phones are set to silent mode. Also, do what you can to minimize sounds such as wind, radio, television, or people talking in the background.

- **Make sure to record some "natural" sound.** If you're shooting video at an event of some kind, make sure you get some background sound that you can add to your audio as desired in post-production.

- **Consider recording audio separately.** Lip-syncing is probably beyond most of the people you're going to be shooting, but there's nothing that says you can't record narration separately and add it later. It's relatively easy if you learn how to use simple software video-editing programs like iMovie (for the Macintosh) or Windows Movie Maker (for Windows PCs). Any time the speaker is off-camera, you can work with separately recorded narration rather than recording the speaker on-camera. This can produce much cleaner sound.

External Microphones

The single-most important thing you can do to improve your audio quality is to use an external microphone. The internal stereo microphones with openings on top of the camera will do a decent job, but they have some significant drawbacks, partially spelled out in the previous section:

- **Camera noise.** There are plenty of noise sources emanating from the camera, including your own breathing and rustling around as the camera shifts in your hand. Manual zooming is bound to affect your sound, and sounds of your fingers may be picked up by the built-in mics as you change focal lengths. An external microphone isolates the sound recording from camera noise.

- **Distance.** Anytime your camera is located more than 6 to 8 feet from your subjects or sound source, the audio will suffer. An external unit allows you to place the mic right next to your subject.

- **Improved quality.** Obviously, Nikon didn't have room for a super-expensive, super-high-quality microphone on your compact mirrorless camera. Not all owners would appreciate the bulk or be willing to pay the premium, especially if they didn't plan to shoot much video themselves. An external microphone will almost always be of better quality.

- **Directionality.** The internal microphone generally records only sounds directly in front of it. An external microphone can be either of the directional type or omnidirectional, depending on whether you want to "shotgun" your sound or record more ambient sound.

You can choose from several different types of microphones, each of which has its own advantages and disadvantages. If you're serious about movie making, you might want to own more than one. Common configurations include:

- **Shotgun microphones.** These can be mounted directly on your camera, although, if the mic uses an accessory shoe mount, you'll need the optional adapter to convert the camera's shoe to a standard hot shoe. I prefer to use a bracket, which further isolates the microphone from any camera noise. One thing to keep in mind is that while the shotgun mic will generally ignore any sound coming from *behind* it, it will pick up any sound it is pointed at, even *behind* your subject. You may be capturing video and audio of someone you're interviewing in a restaurant and not realize you're picking up the lunchtime conversation of the diners seated in the table behind your subject. Outdoors, you may record your speaker, as well as the traffic on a busy street or freeway in the background.

- **Lapel microphones.** Also called *lavalieres*, these microphones attach to the subject's clothing and pick up their voice with the best quality. You'll need a long enough cord or a wireless mic. These are especially good for video interviews, so whether you're producing a documentary or grilling relatives for a family history, you'll want one of these.

- **Hand-held microphones.** If you're capturing a singer crooning a tune or want your subject to mimic famed faux newscaster Wally Ballou, a hand-held mic may be your best choice. They serve much the same purpose as a lapel microphone, and they're more intrusive—but that may be the point. A hand-held microphone can make a great prop for your fake newscast! The speaker can talk right into the microphone, point it at another person, or use it to record ambient sound. If your narrator is not going to appear on-camera, one of these can be an inexpensive way to improve sound.

- **Wired and wireless external microphones.** This option is the most expensive, but you get a receiver and a transmitter (both battery-powered, so you'll need to make sure you have enough batteries). The transmitter is connected to the microphone, and the receiver is connected to your camera. In addition to being less klutzy and enabling you to avoid having wires on view in your scene, wireless mics let you record sounds that are physically located some distance from your camera. Of course, you need to keep in mind the range of your device and be aware of possible signal interference from other electronic components in the vicinity.

WIND NOISE REDUCTION

Always use the wind screen provided with an external microphone (especially the popular fuzzy "dead-cat" covering) to reduce the effect of noise produced by even light breezes blowing over the microphone. Many mics, such as the Nikon ME-1, include a low-cut filter to further reduce wind noise. However, these can also affect other sounds. You can disable the low-cut filters for the ME-1 by changing a switch on the back from L-cut (low cutoff) to Flat. Other external mics also have their own low-cut filter switch.

Special Features

The Z5 II also has two audio frequency response ranges (Wide and Vocal Range) and an Attenuator—both settings found near the bottom of the Video Recording menu, so you can tailor your microphone capture to your subject matter (for ambient sound or voice recording). Audio levels can be adjusted while recording, and the internal microphones have improved wind noise reduction.

Focus on Lenses 11

This chapter provides basic information on the lens options for your Nikon Z5 II when this book was written. Because Nikon introduces new optics at a relentless pace, online forums like DPReview are an excellent source for additional information on the latest lenses and accessories, including reviews that provide rigorous testing data. You may appreciate that I love my 135mm f/1.8 Plena S-series lens, but I think you'll find the aggregate views and testing offered by online blogs and forums useful, too. The discussions of individual lenses in this chapter represent nothing more than my personal take on those lenses and suggestions on how you might want to use them.

Your choice of lenses can have a significant impact on your creative options, including field of view, use of selective focus and perspective, along with operational benefits/restraints in terms of your low-light shooting opportunities or image quality. Fortunately, in the years since the first Z-series cameras were announced in August 2018, the arsenal of available optics has expanded from the initial handful at an amazing rate. It's not an overstatement to say that Nikon has built its reputation on its expertise in lenses. Founded in 1917 as Nippon Kogaku, K.K. (Japan Optical Industries Co., Ltd.), the company specialized in optics for many years before it began producing cameras. In fact, all Canon cameras through mid-1947 used Nikkor lenses!

In the ensuing years, Nikon has developed advanced camera technology, too, combining its proficiency in both arenas to produce the Z-series mirrorless cameras and an outstanding series of lenses. At the time this book was written, there were more than 40 different Z-mount lenses and teleconverters available. Table 11.1 lists the Z-mount lenses available when this book was developed.

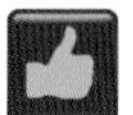 **NOTE** Nikon's APS-C lenses for its crop sensor Z-series cameras (like the Z50 II), are listed, but I won't be discussing those optics in this chapter. They can be used with your camera, but it will automatically provide cropped, DX mode lower-resolution 10.6MP images. I expect only a small number of Z5 II owners will be using DX lenses.

Of course, these, and other Z-mount lenses available from third parties, are not the only lenses available to you. Photographers who started out using Nikon camera bodies and optics have tended to hang onto their lenses for many years, even as they upgraded to newer camera bodies with more features. Many of us have stuck with the Nikon brand at least partially because we were able to use our existing collection of lenses with our latest and greatest cameras. After all, an enthusiast's optics collection can easily cost many times the price of the body itself. So, a large number of Z5 II owners already possess a stable of legacy F-mount optics.

TABLE 11.1 Nikon Z-mount Lenses

DX LENSES	S-LINE PRIME	S-LINE ZOOM	ZOOM
24mm f/1.7 DX	20mm f/1.8 S	14-30mm f/4 S	17-28mm f/2.8
12-28mm f/3.5-5.6 PZ VR DX	24mm f/1.8 S	14-24mm f/2.8 S	24-50mm f/4-6.3
16-50mm f/3.5-6.3 VR DX	35mm f/1.8 S	24-70mm f/4 S	28-75mm f/2.8
50-250mm f/4.5-6.3 VR DX	50mm f/1.8 S	24-70mm f/2.8 S	24-200mm f/4-6.3 VR
18-140mm f/3.5-6.3 VR DX	50mm f/1.2 S	24-120mm f/4 S	70-180mm f/2.8
	58mm f/0.95 S	70-200mm f/2.8 VR S	28-400mm f/4-8 VR
	85mm f/1.8 S	100-400mm f/4.5-5.6 VR S	180-600mm f/5.6-6.3 VR
MACRO PRIME	35mm f/1.2 S		28-135mm f/4 PZ VR
50mm f/2.8 MC	85mm f/1.2 S		
105mm f/2.8 S MC VR	135mm f/1.8 S	**PRIME**	
	400mm f/4.5 VR S	35mm f/1.4	**TELECONVERTERS**
	400mm f/2.8 TC VR S	50mm f/1.4	TC 1.4X
	600mm f/4 TC VR S	26mm f/2.8	TC 2.0X
	800mm f/6.3 VR S	28mm f/2.8	
		40mm f/2	

That's because backward compatibility of lenses is a six-decade-plus tradition for Nikon. The company's SLR and dSLR product lines have always, with few exceptions, been able to work surprisingly well with virtually all Nikkor F-mount lenses dating back to the very first, introduced with the Nikon F itself in April 1959, and emblazoned *Nikkor-S Auto 1:2 f=5cm* (a 50mm f/2 lens). Since then, Nikon has sold well over 120 million F- and Z-mount lenses, and millions more are available from third parties like Tamron, Sigma, and Tokina. Nearly all are compatible with every Nikon single-lens reflex built since then, although those made before 1977 may need an inexpensive $35 modification to be used safely on bodies that debuted after that.

Many of them can be used with the Z5 II, too. Some F-mount lenses offer full autofocus/autoexposure and vibration reduction features when mounted on Z-series cameras. The availability of the FTZ adapter, and its successor the FTZ II, was essential to the success of Z-series cameras for these three reasons:

- **Dearth of native lenses.** The adapter compensated for the original tiny number of native Z-mount lenses that were initially available for the Z-series cameras at introduction. The availability of the first FTZ adapter at introduction meant that, right out of the gate, a huge selection of F-mount lenses were readily available for use with the Z-series cameras. Veteran Nikon owners were delighted to find our favorite F-mount lenses were compatible. My Fisheye Nikkor 8-15mm f/3.5-4.5E (shown in Figure 11.1) is a favorite lens of mine that, because of its specialized applications, I don't expect to be available in Z-mount any time soon.

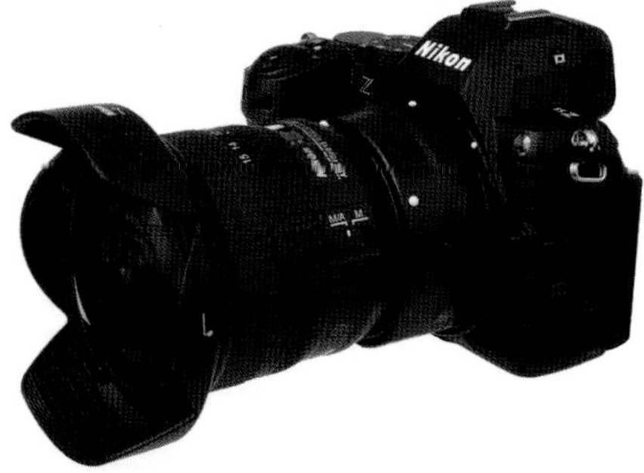

Figure 11.1 Nikon's excellent 8-15mm f/3.5-45E fisheye lens works great on the Z5 II.

- **Current owner loyalty.** At launch, Nikon expected current Nikon dSLR fans to make up the bulk of purchases for the Z-series cameras. The FTZ adapters made the adoption of any Z-mount camera much more seamless and less painful.

- **Technical innovations.** Nikon could have, perhaps, provided the Z-series cameras with a lens mount that would accept F-mount lenses without an adapter. However, that would have meant larger lenses, and the submitting to the technical restrictions imposed by the venerable 60-plus-year-old lens system. The F-mount, designed for film cameras, has a 44mm "throat" and a flange-to-focal plane (*registration*) distance of 46.5mm. These dimensions impose severe restrictions on lens design, including the maximum size of the largest aperture, and the angles at which photons can approach the sensor.

  In contrast, the Z-mount's diameter is a generous 55mm, and the flange/registration distance a mere 16mm, the least of any competing camera from Nikon, Canon, Sony, Panasonic, Olympus, or Fujifilm. Nikon says it can use the mount's flexibility to design lenses that are both faster and optically superior. Indeed, the "S" moniker is said to *represent* Superior.

  As a bonus, the reduced flange dimension means there is plenty of room between the sensor and the rear mount of many lenses designed for other camera platforms to be accommodated by additional adapters. Third-party manufacturers have already announced such add-ons to allow using certain Canon, Yashica/Contax, Leica, Minolta, Nikon, Pentax, and Olympus lenses in manual focus and exposure mode on the Z-series cameras. Although Nikon would prefer you purchase Nikkor lenses, it knows that the ability to use other optics on their cameras—even in manual focus mode—can allay some of the reservations of those considering a switch.

Later on, I'll have more details on how adapted F-mount lenses work with FTZ adapters. This chapter also provides some advice on how to select the best lenses for the kinds of photography you want to do.

Sensor Sensibilities

Ever since Nikon introduced its first digital camera with a full-frame sensor (the Nikon D3, in August 2007), the debate over full-frame versus cropped-sensor DX cameras has been hot and heavy in the Nikon community. Full-frame cameras have a sensor that measures roughly 24 × 36mm, while APS-C (DX) cameras like the Z50 II, Z fc, or Z30 have a sensor that measures about 24 × 16mm. Each type of sensor has its own advantages. Full-frame sensors, especially the back-side illuminated (BSI) stacked sensor variety, typically have larger pixels than their counterparts with equivalent resolution, and better low-light performance, while DX models offer extra telephoto "reach" thanks to their cropped sensors, which create an image from a smaller center portion of the image transmitted by the lens.

Because many enthusiasts have been confused by the full-frame/crop debate, it's useful to look at exactly what the "crop factor" means. In addition to the term *crop factor*, you've probably also heard the term *lens multiplier*. In truth, both are misleading and inaccurate terms used to describe the same phenomenon: the fact that cameras like the Nikon Z50 II, Z30, and Z fc provide a field of view that's smaller and narrower than that produced by so-called FX (full-frame) cameras when fitted with the same lens.

ARCHAIC NOMENCLATURE?

The common industry term for cameras with this smaller sensor is *APS-C*, which stands for Advanced Photo System—Classic. It refers to an ill-fated snapshot film format for cameras offered by Kodak and others from 1996 to about 2004. APS-C is one of many film-era terms that live on, including bulb exposure, rangefinder focus, and the designation "full frame" itself. You'll want to remember the APS-C designation when evaluating lenses from third-party vendors, as Nikon is the only company that uses the term *DX*.

Figure 11.2 quite clearly shows the phenomenon at work. At top in the figure you can see a comparison of the field of view of the FX and DX formats. At upper left, you can see the view you might expect with a 28mm lens mounted on the Z5 II in FX mode. At upper right is shown the equivalent scene in DX mode. For comparison, you can see at lower left the cropped 16:9 proportions available in still photo mode and when you're capturing video. Shown at lower right is one of the other available still photo crops, a square 1:1 aspect ratio.

The cropping effect is produced because the sensors of DX cameras and the full-frame Z-series cameras in their crop modes capture a smaller amount of area than full-frame sensors. As I mentioned earlier, all Nikon "full-frame" cameras have a sensor that's approximately the size of the standard 35mm film frame, 24mm × 36mm. Any DX sensor does *not* measure 24mm × 36mm; instead, it specs out at approximately 15.7mm × 23.5mm. You can calculate the relative field of view by multiplying the actual focal length by 1.5.

In the past, this translation was generally necessary only if you happened to use your full-frame camera accompanied by a DX model. It also comes in handy today if you are working with any lens using one of the camera's crop modes and want to know how a familiar lens will perform. I strongly prefer *crop factor* over the old term *lens multiplier* because nothing is being multiplied; a 100mm lens

Figure 11.2 The full-frame field of view (top left); DX crop (top right); 16:9 crop (bottom left); and 1:1 crop (bottom right).

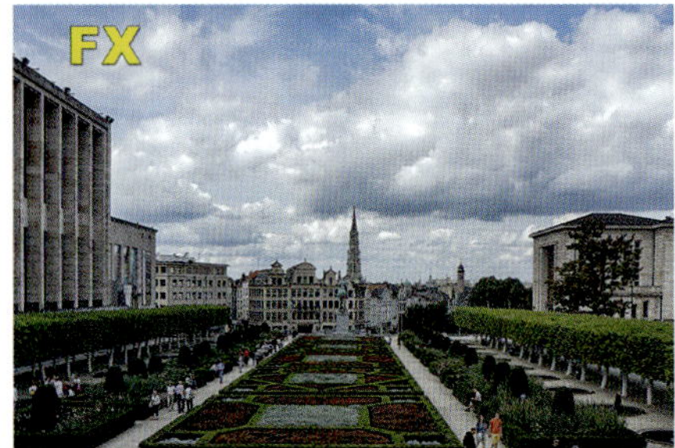

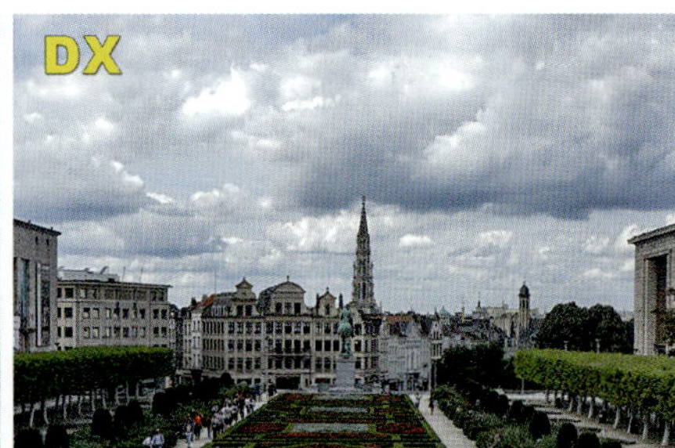

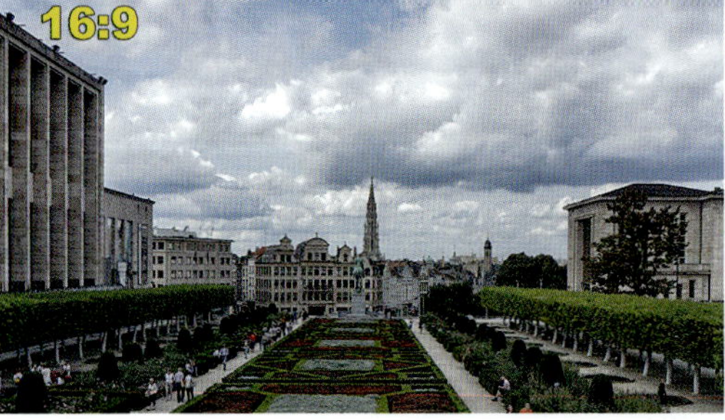

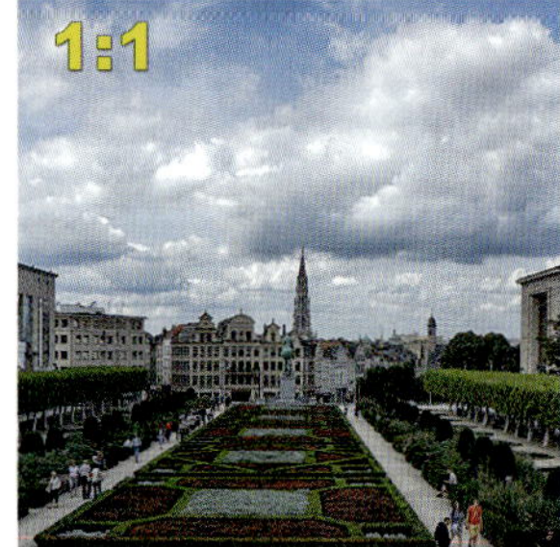

doesn't "become" a 150mm lens—the depth-of-field and lens aperture remain the same, despite what you may have read elsewhere. Only the field of view is cropped. But *crop factor* isn't much better, as it implies that the 24mm × 36mm frame is "full" and anything else is "less." I get e-mails all the time from photographers who point out that they own full-frame cameras with 33mm × 44mm sensors (like the Hasselblad X1D medium-format digital). By their reckoning, the "half-size" sensors found in Nikon FX cameras are "cropped."

If you work with both FX and DX cameras, or you use DX lenses on your camera (either F-mount or Z-mount versions), you might sometimes find it helpful to use the crop factor "multiplier" to translate a lens's real focal length into the full-frame equivalent, even though, as I said, nothing is being multiplied. Lenses designed for the DX format may or may not be usable for full-frame images on your camera, so Nikon automatically switches to DX mode when it detects that a DX lens has been attached. If the camera is unable to discern that an APS-C lens has been mounted (although in my tests of a few Tamron and Sigma lenses it did a pretty good job), you can manually choose the DX crop in the Image Area entry of the Photo Shooting and Video Recording menus.

The main drawback in using DX lenses on the Z5 II is that the cropped image is only 3984 × 2656 pixels—just 10.6 megapixels. You end up with that same resolution penalty when using full-frame lenses in DX crop mode, too, and many will point out that when using full-frame lenses, a crop mode doesn't do anything you can't do in an image editor. In one sense, that's true. You could always shoot in FX mode, and then trim to the DX format—or any other crop—in an image editor, with a bit more flexibility over what part of the frame is cropped. But consider the other side of the coin: if you're shooting a field sports event, such as football or soccer, and need the telephoto reach crop mode provides, would you prefer to manually crop each and every image you select, or would it be more efficient to let the camera crop the frame to match what you're seeing with the viewfinder or monitor?

Choosing Native Z-mount Lenses

If you're new to FX photography or to the Nikon system, you're probably wondering which lenses from the vast array of available optics can be added to your growing collection (trust me, it will grow). You need to know which lenses are suitable and, most importantly, which lenses are fully compatible with your Nikon camera. Nikon's current roster of Z-mount lenses is, of course, fully compatible. Here are some features common to most lenses using the Z5 II's native lens mount:

- **Nikon Z-mount bayonet.** Designed exclusively for attaching Z-series lenses, the lens mount has 11 electrical *CPU contacts* that allow two-way communication with the camera. The data flow includes lens focal length, current and maximum f/stop, distance information supplied by the lens to the camera, autofocus functions, and aperture control.

  Unlike Nikon F-mount lenses, the Nikon Z cameras do not have a physical aperture lever to change the f/stop from wide open (for viewing and focusing) to the aperture used to take the picture (in common photo parlance, the *taking aperture*). Your f/stop is set electronically by the camera based on its autoexposure calculation, or as specified by you (in A and M modes).

  One byproduct of this system is that Z lenses need to have electrically compatible extension tubes and similar accessories; unless they have a manual aperture ring, lower-cost manual alternatives have no way of physically setting the aperture.

- **Programmable lens rings.** Your lens's focus ring is not just for focusing anymore! Indeed, many Z-mount lenses have *two* programmable rings (in addition to the zoom ring on zoom lenses). In addition to the traditional focus ring, a second rotating band dubbed the *control ring* or *lens function ring* is available on some lenses, particularly the higher-end optics. With the Custom Setting f2: Custom Controls (Shooting) entry, you can define various lens ring behaviors, including aperture setting, exposure compensation, or ISO sensitivity, and even assign *different* actions for clockwise/counterclockwise rotation.

- **Stepping motor technology.** All the Z-series lenses with AF capabilities announced to date feature stepping motors for fast, quiet automatic focus. Fast is required for shooting sports or subjects that move unpredictably or rapidly, while quiet is desirable for both movie making (to avoid recording the sound of the AF motor in your video) and stealth shooting.

  A stepper motor is a brushless DC motor that divides one rotation into equal steps, allowing the camera to move quickly to one of those fixed steps without the need for electronic feedback or a sensor to confirm the amount of rotation. Nikon has been using stepper motors in its AF-P lenses for its dSLRs for several years (the "P" stands for the electronic pulse used to drive the motor). The technology allows changing focus mode (autofocus or manual) without the need to flip a physical A/M switch on the lens or camera body; you can do it within a menu.

- **Electromagnetic diaphragm mechanism.** Unlike conventional lenses, in which the blades of the lens diaphragm are operated by mechanical linkages, the aperture blades of Z-mount autofocus lenses are controlled by electronics for extra accuracy under demanding conditions.

- **Special lens coatings.** Z-mount lenses can include what Nikon calls Super Integrated Coatings, and the S-line lenses have an additional Nano Crystal coating. Light is your friend when you're creating an image—except when unwanted photons (say, from illumination coming from backlighting or entering the lens diagonally) cause flare, glare, ghost images, or reduced contrast. Vendors try to counter these effects by applying coatings to lenses, filters, and other optical devices. Often, multiple layers of anti-reflection coatings, such as those found in Nikon's Super Integrated Coatings, are needed to handle all the various wavelengths of light.

  Nikon's additional Nano Crystal Coat's nanometer-sized (one millionth of a millimeter) particles work with *all* wavelengths of light and allow more of the desirable photons to pass unheeded. A complex lens with more than a dozen elements suffers only a 0.75 percent reduction in light, compared with a 15 percent loss with older coating technologies. The S-line lenses also benefit from rugged fluorine coatings on the front element that repel dust, dirt, water, and even grease, making them easier to remove. The coatings have anti-reflective properties of their own.

- **Weather-sealed construction.** Moisture is unavoidable, especially when you must capture images in inclement weather. The Z5 II camera has good weather sealing, and many lenses offer a significant amount of resistance to less-than-ideal shooting conditions (don't dunk your camera in water, however!).

- **Vibration reduction.** Nikon has added vibration reduction (VR) anti-shake capabilities to many of its lenses, including all of the DX zooms. That's especially useful for owners of APS-C Z-mount cameras like the Z50 II, which do not have in-body image stabilization (IBIS) like your Z5 II and other full-frame Z-series models. Keep in mind that some S-series lenses do *not* have VR, which is usually added only to longer focal length prime and zoom lenses, so you will lose that facility when using those optics.

Better Lenses with Z-mount?

There's been a great deal of discussion about the advantages of Nikon's Z-mount lenses. Much of it seems to assume that the larger 55mm diameter (and 52mm throat size) will make it possible to design lenses with faster maximum apertures, such as the 58mm f/0.95 Nikkor Noct. However, it's *not* simply that the larger opening lets in more light and they can now magically make lenses with larger f/stops. If that were true, there wouldn't already be lenses faster than f/1.4 for cameras with smaller "throats." An f/0.95 lens is available in Leica's 40.5mm diameter mount, for example.

What the wider opening does is give lens designers more freedom in creating optics that are sharper, faster, and with fewer aberrations. For example, typical wide-angle lenses for dSLRs use a retrofocus design to move the optical center of the lens so the rear element does not protrude into the mirror chamber. To do that, the rear element must be very large in order to avoid vignetting and other forms of distortion. The Z-mount's 16mm registration distance and wider throat makes it easier to optimize the convergent and divergent elements without worrying about long exit pupil distances between the rear element and sensor plane.

Digital sensors, compared to film, have their particular challenges for lens designers, including the need for a less steep angle of incidence emerging from the rear element, because of the need to send photons down those deep "wells" in non-BSI sensors. Microlenses added on top of the sensor were the primary solution, especially when so many lenses designed for film (which is more tolerant of the angles) were in use. But, with the Z-mount's advantages we can expect much better lenses for our Z-series cameras.

Nikon Lens Overview

I'm dividing the rest of this chapter into several parts, generally arranged in order of relevance to new camera owners. First up, I'm going to list and describe the best native full-frame Z-mount lenses announced or available from Nikon at the time this book was written. As I noted earlier, I am not going to include DX lenses; they are *compatible*, but not recommended because of the reduction in resolution from the 1.5X crop. This initial section will help you decide which lenses to add as your collection of optics inevitably grows.

As I mentioned earlier, for more detailed data, including up-to-date reviews and comparisons, you'll want to consult online resources like DPReview.com. I'm only going to give you my personal take on most of these lenses. I don't do lens testing, pixel peeping, or extensive checking for coma, either type of chromatic aberration, or modulation transfer function. If I like the pictures I take with a particular lens, I use it more. In general, I'll discuss pricing only to point out that certain lenses are relatively affordable, while others are likely to be of interest only to well-heeled photographers.

For the benefit of those new to photography, I'm going to describe the different classes of lenses available, from the focal length ranges wide, normal, and telephoto to those with more special-ized features, such as macro and perspective control lenses. If you're a veteran photographer, you can review or skim that section if you like; it's my attempt to address the needs of a broad range of enthusiasts in one book. Keep in mind that all of us were beginners at one point. I promise I didn't charge you extra for that section.

Finally, I'm going to mention the variety of different F-mount lenses that many of you may already own or wish to use with your camera using adapters. You can trust Nikon to expand its native Z-mount product line to include most or all those optics eventually, but until then, the large array of F-mount lenses remain an important resource for Nikon mirrorless camera owners. Because so many dSLR owners are migrating to the mirrorless world, you'll find some real bargains among the used F-mount lenses that are for sale.

Ingredients of Nikon's Alphanumeric Soup

Before we begin looking at the individual Z-mount lenses available, I want to address the cryptic letters and descriptors that Nikon applies to the names of its lenses, both Z-mount and F-mount. A detailed nomenclature listing like this one was more important in the early days following the introduction of Nikon's Z-series mirrorless cameras, because so many early adopters relied on legacy F-mount lenses and the original FTZ adapter until Nikon's stable of native lenses reached critical numbers.

Even so, I'm including this alphabetical list of the lens terms you're most likely to encounter, as a resource for those exploring the full extent of the Nikon optical world. Not all of these are used as parts of a lens's name, but you may come across some of these terms in discussions of Nikon lenses. Most of these apply only to F-mount lenses; I'll note those that apply exclusively to Z-mount lenses:

- **AF, AF-D, AF-I, AF-P, AF-S.** In all cases, AF stands for *autofocus* when appended to the name of a Nikon F-mount lens. An extra letter is added to provide additional information. A plain old AF lens is an autofocus lens that uses a screw-drive motor in the camera body to provide autofocus functions (and so cannot be used in AF mode on Z-series cameras, which lack that motor). The D means that it's a D-type lens (described later in this listing); the I indicates that focus is through a motor inside the lens; and AF-P is used to designate lenses with that very quiet stepper motor that's especially useful for sound video applications. The most common Nikon focus designation for F-mount lenses is still AF-S, and the S means that a Silent Wave motor in the lens provides focusing. (Don't confuse a Nikon AF-S lens with the AF-S [Single-Servo Autofocus] mode.) Nikon has upgraded most of its older AF lenses in F-mount with AF-S (or AF-P) versions, but it's not safe to assume that *all* newer F-mount Nikkors are AF-S/AF-P, or even offer autofocus. For example, the PC-E Nikkor 24mm f/3.5D ED perspective control lens must be focused manually, and Nikon offers a surprising collection of other manual focus lenses to meet specialized needs.

- **AI, AI-S.** All Nikkor F-mount lenses produced after 1977 have either automatic aperture indexing (AI) or automatic indexing-shutter (AI-S) features that eliminate the previous requirement to manually align the aperture ring on the camera when mounting a lens. Within a few years, all Nikkors had this automatic aperture indexing feature (except for G-type lenses, which have no aperture ring at all), including Nikon's budget-priced Series E lenses, so the designation was dropped at the time the first autofocus (AF) lenses were introduced.

- **ARN (ARNEO Coat).** Included with some lenses, including the Nikkor Z 14-24mm, 24-70mm, and 70-200mm f/2.8 S-series optics. It complements Nano Crystal Coat (described below) to further reduce ghosting and flare produced by incident light entering the lens from a vertical angle.

- **CRC (Close Range Correction).** These optics are optimized for distances encountered in macro photography.
- **D.** Appended to the maximum f/stop of the lens (as in f/2.8D), a D-Series lens is able to send focus distance data to the camera, which uses the information for flash exposure calculation and metering.
- **DC.** The DC stands for defocus control, which allows managing the out-of-focus parts of an image to produce better-looking portraits and close-ups.
- **DX.** The DX lenses are designed for use with digital cameras using the APS-C–sized sensor having the 1.5X crop factor. The image circle they produce isn't large enough to fill up a full 35mm frame at all focal lengths, but they can be used on Nikon's full-frame dSLR models using the automatic/manual DX crop mode. DX lenses are available in both Z- and F-mounts.
- **E.** The E designation was used for Nikon's budget-priced E-Series F-mount optics, five prime and three zoom manual focus lenses built using aluminum or plastic parts rather than the preferred brass parts of that era, so they were considered less rugged. All are effectively AI-S lenses. They do have good image quality, which makes them a bargain for those who treat their lenses gently and don't need the latest autofocus features. They were available in 28mm f/2.8, 35mm f/2.5, 50mm f/1.8, 100mm f/2.8, and 135mm f/2.8 focal lengths, plus 36-72mm f/3.5, 75-150mm f/3.5, and 70-210mm f/4 zooms. (All these would be considered fairly "fast" today.)

  However, today the E designation is applied to lenses to represent those that stop down the lens to the "taking" aperture electronically. Non-E lenses use a lever (missing in mirrorless cameras) in the camera body that mates with a lever in the lens mount. Lenses with an E in their names, such as the F-mount 16-80mm f/2.8-4E ED VR optic, use an electronic mechanism instead.
- **ED (or LD/UD).** The ED (extra-low dispersion) designation indicates that some lens elements are made of a special hard and scratch-resistant glass that minimizes the divergence of the different colors of light as they pass through, thus reducing chromatic aberration (color "fringing") and other image defects. A gold band around the front of the lens indicates an optic with ED elements. You sometimes find LD (low dispersion) or UD (ultra-low dispersion) designations.
- **FL.** Indicates a lens has fluorite lens elements, which have special optical properties, including low dispersion.
- **FX.** When Nikon introduced the Nikon D3 as its first digital full-frame camera, it coined the term *FX*, representing the nominal 24mm × 36mm sensor format as a counterpart to *DX*, which was used for its 16mm × 24mm APS-C-sized sensors. Although FX hasn't been officially applied to any Nikon lenses so far, expect to see the designation used more often to differentiate between lenses that are compatible with any Nikon digital SLR (FX) and those that operate only on DX-format cameras, or in DX mode when used on an FX camera.
- **G.** G-type lenses have no aperture ring, and you can use them at other than the maximum aperture only with electronic cameras that can set the aperture automatically.
- **HRI (High Refractive Index).** This is a term applied to lenses with excellent correction for spherical aberrations and distortion caused by curvature of field.
- **IF.** Nikon's *internal-focusing* lenses change focus by shifting only small internal lens groups with no change required in the lens's physical length, unlike conventional double-helicoid focusing systems that move all lens groups toward the front or rear during focusing. IF lenses are more

compact and lighter in weight, provide better balance, focus more closely, and can be focused more quickly.

- **IX.** These lenses were produced for Nikon's long-discontinued Pronea 6i and S APS film cameras. While the Pronea could use many standard Nikon lenses, IX lenses cannot be mounted on any Nikon digital SLR.

- **Micro/MC.** Nikon uses the term *micro* to designate its close-up lenses for F-mount, and MC for Z-mount. Most other vendors use *macro* instead.

- **N (Nano Crystal Coat).** Nano Crystal lens coating virtually eliminates internal lens element reflections across a wide range of wavelengths and is particularly effective in reducing ghost and flare peculiar to ultra-wide-angle lenses. Nano Crystal Coat employs multiple layers of Nikon's extra-low refractive index coating, which features ultra-fine crystallized particles of nano size (one nanometer equals one millionth of a millimeter).

- **NAI.** This is not an official Nikon term, but it is widely used to indicate that a manual focus lens is *Non-AI*, which means that it was manufactured before 1977, and therefore cannot be used safely on modern digital Nikon SLRs (other than the retro Df model) without modification.

- **NOCT (Nocturne).** Used originally to refer to the prized Nikkor AI-S Noct 58mm f/1.2, a "fast" (wide aperture) prime lens, with aspherical elements, capable of taking photographs in very low light. It's been revived to describe the 58mm f/0.95 Noct lens for Nikon's Z-series mirrorless cameras.

- **PC (Perspective Control)/PC-E.** A PC lens is capable of shifting the lens from side to side (and up/down) to provide a more realistic perspective when photographing architecture and other subjects that otherwise require tilting the camera so that the sensor plane is not parallel to the subject. Older Nikkor PC lenses offered shifting only and manually adjusted f/stops, but more modern models, such as the PC-E Nikkor 24mm f/3.5D ED lens allow both shifting and tilting. Those with the PC-E designation have electronically controlled diaphragms.

- **PF (Phase Fresnel).** A type of lens design that allows using fewer elements to provide excellent compensation of chromatic aberration, for a more compact and lightweight lens form factor.

- **S.** Denotes the top-of-the-line Z-mount lenses and is said to stand for "Superior."

- **SE (Special Edition).** This designation is usually applied to lenses with slightly different finishes, such as silver trim, generally to add a cool appearance when mounted on Nikon's "retro" cameras like the Nikon Zf and Z fc. The lenses are optically identical to their non-SE counterparts.

- **SWM (Silent Wave Motor).** This is a term Nikon applies to F-mount AF-S lenses that allow manual focus adjustment while in autofocus mode. Earlier AF-D lenses had to be switched to manual mode for focus fine-tuning.

- **UV.** This term is applied to special (and expensive) lenses designed to pass ultraviolet light.

- **UW.** Lenses with this designation are designed for underwater photography with Nikonos camera bodies and cannot be used with Nikon digital SLRs.

- **VR.** While VR initially was applied only to F-mount optics, Nikon now has an expanding line of vibration reduction (VR) FX and DX Z-mount lenses. These shift optical elements internally to counteract camera shake and, thanks to what Nikon calls "synchro VR," can take over anti-shake functions for pitch and yaw from the Z5 II's in-body image stabilization.

Wide-to-Normal Zoom Lenses

Lenses are commonly categorized based on their focal length. *Rectilinear* lenses—that is, those that render straight lines without bending (as fisheye optics do)—are considered *ultra-wide-angle* if they have a focal length of about 12mm to 20mm. Those in the 20–35mm range are said to be *wide-angle* lenses. *Normal lenses* have a focal length roughly equivalent to the diagonal of the film or sensor, in millimeters, and so fall into the range of about 45mm to 60mm on a full-frame camera. The boundaries between types of lenses are considered fuzzy, especially when describing zoom lenses that overlap focal lengths and types.

As I'll describe later in this chapter, lenses can also be classified either as *prime* (fixed focal length) or *zoom* (variable focal length) optics. I'm beginning the roster of native Z-mount lenses with the wide-to-normal zoom lenses first.

Nikkor Z 24-50mm f/4-6.3

This is the most popular kit lens offered for Nikon's entry-level full-frame Z-mount cameras like the Z5 II. Although I have other options, I like to use mine on my Z5 II sometimes because of its size. I snapped up this lens, which was an irresistible bargain that offered something my other full-frame Z-mount lenses lacked: it's super compact.

The retractable design of this 24-50mm lens mimics the popular "pancake" form factor that many favor in a walk-around lens, making it a great option for on-the-go travel photography. Retracted, it is less than three inches long. It is dust and moisture resistant, which can be especially useful when capturing images under less-than-ideal weather conditions (seasoned travelers know what I am talking about). The kit lens has a stepping motor that offers quiet, accurate autofocus suitable for candid street photography and general shooting. Despite its low cost, it includes three aspherical elements and two low-dispersion elements for low distortion, excellent sharpness, and clarity.

Enthusiasts tend to dismiss kit lenses as cheap-o optics intended to keep the cost of entry-level cameras low. Even though this 24-50mm lens doesn't merit the "S" (superior) nomenclature, it's an excellent basic lens that's worth having, even if only as a compact spare to use when you want to travel especially light.

Nikkor Z 14-24mm f/2.8 S

Lens manufacturers frequently sell zooms with a given focal length range in tandems: an expensive f/2.8 version and a more affordable offering with an f/4 maximum aperture. If the 14-30mm lens described next is Nikon's full-frame Z-mount affordable ultra-wide/wide lens, this one—which has a slightly less ambitious 24mm maximum focal length—is the premium version with a higher price tag. I hesitate to use the term "pro version" because both are S-series lenses and are incredibly sharp.

The 14-24mm lens is quite a bit heavier than its 14-30mm counterpart, and about one-third longer, making it not your best choice as a walk-around lens if you don't need the fast f/2.8 maximum aperture. I expect it to be part of Nikon's Z-mount "magic trinity," along with the Nikkor Z 24-70mm f/2.8 S and Nikkor Z 70-200mm f/2.8 S, to supply full coverage of the focal lengths from 14mm to 200mm with no overlap.

Nikkor Z 14-30mm f/4 S

I love this lens! It was the first lens I got for my Z-series cameras beyond the initial three (50mm f/1.8, 35mm f/1.8, and 24-70mm f/4), because I needed something wider for architecture and landscape photography. It has a useful f/4 maximum aperture and it extends from its most compact retracted form when zoomed. It's such a basic component I expect many Z5 II owners to at least consider one, especially since no wider zoom from Nikon is currently on the horizon as I write this. If you don't need the extra speed of its 14-24mm f/2.8 stablemate, this lens is an affordable fun-sized option. (See Figure 11.3, left.)

Nikkor Z 17-28mm f/2.8

This lens is a top choice for those who want an f/2.8 constant maximum aperture and can accept a 17mm widest focal length to save half the cost of the Nikon 14-24mm optic. It's a re-configured Tamron lens that uses the same optical formula as its Tamron counterpart, but conforms to Nikon's outer design appearance. Although it's not an S-series lens, this compact lens focuses down to 8 to 10 inches (at 17 and 28mm, respectively) and does not change its four-inch length when focusing or zooming. This lens is a good candidate for a "budget" trinity as an alternative to the 14-30mm optic described above.

Nikkor Z 24-70mm f/4 S

At the unveiling of the original Z-series cameras, Nikon had several challenging requirements to fulfill. In order to attract both existing Nikon dSLR owners and those currently using other platforms, it offered this optic as the basic lens. As a kit lens, it had to be exceptionally sharp, versatile, compact, and, most of all, affordable. The 24-70mm focal length is also quite popular and considered versatile enough to use for everything from landscapes to portraits (despite its limited zoom range).

The lens is reasonably affordable and compact enough to please those who turned to the Nikon mirrorless realm in search of reduced size and weight. This lens weighs less than 18 ounces and measures about 3 × 3.5 inches when collapsed. (See Figure 11.3, right.) In a brilliant stroke, Nikon designed

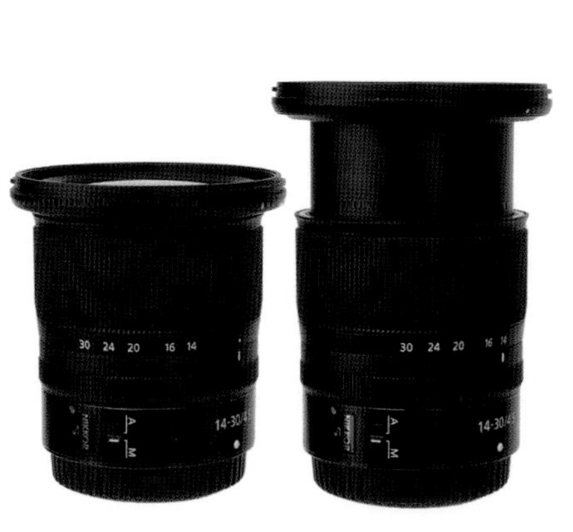
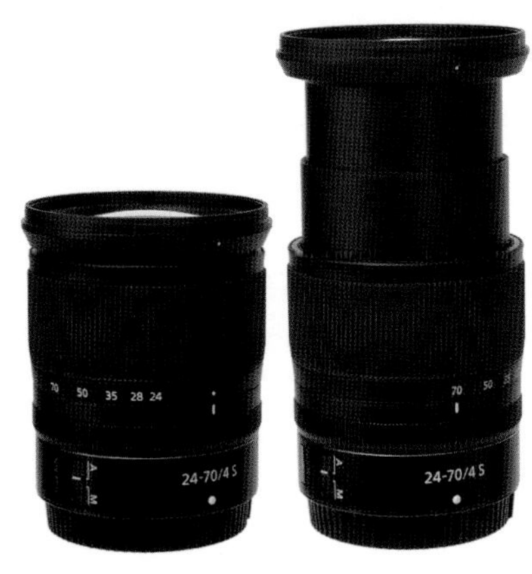

Figure 11.3 The Nikkor Z 14-30mm f/4 S retracted and extended (left). Relatively inexpensive, the 24-70mm lens (shown retracted/extended) is an impressive performer (right).

the lens so that you don't need to press a button to retract it into its most compact configuration; just rotate the zoom ring past its widest 24mm setting, and you feel a brief resistance before the ring continues rotating while the lens retracts fully. However, it does get longer as you zoom, as you can see in the figure. This button-free retractable behavior has carried over to other zoom lenses introduced after launch.

This zoom, like all the Z-mount optics, is sufficiently sharp even wide open, and gets even better as you stop down. It focuses down to about 12 inches (for a reproduction ratio of 1:33) and has a minimum aperture of f/22 for a bit of extra depth-of-field if you need it.

Nikkor Z 24-70mm f/2.8 S

Priced at roughly double the price of the f/4 version, this 24-70mm f/2.8 lens should become the workhorse of professional photographers and enthusiasts who use this focal range a lot and value a large constant maximum aperture and superb sharpness for subjects ranging from landscapes to portraits. It features an innovative "multi-focus" system with *two* stepping motors for very fast, accurate, and quiet focus, making it ideal for movie shooting as well as stills.

Like other S-mount lenses, this one has three separate coatings on individual lens elements to suppress flare, ghosting, and reflections while optimizing contrast and color fidelity. The ARNEO coating minimizes ghost and flare effects from illumination reaching the lens surface in a vertical direction, even when the light source is contained within the frame. The Nano Crystal coating eliminates reflections inside the lens from visible light, reducing ghosting and flare from light entering the lens diagonally. Super Integrated multicoating improves color and contrast from internal reflections and is especially helpful in backlit situations and with lenses having a larger number of glass elements.

Another innovation is an organic LED (OLED) information panel on the top surface of the lens that displays aperture, focus distance, or depth-of-field. A Lens Function button can be assigned custom behaviors and used in tandem with the control ring to make various exposure and other adjustments using controls on the lens itself. While the control ring is set, by default, to adjust manual focus, it can be redefined to control aperture or exposure compensation instead. This is a hefty lens, measuring 3.5 × 5 inches and tipping the scales at a tad more than 28 ounces.

Nikkor Z 28-70mm f/2.8

If you're looking to assemble a budget "trinity," Nikon's licensed version of Tamron's original 28-70mm f/2.8 optical design may fill the bill as your wide-to-short-tele lens. Like several of the lenses already described, this one gains in length when zoomed to its longest focal length. Close focusing is not bad, with a minimum focus distance of 7.5 inches at 28mm but only down to 15 inches at 70mm. This lens is certainly sharp enough, but I find its 28mm perspective not as wide as I'd like for landscape and architectural photography. Unless you need the f/2.8 maximum aperture for something like street photography, I recommend going with the S-series 24-70mm f/4 Nikkor instead.

Wide-Angle/Normal Prime Lenses

When the Nikon Z-series cameras were introduced, the company unveiled an array of high-quality "prime" (fixed focal length) lenses and rolled out zooms a little more slowly. Indeed, three of the first four lenses announced were fast wide-angle or normal prime lenses: 35mm and 50mm f/1.8 lenses and the exotic 58mm f/0.95 Noct. Only one zoom, the 24-70mm f/4 lens described earlier, was available at launch.

Since then, the selection of both prime and zoom Z-mount lenses has grown, with Nikon offering more than 40 lenses (including DX optics) at the time this book was written. So, you'll have a broad selection of both prime and zoom lenses to choose from, with the wide-angle/normal primes covered in this section.

There are several considerations to ponder when choosing between prime and zoom lenses in any range. Here's a checklist of the most important factors, in addition to image quality and maximum aperture; those aspects take on additional meaning when comparing zooms versus primes:

- **Logistics.** As prime lenses offer just a single focal length, you'll need more of them to encompass the full range offered by a single zoom. More lenses mean additional slots in your camera bag, and extra weight to carry. Within Nikon's Z-mount product line, you can choose from a good selection of prime lenses in 20mm, 24mm, 26mm, 28mm, 35mm, 40mm, 50mm, 58mm, 85mm, 105mm, 135mm, 200mm, 300mm, 400mm, 600mm, and 800mm focal lengths. That's a lot of choices!

- **Image quality.** Prime lenses usually produce better image quality at their focal length than even the most sophisticated zoom lenses at the same magnification. Zoom lenses, with their shifting elements and f/stops that can vary from zoom position to zoom position, are, in general, more complex to design than fixed focal length lenses. That's not to say that the very best prime lenses can't be complicated as well. However, the exotic designs, aspheric elements, and low-dispersion glass can be applied to improving the quality of the lens, rather than wasting a lot of it on compensating for problems caused by the zoom process itself.

- **Maximum aperture.** Because of the same design constraints, zoom lenses usually have smaller maximum apertures than prime lenses, and the most affordable zooms have a lens opening that effectively grows smaller as you zoom in. The difference in lens speed verges on the ridiculous at some focal lengths. For example, the 24-50mm f/4-6.3 super-bargain kit lens Nikon offers for the camera gives you a 50mm f/6.3 lens when zoomed to its maximum focal length, while prime lenses in that focal length commonly have f/1.8 or faster maximum apertures. Indeed, the fastest f/2, f/1.8, f/1.2, and f/0.95 lenses are all primes, and if you require a large maximum aperture, a fixed focal length lens is what you should rely on.

- **Speed.** Using prime lenses takes time and slows you down. It takes a few seconds to remove your current lens and mount a new one, and the more often you need to do that, the more time is wasted. If you choose not to swap lenses, when using a fixed focal length lens, you'll still have to move closer or farther away from your subject to get the field of view you want. A zoom lens allows you to change magnifications and focal lengths with the twist of a ring and generally saves a great deal of time.

Let's move on to the prime lenses available in the wide-angle to normal range in Z-mount for the camera.

Nikkor Z 20mm f/1.8 S

Super-sharp wide-angle prime lenses are a favorite of landscape photographers, and those doing street photography prefer wide-angle lenses that are fast enough to capture candid images at night or in murky surroundings. This lens fills the bill for both types of photography, and other applications—such as interior and exterior architectural shots—as well. On a recent trip to Venice, Italy and Sofia, Bulgaria, I was traveling light and carried only my Nikon 28-400mm f/4-8 VR lens (for most outdoor shots), a Laowa 10mm f/2.8 (non-fisheye) wide angle, and the 20mm f/1.8 for landscapes and available light/interiors. This fast wide-angle lens was perfect for night shots and distortion-free indoor architectural work.

It's a compact ultra-wide lens with two synchronized stepping motors to provide fast and accurate autofocus while remaining quiet enough for video or shooting stills in stealth mode. It has full-time manual focus override so you can fine-tune focus easily and uses Nikon's advanced lens coatings to suppress flare and ghosting under demanding conditions. Dust- and moisture-resistant (helpful for street shooting), it focuses a tad closer than eight inches, weighs about 18 ounces, and measures 3.33 × 4.27 inches.

Nikkor Z 24mm f/1.8 S

Like most of the non-zoom (prime) Z-mount autofocus lenses, this one has a maximum aperture of f/1.8. It makes an excellent lens for landscapes, architecture, and candid street photography when you have enough room to step back that the 20mm f/1.8 isn't needed. Its advanced optical system provides great sharpness even wide open, and it has both Nano Crystal and Super Integrated Coatings to minimize flare and ghosting for improved color fidelity and contrast. Those who need a fast, moderately wide lens will prize its compactness and excellent image quality.

Nikkor Z 35mm f/1.8 S

The Nikkor Z 35mm f/1.8 S lens is an exceptionally sharp basic wide-angle lens, suitable for landscapes, street photography, exterior architecture, and shooting interiors that aren't so cramped that they call for a wider lens. You can use it for photographing small groups, and it's especially valuable for available-light photography because of its fast f/1.8 maximum aperture.

It focuses down to 9.84 inches, not particularly close enough for true macro work with its 1:5.25 reproduction ratio (true macro lenses have a 1:2 or 1:1 or better reproduction ratio). Its minimum aperture is just f/16 if you're looking for a lens with extra depth-of-field. But this lens's nine-bladed rounded diaphragm produces pleasing bokeh wide open. (I explain bokeh later in this chapter.)

Overall, this lens (shown in Figure 11.4, left) is an excellent performer with two ED (extra-low-dispersion) and three aspherical elements with plenty of sharpness to match the camera's resolution, so there's little need to

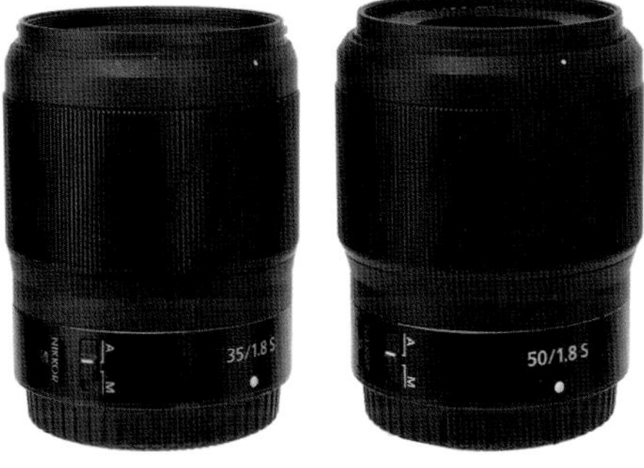

Figure 11.4 The Nikkor Z 35mm f/1.8 S is a fast wide-angle lens (left). The Nikkor Z 50mm f/1.8 S is an exceptionally sharp "normal" lens (right).

consider an adapted F-mount 35mm lens, unless you already own one, or need the extra speed of Nikon's phenomenal 35mm f/1.4G optic, which costs almost exactly twice as much.

Nikkor Z 35mm f/1.4

Introduced in June 2024, this was the first autofocus prime lens in Z-mount with an f/1.4 maximum aperture. It's not an S-series lens and is priced about $100 less than the f/1.8 version above, giving you a cheaper alternative with decent image quality and a maximum aperture that's 2/3 stops faster. In most other respects it's similar in size, weight, and close-focusing distance to its more costly stablemate.

Nikkor Z 35mm f/1.2 S

Why would Nikon's lens wizards introduce a third full-frame optic with a 35mm focal length? Because they can. Make no mistake: this is a specialized lens with a substantial price tag (nearly $3,000), and probably beyond the needs (and means) of the average Z5 II owner. But those who need its features highly anticipated the introduction of this lens when it finally emerged in February 2025.

For the roughly $2,100 premium over Nikon's 35mm f/1.8 lens, you get an optic that is one full stop faster and, importantly, eminently usable wide open, offering the triple advantages of great low-light performance, pleasing bokeh, and selective focus tools uncommon in wide-angle lenses. Photojournalists, wedding and fashion photographers, and those capturing events will love this lens. It's also ideal for videography for the same reasons, but also because it boasts a clickless control ring that can be programmed for smooth aperture changes while shooting. It includes two function buttons.

It's a large lens, at 2.3 pounds, is nearly six inches long, and uses expensive 82mm filters. Rounding out a lineup that includes Nikon's 50mm f/1.2 and 85mm f/1.2 lenses, this is one lens that won't disappoint those who need it.

Nikkor Z 50mm f/1.8 S

Traditionally, 50mm f/1.8 "normal" lenses tended to be inexpensive "starter" prime lenses for those who need a lens faster than the typical zoom, but who can't afford pricier 50mm f/1.4 alternatives. This lens is inexpensive only in comparison with the other S-Line lenses, but for its price you get a super-sharp lens worthy of Nikon's "superior" classification. (See Figure 11.4, right.)

Lenses of this focal length lend themselves to general photography, and, with the automatic extension tubes for the Z-series, for macro work with subjects at distances closer than the 15.7 inches this lens can focus. You can also use it as a portrait lens with an f/1.8 maximum aperture that's excellent for selective focus three-quarter-length and head-and-shoulders portraits of individuals or twosomes. Its nine-blade aperture produces good bokeh. Even those new to photography will have heard the phrase "nifty 50" that is often applied to lenses of this focal length. Lodged between the realms of wide-angle and short telephoto focal lengths, a fast and sharp 50mm lens is an important tool for those looking for versatility at a (relatively) affordable price.

Nikkor Z 50mm f/1.4

This lens caused quite a bit of excitement when introduced among those who wanted a fast 50mm lens and couldn't afford to spring for Nikon's faster alternatives (described shortly). The thrill was lost on me, as this optic is only a little less expensive than its S-Line counterparts, although it is a more affordable alternative to the two lenses discussed next. Its main claim to fame is that this lens is actually sharper than Nikon's super popular 50mm f/1.4G lens that dominated this focal range in the dSLR realm. Many tout its pleasing bokeh and programmable control ring (something the Z-mount 35mm f/1.8 and 50mm f/1.8 lenses lack).

Nikkor Z 50mm f/1.2 S

Only real speed demons will be willing to pay 4X the price tag of the 50mm f/1.4 described above to obtain this monster (2.4 pound/3.5 × 6-inch) optic that weighs twice as much as the Z5 II body itself and is almost as bulky. However, it is *sharp*, I mean *very sharp* wide open, and despite the hefty price tag, is a more affordable alternative to the super-exotic 58mm f/0.95 S Noct discussed next. It's about one-quarter the price of its more glamorous f/0.95 sibling, which will allow you to buy several other lenses, or an extra Z-mount body. Because of its wide maximum aperture, it's a large-ish lens, a bit longer and wider than the 24-70mm f/2.8 S-series zoom. It should be the mainstream king of available-light shooting, great for indoor sports, portraiture, and any illustrative photography where selective focus is desirable. Its f/1.2 is "only" two-thirds of a stop less bright than the 58mm f/0.95 S Noct, but one full stop faster than its 50mm f/1.8 stablemate.

Nikkor Z 58mm f/0.95 S Noct

While I doubt that the average user will be seriously interested in this expensive lens, I concede that most of us who will never be able to afford one give it the same degree of interest we Hyundai drivers (like me) sinfully have toward Lamborghinis. Surprisingly, when this lens was released, a rather large number of well-heeled Z-series owners lined up to purchase one.

Yes, it is almost two full f/stops faster than a 50mm f/1.8 lens, meaning, on your average city street at night at ISO 1600 you could shoot wide open at 1/125th second instead of 1/30th second. Or, in full daylight and ISO 64 you'd need a shutter speed of 1/8000th second for your selective focus images at f/0.95. This lens is purported to be exceptionally sharp wide open, thanks to the Z-series cameras' wide "throat" that loosened many of the chains facing Nikon's lens designers.

Before you available-light photographers add this lens to your birthday "fantasy" list, keep in mind that it is a *manual focus* lens. Most folks buying such a lens would expect autofocus, at least, if not the ability to slice Julienne fries and run a few Android apps as a bonus.

Nikon claims exceptional performance, even wide open, using ultra-high refractive index aspherical (non-spherical) lens elements, and two (count 'em) different reflective coatings to combat glare: ARNEO (I'm still trying to find out what the acronym means), which reduces vertical incidental light, and Nano Crystal coating to counter photons reaching the lens from a diagonal direction.

Its controls are as unconventional as its other design elements. In addition to the control ring found on other Z-mount lenses, it includes what Nikon calls a high-precision focus ring with "extreme accuracy and natural torque." On a manual focus lens with such a large maximum aperture and resulting shallow depth-of-field, you can bet that correct focus will be critical. It also includes a programmable Lens Fn button, and an LCD display (and accompanying DISP button) that can provide information on aperture, focal length, and depth-of-field.

Compact Prime Lenses

I'm going to include brief descriptions of Nikon's trio of compact prime lenses. They are all full-frame lenses, aimed primarily at those who want to combine them with any of the smaller Z-series cameras, giving them a lighter, more portable and discreet shooting package for street photography or casual shooting. Nikon Z5 II owners will appreciate their modest price and small size.

Nikkor Z 26mm f/2.8

This is considered a *pancake* lens because of its form factor. Weighing just 4.4 ounces, it extends less than an inch from the front of the camera, producing a virtually pocketable configuration when mounted on an APS-C camera like the Nikon Z30. In DX mode it effectively becomes a 40mm f/2.8 normal lens and is a moderate wide-angle on a full-frame camera like the Z5 II.

Nikkor Z 28mm f/2.8 (SE)

Why does Nikon offer both a 26mm f/2.8 full-frame compact lens *and* this 28mm f/2.8 full-frame compact lens, available in both SE and non-SE versions? The main reason is that Nikon felt there was a need for an affordable but cool-looking basic lens for its retro-styled Nikon Zf full-frame camera. It's available in both conventional Z-series configuration as well as a classic SE design that resembles Nikkor lenses used with Nikon FM2 film cameras.

With dual stepping motors and a programmable control ring accompanying the focus ring, the SE version includes up-to-date technology underneath its retro exterior. Both the traditional and SE models focus down to about 7.5 inches, are about 2.8 inches long, and weigh roughly 5.5 ounces.

Nikkor Z 40mm f/2 (SE)

This is another compact prime lens, faster than the other two with an f/2 maximum aperture. It's available in both standard and SE designs, which are optically identical. You can consider it a short "normal" lens on the Z5 II and other full-frame Z-series cameras, or a longer "normal" lens (60mm equivalent) if you also own an APS-C model like the Z50 II, Z50, Z30, or Z fc. Its key shortcoming is its ability to focus no closer than about a foot. It doesn't have much to attract Z5 II owners other than compact size and reasonably wide maximum aperture.

Telephoto Prime Lenses

Telephoto lenses also can have a dramatic effect on your photography, and Nikon is especially strong in the long-lens arena, with lots of choices in many focal lengths and zoom ranges. You should be able to find an affordable telephoto prime or tele-zoom to enhance your photography in several different ways. This section will outline your Z-mount options.

Nikkor 85mm f/1.8 S

If you shoot a great many portraits, you may want to invest in this lens, especially for its great rendition of out-of-focus backgrounds (called "bokeh") and excellent image quality wide open. You'll find it provides a pleasing perspective with human subjects, with minimal face "flattening" effects that longer effective focal lengths produce. It shares the same f/1.8 maximum aperture, special coatings, multiple autofocus drive motors, manual focus override, and programmable control ring found in the other Z-mount full-frame prime AF lenses.

As you can see from the listings so far, Nikon's early emphasis in its S-line lenses was to provide the best image quality it can in prime (non-zoom) lenses with reasonably fast maximum apertures. If your budget can afford to go with the flow, you won't be disappointed.

Nikkor 85mm f/1.2 S

It's hard to understate just how much portrait photographers and others using selective focus as a creative tool anticipated the introduction of this lens. If you earn your living through fashion, boudoir, wedding, and maternity shoots; create headshots or other portraits; or want a versatile lens for the most intimate street photography, you need (or want) this lens. The difference between f/1.8 and f/1.2 doesn't seem like much in decimal terms (just 0.6), but in photographic terms, this lens is one full stop faster than the 85mm f/1.8 S lens described above; the bokeh of out-of-focus highlights produced is sensational, and its range of sharp focus wide open is about half as deep at a typical 8-foot shooting distance. (I used one of the many online depth-of-field calculators for my DOF comparison—your mileage may differ.)

In sum, if you can afford it, this lens can quickly become your go-to optic for the types of photography I listed—and it's versatile and even sharper stopped down a bit. It quickly displaced my beloved F-mount AF Nikkor 85mm f/1.4D IF (the legendary "Cream Machine") as my favorite portrait lens, allowing me to capture images—hand-held—like the one shown in Figure 11.5. Although I am currently

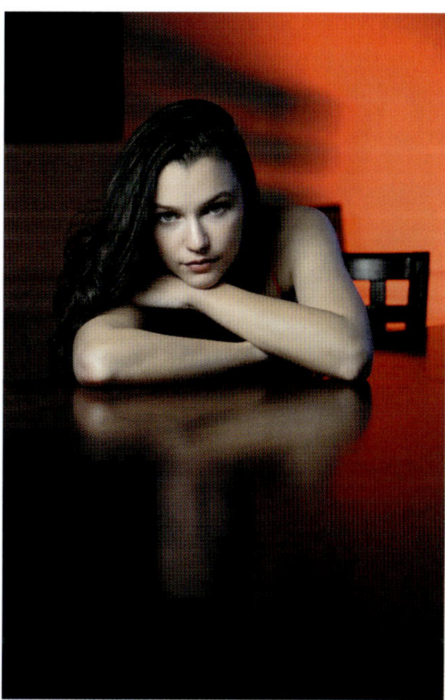

Figure 11.5 A fast 85mm lens is the perfect focal length for portraiture.

crushing on my current obsession—the Nikkor Z 135mm f/1.8 S—they will have to pry this optic out of my cold, dead, hands.

With 15 innovative elements in 10 groups (including two aspherical and one ED element), this lens has been optimized to produce excellent image quality wide open down to f/16, and focuses down to 33 inches (which is generally the closest you'll need to get for portraiture and the like). As good as the 85mm f/1.8 S lens is, this one is even better for those who can justify it.

Nikkor 135mm f/1.8 S Plena

When I got my Nikon Z7 and Z6 cameras back in 2018, one of the first F-mount lenses I slapped on an FTZ adapter was my Nikkor AF-S 105mm f/1.4E ED. It was never removed from my traveling kit until I succumbed to this lens. I resisted as long as I could. The 135mm f/1.8 S Plena's focal length was a bit longer than I like for head-and-shoulders portraits, and it was a third-stop slower (although depth-of-field at comparable subject magnifications is similar); but the results some of my more daring friends were achieving were so spectacular I gave in, purchased this lens, and never looked back.

I normally rely on my Nikkor Z 70-200mm f/2.8 S lens for the two or three concerts I shoot each month. When I can get close to the stage, I love using this lens for its ability to separate a subject from the background. Shooting vocalist Karin Bergquist of Over the Rhine, I was very pleased with the results I got wide open at ISO 1600 (see Figure 11.6, left) and was amazed at the amount of cropping I could do to produce a more intimate look at this performer (see Figure 11.6, right). The Plena is very sharp wide open, edge-to-edge, with virtually no vignetting. (I sometimes *add* vignetting to candid portraits, however; it's nice to have a choice.) Although bokeh wasn't much of a consideration in this case, subsequent shooting has proved this lens produces creamy out-of-focus highlights and is highly resistant to flare (which can be a problem with backlighting at concerts).

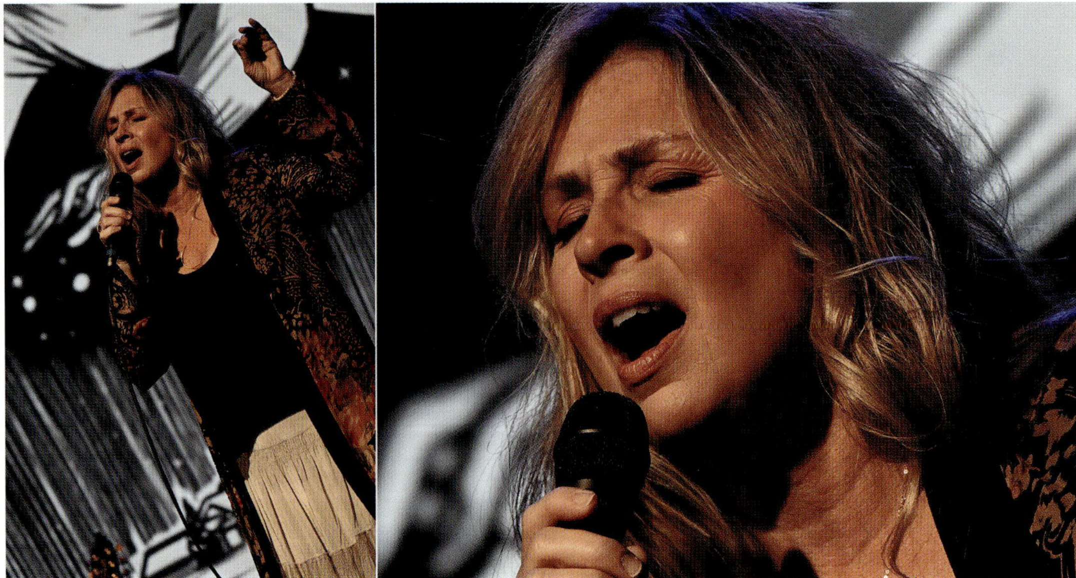

Figure 11.6 The 135mm f/1.8 S Plena is a great lens for intimate photos at concerts.

Nikon deployed 16 elements in 14 groups, with six "exotic" aspherical, ED (extra-low dispersion), and SR (short-wave refractive) elements. (The SR glass provides highly precise chromatic aberration correction.) Focusing down to 2.7 feet, this is a hefty lens at 2.2 pounds, and measures about 4 × 5.5 inches. (See Figure 11.7.) If you're looking for a portrait lens, want to experiment with selective focus, or just need a fast medium telephoto, this lens deserves consideration. If you're torn between this one and the 85mm f/1.2, keep in mind that the 135mm focal length tends to flatten faces a bit when compared to the shorter lens and may not produce the results you want with female subjects or those who already have wide faces. The simplest solution, though, is to get both.

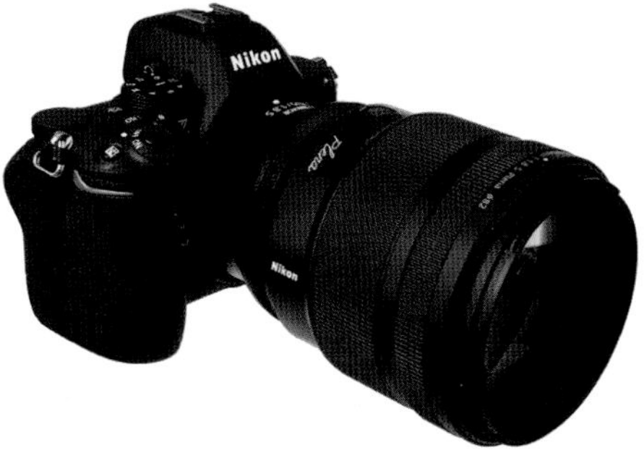

Figure 11.7 The premium Plena lens is not small, but it balances well.

Nikkor Z 400mm f/4.5 VR S

The focal lengths of super telephoto lenses start at 400mm and up, and their prices often start at $5,000 and ascend into the stratosphere. Such lenses are mostly used by sports and wildlife photographers, and in the past those shooters most often belonged to organizations—especially broadcast and print news media—that could afford to keep their equipment lockers stocked with them. Today, however, many of those organizations are trimming their staff and relying on freelancers (in best-case scenarios) or handing reporters iPhones and telling them to capture stills and video. So, there's been a growing need for more affordable super telephoto lenses for professionals, along with the increasing number of photo enthusiasts eager to add longer lenses to their kits for their non-paying work.

The Nikon Z 400mm f/4.5 VR S has become the entry-level super tele prime for the masses. While its $3,000-plus price seems like a lot of money, that's only a fifth of what Nikon asks for its Nikkor Z 400mm f/2.8 TC VR S optic. The company achieved its "bargain" pricing by giving you a maximum aperture that's 1 1/3 stop slower, while using ED/Super ED and SR lens elements instead of more expensive designs with FL (fluorite) or PF (phase fresnel) elements. The lens is compatible with Nikon's 1.4X and 2.0X Z-mount teleconverters (giving you a 560mm f/6.3 and 800mm f/9 equivalent super telephoto lenses), where the high-end 400mm f/2.8 alternative has a 1.4X converter built-in.

Considering its (relative) speed and focal length, the 400mm f/4.5 optic is relatively compact at 9.3 inches in length and 4.1 inches across, and even at a little over three pounds in total weight (with the included tripod foot), it's easier to tote around than many other super telephoto prime lenses, which can easily tip the scales at more than 10 pounds. This lens has handy lens function buttons you can trigger with a thumb press. It's easily usable hand-held (you can remove the tripod foot from the collar if you don't need it), but adapts well to a monopod, which I prefer for shooting sports. It's one of the lenses compatible with Nikon's Synchro-VR feature to integrate its in-lens vibration reduction with the Z5 II's IBIS (in-body image stabilization).

> **FOOT LOOSE?**
>
> One thing to consider with this lens, as well as other Z-mount telephotos discussed in this chapter, is a replacement tripod foot mount that is compatible with standard Arca-Swiss type mounting plates. I use the Kirk alternatives to the Nikon-supplied foot, as the Kirk LP-70 is compatible with the 400mm f/4.5 VR S, 70-200m f/2.8 VR S, and 100-400mm f/4.5-5.6 VR S lenses.

Nikkor Z 400mm f/2.8 TC VR S / Nikkor Z 600mm f/4 TC VR S

These ultimate super-telephoto lenses with leading-edge features also sport bleeding-edge prices. At around $14,000 and $15,500, respectively (as this is written), these optics are likely to be only within the reach of full-time sports photographers and the equipment cabinets of news organizations, and perhaps a few wildlife photographers and businesses able to justify buying or renting them. The executive summary for those who want to skim past this description and return to the real world is this:

- **Nikkor Z 400mm f/2.8 TC VR S.** A superb 6.5-pound lens with vibration reduction that focuses down to 8.2 feet, with a built-in 1.4x teleconverter that transforms it into a 560mm f/4optic at the flip of a switch. It's also compatible with the Nikkor Z 1.4x and 2.0x teleconverters if you're insane enough to want to further extend its range.

- **Nikkor Z 600mm f/4 TC VR S.** An equally excellent 7.2-pound VR lens that focuses to 14 feet, with a built-in 1.4x teleconverter that transforms it into an 840mm f/5.6 lens. It too can be used by overly optimistic photographers with the Nikkor Z 1.4x and 2.0x teleconverters.

The built-in teleconverter is a huge advantage, because Nikon was able to optimize it for these lenses. In addition, sports and wildlife photographers frequently shoot in inclement weather, and an integrated converter preserves the main lens housing's weather sealing, which may not be the case with an add-on converter. These lenses have ED, Super ED, fluorite, and SR lens elements for superior elimination of chromatic aberrations, color fringing, coma, and other distortion. Nikon's literature touts the advanced coatings used for anti-reflection/anti-glare suppression, including an additional *Meso Amorphous* supplement to their venerable Nano Crystal and ARNEO coatings.

Autofocus is said to be extremely fast and accurate, thanks to what Nikon calls its *Silky Swift Voice Coil Motor* (I am not making this up). The SSVCM replaces traditional gearing with magnets that are able to move lens focusing groups smoothly at higher initial speeds, while maintaining the quiet operation required for video shooting. (If you've ever ridden a roller coaster that launches through electromagnetic propulsion, you'll know what I am talking about.)

Physically, these lenses are more compact and lower in weight than their F-mount counterparts, even with the built-in teleconverter. A nice touch was to place their center of gravity at the tripod mounting point, which makes for smoother panning. The mount rotates to allow switching from horizontal to vertical shooting. The sophisticated weather sealing uses rubber gaskets to block dust and moisture, and the front and rear elements have fluorine coating to protect from dirt, moisture, and oily deposits. Both lenses use 46mm filters that drop into the included filter holder.

Nikkor Z 600mm f/6.3 VR S / Nikkor Z 800mm f/6.3 VR S

Nikon is to be commended for recognizing that the majority of Z5 II owners can't afford telephoto prime lenses that cost more than a Rolex Submariner and aren't half as spiffy. The Nikkor Z 400mm f/4.5 VR S makes a great initial purchase for your long lens arsenal, but this pair of optics takes you deep into super-telephoto territory as remarkably hand-holdable and lightweight options.

At less than half the cost of the fast 400mm/600mm lenses described above, these two have less heft, too, at 3.24 and 5.2 pounds, respectively, and are roughly 11 and 15 inches long. Much of the size and weight savings come from the use of the PF (Phase Fresnel) lens elements and f/6.3 maximum apertures (making them best suited for photography under bright lighting conditions). The 600mm version takes 95mm front-mounted filters, while the 800mm lens uses the more affordable 46mm drop-in variety. You can focus on subjects as close as 13.1 and 16.4 feet, respectively, which will typically be of most use for courageous photographers willing to stand their ground when confronted with a fast-approaching wide receiver or charging grizzly bear.

Hand-held lenses particularly benefit from effective vibration reduction, and these lenses offer 5 to 5.5 stops of image stabilization, and each add an additional half-stop with the Synchro VR available with the Z5 II. The center of gravity of both lenses is placed for optimum use without a tripod or monopod. I like the Memory Set button that allows storing a focus position that can be instantly returned to with a turn of the programmable ring. As with the other Z-mount super-tele lenses, you can use the 1.4x and 2.0x teleconverters to increase the focal length to insane lengths (if you can accept the one- and two-stop reduction in effective aperture).

Telephoto Zoom Lenses

Telephoto lenses also can have a dramatic effect on your photography, and Nikon is especially strong in the long-lens arena, with lots of choices in many focal lengths and zoom ranges.

Nikkor Z 24-120mm f/4 S

This is unequivocally my favorite walk-around lens, as was its F-mount counterpart with my Nikon dSLRs. I complemented my Z5 II with a ton of equipment when I drove the length of Route 66 recently, and probably used this lens (plus one of my drones) for 80 percent of the pictures I took. Most of the vast panoramas, including the Painted Desert at Petrified Forest National Park, didn't lend themselves to anything wider than 24mm, and distant wildlife was not often encountered, so 120mm was sufficient for tight compositions and selective focus.

It's quite a versatile lens, ideal for everything from indoor or outdoor sports, weddings, portraits, video, and many other types of subject matter. This zoom focuses down to 1.1 feet, uses internal focusing, and, at about 22 ounces, is one of the lightest everyday lenses you can mount on your camera. It does get longer as you zoom, however (see Figure 11.8, left and center), and lacks built-in VR. Fortunately, the Z5 II's IBIS does a good job of countering camera shake throughout this lens's focal length range.

Nikkor Z 28-135mm f/4 PZ

This lens was developed as part of Nikon's increasing commitment to professional digital video production, reflected by its acquisition of RED LLC in 2024. The new subsidiary is increasing compatibility with Z-mount lenses, and this cinema optic becomes the second power zoom lens offered by Nikon in Z-mount, and the first covering a full 24 × 36mm frame. Priced at $2,600, this lens is likely to be too rich for the pocketbooks of most Z5 II users, and beyond their needs as well. It's really intended for videographers.

As a lens built specifically for video, it includes nifty features like a rectangular lens hood with a filter window for use with polarizers, neutral-density filters, and special effects add-ons; a zoom lever for smooth focal length changes; and the ability to operate the zoom function using the MC-N10 remote grip, or from a computer, smartphone, or tablet through NX Tether or SnapBridge software.

Nikkor Z 24-200mm f4-6.3 VR

Nikon knew Z-series shooters on a budget would need a less pricey, less hefty zoom lens with a 200mm long end and would accept a slower maximum aperture to get one. However, the company opted to expand the zoom range a bit to improve the versatility of its budget zoom option. This lens is an all-in-one 8.3X zoom that extends from wide-angle to telephoto focal lengths, with a variable maximum aperture of f/4 at 24mm to f/6.3 at the 200mm end of its range. But don't confuse it as a budget version of the 70-200mm f/2.8 S-series optic. Here are some important considerations that can get lost in a crowded specifications list:

- **Not an S-series lens.** As you might expect from its modest price tag, this lens is not part of Nikon's S lineup. However, like all Z-mount lenses, it benefits from the freedom afforded lens designers by the new lens mount to use more advanced optical designs. The 24-200mm is plenty sharp.

- **Includes VR.** Note that this lens *does* include VR, which improves image stabilization along two of the five axes, an extra-important feature with longer lenses that tend to magnify camera motion because of their length and telephoto focal lengths.

- **It's not tiny.** While an affordable 70-200mm lens with, say, an f/4 maximum aperture would be significantly smaller than its f/2.8 counterpart, by extending this lens's focal length range to 24mm at the wide end Nikon necessarily produced a slightly larger product. However, this lens is still somewhat smaller than the 70-200mm f/2.8 Z-mount optic, measuring 3.1 × 4.5 inches and weighing 20.2 ounces.

- **Closest focus.** It focuses down to 1.64 feet at 24mm and 2.3 feet at 200mm. With a minimum aperture of f/22 to f/36 (depending on zoom setting), you can actually use this lens as a macro lens, assuming the camera/lens are mounted on a tripod and you don't mind the slight loss in image quality that diffraction effects produce at the smallest f/stops.

I admit I find myself using this lens (shown in Figure 11.8, right) as a walk-around lens sometimes more than its upscale sibling, but I prefer the better bokeh the latter produces. The 24-200mm lens has a rounded seven-blade diaphragm, which offers pleasing out-of-focus highlights, but the 70-200mm optic's nine-blade design gives better results.

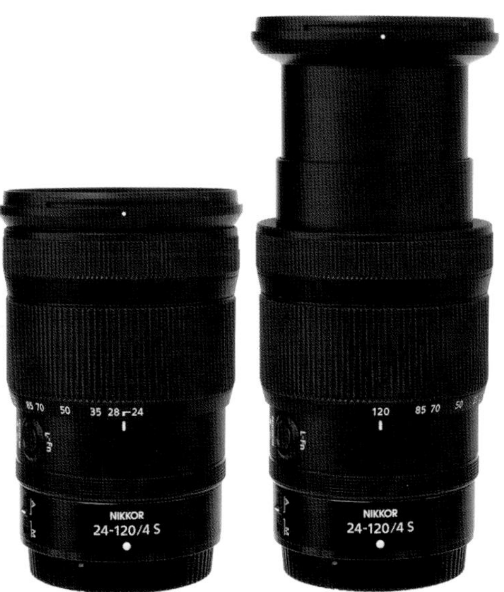

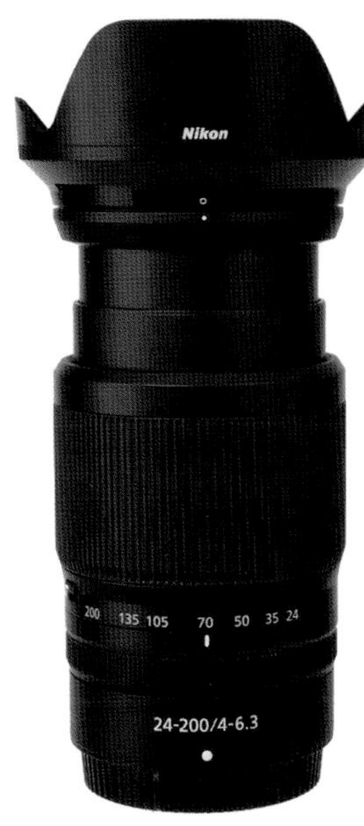

Figure 11.8 The Nikkor Z 24-120mm f/4 S gets longer as you zoom (left). The affordable Nikkor Z 24-200mm f/4-6.3 VR zoom lens (right).

Nikkor Z 70-200mm f/2.8 S VR

This lens will end up being one of the most versatile optics in Nikon's Z-mount lineup, and your best bet for a high-end "magic trinity." It's well worth its price because it can effectively replace three prime lenses while serving as a triple threat for portrait, sports, and event photography. It's sharp wide-open and the combination of in-body image stabilization and lens-based vibration reduction make it ideal for concert photography. (I routinely shoot performances like those illustrated in this book hand-held at 1/180th second at f/2.8 or f/4 and am amazed at the results.)

I also like it for portraits, both formal and candid, often going against conventional wisdom and zooming beyond 100-135mm for tight head-and-shoulders shots. The longer focal lengths (which many discourage because they tend to widen or flatten faces) afford great selective focus control and bokeh when shot wide open or at f/4.

As I'll explain later in this chapter, lens-based VR designed for cameras with IBIS is *not* overkill. When this lens (and other VR optics) is mounted on the camera, the camera hands off image stabilization for pitch (tilting the lens up or down) and yaw (rotating from side to side) to the lens VR, because that system is better able to compensate for that type of movement.

This is another lens with the high-tech coatings and dual stepping motor multi-focus features described earlier. It also has the cool OLED information panel I mentioned in the description of the 24-70mm f/2.8 lens for display of aperture, focus distance, and depth-of field. It has two lens function (L. Fn) buttons that can be assigned behaviors. Focusing down to 1.64 feet, while the 70-200mm f/2.8 Z-mount lens is a sturdy three pounds and measures 3.5 × 8.7 inches, it balances well. Its rotating tripod collar can be removed to trim a bit of weight when you know you'll be shooting exclusively hand-held. (I advise using the lens tripod collar to mount your camera to a tripod when working with this lens to improve balance and avoid putting excess weight on the lens mount.)

Nikkor Z 70-180mm f/2.8

This lens is the "budget trinity" version of the 70-200mm f/2.8 S lens described above. It's half the price, and though derived from a Tamron design, it uses a different focus motor and appearance. It's a worthy alternative, a compact lens (at just 28 ounces) and has the constant f/2.8 maximum aperture sports photographers demand. The six low-dispersion lens elements (plus three aspherical elements) provide excellent color accuracy, sharpness, and clarity. It focuses down to roughly one foot at the 70mm zoom position, and 2.8 feet at 180mm. Nikon says this lens is compatible with its 1.4x and 2.0x teleconverters, giving up to 360mm of telephoto "reach" at a (relatively) low cost. (Nikon's converters cost almost half as much as this lens alone.)

Nikkor Z 28-400mm f/4-8 VR

Dollar-for-dollar, this lens is probably the top bargain do-everything zoom available from Nikon. For about $1,300, you can own one lens that embraces every focal length from 28mm to 400mm, with the vibration reduction that's essential for hand-holding an optic with this much reach. The downside? Its *maximum* aperture (at the 28mm setting) is f/4, and zoomed all the way out to 400mm, your widest f/stop is f/8. That means this lens performs best outdoors in sunny weather, when you can combine an f/11 or f/16 aperture with a shutter speed of at least 1/500th second to supplement the 5.5-stop VR.

However, don't write this lens off for available light photography. When I first received mine, I decided to shoot an entire concert with it when Elvin Bishop (formerly of the Paul Butterfield Blues Band) and Charlie Musselwhite came to town. I was impressed by its performance on the Z5 II and loved the extra-long reach at 400mm. Figure 11.9 shows Elvin captured at 1/200th second and f/13 at ISO 6400, at the lens's 310mm zoom setting.

There's a lot to like and a lot more to love about this 14.2X zoom lens. It's remarkably light at 1.6 pounds and, when collapsed, super-compact, extending just 5.6 inches from the front of the Z5 II, as shown at top in Figure 11.10. Unlike my Nikkor Z 100-400mm f/4.5-5.6 VR S (superior, but at

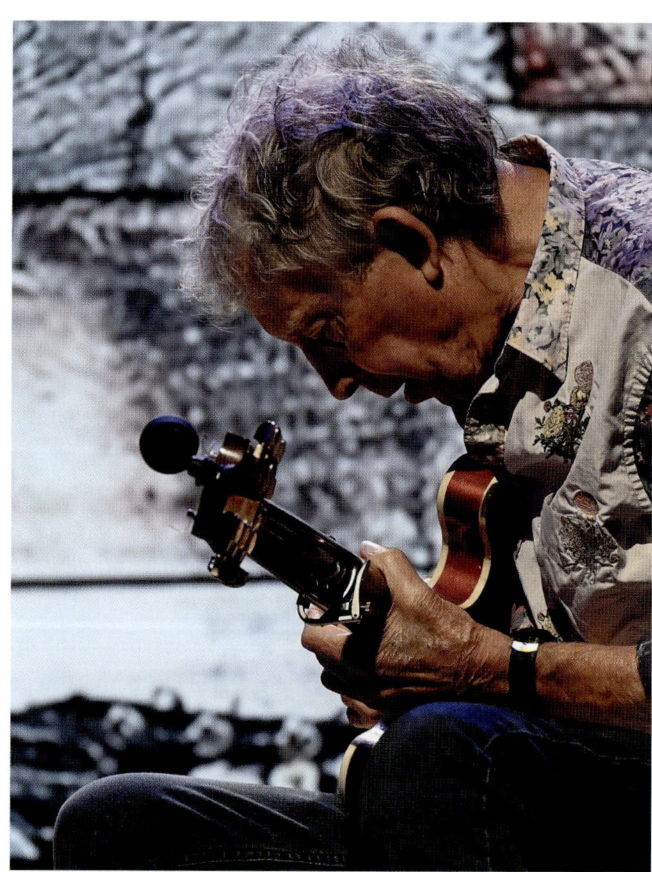

Figure 11.9 VR allows shooting indoors even with "slow" lenses.

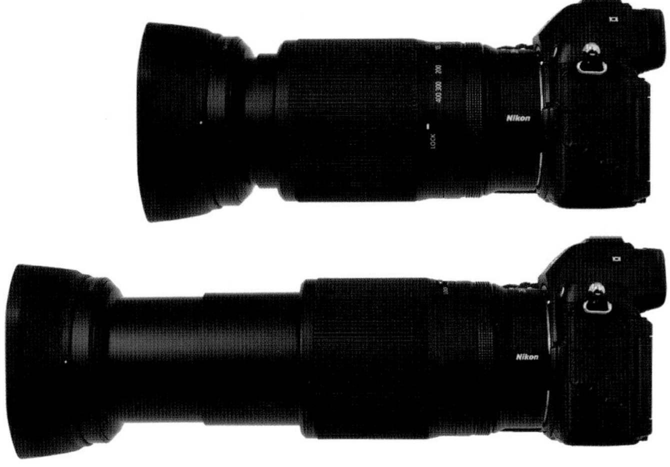

Figure 11.10 The Nikkor Z 28-400mm f/4-8 VR lens collapsed (top) and extended to 400mm (bottom).

twice the price), this one actually can be used as a walk-around lens. However, it does stretch out to 9.8 inches at the maximum zoom setting, so you may find yourself going from wielding a telephoto to brandishing a bazooka when zeroing in on wildlife or other distant subjects. (See Figure 11.10, bottom.)

Well weather-sealed, it focuses down to 7.9 inches at 28mm and 4 feet at 400mm. Thankfully, there's a lock switch that eliminates possible zoom creep when you're toting this lens around. The 28-400mm lens is not compatible with Nikon's teleconverters, but given the limited maximum aperture, you probably wouldn't want to lose another stop or two in any case.

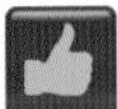

TIP Nikon notes that the included compact square lens hood allows zoom operation when mounted on the lens inverted. Except in the case of emergencies, you should *never* be shooting without having your lens hood in its proper forward-facing position. Even if you think you can do without the reduction in flare and ghosting the hood provides, you don't want to lose your front element's first line of defense against bumps and scrapes.

Nikkor Z 100-400mm f/4.5-5.6 VR S

One of the advantages of my day job (writing these books) is that I get to own and use a broad range of equipment, including lenses, so that for each shoot I can select the gear, from among overlapping choices, that will do the best job for me. When I need a telephoto, this lens, out of all the others mentioned in this chapter, is the one I use most often. (See Figure 11.11.) It covers a useful telephoto

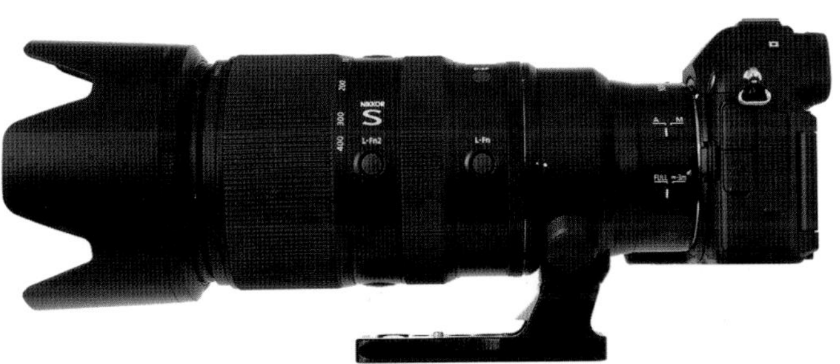

Figure 11.11 The Nikkor Z 100-400mm f/4.5-5.6 VR S lens.

range and has a fast enough aperture, and as an S-series optic, offers superior resolution. Best of all, it doesn't cost an arm and a leg. Most of the photographers I hang out with have opted for the Nikkor Z 180-600mm f/5.6-6.3 VR, described next, but I'm usually willing to give up 200mm of reach in exchange for the more reasonable size and 3.2-pound weight of this lens.

It uses internal focusing, extends only a few inches as you zoom out, and is designed to avoid lens creep so you don't need a lock switch. It includes two separate synchronized autofocus stepping motors for fast focus down to 2.5 feet. Zooming is fast, too, requiring just an 80-degree rotation to go from 100mm to 400mm. There's that integrated OLED information panel described earlier to show aperture, focus distance, and depth-of-field, and two definable lens function (L. Fn) buttons.

Nikkor Z 180-600mm f/5.6-6.3 VR

This is Nikon's more ambitious bargain super-zoom lens with an emphasis on super. In this case, for less than $2,000 (as I write this), you can cover every focal length from 180mm to 600mm with vibration reduction that actually allows using this optic hand-held. Like the 28-400mm zoom, it has a variable maximum aperture, but starts at f/5.6 at the 180mm mark, and loses only *one-third* stop when you zoom all the way to 600mm. For a lens with such an ambitious zoom range, it's relatively compact and lightweight at 4.3 pounds and 12.4 inches long. That's three pounds lighter and five inches shorter than the super-pricey Nikkor Z 600mm f/4 TC VR S I described earlier.

This lens gives you an affordable option for sports and wildlife photography. Zooming is fast, requiring only a 70-degree rotation to go from 180mm to 600mm, and focus is down to 4.3 feet. Slap on one of Nikon's teleconverters, and your reach increases to either 840mm or 1200mm at the long end. No inexpensive drop-in filters with this lens; you'll need 95mm filters.

Macro Lenses

As I've noted previously, some telephotos and telephoto zooms available for the Z5 II have particularly close focusing capabilities, making them *virtual* close-up lenses, rather than true macro optics. In most cases, however, you'll be better served by a lens that is designed specifically to produce sharp images at relatively high magnifications.

Keep in mind that with macro lenses, the object is not necessarily to get as close as possible to your subject. If you get *too* close, you'll find it difficult to light your subject, because the camera and lens will tend to block the light from some angles. What you're really looking for in a macro lens is to magnify the *apparent size* of the subject in the final image while maintaining an appropriate working distance. Camera-to-subject distance is most important when you want to back up farther from your subject (say, to avoid spooking skittish insects or small animals). In that case, you'll want a macro lens with a longer focal length to allow that distance while retaining the desired magnification. Nikon currently has just two true macro options available in Z-mount: 50mm f/2.8 and 105mm f/2.8 lenses, described next.

However, if you don't do enough close-up photography to justify one of them, you have several alternatives. The least-expensive route is to purchase a set of automatic extension tubes available from third parties that can convert one of your existing lenses into a workable macro lens. Figure 11.12,

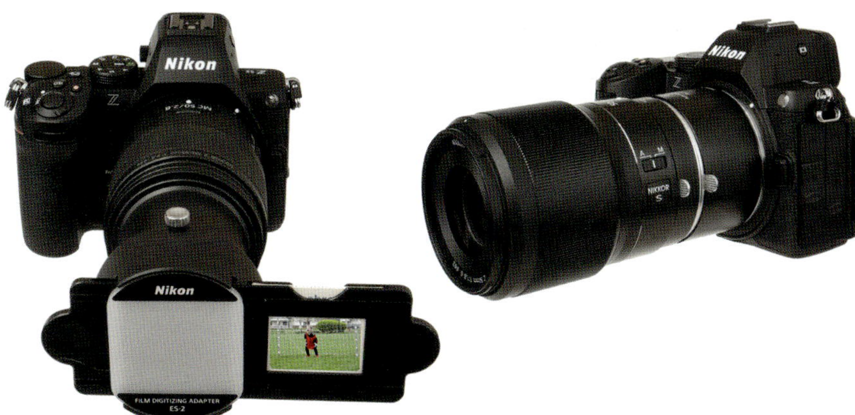

Figure 11.12 Left: Digitize slides with the Nikon ES-2 Film Digitizing kit, using the slide attachment shown or one of the included film strip adapters (not shown). Right: Extension tubes turn a 50mm lens into a macro optic.

right, shows the Nikkor Z 50mm f/1.8 S lens mounted on a pair of FotoDiox Pro automatic extension tubes, which allow that lens to focus down to mere inches from your subject. It's an inherently sharp lens, and works quite well in macro mode. The same tubes can be used with other Z-mount lenses to beef up their close-focusing capabilities.

Another option is to use any of several Nikon F-mount macro lenses, which are given the *Micro-Nikkor* designation, with one of the FTZ adapters. Third-party manual focus lenses, or inexpensive older Nikon manual focus macro lenses can be used with cheap non-auto adapters. My own favorite is a 55mm f/3.5 Micro-Nikkor-P I purchased in the mid-1960s for my first Nikon F; it's super sharp, and I've seen them in excellent condition at keh.com for less than $60.

Nikkor Z 50mm f/2.8 MC

I got this lens only recently, as my F-mount AF-S Micro Nikkor 60mm f/2.8G ED mated with an FTZ adapter had served more than adequately as my general-purpose macro lens for many years. However, once I switched almost completely to mirrorless shooting, I dedicated the older F-mount lens and a Nikon D4s to a permanent setup in my studio that I use for product photography, including the camera/lens/flash/accessories illustrations for my books. This versatile 50mm f/2.8 lens is now a permanent part of my traveling kit, used for a variety of close-up subjects.

It is capable of producing 1:1 ("lifesize") images (that is, the image on the sensor is the same size as the original subject) without needing an extension tube. It focuses down to 6.3 inches and provides edge-to-edge sharpness with excellent out-of-focus highlights (bokeh), which can be a concern because of the shallow depth-of-field commonly encountered in macro photography.

Accurate focus is a special concern for macro photography. Some types of close-up photography benefit from the fast and precise autofocus this lens offers. If you're hand-holding the camera, keeping the exact same subject distance can be iffy, so the ability of the Z5 II to "track" a static subject and maintain focus without undue back-and-forth "hunting" as the camera wavers is valuable. A focus-limiter switch allows focusing to a confined 11.8-to-6.3 inch range when needed for speed and accuracy. In other situations, you'll have the camera firmly mounted on a tripod and may want to focus exactly on a particular plane using manual adjustments. As you rotate the focus ring, a scale appears on the lens barrel with markings at 0.63, 0.56, and 0.53 feet (1:2, 1:1.4, and 1:1 magnifications).

I've been using this lens to digitize my large collection of 35mm slides and film negatives, using the ES-2 Film Digitizing set shown in Figure 11.12, left. Unfortunately, the Z5 II lacks the Nikon D850's in-camera film digitizing feature, which was able to automatically correct for the orange mask overlaid on color negative films. Many have had success using three Rosco gelatine filters over their light source (Cinegel #3202: Full Blue (CTB), Cinegel #3204: Half Blue (1/2 CTB), and Cinegel #4415: 15 Green), but I haven't tried this personally.

Nikkor Z 105mm f/2.8 MC VR S

This lens was my first Z-mount macro purchase for several reasons. My F-mount Nikon 105mm f/2.8 AF-D lens was an older model without a built-in autofocus motor and so would not focus on the Z5 II even when mounted on an FTZ adapter. The 105mm f/2.8 MC VR S boasted excellent autofocus, had VR, was an upscale "S" lens, and, at about $1,000, didn't cost an arm and a leg. Moreover, its focal length and f/2.8 maximum aperture meant it could easily double as a short telephoto/portrait lens.

Its 105mm focal length is better suited for some types of subjects, because you can back off slightly and shoot from a greater distance. Skittish insects and other creatures are less intimidated, and it's easier to arrange lighting on your subject without worrying that the lens itself will cast shadows or block light. Like its 50mm counterpart, it provides a 1:1 reproduction ratio, and, often, a more pleasing look with less apparent perspective distortion. It's great for everything from food and flower photography to jewelry and other product photography.

It focuses down to 11.4 inches and includes an 11.4- to 19.7-inch focus-limiter switch. This lens also has a customizable L-Fn button and control ring (to change aperture, exposure compensation, or ISO at your option) and that interesting OLED information panel described earlier that can display aperture, focus distance, and depth-of field at the press of the DISP button. It's well-corrected for many types of aberrations and distortions, for edge-to-edge sharpness. At 1.4 pounds, it's not a lightweight lens, but it tends to stay in my overloaded bag anyway just for its versatility.

Nikkor Z Teleconverter TC-1.4x/TC-2.0x

I've long used Nikon teleconverters for my F-mount lenses, generally the 1.4X and 1.7X versions with my Nikkor 200-500mm f/5.6 telephoto. I use these because they were *designed specifically for* the Nikon lenses they are compatible with and produce results that are superior to those of third-party lens/teleconverter manufacturers.

The good news is that Nikon offers both 1.4x and 2.0x converters in Z mount, each with excellent optical performance, and hefty price tags. Their performance is virtually as good as that of the built-in converters included with Nikon's TC-series super telephotos described above. The other good news is that Nikon says these teleconverters can be used with no less than eight different lenses (at the time I write this):

Nikkor Z 70-180mm f/2.8	Nikkor Z 400mm f/2.8 TC VR S
Nikkor Z 70-200mm f/2.8 VR S	Nikkor Z 400mm f/4.5 VR S
Nikkor Z 100-400mm f/4.5-5.6 VR S	Nikkor Z 600mm f/4 TC VR S
Nikkor Z 180-600mm f/5.6-6.3 VR	Nikkor Z 800mm f/6.3 VR S

Both of these teleconverters are designed for sports and wildlife photography and include fluorine coatings that harden the surface of the outermost lens elements to protect them when working in inclement conditions (even though converters are only directly exposed to the elements when changing lenses) and to simplify cleaning. With the TC-1.4x, you'll notice almost no loss of optical quality; the teleconverter uses the center portion of the host lens, effectively cropping out any optical defects at the edges of the frame. The image quality loss with the 2.0x converter isn't large.

The main cost is in maximum aperture—one or two f/stops. Your 70-200mm f/2.8 lens is transformed into a 98-280mm f/4 telephoto with the 1.4x converter, and the 2.0x converter gives you a 140-400mm f/5.6 super zoom. The light loss is a small price to pay for the versatility you gain.

Using the FTZ/FTZ II Adapters

Nikon has offered two different versions of its FTZ adapter. The most recent adapter, dubbed the FTZ II, is shown in Figure 11.13. The original FTZ adapter had a built-in tripod socket, which few actually used, many felt wasn't strong enough to withstand the rigors of supporting most hefty F-mount telephoto lenses, and was uncomfortable to use with the Nikon Z9, which has a built-in vertical grip.

When the original Z-series cameras were introduced, there weren't many native lenses available, and I had 30 or so F-mount optics, so I went all in on FTZ adapters, so I could attach one semi-permanently to my favorite F-mount lenses and not have to scramble to find one. I currently have four, plus one FTZ II adapter, each attached to an

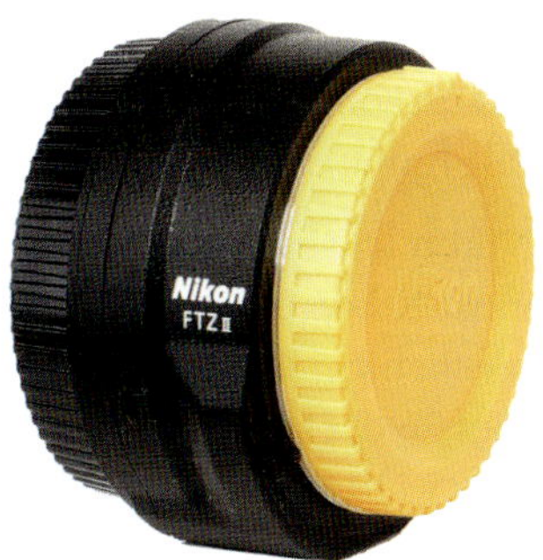

Figure 11.13 The FTZ II adapter.

F-mount lens, such as my Nikkor 8-15mm f/3.5-4.5E fisheye shown earlier in Figure 11.1. I find the FTZ adapters very useful, particularly for legacy F-mount lenses, like the fisheye, that Nikon may never release for Z-series cameras. Optics like the AF-S Nikkor 200-500mm f/5.6E ED VR telephoto zoom have become particularly popular as "bargain" lenses, because dSLR owners switching to mirrorless models are offering them used at surprisingly low prices.

Other than form factor, the two FTZ adapters are functionally identical, and compatible with more than 360 F-mount lenses. This includes more than 90 lenses that have full autofocus and autoexposure compatibility when using AF-S type G/D/E, AF-P type G/E, AF-I type D, and AF-S/AF-I teleconverters. As for other lenses:

- **AF, AF-D lenses.** You must focus these optics manually, but with AF-D lenses the electronic rangefinder will assist in determining correct focus, and focus peaking works with either type. You can adjust the aperture electronically and use Aperture-priority autoexposure.

- **AI-P and all lenses with a CPU chip.** You get manual focus only (with focus peaking) and Aperture-priority exposure.

- **AI, AI-S, and Series E lenses.** Manual focus and manual exposure only, but you can use the non-CPU Lens Data entry in the Setup menu to specify the maximum aperture and focal length of the lens, as described in Chapter 9. However, zoom focal length ranges are not supported. You may also be able to mount and use non-AI F-mount lenses (pre-1977) but may have mechanical interference problems.

As I noted earlier, DX lenses must be used in one of the camera's crop modes if you want some assurance that the entire image area will be filled. Spotting DX lenses is easy: Nikon's versions all have the letters DX in their names. The process is a bit more complicated when it comes to third-party manufacturers. Tamron uses the Di (Digitally integrated) designation for its lenses that are compatible with full-frame digital (and film) cameras and applies the Di II label to lenses suitable only for cropped-sensor models. With Sigma lenses, DG is used for lenses suitable for both FX and DX cameras, and DC indicates a DX-only model. Tokina seems to use the D (for FX) and DX (for DX) nomenclature. All three vendors have been making lenses for (full-frame) film cameras for many years, well before the digital/DX factor became a factor, so when purchasing one of their lenses you may not see a special designation, but, if the lens was introduced prior to about 2004, it's almost certainly a full-frame model.

That's the case with Nikon's older lenses, too, such as the Nikon AI, AI-S, or AI-P lenses, which are manual focus lenses produced starting in 1977 and effectively through the present day, because Nikon continues to offer a limited number of manual focus lenses for those who need them. All are full-frame models.

Nikon lenses produced prior to 1977 must have a minor conversion done to be used safely with most Nikon dSLRs and is recommended for mirrorless camera owners as well, because of possible mechanical issues. John White at www.aiconversions.com will do the work for about $35 to allow these older lenses to be safely used on any Nikon digital camera. **Note:** White was transitioning to a new website as of mid-2025, but the URL I listed will be redirected to the correct page as required.

Other Adapters

As I've noted, because of the camera's 16mm flange distance, there is plenty of room for other adapters to allow the use of lenses from other manufacturers on your camera. Here are my recommendations:

- **Manual adapters.** You'll find inexpensive all-manual adapters for many different "foreign" camera mounts available. I like those offered by FotoDiox and other vendors and use them to attach manual focus Sony and Canon lenses to my Z-series cameras. I also use such manual adapters, priced at $15–$30 to attach *manual focus Nikon* lenses to my Z-series bodies.
- **Auto adapters.** Several companies offer fully automatic adapters that let you use Sony mirrorless camera lenses and Canon EF lenses on the Z5 II, and other Z-series cameras. These adapters (roughly) retain full autoexposure/autofocus features. I've added a few Canon autofocus lenses to my kit because they are plentiful and cheap but produce sharp images. I also used some Sony E-mount lenses on my camera with an auto adapter for a different reason: I already own some very good lenses in focal length ranges Nikon didn't support. I actually used a Sigma 100-400mm f/5-6.3 DG DN OS lens (originally purchased for my Sony a1) with my Z-mount cameras until I purchased Nikon's version.

Third-Party Options

When the great migration from dSLRs to mirrorless cameras changed from a trickle to a surge, third-party lens manufacturers saw the writing on the wall sooner than most of us and stampeded to begin offering lenses in the native Z mount. Virtually all of these early optics were manual focus lenses, often manufactured by startups with only a few years of lens manufacturing under their belts. These include Sirui (2001), Viltrox (2009), Venus Optics-Laowa (2013), Yongnu (2014), 7Artisans (2015), AstrHori (2018), and TTartisans (2019). Then Old Guard companies, which had been making lenses for decades, got into the Act. They included Samyang, Meike, Zhongyi Optics (Mitakon), and others.

Building Z-mount lenses was easy, because, in many cases, the only thing required was to graft on a compatible Z-type lens mount to a manual focus lens and, if you wanted to get fancy, include a chip that would supply focal length and aperture information to the camera's processor. An automatic diaphragm wasn't even required for aperture-priority autoexposure or manual exposure. Ironically, the most successful third-party vendors of the day, such as Tamron, Sigma, and Tokina, lagged behind, because most of their offerings were autofocus lenses designed for existing Nikon, Canon, Sony, or other dSLRs. A few, like Cosina, were well-positioned because they had long been successfully producing manual focus lenses under a variety of established brands, such as Voigtlander.

It's only recently that we've begun to see third-party lenses with autofocus and autoaperture control trickle onto the market, largely from 7Artisans, AstrHori, Laowa, Meike, Sigma, Sirui, and Tamron. As mirrorless models completely dominate the lens market, you can expect to see even more lenses fully compatible with your Z5 II. Some are designed under license from Nikon, while others are developed by companies that reverse-engineer Nikon's technology as best they can. Budget-conscious Z5 II owners can save a few bucks at times, because all of these organizations are capable of providing excellent-quality optics.

My day job requires buying and trying out as many of these as I can, although rigorous testing and evaluation is best left to the YouTubers who make their living from click-throughs and the legitimate gear testing websites. I tend to purchase and use lenses that offer something I can't get from current Nikon lenses. I have to buy as many Nikon-brand lenses as I can to write these books; those from other vendors must offer something special. So, I have in my arsenal a Mitakon Zhongyi 20mm f/2 4.5x Super Macro lens for extreme close-ups, a clutch of Lensbaby special effects optics, a unique Thingify Pinhole Pro X, a 7Artisans 50mm f/0.95, and a Rockstar 27mm f/2.8 (all manual focus lenses).

My latest prize is the Laowa 10mm f/2.8 Zero D rectilinear ultra-wide-angle full-frame lens. (It replaced my Voigtlander 10mm f/5.6 optic, which was manual focus and suffered from distortion at the edges.) Figure 11.14 is a snapshot I took in the Piazza San Marco in Venice. (**Note:** The lens really is Zero-D, optically; the leaning lines you see are considered *apparent*, not *optical* distortion, and is caused by perspective, not the lens. I'll explain this phenomenon further in the next section.) So, although I am unable to cover third-party lenses extensively in this book, I recommend keeping an eye out for interesting optics as you browse the world-wide web.

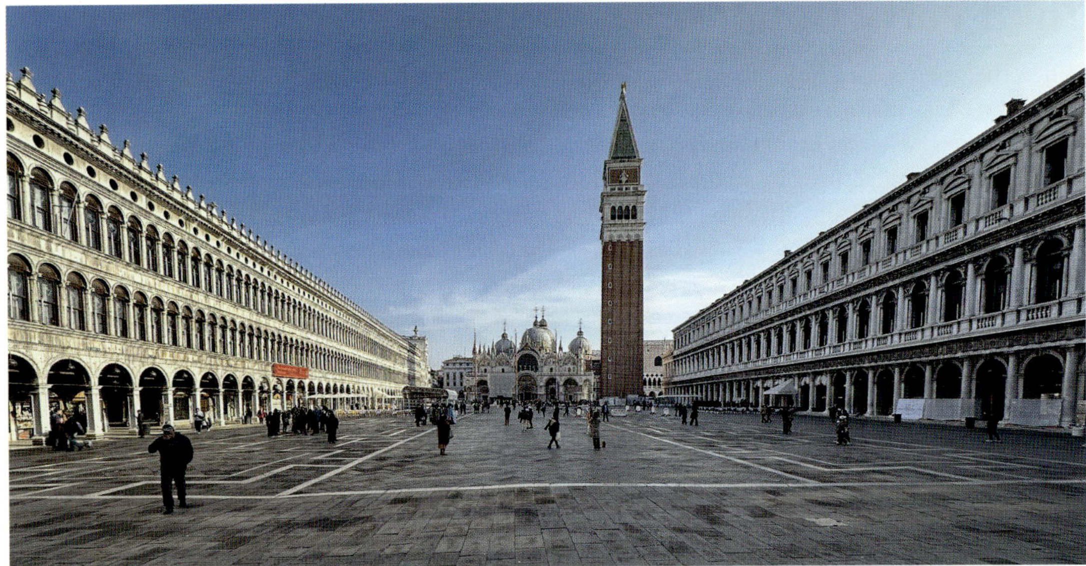

Figure 11.14 To avoid the crowds in Venice, drop by the most popular sites at 6 a.m.

Categories of Lenses

Although I described the native Z-mount lenses earlier, I know that some new enthusiasts need a bit more general information on what lenses can do for them. Even old hands can use a refresher from time to time. So, in this section, I'm going to provide an overview of the key aspects of lenses of various types.

Lenses can be categorized by their intended purpose—general photography, macro photography, and so forth—or by their focal length. The range of available focal lengths is usually divided into three main groups: wide angle, normal, and telephoto. Prime lenses fall neatly into one of these classifications. Zooms can overlap designations, with a significant number falling into the catch-all, wide-to-telephoto zoom range. This section provides more information about focal length ranges, and how they are used.

As I mentioned earlier, any lens with a focal length of 12mm to 20mm is said to be an *ultra-wide-angle lens*; from about 20mm to 35mm is said to be a *wide-angle lens*. *Normal lenses* have a focal length roughly equivalent to the diagonal of the film or sensor, in millimeters, and so fall into the range of about 45mm to 60mm on a full-frame camera. *Short telephoto lenses* start at about 70mm to 105mm, with anything from 135mm to 300mm qualifying as a conventional *telephoto*. For the Nikon Z5 II, anything from about 300mm to 400mm or longer can be considered a *super-telephoto*.

Using Wide-Angle and Wide-Zoom Lenses

To use wide-angle prime lenses and wide zooms, you need to understand how they affect your photography. Here's a quick summary of the things you need to know:

- **More depth-of-field.** Practically speaking, wide-angle lenses offer more depth-of-field at a particular subject distance and aperture. You'll find that helpful when you want to maximize sharpness of a large zone, but not very useful when you'd rather isolate your subject using selective focus (telephoto lenses are better for that).

- **Stepping back.** Wide-angle lenses have the effect of making it seem that you are standing farther from your subject than you really are. They're helpful when you don't want to back up or can't because there are impediments in your way.

- **Wider field of view.** While making your subject seem farther away, as implied above, a wide-angle lens also provides a larger field of view, including more of the subject in your photos.

- **More foreground.** As background objects retreat, more of the foreground is brought into view by a wide-angle lens. That gives you extra emphasis on the area that's closest to the camera. Photograph your home with a normal lens/normal zoom setting, and the front yard probably looks fairly conventional in your photo (that's why they're called "normal" lenses). Switch to a wider lens and you'll discover that your lawn now makes up much more of the photo. So, wide-angle lenses are great when you want to emphasize that lake in the foreground, but problematic when your intended subject is located farther in the distance.

- **Perspective distortion.** When you tilt the camera so the plane of the sensor is no longer perpendicular to the vertical plane of your subject, some parts of the subject are now closer to the sensor than they were before, while other parts are farther away. So, buildings, flagpoles, or NBA players appear to be falling backward. While this kind of apparent distortion (it's not caused by a defect in the lens) can happen with any lens, it's most apparent when a wide angle is used. The "falling-back" look is particularly troublesome with subjects that actually do get narrower toward the top, such as pyramids, and the worst-case scenario, the Nova Scotia lighthouse seen in Figure 11.15.

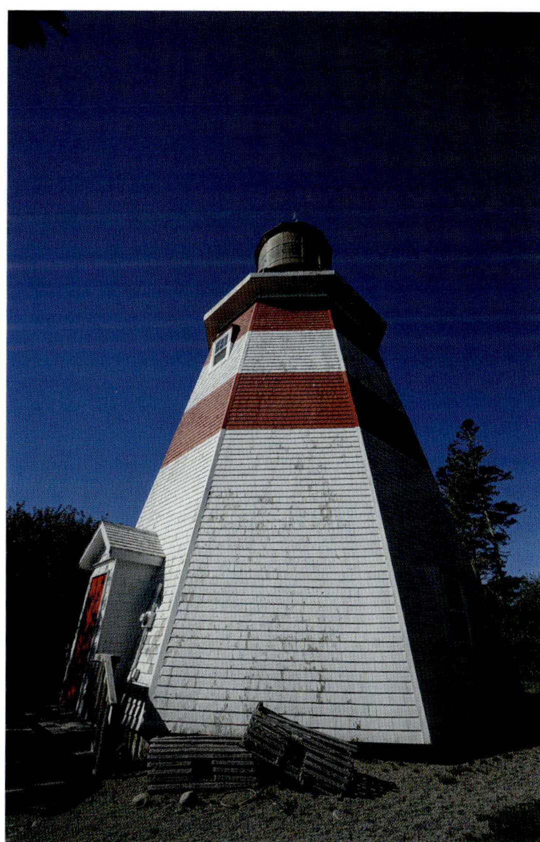

Figure 11.15 Tilting the camera back produces or accentuates this "falling-back" look in architectural photos.

- **Super-sized subjects.** The tendency of a wide-angle lens to emphasize objects in the foreground, while de-emphasizing objects in the background, can lead to a kind of size distortion that may be more objectionable for some types of subjects than others. Shoot a bed of flowers up close with a wide angle, and you might like the distorted effect of the larger blossoms nearer the lens. Take a photo of a family member with the same lens from the same distance, and you're likely to get some complaints about that gigantic nose in the foreground.

- **Steady cam.** Hand-holding a wide-angle lens at slower shutter speeds, without vibration reduction, produces steadier results than with a telephoto lens. The reduced magnification of the wide-lens or wide-zoom setting doesn't emphasize camera shake like a telephoto lens does.

- **Interesting angles.** Many of the factors already listed combine to produce more interesting angles when shooting with wide-angle lenses. Raising or lowering a telephoto lens a few feet probably will have little effect on the appearance of the distant subjects you're shooting. The same change in elevation can produce a dramatic effect for the much-closer subjects typically captured with a wide-angle lens or wide-zoom setting.

Avoiding Potential Wide-Angle Problems

Wide-angle lenses have a few quirks that you'll want to keep in mind when shooting so you can avoid falling into some common traps. Here's a checklist of tips for avoiding common problems:

- **Symptom: converging lines.** Unless you want to use wildly diverging lines as a creative effect, it's a good idea to keep horizontal and vertical lines in landscapes, architecture, and other subjects carefully aligned with the sides, top, and bottom of the frame. That will help you avoid undesired perspective distortion. Sometimes it helps to shoot from a slightly elevated position, so you don't have to tilt the camera up or down.

- **Symptom: excessive foreground.** The tendency of very wide-angle lenses to make foreground subjects appear large can be a problem with landscape and architectural photographs. Your landscape may have majestic mountains in the background, but most of your frame may be filled with the nearby terrain. Limited space forced me to use a wide-angle lens to capture Église Sainte-Marie in Nova Scotia—at 184 feet, the tallest wooden building in North America. With my back at the edge of the roadway that passed in front of the structure, the edifice's parking lot occupied an excessive amount of space in my original uncropped shot (see Figure 11.16).

- **Symptom: color fringes around objects.** Lenses are often plagued with fringes of color around backlit objects, produced by *chromatic aberration*, which is produced when all the colors of light don't focus in the same plane or same lateral position (that is, the colors are offset to one side). This phenomenon is more common in wide-angle lenses and in photos of subjects with contrasty edges. Some kinds of chromatic aberration can be reduced by stopping down the lens, while all sorts can be reduced by using lenses with low diffraction index glass (or ED elements, in Nikon nomenclature) and by incorporating elements that cancel the chromatic aberration of other glass in the lens.

- **Symptom: lines that bow outward.** Some wide-angle lenses cause straight lines to bow outward, with the strongest effect at the edges. In fisheye (or *curvilinear*) lenses, this defect is a feature. When distortion is not desired, you'll need to use a lens that has corrected barrel distortion.

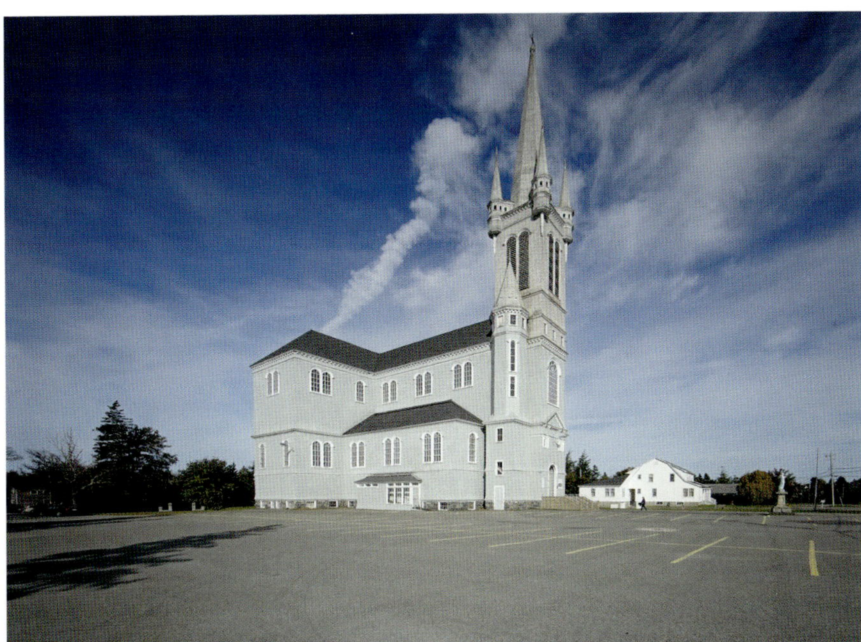

Figure 11.16 Wide-angle lenses can overemphasize the foreground in landscape and architectural shots.

Manufacturers like Nikon do their best to minimize or eliminate it (producing a *rectilinear* lens), often using *aspherical* lens elements (which are not cross-sections of a sphere). You can also minimize barrel distortion simply by framing your photo with some extra space all around, so the edges where the defect is most obvious can be cropped out of the picture. Most image editors have a lens distortion correction feature.

- **Symptom: dark corners and shadows in flash photos.** The optional external electronic flash are generally designed to provide even coverage for lenses as wide as 17mm. If you use a wider lens, you can expect darkening, or *vignetting*, in the corners of the frame.

Using Telephoto and Tele-Zoom Lenses

Here are the most important things you need to know about telephoto and tele-zoom lenses. In the next section, I'll concentrate on telephoto considerations that can be problematic—and how to avoid those problems.

- **Selective focus.** Long lenses have reduced depth-of-field within the frame, allowing you to use selective focus to isolate your subject. You can open the aperture to create shallow depth-of-field or close it down a bit to allow more to be in focus. The flip side of the coin is that when you *want* to make a range of objects sharp, you'll need to use a smaller f/stop to get the depth-of-field you need. Like fire, the depth-of-field of a telephoto lens can be friend or foe. Figure 11.17 shows a photo of a Zebra Finch shot with the Nikkor Z 85mm f/1.8 lens with a wide f/2.8 f/stop to de-emphasize the background.

Figure 11.17 A wide f/stop helped isolate the bird against its background.

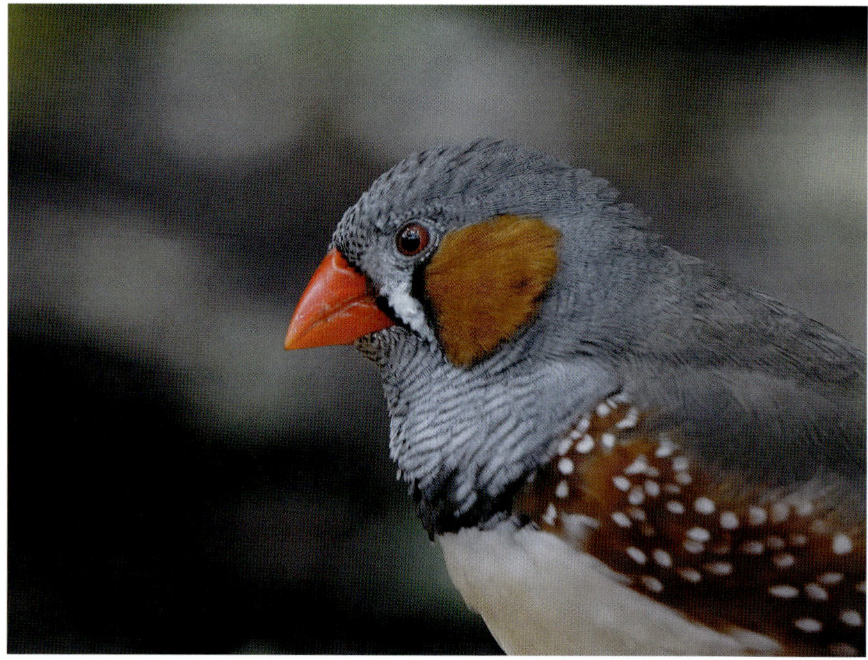

- **Getting closer.** Telephoto lenses bring you closer to wildlife, sports action, and candid subjects. No one wants to get a reputation as a surreptitious or "sneaky" photographer (except for paparazzi), but when applied to candids in an open and honest way, a long lens can help you capture memorable moments while retaining enough distance to stay out of the way of events as they transpire.

- **Reduced foreground/increased compression.** Telephoto lenses have the opposite effect of wide angles: they reduce the importance of things in the foreground by squeezing everything together. This compression even makes distant objects appear to be closer to subjects in the foreground and middle ranges. You can use this effect as a creative tool to squeeze subjects together. You'll find the effect used all the time in TV shows, where the hero dashes toward the camera while racing between slow-moving automobiles, seemingly each just a foot or two apart.

- **Accentuates camera shakiness.** Telephoto focal lengths hit you with a double whammy in terms of camera/photographer shake. The lenses themselves are bulkier, more difficult to hold steady, and may even produce a barely perceptible see-saw rocking effect when you support them with one hand halfway down the lens barrel. Telephotos also magnify any camera shake. It's no wonder that vibration reduction is a popular feature when using longer focal lengths.

- **Interesting angles require creativity.** Telephoto lenses require more imagination in selecting interesting angles, because the "angle" you do get on your subjects is so narrow. Moving from side to side or a bit higher or lower can make a dramatic difference in a wide-angle shot but raising or lowering a telephoto lens a few feet probably will have little effect on the appearance of the distant subjects you're shooting.

Avoiding Telephoto Lens Problems

Many of the "problems" that telephoto lenses pose are really just challenges and are not that difficult to overcome. Here is a list of the seven most common picture maladies and suggested solutions:

- **Symptom: flat faces in portraits.** Head-and-shoulders portraits of humans tend to be more flattering when a focal length of 85mm to 105mm is used. Longer focal lengths compress the distance between features like noses and ears, making the face look wider and flat. A wide angle might make noses look huge and ears tiny when you fill the frame with a face. So, stick with 85mm to 105mm focal lengths, going longer only when you're forced to shoot from a greater distance, and wider only when shooting three-quarters/full-length portraits, or group shots.

- **Symptom: blur due to camera shake.** Use a higher shutter speed (boosting ISO if necessary), consider an image-stabilized lens, or mount your camera on a tripod, monopod, or brace it with some other support. Of those three solutions, only the first will reduce blur caused by *subject* motion; vibration reduction/image stabilization or a tripod won't help you freeze a race car in mid-lap.

- **Symptom: color fringes.** Chromatic aberration is the most pernicious optical problem found in telephoto lenses. There are others, including spherical aberration, astigmatism, coma, curvature of field, and similarly scary-sounding phenomena. The best solution for any of these is to use a better lens that offers the proper degree of correction or stop down the lens to minimize the problem. But that's not always possible. Your second-best choice may be to correct the fringing with your favorite RAW-conversion tool or image editor. Photoshop's Lens Correction filter offers sliders that minimize both red/cyan and blue/yellow fringing.

- **Symptom: lines that curve inward.** Pincushion distortion is found in many telephoto lenses. You might find after a bit of testing that it is worse at certain focal lengths with your zoom lens. Like chromatic aberration, it can be partially corrected using tools like the correction tools built into Photoshop and Photoshop Elements. You can see an exaggerated example in Figure 11.18, especially at the edge; pincushion distortion isn't always this obvious.

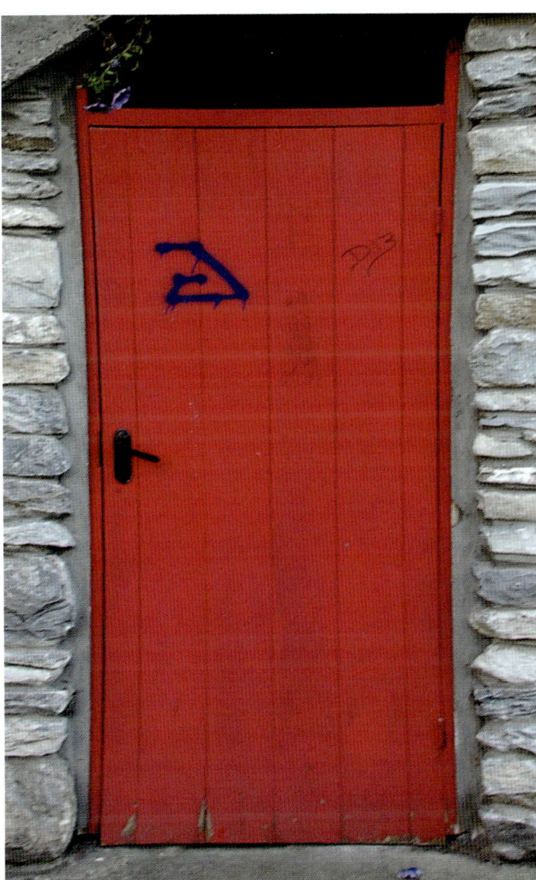

Figure 11.18 Pincushion distortion in telephoto lenses causes lines to bow inward from the edges.

- **Symptom: low contrast from haze or fog.** When you're photographing distant objects, a long lens shoots through a lot more atmosphere, which generally is muddied up with extra haze and fog. That dirt or moisture in the atmosphere can reduce contrast and mute colors. Some feel that a skylight or UV filter can help, but this practice is mostly a holdover from the film days. Digital sensors are not sensitive enough to UV light for a UV filter to have much effect, but a circular polarizer may help in some cases. So, you should be prepared to boost contrast and color saturation in your Set Picture Controls menu or image editor if necessary.

- **Symptom: low contrast from flare.** Lenses are furnished with lens hoods for a good reason: to reduce flare from bright light sources at the periphery of the picture area, or completely outside it. Because telephoto lenses often create images that are lower in contrast in the first place, you'll want to be especially careful to use a lens hood to prevent further effects on your image (or shade the front of the lens with your hand or a hat).

- **Symptom: dark flash photos.** Edge-to-edge flash coverage isn't a problem with telephoto lenses as it is with wide angles. The shooting distance is. A long lens might make a subject that's 50 feet away look as if it's right next to you, but your camera's flash isn't fooled. You'll need extra power for distant flash shots. The Nikon SB-5000 and SB-910 Speedlights, for example, can automatically zoom coverage to illuminate the area captured by a 200mm telephoto lens, with three light distribution patterns (Standard, Center-weighted, and Even).

Telephotos and Bokeh

Bokeh describes the aesthetic qualities of the out-of-focus parts of an image and whether out-of-focus points of light—circles of confusion—are rendered as distracting fuzzy discs or smoothly fade into the background. *Boke* is a Japanese word for "blur," and the "h" was added to keep English speakers from rendering it monosyllabically to rhyme with *broke*. Although bokeh is visible in blurry portions of any image, it's of particular concern with telephoto lenses, which, thanks to the magic of reduced depth-of-field, produce more obviously out-of-focus areas.

Bokeh can vary from lens to lens, or even within a given lens depending on the f/stop in use. Bokeh becomes objectionable when the circles of confusion are evenly illuminated, making them stand out as distinct discs (see Figure 11.19, top), or, worse, when these circles are darker in the center, producing an ugly "doughnut" effect. A lens defect called spherical aberration may produce out-of-focus discs that are brighter on the edges and darker in the center, because the lens doesn't focus light passing through the edges of the lens exactly as it does light going through the center. (Mirror or *catadioptric* lenses also produce this effect.)

Other kinds of spherical aberration generate circles of confusion that are brightest in the center and fade out at the edges, producing a smooth blending effect, as you can see at bottom in Figure 11.19. Ironically, when no spherical aberration is present at all, the discs are a uniform shade, which, while better than the doughnut effect, is not as pleasing as the bright-center/dark-edge rendition. The shape of the disc also comes into play, with round smooth circles considered the best, and nonagonal or some other polygon (determined by the shape of the lens diaphragm) considered less desirable.

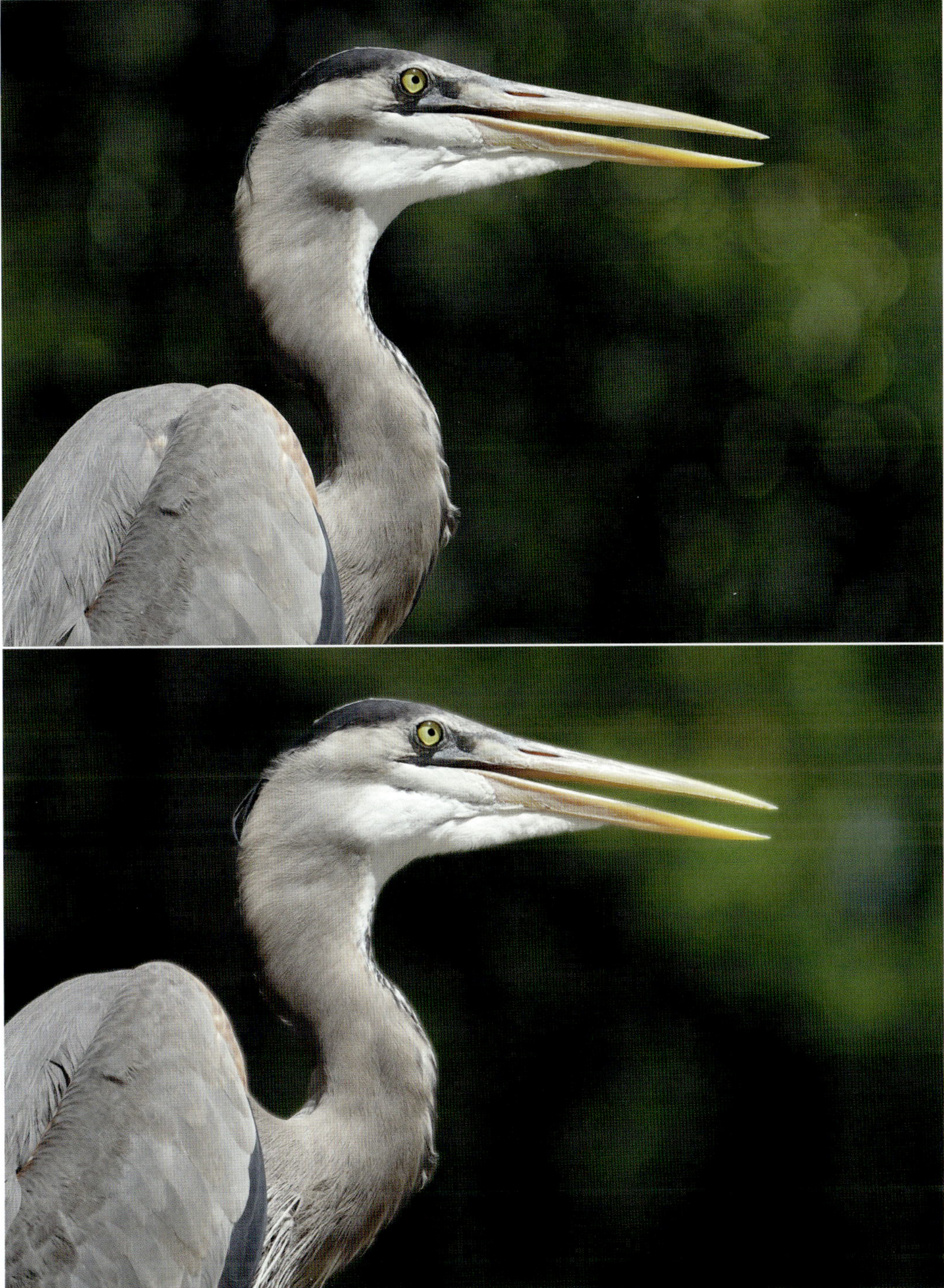

Figure 11.19 Bokeh is less pleasing when the discs are prominent (top), and less obtrusive when they blend into the background (bottom).

If you plan to use selective focus a lot, you should investigate the bokeh characteristics of a particular lens before you buy. Nikon user groups and forums will usually be full of comments and questions about bokeh, so the research is fairly easy.

BOKEH AND SPHERICAL ABBERATION

The characteristics of out-of-focus discs in your image are affected both by the number of blades in the aperture (rounder is better; sharp-sided polygons are worse), and the evenness of illumination of those discs. Highlights may be brighter on the edges and darker in the center because the lens doesn't focus light passing through the edges of the lens exactly as it does light going through the center.

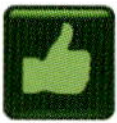

NOTE If you are reading the print version of this title, you can download Chapter 12 here: https://rockynook.com/nikon-z5-ii/